DownBeat — The Great Jazz Interviews

A 75th Anniversary Anthology

DownBeat — The Great Jazz Interviews

A 75th Anniversary Anthology

Edited and Compiled by

Frank Alkyer
Ed Enright
Jason Koransky
Aaron Cohen
Jeff Cagle

HAL•LEONARD®

An Imprint of Hal Leonard Corporation
New York

Published in 2009 by Hal Leonard Books
An Imprint of Hal Leonard Corporation
7777 West Bluemound Road
Milwaukee, WI 53213

Trade Book Division Editorial Offices
19 West 21st Street, New York, NY 10010

Library of Congress Cataloging-in-Publication Data

DownBeat, the great jazz interviews : a 75th anniversary anthology / edited
and compiled by Frank Alkyer ... [et al.].
    p. cm.
ISBN 978-1-4234-6384-9 (pbk.)
1. Jazz musicians--Interviews. I. Alkyer, Frank. II. Down beat. III.
Title: Great jazz interviews.
ML3506.D69 2009
781.65092'2--dc22

2009033018

Book design by Damien Castaneda

Every reasonable effort has been made to contact copyright holders and secure permissions.
Omissions can be remedied in future editions.

Owing to limitations of space, acknowledgments of permission to quote from previously
published materials will be found on page 340.

Printed in the United States of America

ISBN 978-1-4234-6384-9

www.halleonard.com

This book is a labor of love, one that spans 75 years of jazz journalism. It could never have come together so beautifully without the contributions of writers, photographers, editors, designers, sales professionals, circulation managers and the magazine's ownership. Every one of these people have looked at *DownBeat* as something more important than just a magazine, or just a job. And then there are the artists who have given their time, energy, thoughts and even writing talents to *DownBeat* over the years. And finally, none of it matters without the readers. They cheer us when we do it right and set us straight when we do it wrong. Given the fact that we're still around through 75 years and several generations of readers, we get a lot more cheers than canceled subscriptions.

Without all of these folks, *DownBeat* is nothing. This book is dedicated to all of them—the *DownBeat* family.

OCTOBER 28, 1971   50c

own
beat ®

zz-blues-rock

NK TALK!
UNCOMMON
ERVIEW

RGE DUKE:
NNON'S NEW
NO ACE

CK COREA'S CREED

E VERSATILE
OLD MABERN

Contents

Preface

The history of *DownBeat* is the history of the last 75 years, just told through the lens of jazz and blues musicians as well as the journalists who cover them. Race relations, sexual equality, unionism, wars, recessions, birth, life, death, the triumph of the will, the battle of the soul: it spills across the pages of *DownBeat*.

But the aspect of this dense history that holds up best, that truly endures, is the voice of the artist. The editors of *DownBeat* get a lot of opportunities to go back and look through the archives for research. It's one of the great privileges of working for the magazine, and one of the real occupational hazards. Plan for an hour of research, then lose the better part of the day reading through all of those terrific pages from bygone eras.

Whenever I have an opportunity to go into the archives, the items that really draw my attention are the articles written by musicians, or those heavily spiced with quotes from musicians. The music criticism in *DownBeat* is fantastic, second to none, an essential guide to music that is being made. Record and concert reviews provide a glimpse into how a piece of music is received at the time it's presented. The critics may not always be right, but they do give you a sense of how that work fit into the critic's personal tastes as well as into the realm of other music being created at that time.

But the opportunity to read about Ellington, Armstrong, Miles, Bird, Dizzy, Coltrane, Brubeck, Eldridge, Lester Young, Ella, Lady Day—all the greats—to hear them talk about their lives and their careers—in their voices— that's what paints a lasting picture, and delivers a glimpse inside the artist's world. That's the essence of *DownBeat*.

So, when our editorial staff began researching in anticipation of this 75th anniversary anthology, we had to set up some ground rules, because there is so much great material. First, we decided to focus on articles that were either written by artists, or were chock-full of quotes from the artists. Second, we decided to focus on folks who are in the *DownBeat* Hall of Fame, which is voted on by the readers and the critics in our annual polls, or someone we felt should be in the Hall of Fame. And, of course, the writing had to be the best of the best.

The result is before you, 124 of the best interviews or artist-written articles that this magazine has ever produced. The writers serve as a Mount Rushmore of jazz journalism—Dave Dexter Jr., John S. Wilson, Bill Gottlieb, Leonard Feather, Nat Hentoff, Ira Gitler, Ralph J. Gleason, Gene Lees, Stanley Dance, Don DeMicheal, Dan Morgenstern, John McDonough, Michael Bourne, Howard Mandel, and Paul de Barros, to name just a few.

But moreover, the list of musicians who have written for the magazine is nothing short of crazy. Louis Armstrong, Gene Krupa, Jelly Roll Morton, W.C. Handy, Count Basie, Harry James, Woody Herman, Lionel Hampton, Duke Ellington, Les Paul, Benny Goodman, Chet Baker, Jon Hendricks, Cannonball Adderley, Charles Mingus, Marian McPartland, Dizzy Gillespie, Rex Stewart, Joe Williams, Wayne Shorter, Jon Faddis, Greg Osby and Joe Lovano all have bylines in this anthology. Dizzy's article on Charlie Parker is a rare, touching treat. Cannonball and Mingus each offer their surprising insights into the music and phenomenon of Ornette Coleman. Marian McPartland offers a glimpse into the life of Paul Desmond that only she, as a friend of Desmond's, could deliver. Rex Stewart's piece on the life and times of Art Tatum, again, could have only been written by a friend and fellow musician. And Jon Faddis' interview with Milt Jackson, just weeks before Jackson passed on, is nothing short of a breathtaking passing of the torch from one generation of jazz to another.

I believe that's why *DownBeat* has lasted and remains fresh after 75 years. It's a magazine for jazz musicians, written by jazz musicians and the best jazz journalists in the world. Everyone who gets involved, from the musicians to the writers to the photographers, does so with an amazing dedication to the art form of jazz and the craft of making a great jazz magazine. It's magic.

We hope you enjoy it.

Before you dive headlong into the real text, there are a few housekeeping details that must be highlighted. We worked to keep all articles as close to the originally published versions as possible, but we did create a style guide to stop the copy editors from quitting. Every editor who has ever worked for *DownBeat* has developed their own editing quirks and "improvements" to the style guide. You will notice how jargon, colloquialisms, language and writing tastes changed over the course of 75 years. You will also notice how words that were considered fine to use in the 1930s and 1940s make us cringe today. Case in point, the word "Negro." You'll first encounter the word in the Duke Ellington article from 1936, and in a few articles after that. We did not change it. The word was acceptable in that era.

Because we're dealing with musicians and their colorful language, you may come across a swear word or two that make you uncomfortable. We're sorry, but again, we wanted to stay true to the original text and did not change these, either.

Finally, the book title is *DownBeat, The Great Jazz Interviews, A 75th Anniversary Anthology*, but there are articles on Frank Zappa, Muddy Waters and Paul Butterfield, T-Bone Walker, Stevie Wonder, Captain Beefheart, Al Green, Ike and Tina Turner, Brian Eno, Van Morrison, James Brown, Elvis Costello and Alan Toussaint, and probably a few more folks you wouldn't consider jazz. All we can say is we're sorry. We cast a wide net at DownBeat. These folks either were seriously influenced by jazz or had a serious influence on jazz. For that, we'll gladly take the heat because in our world they belong. In the end, as Duke Ellington said, there are only two kinds of music—good and bad. Actually, we'll add one more kind— great. Every artist in this book made *great* music.

Acknowledgments

Pulling this book together has been a Herculean task for our small, dedicated staff at *DownBeat*. First, Jason Koransky, our former editor, Aaron Cohen, our associate editor, and I went through every issue of *DownBeat*, divvying the work up by decade. We poured over pages, selected articles and Xeroxed those old, frail pages, being as careful as we possibly could—and feeling like criminals every time one would decay a little in our hands. Some older issues are so fragile. Even being very selective, we had about three times more content than space. So, I took the responsibility (which means I took the hit) of paring the book down to 120 or so of the best articles we have ever published. It was a painful process, like choosing favorite albums… like choosing favorite children.

From there, every article created before the digital era (which is the vast majority), had to be scanned using optical character recognition software, then seriously edited. The software comes up with some odd and unusual interpretations. So, Ed Enright, our new editor, and Jeff Cagle, a trusted freelancer, went through each article with a fine-tooth comb. It was great work to change every "tIIe" to "the," and the like. And then there are our amazing designers, Ara Tirado and Andy Williams. Both do yeoman's work on our magazines and Web sites, and both helped tremendously by scanning photos and text without the slightest whimper, even though the task was well below their skill set.

Because we were pulling this together between issues of the magazine, Web site updates, newsletter deadlines and everything else involved in being a modern publishing company, someone had to crack the whip on me to make sure we didn't flake out and forget the book. Enter Hal Leonard's Marybeth Keating and John Cerullo. They were able to strike the perfect tone when they'd ask, "When might we expect the copy?" or "When can you get us those photos." They hung with us and encouraged us through every missed deadline and slight hiccup. In short, gentle guilt is a powerful tool and they used it like professional carpenters. On their end, they did an important editing and cleaning job from a distance to ensure this reads like a book with some distinction. For that, thanks to the detailed Godwin Chu for his copy editing contributions. Also, the design of the book is incredible. Thanks to Damien Castaneda for the look of this project, and Ara Tirado for the cover design.

Finally, thanks to Kevin Maher, our president, for recognizing the opportunity we have in creating books like this and giving us an amazing amount of freedom to make *DownBeat* a great publishing brand. His management style gives our entire staff tremendous ownership in the work we do. And thanks to Keith Mardak, Larry Morton and Brad Smith at Hal Leonard for being terrific business partners who help us deliver these books to readers around the world.

—Frank Alkyer

Blister

FANNING THE
FLAMES OF
JOHN
COLTRANE
LEGACY

Louis Armstrong
publicity photo
from the 1930s.
(DownBeat Archive)

June 1935

"My Chops Was Beat," Says Louis, "but I'm Dyin' to Swing Again"

Armstrong to Open Series of One-Nighters

Louis Armstrong and his newly formed orchestra begin a tour of one-nighters, opening at Indianapolis the first week in July. Joe Glaser, Louis' newly acquired personal manager, is handling the details of the bookings.

Louis Armstrong, king of the trumpet, whose freak lip and "hot" solos have amazed and delighted musicians for 10 years, will definitely resume his career the first week in July.

"My chops was beat when I got back from Europe," said the leather-lipped, balloon-lunged Louis. "My manager worked me too hard, and I was so tired when I got back that I didn't even want to see the points of my horn. And 'pops,' he wouldn't even let the 'cats' come backstage to visit me, and you know I'm always glad to see everybody."

All musicians are "cats" to Armstrong. He usually addresses his acquaintances as "pops" or "gate."

Armstrong has been resting in the Chicago home of his mother-in-law waiting for his contract with manager Collins to expire.

His inactivity and seclusion has started a score of rumors that he had "lost his lip," that he had a split lip, that his former wife [Lil Hardin Armstrong]—now leading her own band—had tied up his earnings to satisfy the demands of her suit for alimony, and so on. Musicians all over the world wondered what the real truth was in Louis' "solitude."

"My chops is fine, now," Armstrong said, "and I'm dyin' to swing out again. They gave me a new trumpet over in Europe, and I've got a smaller mouthpiece than I had on my old horn. And my old first-trumpet man, Randolph, is making some swell arrangements. I'm all rested up and dyin' to get going again."

Asked what he thought of American dance bands after his two-year absence from the States, Louis said, "I think Benny Goodman and Casa Loma have mighty fine bands." His attention was called to Louis Prima, an Italian youth from his hometown of New Orleans, who is creating something of a sensation at the Famous Door in New York.

"I don't know Prima," Louis replied, "but his voice on phonograph records tells you that he's a mighty sweet boy. And say," Louis replied with a great deal of enthusiasm, "my old drummer, Zutty Singleton, has a nice little band right here in Chicago." Zutty plays nightly at the famous Three Deuces.

The 1930s

July 1936

A Black Genius in a White Man's World

Much Nonsense Has Been Written About the Duke

A Frank Interview Revealing Many Unheretofore Known Facts About Edward Kennedy Ellington

by Carl Cons

[Editor's Note: May it be to the white man's eternal credit that a black man's genius is so universally recognized and acclaimed in a white man's world. The color line that has built so many racial barriers in the social world and other lines of endeavor have not corralled or subdued the Duke's great talent, although it of course has influenced him. The following remarks are an honest attempt to get THE MAN on paper. The sketch is the result of an interview from midnight to sun-up, and a search for the tangible in a brilliant talent. The key to understanding and appreciating fully his unusual compositions and his brilliant scoring is to UNDERSTAND THE MAN. Because of the short acquaintance and the limited time to probe his genius, necessarily this must be a portrait in miniature.]

The Duke is a Negro!

He is a black man fully conscious of the extraordinary talents of his race AND PROUD BECAUSE HE IS A BLACK MAN.

He thinks and acts in Negroid ways. He is not a black edition of a white man, and he is not trying to imitate a white man as is the case with many Negroes who prostitute their own fine talents trying to copy or emulate those of the white.

His inspiration comes from within. He and his music is written in what he calls the Negro idiom. Every race has its own characteristic feelings and ways of expressing them. For instance, the colored man makes love, dresses with different ideas, sings and pouts, etc., quite differently than his white brother.

All these the Duke has grown up with and been a part of, and his genius is the first to translate in music all the rich color and personality of the American Negro. Their feelings are of a racial minority, their hopes and ideals, their tremendous vitality and good humor, their possibilities and their limitations.

Remember then that when a colored man is full of jive, he isn't always that way because he wants to be, but because when he is sincere he usually isn't taken seriously. Remember when he is sad that he still isn't completely free. Remember that he lives in a world that has boundary lines that he cannot cross. That when he gets out of line he may be trampled by the cruel feet of race hatred. Yes, there are many overtones in Negro music.

His Early Life— How He Got His Start

Duke was born in Washington, D.C., as Edward Kennedy Ellington on the 29th day of April, 1899. He was a talented child, and like many composers before him, it was a toss-up whether he would distinguish himself as a musician or as a painter. Duke majored in art in school, and won a scholarship in fine art to the Pratt Institute. At 14 he played piano by ear for his own amusement, and for house-rent parties. His first money was 75 cents from 8 [p.m.] to 1 [a.m.], and he was so elated that the moment the job was over he broke for home with it.

His first real chance in fast company was at the Abbott House as relief pianist for Doc Perry, and it brought an awakening to his first need for study. Duke comments jovially "that now I was recognized as a musician I had to live up to it—and protect that reputation!" So he studied harmony with Henry Grant.

Married at 19

At 19, Duke got married. The world against two gave him more of the fighting spirit. So he went into business for himself, took a big sized ad in the telephone directory and waited for the phone to ring. There were many parties in Washington then during the war, and between them and "these Virginia gigs" Edward Kennedy did well. Well, well enough to buy a home. It was a four-piece band that got so good the horseshows in that part of the country stopped hiring those 30-piece bands and hired Edward Kennedy. Bill Miller played banjo; Lloyd Stewart, drums; Duke on the piano; and a fellow by the name of Tobin played C melody sax.

Deserted the Barnyard Blues for the Rosary

In 1923, Duke went to New York with Sonny and "Tobie" and Otto Hardwick to join Wilbur Sweatman, a terrific clarinet player and the source of the many of Ted Lewis' licks at the time. But they found they had just deserted the Barnyard Blues for three clarinets on the Rosary. So they Sunday-concerted until the Biscuits called them back to Washington. Duke said, "It was all right to be ragged, but it's bad to have your feet on the ground."

After they got fat, Elmer Snowden, banjo; Sonny Greer, drums; Art Whetsel on trumpet; and Hardwick on sax and clarinet joined "Fats" Waller in New York. Sometime later they sent word to Duke to join them to take Fats' place on a vaudeville tour, and that everything was "ducky." Well, when the Duke arrived, they met him with a "Well, lend me a quarter, pal," and a story that bookings had been temporarily cancelled. "We starved for five weeks," Duke said, "and once we split a hot dog five ways."

Wins on a 6-Ball Game

"Then we got a break, playing in Montmarte, France, and after that worked three months in Barrens," Duke went on. "Then five years in the Kentucky Club. Sonny and I—we lived on the street. We wouldn't eat those hot dogs anymore, so we would shoot up a '6-ball'—win $2 on a deuce, spend 75 cents each on dinner, tip the waiter 25 cents and keep a quarter to start another game.

"In 1927, on December 4th we opened the Cotton Club, and on February 3rd in 1931 we closed it. And we have been on the road ever since. Friday, June the 3rd, we sailed for Europe and the Blue Mills Rhythm Band came down and played 'Stormy Weather.' Yes, the world is full of jive, but we have never been bored."

His Philosophy

Duke is a Baptist and a Methodist. And believes in a hereafter. Definitely so. He is kind and forgiving, and believes that there is a leniency in the afterworld. And, believe it or not, Duke said, "I read the Bible every night before retiring whether I'm 'tight' or not, I got a lotta things to answer for!" He also returns thanks before each meal.

There is a lot of the passive resignation of his race in the Duke and an engaging modest charm that amazes when you consider the amount of attention that has been showered upon him. He is a perfect gentleman, and leans backward in his efforts to be courteous and considerate. He will not even talk to a white woman without his manager. He knows too well the inflammatory moods of a dominant race.

Refused to Study Composition

It is significant to know that Duke refused to study composition because he felt he had something essentially Negro to express in his music, an intangible something he felt academic training would stifle rather than encourage. He does not like mathematical problems and avoids the mechanical in music.

Duke is highly imaginative and extremely sensitive to close and weirdly beautiful harmonies. He has a mirror type of mind that catches all the brilliant, colorful and vivid images of living and reflects them in tonal pictures. He is reflective rather than interpretive in that he is interested principally in reproducing all of his experiences rather than accounting for them. He is a tone painter who tries to catch all the warmth and color of a setting sun on his canvas keyboard, translating sight into sound, and using chords as his pigments.

His Musical Ideas

Many critics read a great deal of their own personalities into Duke's music when they start interpreting it for us—and usually miss the central idea. This is regrettable, but a simple mistake that would not be made over and over again if they understood one fundamental characteristic of the Duke. He is a narrator, and a describer. "Lightnin'" is the description of a train journey with all the excitement and variety of scenes and sounds. "Mood Indigo" is an innocent little girl longing—soliloquizing. "Toodleo," the picture of an old Negro man broken down with hard work in the field coming up a road at sunset, his broken walk in rhythm.

One critic described his composition "Monkey" as an experimental exercise in whole tone scales, and a weaving of rhythmic and melodic patterns. Duke said, "It's just a bunch of monkeys, that's all! It sounds like a jungle because it doesn't

Duke Ellington.
(DownBeat Archive)

sound like anything else." And he received his inspiration one day at the zoo!

What He Strives For

"I like to work alone, and to reach for intricate figures," he said. "I always figure cluster: never any of that single jive! And I always try to get a lift in my music—that part of rhythm that causes a bouncing, buoyant, terpsichorean urge. My idea of real Negro music is getting the different Negro idioms in cluster forms, and the distribution of those idioms in arrangement and still retain their Negroid quality.

"I don't like to trifle with another man's idea, unless I can finish it in the same manner and style that it was conceived. It's bad to interfere with another man because you interrupt his inspiration and spoil the flow of his thoughts.

"I stop writing when I stop feeling, because if you continue after that you become an observer rather than the participator. Many of the boys in the band get good ideas, and I always try to let them finish them out themselves, unless I, too, can feel it, and can help them by suggesting."

His Ambitions

"I never have caught a vine swinging in a forest, but I think that would be a real moment in musical literature when the gentle swaying to and fro of that vine, and the rhythmic swish of the leaves as they were caressed by it, could be captured in orchestral sound!"

Duke is living for the day when he can write an opera. He has already planned a suite of numbers depicting the history and accomplishments of his race from their origin in Africa to their present day status, catching all the violence, misery, torture and the yearning of their trials and tribulations.

It is a gigantic task but one that challenges and inspires him, and the type of thing that should interest and intrigue our more commercial white maestros into some genuine creative musical enterprise.

Aug. 1937

"Musicians Killed Bix Beiderbecke!"

"Bix Died of a Broken Heart," Says Famous Leader of Five Pennies

by Carl Cons

Between sets at the College Inn, CHICAGO—Sober as a grim-pussed judge on election day, carrot-topped, world-famous Red Nichols fortified himself behind a glass of beer. He didn't touch it. But six cigarette butts and two dance sets later he exploded.

"Gin and weed? Hell! They didn't kill him. MUSICIANS KILLED BIX BEIDERBECKE!

"Some of those same musicians living today know what I mean. Bix died of a broken heart. And it was broken by the professional jealousy of musicians who couldn't stand to be outplayed by him so easily.

"Bix was a wonderful and sensitive musician and wanted to be friends with everyone. He could do more on one note than any group of 100 cornet players and you can put me at the last.

"After he died, and jealous musicians had nothing to fear, they began to realize what a great artist he was.

"Yes, Bix was appreciated after he was dead. But when he needed a lift, they wouldn't give it. Many a night they got him drunk and if he slipped or didn't play up to his best, they would pan the hell out of him."

Red shrugged his shoulders resignedly. He has a sense of sportsmanship, and a keen admiration for the great Beiderbecke. "It's a dirty shame, isn't it," he went on, "that a man's own kind can be so bitter toward him? The very guys that should have been the first to appreciate his talent and encourage him were the ones who were most eager to discredit him."

Nichols, who plays in the Bix tradition and who has recorded some of the most polished classics of jazz with his famous Five Pennies, has been the unhappy recipient of much severe and unintelligent criticism by the "great unwashed" or the "not-dry-behind-the-ears" tribe of critics who swarm over the country today mouthing authoritative nonsense about everything.

Hardened by Criticism

Their unknowing "bull-in-the-china-shop" remarks have had their effect and though they come from outsiders, they have unwittingly handicapped another great musician. Red is hardened by a life full of criticism and attacks but it has made him, nevertheless, reticent and word-shy.

The man is one of the few remaining great musicians of the so-called golden era of swing, and it is a damn dirty shame if the same blind jealousy of fellow musicians and the inane remarks of trigger-mouth critics should parallel Bix's tragedy by making Red so self-conscious and discouraged as to affect and spoil his own artistry and inspiration for playing.

Feb. 1938

Carnegie Hall Gets First Taste of Swing

Benny's Clarinet Sounds Good to Lorgnettes— Band a Bit Shaky

by Annemarie Ewing

The boys were nervous.

After all, it was Carnegie Hall and the pile of the red plush seats was still ruffled from contact with the devotees who had listened to the Beethoven Fourth Symphony, the Mozart Haffner Symphony and the violin of Georges Enesco playing the Saint Saens concerto that afternoon. Even the New York Philharmonic Symphony microphone still hung in austere silence 20 feet above the first rows of the orchestra.

And supposing you were Harry James or Gene Krupa or Babe Russin, with a nervous grin on your face and the knowledge of a vast concert hall filled with 3,900 people, more than 100 of them sitting on the stage (at $2.20 a chair), and the space in the rear crowded with the dim shadows of people who had waited in line since 2 p.m. that afternoon for standing room to go on sale.

It isn't the same as playing for the crowd at the Manhattan Room, or even the hysterical audiences in the CBS Playhouse.

"Sure, I'm nervous," Harry James said. "You know, Carnegie Hall, after all."

Later he went out to take the first big hand of the evening!

And "Sure, I'm nervous," Gene said. "But gee! I always get nervous. Every time we change hotels I get nervous!"

Then he went out to take the second big hand of the evening.

Babe Russin said he'd prepared himself with a half gallon of blackberry wine. And Gordon Griffin with lobster and whiskey.

Only the inscrutable Teddy Wilson, with a face like an East Indian deity, and Lionel Hampton, last arrival, shrugged as if to say, "It's only another performance after all."

Then all of them lost themselves, discussing degrees of nervousness with Ivy Anderson, who came down in a Persian lamb coat and her customary breezy camaraderie to cheer the boys on.

"I guess this is the top," Ivy said. "Say, I was so nervous when I made my first movie, my knees knocked together!"

She demonstrated how her knees behaved in Hollywood.

"And on our first European tour—boy, was I nervous!"

At this point, Sam, the major domo of backstage Philharmonic Symphony proceedings, warmed up to the whole business. Out of the vest pocket of his tuxedo, he produced the key to that holy of holies, the door marked with a plaque "For Members of the Philharmonic Symphony Society Only." Sam conducted a personal tour through the big club room where the Philharmonic Symphony musicians play chess, smoke or gossip during intermissions. Gene and Teddy and Ivy and one of the Philharmonic violinists who had come over to see what all the shouting was for, looked around in awe, stretching their necks at the pictures on the wall.

Everybody was impressed with the Toscanini pictures—a photograph of him with the orchestra on its European tour, a portrait, and a drawing by a Philharmonic flutist, very moderne.

"I guess he's about the biggest musician of all," Ivy said.

"He's even considered greater than Stokowski," Teddy said with amiable deference. He seemed surprised to learn that Stokowski is at least 55 years old.

Sam showed them the old lithograph of Wagner's dream of "Tannhauser." They all recognized it—but Ivy called him "Vogner" to Philharmonic Sam's "Waggonner."

When the sacred door was again locked, we heard music seeping through the dressing room section of Carnegie Hall—rhythmic, pulsating music, not much like the kind that comes from a concert meister's bow.

It came from the sanctum sanctorum of Philharmonic conductors, the chamber with ante room just to the right of the backstage stairway. And it was your swing man's cure for all evils—a jam session!

As I live and breathe, Jess Stacy started playing the piano back there. And it wasn't long before Benny himself—complete with that blue carnation, and not nervous (oh, no! except that those papers in his hands were trembling like the "Lullaby of the Leaves"!)—Benny who immediately got the point and set in with the clarinet. Pretty soon there was a trumpet or two. And a sax. And the feet of the artists of the evening, tapping with as many rhythms as there were feet.

By the time Martha Tilton skipped up the steps looking like a blushing version of Snow White in pale pink tulle, full and fresh as a little girl's first party dress, with pink roses in her blonde hair, the jam session was going full tilt. Martha trucked into the same room in which Enesco, five hours earlier, had tuned the famous violin which the Frenchman, Coll, made specially for him.

"Martha! Honey!" everybody shouted—showing that everybody was set.

"They just start playing," said the violinist who had come over the see what all the shouting was for, a little wistfully, "and it all synchronizes!"

Then, all of a sudden, it was 8:45 and Benny, pale as a ghost, was instructing everybody to go on together, and the boys pushing each other around in the wing space—about four square feet, filled with photographers, musicians, ticket holders with seats on the stage, a curly headed usher, trying to be dignified, and the press. And all the boys refusing to be the first one out. And Gene asking if there was anybody in the house, and grinning. And Benny

Benny Goodman.
(DownBeat Archive)

instructing his man Godfrey ("Benny calls me Godfrey, but mah name's Jimmie," he said later at the Savoy) to call the boys from Ellington's band and the boys from Basie's band as soon as he finished with "Sometimes I'm Happy." And Gordon Griffin finally being pushed out first. And the applause welling up. And nobody being able to forget the way "Godfrey" (or Jimmie, as you will) leaned down and polished off the tips of Benny's shoes before he went on!

Much of what followed is by now, as the man says, history.

The unassuming way that American swing took the platform, plain and unadorned and panicking them. The way Bobby Hackett dreamed through the Beiderbecke chorus of "I'm Comin' Virginia." The way Benny took off Ted Lewis, even to the angle of the clarinet, with a nuance that

said, louder than words, that he was playing a caricature. The way Harry Carney, Cootie [Williams] and Johnny Hodges made "Blue Reverie" everything that Duke Ellington had in mind when he created it.

The way Teddy grinned with appreciation when his audience lifted him on the palms of its applause after "Body and Soul." The way dignified, gray-haired gentlemen in the orchestra seats laughed as they have not laughed this side of a smoking car to hear Lionel Hampton's "Yeah, yeah"s in "Nobody's Baby Now" and "I Got Rhythm." The way the hush fell, more poignant than any of the Gershwin eulogies, as Benny, unaccompanied, set into the opening phrase of "The Man I Love."

Well, by the time they had polished off the program's jam session—with Benny sitting happily in the back row like one of the boys, and such artists as Lester Young, Buck Clayton, Johnny Hodges, Bobby Hackett, Harry Carney, Cootie Williams, and Count Basie himself giving performances that surely would have been approved by the master improvisers of 100 years ago, by the man Beethoven himself—it was time to see what was going on out in front.

And don't get the idea that the audience was all jitterbug. There were lots of collegians or their equivalent, naturally. But there were also gray-haired gentlewomen in the Dress Circle whose white gloves clapped in time to the rhythm during "Bei Mir Bist du Schoen" like any debutante, of whom there were also plenty.

Not to mention the lady with the lorgnette who sat in the Dress Circle, right, and put down the lorgnette to clap as hard as the little crippled boy whose father helped him up the steep steps to the balcony.

It was that lorgnette that made Whiteman's wire to Benny seem almost prophetic. The wire said simply, "Congratulations on your coronation! And remember, son, a clarinet sounds just as good to a lorgnette."

And don't forget Yella Pessl, the Viennese harpsichordist who has not yet got over the way Teddy Wilson plays Bach on her harpsichord, as well as swing. And who tells you, in a delightful Viennese accent, impossible to reproduce on paper, how Teddy comes to her house Friday nights and swings on her delicately classical instrument.

"Such a clarity of tone," Miss Pessl says. "So much nicer to hear swing music well played than classical music played badly!"

And Rose Bampton, Metropolitan singing star, who is so glad that these swing musicians can reach out to a new audience, the concert hall audience, and considers it a fine idea to preach swing to a brand-new public.

Of course, there is Deems Taylor's opinion that jam sessions are only one long cadenza—and cadenzas bore him. But he will still admit that anything is worth trying once—and that a swing concert in Carnegie Hall may turn out to be more worthwhile than it seems on the surface to the Philharmonic broadcasting commentator.

One of the most interesting listeners was Shiraly, drummer with Shan-Kar, the Hindu dancer. Shiraly attracted some attention in the audience with his delicate brown profile and long, curling hair, as well as with his absorption in Krupa's playing.

"The man has a genius for rhythm," Shiraly said. "It's quite different from our Indian way of drumming, of course. He beats in multiples of two, whereas we think of rhythm in multiples of three. But I am amazed to find he makes an almost melodic instrument out of the drums. His variations are so intricate that they seem to have an absolute melodic line."

Shiraly's comment didn't differ very much from that of Sol Goodman, tympanist with the Philharmonic, who was among the many Philharmonic musicians who dropped in backstage near the end.

Sol Goodman is the man who took the pictures of Toscanini that appeared in *Life* a month or so ago. He made a special enlargement of one of his shots as a present to Benny, whose admiration for the great symphonic conductor Sol appreciates.

"There isn't a drummer I know that has the feeling for rhythm that Gene has," Sol said. "Even when he sets into a chorus cold, he seems to have some subconscious idea of a pattern that is perfect for what he's playing."

And perhaps some of the highest praise came from Nicholas Moldavan, viola player with the Coolidge String Quartet, who were Benny's guests on his broadcast the Tuesday following the Carnegie Hall concert.

Benny played the Mozart Quintet for Clarinet and Strings with the Collidge group and Mr. Moldavan.

"I consider Benny Goodman one of the great musicians of our time," Moldavan said.

With string music generally conceded to be the highest form of musical art because of its abstract purity—it's pretty hard to get higher praise than that!

But nobody is trying to insist that we make an honest woman of swing. It's enough for the moment that 3,900 people were made ostensibly joyous while a swing band made music in the nation's number one concert hall, and still left the hall intact for the enjoyment of Beethoven, Tchaikovsky, Stravinsky, et al.

There was a little holy roller enthusiasm, certainly. There were intermittent shouts, screams, and reckless hoopla, of course. There was even sporadic trucking going on up in the Dress Circle as the boys got their teeth into "Sing, Sing, Sing."

But for the most part, the audience did just what the music indicated. When it was noisy, they were noisy. In fact, at one point, during "Bei Mir Bist du Schoen," they all began clapping in time to the music—even the woman with the long white gloves and

the woman with the lorgnette. And because of the size of the hall, they were inevitably a little off the beat—a circumstance which filled the boys with momentary consternation, until Gene set in on all the drums he had to drown them out and keep the rhythm intact.

And when the music lowered to a quiet passage, folks sat rapt and quiet, too. Sometimes it seemed almost as if Benny were directing the audience.

But the payoff came when somebody asked Jimmy Mundy if he felt anything like George Gershwin, having his music played in Carnegie Hall. It might have been Whiteman's press agent, sitting on the stage, and remembering the famous Rhapsody in Blue concert.

But Mr. Mundy said, "No, I just feel like tapping mah feet!"

If that be musical treason, can anybody be blamed for wanting to make the most of it?

May 1938

No Squawks on Criticism Before—Why Start Now?

by Gene Krupa

CHICAGO—"The stories about my split-up with Benny Goodman have been exaggerated," declared Gene Krupa in a long-distance call from New York.

"John Hammond and the other critics have made too much out of our differences," he went on. "It's not dramatic at all, but simply a case of ragged nerves, the strain of 40 shows a week, riding trains, etc.—which can happen to any musician.

"I've always wanted a band, and my new venture has been more successful than I ever dreamed, and I'm very grateful to everyone."

Krupa then very sportingly added, "I've never squawked about a criticism before, so why start now? Everyone is entitled to say what he thinks."

Willet and Mundy Arrange

"Chappie Willett and Jimmy Mundy are making special arrangements for me, and I have five arrangers in the band. We have about 70 arrangements now, and we're planning to organize a little jam session group with Leo Watson beating it out on a suitcase."

Gene then informed, "Promoters seem tickled with the band, and we've been getting $1,100 to $1,400 per date on one-nighters."

Interesting to cats is the unusual fact that Helen Ward, Benny's former vocalist, came out of retirement to make some Brunswick records with Gene's new band. Krupa opens Philadelphia's Arcadia International on May 7 for three weeks.

June 1938
· ·

"Ah'm Mahty Glad to See Gene," Says Goodman as They Make Up

Gene Krupa behind the drums and Benny Goodman from an all-star band engagement.
(DownBeat Archive)

PHILADELPHIA—The break between Benny Goodman and Gene Krupa has finally been healed and sealed.

There will be no more fights with fists or words in public or in private between the two rival swing band leaders, because they have shaken hands, patted each other on the back, set up drinks for each other and offered mutual wishes for the best of luck.

Benny played a job at Convention Hall Wednesday night and afterward dropped in at the Arcadia International Restaurant with his band to hear Gene's new orchestra. Goodman sat in the background until the emcee spotted him with a light, whereupon he came bashfully up to the mike and made a little speech:

"Ah'm mighty glad to be heah. It's the first time Ah've seen Gene since he left, and

the first time Ah've heard his band. It really sounds fine." And he shook hands with Gene, who was grinning from ear to ear.

When Gene finished the set, the two bands and the two leaders went back to the bar to exchange the latest news and renew old friendships. Gene and Benny put their arms around each other's shoulders, and there was no doubt in the minds of observers that the two men were really glad to be together again.

Later on Gene commented on Benny's unexpected visit. "See, I told you," he laughed. "No bad blood at all. You see how everything went between us the first time we met since I left the band. If Benny was still hot about it, he certainly wouldn't come down to see us after playing a hard job. I got

a terrific kick out of seeing Benny and all the guys. It was just like old home week."

Today the two bands got together with true English sporting spirit for a fast game of softball. Goodman's team, functioning smoothly, left the Krupa boys in the dust with a final score of 19–7. Unfortunately, Benny had been called to New York and couldn't lead his band for that performance.

Krupa sprained an ankle badly while doing a sandlot slide to third, and Harry Goodman is sporting a black eye caused by a foul tip. Chris Griffin slugged two homers, Bud Freeman got one and did some brilliant fielding, and Bruce Squires starred with a homer and two hits for Gene's team. Goodman's gang beat out 21 hits to Krupa's 15.

Harry James, Benny Goodman and Gene Krupa cut up in a photo from 1951. (DownBeat Archive)

ship swishes away from the dock. Acquaintances are made quickly among the holiday-bound passengers, and the inevitable cocktail party with its growing hilarity takes place. Excitement reaches its peak... only to be halted by the sobering dawn, as the liner quietly heads for home.

"Dinner Music for a Pack of Hungry Cannibals"
Dinner music... dinner jackets and décolleté dresses... dinner music... odd dinners, odd music... wonder what kind cannibals have? It was this sort of mental fantasy that gave me a starting point for this composition... and provided musically inclined cannibals with a dinner-time tune.

July 1938

Raymond Scott Explains His Compositions

Descriptive Jazz Composer Tells Ideas Behind Each Tune

by Raymond Scott

"The Toy Trumpet"
A very modern little boy, brought up in a metropolitan city, hears swing trumpeters on the radio, blues trumpeters on recordings, the hunter's trumpet in news reels, and one Christmas is given a toy trumpet as a gift. This composition is an impression in music of the youngster's antics as he attempts to emulate the examples he has

heard—with the addition of a few of the to-be-expected wrong notes.

"Twilight in Turkey"
The Orient... adventure... mystery... combine to form the background for this Oriental adventure in jazz with a setting of the most exotic time of day in the most exotic part of the world. What happens between the setting of the sun and the coming of complete darkness? Dusk settles over the Orient... Dancing girls make their appearance... An Englishman gets lost... A camel takes a drink. All combine to suggest a visual representation of "Twilight in Turkey."

"Power House"
Did you ever poke your head into a power house? Here is a jazz impression of a person who pokes his head into a power house... the smooth, electric hum of dynamos... the droning rise and fall of surging power... the rhythmical noise of levers and machines... the imposing sight of gigantic generators.

"Reckless Night on Board an Ocean Liner"
Pleasure cruise... an overnight trip on an ocean liner... to nowhere. The crowd-murmur of anticipated pleasure is heard as the

Aug./Sept. 1938

"I Created Jazz in 1902, Not W.C. Handy"

by Jelly Roll Morton

Dear Mr. Ripley:

For many years I have a been a constant reader of your *Believe It or Not* cartoon. I have listened to your broadcast with keen interest. I frankly believe your work is a great contribution to natural science.

In your broadcast of March 26, 1938, you introduced W.C. Handy as the originator of jazz, stomps and blues. By this announcement you have done me a great injustice, and you have also misled many of your fans.

It is evidently known, beyond contradiction, that New Orleans is the cradle of jazz, and I myself happened to be the creator in the year 1902, many years before the Dixieland Band organized. Jazz music is a style, not compositions; any kind of music may be played in jazz, if one has the knowledge. The first stomp was written in 1906, namely, "King Porter Stomp." "Georgia Swing" was the first to be named swing, in 1907. You may be informed by leading record companies. "New Orleans Blues" was written in 1905, the same year "Jelly Roll Blues" was mapped out, but not published at that time. New Orleans was the headquarters for the greatest ragtime musicians on earth. There was more work than musicians, everyone had their individual style. My style seemed to be the attraction. I decided to travel and tried Mississippi, Alabama, Florida, Tennessee, Kentucky, Illinois and many other states during 1903–'04, and was accepted as sensational.

Whoever Heard of a Professor Advocating Ragtime?

In the year of 1908, I was brought to Memphis by a small theater owner, Fred Barasso, as a feature attraction and to be with his number one company for his circuit, which consisted of four houses, namely Memphis, Tenn., Greenville, Vicksburg and Jackson, Miss. That was the birth of the Negro theatrical circuit in the USA. It was that year I met Handy in Memphis. I learned that he had just arrived from his hometown, Henderson, Ky. He was introduced to me as Prof. Handy. Whoever heard of anyone wearing the name of Professor advocate ragtime, jazz, stomps, blues, etc.? Of course, Handy could not play either of these types, and I can assure you he has never learned them as yet (meaning freak tunes, plenty of finger work in the groove of harmonies, great improvisations, accurate, exciting tempos with a kick). I know Mr. Handy's ability, and it is the type of folk songs, hymns, anthems, etc. If you believe I am wrong, challenge his ability.

Williams Wrote Original Tune of "St. Louis Blues"

Prof. Handy as his band played several days a week at a colored amusement park in Memphis, namely, Dixie Park. Guy Williams, a guitarist, worked in the band in 1911. He had a blues tune he wrote, called "Jogo Blues." This tune was published by Pace and Handy under the same title, and later changed to "St. Louis Blues." Williams had no copyright as yet. In 1912 I happened to be in Texas, and one of my fellow musicians brought me a number to play—"Memphis Blues." The minute I started playing it, I recognized it. I said to James Miles, the one who presented it to me (trombonist, still in Houston, playing with me at that time), "The first strain is a Black Butts strain all dressed up." Butts was strictly blues (or what they called a boogie-woogie player), with no knowledge of music. I said the second strain was mine. I practically assembled the tune. The last strain was Tony Jackson's strain, "Whoa

Jelly Roll Morton.
(DownBeat Archive)

B- Whoa." At that time no one knew the meaning of the word "jazz" or "stomps" but me. This also added a new word to the dictionary, which they gave the wrong definition. The word "blues" was known to everyone. For instance, when I was eight or nine years of age, I heard blues tunes entitled "Alice Fields," "Isn't It Hard to Love," "Make Me a Palate on the Floor"—the latter which I played myself on my guitar. Handy also retitled his catalogue "Atlanta Blues." Mr. Handy cannot prove anything is music that he has created. He has possibly taken advantage of some unprotected

material that sometimes floats around. I would like to know how a person could be an originator of anything without being able to do at least some of what he created.

I still claim that jazz hasn't gotten to its peak as yet. I may be the only perfect specimen in jazz today that's living. It may be because of my contributions that gives me authority to know what is correct or incorrect. I guess I am 100 years ahead of my time. Jazz is a style, not a type of composition. Jazz may be transformed to any type of tune; if the transformer has doubt, measure arms with any of my dispensers, on any instrument (of course I'll take the piano). If a contest is necessary, I am ready.

Public Wants the Truth

Please do not misunderstand me. I do not claim any of the creation of the blues, although I have written many of them even before Mr. Handy had any blues published. I had heard them when I was knee-high to a duck. For instance, when I first started going to school, at different times I would visit some of my relatives per permission in the Garden District. I used to hear a few of the following blues players, who could play nothing else—Buddie Canter, Josky Adams, Game Kid, Frank Richards, Sam Henry, and many more too numerous to mention—they were what we call "ragmen" in New Orleans. They can take a 10-cent Xmas horn, take the wooden mouthpiece off, having only the metal for a mouthpiece, and play more blues with that instrument than any trumpeter I have ever met through the country imitating the New Orleans trumpeters. Of course, Handy played mostly violin when I first arrived in Memphis. Violinists weren't known to play anything illegitimate even in New Orleans.

Chris Smith Wrote First Tune Titled "Blues"

I hope this letter will familiarize you more with real facts. You may display this in the most conspicuous places, it matters not to me. I played all Berlin's tunes in jazz, which helped their possibilities greatly. I am enclosing you one of my many write-ups, hoping this may help you in the authenticity of my statements. I am able to hold up any of my statements against any that may contradict. I barnstormed from coast to coast before Art Hickman made his first trip from San Francisco to New York. That was long before Handy's name was in the picture. The first publication with a title "blues" as far as I can remember was a tune written by Chris Smith, who still resides in New York and may be located through Shapiro-Bernstein, publishers, located one flight above the Capitol Theater Building.

Tony Jackson used to play the blues in 1905, entitled "Michigan Water Tastes Like Sherry Wine." He never sang anything on the stage but blues, such as "Elgin Movements in My Hips, with 20 Years' Guarantee." Blues just wasn't considered music—there were hundreds, maybe thousands, who could play blues and not another single tune.

Music is such a tremendous proposition that it probably needs government supervision. There does not seem to be any proper protection for anything in this line. I think one should have conclusive proof before being able to claim a title. I also advocate much more rigid laws so thieves may get their just deserts. There are many who enjoy glory plus financial gain's abundance, even in the millions, who should be digging ditches or sweeping the streets. Lack of proper protection causes this.

Thief Got the Cash

I could dig up many tunes that were published, and benefits reaped accredited to one who never wrote the first note, no arranger who got paid for his work, and the cash went to the one who was the actual thief. The original writer is then afraid to open his mouth for fear that he may be made to do a jail term (negligence of the law excuses no one). These are words of many would-be writers. (What is the use in worrying yourself to death, when you can steal a little bit here and a little bit there?) I laid the foundation of jazz and am still the flowing fountain. Now everyone wants to claim it. They take different names for it in order to baffle their public and gain a false reputation, but they all must serve the same foundations to give satisfaction. As with religion, there are many denominations, but only one God.

Speaking of jazz music, anytime it is mentioned musicians usually hate to give credit but they will say, "I heard Jelly Roll play it first." I also refer you to Clarence Jones. I'm sure he remembers when different musicians would say, "There's something peculiar," referring to my playing and arranging, but all who heard me play would immediately become copycats, regardless of what instrument they played. My figurations—well—I guess, were impossible at that time, and arguments would arise, stating that no one could put this idea on a sheet. It really proved to be the fact for years. Even Will Rossiter's crack arranger, Henri Klickman, was baffled. But I myself figured out the peculiar form of mathematics and harmonics that was strange to all the world but me.

New York's Just Getting Wise to Jazz

My dear Mr. Ripley, I also ask you for conclusive proof, which I am sure that you will never be able to offer, due to the fact that the one who inveigled you into this announcement cannot give you any. He doesn't know anything about the foundation. New York itself is just beginning to get wise to jazz, and all the decent dispensers came from parts that I have educated or from tutors of the good New York musicians. Not until 1926 did they get a faint idea of real jazz, when I decided to live in New York. In spite of the fact that there were a few great dispensers—such as Sidney Bechet, clarinet, and William Brand, bass—New York's idea of jazz was taken from the dictionary's definition—loud, blaring, noise, discordant tones, etc., which really doesn't spell jazz music. Music is supposed to be soothing, not unbearable—which was a specialty with most of them.

It is great to have ability from extreme to extreme, but it is terrible to have this kind of ability without the correct knowledge of how to use it. Very often you could hear the New York (supposed-to-be) jazz bands with 12 to 15 men. They would blaze away with all the volume that they had. Sometimes customers would have to hold their ears to protect their eardrums from a forced collision with their brains. Later in the same tune, without notification, you could hear only drums and trumpet. Piano and guitar would be going but not heard. The others would be holding their instruments leisurely, talking, smoking reefers, chatting scandals, etc.

Musicians of all nationalities watched the way I played; then soon I would hear my material everywhere I trod, but in an incorrect way, using figures behind a conglomeration of variations sometimes discordant, instead of hot swing melodies.

My contributions were many: First clown director, with witty sayings and flashily dressed, now called master of ceremonies; first glee club in orchestra; the first washboard was recorded by me; bass fiddle, drums—which was supposed to be impossible to record. I produced the fly swatter (they now call them brushes). Of course many imitators arose after my being fired or quitting. I do not hold you responsible for this. I only give you facts that you may use for ammunition to force your pal to his rightful position in fair life. Lord protect us from more Hitlers and Mussolinis.

Very truly yours,
Jelly Roll Morton
Originator of Jazz and Stomps
Victor Artist
World's Greatest Hot Tune Writer

Sept. 1938

"I Would Not Play Jazz If I Could"

W.C. Handy Says Jelly Roll's Attack Is the "Act of a Crazy Man"

W.C. Handy.
(DownBeat Archive)

Gentlemen:

In looking over *DownBeat* I came across an article by Jelly Roll Morton captioned: "W.C. Handy Is a Liar!"

For your information: Ripley had me on his program, *Believe It or Not*, and Mr. Jelly Roll Morton wrote a similar article in the *Baltimore Afro-American*—a Negro journal. In order to refute such statements by Jelly Roll Morton in the future, we obtained letters and statistics, etc., to make available to any newspaper that would carry such a scurrilous article. We have nothing much to fear from the Negro newspaper, but when a paper like yours circulates lies of Jelly Roll's concoction to musicians and other professional people, it is doing me not only an injustice but an injury that is irreparable.

If you want to be fair, I am giving you material in this letter which you can assemble and use as a denial. I feel perfectly sure of my position in the musical world and of my ability as a pioneer, creative musician and composer.

I brought the quartet from Alabama to Chicago for the World's Fair in 1893, which sang native songs of my arrangement. I traveled with Maharas' Minstrels that had its headquarters at the Winterburn Show Printing Co. of Chicago in 1896, in which I arranged and played unusual unpublished Negro music. In 1897, I led the band that started from the same address, giving our first performance at Belvidere, Ill., on Aug. 4, 1896, and in Joliet, Ill., in 1897. I was then arranging music for my band, orchestra and singers with my pen and later played Chicago at the Alhambra theaters, where some of Chicago's ablest musicians followed my

band to hear us play original compositions like "Armour Avenue." This minstrel show traveled throughout the United States, Canada, Cuba and Mexico. I had a great opportunity to hear what Negroes were playing in every city and hamlet. I lived and traveled all over the South, and because of a knowledge of Negro music and because of my exceptional ability to write down the things peculiar to him, I created a new style of music which we now know as the "blues," and no one contested in these 25 years my copyrights which I own, nor challenged my ability until this jealous man comes along 25 years later.

I am sending you a copy of the "Jogo Blues," which I as a musician and composer wrote, which was an instrumental following up the success of the "Memphis

Blues," which I composed and wrote. In my early compositions I didn't allow anyone to dot an "I" or cross a "T" other than myself. Now, out of this "Jogo Blues" I took a strain and put words to it and composed the "St. Louis Blues." Wrote the words and music myself. Made the orchestration myself and, contrary to Mr. Morton's statement that I was playing for colored people at Dixie Park, I played this composition atop of the Falls Building in Memphis, at the Alaskan Roof Garden, which was an exclusive spot. My band played for the elite of Memphis throughout the South. Almost every state in the South, every society affair. I did control the music at Dixie Park and played there on Sundays but substituted musicians for other days. The records of every steamboat, amusement park, dance hall, exclusive club in Memphis will reveal these facts. The Universities of Mississippi, Arkansas, Tennessee, Alabama, Georgia, Virginia, North Carolina and Kentucky will also substantiate these claims. Handy's band was a household word throughout the Southland because we could play this music that we now call jazz better than any competitor.

Yes, I Remember Jelly Roll

Yes, I remember when Jelly Roll played for Barrasso in Memphis on what we call T.O.B.A. time. But we were too busy to take notice of his great musicianship. Guy Williams, to whom he refers as the originator of the "Jogo Blues," which I stole and called "St. Louis Blues," was the guitarist in my No. 2 band. I never heard him create or play anything creative, and if I had heard him and plagiarized his idea, he himself would have sought satisfaction 25 years ago.

When A&C Bony Inc. published my *"Blues"—An Anthology*, I was invited to St. Louis to the convention of the American Book Publishers and autographed 300 copies to guests. Guy Williams invited me to his home, where I spent one week with him and his family, which proved our friendly relationship, and he always takes advantage of my visits to St. Louis to extend such hospitality. Never once has he referred to my work other than original.

Morton says that up to 1925, "St. Louis Blues" was as dead as a doornail. I am sending you proof contradicting this statement in the form of a letter from Otto Zimmerman. He printed the first copies in 1914, and you will see that they printed 37,000 the first two years when I was down in Memphis.

In 1921, the Dixieland Jazz Band recorded "St. Louis Blues" on Victor Records, and their first statement (which I am sending you) was 179,440, plus 25,521, plus their third statement of 5,243—records. That's almost a quarter of a million records in 1921 from one phonograph company.

The Brunswick, in 1921, paid me for 39,981 records. In 1923 the Columbia Co. recorded 94,071 records by Ted Lewis. In 1924 the Brunswick recorded 30,472 records. In 1925 Columbia recorded 17,945; also in 1925, Columbia recorded 36,870 records by Bessie Smith. Add to these recordings on the Arto, Edison, Emerson, Pathe, Autophone, Grey Gull, Paramount, Pace Phonograph Co., Banner, Regal, Little Wonder, etc., of the records they made and you will find that "St. Louis Blues" has had

more recordings, sold more records, than any other American composition.

With all these records being played in people's homes before 1925 and with our tremendous sales of sheet music from 1914 on—say nothing about the piano rolls and vaudeville artists singing it from coast to coast on every stage and in every cabaret—how could he say that "St. Louis Blues" was dead? It was because of the popularity of "St. Louis Blues" that Mr. Melrose sent his representative, Henry Teller, to New York in an effort to acquire the dance orchestration rights only for "St. Louis Blues" for the existing term of its copyright, which expires in 1942.

We reserved the symphonic rights and have ready for publication now a symphonic suite in three movements for a standard orchestra. Mr. Melrose was kind enough to write us a letter that we could use with the Afro-American. He refuted Jelly Roll's statement, which we are sending you herewith attached.

For the public's information, you must know that I own the copyright to "St. Louis Blues" but have permitted arrangements for piano, accordion, all kinds of guitars, organs, etc., to be made and sold by firms that specialize along these lines. But they do not own the copyright to "St. Louis Blues." I own that.

I Would Not Play Jazz, Even if I Could

Jelly Roll Morton says I cannot play "jazz." I am 65 years old and would not play it if I could, but I did have the good sense to write down the laws of jazz and the music that lends itself to jazz and had vision enough to copyright and publish all the music I wrote so I don't have to go around saying I made up this piece and that piece in such and such a year like Jelly Roll and then say somebody swiped it. Nobody has swiped anything from me. And, if he is as good as he says he is, he should have copyrighted and published his music so that he could not be running down deserving composers. If I didn't know him, I would think he is crazy and it is the act of a crazy man to attack such fine men who have done outstanding work like Paul Whiteman and Duke Ellington. He reminds me of Captain Higginson, who wrote articles for the *Saturday Evening Post*. He said in one of these articles: "There was an old Negro on the Mississippi River who played the fiddle away back before the Civil War and played the 'Memphis Blues' and 'St. Louis Blues'

before Handy was born," which, of course, was fiction. I expect to hear such tirades as long as I am living, but I don't expect to see you print them and under such captions as the one in this issue.

Jelly Roll Morton is running true to form. Booker Washington always told a story in which he likened Negroes to crabs in a basket: when one was about to get out of the basket, the other grabbed a hold of him and pulled him back.

Very truly yours,
W.C. Handy

July 1939

Critics in the Doghouse: Basie Examines Basie

by Count Basie (as told to Dave Dexter Jr.)

Criticizing one's own band isn't the easiest thing to do, and yet I welcome the opportunity. Sometimes, you know, we form snap judgments of bands on broadcasts, in theaters and even on one-night stands, which is not quite fair. Unless the listener hears and studies a band seriously, there's a chance that he will form his own opinion of that organization's ability and worth. And sometimes that's not so good.

Tate Fits in OK

Some of you know that our band features a "heavy" brass section. I guess the word "heavy" is OK in this instance because our brass includes four trumpets and three trombones. Frankly, I think the brass is our problem, but—and I'm being just candid in my opinion—I also think we have that particular section just where we want it now. My problem, of course, is keeping it that way.

The saxes, four of them, are also phrasing the way I want them to phrase, and their intonation—which gave us a little

Count Basie, right, with boxer Al Hooseman from the late 1940s. (DownBeat Archive)

trouble back in the days when the band was first organized—apparently is up to the par we set. Of course we were a little rough a few months ago when we made a change as a result of Herschel Evans' death, but George "Buddy" Tate caught on in a hurry and fits right in now.

No Rhythm Worries
I am sure that the rhythm section is right as it is. It's the one section that has given us no trouble at any time. And when I speak of the rhythm, I mean bass, drums and guitar. You can count me out.

Am I satisfied with the band today?

Follows His Old Ideas
Not by a long shot, Jack. I have a purpose in everything I try to do with the band. A few years ago I was using nine pieces in a little club called The Reno in Kansas City. We worked together a long while. We got so we coordinated every move, every solo, perfectly. That was how Walter Bales, John Schilling, Don Davis and a few other Kansas City cats found us playing; that's how we got to broadcast every night. It was nine pieces that saw Basie get his biggest break with Benny Goodman, John Hammond and Willard Alexander, as a result of that radio wire and the raves of the men I

just mentioned.

Now—and this is the point I want understood most, if you don't mind—I want my 15-piece band today to work together just like those nine pieces did. I want 15 men to think and play the same way. I want those four trumpets and three trombones to bite with real guts. BUT I want that bite to be just as tasty and subtle as if it were the three brass I used to use. In fact, the only reason I enlarged the brass was to get a richer harmonic structure. The minute the brass gets out of hand and blares and screeches instead of making every note mean something, there'll be some changes made.

Not Too Much Piano
I, of course, wanted to play real jazz. When we play pop tunes, and naturally we must, I want those pops to kick! Not loud and fast, understand, but smoothly and with a definite punch. As for vocals, Jimmy Rushing and Helen Humes are handling them the way we feel they can best be handled. Earl Warren, who plays lead alto, also sings occasionally. That's all the comment I have on our purposes, style and our vocalists.

My piano?

Well, I don't want to "run it into the ground," as they say. I love to play, but this

idea of one man taking one chorus after another is not wise, in my opinion. Therefore, I feed dancers my own piano in short doses, and when I come in for a solo, I do it unexpectedly, using a strong rhythm background behind me. That way, we figure the Count's piano isn't going to become monotonous.

Eight Original Men Remain
We get a lot of questions about personnel. It includes Earl Warren, alto; Lester Young, tenor; Jack Washington, alto and baritone; Tate, tenor; Ed Louis, Wilbur (Buck) Clayton, Shad Collins and Harry Edison, trumpets, in that order; Benny Morton, Dickie Wells and Dan "Slamfoot" Minor, trombones, in that order; and Jo Jones, drums; Walter Page, bass; Freddie Green, guitar; and Basie, piano. That's it. Of that number, Louis, Clayton, Washington, Young, Jones, Page, Minor and Jimmy Rushing all have been with me since the old Reno Club days in Kansas City. They are a great bunch, and any success we have had is due entirely to the grand spirit among us all.

Most Arrangements "On Spot"
We recently hired Lloyd Martin, an Indiana youth, who is turning out some good arrangements. Buck Clayton's also are

used a lot. But with most of our arrangements, one of the boys or I will get an idea for a tune, like "Every Tub," for instance, and at rehearsal we just sorta start it off and the others fall in. First thing you know, we've got it. We don't use paper on a lot of our standards. In that way, we all have more freedom for improvisations.

That's about the best I can do as a reviewer, I'm afraid. I'd like it known that the band works hard—rehearsals three hours long are held three times a week, on the average—and that we get our kicks from playing.

Oct. 15, 1939

Artie Shaw.
(DownBeat Archive)

Artie Shaw Fed Up with Music Racket

by Dave Dexter Jr.

"I hate the music business," said Artie Shaw last week, "and I'll tell you why. In a

month and a half they haven't given me a minute to work out something worthwhile with my band."

No Time to Breathe

With his customary candor—which too many times has been misinterpreted by listeners and reporters as "snootiness"—Shaw in an interview given with Michael Mok of the *New York Post* honestly gave forth his views on the dance music industry.

"I have been at the top, God help me, only since last November," Shaw declared. "Before that, when we were not in demand we had time to rehearse, prepare things, create nice effects. On the strength of that, we arrived. But they won't let you stay at the top. They won't give you a chance to breathe. That's why dance bands shoot up like rockets and plunk down again."

Shaw told Mok, without pulling any punches, that he does not like crowds. "I'm not interested in giving people what they want—I'm interested in making music. Autograph hunters? To hell with them! Often I've played for 2,500 or 3,000 people and 1,000 would stand around the stand staring at me. They aren't listening—only gawking. Then they want autographs. Nothing doing! I'm too busy with my job. Sometimes I let my valet sign my name and they're just as satisfied.

"My friends, my advisers tell me, say I'm a damned fool. 'Look here,' they shout at me, 'you can't do that—those people MADE you!' Want to know my answer? I tell them that if I was made by a bunch of morons, that's just too bad. And besides, if they made me, what do they want my autograph for? You don't worship your own creation, do you?"

Doesn't Claim to Be Leader

Artie told Mok how the motion picture industry is run by a bunch of stooges who tell you what to say, when to say it, and how to say it. He said he even got bad publicity because he refused to say silly lines that actually didn't make sense. And he was right. Because Shaw refused to be a jackass, everybody called him temperamental.

"They also said I stole scenes," Artie said. "I don't steal scenes. I'm not an actor. I'm not even a band leader. I'm a clarinet player who leads a band."

May Junk Band Shortly

Shaw, most musicians who know him agree, has been kicked around unjustly of

late. He has been criticized for dozens of things over which he had no control. Even *DownBeat* has not been hesitant to publish stories about his band appearing late on the bandstand, about Artie refusing to talk to reporters, and how he snubs dancers and news hawks alike wherever he goes. What isn't generally known is that Artie is fed up with the whole business, and he's honest enough to act as he feels—being frank and candid all the time. You ask why he doesn't get out of the business if he dislikes it so much?

He's going to. Just as soon as he is fixed for life financially. And that time isn't far off.

Oct. 15, 1939

Here's Why Louise Tobin Is with B.G.

by Harry James

Right off the bat, I'd like to answer the question that most everybody asks us constantly: "Why does your wife sing with Benny Goodman instead of you?"

Saxes Are My Problem

The answer's pretty simple. Louise can learn more from Benny, she can make more money and naturally she can become better known. She is very happy right now with Benny.

Our band is now about 10 months old. And when Dave Dexter asked me to review the outfit I was only too glad to jot down my ideas. In reading other leaders' reviews in *DownBeat*, I have noticed that most of them swear they are satisfied with their band as it is. Well, I'm not. And here's why:

The saxes are my problem. Now don't take the idea that they aren't any good and are not working together right. I mean, they are just a little slower at grasping new arrangements, and new ideas the arrangers and I get. I haven't made a change in my sax or rhythm sections since I started out on my own. I have the utmost confidence in every man in the band. And I think the saxes are doing OK—another couple of months and they'll be up to the level of the trumpets, trombones and rhythm.

Squires Helps Band

The rhythm section is our pride. I feel it is the best white rhythm section in the business. Red Kent, guitar; Ralph Hawkins, drums; Jack Gardener, piano; and Thurman Teague, bass, form the section.

Bruce Squires, an old "podner" of mine in the Ben Pollack band, is helping plenty since he joined on trombone. He shares solos with Dalton Rizzotto. The trumpets are just about the way I want them.

Our hot tenor is played by Claude Lakey. Dave Matthews, who gave up a good job with Goodman to help me organize last winter, is featured a lot on alto. I think he plays the finest alto in the business. Eight of my boys, including myself, are from Texas. And we've known each other a long while. I had the band all picked two months before I left Benny.

Born Under "Big Top"

It seems to be the custom to give a little background on the leader, so I'll sum it up briefly by saying Louis Armstrong has influenced my style most, and that my parents, Mabell and Everette James, gave me my professional start when I was a baby. They were featured in a circus—my mom played calliope and my father still is a fine cornetist and teacher. And I was playing drums when I was in rompers. Then I played cornet a long time, until I started playing dance music. Then I got a trumpet.

Jack Mathis and Andy Gibson do most of our arrangements. Both are serious students of Sibelius and Debussy, and on our pop tunes you can often tell they are. I've been asked why we don't feature a clarinet a lot. I don't because most dancers would waltz by and say, "That guy isn't as good as Benny Goodman or Artie Shaw." Our style doesn't need hot clarinet. My trumpet, if I may say so, takes most of the solos, and Drew Page handles the clarinet when we need a few bars of solo.

Swell Morale in Band

Vocalists? This young Frank Sinatra handles the ballads. We think he is doing a fine job. Jack Palmer, the trumpeter, steps down to handle the comedy and novelty stuff. We do not use a girl singer because everyone we've had yet has been unsatisfactory, and until we can find one who stacks up as strong as the band, we won't worry. Sinatra

Harry James from the movie *Private Buckaroo*.
(DownBeat Archive)

and Palmer, with Kent helping occasionally, can carry the load OK in our opinion.

We have a wonderful morale; swell spirit, no cliques. The guys get along swell. We know we aren't the best in the business yet. But we think we can be. Our records

(Columbia) are selling fast, we have had plenty of radio time, the fan mail is coming in, the bookings are good and we are all hustling. That's about all a leader can ask. The future will reveal just how far my gang of Texans is going to go.

Feb. 1, 1940

"I Don't Want a Jazz Band" —Glenn Miller

He Claims Harmony, Not a Beat, Is What Counts with the Public

by Dave Dexter Jr.

NEW YORK—"I haven't a great jazz band, and I don't want one."

Glenn Miller isn't one to waste words. And he doesn't waste any describing the music his band is playing these nights at the Hotel Pennsylvania. Soft-spoken, sincere and earnest in his conversation, Miller is now finding himself at the top of the nation's long list of favorite maestri.

"We leaders are criticized for a lot of things," Miller says. "It's always true after a band gets up there and is recognized by the public. Some of the critics, *DownBeat*'s among them, point their fingers at us and charge us with forsaking the real jazz. Maybe so. Maybe not. It's all in what you define as 'real jazz.' It happens that to our ears harmony comes first. A dozen colored bands have a better beat than mine."

"We Stress Harmony"

"Our band stresses harmony. Eight brass gives us a lot of leeway to put to use scores of ideas we've had in mind for a long time. The years of serious study I've had with legitimate teachers finally is paying off in enabling me to write arrangements employing unusual, rich harmonies, many never before used in dance bands."

Glenn isn't fooling either. How he was the first to use a clarinet lead above four saxes is fairly old stuff at this late date. And

From left, Glenn Miller
Jimmy Abato, Wilber
Schwartz, Tex Beneke, Al
Klink and Hal McIntyre
from 1940. (DownBeat Archive)

how he went on from there to experiment with trombone-trumpet combinations to achieve entirely original ensemble effects is what is keeping the Miller band a step ahead of competition.

Do Not Gripe About Chester

In recent weeks reports blossomed forth that Miller, hearing Bob Chester's band, which employs a similar instrumental style, "hit the roof" and demanded that RCA-Victor drop the Chester band from its list of recording combos. No report could be more untrue. Leonard Joy, Victor chieftain, was checked and denounced the rumor.

"Neither Glenn nor any members of his orchestra have ever approached RCA-Victor regarding the Chester band," Joy said.

Small talk irks Glenn. He's no tin god, and he has his faults like all of us, but he isn't the kind to bellyache about competition. He's had plenty of it, all down the line, and until eight months ago, when his platters started clicking and sent the band's stock up bullishly to the heights, he was a pretty sad and disillusioned guy.

"I thought I had swell ideas, and wonderful musicians," he recalls, "but the hell of it, no one else did."

Then All of a Sudden—

Then it happened. Glenn remembers the night, and so does his wife. "We were playing the Meadowbrook early that spring," he says, "and up front, all of a sudden, the band hit me. It was clicking. For the first time I knew it was playing like I wanted it to. It sounded wonderful. I didn't say anything—just drove home and told the wife. But I prayed it would last."

It did.

Later on, the second spurt hit the band the same way.

"We were then at Glen Island Casino, and it hasn't been long ago," Glenn says. "Bang; again the boys hit me hard. They sounded wonderful; better than ever before, better than any band I had ever heard. When I drove home that night, I knew we had hit the top. And believe me, from that night on everything broke right. My problem now is to keep it there. I don't expect any more bangs coming right off the stand at me anymore."

Glenn thinks Benny Goodman is the hardest working leader in the business. His admiration for Benny, as a friend and as a clarinet-playing leader, isn't easy to restrain. Glenn today will do battle arguing that B.G. is the greatest clarinetist ever to

lick a reed. And he doesn't hide his admiration for Benny. The two get along great, and why not? They've known each other 15 years, shared rooms, split dimes to eat, and risen to fame similarly.

Actually, this Miller man is a quiet sort of guy. He does little back-slapping; employs less loud talk. When he discusses his band, you feel a subtle sarcasm behind his words, because for nearly two years he worked like a fool, borrowed money, traveled constantly and fought like a wild man to keep his band—and his ideas on music—intact. He doesn't gloat about his victory today. He's too big a man, and he is wise enough to know that a great group can slip fast in a hurry. He's proud that he has a band of virtual "unknown" kids in his crew; kids that he found himself and that he has taught personally. Most of them are in their early 20s; all of them have become professionals since Goodman made his historic rise.

Trouble with "Styles"

"I had a time with some of them," he declares. "Take Hal McIntyre on alto. He phrased, breathed and played in every respect like he was playing with Benny's band. I pointed out that maybe there was another way to play sax in a section, and we slowly worked out the style we use now. Sure it was tough, but all the boys know what I want and they're fast to learn."

Result? Miller's saxes are the most famous in the land today.

For the records, Miller was born March 1, 1905, in Clarinda, Iowa. But he didn't stay in the corn country long. His parents moved to Denver, and out there, in the land of the Rockies and "tall" air, Glenn learned to play trombone. He was still a moppet when he started playing professionally.

Rose from Noble Band

Glenn first became prominent, nationally, while with Ray Noble's first American dance band five years ago in New York. It was a great outfit—Miller, Spivak, Mince, Cannon, Freeman, Irwin, Thornhill, D'Andrea, and a lot of other terrific musicians all were members. And it was with Noble that Glenn worked out his early ideas on harmony. He also played with the Dorsey Brothers band. His decision to form his own crew was somewhat sudden; he hadn't, as the storybooks say, "always dreamed" of leading his own outfit.

Glenn doesn't claim to be a star soloist on his horn. Not as long as Tommy Dorsey

lives. Tommy, to Glenn, plays the greatest tram in the business. But as a section man, Glenn Millers on trombone don't bob up often. That's why Glenn chose to organize a band that stresses excellent musicianship and perfect ensembles rather than a band that gets by on one hot soloist jumping up after another to take hot choruses.

Men All "Great" Guys

The men in the Miller band? Once he starts talking, Miller won't stop. They're all great. And they were "great" before last Christmas Eve when they all got together, pooled their money, purchased a huge shiny new Buick Roadmaster for their boss and presented it to him in the lobby of the Pennsylvania Hotel a few hours after the band had broken a 14-year attendance record up in Harlem at the Savoy Ballroom.

But Gordon "Tex" Beneke—the young and hungry tenor man whose name rhymes with "panicky" except for the "a" in the latter—is Glenn's fair-haired boy. Miller claims Tex, in another year, will be acclaimed by even the righteous guys as great a man as Hawkins. Already Glenn says Tex is the greatest white tenor alive.

Harmony Above Rhythm

But back to the music. Glenn doesn't want a strict jazz band. Of course he likes the pure stuff himself, and he admits Louis Armstrong's old Hot Five and Hot Seven discs of the early 1920s have given him a lot of ideas which he used to advantage. "But the public has to understand music," he says. "By giving the public a rich and full melody, distinctly arranged and well played, all the time creating new tone colors and patterns, I feel we have a better chance of being successful. I want a kick to my band, but I don't want the rhythm to hog the spotlight."

Just one more slant on Glenn Miller's way of thinking. Smart? Not long back he pulled Tommy Mack out of the band to make him manager of the band. Tommy plays trombone. So when Glenn, rehearsing for a record date or a broadcast, wants to step into the control room to check balance, intonation and the like, Tommy drops back, sets up his sliphorn and no time is lost. The band sounds exactly as it will sound with Glenn riding along with the other three trombones later.

Remembers Winchell's Advice

Glenn Miller deserves every break he's gotten. Plenty of the big guys refused him help when he needed it. He's had to fight for every break. Now that he's at the top he can look back and grin, but he doesn't hold a peeve for anyone.

Meanwhile, he's working harder than ever. He remembers reading in Winchell's column a few years back that you meet the same people on the way down that you met on the way up. Some of those people Glenn doesn't want to mix up with again.

March 1, 1940

"Educated Cat Stole My Mute Idea"—Joe "King" Oliver

by Dave Clark

JACKSON, Tenn.—On a hot August day in 1936 as I was sitting under a tree in my yard trying to keep cool and dodge the heat from the blazing sun, a bus rolled up in front of my door and stopped and out stepped Theodore Taylor, former manager of the Royal Knights orchestra, which I had sent out on a successful tour a few months back. Taylor was now kicking the hides and acting as right-hand man for King Joe Oliver and his band.

Taylor advised me that the band was in a tough spot due to some bad booking they had been working on under some guy in North Carolina, who had taken the band for a ride. He asked if I could do anything to help them get off of the rim. I advised that it would be rather hard to get booking without any time for connections and exploitation, but I would do my best to help the band out.

Oliver Tells Sad Story

Taylor then called King Joe Oliver, who came out of the bus to help Taylor explain things. It was a sad story this old fellow told me. He stated that he had tough breaks for two years straight but was still trying to overcome his handicaps.

King started to tell me his plight in this manner:

"Pops, breaks come to cats in this rack-

et only once in a while, and I guess I must have been asleep when mine came. I've made lots of dough in this game, but I didn't know how to take care of it. I have been under the best management in the country, but I didn't know how to stay under it.

"When Fredericks Brothers of K.C. [Kansas City] was handling my business, I didn't have anything to worry about. But I messed up. I couldn't keep my band together. In a way, I was unfair to them and I started down the hill. From that point I haven't had any real breaks since then."

"Educated Cat Made Fortune Off My Ideas"

"I have helped to make some of the best names in the music game, but I am too much of a man to ask those that I have helped to help me. Some of the guys that I have helped are responsible for my downfall in a way. I am the guy who took a pop bottle and a rubber plunger and made the first mute ever used in a horn, but I didn't know how to get the patent for it and some educated cat came along and made a fortune off of my ideas. I have written a lot of numbers that someone else got the credit and the money for. I couldn't help it because I didn't know what to do.

"I am in terrible shape now. I am getting old and my health is failing. Doctors advised me a long time ago to give up and quit, but I can't. I don't have any money and can't do anything else, so here I am.

"I have been under management of both colored and white bookers in the past few years, but I haven't had one yet to deal fair with me. I had one booker who collected deposits on all the dates I played for him and skipped out. I had another who bought a bus for my band and had me to sign papers that put all the fellows' instruments under mortgage. I gave him money to make the payments and he kept it for personal use. The company took the bus and the instruments, but I pleaded with the manager to let me keep the instruments and told him how I had been gypped, and he opened up his heart and gave back the instruments. After this we made jobs for a week in a coal truck, as we didn't have enough money to rent cars or a bus. Then my band broke up and I had contracts for some very nice jobs, so I was lucky enough to get Maurice Morrison and his band to fill the dates for me until I got another band together. Things changed a little for me after this. I got a new and better band and a bus and headed south for Florida, where I became the victim of another

crooked booker, and my band broke up by degrees. I played my last job under him with four men including myself. I then went to Georgia and organized another band, the band I have now, and if you don't do something to help me, I will lose them."

Stakes King to a Room

After hearing King's story, I took the band to a local rooming house and made myself responsible for their room and board for a few days while I got out and worked up some dates for them. Their first date was at the Cotton Club here. With one day's advertising this date was a sellout, with the band making enough money to hold them up for a few days. I then sent the band on a tour through Mississippi, Arkansas, Tennessee and Kentucky, which was very hard to book because so many of the spots' bookers had messed up with King's band. King didn't want me to book his band near New Orleans, as he didn't want the folk in his home town to see him in this plight. He also had me dodge all large cities because he had made a name in most of them and he wanted his reputation to stand. King was down as far as finance was concerned, but the old fellow still had high ideals.

I heard the band only once while I was booking it, and they really sounded nice with King only playing three numbers during the entire program, and these three numbers would make anybody sit up and take notice. When King blasted out on his famous "West End" and "Cedar Street Blues," you could see real art and unexcelled musical background. Although he was about to become a victim of Father Time, the notes were made with perfection and the tone was clear as it ever was.

The "Cedar Street Blues" was the last number written by King Oliver. He wrote this number while playing the Wagon Wheel in Nashville, Tenn. Cedar Street was the hangout for sepias in that city.

Then Oliver Died

After working with me for two months, the old fellow advised me that his band was ready for the East Coast. So he paid me every cent that he owed and pulled out for Georgia to work under another agent. I learned that his band broke up in Savannah, Ga., again a victim of the unfair sharks. I received a card from King about two months before he died stating that he was going to organize again and wanted me to handle his band exclusively. And when I heard from him again, the great

Lionel Hampton.
(DownBeat Archive)

King Joe Oliver was dead, the poor fellow was through worrying about his tough breaks because the booker from Gabriel's band is a fair and square shooter. So King Oliver can hit the high notes hard and clear without worry or care.

Note: Two of the bookers that once handled King's band are doing time in the federal institutions for using the mails to defraud. Another is washing dishes in a hot dog stand over in Virginia.

June 1, 1940

Hampton, Boiling Hot, Shoots at the Critics

by Lionel Hampton

LOS ANGELES—In the past year, while knocking around the country with Benny,

I've taken low more than once on one count. Now I'm going to straighten that out with a lot of folks, many of them who read *DownBeat*, I know. It's this: for a long time now, a lot of people have taken delight in asking me why I don't smoke weeds since "all musicians do."

ALL musicians do NOT smoke weeds, nor do ALL musicians drink!

I know that's going to set a lot of the yokels back on their heels, but they need it. Why the profession has to keep taking black eyes because a few cats here and there believe in living their lives is a little beyond me. And, brother, I'm plenty sick of staring 'em down when they want to know about it.

"Work Harder than Subway Guards"

We musicians are making a living just like anybody else. Being in the groove to keep your roof over your head doesn't stand for much gay-catting around. We work harder in some cases than bricklayers and subway guards. Nowadays competition out there is a killer, and you have to keep off the old beaten path if you want to keep on eating. We're pretty much a level-headed bunch of people, and damned if I, for one, don't resent the popular conception that all we do is get high off our tea, and use grog for chasers.

So, help me, it's a lotta baloney.

"No Time for Hangovers"

Another thing, in this phase of music specialization is hitting its best high. That means if you're lucky enough to be working with a first-class outfit, you hardly have time to drink Cokes. So, I'm going to bat for the boys once and for all. The next time a guy ambles up and asks, confidentially, when are we all going to raise some private hell, I'm going to wrap my vibes around him.

Weeds and pint bottles didn't originate in Harlem, either.

When you spend six months getting on and off trains, planes and buses, eating lousy food, and praying to St. Michael for no more bedbugs in the next three towns, and then, in between, knocking out your expected good stuff with the outfit, you don't give a prelude to a hangover a thought. And anybody out there who says I'm lying, I'll pay their plane fare to Los Angeles so I can knock their block off.

"Not Trying to Reform"

Bandleaders come in for a lot of bad butts, too, from unthinking wise guys. They get accused of everything and back again. Well, in the long run, stick-wavers and bandmen are all the same, and their habits aren't worlds apart. Call one of us a blackguard, and it hits the whole setup.

One thing stands out, words or no long words: musicians are like any other profession, and they're all working for the same old thing. Don't put the finger on us. Give us a break, too.

(Funny thing, too, I seldom ever hear a musician bother to set any of these wrong-thinking folks right!)

"I'm Boiling, Brother"

Nothing I dislike more than somebody trying to reform someone. That's not my point. I just want a lot of cats to really know, once and for all, that they're loud and wrong for hooraying around that musicians are a 100-percent bunch of hopheads and drunken bums. If a man wants to take a drink now and then, that's his right. But I don't see why the Lindbergh beacon has to be put on him if he happens to carry an 802 card in his vest.

Of course, I know some of the boys do over-sport every now and then, and it gets out. But that's natural. That happens in any business. When and if I do break out with a band of my own, I'm going to let every man go right on doing just what he was doing the month before. We're no bunch of adolescents, you know.

Now don't get me wrong, I'm not mad. I'm boiling, brother, I'm BOILING…

"We Were Suckers"

Without a Pot to Cook in We Went Stumbling Along Minus an Angel

by Woody Herman

We were suckers. We did it the hard way. We started out without backing, without an angel to fork over the checkbook when the going got tough; without even the proverbial pot to cook in. We started clean and damn near ended up that way, too.

Would we do it again and go through all the heartache and bad breaks that hit you between the eyes just when you need help desperately? The answer is—No! It's too tough a grind. Besides, bands aren't made that way anymore. Nowadays the road to the top begins when a leader finds himself a backer. The backer can be a millionaire cat on a swing kick or a man of "influence." The latter, according to the book, has a "commercial" in his pocket or some other equally solid "in." We had none of that.

Fished for Their Dinners

Now that we've landed in what is laughingly termed the "big time," we can look back and snicker. We had all the trimmings for a Horatio Alger classic. For instance, there was that time in Biloxi, Miss., when the boys yanked catfish out of the river for dinner. Or that time in Cleveland when we were stranded dead broke, without a job and little hope of getting one in the near future. That time we had to hock the instruments to get back to New York. Those were the good old days. Period.

But during the days when the going was tough, five guys had faith in my band. There were times when I thought they

Woody Herman.
(DownBeat Archive)

were the only five people in the world who liked us. They kept us from falling apart. I'd like to name them—Dave Dexter, Mike Nidorf, George Simon, Bernie Woods and Danny Richman.

Stuck by the Band

With the exception of Mike, the boys are all from the trade press. As critics or reporters or editors, they liked us when no one else did. What's more, they said so in print long enough and often enough until they persuaded others to listen to us—if only to contradict them. And plenty did!

Issue after issue the boys complained that we were underrated—that we had not been given a square deal. *DownBeat* appeared month after month and pointed out that we had a good band that was worth listening to but too few people appreciated it. That was a fact, too. Maybe we weren't the best band in the country, but we weren't the worst, either. The least

we deserved was three squares a day and steady work.

The boys in the press helped build our band almost as much as the men in the organization, because we're playing the same music now that we played when no one liked us. There's a special column in *DownBeat* called "Critics in the Doghouse." That's not for us. The critics took us OUT of the doghouse. We couldn't have built the band to its present successful peak without them.

Nidorf Had Patience

Along with the critics, there's Mike Nidorf. Mike always gave us that word of encouragement when the grind brought us down. Two years ago when things were at their worst, Mike pleaded with us to hold on. Sometimes I would go up to the office to see him alone. Other times Neal Reid would go with me. We'd ask him what was wrong and he invariably told us that there's nothing wrong—"It just takes time."

We have a cooperative band, of course, so that when Neal and I would come back to the boys and give them Mike's answer, it would only confuse them further. Finally, we'd have meetings that would take all night, and the next day we'd all troop up to Mike's office to have the matter straightened out.

That would be a scene. The receptionist would look with amazement at us as we came into the office—seven sad-faced musicians. She'd buzz Mike and say: "The Woody Herman corporation is here again."

Then through the telephone receiver, we'd hear Mike roar, "What? Again? Send in only one of them. I'll speak to Woody. Holy smoke, what an outfit!"

He wasn't kidding, either.

Oct. 15, 1942

"Gotta Feel the Blues to Play 'Em," Asserts T-Bone

by Dixon Gayer

CHICAGO—"The blues? Man, I didn't start playing the blues ever. That was in me before I was born, and I've been playing and living the blues ever since. That's the way you've gotta play them. You have to live those blues, and with us that's natural… it's born in us to live the blues."

T-Bone Walker, one of the most revered blues singers in the business today, who stops shows cold wherever he plays his blues for his people, told me that the other day when I asked him when he started playing the blues.

"I think that the first thing I can remember was my mother singing the blues as she would sit alone in the evenings in our place in Dallas where I was born. I can't remember the words to those blues, but she could sing you the blues right now like you never heard before. I used to listen to her singing there at night and I knew then that

the blues was in me, too. Everyone down there sang the blues. In fact, they still do. Go any place where there's a group of Negroes and you'll hear them singing blues you never heard of… wonderful blues."

Just Makes 'Em Up

"After I heard my mother play the blues and sing them, then I started in. I didn't know the words because there weren't any set words. I made them up as I went along. That's the way we do, you know. Right today I can make up blues faster than I can sing them. I could sing blues for you for a whole day and never repeat a verse. Anyhow, when I first started singing, I used to take an old Prince Albert tobacco can that I had and strum it like a guitar. There wasn't much tone, you know, but the bluesy beat was there and a kind of melancholy note, too, that I liked when I sang the blues.

"You know, there's only one blues, though. That's the regular 12-bar pattern, and then you interpret over that. Just write new words or improvise different and you've got a new blues. Now, you take a piece like 'St. Louis Blues.' That's a pretty tune and it has kind of a bluesy tone, but that's not the blues. You can't dress up the blues. The only blues is the kind that I sing and the kind that Jimmy Rushing sings and Basie plays. I'm not saying that 'St. Louis Blues' isn't fine music, you understand. But it just isn't blues. Now, 'Blues in the Night' is a lot better blues than 'St. Louis.' That's because the first part in 'Blues in the Night' is really blues on the right pattern. Of course, when they get to the bridge of the tune, it isn't blues anymore. It's pretty but it isn't blues. It's even more spiritual than it is bluesy, with that whistle cry in it. Blues is all by itself."

You Gotta Feel the Blues

"Blues is all in the way that you feel it. One person can feel it and another can't. Count Basie's band can play wonderful blues because he and all the band feel the blues. Duke Ellington, with all his fine musicians, can't play good band blues. Some of his men can, but the band can't. The way it is with bands is the same with singers. Louis Jordan, for instance, plays good blues and he sings them like they were originally sung, too. Take his 'Outskirts of Town,' that's really fine old blues. But then you listen to Dan Grissom sing 'Outskirts' and that isn't blues, with the same melody and everything. It takes a bluesy feeling and the old 12 bars. Grissom sings it sweet, but the

blues aren't sweet. You've gotta feel the blues to make them right.

"That kind of music really affects people, too. It's played from the heart and if the person listening understands the blues and is in the right mood, why, man, I've seen them just bust out and cry like a baby. In fact, there's a girl out in California in a hospital right now because I was playing a blues that affected her so much that she lost control of herself and started crying, and she stood up and fell over backwards and fell on another table and injured her spine. That's the way the blues affects some people."

Some Preach the Blues

"Of course the blues comes a lot from the church, too. The first time I ever heard a boogie-woogie piano was the first time I went to church. That was the Holy Ghost Church in Dallas. That boogie-woogie was a kind of a blues, I guess. Then the preachers used to preach in a bluesy tone sometimes. You even got the congregation yelling 'Amen' all the time when his preaching would stir them up… his preaching and his bluesy tone. In fact, that's the same tone that you have in this new tune 'Amen.' Lots of people think I'm going to be a preacher when I quit this business because of the way I sing the blues. They say it sounds like a sermon."

I asked T-Bone about the obscenity that has arisen in the verses of the blues.

"Well, the real blues doesn't have that so much. The first blues that I heard—the ones my mother used to sing—weren't like that. They were always homey things or things that were troubling her. She might sing about the dinner burning or anything like that. I guess that the obscenity was built up with commercial playing of the blues. Usually I don't think it's bad because a good blues singer is so sincere in the thing that he sings that he has a feeling and a meaning beyond the dirty words of his song. Some people just go to hear that kind of stuff, but anyone who understands blues goes beyond that to the real blues that's there. And people are beginning to really understand blues now; the whites are getting it, and I'm glad. They're missing something without the blues."

That's T-Bone's Blues

T-Bone has been playing blues commercially since his teens and, in that time, has written more than he can count. He recorded "T-Bone Blues" with Les Hite for Bluebird but has generally worked as a solo act. Capitol Records will soon release some new sides that he cut with Freddy Slack and some others on which he played guitar with the Slack band. He has refused offers to play guitar with a host of name bands in order to continue his blues work. He has a tremendous following, principally on the Pacific coast, where he has concentrated his work and where he lives with his wife and their child.

And, another thing. Let's get his name straight. It isn't Teabone, as it is so often spelled. It's T-Bone. The former indicates a delicate little chicken bone upon which you might nibble at a society tea. The latter is a good, he-man-sized steak that has a bone cross-section that looks like the letter "T." And that's the way T-Bone plays the blues and sings them... not dainty and delicate like a society tea, but strong and meaty like a good thick T-Bone steak. That's T-Bone's blues.

Jan. 1, 1947

Willie "The Lion" Smith. (©William P. Gottlieb, www.jazzphotos.com)

Lion Tracked to His Lair—or Willie Smith's Story

by Bill Gottlieb

NEW YORK—I first met the Lion in 1938, down on 52nd Street. Wingie Manone's band was working the spot and Willie Smith, the Lion, was playing during intermissions.

"Just to help out the owner," the Lion assured me. "We're old friends."

It was repugnant for the Lion to be anything but head man. I never heard the Lion say he worked for anyone. He was always helping a friend.

Once he went into Nick's in the Village "to help out Eddie Condon, who led a band there." The Lion lasted one set. It seems shortly after he began playing, the late Nick, as was his wont, sat at another keyboard for some two-part harmony. The boss was known as a good guy but a sad pianist. The gesture so humiliated the Lion that, after deliberately screwing up Nick by constantly changing keys (Nick played only in G), he disappeared. Two hours later, Condon got a call: "Eddie, this is the Lion. The Lion is home and he's quit."

Willie, in God-like third person, refers to himself as the Lion, even in his most private moments. When I recently tracked him to his 151st Street lair to learn what he's been doing with himself, I peeked at a note lying near his phone. "At three," he had written himself, "Bill will come to interview the Lion."

Ill for Past Year

On my visit I learned that the Lion hadn't been tossing his shaggy mane around the jazz spots for the past year because he had been seriously ill. High blood pressure, infected teeth and miscellaneous complications had cost him more than 25 pounds. Though he had regained half, the missing pounds still gave his suit a floppy, oversized look.

My first formal question concerned the origin of his name, the Lion. I've asked him this every time I've ever seen him. But he forgets and, each time, obliges anew— with a different explanation. This time, he said, simply, that he got the name from Jimmie Johnson (the great James P., who is now at Bellevue with a brain tumor).

"Jimmie gave me the title (he doesn't refer to it as a nickname) because of my spunk and enterprise. The Lion named him the Brute. Later, we gave Fats Waller the name Filthy. The three of us, the Lion, the Brute and Filthy, plus a guy called Lippy, used to run all over town playing piano."

Lion's Other Versions

Here are a couple of other sagas concerning his name that he's given me: "During the first war, I was one of the few to volunteer to go to the front and fire a French 75—and of those who did, few returned. I stayed at the front for 51 days without relief. I was known from that time on as Sgt. William H. Smith, the Lion."

And another time: "I wanted to become a rabbi. (He's part of a congregation of Jewish Negroes living in Harlem.) I got as far as becoming a cantor. Because of my devotion to Judaism, I was called 'the Lion of Judea,' later abbreviated to 'the Lion.'"

With this, he showed me his calling card. It was printed in Hebrew, except for the words "Willie 'the Lion' Smith, Greatest Piano Player in the World."

Writing Jewish Numbers

Willie, incidentally, is very religious. I first tried to arrange an appointment with him on what proved to be Yom Kippur eve. He was home when I called but, because of his orthodoxy, didn't pick up the phone. The Lion once played the Jewish theaters and got to know Paul Muni well. Right now, he occasionally collaborates with a Cantor Goldman on Yiddish compositions. His latest, the Lion tells me, is "Wus Geven Is Geven," which Willie translates as "Gone—Never to Return."

Willie Smith has always been more "the lion regal" than "the lion ferocious." His pomp and dignity are impregnable. I once watched him conduct his orchestra on a Potomac River boat cruise on which a riot had broken loose. The president of the Midwestern state society sponsoring the trip had his head opened by a flying bottle. Yet, as the bottles flew in the melee, the Lion stood poised on the podium, one arm bent across his vest in studied grace, the other deliberately raised to indicate the beat. His mien refused to take cognizance of the disrespectful fracas. He simply ducked bottles with a dignified stoop, straightened his crown and wrapped his ermine more closely about him.

Never Rolled in Dough

Though unquestionably one of the giants of the piano and a composer of ASCAP standing, the Lion has never hit big money. The preceptor and paragon of a distinguished line of keyboard men from Duke Ellington through Mel Powell, Willie has never had the commercial success of any of a dozen protégés.

Pianists as diverse in style as Walter Gross and Joe Bushkin swear by the Lion. Gross calls him "one of the real greats, a man who started so much of the things we have now, up in a class with Louis Armstrong."

Duke Ellington, when referring to his early struggles in New York, always talks reverently of tagging after the Lion.

Pianists Acknowledge Debt

In a book about famous pianists, *88 Keys to Fame*, written by *DownBeat*'s Sharon Pease, man after man—Joe Bushkin, Milt Raskin, Howard Smith—trace their beginnings to the Lion.

Mel Powell tells me of the Lion's role in taking him in hand and getting him on the right track. "He spent months on me. Never cared about getting paid for the lessons. Just an occasional small bottle of absinthe with a lump of sugar."

Newest of the Lion's charges is Jack O'Brien of Hartford, "A terrific piano player; but he doesn't want to leave Hartford."

It was the Lion who gave a big push to early Decca musical units when the Lion worked as a kind of "house" pianist. Milt Herth has told me he was floundering for a good idea when Willie passed his studio, suggested a trio with himself on piano and the late O'Neill Spencer on drums. That was the first Milt Herth Trio. The Kirby band got a big push as the cubs of The Lion and His Cubs, a Decca recording unit.

Willie was leader of the Jazz Hounds, who backed Maimie Smith in 1921, and led the rhythm section on Mezzrow's collectors' classics like "Apologies."

Got Fats His Break

Artie Shaw, Claude Thornhill, Mary Lou Williams and Shorty Sherock are a few of the others who were in the Lion's court at one time or other. It was Willie who got Fats Waller his break, too. Fats once came along with the Lion to some party attended by an NBC executive. The exec was struck by Fats' boisterous delivery and, after due apologies, told Willie that although he realized the Lion wanted a radio spot, he thought Fats was his man. "And would you try to see that Fats gets to rehearsals and broadcasts? I hear he's not too dependable."

"If that's the man you want," the Lion said, "that's the man you'll get." For months he saw to it that Fats toed the line.

Willie Smith, the Lion, finds solace for his lack of commercial success in a strange pair of forces: religion and astrology. The former gives him patience, faith and an acceptance of fate. "Why, the Lion might have been dead," he explains, referring to a recent illness.

Astrology Hound

Astrology gives Willie his optimistic outlook. "This will be the Lion's year," he guarantees. "The planet Mars has been in my house since 1918. It runs in 30-year cycles and is now on the way out. Nothing happens when Mars is around, especially when you were born under Saturn, the get-it-the-hard-way planet. Jupiter will be with me the next two years. That's the money planet. Look out, now, for the Lion."

There's a good chance Willie may be reading his stars right. A private piano recital in his third-floor apartment convinced me of what my memories of Willie, and my re-hearings of his old Commodore album of piano solos made me suspect, that the Lion, though still playing as he always has, is still more advanced harmonically and technically than most of the present big names. And with his characteristic delicacy, he's right in line with the move in swing toward softer and sweeter sounds.

Beauty in Works

The Lion's fragile music, so much in contrast with his bombastic personality, is startling in its melodic beauty. As lovely as the titles of the songs he writes in his playing on "Passionette," "Echo of Spring," "Fading Star," "Rippling Waters," "Morning Air" and the less euphonious "The Boy in the Boat."

His inventions on standards like "Tea for Two" are remarkable; though, sometimes, as in "The Devil and the Deep Blue Sea," his over-developments have him falling off the deep end. Willie can be robust, too, on his "Finger Buster" and especially when he's playing rhythm for a big band.

The Lion hopes to soon get set with a band at some location. Meantime, while regaining his health, he's been active leading pick-up bands at jazz concerts in Canada. A devoted Canadian fan named Dave Gerrand, who fortunately happens to be a promoter, has been keeping him in bookings.

Composing Again

The Lion has also returned to composing with renewed vigor. His newest composition, "A New Kind of Song," is being waxed by Walter Gross on Musicraft. Shorty Sherock has it, too.

His most active collaborator right now is Mrs. Rosalind Freeman, a New York City school teacher who respectfully addresses letters to: "Mr. William H. Smith, the Lion; Composer, Artist and Lecturer; 300 W. 151st Street." Their latest joint

effort is "One Little Tear Drop."

The Lion's most lush period came after the First World War in a speakeasy named Pod's and Jerry's, up on 133rd Street in Harlem. As Mohammedans go to Mecca, jazz musicians went to hear the Lion—Benny Goodman, the Dorseys (his favorite band, incidentally, has always been T.D.'s), Bix Biederbecke, Eddie Condon—the whole gang.

Show people came, too, like Talullah Bankhead. Writer Howard Deitz did his first musical comedy at a table in Pod's and Jerry's. He listened nightly to Willie, wrote a little and left a $5 tip.

He Left an Influence

Next to his pretty ideas, the thing that most drew the musicians was the Lion's mighty left paw. (The emphasis on the left hand was Willie's biggest contribution to his many disciples.) The Lion says he developed his left "because I was always using my right for drinking."

The Lion's drunks were protracted and chronic. "If all the Sixth Avenue subway conductors didn't know the Lion and where to dump him off, he never would have gotten home nights."

He stopped heavy drinking when, one night on a subway train, "The Lion cracked his eyes open wide enough to see some bum switching shoes on him!"

Willie is still immoderate about cigars, which he takes with him to bed, showers and work. He says he started smoking cigars at 12 and swears he sings better when one is in his mouth.

June 4, 1947

"Don't Blame Show Biz!"— Billie

Daily Press Taking Usual Rap at Trade with Holiday Case

by Michael Levin

BULLETIN—At press time, Billie Holiday was released on $1,000 bail by U.S.

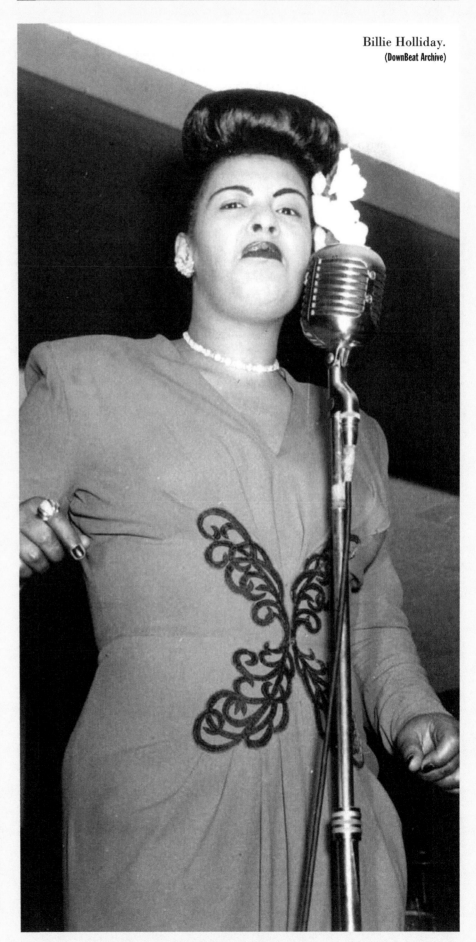

Billie Holliday.
(DownBeat Archive)

Commissioner Norman J. Griffith in Philadelphia to return for further hearing today, June 4. *DownBeat* learned from an unimpeachable source that in all probability charges would not be pressed against her, she would be allowed to finish out her present run at the Club 18 in New York and other work presently contracted, and then would probably go to Lexington, Ky., for medical treatment of some months' duration.

NEW YORK—"When you're writing, straighten them out about my people. Tell 'em I made my mistake but show people aren't all like that. Whatever I did wrong, nobody else but me was to blame—and show people aren't wrong."

That's what Billie Holiday said 10 days ago before arraignment in Philadelphia federal court on charges of possessing heroin in her Attucks hotel room there.

"I'm not offering an alibi, I'm not singing the blues. Things weren't easy. There were a lot of things I didn't have when I was a kid. My mother died 18 months ago, the only relative I had in the world. I guess I flipped, run through more than $100,000 since then.

"But I was trying to go straight. It just seems as though I have a jinx over me. I was with Count Basie when things were really rough, then I had a fight with John Hammond and got fired. I stuck with Artie Shaw through that Southern road tour; we got back to New York and they had to let me go. It's been one thing after another.

"This year I made a picture, my records were really selling, it was going to be my time."

Says She's Through

"Now it looks finished. I'm through—at least for a while. After all this is over, maybe I'll go to Europe, perhaps Paris, and try to start all over. Sure, I know about Gene Krupa—but don't forget he's white and I'm a Negro. I've got two strikes against me, and don't you forget it.

"I'm proud of those two strikes. I'm as good as a lot of people of all kinds—I'm proud I'm a Negro. And you know the funniest thing: the people that are going to be the hardest on me will be my own race. Look what they did to Billy Eckstine for three weeks in two of the big Negro papers—and you know that was a frame-up.

"You know, I just spent $3,000 of my own money taking the cure for three weeks. Maybe I was a fool to do it. It put me on record. They may have suspected before, but they were never sure of it. Now the federal people tell me they may send me away for another cure—and they never tell you how long it will be.

"Just when things were going to be so big and I was trying so hard to straighten myself out. Funny, isn't it?"

Tucker Not Involved

"Bobby Tucker? My piano player? Baby, the strongest thing he ever had in his life was a Camel cigarette. Believe me he is the most innocent thing that ever was. [Editor's Note: Tucker has been released due to lack of evidence.]

"You know what actually happened? I was coming back to the hotel and we noticed a lot of people around it, and my driver, Bill, said it looked like it had been raided. I told him he was crazy, but we parked by the side of the hotel, and he went up to see what was going on. He saw some agents and came running back to the car. Evidently he had one offense against him for something and they had told him he would lose his car if he did anything else. Well, he started the car like it was a jackrabbit, and we tore by a couple of policemen on the sidewalk.

"I heard a couple of sounds like shots, and I asked him and he said yes, they were shots but that he was afraid to stop, he didn't know what was going on. So we came back to New York City.

"Don't believe that business about our trying to run down an agent. Were we driving over the sidewalk? You know another funny thing: one of those officers mixed up in the case is Lt. Anderson, Marian Anderson's nephew."

Husband Held

"They're sitting on my Joe Guy downtown right now. They're holding him on $3,000 bail, claim he was mixed up with some of the stuff they found there. Joe's been a headstrong boy. When I first knew him, he was just playing horn for Lucky Millinder. I gave him a lot of clothes and a band. Guess it turned his head, he ran through $35,000 with the band and nothing ever happened.

"But don't let anyone tell you it's his fault. My manager Joe Glaser hates him, says he's responsible for everything that has happened to me. Don't you believe it. I'm grown-up. I knew what I was doing. Joe may have done things he shouldn't, but I did them of my own accord, too. And I never tried to influence anybody else or do

anything to hurt anyone. Joe didn't make it any easier for me at times—but then I haven't been an easy gal, either.

"I've made lots of enemies, too. Singing that 'Strange Fruit' hasn't helped any, you know. I was doing it at the Earle (Philadelphia) 'til they made me stop. Tonight they're already talking about me. When I did 'The Man I Love' (at NYC's Club 18), I heard some woman say, 'Hear he's in the jug downtown.'"

Won't Divulge Info

"Jimmy Asendio? They grabbed him for bringing some stuff wrapped in a stocking he said was mine. Actually what they want me and Joe to do is tell them where—and that is something I would never be sure about. I'm just not cut out for that.

"Of course my singing was never better because of it. I was unhappy and a Negro and a lot of other things. But that was still no excuse—you don't have to tell me that. It's just wrong somehow that it happened when I was trying to turn around.

"I guess *DownBeat* is going to chew me to shreds like the papers are doing. Ned Williams has known me ever since I was a little girl—'bout as old as that 14-year-old picture of me they used in the papers. My eyebrows were all off 'cause I tried to shape 'em and took half of one off by mistake. I never won the *DownBeat* poll. Guess I never will now.

"Don't forget, though. I just want to be straight with people, not have their sympathy. And remember, nobody else in show business has made as many mistakes as me."

Sept. 24, 1947

Thelonious Monk—Genius of Bop
Elusive Pianist Finally Caught in an Interview
by Bill Gottlieb

NEW YORK—I have interviewed Thelonious Sphere Monk.

It's not like having seen Pinetop spit blood or delivering the message to Garcia. But, on the other hand, it's at least equal to a scoop on the true identity of Benny Benzedrine or on who killed Cock Robin.

Thelonious, the George Washington of bebop, is one elusive gent. There's been much talk about him—about his pioneering role at Minton's, where bebop began; about his fantastic musical imagination; about his fine piano playing. But few have ever seen him; except for people like Diz and Mary Lou, I didn't know anyone else who had seen very much of him, either.

Come to think of it, I had seen him once, at the club where Dizzy's band was working some time ago. Even without his music, which was wonderful, you could recognize his cult from his bebop uniform: goatee, beret and heavy shell glasses, only his were done half in gold.

I listened in fascination until he got up from the keyboard. "And who," I finally inquired, "was that bundle of bop?"

"Why, Thelonious Monk."

But by that time the quarry had disappeared.

Meeting Is Arranged

Finally, through the good offices of Mary Lou Williams, I was arranged with Thelonious. In order to take some pictures in the right setting, we went up to Minton's Playhouse at 208 W. 118th St.

In the taxi, on the way up, Thelonious spoke with singular modesty. He wouldn't go on record as insisting HE started bebop; but, as the story books have long since related, he admitted he was at least one of the originators. Yes, he continued, verifying the oft-told tale, it all began up at Minton's in early 1941.

Orchestra leader Teddy Hill had broken up his great orchestra because of problems brought on by the draft, poor transportation facilities and the like. He had bought into the tavern owned by Morris Milton (who had been the first colored delegate to the New York local of the musicians' union). Teddy eventually took over active management and instituted a policy of good music.

Guys in Band

As a starter, Teddy called together some of the boys who had played in his last band, including John Birks Gillespie (by then with Calloway) and Joe Guy, trumpets; and Kenny Clarke, drums. There was also Nick Fenton on bass. Monday night was the big night at Minton's. Bandleaders like Goodman, Dorsey and Johnny Long would come in to visit. And practically every jazz man of merit in town sat in at one time or other. Charlie Parker, who had come to New York with the Jay McShann ork, appeared often and became a regular at Minton's.

"Bebop wasn't developed in any deliberate way," Thelonious continued. "For my part, I'll say it was just the style of music I happened to play. We all contributed ideas, the men you know plus a fellow called Vic Couslen, who had been with Parker and Al Hibbler in the McShann band. Vic had a lot to do with our way of phrasing."

Piano Focal Point

"If my own work had more importance than any others, it's because the piano is the key instrument in music. I think all styles are built around piano developments. The piano lays the chord foundation and the rhythm foundation, too. Along with bass and piano, I was always at the spot, and could keep working on the music. The rest, like Diz and Charlie, came in only from time to time, at first."

By the time we'd gotten that far, we had arrived at Minton's, where Thelonious headed right for the piano. Roy Eldridge, Teddy Hill and Howard McGhee dropped around. McGhee, fascinated, got Thelonious to dream up some trumpet passages and then conned Thelonious into writing them down on some score sheets that happened to be in the club.

Hill Gives Credit

Teddy Hill began to talk. Looking at Thelonious Monk, he said:

"There, my good man, is the guy who deserves the most credit for starting bebop. Though he won't admit it, I think he feels he got a bum break in not getting some of the glory that went to others. Rather than go out now and have people think he's just an imitator, Thelonious is thinking up new things. I believe he hopes one day to come out with something as far ahead of bop as bop is ahead of the music that went before it.

"He's so absorbed in his task, he's become almost mysterious. Maybe he's on the way to meet you. An idea comes to him. He begins to work on it. Mop! Two days go by and he's still at it. He's forgotten all about you and everything else but that idea."

While he was at it, Teddy told me about Diz, who worked in his band follow-

Thelonious Monk.
(Joe Alper)

ing Roy Eldridge. Right off, John Birks G. showed up at rehearsal and began to play in an overcoat, hat and gloves! For a while everyone was set against this wild maniac. Teddy nicknamed him Dizzy.

Dizzy Like a Fox

"But he was Dizzy like a fox," Hill said. "When I took my band to Europe, some of the guys threatened not to go if the frantic one went, too. But it developed that youthful Dizzy, with all his eccentricities and practical jokes, was the most stable man of the group. He had unusually clean habits and was able to save so much money that he encouraged the others to borrow from him so that he'd have an income in case things got rough in the States!"

Stan Kenton.
(DownBeat Archive)

Nov. 19, 1947

"World Needs Strong Music!" Cries Kenton, "So Let 'Em Have It!"

by Ted Hallock

SEATTLE—At 7 a.m. on a bright April 19, 1947, morning, Stanley Newcomb Kenton came within one psychiatrist of becoming a sawmill worker! Kenton, interviewed before a one-nighter in Eugene, Ore., on

Oct. 17, tells it this way:

"I was three days out of the Tuscaloosa hospital, driving to L.A., when I hit a small town in Arkansas early in the morning.

"Some guys were sawing and hauling wood. It looked nice. About like the nicest job I could have had then. Whereupon I applied for work, and got turned down. I guess they weren't in the market for long collars."

Kenton, now fit, on what he refuses to use in his ork, admits having been temporarily out of his head—worried at the time about suits from ballroom ops indignant over dates cancelled because of the band's sudden demise. But he's OK now, and leading a gangbusters outfit.

Lambasts Traditions

Stan very readily devoted 45 minutes to this scribe, during which verbally explosive period he lambasted almost every tradition, and leader, in the business.

"Public likes and dislikes have nothing to do with the progress of the business,"

Kenton said. "Bands, with guts, will play what they like; a tonal picture of the American way of life… everyday sounds put to music. In two years no one will remember what 'Home on the Range' was like."

Kenton revealed plans for a forthcoming performance with the Detroit Symphony, in which his band will play the jazz movement off a recently completed work by a new composer. The Kenton crew "will work on the same stand." The White House, Stan also disclosed, has contacted Carlos Gastel (Kenton's manager) for a Presidential "command performance," date unknown. To this Kenton tacked, "I hope they know what they're getting!"

Says Band Isn't "New"

Thrilled by the abilities of replacement sidemen, and the band in general, Stan preferred not to use the expression "new band" in discussing his plans, just as he abhorred references to his music as "jazz," himself using the descriptive phrase "progressive jazz."

Milt Bernhardt has been given the ex-Winding, or "mood," chair in the trombone section, with Eddie Bert subbing for Layton—the "mad" seat, in Kenton's words. Bert, incidentally, looks like a mouse and plays like a lion. New lead alto George Weidler plays little take-off, unlike his predecessor, Mussulli. Also-new Art Pepper does all the solo work.

Bob Cooper, who slid leisurely but not with a great degree of certainty (in this writer's opinion) into Vido's chair, may leave the band soon, with wife, June Christy.

"No," Stanley said emphatically, "I will not take Musso back, under any circumstances." To which the leader added several unprintable but otherwise choice quotes.

Good Album Coming

Kenton waxed profuse and profound over his two to-be-released Capitol albums, *Concert in Progressive Jazz* and *Prologue Suite*, both penned by the leader. The former will contain one side featuring guitarist Laurindo Almeida, who otherwise does little with the band save contribute four beats per bar to the somewhat odd rhythm section. Also in the Concerto waxings will be an "Elegy for Alto," featuring Weidler, not Pepper. A Eugene artist, Don Shirley, has been given tentative carte blanche to proceed with ideas for the albums' covers.

Also given more than an "it may happen" go-ahead signal was Eugenian Bob Ramsey, whose new foot-pedal so excited drummer Shelly Manne and Kenton that the leader plans to endorse some nationally. It is rumored that the pedal's construction is definitely simpler than that of the atom bomb.

Kenton did not apologize for having let the Pastels go. "So few, if any, vocal groups today can even sing jazz phrasing. The Mel-Tones are one such unit. We could have had them a while ago, but avoided the inevitable label hassle that would have ensued."

Praises Herman Herd

Stan was happy that Woody Herman's reorganization plans were succeeding. "His music is a definite force. While James and Beneke always fight each other, our type of orchestra helps each other—maintaining interest in music.

"There's no hope for so-called sweet bands. Two years will tell the tale. People are tired of the old 'drone' chords. Dissonances are required. I think the greatest contemporary composer is Stravinsky, with Milhaud a close second. The generation that makes my band known will make Stravinsky's music as popular as Beethoven's.

"It's hard to accept that theory today, but the Lord help the Mickey bands tomorrow. I am not, however, influenced by Stravinsky, nor by Dizzy, as many think. I like to feel that the band isn't influenced by anybody or anything, except perhaps sound."

Music Typed to Sounds

"My music is typed to sounds—not necessarily to emotion. Though I believe the world needs psychiatry for its present neurosis, I don't believe my, or anybody's music, is a part of that treatment. The world needs stronger music. Before the war they yelled, 'Things are too upset, no jazz.' During the war, they screamed, 'The time is for patriotism, not jazz,' and now, after the war is over, they insist, 'It's so peaceful in the country, stifle the jazz.'

"Some of the wise boys who say my music is loud, blatant and that's all should see the faces of kids who have driven a hundred miles, through the snow, to see the band—to stand in front of the stand in ecstasy all their own."

To give credence to his beliefs, Kenton is planning a Modern Music Week, during which jocks and live bands will feature no music written earlier than 30 years ago.

It all sounds like a surrealist's dream. But that's what the man said. And he meant it, too!

Pres Talks About Himself, Copycats

by Pat Harris

CHICAGO—"The trouble with most musicians today is that they are copycats. Of course, you have to start playing like someone else. You have a model, or a teacher, and you learn all that he can show you. But then you start playing for yourself. Show them that you're an individual. And I can count those who are doing that today on the fingers of one hand."

It was the Pres talking. Lester Young, a pioneer of the "new" jazz, whose friends find themselves in the peculiar position of trying to persuade him to tolerate the majority of musicians who can't meet his standards, and, on the other hand, getting others to try and understand the Pres.

"Lester Young has been so misunderstood, underestimated, and generally shoved around," one of them said, "that he almost was pushed out of the field of top active jazz musicians." The tendency is to relegate him to the position of a historical "influence."

Not Ready to Settle

"I'm not ready to settle down yet," Lester said. "When I do, I'll stay in California. I have a house there, and I like the weather. My mother, brother and sister live there, too. I like traveling, though. There's always something new."

The tenor saxist was almost something new himself in Chicago, his four weeks at the Blue Note opposite Sarah Vaughan being the first time in several years that the town really had a chance to hear him.

Rarer than hearing Lester play, however, is getting him to talk about himself. He has the well-deserved reputation of being comfortably shy, and would be content to gaze silently at his pigeon-turned feet rather than talk. Shy about everything except playing that horn.

"My father, William H. Young, was a

carnival musician. He could play all the instruments, although he liked the trumpet best. He taught voice, too, and kept up traveling with carnival minstrel shows and teaching music until he died in the '40s.

"I was born in New Orleans, Aug. 27, 1909. My mother, Lizetta Grey, lives in Los Angeles now. I stayed in New Orleans until I was 10, when my sister Irma, brother Lee and I went to live with my father. He took us to Minneapolis, where we went to school. During the carnival season we all traveled with the minstrel show through Kansas, Nebraska, South Dakota, all through there."

Plays Drums

"I played drums from the time I was 10 to about 13. Quit them because I got tired of packing them up. I'd take a look at the girls after the show, and before I'd get the drums packed, they'd all be gone.

"For a good five or six years after that [Editor's Note: Don't try to make Lester's time estimates jibe. They don't.] I played the alto, and then the baritone when I joined Art Bronson's band.

"Ran away from my father when I was about 18. We were in Salina, Kansas, and he had a string of dates down through Texas and the South. I told him how it would be down there, and that we could have some fine jobs back through Nebraska, Kansas and Iowa, but he didn't have eyes for that. He was set to go.

"Art Bronson and his Bostonians. Played with them two or three or four years. He lives in Denver now, and all the men in the band have got families, like to stay close to home—all except me. Anyway, I was playing the baritone and it was weighing me down.

"I'm real lazy, you know. So when the tenor man left, I took over his instrument. But we stuck to Nebraska and North Dakota. Only time I went through the South was with Basie, and it was different then.

"I worked at the Nest club in Minneapolis when I first heard Basie's band. Band at the Nest wasn't anyone's, really; they gave it to different people every week.

"Used to hear the Basie band all the time on the radio and figured they needed a tenor player. They were at the Reno club in Kansas City. It was crazy, the whole band was gone, but just this tenor player. I figured it was about time, so I sent Basie a telegram.

"He had heard me before. We used to go back and forth between Minneapolis and Kansas City. When I joined the band

Lester Young.
(DownBeat Archive)

he had three brass, three reeds, and three rhythm. I'd sit up all night and wait to go to work.

"But Basie was like school. I used to fall asleep in school, because I had my lesson, and there was nothing else to do. The teacher would be teaching those who hadn't studied at home, but I had to, so I'd go to sleep. Then the teacher would go home and tell my mother. So I put that down.

"In Basie's band, there always would be someone who didn't know his part. Seems to me that if a musician can't read, he should say so, and then you help him. Or you give him his part before. But Basie wouldn't. I used to talk to him about it, but he had no eyes for it. You had to sit there and play it over and over and over again. Just sit in that chair."

And Then Henderson

"I joined Fletcher Henderson in Detroit in 1934. Basie was in Little Rock then, and Henderson offered me more money. Basie said I could go.

"Was with Henderson only about six months. The band wasn't working very much. Was with Andy Kirk for six months about that time, too. Kirk was wonderful to work for. Then back to Basie until 1944 and the Army.

"What else happened during that time? You mean like the Condon book? No, it was all music; that's all there was."

Sept. 9, 1949

"No Bop Roots in Jazz" — Parker

*by Michael Levin
and John S. Wilson*

NEW YORK—"Bop is no love-child of jazz," says Charlie Parker. The creator of bop, in a series of interviews that took more than two weeks, told us he felt that "bop is something entirely separate and apart" from the older tradition; that it drew little from jazz, has no roots in it. The chubby little alto man, who has made himself an international music name in the last five years, added that bop, for the most part, had to be played by small bands.

"Gillespie's playing has changed from being stuck in front of a big band. Anybody's does. He's a fine musician. The leopard coats and the wild hats are just another part of the managers' routines to make him box office. The same thing happened a couple of years ago when they stuck his name on some tunes of mine to give him a better commercial reputation."

Asked to define bop, after several evenings of arguing, Charlie still was not precise in his definition.

"It's just music," he said. "It's trying to play clean and looking for the pretty notes."

Pushed further, he said that a distinctive feature of bop is its strong feeling for beat.

"The beat in a bop band is with the music, against it, behind it," Charlie said. "It pushes it. It helps it. Help is the big thing. It has no continuity of beat, no steady chug-chug. Jazz has, and that's why bop is more flexible."

He admits the music eventually may be atonal. Parker himself is a devout admirer of Paul Hindemith, the German neo-classicist. He raves about his Kammermusik and Sonata for Viola and Cello. He insists, however, that bop is not moving in the same direction as modern classical. He feels that it will be more flexible, more emotional, more colorful.

He reiterates constantly that bop is only just beginning to form as a school, that it can barely label its present trends, much less make prognostications about the future.

The closest Parker will come to an exact, technical description of what may happen is to say that he would like to emulate the precise, complex harmonic structures of Hindemith, but with an emotional coloring and dynamic shading that he feels modern classical lacks.

Parker's indifference to the revered jazz tradition certainly will leave some of his own devotees in a state of surprise. But, actually, he himself has no roots in traditional jazz. During the few years he worked with traditional jazzmen he wandered like a lost soul. In his formative years, he never heard any of the music that is traditionally supposed to inspire young jazzists—no Louis, no Bix, no Hawk, no Benny, no nothing. His first musical idol, the musician who so moved and inspired him that he went out and bought his first saxophone at the age of 11, was Rudy Vallee.

Tossed into the jazz world of the mid-'30s with this kind of background, he had no familiar ground on which to stand. For three years he fumbled unhappily until he suddenly stumbled on the music that appealed to him, which had meaning to him. For Charlie insists, "Music is your own experience, your thoughts, your wisdom. If you don't live it, it won't come out of your horn."

Charlie's horn first came alive in a chili house on Seventh Avenue between 139th Street and 140th Street in December 1939. He was jamming there with a guitarist named Biddy Fleet. At the time, Charlie says, he was bored with the stereotyped changes being used then.

"I kept thinking there's bound to be something else," he recalls. "I could hear it sometimes, but I couldn't play it."

Working over "Cherokee" with Fleet, Charlie suddenly found that by using higher intervals of a chord as a melody line and backing them with appropriately related changes, he could play this thing he had been "hearing." Fleet picked it up behind him and bop was born.

Or, at least, it is reasonable to assume that this was the birth of bop. All available facts indicate this is true. But Parker, an unassuming character who carries self-effacement to fantastic lengths, will not say this in so many words. The closest Charlie will come to such a statement is, "I'm accused of having been one of the pioneers."

But inescapable facts pin him down. He says he always has tried to play in more or less the same way he does now. His earliest records, which were cut with Jay McShann in 1940 (on Decca), back him up on this. They reveal a style that is rudimentary compared to his present work, but definitely along the same lines: light, vibratoless tone; running phrases, perkily turned; complex rhythmic and harmonic structures.

From 1939 to 1942, Charlie worked on his discovery. He admits he thought he was playing differently from other jazzmen during this period. Indicative of his queasiness about saying who did what before with which to whom is his answer to our query: Did Dizzy also play differently from the rest during the same period?

"I don't think so," Charlie replied. Then, after a moment, he added, "I don't know. He could have been. Quote me as saying, 'Yeah.'"

Dizzy himself has said that he wasn't aware of playing bop changes before 1942. Whether he'll admit it or not, the cal-

endar shows that Charlie inaugurated what has come to be known as bop. In some circles he is considered to be the only legitimate boppist.

"There's only one man who really plays bop," one New York reed musician said recently. "That's Charlie Parker. All the others who say they're playing bop are only trying to imitate him."

Despite his unwillingness to put anybody down, a slight note of irritation creeps into Charlie's usual bland mien when he considers the things that have been done by others in an attempt to give his music a flamboyant, commercial appeal. The fact that Dizzy Gillespie's extroversion led the commercially minded to his door irks Charlie in more ways than one. As part of Dizzy's buildup, he was forced to add his name to several of Charlie's numbers, among them "Anthropology," "Confirmation" and "Shaw Nuff." Dizzy had nothing to do with any of them, according to Charlie.

As for the accompanying gimmicks that, to many people, represent bop, Charlie views them with a cynical eye.

"Some guys said, 'Here's bop,'" he explains. "Wham! They said, 'Here's something we can make money on.' Wham! 'Here's a comedian.' Wham! 'Here's a guy who talks funny talk.'" Charlie shakes his head sadly.

Charlie himself has stayed away from a big band because the proper place for bop, he feels, is a small group. Big bands tend to get over-scored, he says, and bop goes out the window. The only big band that managed to play bop in 1944, in Charlie's estimation, was Billy Eckstine's. Dizzy's present band, he says, plays bop, [but it] could be better with more settling down and less personnel shifting.

"That big band is a bad thing for Diz," he says. "A big band slows anybody down because you don't get a chance to play enough. Diz has an awful lot of ideas when he wants to, but if he stays with the big band he'll forget everything he ever played. He isn't repeating notes yet, but he is repeating patterns."

The only possibility for a big band, he feels, is to get really big, practically on a symphonic scale with loads of strings.

"This has more chance than the standard jazz instrumentation," he says. "You can pull away some of the harshness with the strings and get a variety of coloration."

Born in Kansas City, Kan., in 1921, to a family that was in relatively comfortable circumstances at the time, Charlie moved

Charlie Parker and
Dizzy Gillespie. (Ted Williams)

with his parents to Olive Street, in Kansas City, Mo., when he was seven. There were no musicians in his family, but Charlie got into his high school band playing baritone horn and clarinet. He had a special fondness for the baritone horn because it helped him win medals awarded to outstanding musicians in the band. Not that he played the horn particularly well, but it was loud and boisterous and dominated the band so much the judges scarcely ignore it.

In 1931, Charlie discovered jazz, heavily disguised as Rudy Vallee. So that he could emulate Rudy, his mother bought him an alto for $45. Charlie settled on the alto because he felt the C melody wasn't stylish and a tenor didn't look good. His interest in the alto was short-lived, however, for a sax-playing friend in high school borrowed it and kept it for two years. Charlie forgot all about it until he was out of school and needed it to earn a living.

It was back in his school days, he says, that his name started to go through a series

of mutations that finally resulted in Bird. As Charlie reconstructs it, it went from Charlie to Yarlie to Yarl to Yard to Yard-bird to Bird.

After his brief exhilaration over Vallee, Charlie heard no music that interested him, outside of boogie-woogie records, until he quit high school in 1935 and went out to make a living with his alto horn at the age of 14. As has been mentioned, he was under the influence of none of the jazz greats. He had never heard them. He was influenced only by the necessity of making a living, and he chose music because it seemed glamorous, looked easy and there was nothing else around.

This primary lack of influence continued as the years went by. The sax men he listened to and admired—Herschel Evans, Johnny Hodges, Willie Smith, Ben Webster, Don Byas, Budd Johnson—all played with a pronounced vibrato, but no semblance of a vibrato ever crept into Charlie's style.

"I never cared for vibrato," he says,

"because they used to get a chin vibrato in Kansas City (opposed to the hand vibrato popular with white bands) and I didn't like it. I don't think I'll ever use vibrato."

"The only reed man on Charlie's list of favorites who approached the Bird's vibrato-less style was Lester Young.

"I was crazy about Lester," he says. "He played so clean and beautiful. But I wasn't influenced by Lester. Our ideas ran on differently."

When Charlie first ventured onto the music scene in Kansas City, the joints were running full blast from 9 p.m. to 5 a.m. Usual pay was $1.25 a night, although somebody special could command $1.50. There were about 15 bands in town, with Pete Johnson's crew at the Sunset cafe one of the most popular. Harlan Leonard was in town then, along with George Lee's and Bus Mosten's little bands. Lester Young, Herschel Evans, and Eddie Barefield were playing around. Top local pianists were Roselle Claxton, Mary Lou Williams, Edith Williams and Basie.

Charlie spent several months picking up on his alto. On Thanksgiving night, 1935, he got his first chance to play for pay when he was rounded up with a small group of others to do a gig in Eldon, Mo. He was offered $7 for the night, not because he was any good but because practically every musician in Kansas City was working that night and the guy who hired him was going crazy trying to find men to fill the date. Driving to Eldon, they had a crackup. Two of the men were killed, and Charlie got out of it with three broken ribs and a broken horn. The man who had hired him paid his medical expenses and bought him a new horn.

In February 1936, Charlie started out for Eldon again with another group, and this time he made it. The rest of the combo was a shade older than Charlie. J.K. William, the bass player, was 72. The rest were in their 30s and 40s. Charlie was 15. But, as the baby of the group, he got a lot of attention and advice. He had taken guitar, piano and sax books with him and set about learning to read seriously. The pianist, Carrie Powell, played for him and taught him simple major, minor, seventh and diminished chords.

By the end of the Eldon job, in April, he could read fairly well but not quickly. He went back to Kansas City and got his first club job at 18th and Lydia at either the Panama or the Florida Blossom (he can't remember which). It paid him 75 cents a night.

"The main idea of the job," Charlie recalls, "was to be there and hold a note."

Soon after this, he tried jamming for the first time at High Hat, at 22nd and Vine. He knew a little of "Lazy River" and "Honeysuckle Rose" and played what he could. He didn't find it difficult to hear the changes because the numbers were easy and the reedmen set a riff only for the brass, never behind a reedman. No two horns jammed at the same time.

"I was doing all right until I tried doing some double tempo on 'Body and Soul,' Charlie says. "Everybody fell out laughing. I went home and cried and didn't play again for three months."

In 1937 he joined Jay McShann's band, but left after two weeks. Later he was arrested for refusing to pay a cab fare. His mother, who didn't approve of his conduct then, wouldn't help him out, and he was jugged for 22 days. When he got out, he left his saxophone behind and bummed his way to New York.

For three months he washed dishes in Jimmy's Chicken Shack in Harlem. This was at the time Art Tatum was spellbinding late-hour Shack habitues. Charlie got $9 a week and meals. Then he quit and bummed around a while, sleeping where he could.

"I didn't have any trouble with cops," he recalls. "I was lucky. I guess it was because I looked so young." He was 17.

After he had been in New York for eight months, some guys at a jam session bought him a horn. With it he got a job in Kew Gardens that lasted for four months, even though he hadn't touched a horn in one and a half years. Then he moved into Monroe's Uptown House with Ebenezer Paul on drums, Dave Riddick on trumpet, and two or three other guys. There was no scale at Monroe's. Sometimes Charlie got 40 or 50 cents a night. If business was good, he might get up to $6.

"Nobody paid me much mind then except Bobby Moore, one of Count Basie's trumpet players," Charlie says. "He liked me. Everybody else was trying to get me to sound like Benny Carter."

Around this time, the middle of 1939, he heard some Bach and Beethoven for the first time. He was impressed with Bach's patterns.

"I found out that what the guys were jamming then already had been put down and, in most cases, a lot better."

At the end of 1939, shortly after his chili house session with Biddy Fleet, he

went to Annapolis, Md., to play a hotel job with Banjo Burney. Then his father died and he went back to Kansas City, where he rejoined McShann.

Charlie cut his first records in Dallas, in the summer of 1940, with McShann. His first sides were "Confessin'," "Hootie Blues" (which he wrote), "Swingmatism" and "Vine Street Boogie."

His solos with McShann are on "Hootie," "Swingmatism," "Sepian Bounce," "Lonely Boy Blues" and "Jumpin' Boy Blues." He tried doing a little arranging then but he didn't know much about it.

"I used to end up with the reeds blowin' above the trumpets," he explains.

The McShann band went from Texas to the Carolinas to Chicago, back to Kansas City headed east through Indiana and then to New York and the Savoy. Charlie drove the instrument truck all the way from Kansas City. While they were at the Savoy, Charlie doubled into Monroe's, where he played with Allen Terry, piano; George Treadwell (Sarah Vaughan's husband) and Victor Coulsen, trumpets; Ebenezer Paul, bass; and Mole, drums.

He left McShann at the end of 1941 and joined Earl Hines in New York early in 1942. This was the Hines band that also had Dizzy, Billy Eckstine and Sarah Vaughan. Charlie had known Dizzy vaguely before this, and it was about this time they both started getting into the sessions at Minton's.

It was on this visit to New York, in late 1942 after he had worked out his basic approach to complex harmony, that Charlie heard Stravinsky for the first time when Ziggy Kelly played Firebird for him.

Charlie played tenor for the next 10 months he was with Hines. He started out getting more money than he had ever seen before—$105 a week. With McShann he had gotten $55 to $60. But the Bird was sent on an Army camp tour in a Pabst Blue Ribbon Salute package put together by Ralph Cooper, and their salaries started going down. This, with ongoing hassles, eventually broke up the band. Charlie dropped out in Washington, in 1943, and joined with Charles Thompson ("Robbins Nest" composer) at the Chrystal Caverns.

Later he came back to New York and cut his first sides since the McShann discs—the Tiny Grimes "Red Cross" and "Romance Without Finance" session for Savoy. Charlie worked off and on around New York during 1943 and 1944. In the spring of 1944 he was playing the Spotlite on 52nd Street, managed by Clark Monroe

of Monroe's and on the site of the old Famous Door, when Doris Sydnor, the hatcheck girl there, raised an interested eye at him. Charlie, according to Doris, didn't notice it.

"He ignored me very coldly," she reports.

But Doris was a persistent girl. She didn't even know what instrument Charlie played when she first met him, but she stacked records by the Bird and Lester Young on her phonograph and listened and listened until she caught on to what they were doing. She and Charlie were married on Nov. 18, 1945, in New York.

Right after his wedding, Charlie went out to the coast with Dizzy to play at Billy Berg's. He stayed there after the Berg's date was finished.

On the coast he started cutting sides for Ross Russell's Dial label until his physical breakdown in August 1946 landed him in a hospital. His opinion of these Dial discs is low.

"'Bird Lore' and 'Lover Man' should be stomped into the ground," he says. "I made them the day before I went into the hospital. I had to drink a quart of whiskey to make the date."

Charlie stayed in the hospital until January 1947. Russell, who had hired a psychiatrist and a lawyer, got him released then into his custody and staged a benefit for the Bird, which produced some cash and two plane tickets back east.

But Parker is bitter about Russell's role in this. He says that Charlie Emge of *DownBeat* was equally helpful, that Russell refused to sign the papers releasing him unless he, Parker, renewed his contract with Dial. Later, Parker claims, he found that he had needed no outside help to get out.

When he originally signed with Russell, Charlie was already under contract to Herman Lubinsky, of Savoy records. Before leaving New York, he had signed with Lubinsky to cut some 30 sides. Four of these were done before he went to the coast—"Ko-Ko," "Billie's Bounce," "Now's the Time" and "Anthropology." Lubinsky bought all four tunes from Charlie for $50 apiece.

Today Charlie has come full cycle. As he did in 1939, when he kicked off bop in the Seventh Avenue chili house, he's beginning to think there's bound to be something more. He's hearing things again, things that he can't play yet. Just what these new things are, Charlie isn't sure yet. But from the direction of his present musical interests—Hindemith, etc.—it seems likely he's heading toward atonality. Charlie protests when he is mentioned in the same sentence with Hindemith, but, despite their vastly different starting points, he admits he might be working toward the same end.

This doesn't mean Charlie is through with bop. He thinks bop still is far from perfection and looks on any further steps he may take as further developments of bop.

"They teach you there's a boundary line to music," he says, "but, man, there's no boundary line to art."

For the future, he'd like to go to the Academy of Music in Paris for a couple of years, then relax for a while and then write. The things he writes all will be concentrated toward one point: warmth. While he's writing, he also wants to play experimentally with small groups. Ideally, he'd like to spend six months to a year in France and six months here.

"You've got to do it that way," he explains. "You've got to be here for the commercial things and in France for relaxing facilities."

Relaxation is something Charlie constantly has missed. Lack of relaxation, he thinks, has spoiled most of the records he has made. To hear him tell it, he has never cut a good side. Some of the things he did on the Continental label he considers more relaxed than the rest. But every record he has made could stand improvement, he says. We tried to pin him down, to get him to name a few sides that were at least better than the rest.

"Suppose a guy came up to us," we said, "and said, 'I've got four bucks and I want to buy three Charlie Parker records. What'll I buy?' What should we tell him?"

Charlie laughed.

"Tell him to keep his money," he said.

Coda

We both were tremendously impressed by the cogency and clarity of Parker's thinking about music. Musicians, classical or jazz, are traditionally unanalytical about the things they create. Parker, however, has a definite idea of where he wants to go and what he wants to do, though he is properly vague as to the results.

His insistent vagueness as to exactly what bop is to him is no pose. Parker is a musician fighting for his proper mode of expression, a vastly talented man who hasn't the schooling yet to expand as completely and properly as his musical instincts would have him do.

If we understand his crypticisms correctly, Parker feels that traditional jazz has strongly lacked variety and economy of form as well as the wealth of discipline and control of ideas to be found in modern formalistic music. On the other hand, he feels the symphonic score of today lacks drive (contained, perhaps, in his concept of dynamics) and warmth, and that his group of musicians will help inject these aspects traditional to the jazz scene.

Parker's insistence that bop has no connection with jazz is interesting as an example of a younger musician bursting through forms that he finds constricting and that he feels have outlived their usefulness. We suspect his position might be difficult to maintain.

He undoubtedly is seriously searching for a synthesis of the best in formalistic and folk music. If he can achieve it, he will pull off a feat seldom before accomplished in music. Many composers have utilized folk themes and folk feeling, but none has completely integrated the colors and emotional patterns into scored music.

He is, like all good musicians, inordinately impressed with technique. He has a fondness for lush string tones that, as he uses more of it, will settle more into balance, as will his taste for such technical musicians as Jimmy Dorsey.

Parker feels very strongly on the subject of dope in all its forms. He told us that while he was still a young boy in Kansas City he was offered some in a men's room by a stranger, when he hardly knew what it was. He continued to use it off and on for years until his crackup in 1946, and says bitterly that people who prey on kids this way should be shot.

Parker told us flatly: "Any musician who says he is playing better either on tea, the needle or when he is juiced is a plain, straight liar. When I get too much to drink, I can't even finger well, let alone play decent ideas. And in the days when I was on the stuff, I may have thought I was playing better, but listening to some of the records now, I know I wasn't. Some of these smart kids who think you have to be completely knocked out to be a good hornman are just plain crazy. It isn't true. I know, believe me."

Parker struck us as being direct, honest and searching. He is constantly dissatisfied with his own work and with the music he hears around him. What will come of it, where his quite prodigious talent will take him, even he doesn't know at this stage.

But his ceaseless efforts to find out, to correct, to improve, only bode well for himself and that elderly progenitor, jazz.

Oct. 7, 1949

"Bird Wrong; Bop Must Get a Beat"—Diz

by John S. Wilson

NEW YORK—The Bird is wrong about the relationship of bop and jazz, says Dizzy Gillespie. "Bop is an interpretation of jazz," Diz told *DownBeat*. "It's all part of the same thing." Last month, Charlie Parker said that bop had no roots in jazz, was something entirely separate and apart from the older tradition. Parker identified the beat as the distinguishing factor of bop.

"It [bop] has no continuity of beat, no steady chug-chug," Parker said.

This lack of a steady beat, according to Dizzy, is what is wrong with bop today.

"Bop is part of jazz," Dizzy said, "And jazz music is to dance to. The trouble with bop as it's played now is that people can't dance to it. They don't hear those four beats. We'll never get bop across to a wide audience until they can dance to it. They're not particular about whether you're playing a flatted fifth or a ruptured 129th as long as they can dance."

The important characteristics of bop, Dizzy says, are the harmonics and the phrasing. Tossing in a variety of beats isn't essential.

These are conclusions that Dizzy has reached after dragging his big band around the country for more than a year. As a result, he's revising his book so as to turn his outfit into a band that can be danced to.

"We'll use the same harmonics," he said, "but with a beat, so that people can understand where the beat is. We'll use a lot of things which are in the book now, but we'll cut them and splice them together again like you would a movie so as to leave out the variations in beat.

"I'm not turning my back on bop. My band has a distinctive sound and I want to keep that. But I want to make bop bigger, get it a wider audience. I think [pianist] George Shearing is the greatest thing that's happened to bop in the past year. He's the only one who has helped it along. He plays bop so the average person can understand it.

"Anybody can dance to Shearing's music. By doing that, he has made it easier for me and for everybody else who plays bop."

They Were Unhappy

The main pressure on Dizzy to make the switch has come from his wife, Lorraine, a former dancer, and his manager, Willard Alexander. For the last year, Lorraine has circulated in the audience on his one-nighters, getting audience reaction and trying to impress him that a lot of his numbers were making the dancers unhappy.

From Alexander's point of view, the big hurdle with Dizzy's band, as it was, was scarcity of places where a big band that didn't draw dancers could be booked.

"We can't play small places that hold 100 or 200 persons," Dizzy pointed out. "We're playing big auditoriums that hold a couple of thousand, and you can't rely on the extremists to support you there."

Alexander says he isn't asking Dizzy to become commercial.

Duke Did

"Ellington has always made it as a dance band, and nobody accused him of being commercial," he said. "I don't want Dizzy's men to bastardize their instruments or be corny. But I think they should perform and not look bored. Unless bop is improved in the next six months, I think it will die. Shearing is the only thing that's holding it up now."

Under the new setup, Dizzy will carry a dance book, a concert book, and a theater book. New arrangements are being turned out for him by Garland Wilson and Buster Harding. J.J. Johnson has done a pair of medleys for him, each medley consisting of three standards and winding up with a current pop tune. As part of the switch, Dizzy has dropped singer Johnny Hartman and taken on a girl, Tiny Irvin, whom he found in Pittsburgh.

Big Surprise

The first tryout of the new Gillespie dance book was made on a late August date in Mahoney City, Pa., a big Mickey stronghold. The operator, who reluctantly set the date as a favor to Alexander, was so

Dizzy Gillespie.
(DownBeat Archive)

impressed with the results that he burned up the wires to New York with reports of Dizzy's "sensational" success.

"As long as they say I've got a great band," said Dizzy, "I don't care if they say it's bop or what."

Louis Armstrong.
(DownBeat Archive)

July 14, 1950

Ulceratedly Yours

by Louis Armstrong

Howdy, folks:

Here I am in my dressing room after beating out one of those fine shows, "killing the cats," and now I'm getting ready to knock out a big delicious malted milk with two eggs in it—much different from those Schnapps I was devouring over in Europe with the natives… tee-hee. Yessir, every time they raised their arm and said, "Skol," I said it right along with them.

And one morning I went to get out of bed and fell flat on my face… ha-ha-ha. So, after a few stomach aches and stuff, I am back on my baby diet again. That includes milk and cream, constantly, or, should I say, disgustingly. Anyways, I had a whole gang of fun everywhere we went in Europe. Although I nixed out the nips, I still kept my appetite for that good food they served us.

After each concert, we were invited out to big hotels for dinner, and they would serve us everything but the kitchen stove. One place we ate—in Lyon, France—we started eating at 11:30 that night after the concert, and we ended up at 4 o'clock in the morning. Velma Middleton (my vocalist), Lucille (my wife) and myself, we all but cried when they served the last dish. The whole evening we had been dilly-dallying with those nice little tasty things each waitress would bring around to you and you couldn't refuse to save your life, figuring, well, maybe this is it.

But at 3:30 in the morning when they brought in that good Creole chicken and rice—mmm—all we could do was look at it with tears in our eyes and say, "No, thank you." I'm tellin' you, I've never felt so bad in all my life as of that time. Just think,

stewed chicken… my birthmark.

I get started talking about my trip abroad and I almost forgot what I actually sat down here at this li'l ol' Swiss typewriter to talk about. What I really want to say is I am so happy, at the age of 50, still blowing my little Satchmo trumpet, still enjoying the fine things in life, still love everybody, and everybody still loves me, and from one end of the world to the other, to me, everybody's just like one happy family.

And, folks, that's the way it has been with me (inwardly) all of my life. And musically everybody's been all reet with me at all times. Of course we all have had our little say as to what they liked and what they didn't particularly like (musically, I said), but when one would hear the other fellow play, deep down in their hearts they would say, gee, that's great.

I have been quoted as saying this and that about bop, etc., and they've given me hell to boot. But any time we would run across each other, there would always be a lot of warmth amongst us, ya dig? And the public, they'd think, My Gawd, those guys pan each other

so bad, they really must be enemies. Shucks, pay it no mind. We musicians have always loved each other.

Ever since I can remember playing music, way back in the days in New Orleans, the white musicians always were glad to see colored musicians. And, you know, the colored guys were always the same. The last time I was in New Orleans, the night just before Mardi Gras day, we played a concert for the high school kids. And after the concert, our boy Turk—a white boy tavern owner from down in the Creole section, a racehorse big-shot who has horses the same as Louis Prima and who is a friend of the Primas, Louis and Leon—came by the concert and waited for me to get dressed… you know, take off my uniform and put on one of those fine Vines just made by Abe Sherer in Chicago. After I got dressed, we trucked on down to Leon Prima's place down in the swing section of New Orleans, on Bourbon Street. Louis Prima happened to be in town also. He usually appears at his brother's place when he's down there for the races. So, we dropped in on those cats, and Louis was swinging that band down to a low gravy when we entered.

When he spied me, I just walked away from Turk and the gang, and just kept walking right straight to the bandstand, and ordered a li'l taste of "I'm Confessin' I Love Ya." Oh, and it was really "on." Yea, man—we really had a ball. The next day, I was on the float in the Zulus parade, the King of the Zulus. Moments such as those, how in the world can one forget them… huh?

For my 50th birthday present, I shall receive a nice, very fine operation for those two devilish ulcers of mine. I am sure if I can tolerate those two boys for more than five years, blowing that horn, hitting those high notes every time they were supposed to be hit—just think, I will knock out 50 more (very easily) with those boys removed. I was talking to Lil Armstrong (my second wife), whom I lived with through my real wild days, and she and I had so much in common, especially musically.

Lil told me the other day in my dressing room here at the Oriental Theatre, when she came to visit me and spend the day with me as she always does, that I have had trouble with my stomach for more than 10 years. As far back as 1926, when I was playing at the Sunset Cafe for my manager, Mr. Joe Glaser, I used to get those heartburns (the old word for ulcers—tee-hee).

Lil, who was on the mound as Mrs. Satchmo Armstrong, put me on a strict diet. That's when I first realized that I could eat all sorts of dainty foods instead of so much ham hock and cabbage and my favorite dish, red beans and rice. So, you see, from what Lil sez—I've been blowing trumpet a long time on ulcers.

Well, the reason for that was—I love my horn and my public, now you can figure it out for yourself. So, folks, as I said before, I am a very happy man, indeed, at 50, still blowing and feeling like a 10-year-old. B'lieve me. So, all I have to do is to disband these two bad boys (ulcers, that is) and all will be well on the Satchmo front… YARSUH. And a many thanks to all of my friends and fans who wished me a happy birthday.

Am Ulceratedly Yours,
Louis Armstrong

June 29, 1951

"I Finally Know What I Want to Do," Says Shaw

by Leonard Feather

NEW YORK—Recently I spent a quiet and pleasant day at Shekomeko, N.Y., visiting a friend up there who is a dairy farmer. His 240 acres, known as Picardy Farm, are in a remote spot three train hours from Manhattan. It was a rewarding visit. Not because my farmer friend sold me any milk, but because I learned a lot more about him and about his book, which is called *The Trouble with Cinderella* and is scheduled for Farrar Straus' fall list.

And because this farmer, whose name is Artie Shaw, is quite a guy to sit around and chat with.

This is not the same Artie Shaw you have seen on the bandstand or heard on records. He looks the same outside, except for informal clothes, but he is a very different man inside. A happier, better-adjusted Artie Shaw than you could ever have known when his main concern was the music business.

Learned Many Things

During this day at the farm I learned many things Artie had never previously discussed about his background. He also read me, off the record, several chapters of his book, which is a mixture of philosophy, psychology and autobiography, and which gets its title from the author's disbelief that people "live happily ever after."

"Too many people live by that Cinderella myth and expect the prince to lead them into permanent happiness," he explained as we sat in the big, bright, cool living room surrounded by several thousand books and almost as many thousands records.

I asked him his main motive in giving up so many things—fame, the public eye, and possibly a great deal of money— just to divide his time between farming and writing.

Not Just Autobiography

"A man reaches a stage in his life," he said, "when he ought to review where he has gone, see just where he is and figure out where he is going. I could just write a straight autobiography and that would be that, one book and finished. I want this book to be the first of a series. The first draft ran to around 70,000 words. I work on it every day from 7:30 in the morning until 12:30."

Through the subsequent conversation, readings from the book and chats I had later with several old friends of Artie's, I was able to reconstruct an accurate picture of his childhood. An only child, born May 23, 1910, to a poor family on New York's Lower East Side, he moved with them to New Haven, Conn., in his eighth year.

It was there, while he was still too young to even know there was such a word as anti-Semitism, that he found out there was something strange about having a name like Arthur Arshawsky, which on Manhattan's east side had not been considered unusual.

Shy, Withdrawn

Because the other kids said things that made him, as a Jew, feel like an outcast, Artie became a shy and withdrawn youngster, one who found refuge in reading and music. Musically and mentally he was always years ahead of his contemporaries. As a result, when he skipped a grade and found himself smaller than the other boys in his class, he would be subject to further frustrations.

By the time he was 10 or 11, Artie had

a reputation as a wizard with a ukelele. A couple of years later he took up the saxophone, and after a few months of lessons was able to stop because his teacher said, "Why should I go on? He already plays better than I do."

When Artie joined the high school band, its leader at first was Bernie Disken; other members were pianist Johnny Ferdinandus, guitarist Gene Beecher, drummer Ted Pearlman, and trumpeter Billy Berman, who, like his brother Sonny Berman, was to meet a tragic and early death: he was killed in an accident at 16.

Became Leader

Later, Artie became the leader and decided to shorten his name: it was Artie Shaw's Bellevue Ramblers, who played after the basketball games and later on the Liberty Pier at Savin Rock. While he was working his way into $5 gigs, his mother, a dressmaker, struggled to support him. (His father had quit the family circle when Artie was 14.)

Still a studious youngster who would be engrossed in Dumas while the others were busy with dime novels, he had by now acquired a certain standing in his juvenile community, and was always the center of attraction whenever his little band played summer jobs up at Banham Lake, along with Charlie Spivak and drummer Johnny Morris.

When these two last New Haven boys went off to join Paul Specht, they became objects of great admiration among their former colleagues. Spivak and Morris were in the big time.

Artie never graduated from New Haven High. Ted Pearlman recalls it as a spat between Artie and the music supervisor; whatever the cause, Shaw ran away from home at age 15 and rattled off to Kentucky in an old jalopy with Ralph Platt for a job that folded up on them before they got there.

Stranded in Kentucky, his horns in hock, he finally earned enough money to get home by joining a band that passed through town—he thinks it was Blue Steele's.

The next job he recalls was with Johnny Cavallaro, who worked at the Cinderella Ballroom locally and at a gambling joint in Florida.

Makes Good

It was while he was working New Haven's Olympia Theater, doubling between stage and pit and pretty tired of it, that he was

Artie Shaw and his orchestra from 1951. (DownBeat Archive)

auditioned by a visitor from Cleveland for a job with Joe Cantor. When he left town in triumph to take the job, his friends marched to the railroad station carrying his baggage. The local boy had made good.

"I went out to Cleveland," Artie recalls, "and that was where I started learning to arrange. Everything came out very badly, all mixed up, but they were a friendly bunch of guys and they taught me more than I'd ever learned in school. Then I got a job there with Austin Wylie, and more or less ran the band for him—he was a nominal leader, held a fiddle. That was back in the days when leaders were mainly businessmen.

"A typical set with Wylie would consist of three sweet tunes and a hot number like 'Tiger Rag' or 'San.' We had a 'big' band: three saxes, three brass, banjo, piano, bass and tuba."

Also Arranged

"While I was in Cleveland I did some arranging, too, for the house band at WTAM, in the grandiose style of the day. I left Cleveland through an odd thing that happened: a local paper was running a contest tying up with the National Air Races that were being run locally. You were supposed to write 150 words on how the races

would benefit the city.

"Well, I sent mine in and forgot it, just as you would a lottery ticket. Then one day I got back from work and my mother said a man was there from the newspaper—I'd won first prize, a free two-week trip by air to Hollywood.

"I was 18 years old and very impressed by seeing people like Charlie Chaplin, Jean Harlow and all the celebrities who hung out at the Roosevelt Hotel where I stayed.

"The band in that Hollywood hotel was Irving Aaronson's Commanders, and Chummy MacGregor, the pianist, really ran the band. Two of the men were friends of mine from New Haven—Charlie Trotta on trumpet and Tony Pestritto (Pastor) on sax. We found we had a lot in common, chiefly our admiration for Louis Armstrong, who was then a more-or-less unknown artist on race records."

Playing Great

Six months later, back in Cleveland, Artie saw his friends again in the Aaronson band. By now he was playing "terrific" clarinet, according to Trotta, and had helped get Claude Thornhill into the Wylie band. After the Aaronson band returned to the coast they sent for Artie, who drove out there to join them. Toots Mondello played first alto in the band, and Artie switched to tenor.

Artie was 19 years old when the crash hit. It was another crash, of a very different nature, that was to hit him much more personally. After working Chicago, where he learned a lot by sitting in after hours with Louis, Earl and others at the Grand Terrace, he came to New York, where the Aaronson band played the Beacon Theater at 74th and Broadway.

One night, while he was driving up Broadway, a pedestrian stepped in front of the car; Artie could not avoid knocking him down. The pedestrian died instantly. This was the beginning of a long nightmare for Artie. He was to be tried for manslaughter and had to be held on bail while the band left town. The case dragged on and on, dragging a small fortune in lawyers' fees and the bulk of Artie's mother's worldly goods along with it.

It was almost four years before this ordeal ended, when it had finally been established that the victim had been at fault.

Rough Existence

For a while things were tough as Artie hung around New York. At one time he lived in the Roxwell apartments at 50th and Seventh Avenue, where Harry Bluestone and Artie Bernstein also lived and where Bix and Eddie Condon and Will Bradley often hung around. Sometimes they would all sit around in a circle for a jam session, taking several choruses each; other nights they'd go out and sit in at various gangster joints.

At another period, Artie stayed at the President Hotel. "Charlie Spivak and Artie and I shared a room, with Artie sleeping on the floor," says Johnny Morris. "Then I went with Vincent Lopez and got him on the band at the St. Regis." Charlie Trotta, then with Lopez, also helped to get Artie that job.

Artie, it seems, didn't abound with respect for Lopez. "He blew out his cheeks, made all sorts of icky faces and called Lopez 'The Seal,'" says Morris. "After we'd gone as far as Milwaukee, he got an offer from Roger Wolfe Kahn and gave Lopez his notice."

Waited Out Card

Around this time, Artie decided to wait out his six months for his 802 card. During the first three months, when he couldn't take any work at all, the only playing he did took place at a little after-hours spot called the Catagonia Club, better known as Pod's

and Jerry's, where Willie "the Lion" Smith was at the piano.

"The Lion was a great friend to me. I'd get in there at 1 a.m., sit around and play until the joint closed at 6 in the morning, then maybe the Lion would buy me breakfast."

Artie's first job after he got his 802 card was with Paul Specht. He made his first records with Roger Wolfe Kahn and with Specht, playing alto on the latter's "Dancing in the Dark" and "You Forgot Your Gloves."

Called for Audition

While working with Red Nichols' newly organized Five Pennies group, shortly after the Specht job, Artie ran into Freddie Rich, then a music director at CBS, who said he wanted Artie to audition for a first alto chair.

"It was the most peculiar audition I ever played," reminisces Artie. "They stuck me in the middle of a room all by myself and gave me a third alto part taken out of stock orchestration. I had to read this, unaccompanied, while they listened in another room. Of course, I didn't get the job."

Later, however, when a call came from Rich with a definite offer for the first alto job, Artie asked for $125 a week instead of the $100 scale, and, to his surprise, got it.

Double Life

"This was the beginning of a double life for me," he says. "During my idle months I had started some literature courses. I had now gone as far as I could as an instrumentalist, and the music I had to play made very little sense to me, so I decided to go to school. I took some extension courses at Columbia. Around this time, too, I got married—to a very nice girl." (A previous attempt at matrimony credited to Artie by some writers doesn't even count, he says, since both parties were underage and there was an immediate annulment.)

Artie also discovered "serious" music during his year with CBS. His colleagues thought it a little odd for him to be so engrossed in Stravinsky, Bartok and Debussy. After the CBS year, while he was freelancing successfully in radio and recording studios, a literary mentor told him about a group of intellectuals who had bought small farms in Bucks County, Pa. Having saved up enough to buy a little land, and having decided he was through with music and wanted to write, Artie moved up there with Margie and lived fru-

gally, without electricity, even taking a job chopping wood to fill out the simple, regular life he wanted. Claude Thornhill was among the few friends who visited him during this hibernation period.

There was one hitch, though: during that year, Artie realized that he didn't quite know what he wanted to write about. Returning to New York, he went "back into music with one toe," as he puts it, "while the rest of me was immersed in study." He studied independently with tutors or by reading, acquired a smattering of science with the help of a biophysicist friend and enrolled in a preparatory school while his wife took a medical course at Columbia, later going to work as a hospital nurse.

Making Money

While the intellectual side of him was "trying to formulate a philosophy," Artie recalls that the financial side was formulating a pretty fair bank account. He reached the stage where, if a clarinet man was wanted to do a radio or recording job, the contractor would automatically send for either Benny Goodman or Artie.

Often they subbed for each other or worked together on various jobs. Toward the end of 1934, he started to make a name for himself with jazz record fans by making a couple of sessions with Red Norvo and Frankie Trumbauer. In the summer of 1935, Joe Helbock, then owner of the Onyx Club, decided to put on a concert featuring that red-hot novelty, "swing," at the Imperial Theater. Approached to participate along with a bunch of bigger swing names, Artie decided to do something different by writing a jazz piece for clarinet and string quartet.

Broke It Up

They almost canceled him out of the concert at the last minute; if they had, it would surely have left a big gap in jazz history, for Artie's one number, "Interlude in B Flat," broke the show. Tommy Rockwell, head of what is now GAC, approached him about forming a band along similar lines. Artie said he wasn't interested, wasn't sure what he wanted to do.

Rockwell pointed out that whatever it was he was groping for, a little money wouldn't do any harm in getting him there, and he could always go back to whatever he wanted to do after making his killing.

At the same time, Brunswick offered Artie a deal, and by adding trumpet, trombone and tenor he managed to get something approximating a full band sound for the first session, using pickup personnel. A few weeks later he was on the road with a band that included Jerry Gray leading the string quartet and assisting on the arrangements, Lee Castaldo (Castle) on trumpet, Tony Pastor on tenor, Joe Lippman on piano and Peg LaCentra on vocals.

Hard to Beat

Artie and Jerry battled hard to make this thing work, but as Artie recalls now, "We were bucking a tide that was impossible to beat—the chewing gum drummers and the loud-swing fanaticism. That kind of band would actually have a better chance today. We needed a band that was flexible enough for theaters, one-nighters and hotel rooms."

Even on its location at the Lexington Hotel in New York, there was trouble getting the right mike setup for the fiddles. One of the more successful jobs was the Paramount Theater booking in December 1936. Short of a guitar player, Artie decided to help out Eddie Condon by giving him the job, even though Eddie read so little music that he didn't know what a repeat sign meant, and consequently got to the end of each engagement about a minute ahead of everyone else.

He also showed up at the Paramount wearing one brown suede shoe and one black shoe. "Who cares?" said Condon when this was pointed out to him. "I keep one foot under the chair—they'll never notice." When he had to come front and center for a solo on "Streamline" (yes, a solo by Condon!), the discrepancy was a little harder to hide.

Hectic Date

The night after they closed the Paramount, the band took off for Dallas, where they played a hectic engagement at the Adolphus Hotel calling for lunch sessions, floor shows, broadcasts, more shows. When Artie finally managed to get money to bring the band back to New York, he decided the time had come to stop pioneering.

Jerry Gray stayed on as arranger and, working from Artie's sketches, built a new book for the regular swing band instrumentation. In May 1937, "Art Shaw and His New Music" made its first session for Brunswick.

It was still a hassle. Borrowing money to keep going, Artie rehearsed in cellars and barns, using young kids who took two weeks to learn a new arrangement but would work for $10 a man a night and sometimes only got two nights a week.

"When we went into the Raynor Ballroom in Boston," Artie recollects, "we had

to pay off everybody—sidemen, singer, arranger, valet, everything—a total of 18 people, on $1,000 a week."

Air Shots

"Finally in Boston we met Si Shribman, and those being days when you could still make a band with air time, I gave him a piece of the band in exchange for two nights a week broadcasting from the Roseland State Ballroom."

Around this time Artie had been experimenting with the idea of building up an Americana library—tunes like "Sweet Adeline" and "How Dry I Am" done up in swing style. He had also been experimenting, with an equal lack of success, in the girl vocal department.

Finally he decided the hell with the Americana idea, he would try a policy of the best music by the best composers of standards—Gershwin, Kern, Porter, Youmans, Rodgers. Also, the hell with indifferent girl singers; if he wanted to hire a Negro girl he defied anyone to stop him. And he hired Billie Holiday.

Revolutionary Move

It was a revolutionary move at the time; the nearest thing to a mixed band had been Benny Goodman's use of Teddy Wilson and Lionel Hampton as specialty acts. Billie Holiday, lending her fresh approach to great standards and pops, gave the Shaw band something unique, but when they hit St. Louis the Chase Hotel informed him he must hire a white singer, too. Artie hired the then-plump and unknown Helen Forrest, and paid both girls $60 a week, the same money the sidemen were getting.

Early in 1938 he had broken away from Brunswick, and it was almost seven months before he started recording again, this time for Victor's 35-cent Bluebird label. The first side they cut on the first session was "Begin the Beguine," which, Artie says, Eli Oberstein was not anxious to record since it came from a flop show. They put it out on the back of "Indian Love Call," which they were sure the novel swing treatment would help to sell.

On the way back from St. Louis, Artie began to get calls for "Beguine" and a bafflingly strong reaction at the end of the number. He didn't realize that the record had just come out, and was even less aware of the sensation it had caused.

A Madhouse

"By the time we hit New York and got to

the Lincoln Hotel," said Artie, "our opening night there was a madhouse. From then on I couldn't think straight. My life wasn't my own. Photographers from *Life* magazine, autograph hunters, everything all at once, plus all kinds of disagreeable pressures being put on me.

"The bigger our success, the more dissatisfaction there seemed to be in the band. Billie Holiday, who had gotten along fine with Helen Forrest, began to resent her. Georgie Auld came in for $125 while the rest of the band, getting scale, objected. Buddy Rich joined us, and the older guys didn't like it when he got so much applause. Instead of a bunch of guys that were happy to be struggling toward a common objective, we became a bunch of cliques, and I became gradually estranged from the men.

"When we went into the Strand Theater, it was even worse. People jumping up on the stage, cops, riots—things that were almost impossible to live through. I was making more money than I had ever thought existed, and I guess I got carried away by it."

Was "Glamor-Struck"

Artie admits that he was "glamor-stuck" by the time the band got out to Hollywood and made its first picture, *Dancing Co-Ed*. There was an inner turmoil going on between his artistic and commercial values that added to his trouble in coping with audiences and frantic fans.

Finally, one night back in New York at the Pennsylvania Hotel, the last thread of his resistance snapped. He walked out on the band, never to return. Georgie Auld took over the leadership temporarily; later Tony Pastor, using some of the same men, started his own band. Meanwhile, Artie had escaped to Mexico, leaving the music world stunned at his running out on a million-dollar career.

By the time he returned the following spring, he made headlines again by marrying the teenaged movie starlet Lana Turner. In Hollywood, switching from Bluebird to RCA's 75-cent Victor label, he recorded with what was then the biggest swing band ever heard—brass, woodwinds, rhythm and 13 strings—and, paralleling his Bluebird career, he made a hit out of the first tune waxed at the first session, a number he had picked up in Mexico called "Frenesi."

Common Property

This was March 1940. Artie's career since then has been pretty much common property in the press, with an undue accent on his matrimonial misadventures. He himself blames his marital troubles on his psychological maladjustments, which have not prevented him from retaining a pretty firm friendship with a couple of his ex-wives, notably Ava Gardner, for whom he has considerable respect as a human being. Ava was preceded by Betty Kern, the late Jerome Kern's daughter, who bore Artie a son; she was followed by Kathleen Winsor.

Among highlights of the past Shaw decade or so were the big acting and playing role in *Second Chorus*, with Fred Astaire and Paulette Goddard; the birth of the Gramercy Five, with Johnny Guarnieri on harpsichord, in a Victor session, Sept. 3, 1940; his enlistment in the Navy in January 1942 and subsequent tours to Guadalcanal, New Zealand, Australia and all over the Pacific; his first post-discharge civilian band, with Roy Eldridge, in the fall of '44; his 1945–'46 skirmish with Musicraft Records, using Mel Torme, Kitty Kallen and Teddy Walters as vocalists; his still-discussed week at the brand-new Bop City early in 1949, leading a concert orchestra and eschewing jazz entirely; his interesting classics-and-concert jazz LP for Columbia; and his retreat into semi-retirement with the acquisition in 1949 of the Shekomeko farm.

Lives Alone
Artie lives alone now in a big, handsome house, with several household and farm employees living on his land. He is glad that dairy farming, unlike the music business, involves a community where you don't have to deal directly with the customers. The milk cans are picked up and taken away regularly, and he expects to make a nice modest profit this year.

Between this and his royalties, he can live comfortably, and if he wants anything more, he can always use music to help his plans, as he did last fall when, to pay for the addition of a new wing on a barn, he worked a few weeks at Iceland.

His views on music have not changed, basically. He says the American public is getting better music than it deserves, and points out that the best-selling record he has made so far under his Decca contract is a "real piece of crap" that sold 250,000 copies while the record that he considers his best musically on Decca sold exactly 415.

Cynicism Rewarded
His cynicism increased when he went out

with his last band in 1950. After getting together a band of talented youngsters, using kids like Dodo Marmarosa and arrangers like Johnny Mandel, he gave up hope, and sometime later, when he had a few weeks of commitments to fill, he had someone hire the first 12 musicians available at random and went out on some dates playing nothing but stocks, with men who could hardly read.

The reaction was the crowning insult. Almost everybody thought it was great; one promoter even called it "the greatest thing I've heard since Blue Barron worked for me."

Despite the apparently anti-jazz nature of his philosophy after Bop City in 1949, Artie is aware of, and interested in, new trends in jazz. He says he has Lennie Tristano's records and has great respect for Lennie's freshness of ideas and uncompromising musical integrity.

Writing Chief Impulse
But music has never, he claims now, been the mainstream of his life. The writing compulsion is very strong in him. Artie Shaw, who has been called everything from an egomaniac and a psychotic to a Bluebeard and a Communist, is none of these things. He is the possessor of one of the keenest minds ever applied to jazz; his intellectualism, sometimes called false, is so genuine that it puts a barrier between him and the less sensitive people he has had to deal with in the music business.

Neurotically confused by the conflicting urges of music, books, glamour and money, he sought help through psychiatry and derived great benefits from it.

"The only people Artie dislikes," as an old friend put it recently, "are leeches and stupid people. He's always cordial to everybody else and has never fluffed off his old friends."

Summation Simple
Artie's own summation of his present life is simple and succinct. "I'm doing Bucks County again," he says, "but this time on the right scale. A dairy farm in those days was out of my reach. Now I know what I want to write, and I have the conditions in which to write.

"Bucks County was in 1933, and it'll be a couple of years before I've rounded out this writing job. It will have taken me just 20 years to get back to where I wanted to go. I sure went a long way around!"

Nov. 5, 1952

Duke Tells of 10 Top Thrills in 25 Years

by Duke Ellington

NEW YORK—I have been asked to list the 10 events that seem most memorable to me out of everything that has happened since we originally opened at the Cotton Club.

This is a task of considerable magnitude, since we have been fortunate enough to be on the receiving end of a large variety of honors. If I recall certain events and pay tribute to certain beautiful people, I may be unconsciously offending certain other beautiful people. However, I shall search my mind for the 10 occasions that stand out as personal memories.

Main Stem
Of course, our values today are greatly changed, but in those days there were certain things you had heard about that you always wanted to experience, and one of these was playing the Palace Theatre on Broadway. It meant reaching the peak for any artist who worked vaudeville, since the Palace was the ultimate in that field. So perhaps our first very big moment after the Cotton Club opening was the day we first played the Palace, in 1929.

Lights Out!
We opened the show with "Dear Old Southland." I remember the men hadn't memorized their parts on this, and the show opened on a darkened stage. When I gave the downbeat, nothing happened—the men couldn't see a note! Then somebody called for the lights and the show went on.

The next highlight, I believe, was our trip to the West Coast to make our film movie. It was the Amos and Andy feature *Check and Double Check*, and we did "Ring Dem Bells" and "Three Little Words." Later, of course, we were in Hollywood for *Murder at the Vanities*, Mae West's *Belle of the Nineties* and several other pictures; but there was a special kick out of making our screen debut.

We took time out from the Cotton Club to make *Check and Double Check*. Aside from that, we were at the club right along from our opening in December 1927 until early 1931. We doubled into Ziegfeld's Show Girl and various other theater dates. All that time, we were on the air from the Cotton Club.

On the Air

Broadcasting was a lot simpler in those days; you didn't have to clear all your numbers a day or two in advance. I can remember times when Ted Husing would turn around to me in the middle of a broadcast and say, "Duke, how about playing so-and-so?" and we'd go right into it.

The next big moment was our opening night at the London Palladium. This was a night that scared the devil out of the whole band, the applause was so terrifying—it was applause beyond applause. On our first show there was 10 minutes of continuous applause. It was a tremendous thrill. In fact, that entire first European tour in 1933 was a tremendous uplift for all our spirits.

Europe was responsible for the next big kick I can recall, too. It was my birthday celebration in Stockholm, Sweden, April 29, 1939. I was awakened by a 16-piece band from the local radio station that marched into my hotel room serenading me with "Happy Birthday." All day long, at the hotel and at the concert house where we were playing, huge bouquets of flowers kept arriving, and hundreds of people flocked to the dressing room. The whole audience rose to sing "Happy Birthday" and there was a ceremony onstage, followed by a big banquet for the entire orchestra and numerous guests at the Crown Prince Cafe. It all brought a very glowing ending to our second European tour.

Two years later, in 1941, we got a very special kick out of *Jump for Joy*. This was the revue in which the whole band took part. A number of critics felt this was the hippest Negro musical and has remained so to this day. We had some great lyrics to our songs, thanks largely to Paul Francis Webster; some fine writing by Sid Kuller, and such artists as Marie Bryant and Paul White, Joe Turner, Herb Jeffries, Dorothy Dandridge and Wonderful Smith.

The Three B's

The sixth important occasion was the first Carnegie Hall concert—first of what

Duke Ellington.
(DownBeat Archive)

turned out to be an annual series. This enabled me to present my *Tone Parallel to the History of the American Negro, Black, Brown and Beige*, which was originally presented at Carnegie and ran about 50 minutes. We only recorded excerpts from it for the RCA Victor album, but the entire concert was recorded privately and we hope to someday have this recording released generally so that everybody can hear *B, B & B* in its original form.

That first night at Carnegie was the only time in my life that I didn't have stage fright. I just didn't have time—I couldn't afford the luxury of being scared. Dr. Arthur Logan, an old friend and our personal physician, was standing around backstage handing out pills to everyone in the band. He even took one himself. He offered one to me and I refused it. I wasn't nervous—not at all. But I did walk onstage without my music. Someone signaled to me from the wings that they had it—but I didn't need it anyway; I remembered it all.

Carnegie Annual

This first concert, in January 1943, turned out to be a milestone that paved the way for other regular concert series, so that by now an annual jazz concert at Carnegie has become a permanent thing for several other organizations. One thing that hasn't been

duplicated, however, is the audience we had on that opening night and at our subsequent concerts. The quality of the appreciation, the attentiveness of the entire crowd of 3,000 people to every note we played, was a model of audience reaction that has proved hard to duplicate.

At the time of that concert, too, the music business celebrated a national Ellington week, and during the performance at Carnegie we were privileged to receive a plaque inscribed by some of our well-wishers from every branch of music—among them John Charles Thomas, William Grant Sill, Deems Taylor, Marian Anderson, Albert Coates, Kurt Weill, Dea Dixon, Aaron Copland, Paul Whiteman, Benny Goodman, Count Basie, Earl Hines, Artie Shaw, Morton Gould and Marjorie Lawrence.

Esquire Jazz

There was a similarly jubilant occasion in 1945, when we took part in the annual *Esquire* jazz awards concert at the Philharmonic Auditorium in Los Angeles. Most of the presentation of "Eskies" to individual winners were made by Hollywood personalities. Billy Strayhorn received his from Lena Horne; mine was presented by Lionel Barrymore.

There was another great evening, in

1949, when we played at Robin Hood Dell in Philadelphia with this beautiful 96-piece symphony orchestra, conducted by Russ Case, wrapped around ours.

I spent a lot of time listening that evening, when I should have been playing. I wrote a bop thing for them, using the same jump-blues theme we recorded on one of the small band dates as "Who Struck John." They played it perfectly.

Harlem

Ninth on our list of significant moments would be the concert at the Metropolitan Opera House early last year. Our audience numbered more than 3,500, including Mayor Impellitteri, who paid a special tribute to us onstage, and we introduced a new concert work, "Harlem," which I later performed with the NBC Symphony Orchestra.

Tenth and last, I recall with special delight another Philadelphia story—this one was the annual musical festival held by the *Philadelphia Inquirer* at the Municipal Stadium, with a tremendous show for an audience of 125,000 people, all admitted free. There were, if I remember right, three symphony orchestras, as well as Benny Goodman, Perry Como, Mindy Carson and a big Indian war dance routine. I was especially impressed by the fact that when I did "Monologue" I had the whole audience giggling—and believe me, it's quite impressive to hear 125,000 people giggling.

Then There Was...

It is a somewhat arbitrary decision to select 10 events over a 25-year span, but these are the ones that came to mind. Of course, I could go into many details about some of the great people we've met through the years.

There was my meeting with the Pope on my last visit to Europe, when the Pope had a great deal to say to me, but I must have been overawed because later I didn't remember a single thing he had said. There was my private audience with President Truman, whom I found very affable and very musically informed. There was the party in London when I fluffed off the guy who kept asking me to play "Swampy River," and then found that he was Prince George. Later that evening the Duke of Windsor (then Prince of Wales) sat in with us on drums and surprised everybody, including Sonny Greer.

Sincerity

There was the time we were playing the downtown Cotton Club in 1937 when Leopold Stokowski came in alone and listened to our band. Later he discussed our music and invited me to attend his concert the next evening, when I heard him conducting the Philadelphia Orchestra at Carnegie hall.

But I don't want to go on name-dropping, because what has impressed me most through all these years has been not the renown of these people, but the sincerity of their interest in our music, and the interest of all the audiences who have helped to make our achievements possible. I can best sum it up by saying that the days since that long-ago Cotton Club opening have provided 25 years of eminently happy memories.

March 25, 1953

Frank Sinatra.
(United Artists)

Hokey Tunes "Bug" Frank

by Nat Hentoff

BOSTON—"Do I still think it's hard to find a decent new pop tune these days?" echoed Frank Sinatra. "Man, it's worse than ever. These trick songs are coming out of my ears. But the situation isn't hopeless.

"First of all, we've got to convince the accepted songwriters to come out of hiding and write again. The way things are now, they feel they'd be wasting their time. Another way is to record and revive more of the standards—like 'The Birth of the Blues' on my last release—that way we can at least balance the hokey tunes. It's murder now."

Public Not Square

"And I don't think the reason for the low caliber is the public, primarily. They're not that square. They certainly weren't five and 10 years ago when at least four out of five of the first 10 on the Hit Parade were good tunes.

"I think it's all part of a cycle—including the echo chambers and the other gimmicks—that will exhaust itself. Everybody now wants to take the easiest way out, but eventually the people who have something to say musically will be the ones who survive.

"Future plans? Well, I've been awarded the wonderful part of Maggio in the film version of *From Here to Eternity*. Montgomery Clift, Burt Lancaster and Deborah Kerr will be in the cast, and Fred Zinnemann will direct. I expect to be making more pictures than before but not all straight dramatic ones. Roles like this don't come along that often."

Sinatra then spoke long and feelingly about the band business and the prospect of its full-scale revival. "As you know, the band business was at its height when I was with Harry James and Tommy Dorsey. It was great training for me. I learned about tempos—which ones for what tunes—and how to mix them up and how to pace a show."

Inflation to Blame

"Somebody—Tony Bennett, I think—said I was the first singer to make it on a popular-enough kick so that the way was cleared for other singers. Well, whether that's so or not, it's true that the emphasis on singing certainly hurt the band business. But inflation had a lot to do with it, too. These bands began to ask for higher guarantees, the promoters passed the increased cost on to the kids and they couldn't afford it.

"I'd surely like to see the bands come back. One way would be to get men like Norvo and Goodman (and I'm glad to hear about his tour), who know how to put a band together, to go on the road. After all, there are only a handful of real dance bands on the road now, so how can you hope to make the kids dance-conscious?

"I know it's a problem. It's hard to get good sidemen to go on the road, what with studio jobs and the like. And Kenton may have a point when he says the kids have forgotten how to dance. Because there hasn't been enough sound dance music to which they could lean. They're so busy listening to gimmick records without any good dance music on them.

"There don't seem to be any parties anymore, like when I was a kid, where we used to dance to records or go out to dance to bands. But if the bands are to come back, Les Brown is the model. Not this 55-piece concert band stuff. Les has stayed with dance music all along. But your guess is as good as mine as to whether they'll come back. This is a crazy business."

Jan. 27, 1954

Can't Sing Any Way but Soft, Explains Nat Cole

by Nat Hentoff

Nat "King" Cole.
(DownBeat Archive)

NEW YORK—Nat Cole, beaming at having won the *DownBeat* poll as the nation's most popular male singer, was discussing his personal style. It was a few minutes before his first show of the evening at La Vie En Rose, and the room was filled with those who had come to hear him.

"Mine is a casual approach to a song; I lean heavily on the lyrics. By that I mean I try to tell a story with the melody as the background. I pick songs with lyrics that will make a guy think of his life, of his experiences, that will start him reminiscing. And I sing soft—because I can't sing any other way.

"I suppose those have been the ingredients to my commercial success. Vocally, I guess I do everything contrary. I smoke. I don't go through the typical warm-up routine unless I have a cold or something, and I've had no vocal lessons. A lot of people with well-trained voices can out-sing me, but trained singers generally learn a certain way of projecting, and when they sing a popular song that way, they can't come down and communicate, just as we couldn't sing an opera song."

Soul Does It

"If you think about it, 90 percent of the popular stars today, including myself, have no voice, but they have soul, that appeal that will touch the average guy. I don't mean this at all as an affront to trained singers, but this is a different thing.

"And many popular singers, especially some of the young ones, forget the important thing in our type of singing is a certain amount of emotion. You can't buy it, you can't learn it. You have it, or you haven't. And if you have it, you won't be so carried away by your voice—as some singers are—that you forget to sell the song."

What About Songs?

What about the songs that are to be sold with emotion these days? Did Nat agree

with Johnny Mercer about the low quality of most present day pop tunes? "I'll agree to a certain extent," Nat said seriously, "but I don't blame it on the songwriters.

"I blame it on the publishers, because they won't generally accept what I call smart songs. They discourage writers from writing good songs. When they say a song is too pretty to sell, they put a psychological thought into the writer's mind and into the whole trade. And it's not so. I'm positive that if the public were to get a dose of beautiful songs on the air all the time, they'd buy them."

Artist's Responsibility

"The artist has a responsibility, too," Nat went on animatedly. "A lot of artists haven't the courage to try a good song. I will, and that's why I have so many friends in the music business. I'll experiment, and I'll take a chance on a song.

"Just take four songs I've done that with—'Too Young,' 'The Christmas Song' (which is now a standard), 'Nature Boy' and 'Mona Lisa.' I'd call them smart songs, but they sold. And other artists and companies latched on to them after the public showed they liked them.

"In any case, I'll continue to choose my own material and continue to experiment. I'm lucky at Capitol, because Lee Gillette, when he does suggest songs, suggests those I'll like. He never tries to shove a song down my throat. We meet on even grounds, we respect each other and that leads to a very harmonious relationship."

Nat then began to talk about his favorite jazz pianists and his enjoyment of jamming, which he still does frequently. But it was time to go on. He looked around the room and emphasized, "You know I'm still as interested in jazz as I ever was, because that's my basic background. And I certainly haven't turned my back on it, which is why, I guess, I haven't lost my original jazz fans. Of course, some people say I've gone so-called commercial, but I challenge them to say I'm corny."

June 30, 1954

I Try to Make Perfect Records

by Les Paul

I try to make what I consider perfect recordings by myself. (I'm using the term "perfect" loosely, because outside of Mary I haven't found anything perfect. Even the Liberty Bell has a crack in it.)

To make a recording on a disc from tape, you must first of all have a room that has good acoustics—a room where the surfaces are not alike and where the walls are not directly opposite each other. Try to establish a room where standing waves are at the minimum, and you can do this with irregular walls and surfaces.

Use Several Mikes

Then pick several different microphones to be used for separate purposes. If you are recording a jazz orchestra, you would place different types of microphones on different sections of the orchestra so that each mike would be complementary to the particular instrument it was picking up.

For example, you might play up the brass section if this section was being featured. But if the orchestra being recorded was a Guy Lombardo–type of band, and the brass section was being featured, you would probably use a different set of microphones than you would if you were recording a Stan Kenton–type orchestra featuring the brass section. The selection of microphones, then, depends upon the type of music, the room and the arrangement.

Vocals Are the Same

The same thing applies to vocals. Again, for an example, one vocalist may be on top of the mike and sound perfectly normal, whereas another vocalist using the same mike might have to stand a foot and a half away because of a different characteristic in the voice. So microphones are variable subjects to be used variably.

Now Comes the Mixer

After you have supplied the mikes and the room, the next element is a mixer. A mixer is a way of taking one or more mikes and blending them together. The mixer should be flat, frequency-wise, and as low as possible in the inter-modulation and harmonic distortion. Here again there arises the problem of equalizing the different inputs, because of the mystery involved in the microphones versus the speaker, the speaker versus the person listening and the room.

Monitoring Amplifier

After the sound goes through the mixer, it looks into a monitoring amplifier, which feeds the monitor speaker. The monitoring amplifier and speaker must be capable of handling the sounds you put in with a minimum of distortion. The monitoring amplifier should be flat in frequency response, about 50–15,000 cycles. The speaker, however, is still the biggest problem.

Why It's a Problem

Some of the reasons that the speaker is such a problem: to re-create all sounds in the audible range would mean having a speaker mounted in a very large baffle. This is necessary to reproduce the low frequencies,

because it has become quite a problem to condense the baffle. The speaker manufacturers tried to re-create the low frequency by different methods of speaker enclosures. Another problem is trying to make the speaker flat in frequency response through the audible range. Today, one of the most popular methods is to employ two, three or four types of speakers in one enclosure to reproduce different sections of the audible frequencies. For instance: one speaker would be used to reproduce from 40 cycles to 400 cycles, the second speaker to reproduce 2,000 cycles, another speaker to reproduce 7,000 cycles and maybe a fourth one to reproduce to 15,000 cycles. This entails crossover networks, resonant points and many other unpleasant problems. This could go on for years with no simple definite solution in sight. Without going further this seems to answer one of the reasons that the speaker is so inefficient. A different kind of speaker design will probably be the answer someday.

Going back from the mixer, the signal or sound should be picked up by a tape or disc machine. The tape machine should be of the highest standard, which means the least amount of distortion from wow and flutter. It should also have flat frequency response, etc.

Disc Machine Requirements

As for the disc machine, it should be as free as possible mechanically from wow and flutter, turntable rumble, lead screw patterns. One of the toughest parts of disc recording involves the cutting head. We have found that to have the head equalized complementary to the Audio Engineering Society playback curve is a pretty good arrangement.

The equalization should be approximately +13 dB at 10,000 cycles, flat at 500 and −20 at 50 cycles. We have found that it is better to get a clean record flat to 8,000 cycles than it is to get 12,000 cycles on the record, because the latter leads to more distortion.

We must always keep in mind that, although electronically many of the components are flat, frequency-wise the microphones and the placing of the subjects looking into the system (plus the speaker, the room acoustics and the human ear) make you the judge as to what makes a good recording good. We believe it wise to have the system flat from input to mixer to the output of the monitoring amplifier or tape machine and to do the equalizing with different types of mikes or with equalizers. For critical monitoring, we prefer to have our speaker in a room considered quite dead.

In playback for disc recording we have found that it is one thing to put sound on a disc, but—here we go again—it's generally a lot tougher to get it off than on. The playback system should be as free as possible from table rumble, wow and flutter. The pickup's toughest problems are compliance, tracking, minimum distortion, etc.

Echo Chambers

Quite a few years back, listening to the Ambrose Orchestra, Jack Hylton, Ray Noble and others from England, we became acquainted with echo or delay—which, when used properly, enhanced certain musical passages. It can also take away ugliness in certain other cases. This also works in reverse, however, in that echo can destroy intimate sound, and intimate sound is, to say the least, very hard to capture. This becomes a matter of personal taste as to which sounds should have echo and which should be intimate.

In making our records, we have found that using echo of various types creates entirely different overall sound. This can be achieved many ways—by actually recording in a large hall, in an echo chamber or by forming a loop with a tape or disc machine. The echo chamber is a world of its own.

This, again, is our personal belief, and probably no one will agree with us, but we feel you must have at least 3,000 feet—which, incidentally, we built in a hole on the side of our mountain. Again I warn you this becomes a matter of personal taste. After experimenting with angled walls, different speakers, microphones and the distance between the speaker and the microphone, the problems change with the subject of sound looking in.

Again we are faced with two of the deadliest of all components in recording—the mike and the speaker, not to mention the echo chamber. It takes lots of hard work to hand-tailor the echo chamber and, by compromise, to reach a happy medium so that the echo chamber works properly with a different type of sound looking into it to be fed back to the original source. You could go on with this subject for 499 pages, and I think it would prove that I am searching like everybody else to make a perfect home recording.

In present-day speakers, the method used to reproduce sound from electrical to

Les Paul and Mary Ford with a variety of awards, including several from DownBeat.
(Capitol Records)

mechanical creates the problem of uniform frequency response. For example, the toughest problem is to get all frequencies alike in volume. Transient distortion and unwanted disturbances are like the lens of a camera out of focus.

One thing I will always remember is that four or five years ago I paid $200 for a big pickup and felt so happy to get good reproduction. Along came a fellow who walked into the backyard and asked if I wanted a handful of pickups for $6 apiece. Those $6 pickups remain today among the finest. No matter what the advancements have been, it isn't all a matter of spending money or assembling elaborate equipment. In many cases, as our own, it is a wedding of different components that are used. To explain this further—one thing might be right in one specific case and the other wrong, or vice versa.

Above all, the most important link in an automobile is the guy driving it. We still feel that some of the old records made 10 years ago without amplifier, echo, equalizers and frequency response to 15 KC in

many respects were better than some made today with 372 knobs on them.

June 30, 1954

B.G. Sheds a Tear in the Beer for Yesteryear

by Benny Goodman

I was asked to write about the past, to reminisce about the last 20 years in music. This is a rather difficult assignment for me, for as glorious as these years were for me, I am

From left, Jess Stacy, Benny Goodman, Sid Weiss and Morey Feld from the film *Sweet And Low-Down*. (20th Century-Fox)

still living in the present and am more concerned about what's going on right now than I am about reflecting over memories, as wonderful as they may be.

It seems to me that conditions in the music world today are rather frightening. I'm not what you'd call a gadabout, but I do occasionally like to get around to hear what might be labeled by initiates as "new" sounds and an occasional "old" sound or two. My problem has been where to find these sounds. "New" or "old," they seem to be hiding, almost as though jazz music, and even good dance music, has gone into an underground of sorts.

Problem of Plenty

Not too many years ago, it was more a problem of plenty when a person felt like making a night of it in musical nightlife. At that time there were two dozen assorted places in midtown Manhattan alone where one could find "good" music in one form or another. What's happened to the New Yorkers, the Cocoanut Groves, the Famous Doors, the Onyx Clubs, the Blue Rooms,

the Commodores, and the many other good old musical haunts? Obviously they aren't with us, and there must be some good reasons why.

Actually, I think I know one good reason. It boils down to something like this: the musicians (and in this category I must include the leaders) made such a tremendous inroad with the public through the late '30s and early '40s that they became bold enough to attempt either consciously or unconsciously to take the music away from the people. The modern musicians made what could be termed tremendous technical advances and tried to press these advances on a public whose musical knowledge extends (at least in 90 percent of the cases) to little more than a tapping of the toe, the clapping of hands and the whistling of a tune. Actually, in their quest to make musical progress, they forgot that the public was primarily interested in dancing to music.

Waged War on Squares

What it amounts to is that the modern jazz musician waged a cold war with a genera-

tion of squares, and the musicians got the daylights kicked out of them. That's pretty obvious, because the jazz musician can hardly be found, least of all heard. Occasionally, you can hear him on a disc jockey show and on a phonograph record. But then again, the phonograph record is beginning to waste away as an outlet of expression for the modern musician.

I just heard a few weeks ago that Decca and Coral and Brunswick, related record companies and heretofore quite active in all forms of jazz recordings, have all but cut out jazz recordings and releases, the latter category even including reissues from a fabulous catalog that included Count Basie's greatest, Louis Armstrong, Mildred Bailey, Nat Cole, Charlie Barnet, Jimmie Lunceford and many more. Reason: The Decca-Coral jazz issues weren't being bought, "new" sounds as well as "old" sounds. In other words, the pubic is not supporting the contemporary jazz musician. And if I know musicians, they would never in a million years conceive that possibly they were to blame.

Some Emotional Moments

Certainly there have been those in modern music circles who have transmitted some genuine emotional moments along with their technicalities. The so-called founders of modern jazz, Charlie Parker and Dizzy Gillespie, and maybe George Shearing and Erroll Garner, Stan Getz and Oscar Peterson, have reached the people from time to time from their hearts as well as their minds. But fundamentally, the rest of the modern school have fumbled in the shadows of their founders and have succeeded in removing the emotional factor in music in favor of mimicry and experimenting with technical prowess.

Of course, there is other evidence that I can see. From what I've heard and from what I've gathered in the various polls and from what I occasionally pick up in trade reports from the grapevine, the best jazz bands around the world are also the oldest: Count Basie, Woody Herman and Duke Ellington. And the finest all-around dance band in the country still belongs to the Dorsey family, from what I've been able to gather. Of course, you've got to hand it to a newcomer like Ray Anthony, who at least tries to give the public a go for their money with slick performance, precision musicianship and a touch of showmanship.

Miller Still Hottest

One thing alone can speak, unfortunately, not very well for the modern music generation. The "hottest" bandleader in the trade at the moment is the late Glenn Miller. Sure, it's because they made a movie of his life, and a very good movie at that, but, nonetheless, if there were anything else worthwhile around, half the disc jockey time available would certainly not be composed of Glenn Miller recordings. Nor, for that matter, would those concert albums made by my band in 1938 turn out to be among the biggest-selling dance and jazz records of all time in 1952 and 1953.

The plain fact of the matter is that the spark of originality that made the swing era swing has given way to imitation or to technically progressive but mentally oppressive jazz.

People fundamentally turn to music for relaxation, to forget their griefs and taxes. They want to be made happy or moodily sublime. They don't think about it, they don't want to digest their music. They want to sing to it, or dance to it, or laugh to it, or love to it, or tap toes to it, or whistle with it, or clap hands on the beat to

Tito Puente.
(PoPsie)

it, or even play it.

If the people got this kind of musical diet, it would make it a lot simpler for me to find places to go to on those nights I feel the urge.

Oct. 6, 1954

The Mambo!! They Shake A-Plenty with Tito Puente

by Nat Hentoff

NEW YORK—Though the tender pop vocalists still reign, music with a beat is relentlessly returning to a national popularity. Evidences include the steadily widening audience for jazz and rhythm and blues—and the growth of the mambo!

Dance studios find a course in mambo these days is as essential as a time payment plan. And almost all dance halls and nightclubs now require bands to have at least some mambos in their books. Columbia

records, prodded by its distributors and district sales managers, has started a special series of mambo sessions. Victor, in answer to disc jockey requests for more mambo material, sent out a mambo kit with 25 of the label's most popular mambo sides. Significantly, many of those disc jockey requests came from the smaller towns as well as the major cities that already are confirmed mambo centers.

Although there are several major mambo leaders, Tito Puente "El Rey Del Timbal" particularly reflects in his success the many signs of the rise in mambo popularity. Tito, who is featured on vibes and timbales and also plays piano, bongos, conga drum and alto, starred recently in the first Mambo-Rhumba Festival tour. Covering 16 cities, the tour did better than even the more optimistic of its backers had hoped. Tito is also a major attraction of Tico Records, and his strongly selling mambo sides are one of the chief reasons for that firm's sturdy growth in the past few years. And these Puente records on Tico are used by Arthur Murray and many other dance studios around the country to teach the mambo.

Tito's career, furthermore, has paralleled the appearance of more and more nightclubs that are solely devoted to the mambo and its polyrhythmic allies. The chief of these is Broadway's Palladium, a few doors up from Birdland, and the head bandman at the Palladium is Tito Puente.

Tito is at the Palladium about five

months every year, spending the rest of his time at mambo dates, private parties, jazz clubs and plush resort hotels around the country. Tito's association with the Palladium began about four years ago. When he's there, Tito plays for the enthusiasts Friday, Saturday, Sunday and Wednesday. The uninhibited home of mambo feet holds about 1,500, and they're all there during the four nights. Even more, it seems, crowded in on the climactic Wednesday evenings.

At these memorable Wednesday festivals, the $1.75 admission entitles the adventurous patron to mambo instructions early in the evening, plus an amateur contest for mambo dancers, plus a professional mambo show from 11 to 12, plus dancing to Tito and a relief band. The consensus of the clientele seems to be that this is far better exercise than bowling or turning off the TV commercials.

This Wednesday bacchanal at the Palladium is called Mamboscore. Neighboring Roseland has a Rhumbarama on Tuesday, and the Arcadia ballroom has its special revels on Thursday. Meanwhile, La Bamba (which used to be the jazz-based Music Box) is also prospering several nights a week on the mambo beat.

Surveying this disarming spectacle of Broadway-turned-offbeat, Tito explains the rise of the mambo this way: "Rhythm is what you dance to, and the mambo is popular because its strong rhythms make for good dance music. What is making it even more successful is the combination of jazz elements with the mambo. Bop, for example, by itself has crazy sounds harmonically, but rhythmically, it is not easy to dance to. That's why bop bands are putting in conga drums and adding mambo flavor to their work.

"Similarly, in my band, I use certain aspects of jazz. In our arranging, we use some of the modern sounds in the manner of Gillespie and Kenton, but we never lose the authenticity of the Latin rhythm." Tito confirmed that among the frequent famous visitors at the Palladium to absorb his fusion of mambo and jazz are such jazz vanguardists as Kenton, Gillespie, Duke Ellington and Woody Herman, as well as innocent bystanders like Henry Fonda and Mel Ferrer.

"The popularity of the mambo," Tito believes, "is still in its early stages. All the major record companies will soon be organizing mambo sessions. More clubs and theaters will introduce special mambo evenings. Already the Savoy Ballroom and

the Apollo have Monday mambo nights. And the mambo itself is capable of more and more variations. Like the cha-cha-cha we've been introducing. It came over from Cuba a little over a year ago, and it's a mambo in a slow, rocking tempo.

"The mambo itself, you know," continued Professor Puente, "is basically a rhythm from Africa. Some of the slaves introduced it to Cuba and it became mingled with Cuban rhythms in the rituals and ceremonies that took place in the jungles of Cuba. The mambo became modified through the centuries in Cuba, and came to the United States about seven years ago, though its main rise has been within the past two years.

"The mambo," Puente explained, "differs, let's say, from the rhumba in that it concentrates more on the offbeat, the after beat, like modern jazz, whereas the rhumba is mostly on the beat. And the mambo has more syncopation in its melodic forms than the rhumba. Any person, I think, who digs jazz, will dig the mambo."

As the joyously waving bodies at the Palladium indicate, the essential reason for the mambo's popularity is that these particular musical ingredients make it so exhilarating to dance to. Or, as a friend of Tito said one evening at the Palladium as he watched the swirling multitude, "The reason the mambo is tremendous is that it's a great exhibition dance—everybody who dances is a star."

Feb. 22, 1956
. . . .

Jazz Messengers Blazing a Spirited Trail

by Nat Hentoff

The Jazz Messengers are a blazing band of jazz evangelists who believe that jazzmen advance most surely when their roots in the jazz tradition are deepest. The Messengers, a co-operative unit in which everyone

shares both sides of the ledger, consist of Art Blakey, drums; Horace Silver, piano; Donald Byrd, trumpet; Hank Mobley, tenor; and Doug Watkins, bass.

Blakey and Silver are by now veterans of the modern jazz scene. Byrd and Watkins are two of several young Detroit jazzmen who have become valuable members of the New York jazz fraternity in recent months. Mobley is from New Jersey, and worked with Max Roach and Dizzy Gillespie before becoming a Messenger.

Byrd, incidentally, recently replaced Kenny Dorham, who had been with the Messengers from their start. Kenny is now part of the all-star east/west jazz septet on the February Birdland tour and hopes thereafter to form his own unit with Jackie McLean.

The group was formed as a result of a record date. During the 1954 Christmas holidays, Horace, Watkins, Mobley and drummer Arthur Edgehill were working uptown at Minton's. Horace had a record session coming up, and asked Blakey and Dorham to make it along with Mobley and Watkins. The five liked the way they sounded on that session (Blue Note BLP 5058 under Horace Silver's name) and decided to stay together. They were co-op from the beginning.

Around the beginning of February, the Messengers played their first gig as a unit at the Blue Note in Philadelphia and since have played many of the key jazz clubs in the East and Midwest. The title of the unit came from a big band called the Messengers that Art Blakey led at times from 1948–'50.

Art explains his liking for that title for a jazz unit by reminiscing: "When I was a kid, I went to church mainly to relieve myself of problems and hardships. We did it by singing and clapping our hands. We called this way of relieving trouble having the spirit hit you. I get that same feeling, even more powerfully, when I'm playing jazz. I agree with Reverend Kershaw (who answered the $32,000 television question on jazz) that the spirit in good music is sometimes stronger than the spirit in a church meeting.

"Well, in jazz," Art continued, "you get the message when you hear the music. And when we're on the stand, and we see that there are people in the audience who aren't patting their feet and who aren't nodding their heads to our music, we know we're doing something wrong. Because when we do get our message across, those heads and feet do move."

Silver, too, feels the importance of keeping the mainstream jazz tradition in the group's playing so that the Messengers can firmly go as far back and as far forward as they feel. "Sometimes," Horace said, "we can reach way back and get that old-time, gutbucket barroom feeling with just a taste of the backbeat, as in 'Doodlin'' and 'The Preacher.' And in one number, the medium tempo 'Funky Blues,' we even include some boogie-woogie. And then we come around in numbers like Kenny Dorham's 'Minor Holiday' and Hank Mobley's 'Avila and Tequila' to more intellectual, more up-to-date forms, but still with feeling. And we can just as easily switch to a ballad. We can just adapt to any audience, and to the way any audience feels at a given time."

A large part of the Messengers' book comes from within the band. Everyone writes, and Art, too, has a compositional hand in the numbers in that he's consulted with regard to the percussion effects. "Basically," Horace said, "we just let him play. He can fill in better then we can tell him. Sometimes we do give him suggestions that provide him with ideas."

About three-fourths of the Messengers' library consists of originals by the men themselves, along with such modern jazz standards as "Confirmation," "Woodyn' You," "Night in Tunisia" and "Round About Midnight." The rest consists mostly of the more durable popular standards.

"We have emotion and we have a swinging rhythm section," Horace said. "That's the most important thing—swinging. But we're also trying to create our own arrangements so that they build, so that each one isn't just a first chorus and then blow. We want more meat to our material. That's why I feel more fulfilled in this group than any I've been in. I've always wanted to be part of a unit that stays together, that rehearses and builds. I've gotten sick in recent years where guys just blow, or of having just a week's work with a group that then falls out. But a group like the Messengers makes you more ambitious, makes you want to write more because you have somebody to try out your material."

The Messengers use many devices to structure their arrangements while still leaving large, free spaces for blowing. The scores include interludes, tempo changes, and in some cases, contrapuntal lines. "But we also," Horace added, "don't want to go too far out. We want people to understand what we're doing."

With all of these cross-devices to channel their blowing into fresh, unique structures that at the same time will not inhibit their fiercely driving emotions, the Messengers are building one of the most exciting repertoires in jazz. Currently on another swing of the jazz clubs, the Messengers may also hit the West Coast during the earlier part of the year.

Recording-wise, Blue Note will soon issue a 12-inch LP of the Messengers that was recorded at Cafe Bohemia. The group at press time was considering a new—and quite attractive—contract with Atlantic, under which the Messengers would record as a unit for that label under their name. (Art Blakey as a single is still signed to EmArcy, but would be borrowed from EmArcy for the Atlantic sessions for the Messengers.)

In a jazz era of multiple experimentations and divisions into "schools," the Messengers are a healthy and kicking reminder that if a gifted artist's roots are strong in the history and basic nature of his language, then his own contributions to that language will be all the stronger and more individual because of the nourishment he receives from those roots.

May 2, 1956
. . . .

Chet Baker Letters Tell of Europe Successes

by Chet Baker

[Editor's Note: Touring and recording with his quartet in Europe and Iceland since September 1955, Chet Baker took time out when his hectic schedule permitted to jot a few lines to *DownBeat* on the tour's progress and his impressions of the European jazz scene. Excerpts from the letters follow.]

LONDON, September 1955
Hi, everybody Stateside:

I only wish I could sit down every day and write about things as they happened. You have no idea, though, how we've been kept going, between concerts, recording dates and so on. When we landed in London I thought, "This is going to be a square scene. Bet there's nothing happening in this town." Boy, was I wrong. Not only are the British fans wild about modern jazz from the States, but they have their own fine jazzmen, too. Places like the Feldman Club on Oxford Street have been putting on the best jazz here since the war.

There's a lot happening on records, too. Cats like Johnny Dankworth, Jack Parnell, Ronnie Scott, Jimmy Deucher and a very fine but little-known tenor man, Jack Chilkes, who hasn't been recording lately, help to brighten the scene.

Sorry, but I don't dig this climate. It's supposed to be summer here, but you'd never know it. Can't compare to California!

PARIS, Sept. 22, 1955
Paris! Wow! We're really packing them in everywhere. Really never thought it would go over so well…

Oct. 4, 1955
Tonight we do our first concert in Paris and tomorrow we start touring France. I know this is going to be a ball.

STUTTGART, Oct. 15, 1955
We're doing a concert tonight with Caterina Valente and Lars Gullin—should be good. Best promotion of jazz here is being done by the Armed Forces Radio Service based in this city. It's like listening to Joe Adams at home…

Oct. 16, 1955
Last night's concert was part of the very fine "Week of Light Music" festival, an annual affair that attracts musicians from all parts of Europe. I guess we went over pretty big because the audience didn't want us to go off.

BADEN-BADEN, Dec. 1, 1955
Pardon the long silence, but things have been moving so fast. We were all deeply saddened by the passing of Dick Twardzik. He was a wonderful person and brilliant musician. And only 24.

We're here to do a television show on the Studenwestfunken (I think that's how you spell it) network. They tell me that I'll be the first American musician to appear on a German TV show—that's a kick. We

Chet Baker.
(DownBeat Archive)

did some recordings in Paris that were not too bad, I think. After Germany we return to Paris to clean up the record sessions with Blue Star, Madame Barclay's label. From there we go on to Iceland to play some U.S. bases, then to Denmark and then, if all goes well, we open in Milano, Italy, for two months starting Jan. 3.

MILANO, Jan. 1, 1956

Happy New Year! We opened last night at the Taveno Room in the plush Hotel Duomo here. This is the city's best hotel. But, man, these Italians are hard to please—they want dance music! However, before we finished they sure swung...

Jan. 10, 1956

Just love this crazy town. Just learned I won't be going to Japan till late September, which will give me from May to the

end of September in the U.S. We're going to do a movie for an Italian company before going on tour in Italy and are booked to play in the Italian Jazz Festival at San Remo, Jan. 28–29. After that we go back again to Germany.

ROME, Jan. 18, 1956

Rome is too, too much! It's about the best city I've seen in my life. We do two concerts here later this week.

FRANKFORT AM MAIN, Feb. 1, 1956

Well, back in Germany after four great weeks in Italy. You have no idea how well we went over. Just can't get over it. Joe Napoli [Editor's Note: Chet's manager] had to get the police to get me out of the concert halls, the crowds were so enthusiastic. A ball!

Feb. 23, 1956

We closed last night here in Storyville after three packed nights. I have never seen such a packed nightclub. You know, there's a club in Koln we played that sure brought me back to the Haig. It really swings. Tomorrow we leave to play for the Canadians, then back to our airbase for a few days.

Feb. 28, 1956

Still in Frankfort. What I've seen here regarding the jazz scene would take pages to describe, but I can say now that the jazz scene here in Europe is much bigger than you could ever think. These people are screaming for new records that they are unable to get. The Pacific Jazz stuff (it's "vogue" here) is as hot as a Fourth of July outing. We've played to huge houses and never dreamed we'd go over so big.

BADEN-BADEN, March 15, 1956

We will record with Caterina Valente here March 26. On March 31, we're looking forward to the concert in Berlin with the Stan Getz group. Germany, as always, is too much! See you in May.

Regards,
Chet

May 16, 1956

"Multi-Taping Isn't Phony" —Tristano

by Nat Hentoff

After he made coffee, Lennie Tristano sat and talked in his studio late one afternoon. Except for a small lamp that gave a bare minimum of light by which to scrawl notes, the studio was dark. The room was also curiously peaceful as if it were used to long periods of silence as well as music, and relatively unused to loud, hurried anxiety.

Usually after an interview, I piece together a mosaic of quotes into a monologue that has more continuity than any real conversation short of a visiting clergyman's can really have. This time I decided not to splice the talk as much as usual, and to record instead what an actual conversation with Tristano is like.

I've talked with many people in line of assignments and after hours, and I am rarely as stimulated as by a talk with Tristano. Like the writings of Andre Hodeir, the ideas of Tristano awaken the kind of attention that moves a mind to think for itself. Whether one agrees with all of Lennie's points or not, one is always aware that unusually probing points are being made.

Lennie's Atlantic LP had recently been released, his first recording in some four years. It had immediately detonated controversy, a phenomenon hardly new to Tristano activities. While there was nearly unanimous agreement that the music was absorbing, there were strong objections in some quarters to Lennie's use of multiple taping on several of the tracks, and some suspected that in two of the numbers, the piano tape had also been speeded up. A similar multi-track controversy had been ignited by a Tristano single record a few years before.

"I remember," Lennie said, "that around 1952, when that last record came out—"Juju" and "Pass-Time"—there wasn't one review out of the five or so that the record received that mentioned that those two sides could possibly have been a result of multiple track recording. It was only six months or a year later that somebody got the idea it might be, and then the talk started. I never really told anybody whether it was or not.

"One of the people who got so hung up on the subject," Lennie continued with amused calm, "was Leonard Bernstein. He and Willie Kapell were over here one night, and Bernstein finally decided it was a multiple track recording. He couldn't stand to believe it wasn't. And then Kapell sat down at the piano and started playing Mozart 16 times faster than normal. Lee Konitz tried to save the situation earlier by telling them it was multi-track. But he didn't know for sure, either.

"The reason I mention this background for the present controversy"—Lennie became more animated—"is to illustrate one of the most surprising things prevalent in music today—the element of competition. It's true of the musicians and non-musicians. They can't just listen to the music. They have to compete with it. If it's not in terms of speed—whether they can play as fast as the record—then it's in terms

of finding out what the tune is. It's ridiculous. You can't hear music if you're not able to sit back and listen a few times, just listen. Then, if you can do that, maybe the fourth or the 10th time, you can figure out what the tune is if you want to. It doesn't really matter, anyway. The music does.

"Getting back to an example of competition by speed," Lennie said, "there was a night I was playing at Birdland, and I was playing something pretty frantic. A boy was standing at the bar—he was a pianist—and as he watched me, his hand got paralyzed. He dropped the glass he was holding, and his hand was still paralyzed a half hour later. That's kinesthetic competition, and it's a pitiful commentary on this urge to compete. Some people are affected physically another way. I've seen them get sick and have to leave the room. It gets them in the stomach. They get scared and have to cut out. They can't just enjoy the music; they listen to see if they can do it.

"It's not just me that some people react to that way," Tristano emphasized. "Many piano players, when Bud was playing great, couldn't stand to listen. They gave up, some of them, and became like slaves, like worshippers. That's why the worshipper has to elevate the artist he worships to such a height. If they remove this particular artist from any type of human contact, they feel they no longer have to compete with him. You don't have to compare yourself with God. It's not as if they had kept him on earth, which is where he belongs.

"Another aspect of this whole thing," Lennie reflected, "is the reaction of a lot of people who have played with me. They can't stand to have me pause in my line. The longer I pause, the tenser they get. Once at a concert in Toronto, I'd stopped for 16 bars. The time was going on and I could feel the drummer get tenser and tenser. Finally I hit one chord, and it was as if I'd set off an explosion. He hit everything on that drum set he could, all at once. The drums were all over the stage. It's like he was waiting for me to pounce on him.

"My audience sometimes reacts the same way when I pause. They get tense. What's Lennie going to do now? What's Lennie going to hit us with next? Instead of listening, they're worrying."

The conversation returned to the new LP. According to Barry Ulanov's notes on the set, "Lennie has fooled with the tapes of 'East Thirty-Second' and 'Line Up,' adjusting the bass lines Peter Ind (on bass) and Jeff Morton (on drums) prepared for

him to the piano lines he has superimposed on them." Barry went on to mention the paired piano lines in "Requiem" and "the three lines played—and recorded—one on top of the other in the 'Turkish Mambo'… one track proceeds from 7/8 to 7/4, another from 5/8 to 5/4, the last from 3/8 to 4/4."

"If I do a multiple-tape," Lennie said slowly with determination, "I don't feel I'm a phony thereby. Take the 'Turkish Mambo.' There is no way I could do it so that I could get the rhythms to go together the way I feel them. And as for playing on top of a tape of a rhythm section, that is only second-best admittedly. I'd rather do it 'live,' but this was the best substitute for what I wanted.

"If people want to think I speeded up the piano on 'East Thirty-Second' and 'Line Up,' I don't care. What I care about is that the result sounded good to me. I can't otherwise get that kind of balance on my piano because the section of the piano I was playing on is too similar to the bass sound. That's especially so on the piano I use because it's a big piano and the bass sound is very heavy. But, again, my point is that it's the music that matters."

One of the objections voiced to these particular tracks was that whatever Lennie did to the tape made his playing very fast. "It's really not that fast, though," Lennie said. "There are lots of recordings out there that are much faster. I understand some people say that making a record like the one I made isn't fair because I couldn't play the numbers that fast in a club. Well, I'll learn the record so I can play it at that tempo 'live.' But even as is, it's not that fast. Some people are being misled by the nature of what it feels and sounds like rather than by the tempo itself. The tempo, in most jazz joints, in fact, is faster than on the record. And the record was a little above A-flat. That may account for a little of the speed, too.

"Actually," Lennie said, "we manipulated other things electronically. Am I to be put down for adding a tape echo on the blues and adding a tremolo on the last chorus of that number? In essence, I feel exactly this. When I sit down to do something, I can hear and feel what I want. Instead of trying to have three or four people on hand so I don't have the 'stigma' of multi-track recording, there are some things I'd rather do myself because there are some things I want to do that others are not capable of doing with me.

"If someone objects," Lennie pointed

out, "to, let's say, the sound on 'Line Up,' that's a matter of taste. But why not hear what's happening in the line to see if that's of any value, and why not hear what kind of feeling the performance has? I have absolutely no qualms about multi-tracking. This kind of thing happens all the time in the recording of classical music, for one example. Are we supposed to give up the typewriter because we've had the pencil so long? Or am I not to use the Telefunken mike and rely instead on a dirt old crystal mike? I'm sure other people have done a lot more multi-tracking than I have. There's nothing at all wrong, for another example, in a pianist recording both parts of a two-piano classical work. Why is it wrong when I do it?"

I mentioned at this point that a recorded case in point is the Heifetz recording on both parts of the Bach Concerto in D Minor for Two Violins (Victor LM 1051).

"Anyway," Lennie said, "I will continue to do anything that will produce on a record what I hear and feel."

The conversation then veered to the problem of recording itself. "Right now in jazz," Tristano came on strongly, "everything is being recorded with a lot of echo, with the illusion of a big room. Even if the recording is done close, the full impact doesn't come through. It may be that people don't want that direct an impact, maybe they prefer to have everything softened by the added echo and want to hear their music in a sweet, mushy context like Muzak. I'm not against reverberation as such, but this excess use of echo points to the fact that a lot of people can't really take jazz in its straight, natural form.

"For example," Lennie underlined, "there are the horrible things they've done to some of Bird's records in the remastering process by adding echo to them. Yet the greatest records he made were made with almost no echo. You could feel all the notes.

"A little echo is all right, but now it's no longer being used as an effect," Lennie went on. "Now it's the whole thing.

"As for the Atlantic LP, except for the tracks made at the Confucius, where you really couldn't get a good balance—the engineers did a good job considering everything—the rest of the LP I made here at the studio without an engineer. And those tracks came out pretty good.

"I used a Telefunken, a great mike, maybe a foot or a foot and a half over the strings. On the blues I added a little tape echo. There was no echo, I think, on the

others here. I was trying to get a kind of cathedral sound, and I think I made it. There's quite a difference, incidentally, between a tape echo and echo chambers or reverberation generators. Tape echo, I feel, is a little more pronounced and more natural. With tape echo you can actually hear the echo coming through the second time instead of a big hollow, open sound as with an echo chamber."

Since various aspects of recording had dominated the talk up to this point, I asked Lennie why he had waiting so long to record again, even though he had received offers from almost every label in the field. "For one thing," Lennie explained, "I wasn't able to find a rhythm section. I don't mean, let me make clear, that there aren't any good rhythm section men. I just couldn't find one for myself, and I still can't."

Asked what he wanted in a rhythm section, Lennie detailed his requirements: "I want time that flows. I want people who don't break the rhythm section with figures that are really out of context. What figures are used should be in the context of what's happening, so as not to break continuity. A lot of drummers interpolate figures that break the line. All of a sudden, the line stops, and he plays a cute figure on a snare drum or a tom-tom. Some bass players do that, too. They break time to play a figure that doesn't fit with what's already happened and is happening. With rhythm sections I've played with, I don't have the feeling of a constantly flowing pulse no matter what happens. As soon as I feel the pulse being interrupted, my flow is interrupted whether I'm playing or resting, because it's all the same thing.

"I also need in a rhythm section people with feeling for simultaneous combinations of time—people who are able to perceive 5/4 and 4/4 at the same time. I'll probably be doing more and more of that. Working with 7/4 and 6/4 and the double times of those—5/8, 6/8, 7/8, and maybe sometimes 9/8. Occasionally, I've played something and tried to figure it out afterward, and have maybe done some 13/8."

Lennie continued his description of the rhythm section he's seeking: "I'd like to have a rhythm section with a feeling for dynamics. One of the faults of most jazz today is that it proceeds at one dynamic level.

"What I'm after is not an up and down kind of thing but something pretty subtle. Parenthetically, I think that drummers today are doing too much. They play the bass drums, sock cymbal, snare drum,

top cymbal—four basic instruments right there. Add to that tom-toms, other accessories, and funny noises like tapping on top of the snare, and it's all much more than one man should be doing.

"Then there's the matter of tempo," Lennie said. "Rhythm sections today like to play a real fast tempo—'cooking' as some people call it. A real fast 2/4. As a result, everything is pat and things go by so fast with generally a good feeling that they don't miss the subtleties, subtleties that ought to be there. Another thing is the ridiculous ballad tempo that's prevalent. They try to get it just right so they can play double time on that, too, so they really wind up in the same place. And the in-between tempos are generally very crude.

"I want to play a lot of different tempos and more of the in-between. For example, many of the early Bird records and the early Pres sides with Basie were played at these in-between tempos. A couple of the Pres records—like 'Clap Hands, Here Comes Charlie'—were fast, but he made it. Now 'Ko-Ko' was one of Bird's fastest records, and it wasn't as good as the more in-between 'Warming Up a Riff,' also based on 'Cherokee,' which had more creative Bird.

"Another thing I've missed," Lennie said, "is that people don't seem to have a feeling of playing together. That's a general comment, of course. Some people play together better than others. But a lot of people give the impression of everybody manning his particular gun and shooting wherever he wants to. Remember the old Billie records with Teddy Wilson, Roy and sometimes Pres? The rhythm section on those is sort of old-fashioned now, but they really played together. This is probably true of jazz in general right now. You don't hear the kind of togetherness in the groups that are playing. There's either a neat, commercial jazz sound, or they're trying to improvise and it's a little ragged."

Lennie came back to his specific problems with rhythm sections. "I have trouble with bass players and chord progressions. I've pointed out to them that instead of trying to find out where I'm going, they'd do a lot better and get a better sound by playing the foundation chord instead of trying to get to where I am at the moment. If they're on the fundamental chord, they'll get to relate to what I'm doing and eventually get to where I am sometimes.

"To make another general statement," Lennie said, "everybody's a soloist now.

There are no more sidemen in the world. Everybody is a star. I can't imagine anything more monotonous, for example, than a bass playing two or three choruses on a ballad unless it's a good bass player like Oscar Pettiford who can solo."

"What about the charge," I interjected, "concerning the long time you didn't record, the charge that you didn't want to set down your ideas so people could have them that accessible for copying?"

"I don't think anyone would want to copy me to start with," Lennie answered. "And what I do isn't pat or that perfect anyway. Now the way Bird played his ideas, they were perfect the way they were. Changing some of the notes would have spoiled them. What you can do is mix them up or play them in different sequences but the essential idea was perfect. Another thing you can do with Bird's ideas is play them on a different part of the bar. Instead of one, start the idea on two. Or you can stretch a 4/4 idea into 5/4 or 7/4, lengthen the phrase. I feel that if Bird's situation had been conducive to this sort of thing, he would have done that kind of thing himself. I remember doing a concert with him and we were warming up without a rhythm section. I was playing some chords and he was really stretching out.

"Another factor in my not having recorded in so long a time is that I'm not ambitious. If I don't think I have something to record that means something to me, I don't feel the necessity to release it. At least half the records of mine that are out are rejects from my point of view. A couple of the Capitol sides, for instance, and most of the Prestige, a couple on Disc, and the four on Royale. It's really pretty silly because it means part of my audience likes me because of my bad records. That's why I've felt that as soon as I learned how to play I'd lose a big part of my audience, an audience that's not too big to start with.

"I don't think, by the way," Lennie said, "that I'm the next jazz messiah. The way some people have spoken or written of me pro and con may have created the impression I thought that, but that isn't the way I think, and I've never said it. Maybe that impression is also due to the antagonism against me in some quarters. If enough people put somebody down, he assumes a large proportion in some eyes.

"What I am doing is trying within the limits of my ability to develop my capacity to improvise so that I'm really improvising as much of the time as I can. I think I've done a few things that haven't been done, at least to the extent that I'm doing them, but I don't feel there's anything 'great' about them. It took me a long time, for example, to feel 5/4 and 10/4 on top of 4/4. It's something that can't be done intellectually. It's something you have to get the feel. I am not running some kind of weird laboratory and manipulating scientific gadgets. It's been hard learning how to play what I feel on the piano because the piano is a difficult instrument. There are fingering problems we all have. Other instrumentalists, for example, generally can make the same note with the same finger. With the piano, there are spatial problems…"

There was a visitor downstairs, and this next turn in the conversation had to be postponed. As I was leaving, Lennie said, "There is one other thing I'm looking for, and perhaps the magazine's readers can help. We'll have to be leaving this building soon since they're tearing it down. I haven't found a new location yet. Anybody with an idea can write me at the studio, 317 E. 32nd St.

"I also am thinking of starting a club again. As for working in other clubs, I have offers, but I'm not sure yet what I'll be doing in that regard. Jazz musicians are expected to be entertainers. I'm not. Although I feel I can be very entertaining sometimes among friends."

The Hawk Talks
Coleman Discusses Individuality and Some Young Musicians
by Nat Hentoff

Tenor Budd Johnson, who has been an undiluted jazz-sayer for a long time, was talking to Coleman Hawkins during an intermission recently. "You know," Johnson said, "it's a funny thing. All those fellows who play tenor, most of them give the impression they're pretty much alike. Me too. We give the impression that we're looking for something and can't quite find it. But you're different. You're the one who did it, and when you play, it's altogether different."

The next day when the same subject of originality came up, Hawk shook his head and said, "It seems like it just comes. I guess I've always had my own way of playing. But one thing I'd like to clear up. People always say I invented the jazz tenor, that I was the first who played jazz on the tenor. It isn't true. There was a Happy Cauldwell in Chicago and Stomp Evans out of Kansas City. They were playing like mad.

"What it may have been is that people around here in New York used to hear me all the time at the Roseland with Fletcher Henderson, and that's how that story grew.

"But they didn't realize all those other tenors were around. Why, gangs of tenors would be coming into New York all the time from bands on the road. They used to wake me out of my bed to come down and cut people. Tenors like Prince Robinson, for example.

"I guess it is true," Hawkins paused, "that I introduced a new style, a new way of playing tenor. I had a much heavier tongue, for one thing, than most of the others had. And their tone was kind of thin."

The Hawk laughed. "There's nothing new about thin tones. That's been around for years.

"It's funny about having a big tone," he continued. "A lot of times I can play the exact same thing as someone else, but they swear it's different, but it's only because my tone is bigger. I always did want to be heard. I used to say to myself: it's foolish to be blowing if nobody can hear you. So I fooled a lot with reeds and mouthpieces. I wanted a strong tone. No, I don't think I could advise people how to get a big tone. And I don't believe that's something you can teach. It just comes from the individual way a man blows into a horn. Does it have anything to do with personality? Well, maybe so.

"You take, for instance," Hawkins said intently, "other instruments, like fiddles. Some violinists can get larger sounds than others. They always blame the instrument, but I don't believe it. Stradivarius or not, it's strictly an individual thing."

Hawkins turned to the younger tenors today. "I like a lot of them," he said. "Al Cohn. Zoot Sims. Naturally, I like Budd Johnson. Of course, he's not one of the younger ones, but he's a very good musician whom people have been asleep on for a long time. And he plays a lot of modern tenor, too. And he always will. Yes, I like

Coleman Hawkins.
(William Morris Agency)

Hawkins shook his head, thinking of the strangeness of conformity, and said, "I hear 1,000 players today, and they all sound alike. Maybe a little more jamming might help that some. Very few of them are individuals. I guess maybe they're just satisfied with copying.

"Fats Navarro was quite good," Hawkins said, outlining exceptions. "And Clifford Brown was going to develop into something and to be himself eventually. But he needed a few years. He was a heck of a trumpet player. He could fly all over the horn. He could make a million notes, but you'd heard those notes already. Years and experience would have given him a distinctive thing of his own.

"What has there been original after Dizzy?" Hawkins asked rhetorically. "There should be some other originals. There are so many playing as good as they can play, but they should get another way of playing, more their own way. But maybe they're satisfied with the way they sound.

"There's another trumpet player," Hawkins went on, "who's not so well known but who's developing his own way of playing, and I'd like to bring him out. I may use him on a Capitol date I have coming up. He's Idrees Sulieman. He's having some trouble. He plays an awful lot of trumpet, but he plays too much at times. He needs somebody to say: 'Settle down—wait a minute—wait a minute.' I was talking to Monk about him, and he says the same thing. There's such a thing as playing too much. He gets excited, and off he goes. But he's young. Give him 10 years.

"Monk." Hawkins nodded his head in emphatic approval. "That's originality! That's why I like it when he does it. You haven't heard it before. Other originals? Bird, you know. J.J. Johnson, and some others. But I hate to list names like that. Don't make this article so my friends won't talk to me."

The talk turned to a more general topic, the trend toward writing in jazz.

"I think it's fine for ensemble," Hawk said, "but it's hard to appreciate a person having a solo all written out for him. When you stop and think about it, maybe in 100 years, jazz will be like that, like classical music. But if it does turn out that way, you'll have taken the basic effect of jazz away. Improvisation is the key. Jazz would lose all its originality without it. That's why jazz is a different kind of music from classical.

"But it's also true that if classical music were written like it used to be a cou-

Getz. And there's Sonny Rollins. And Sonny Stitt—except Stitt has been playing alto so much lately.

"I'll tell you something about the young players," he emphasized. "It takes everyone age and experience to find themselves in their horns. Take Dizzy Gillespie. To me he plays 100 percent better today than he did 10 years ago. He's had all that experience. There's a certain amount of wildness in a young player, but they eventually get down to precision, to real artistry."

Talk turned to the scarcity of places for musicians to jam as contrasted with years ago. "There are some places," Hawk said, searching a mental map. "Roy Eldridge finds them. But it's usually not real jamming because there's usually

nobody there but him when he gets there. Like he goes up to Bowman's a lot opposite the Polo Grounds, but he's the only horn playing there with the house rhythm section. Why, there used to be eight to 10 different horns at a session."

On being asked if the current infrequency of jam sessions limits the development of younger musicians, Hawkins' first reaction was that it didn't. But the more he thought, the more he changed his mind.

"The sessions used to be valuable for exchanging ideas," he said. "Today with many fellows it seems to be records. A fellow will steal a whole chorus of a record and go out and play it. Perhaps it may be partially from not jamming enough that so many younger musicians lack originality."

ple centuries ago, there'd be a lot of improvising in it, too.

"A lot of the great composers years ago used to ask people to play their music but to use their own ideas when they did. I read about when Copeland, the pianist, met Debussy. Copeland had been going around America, playing a lot of Debussy in concerts. The first time he met Debussy in Paris, Copeland sat down to play. He was trying to play this particular piece according to all the exact expressions Debussy had written on the score. But Debussy said, impatiently, 'Don't play with it that way. Play it the way you would feel it.'

"For another example, if you listen to the same concerto played by four or five different artists, you'll find several places where they vary. The music would be ruined if the interpretation was always the same. It's the differences, the individuality, that makes people artists in classical music, too."

Hawk went on to talk of his pleasure in listening to classical music and, from there, to the kind of musical settings he himself prefers:

"Would I get a group together to travel? I wouldn't be too eager unless I was very highly paid. I average two to five or six gigs a week staying home, plus record dates, and I go down to Childs on Saturday nights if I'm not booked somewhere else.

"What would I travel with if there were no financial restrictions? What I'd want, nobody could afford. I would want to travel with a lot of strings, a lot of brass, a lot of reeds, a lot of woodwinds, and definitely a harp.

"I don't want an old-time band like seven or eight brass and four or five reeds. For what I want, I'd need a really big group. I would like to carry around the kind of bands I record with, like those on the last two albums for Victor (*The Hawk in Hi-Fi*) and Vik (*The Hawk in Paris*).

"With that kind of background," Hawkins beamed, "there'd be no limit to the ideas you could use and to the different colorations you could make. You could play anything. With a small combo or with the usual kind of big band, you're limited in how much you can play, and the effects you can get. A harp is something I have to have for effect—strictly for effect.

"The strings I would use," Hawk sketched his program, "only on ballads. On a swinging tune, I'd use brass, no strings. As a matter of fact, part of the record date I'm about to make for Capitol will have me

and about 13 brass and a rhythm section. That's all. Then I'll do a session for that LP with strings and woodwinds, and another with just trumpet and four rhythm. I like to get a variety of things onto an LP.

"Yes," Hawk nodded, "I'm freelance now. I prefer it that way—for the time being. I have contracts at home from Victor and Capitol that call for exclusivity. And both promise to put out some singles, too, as well as albums. That's where the money is. I may sign one of them later, but right now, I wanted to do these things and see how they turn out.

"There are a lot of different things that can be done, a lot of different colors you can use. The thing, though, is to be original. To play a way of your own."

Soulful Sarah

A Success as a Pop-Jazz Singer, She Seeks Greater Accomplishment

by Don Gold

Sarah Vaughan has cold feet. She'd like to record an all-piano LP, but she lacks the courage, despite eight years of piano training and experience as vocalist-pianist with the Earl Hines band.

"I've thought of playing more piano, but I always get cold feet. It's always in the back of my mind," she says. "I dig Tatum so much, and Hank Jones, Jimmy Jones, Garner and Shearing. I practice at home, backstage, when there's time. You know, I'd like to do the kind of piano LP Nat Cole has done."

Despite the lucrative, satisfying career she has found, Sarah continues to seek other worlds to conquer, including the world of the spiritual.

"You have to have a little soul in your singing," she says. "The kind of soul that's in the spirituals. That's why I'd like to include spiritual material in the sets I do. It's a part of my life. You know, I'm from a Baptist church. Every now and then, when I'm home in Newark, I sing with the church choir.

"I want so much to do a special album of spirituals, like an Italian wanting to do Italian folk songs. I dig most of the spirituals I know from church, what you'd call the 'old standards,' not too many of the new. I'd like to give an all-spiritual concert, too, with choir. Do it up right, like Marian Anderson. She's always been an idol of mine."

From one aspiration, she moves on to another.

"You know what else I'd like to do? I'd like to have a crazy TV show, like Rosemary Clooney's show. I'd have a variety of things, not just jazz. Something of musical value for young and old. It would be fun for me."

It would be fun, she admits, but not quite like the earlier days, before these large-scale hopes, when she joined the Earl Hines band in 1943 at the age of 19.

"I never had so much fun in my life as I did singing with Earl," she remembers. "Billy (Eckstine), of course, helped me get that job, by telling Earl about my amateur hour appearance at the Apollo Theater. Not only did I learn much about stage presence from Billy, but several other members of the Hines band were like fathers to me. It was a beginning. No money, but much fun. I wouldn't mind going through it one more time."

She and Eckstine left Hines and sang together in Eckstine's band. She began recording first for Continental, then Musicraft. She worked and listened to the jazz innovators. Inspired and encouraged by such people as Charlie Parker and Dizzy Gillespie, she turned to working as a single.

"I thought Bird and Diz were the end," she says. "I still do. At the time I was singing more off-key than on. I think their playing influenced my singing. Horns always influenced me more than voices.

"All of them—Bird, Diz, Pres, Tatum, J.J, Benny Green, Thad Jones—listening to them and others like them, listening to good jazz, inspired me."

Until the late '40s, Sarah went unrecognized by the general public. Then came a Columbia recording contract. The efforts of her unofficial fan club began to pay off. She attributes her success to a combination of influences and loyalties.

"Dave Garroway… People were telling me about him praising me before I knew Dave," she notes. "He praised me so much, some of his listeners thought we were married. It was the kind of support you can't pay for."

Her manager, and husband since

Sarah Vaughan.
((DownBeat Archive)

1947, George Treadwell, played an integral part in her maturation as a singer and increased the number of strolls to the bank.

"Good management has helped me find much of the success I've got. George was the one who helped me all along. There are other loyal ones, too. My right-hand man, John Garry, has been with me for 10 years. If he ever left me, I'd be out of business. And with my secretary, Modina Davis, around, I don't have to worry about a thing. I just have to sing."

Now with Mercury-EmArcy, Sarah can sing. She records pop tunes for Mercury, jazz-flavored sounds for EmArcy. She is aware of happenings in both fields, but devotes most of her listening time to jazz.

"I dig Chico's group, the Modern Jazz Quartet, and some of Mulligan's things," she says. "Doing a 'Pinky'-type tune with such groups would just knock me out.

"I've got quite a record collection at home, jazz and semi-classical. I start listening as soon as I walk in the door. I prefer to have good music around me at all times. Good music? Well, Mahalia Jackson can sing! If she wanted to, she could sing any-

thing well. I dig Doris Day. And I love the way Jo Stafford reads. Clooney can wail... Fitzgerald... Nat Cole... Billie.

"It's singing with soul that counts. Billie has so much soul. When I sing a tune, the lyrics are important to me. Most of the standard lyrics I know well. And as soon as I hear an arrangement, I get ideas, kind of like blowing a horn. I guess I never sing a tune the same way twice. And a recent rehearsal we had in Boston was the first one we had in years. My trio—Jimmy Jones, Richard Davis and Roy Haynes—is always up to tricks onstand. I dig it this way," she concludes.

Those who have known her since the awkward days of the mid-'40s, when her voice showed indications of quality and her gowns and stage presence did not, can best appreciate the transformation that has taken place. Today, as one of the most successful singers, she is poised and chic, and is singing more communicatively than she has in the past.

As a major figure in the evolution of singing in jazz, and as a singer with appreciable fame in the pop field, she finds her-

self in a position quite different from that of the nervous 19-year-old in front of the Hines band. Today, young singers look up to her for inspiration.

Oct. 16, 1958

'Trane on the Track

by Ira Gitler

Asked about being termed an "angry young tenor" in this publication's coverage of the 1958 Newport Jazz Festival, John Coltrane said, "If it is interpreted as angry, it is taken wrong. The only one I'm angry at is myself when I don't make what I'm trying to play."

The 32-year-old native of Hamlet, N.C., has had his melancholy moments, but he feels that they belong to a disjointed, frustrating past. The crucial point in his development came after he joined Dizzy Gillespie's band in 1951.

Prior to that, he had studied music and worked in Philadelphia, assuming many of the fashionable nuances of the Charlie Parker–directed groups. When the offer to join the Gillespie band came, Coltrane felt ready.

The feeling turned out to be illusory.

"What I didn't know with Diz was that what I had to do was really express myself," Coltrane remembered. "I was playing clichés and trying to learn tunes that were hip, so I could play with the guys who played them.

"Earlier, when I had first heard Bird, I wanted to be identified with him... to be consumed by him. But underneath I really wanted to be myself.

"You can only play so much of another man."

Dejected and dissatisfied with his own efforts, Coltrane left Gillespie and returned to Philadelphia in search of a musical ideal and the accompanying integrity. Temporarily, he attempted to find escape in work.

"I just took gigs," he said. "You didn't have to play anything. The less you played, the better it was."

Plagued by economic difficulties, he searched for a steady job. In 1952, he found one, with a group led by Earl Bostic, whom

John Coltrane.
(Lee Tanner)

he admires as a saxophonist even though he disliked the rhythm-and-blues realm the band dwelt in. But this job did not demolish the disillusion and lethargy that had captured him.

"Any time you play your horn, it helps you," he said. "If you get down, you can help yourself even in a rock 'n' roll band. But I didn't help myself."

A more productive step was made in 1953, when Coltrane joined a group headed by Johnny Hodges.

"We played honest music in this band," he recalled. "It was my education to the older generation."

Gradually, Coltrane rationalized the desire to work regularly with the aim of creating forcefully. In 1955, he returned to Philadelphia and, working with a group led by conga drummer Bill Carney, took a stride toward achieving his goal. As he recalled, "We were too musical for certain rooms."

In late 1955, Miles Davis beckoned. Davis had noted Coltrane's playing and wanted him in a new quintet he was forming. He encouraged Coltrane; this encouragement gradually opened adventurous

paths for Coltrane. Other musicians and listeners began to pay close attention to him. When Davis disbanded in 1957, Coltrane joined Thelonious Monk's quartet.

Coltrane will not forget the role Davis and Monk played in assisting his development.

"Miles and Monk are my two musicians," he said. "Miles is the No. 1 influence over most of the modern musicians now. There isn't much harmonic ground he hasn't broken. Just listening to the beauty of his playing opens up doors. By the time I run up on something, I find Miles or Monk has done it already.

"Some things I learn directly from them. Miles has shown me possibilities in choosing substitutions within a chord and also new progressions."

Enveloped in the productive atmosphere of both the Davis and Monk groups, Coltrane emerged more an individualist than ever before. In early '58, he rejoined Davis. In the months since he did so, he has become more of an influence on other jazz instrumentalists. His recordings, on Prestige, Blue Note and with Davis on Colum-

bia, often are matters for passionate debate.

Yet there is no denying his influence. There are traces of his playing in that of Junior Cook, with Horace Silver's group, and in Benny Golson, previously a Don Byas-Lucky-Thompson-out-of-Hawkins tenor man.

Coltrane's teammate in the Davis sextet, Cannonball Adderley, recently said, "Coltrane and Sonny Rollins are introducing us to some new music, each in his own way. I think Monk's acceptance, after all this time, is giving musicians courage to keep playing their original ideas, come what may."

When the jazz audience first heard Coltrane, with Davis in 1955 and '56, he was less an individualist. His style derived from those of Dexter Gordon (vintage mid-'40s), Sonny Stitt, Sonny Rollins (the Rollins of that time and slightly before), Stan Getz (certain facets of sound) and an essence of generalized Charlie Parker.

As he learned harmonically from Davis and Monk, and developed his mechanical skills, a new, more confident Coltrane emerged. He has used long lines and multi-toned figures within these lines, but in 1958 he started playing sections that might be termed "sheets of sound."

When these efforts are successful, they have a cumulative emotional impact, a residual harmonic effect. When they fail, they sound like nothing more than elliptically phrased scales.

This approach, basic to Coltrane's playing today, is not the result of a conscious effort to produce something "new." He has noted that it has developed spontaneously.

"Now it is not a thing of beauty, and the only way it would be justified is if it becomes that," he said. "If I can't work it through, I will drop it."

Although he is satisfied with the progress he's made during the last three years, Coltrane continues to be critical of his own work. Dejection is no longer a major part of this self-criticism. Now, he seeks to improve, knowing he can do so.

"I have more work to do on my tone and articulation," he said. "I must study more general technique and smooth out some harmonic kinks. Sometimes, while playing, I discover two ideas, and instead of working on one, I work on two simultaneously and lose the continuity."

Assured that the vast frustration he felt in the early '50s is gone, Coltrane attempts to behave in terms of a broad code, which he outlined:

"Keep listening. Never become so self-important that you can't listen to other players. Live cleanly… Do right… You can improve as a player by improving as a person. It's a duty we owe to ourselves."

A married man with an eight-year-old daughter, Coltrane hopes to meet the responsibilities of his music and his life without bitterness, for "music is the means of expression with strong emotional content. Jazz used to be happy and joyous. I'd like to be happy and joyous."

Dec. 11, 1958

A Profile of Mahalia

by Studs Terkel

"Mahalia, she was a girl in the slave days. She was dreaming of jubilee all the time.

Of better days to come. My people gave me her name."

The big, handsome woman with the gentle face was weary as she stared out of the window of her South Side Chicago home at the Indian summer afternoon. She was looking out toward the setting sun, miles away and years ago. Her hands were clasped in her lap. They are graceful hands but not dainty, not soft. The calluses are eloquently present.

Mahalia Jackson spoke again:

"You got to work with your hands. All artists should work with their hands. How can you sing of amazing grace, how can you sing of heaven and earth and all God's wonders without using your hands? My hands demonstrate what I feel inside. My hands, my feet. I throw my whole body to say all that is within me. The mind and the voice by themselves are not sufficient."

Her weariness might have been explained by five straight nights of revival singing at Greater Salem's new church, all the proceeds going to the church's young persons fund "so those children wouldn't have to run around in the streets like sick little chickens."

She had just returned from an appearance on Bing Crosby's television program, which one might have thought added to her fatigue. "Oh, no," she said, "it's just that California's too far away for anybody to go."

She had traveled from Chicago, which has been her hometown since the late 1920s. Now 46, Miss Jackson, since her arrival in Chicago, has done her share of manual labor—washerwoman, day factories, domestic.

What about the beauty shop? "Oh, I didn't get to work there 'til I was up on the hog's back," she said, "1943."

When did she get to sing? "Sundays and in the evening," she said. "Prof. Thompson of the Greater Salem Baptist church picked me out of the choir. I sang so loud. I just drowned out the others. Remember, they had no mikes in churches in those days. I just sang out, and with the Lord's help the people in the back rows heard. I got that from David of the Bible. Remember what he said? 'Sing joyfully unto the Lord with a loud voice.' I took his advice.

"When did I first begin to sing? You might as well ask when did I first begin to walk and talk. In New Orleans, where I lived as a child, I remember singing as I scrubbed the floors. It would make the work go easier. When the old people weren't home, I'd turn on a Bessie Smith

record. And play it over and over. 'Careless Love,' that was the blues she sang."

Suddenly her eyes suggested a twinkle, and she added, "That was before I was saved. The blues are fine, but I don't want to sing them. Just remember, all I'm saying about my listening to Bessie and imitating her when I was a little girl; just remember this was before I was saved.

"I'd play that record over and over again, and Bessie's voice would come out so full and round. And I'd make my mouth do the same thing. And before you know, all the people would stand outside the door and listen.

"I didn't know what it was at the time. All I know is it would grip me. It would give me that same feeling as when I'd hear the men singing outside as they worked, laying the ties for the railroad. I liked the way Bessie made her tones."

What was it about Bessie? Mahalia squinted thoughtfully and said:

"Listening to a song by Bessie, it almost fits into your own plane. You have a troubled mind, you sense it in her. She's an oppressed woman, a troubled woman. She's trying to get free from something. It's like a preachment, even though it's the blues. More than words, you feel a troubled heart.

"When I was a little girl, I felt she was having troubles like me. That's why it was such a comfort for the people of the South to hear her. She expressed something they couldn't put into words.

"All you could hear was Bessie. The houses were thin; the phonographs were loud. You could hear her for blocks."

Before she was saved, had the thought of singing the blues occurred to her? Mahalia laughed.

"My father's people were theatrical," she said. "They worked with Ma Rainey and Bessie and the other great blues singers. They wanted me to travel with them. But my mother's people were very religious. They forbade it. My mother was so independent, too. They told her I could make what was good money at the time. But she said no. And she didn't have a dime. It's easy to be independent when you got money. But to be independent when you ain't got a dime, that's the Lord's test.

"Sure, somebody's always coming up to me telling me if I'd sing the blues, they'd get all kinds of money for me. Or if I'd sing in a nightclub, I could have my own price. They won't serve drinks while I'm singin' and all that foolishness.

"They just don't understand. I try to

explain. I don't mean to hurt their feelings; they don't mean bad. But I just wouldn't feel right singing that kind of music. After all, I've been saved. The good Lord has helped me in so many ways, and I can't let Him down. He spared me. Remember?"

Several years ago, Mahalia, gaunt and emaciated, lay in a bed in Billings Memorial Hospital in Chicago. It appeared to be a most critical ailment, affecting her chest and thus the strength of her voice. That she pulled through and now sings—with as much strength as ever—she attributes to God's amazing grace.

Does she have any idea in how many churches she has appeared?

"Hundreds, I guess," she said. "I can't count 'em. All the way from little storefront churches to big ones. Oh, sure, I've sung anywhere people asked me to sing. I've got to have people to sing to. In front of me. I got to see their faces. Their response. Oh, yes, even when I close my eyes I see them. I can't explain why I close my eyes when I sing a soulful song. I suppose it's because I don't want to lose what's inside me all at once."

The feeling. There was a feeling Blind Frank had. He was one of the earliest singers of spirituals she remembers.

"He used to come around the churches in New Orleans and play his guitar. Places where the Holiness folks gathered, the Sanctified people. They sang the way I liked it, with free expression.

"That's where I think jazz caught its beat. From the Holiness people. Long before Buddy Bolden and Bunk Johnson, they were clapping their hands and beating their tambourines and blowing their horns."

On the state of spiritual singing today, she noted, "They can't be sung exactly as they were sung in the slavery days, because today the Negro people have a new type of hope. They don't have to hide anymore, like the slaves or the Jews in Egypt.

"Oh yeah, we still have troubles, plenty of burdens. So it still has to be from-the-heart singing. Not like some of those quartets you heard on the jukeboxes. Making a gimmick out of this music, this music which is the hope of humanity. I'm so tired of these singers who make a mess of things. They don't care about religion or the Lord, taking His name in vain the way they do.

"It's taking our great music, like taking the country's flag and stepping on it. These songs have been the hope and salvation of our people. I get mad."

About jazzmen playing spirituals, she said, "If they play for their own comfort, for

Mahalia Jackson.
(DownBeat Archive)

their real feeling, all right. But if they gimmick it, they're no better than those gimmicky jukebox singers.

Mahalia arose and mimicked a bloodless soprano in what was for a moment a wildly comedic interpretation. But then she was serious about music again:

"When it comes to singing anthems, that's something else. Like the 'Hallelujah Chorus' from The Messiah. But you have to have the right voices, good, strong, young voices. Our older people used to sing them in churches when I first came up to Chicago. They seemed uncomfortable. I know they'd have felt a lot better with spir-

ituals or gospel songs or just plain hymns. They seemed so stiff, not free.

"No matter what kind of songs people sing, it must come natural to them. They shouldn't just because they feel it's the proper thing to do. Then the real person gets lost. He's away from his roots."

A pause. Any feeling about modern jazz?

"I prefer listening to the old style because I'm used to it," she replied. "I don't know which direction they're going today. Maybe I'm wrong, but I feel they've gone too far away from roots.

"When I was small and they played

jazz, the houses just talked, spoke the music. Some of the progressive jazz sounds to me like lost little children who don't know what road they're on or what they're doing or why they're doing it. Maybe they're reaching out for something good, but I just don't understand it.

"Today so many people call gospel songs 'jazz.' They don't know, they just don't know. Just as a spiritual came from the slavery days, the gospel song came from liberation.

"The jubilee songs that sprang up after the Civil War led into what we call gospel songs today. 'Nobody Knows the Trouble I've Seen' or 'Swing Low Sweet Chariot.' They're spirituals. 'What a Friend I Have in Jesus' or 'I'm So Glad Jesus Lifted Me.' They're gospel songs."

The twinkle appeared again.

"You know the Fisk University Choir," she said. "They made lots of those songs popular. They took out the beat that the Holiness people gave them and cultivated it. They concertized them, prettied them up. Not much feeling, but, oh, it sounded so sweet!

"Take 'Hold Me' (a number by Thomas A. Dorsey, America's most prolific writer of gospel songs, formerly known as Georgia Tom, who often had accompanied Ma Rainey). He wrote this out of his trial and tribulation. He was sick; his children were sick; he felt everything was gone. You can sing it as mournfully as Bessie. Then I hear a girl sing it and she sounds like Lily Pons. I said to Mr. Dorsey, how come she sounds so operatic. My, my, it's pretty, wish I could be that operatic."

There came a change in the tempo and tenor of the conversation that—like her songs—is sometimes soft and deeply moving and at other times earthly and exuberant. She offered random observations of people, places and things, the lost and found.

Billie Holiday: "I never knew her, never met her, never knew what made her do the things she did. But when I saw her last year on the CBS show *The Sound of Jazz*—you know that Lively Arts series?— I caught that cry from her. I know everybody who watched that show caught something from her. She looked like she knew trouble. She sounded like it."

Miss Jackson feels strongly about Europe, where she was recognized and accepted long before white America did so. Why were Europeans seemingly able to appreciate her so readily?

"People are people the world over," she said, "and everybody can feel suffering when you sing a spiritual. We all carry different kinds of burdens, and each person interprets the spiritual in his own way. It's more than just the words. It's the feeling. It lingers after the song is ended."

What of tomorrow?

"I hope one day I can teach people to sing songs with the deep feeling they once had," she said. "We shouldn't forget our roots, our history.

"Sometimes I hear how music is supposed to be sung; there are certain notes I want to make. I get to my pianist, Mildred Falls. We put it down. So in this way I'm able to capture the voice within me. Oh, people should study, of course. But they should also listen to what is inside themselves. You first must sing for yourself. When you make that peace within yourself, then you can reach out to the others. If I do nothing else, I hope to teach people that. Each to find his way."

Mahalia Jackson found her way. She found it long before "Move On Up a Little Higher" sold a million in the mid-'40s. Adversities and detours were present.

But always Mahalia has made her own free-wheeling way onto the main road. She'll never get lost.

March 19, 1959
· ·

Roy Eldridge
Little Jazz Goes a Long Way
by Dan Morgenstern

The sign outside the Metropole in New York City reads: "Dixieland." But if signs mean less to you than sounds, and you step inside, what you will hear is jazz. And if it's Sunday afternoon or Monday or Tuesday night, it will be some of the best jazz, these or any days.

That is when a quintet led by two timeless masters of the art of jazz holds postgraduate seminars. The language they speak is informed by the past, which they helped to create, aware of the present, in which they live and listen and hear, and pointing toward the future, which the are

still building.

They are Coleman Hawkins and Roy Eldridge, one of the great partnerships in jazz, a partnership of mutual inspiration, common experience and warm friendship. It currently rests on a solid foundation supplied by J.C. Heard on drums and two new but experienced faces, pianist Joe Knight and bassist Francesco Skeets.

Among those who have been on hand to receive, and perhaps get, the message are students and faculty members from all the schools: Thelonious Monk, Miles Davis, Dizzy Gillespie, John Lewis, Lucky Thompson, Gerry Mulligan and many others. There is a loyal lay audience as well.

"Working with Coleman is just perfect," said David Roy Eldridge. "That's it. Perfect. He'll play something, and it will get to me and make me play. And he's himself. I hope we can stay together for the longest time."

When Roy took a leave of absence this summer to accompany Ella Fitzgerald on a tour, Hawk was impatiently awaiting his return, even though his replacement was a more than capable trumpeter.

"Roy will be back soon," Hawkins was heard to say frequently and with growing expectancy. "Roy and I can get that real good feeling going when we play."

The difference in Eldridge's playing when he worked with clarinetist Sol Yaged, who believes in set routines, from his work with Hawk, who believes in freedom, says more than many words. So do the fresh, original lines Hawkins and he constantly are working up on standard tunes.

Born in Pittsburgh on Jan. 30, 1911, Eldridge has been a professional musician for 32 years. He as earned a large share of acclaim in those decades, but is not inclined to rest on them.

"Your horn," Roy once remarked, "is like a woman. If you're not in shape, you'd better not mess with it."

And if there is a challenge, you respond. "I listen to everything," he said, "and if I hear something that upsets me— well, I get out my horn, warm up and go back in the bin. I don't mean copying what you hear, not that. But if you don't feel that your playing is improving as you go along, you might as well pack up your horn. And one thing: You've got to be yourself."

Himself, Eldridge unquestionably is. The surging vitality and exuberance that long have been characteristics of his style are undiminished, but to them have been added the thoughtfulness and concern for

Roy Eldridge.
(Kjell Tornoe)

structure that are signs of maturity.

The virtuosity that once earned Roy, on 52nd Street, billing as "the Wizard of the Trumpet" enables him to cover the entire expressive range of the trumpet with complete authority and with that singing, vibrant vocal quality that trumpets never had before jazz and Louis Armstrong and seem to have almost lost again in the hands of some current practitioners.

Roy also plays the flugelhorn, a foreshortened, large-belled, mellow-toned sister of the trumpet—and a B-flat instrument.

Eldridge's first instrument was the drums. He still plays them with enough skill to have allowed himself a little drum duet with Jo Jones at the Newport Jazz Festival and to have played Gene Krupa's specialties with the band when Gene was ill. Piano he plays "for kicks," with less pol-

ish but with a driving beat. And he can manage a bass as well.

In the history books, Eldridge generally is referred to as "the link between Louis and Dizzy" or the creator of "saxophone-style trumpeting."

There is something to all of this, but it leaves out more than it conveys. Jazz is a living, growing art, and if time has not stood still since that supposed night at Minton's when Gillespie cut Eldridge, neither has Roy. Neither he nor Gillespie play now the way they played in 1941. And when they get together, it is in a spirit of friendly rivalry, not of historical comparison.

"Dizzy is too much," Roy said. "There has never been any hostility between us, and when we get together, it's a ball."

Jazz is not boxing: Ideas are exchanged, and the music is always the

winner. There are elements in Roy's playing today that would be unthinkable without Gillespie and Charlie Parker ("Bird was the greatest; he had his own," Eldridge said) and he is still himself.

As for the saxophone style, Roy acknowledges Hawkins and Benny Carter among his early and continued influences. But there were also trumpet players: Rex Stewart ("for speed, range and power"), Jabbo Smith and, somewhat later, Armstrong, "who taught me to tell a story, among other things."

Whatever the influences, once Roy found his own voice, he created an idiomatic trumpet style. Roy's elder brother, the late Joe Eldridge, was an alto saxophonist and arranger, unduly underrated in both capacities. It was he who encouraged Roy to stick to music and who gave him his first trumpet.

Eldridge has done his share of big band work. The list includes Horace Henderson, Speed Webb, Charlie Johnson and McKinney's Cotton Pickers, among the pioneer bands of the pre-swing era. Later came work with Teddy Hill and Fletcher Henderson. "We had Chu Berry, and Buster Bailey, Joe Thomas and, of course, Big Sid Catlett. That band was school."

With Krupa and Artie Shaw, Roy played the book as well as his specialties. But he prefers the freedom of small groups now, saying, "You don't get to stretch out in a big band. And things get kind of set." Studio work, as well, is a doubtful pleasure to Roy.

"As far as I know," he said, "I never play a tune the same way twice. Sure, you play a number a lot of times, and certain little things get set. But the overall feeling is never the same. That's why it's such a drag for Coleman when they always ask for 'Body and Soul.' He made a record of it—and now they want him to always play the same thing. It's just not possible. I guess that's why I don't like studio work. I'll play something, and the cat says, 'That sounds good. Write it down and do it that way on the show!' But when the show goes on, I don't feel the same way. So it doesn't come out naturally."

Eldridge's most famous record is probably "Rockin' Chair" with Krupa.

"We had the number scheduled for recording for quite some time," Roy said, "but never got around to it. When we finally did, I didn't feel ready. After we cut it, I ask them to please not release it. Sometime later, we were out on the coast, and Ben Webster and I got together. He loves records, and we got to playing some. When he put on 'Rockin' Chair,' I said, 'Who's that?' Ben smiled. I didn't recognize myself until the chorus—and I'm still surprised."

There was another time, later, when a record surprised Roy. By the late 1940s, he had come to a critical stage in his career. He was nagged by feelings of doubt: that being himself no longer had validity, that his voice was clashing with the voices of newcomers. The jazz scene had changed. "I felt unhappy with the way things were going," he said. "I felt out of place. My playing didn't seem to fit, the way I could hear it. I'd been with *Jazz at the Philharmonic* for quite some time. In 1949, I decided to quit and came back to New York. Norman [Granz] asked me to do one more concert, at Carnegie Hall, and I agreed. Afterwards,

I still felt the same. So when Benny Goodman asked me to go to Europe with him in 1950, I was more than happy to accept."

Perhaps it wasn't just the music. There were many indignities Roy suffered when he was with Krupa and Shaw: the contrast between star billing, acceptance by fellow musicians and audiences and the behavior of hotel clerks, bouncers and others a musician deals with on the road was a contrast that could not fail to affect a man as straightforward and honestly emotional as Eldridge.

In Europe, he found new confidence in his voice, plus the freedom he cherishes. "When the tour with Benny ended, I stayed on in Paris," he recalled. "I had a steady gig in a good place. I had friends, and I had a following. The money wasn't exceptional, but I was happier than I had been in years. Nobody told me how to play, and I began to enjoy my work again.

"Then Norman came to Paris, and we got together. He asked me to go back with him. 'No,' I said. 'I'm happy right here.' He offered me a good contract. And to make it more appealing, he showed me some bills. It was good to see some real money again, and I was tempted. But then I thought for a while, and I still felt 'no.' Then Norman put a record on. It was the one made at the Carnegie Hall concert in '49. I listened, and I couldn't believe it—it sounded good. My playing didn't stick out—it was a statement, the other guys were making their statements, and together it made sense. That record made me go back. That bad feeling was gone." (The record is Vol. 12–13 of *Jazz at the Philharmonic*.)

When Roy returned from a six-week tour of Europe last summer, he was asked how it had been.

"Wonderful," he replied. "That Cannes... if I had the money, I'd buy it and have my friends come around.

Roy looked around for a while. Then he turned and said, "You know what? It feels good to be back home."

In the last few years, Roy has toured here and abroad with the Granz enterprises. New York is his home base now; before the Metropole one could find him at the Central Plaza, where the sledding was often tough, or at the late Bohemia, where it was sometimes drafty.

Now there are weekend gigs in Brooklyn and Long Island, often with Hawkins. And television. The latter is not an unmixed blessing.

"Somehow, you never get a chance,"

Eldridge said. "On Art Ford's show (which has left the air) we got away a few times. But it's gotten so that I don't expect anything to happen. I may have some little thing worked up, but, sure enough, before we go on, they have to cut it. I'm not on a glamour kick. I don't push myself up front. What for? But maybe someday I'll get a chance to do something I like on a show."

The most recent Timex show, on which Eldridge was allotted eight bars—and those eight split in two fours—is a disheartening illustration of Roy's point.

Recording has been more satisfying. In the recent past Roy has made permanent some of his most creative playing, in varied contexts, but always in good company. His associates have included Hawkins, Lester Young, Gillespie, Carter, Art Tatum, Stan Getz, Sonny Stitt, Jo Jones, Oscar Peterson and a string section. The records haven't made the hit charts but will outlast most of the stuff that has.

Roy reflects that today, "Some cat can come along, get himself a hit record and overnight he's a big name and can get any booking. It was never like that in the 'old' days.

"I think that a musician who is a musician should be able to play anywhere," he added, "and shouldn't be limited to one style. Something is wrong if he is."

Eldridge loves music and takes pride in it. This attitude is reflected in his consistently meticulous appearance. His style of dress is not "sharp," but correct. And as Jo Jones has said, "Roy will work just as hard for $25 as for $250. He's a very responsible man."

And a very energetic man as well. At Max, the Mayor's, a large establishment in the Sheepshead Bay section of Brooklyn, where the budget does not allow for a bass, and the crowd does not allow for a letup, Roy would play chorus after chorus, sing, emcee and even back local "talent" on the drums (generating enough steam to drive the Basie band), and somehow educating the rough-and-tumble audience to appreciate the beauty of a passionate rendition of "I Can't Get Started." And when he came off the stand for a brief intermission, he would be warmly received at the bar.

"Roy sure knows how to break the ice," a member of the band commented. "And how to give."

At the Metropole, things are sometimes more relaxed, and Roy may get a chance to play one of his "strollers." A stroller is a muted solo with just walking bass and brushes behind it. After two choruses, the mute comes out and the piano comes in.

The restless searching and energy that is in Roy (but which doesn't prevent him from playing relaxed when he wants) makes him his own severest critic.

"It happens maybe three or four times a year," he said. "You pick up the horn and everything comes out just right—feeling, range, speed—you know just what you want and you can get it. It's a mysterious thing."

But there are many more times when it seems that way to the listener, or to the musician playing with Roy. "When you work with Roy, there's always something new," said bassist Gene Ramey. "The more you can play, the more you've got to play."

Eldridge has a pleasant house on Long Island, where he lives with his wife, Vi; his teenage daughter, Carol; and a large, shaggy dog of indeterminable ancestry named Chico.

He is an enthusiastic amateur photographer and a prolific and exuberant letter writer. He has completed his autobiography and has hopes of finding a publisher in England. There have been interested American parties, but they all found the book too outspoken. Roy, however, wants no compromises. It is his story, and he wants to tell it as honestly in print as he tells it on the horn. He has been himself too long to change now.

Sept. 17, 1959

Lambert, Hendricks and Ross

and How They Grew

by Jon Hendricks

with an introduction by Gene Lees

EDITORS NOTE—In the wee small hours of a morning at Newport this year, I told Jon Hendricks that *DownBeat* would like to do a story on the LHR group. "Why not let me write it?" Jon said. I hedged and hesitated for a moment (perhaps Jon will remember it) and then began running some of his remarkable LHR lyrics over in my mind. "OK," I said.

We kicked the idea around a bit, notably backstage at Chicago's Regal Theater, and I learned that Jon was thinking of doing the article in rhyme, no less. I shook my head a bit, reassured myself that his tremendous taste and talent would not fail, even in the unfamiliar task of writing an article, swallowed hard and said: "Wild."

Jon telephoned from time to time as he worked on the article. I began to get nervous. Deadline was approaching, and I had already scheduled the cover photo to go with the article. "You have to promise me you won't change a thing," Jon said. That made me more nervous.

When the piece at last arrived—right on deadline—I scanned it, still nervously at first, then less nervously, and finally, jubilantly. It was—and is—one of the strangest articles I've ever read. As promised, it rhymed. Not unexpectedly, it sounded like an LHR lyric without the music. It also had in places the delightful flavor of an Ogden Nash poem. And finally, I guessed that some astute reader would look at its last line and think of James Joyce's *Finnegan's Wake*.

Jon didn't say this in the article, but he has done a lot of thinking about the possibilities of true jazz opera. The article tends to validate his theory that it can—and should—be done.

Lambert, Hendricks and Ross is one of the most remarkable groups in jazz today. With their vocals on famous instrumental numbers, they have broken up audiences at every jazz festival they have played this summer—and they have played most of them, with more yet to come, including Monterey. Where their jazz-vocals experiment will lead is something no one, including Jon, pretends to be able to predict with certainty. All that anyone knows for sure is that their popularity is huge and growing, that they deserve it and that the end is not in sight.

In the meantime, here is Jon Hendricks' story on LHR. As Dave Lambert said to me, explaining why when he worked on construction he liked to use jackhammers, "I dug it." I hope you will, too. —Ed.

As to dates, times, names and places, my accuracy ain't apt to be too outstanding. Data's too demanding. I haven't the faintest idea on what date Dave Lambert's birthday occurs, and experience with women and the subject of age gives me better sense than to ask Annie Ross hers, so, on biographical data I won't be too factual. However, on matters of the heart and soul I hope to be very actual, 'cause if you're gonna know how Dave Lambert, Annie Ross and I have such a collective ball while singing our individual parts, you'll have to know that it comes from what we fondly recall, and what is in our hearts.

Some people say our name is a clumsy name for a singing group to be stuck with. They compare it to Merrill, Lynch, Pierce, Fenner and Smith, an overstatement, by far. Actually we call ourselves Lambert, Hendricks and Ross for no other reason than that's who we are! And so that your understanding of our name will gain even more clearance, if you dig what I mean, our name describes the order of our appearance on the scene.

Dave Lambert, ex-everything under the sun and musical truth-seeker, came home from high school in New England one day, heard a Count Basie record on an outside downtown radio-shop-loudspeaker on the way, and the amazement that there could be such a feelin' never left him after that. When I engaged Dave to do the vocal adaptation of Jimmy Giuffre's "Four Brothers" arrangement, he bent my ear about doing a lyricised Basie album in nothin' flat! While we were rehearsing "Four Brothers," or listening to what each other was sayin', Dave made sure some Basie records were playin'. He'd play the old things most, the "good ol' ones" we both grew up listening to, and again we heard the marvel of them all. In this era of "conservatories," we heard the old Basie band full of natural musicians from their heart play more jazz than anybody we've ever heard, no matter how smart. And nary one of 'em knew what the inside of a music school looked like. They just played and had a ball.

Finally I got Dave's subtle message (as subtle as a ton of coal on the head) and stopped listening casually and got t' writing lyrics instead. I soon had words to "Down for the Count" and "Blues Backstage" and Dave adapted Frank Foster's arrangements for voices, then we started making choices of recording company A&R men. (Means "artist and repertory" and they're to blame if the recording output sounds a bit gory. Their judgment of a

From left, Dave Lambert,
Anne Ross & Jon Hendricks.

"hit" often depends on how much a new tune sounds like the last "hit." They often are unable to see any future in a tune because of a single-minded preoccupation with a past hit!)

Creed Taylor, of ABC-Paramount, is a rarity among his kind. He has his own taste and uses his own mind, I'm happy to state.

And besides, he gave Dave and me a recording date.

During the time we were working on *Sing a Song of Basie* for Creed, I lived and wrote in Greenwich Village, which I had always thought of in an artistic way, but which I found retaining only an artistic facade, masking pseudo-intellectual morbidness 'midst moral decay. It may be a good place to stay up late in, but its new, thrill-seeking Freud-spouting population has rendered it no longer a desirable place to create in. (Don't blame *DownBeat*, this is my personal contention—just a little something I thought I'd mention.)

For our first date, Dave contracted 12 experienced singers he had known and used before as the Dave Lambert Singers, some of whom worked on such programs as *The Perry Como Show* and *Your Hit Parade*, and who had reputations something fierce. We also had the Basie rhythm section, Freddy Greene, Sonny Payne and Eddie Jones, with Nat Pierce.

It was during this first date that the spiritual quality that is in all jazz, and prominently so in Basie, made itself manifest; that spiritual quality we—and Ray Charles—got in church, and got so West Coast cool we left in the lurch and got back to for 30 pieces of Horace Silver, after a long, cold search.

Those singers had music and lyrics, but that spiritual quality was missing at the very first test, even though they tried their best. Eddie Jones saw and heard and laid his fiddle gently down and walked amongst them and talked to them and spread the word, and Sonny Payne and Nat Pierce did, too. Freddie sat placidly by and regarded it all with an ever-patient eye and didn't move to get his message through, just sat calm, like he usually do. What Eddie Jones told those singers about "layin' back, but not slowin' down" was beautifully true, but when all the gentle urging was done there was no concealing that those well-trained singers still couldn't sing Basie with that spiritual feeling—except one—a silent, beautiful red-haired girl Dave had introduced me to several days before at Bob Bach's house in Washington Mews, a name I remembered from then-current theatrical news as starring in an imported-from-London Broadway review called *Cranks*. But I remembered more; five years or so earlier than then—a Prestige record given me by Teacho Wiltshire, who recorded "Four Brothers" vocally first, a record of a vocal version of Wardell Gray's "Twisted," excellent lyric by Annie Ross—better than good—boss!

Yes, Annie Ross has that feeling, that feeling you can't learn in no school, that feeling that the men in the old Basie band had from birth and got together in nightclubs and tent shows. And don't get the idea schools, to them, are unknown, 'cause those men started a few schools of their own! Pick a tenor player at random and, no matter what he says, chances are, at one time or another he studied under Pres. And make no bones about it—Jo Jones invented the sock

cymbal, and don't ever doubt about it.

Philly Joe know.

And every trumpet player ever plays through a "bucket" mute oughta know that Buck Clayton's real nickname ain't Buck—it's "Bucket!" (Ain't that cute.)

At any rate, the first *Sing a Song of Basie* was scrapped and, thanks to Creed Taylor, we got another chance—but what to do? Dave Lambert knew. Dave has a talent for putting very large possibilities into a very few words. "Annie feels it," he said. "Let's you, me 'n Annie do it." Coming from anyone else I'd have thought such an idea was for the birds, because of the hard work entailed, but I soon saw the beauty of Dave's suggestion, especially if we all three really wailed.

From the time we started out, Annie knew what she was about. She did everything with ease and a naturalness found only in great artists, I guess. Annie Ross is more than just a singer, to say the least. She is an artiste. Every night, on "Avenue C," she stands up there between Dave and me and hits that last note, F above high C, as though it were any note—and it might as well be! I remember when Dave asked her if she could make that note and she said, "No, never," so Dave said he'd change it, winked at me and left it like it was, and Annie sings it like she's been singing it forever.

So we did *Sing a Song of Basie* alone, Dave, Annie, the Basie rhythm section with Nat Pierce, and me, and the rest is known. When people would congratulate us on our artistic success, it got to be an unfunny joke, cause Dave and I stayed broke. Annie was straight. She was singing on the *Patrice Munsel Show*, which is like a permanent record date. Then, one day at Dave's house, I saw the strangest sight I've ever seen: *Sing a Song of Basie* showed up in *DownBeat* as number thirteen! So Dave and I decided to see if we could get some gigs—just local. We envisioned nothing on a grand scale for an act so unusually vocal. Annie was in Europe then, sendin' messages that everything was dandy, so 'til Annie got back we worked with Flo Handy, wife of George Handy and singer of great skill, and the Great South Bay Jazz Festival put us on last year's bill.

Later, the MJQ's manager, Monte Kay, set us up an audition with Willard Alexander one day. Willard got so excited he made us wonder what we had! We weren't all that sure it was good, but when you knock somebody out like Willard Alexander, you know it ain't all bad. Annie came back from

Europe and joined Dave and me, and Willard signed us immediately.

As to how Basie feels about us, that'll be easy to understand, 'cause he invited us to do an album with his band, yet! (*Sing Along with Basie*, on Roulette.) Our current album, to be specific, is *The Swingers* on Dick Bock's World Pacific, with Zoot Sims, Russ Freeman and Basie's steady three men, Eddie Jones, Sonny Payne and Freddie Greene, the finest rhythm section anybody's ever seen.

We've just been honored by being asked to sign with Columbia Records, under the aegis of Mr. Irving Townsend. "Moanin'," by the pianist with Art Blakey's Jazz Messengers, Bobby Timmons, and "Cloudburst," a Sam-the-Man Taylor saxophone solo, are about ready for single release, and there's an album of Ellingtonia in the works, so who knows where it will cease?

My brother, Jim Hendricks, manages to manage us—an unmanageable task, and as for how we feel about what's happened to us—need you ask? How far Lambert, Hendricks and Ross will go is something I don't pretend to know, but, since I write a lot of the words we sing, I can tell you what message I'll bring: that opera houses dedicated to European musical culture are not the American norm. Jazz is America's cultural art form. To say that our opera houses are the Chicago, the San Francisco and the Metropolitan just doesn't follow. America's real opera houses—as one day, pray, the American people may realize—are the Howard Theater in Washington, D.C., the Regal Theater in Chicago and Harlem's Apollo. And our divas are not singers of the kind of music Europe has, but Billie, and Ella, and Sarah, and they sing jazz!

We are honored anew every time a jazz musician compliments us, because we know they know what it's all about, but to have three great jazz musicians accompany us is something about which to shout. We have the Ike Isaacs Trio—Gildo Mahones, piano; Kahlil Madi, drums; and Ike on bass—and we hope to take them with us every place.

As for me—I'm the ninth child and the seventh son of Rev. and Mrs. A.B. Hendricks. I have eleven brothers and three sisters, all reared in the African Episcopal Church around Toledo, Ohio. All other data can be found in my bio. My musical education consisted of singing Negro spirituals and hymns with my mother in church, singing in bars and grills for whatever people threw me, which, praise be, was never out, singing in nightclubs at thirteen (they used to bill me as "The Sepia Bobby Breen!"), accompanied for one magical spell by a local pianist whose family were our neighbors, whom we knew well—Art Tatum, who started on the violin, but sat down to the piano and never got up again. I was fortunate enough to have learned to listen to him early and I'm glad I paid heed, 'cause I never did learn how to read.

When Bird came through Toledo one night with Max, Tommy Potter (now with "Sweets"), Kenny Dorham and Al Haig to play a dance, I got a long-awaited, unexpected chance to scat a few choruses, after which, while Kenny Dorham blew, I started to split, but Bird motioned me to Kenny's chair next to him and said, with that warm smile, "Sit awhile." I ended up scatting the whole set, and before they left, Bird said, "Look me up when you get to New York. Don't forget."

It was two years later when I got to New York. Bird was playing at the Apollo Bar uptown, and I got up there fast as anyone can. And when I walked past the bandstand, Bird waved at me and spoke my name and thrilled me to kingdom come when he said, "Wanna' sing some?" and two years passed away as though it had been only one day! Roy Haynes was playing drums and I was a drummer (who had just put his drums in pawn), but when I heard Roy with Bird I said to myself, "That's it for my drumming. Them days is gone!"

I knew nothing about the New York scene except what I'd seen or heard, so I decided to judge everybody by "who stood up with Bird," or, if they didn't ever share the same bandstand, how did they stand with the man. Dave Lambert did "Old Folks" and "In the Still of the Night" with Bird, vocal arrangements by Dave, musical arrangements by Gil Evans, among the more beautiful things I've ever heard. Annie Ross sang with Bird a few times. The fact I'm trying not to keep it hid is that, at one time or another, all three of us did. It's a coincidence with a spiritual quality I can't name, but Dave Lambert, Annie Ross and I came together naturally, just at the time when jazz began to receive wide public acclaim.

As a writer of words, this gives me a great responsibility, especially to American youth: Tell the truth! Interpret the compositions and jazz composers, writing today, not three hundred years passed away. And the composers are numerous, most every-body playing, and all I have to do is tell the people what they're saying.

Oct. 29, 1959

The Trouble with Jazz Piano
The Viewpoint of Oscar Peterson
by Gene Lees

Exactly 10 years ago last month, a young Canadian pianist walked onto the stage of Carnegie Hall to make his U.S. debut.

Within minutes, according to Mike Levin's report in *DownBeat*, Oscar Peterson had "stopped the Norman Granz Jazz at the Philharmonic dead cold in its tracks."

The show of technique was astonishing.

"Balancing a large and bulky body at the piano much in the fashion of Earl Hines," Levin wrote, "Peterson displayed a flashy right hand, a load of bop and Shearing-styled ideas, as well as a good sense of harmonic development.

"And, in addition, he scared some of the local modern minions by playing bop figures single-finger in his left hand, which is distinctly not the common practice.

"Further than this, Peterson impressed musicians here by not only having good ideas and making them, but giving them a rhythmic punch and drive, which has been all too lacking in too many of the younger pianists. Whereas some of the bop stars conceive good ideas but sweat to make them, Peterson rips them off with an excess of power, which leaves no doubt about his technical excess in reserve."

The perceptiveness of Levin's report can be seen in the fact that 10 years later, his description of Peterson's playing (and his lament about no-power pianists) still remains remarkably accurate—except that all the virtues he saw then have grown deeper and stronger and have been augmented by several new ones.

Today, Oscar Peterson occupies a position of technical dominance on his instrument. If there are pianists who rival his speed (Andre Previn and Phineas Newborn, for example) they lack his virility and blues-rooted power. If there are those who rival his power (Red Garland, Erroll Garner), they lack his absolute mastery of the instrument.

It is curious, then, that Peterson has not influenced other pianists more strongly than he has—though, of course, slight touches of Peterson turn up in the work of numberless others.

Yet the explanation for it is probably simple. Peterson is in much the same position as Dizzy Gillespie, who also is not imitated widely and, therefore, cannot be considered the present dominant influence on trumpet. As critic Ralph J. Gleason put it (in a conversation with this writer): "If nobody imitates Dizzy, it is because when a trumpeter picks up his horn, he knows he can't imitate Dizzy. So why try?"

This inimitable—in the literal meaning of the word—quality may, therefore, tend to detract from the appreciation of both Peterson and Gillespie. But not among those who know.

Recently, both the Andre Previn Trio and the Oscar Peterson Trio were in Detroit for that city's jazz festival. On a free evening, Previn and his two colleagues, drummer Frank Capp and bassist Red Mitchell, dropped by a club where Peterson and his two colleagues—drummer Ed Thigpen and bassist Ray Brown—were working.

When Peterson saw them, he turned up the gas, as he has a way of doing when good friends walk into a club. When the number was over, Previn turned to his companions and said, "Can I fire all three of us?"

How did Peterson get that way? The answer sounds pretty clichéd: he started early at music and practiced hard. There were, of course, the unacquirable qualities of basic ability and drive.

Born Aug. 15, 1925, in Montreal (not in Toronto, as many biographical notes have it), Peterson is the son of a porter on the Canadian Pacific Railway. He began learning piano when he was scarcely more than a baby. A rumor used to circulate in Canada that Oscar was just a "born talent," a sort of gifted primitive who couldn't read music. The story was totally false. Oscar's training was gruelingly thorough. His first teacher was his sister, and the emphasis was on classical music.

By the time he was five, he was playing trumpet. In all probability he would be playing the instrument still had he not been stricken at the age of seven with tuberculosis.

For 13 months, he was in Children's Memorial Hospital. When he left the

Oscar Peterson Trio, from left, Peterson, Ray Brown and Herb Ellis in 1957. (Bernie Thrasher)

hospital he was cured, and nothing about the huge, powerful Oscar Peterson of today would suggest his early bout with the disease.

But his lungs were weakened, and his father decided he should not go on with trumpet. So the boy was started on piano. He liked the instrument and continued with it, playing hymns and classics.

When Peterson was 14, his sister, Mrs. Daisy Sweeney, took him to meet Ken Soble, who ran an exceptionally good amateur program on the Canadian Broadcasting Corp.

network. (In recent years, singers on the show have found themselves accompanied by an orchestra with full string section, and good tailor-made arrangements.) Soble auditioned the boy. Oscar went through the semifinals and then went on to Toronto to win the finals and a cash prize of $250.

This victory led to a weekly 15-minute spot on Montreal radio station CKAC. There he met Canadian pianist Paul DeMarky, and studied both swing piano and the classics with him.

By this time, he was also a student at

Montreal High School. A schoolmate, Martin Siegerman, recalled that Peterson was already showing signs of the phenomenal skill he would later possess. Boogie-woogie was the fad and, Siegerman said, "Oscar always had a gang of kids around him, asking him to play." When he did play, they heard boogie at faster tempos than most of them knew were possible.

From CKAC, Oscar joined the Johnny Holmes Orchestra, and did another broadcast on CBM, the CBC's English-language outlet in Montreal (the CBC also has a French-language network). Oscar has said Holmes was responsible for building up his technique. He was overdoing boogie-woogie at the time and was finding it harder to play ballads.

One day, Peterson told his mother he'd like to cut some records. She suggested he call one of the record companies and say so. Dubiously, Peterson called Hugh Joseph, who was in charge of RCA Victor recordings in Canada at the time. But Joseph knew all about Peterson and said in fact he had been thinking of calling the pianist.

The first side Peterson recorded was "I Got Rhythm." Later, he was about to add two dozen sides to these early Victor discs. Among them were "Oscar's Boogie" and his theme, Ellington's "Rockin' in Rhythm." They were released in Canada about 14 years ago.

This writer remembers these first Peterson sides well. Oscar does, too. He said, "They weren't too representative of my playing at the time."

Nonetheless, they caused a stir in Canada. They were not deeply jazz-rooted. But they were played at a ferocious speed and demonstrated that Peterson was already one of the most technically accomplished young pianists alive. Canadian jazz fans treated them with some skepticism. For one thing, the artist was Canadian, not American, which was a strike against him. Yet the records enjoyed a vogue as a novelty and disc jockeys occasionally spin them even now.

Peterson by now had his own trio (Clarence Jones, drums, and Ozie Roberts, bass; guitarist Bernard Johnson later replaced Jones), and his reputation was growing. He was beginning to receive tempting offers to come to the United States, including a bid from the late Jimmie Lunceford and several from Norman Granz. He didn't think he was ready.

But at last he agreed to make the move. Granz immediately scheduled him for the aforementioned Carnegie Hall concert. From that time to this, his position in the respect of jazz fans has never known a moment's doubt—despite the occasional forest-and-trees shortsightedness of critics puzzled by his frank eclecticism.

After touring with Granz in 1949, Peterson returned to Montreal, where proud local fans were busy organizing clubs in honor of the first Canadian to make a major splash in U.S. jazz. Various U.S. bands were seeking his services, and Granz made him a permanent offer. But

Peterson didn't think the time was right.

Meanwhile, U.S. musicians such as Coleman Hawkins, Woody Herman and Ella Fitzgerald were making it a point to hear him when they were in Montreal. They always came away raving.

By 1951, Peterson's reputation had reached national-name proportions in the two countries. His style was being described as the best of swing and bop. The occasional tributes to Erroll Garner were there—and, of course, the influence of Art Tatum, who was to become a personal friend and mentor before his death. To this day, the influences of these men can be heard—plus occasional amused little nods to Fats Waller and others. For Oscar Peterson had surveyed the field of jazz styles and, because of his prodigious technique, was able to take something from all of them in the development of what by now is a highly personal, if multi-sourced, style.

And therein, perhaps, lies the secret: technique. It is occasionally fashionable in jazz circles to minimize the importance of technique, emphasizing the roots of jazz to the exclusion of all executive skill. And while it is true that more than a few artists have been ruined by a preoccupation with technique, it is also true that the fullest possible expression is possible to the man who achieved this mastery of his instrument.

"That is about all I can tell you about my approach to piano," Peterson said. "I have always sought to play pianistically.

"I think most of the younger pianists don't want to face up to the job of mastering piano.

"Charlie Parker, of course, was a tremendous influence not only on the horns but on piano. Because so much piano playing is so linear, a great many persons have thought you could eliminate it, as Gerry Mulligan did.

"But as far as I'm concerned, piano is too much instrument to be approached always in terms of horn lines.

"And so who are my influences? I think one should be influenced by a format.

"I listened to Tatum as a listener, but as a pianist I admired his format, the approach. Art played pianistically. Most of the older pianists did—or do, as the case may be.

"And that's why I'm not impressed by most of the crop of younger pianists. I just don't hear what I want to hear from most of them. Consequently, I can't bring myself to admire them. I admire the initial effort, but not the result.

"I can remember hearing most of the

span of Art's records, and I've yet to hear something from the younger pianists that I haven't heard from Art in one vein or another."

Peterson, as it will be seen from these remarks, is an extremely lucid and literate talker. Friendly and warm by nature and inclined not to hurt anyone if he can help it, he nonetheless declines to pussyfoot in talking about piano and pianists.

He is quite specific about those who leave him not completely impressed. For example, among them are Horace Silver, Erroll Garner and Ahmad Jamal.

"Each of these men," Peterson said, "is confined for a certain reason.

"Erroll because he's a stylist. We will never hear what he might have done if he'd studied. Horace pursues primarily the linear approach. Ahmad sticks to the type of abstract singing lines that he uses. All of these men are pursuing one line of the instrument's potential."

What about Bill Evans, New Star winner in *DownBeat*'s International Jazz Critics Poll—one of the pianists with background who does use the whole instrument?

"About Bill, it's hard to say at this point," Oscar replied. "It is like trying to judge the color of a rose when the bud is only half-opened."

"To quote Art again," he continued, "I was very close to him personally, and he used to tell me one thing, 'You have the instrument, so you have nothing to worry about.'

"I think this is why a lot of pianists never grow. One thing that has made me, subconsciously, never want to become as hot (commercially) as Ahmad or Erroll is that I don't want to be confined to only one part of what I do.

"Let's face it. Basically, jazz piano is an instrument that most pianists have forgotten. A piano can be as subtle as a French horn in the distance or as driving as the Basie band.

"When I am working, it's a challenge, not a chore. But I'm not afraid of the instrument. I love it.

"You should be able to build. You shouldn't build to a summit only to fall off. That is another thing wrong with much jazz piano. When the pianist shifts into high, often he's used up all he's got to get there."

Despite his enormous and frank admiration for Tatum, Oscar said he "didn't admire Art as a trio pianist. He never could be subservient enough to be a trio pianist. I'm not trying to make my present group piano with rhythm accompaniment."

An evening of listening to the Peterson group—changed enormously in flavor since Peterson's close personal friend, guitarist Herb Ellis, left the group to be replaced by drummer Ed Thigpen—illustrates what he means.

Whereas the Peterson-Brown-Ellis triumvirate had an incredible rapport, the new group has fully as much rapport as the old one—but of a different kind. Thigpen, whom John Tynan, *DownBeat*'s West Coast editor, has dubbed "the thinking man's drummer," works so closely with Peterson and Brown that there is that three-minds-with-a-single-thought effect that the Basie rhythm section has always been noted for.

So smoothly do they work together that recently, in Chicago, they recorded a total of nine albums in 17 days! The albums will be released by Verve. Most of them were stereo remakes of the composers' series Peterson had done for the label. "We also did our first out-and-out jazz album with this trio," Peterson said. "There aren't many things I'm happy about, but I'm happy about this one."

A further indication of the ease with which the three men work together is the fact that Peterson acted as his own A&R man on the dates. "We just went in there every day," Thigpen said, "and kept playing until we'd had enough. Then we knocked off."

Finally, it has been noted by a number of persons that Peterson's old habit of singing while playing has been diminished somewhat—as if, with the new group, he did not feel so much need for it. (Peterson thinks the habit is a holdover from playing trumpet, and speculated, "It's probably an attempt to get a more legato feeling in my playing.")

In any case, the new trio is a superbly integrated one, and if the melodic variety that Ellis lent is gone, there is a new rhythmic drive that is almost frightening from so small a group.

"There is a danger in trio piano," Peterson said. "Most of the younger men are trio pianists. It means thinking so sympathetically with the other two that you worry about washing yourself away pianistically.

"The last thing I'll decry is this sleep-walking approach to swinging piano. Most pianists don't swing because basically they don't believe the instrument can be swung that hard—which Erroll disproved.

"The problem is that most pianists

today don't think dynamically. They start way up, and then have nowhere to go.

"As Lester Young used to call them, the little kiddies… When I hear them talking, I feel a little more confident about what I'm doing.

"Pianists must be taught.

"If a man has no technique, if he has been self-taught, you'll hear it said that he has an open mind. Not true. On the contrary, he has grooved himself.

"But the classical-trained musician has been trained to take in new aspects, new materials."

Does Peterson, to ask a tired question, therefore recommend classical training for would-be jazz pianists?

"Yes, it's good. You're equipped with the technical tools you need. It is not a matter of blatant change from classical piano to jazz; it's a matter of modification.

"But there are inadequacies when you apply it to jazz. I'm writing a series of jazz piano exercises. Ed Thigpen is working on a series for drums, and Ray has finished the first volume of his book on bass."

All the foregoing could lead the imperceptive to think that Peterson is impressed by his playing. But, on the contrary, there is a considerable modesty in the man, and he says of himself, "I feel basically that I am just on the threshold of gaining command and intuitive sense that I've always wanted."

Peterson was advised that because of his candor, he was likely to enrage the fans (the unconditional fans) of Jamal, Garner, et al. "It's the way I feel about piano," he replied simply.

Nonetheless, admirers of the pianists Peterson discussed are likely to blind themselves to the substantiality of his comments.

Let's look at it this way: jazz trumpeters, trombonists, and reed men all have pushed the horizons of their instruments far beyond the playing of their symphony counterparts. Listen to the trombone and alto solos in Ravel's Bolero, particularly the way in which the average classical trombonist will struggle to make the range and articulation of the part; then listen to, say, J.J. Johnson—or Jack Teagarden or George Brunis—and compare.

Then, in contrast, take a record by almost any jazz pianist and compare it with the playing of such classical pianists as the late Walter Gieseking (in the Debussy Etudes, for example). You find that whereas on most instruments the jazzmen have left the classical musicians

behind, the classical pianists continue to carve the jazzmen up badly.

To those who contend that technique isn't everything (and no one, least of all Peterson, is suggesting that it is), it can only be said that the greater a man's vocabulary and skill in using it, the more fully he can express what it is in his mind and his soul.

This is one reason why Peterson's ballad playing today is so moving. Technique is not a matter of sheer speed; indeed, it is perhaps more difficult to play piano very slowly—and for just about the same reason that in doing setting-up exercises, it is more difficult to execute them slowly.

Upon reflection, it seems strange that Oscar Peterson should refer to "the younger pianists" in the way he does. For he is only 34, a young man himself. It is perhaps the mark of his solid establishment in music that it does not sound strange when he uses the term. Jazz has come to think of him, and he has come to think of himself, as one of its veterans, only 10 years after his Carnegie triumph.

Peterson today lives in Toronto—or, more precisely, in Scarborough, a suburb that overlooks Lake Ontario—with his wife, Lillie (also a Montrealer), his three daughters, who are studying piano, and two sons. In his basement he has his darkroom, for his passion after music is photography. He is an accomplished photographer and has a range of expensive equipment that turns many a professional green.

He and Ray Brown, with whom he has worked since the period following the Carnegie Hall concert when they played as a duo, are, without Thigpen, establishing a school. Thigpen and Brown thus will have the status of emigrants to Canada.

They will teach jazz—and the group playing of jazz. Their plans call for a half-hour lesson for each student with whichever of the three men he is studying with. At the end of the half hour, the other two members of the trio will come in, and the student will work a half hour with them.

"When I was studying piano," Oscar recalled, "I practiced from 9 a.m. to noon, took an hour off for lunch, practiced from 1 to 6 in the afternoon, then went to dinner, and went back to the piano about 7:30. I'd keep practicing until my mother would come in and drag me away from it so the family could get some sleep.

Does he expect that kind of application from his students? "No," he said with a smile, "but I do expect them to practice. A man should know his instrument."

THE 1960s

The Blues Is a Story

by Joe Williams

as told to Barbara J. Gardner

Joe Williams.
(Jack Mahoney)

There is a music, wrung from heavy hearts, shouted defiantly or wailed pitifully—but lasting. Rooted deep in millions of enslaved people, the blues smoldered, sputtered for centuries, and burst into a globe-encompassing flame of recognition. Today, everybody knows the blues, because at one time or another everybody gets the blues—or the blues gets them.

I know about the blues. To me, the blues is a story—a story of heartbreak and sorrow. Yet at time it is a story of hope and faith. I am a blues singer—a storyteller—and I can't tell you why.

I can remember stories, terrible stories from the days of slavery, of children being torn from the arms of their mothers, and families and lovers being separated by force. These yearning, lonely people could speak little English. They could only stammer, parrot-like, jumbled phrases they picked up from their masters.

Lacking even this, they often found expression for their misery through moans and wails, cries and shrieks. This might have been the start of the whole thing, the start of something big, so to speak. The unleashed desire to scream as loud as you could for your loved one to be back with you, and the yearning to be free, helped greatly to lay the foundation of the blues.

The blues have been faithful to that beginning. They have recorded graphically the long, agonizing struggle of a people to adjust, to adapt, to find happiness in an alien land. Yet, not only the hard times and ill treatment have been preserved. The good times and high hopes have maintained their place in the blues.

What began as an expression of the downtrodden Negro now belongs to the world. It is a universal language. The only discriminating feature of blues and blues singers is that the message and the interpretation must have "soul." Until recently, the

tune had to be "funky." I haven't heard "funky" so much lately, so apparently they have "funked" out and "soul" is the new ingredient.

I can't accept the belief that soul is given to one particular group of people. Soul is the feeling that a man or woman imparts either vocally or instrumentally. The ability is not given to everyone. But when it is, it is given irrespective of race or color.

The early blues told of hollow logs, lonesome train whistles, howling dogs, muddy water and loneliness. Of these, only loneliness remains in modern times. The same heartache that drove the old timer to lay his head "on some lonesome railroad track" now drives him to stretch out on the couch of the local psychiatrist.

Of course, there is blues expression in modern tunes. Unfortunately, the writers and critics have failed in the main to recognize it. Ray Charles is the blues master of this age. When he sings about "Maryann," every man listening—whether he is a college boy or a steel worker—understands just what he's saying.

What man has not at one time in his life pleaded with his girl at least once, "Let me take you home tonight, baby, I'll make everything all right." People say these things in the way that is most natural to them, but the same requests are always essentially the same.

This newly found identification has resulted in a sharp surge of interest in the blues. Today, in the fast missile age, blues are becoming more popular because people are beginning to realize that many of these situations in song touch on their own problems.

For years the blues singers were not able to get their stories across because the blues had not been understood. But more and more now, the lyric is becoming clearer and people can understand what is being said; they are getting the story.

The blues have always been a personal vehicle for me. Many people believe that there can be no happy blues. I read all kinds of messages of happiness and hope from the blues. Even when the tune is unhappy, as in the familiar "Trouble in Mind" lyric, there is the anticipation that "the sun's gonna shine in my backdoor some day."

To me, this is strength.

The blues should sound good. It

should sound sincere. Even if it is a happy blues, and the situation in the song itself is preposterous, I think it should ring true and be sung with sincerity. For, after all, sincerity and feeling are the key factors in transforming a ballad or a popular tune into a blues work. Again I must return to Ray. His perfect blues treatment of the ballad "Come Rain or Come Shine" is one of the best examples.

Duke Ellington is another great blues man. He is one of the best blues storytellers you will ever hear. Ellington polishes his blues with shellac and satire, but if you listen to his music and his lyrics, the main ironic, unhappy situations are there.

Unfortunately, there are few women blues singers who are projecting the message today. The queen of these is Dinah Washington.

There are no words to describe the wonderful warm feeling she emits when she sings. The lyric becomes so personal that you remember each and every incident in your own life vaguely similar to the situation she sings about.

It is strange that with the great interest in blues at this time, there is still talk of jazz and blues as a dying art. It is my belief that as long as singers are able to strike a vibrant chord within the hearts of people, the art will live. The blues is like a woman, full of new discoveries every day.

The blues and I have been together for 20 years now. I have had some very good times, some very good days, and I have had some pretty low days, days when I couldn't get a job. But always, singing the blues, I had hopes and dreams of that better tomorrow.

The first inspiration to sing the blues came to me from Big Joe Turner, back in the early 1930s. If you have any doubts about modern-day blues, listen to Big Joe sing "Chains of Love."

The better tomorrow began for me when I joined the Count Basie organization. Here is the swingingest band in the world, and the entire group to the last man enjoys his work. I am sure we all enjoy our work or we could never suffer the hard knock we encounter.

We're forever pulling up roots. We're like a band of gypsies. We have a suitcase packed all the time and usually we never get to everything in the suitcase. We're forever traveling, moving on. Sometimes, we're not ready to move on, but it's our work, and a man has to follow his work. So I go where I'm told to go and sing what I'm told to sing.

Count Basie, his magnificent orchestra and the boy singer constitute a top attraction. People come to hear what we have to say. So the band is still swinging and I am still singing and—there it is!

May 26, 1960

Cannonball Looks at Ornette Coleman

by Julian Adderley

[Editor's Note: In the wave of controversy over the playing of Ornette Coleman, there have been few cool, reasoned attempts to evaluate the work of this startling alto saxophonist and his colleague, trumpeter Don Cherry. *DownBeat* assigned the task to a man who is not only one of the most important jazz musicians of the present era but a calm, analytical and literate commentator as well: Julian (Cannonball) Adderley. The following is his essay on Ornette Coleman.]

Dizzy Gillespie stood in front of the stand at the Five Spot Cafe in New York, folded his arms and looked disdainfully at the musicians as he asked, "Are you cats serious?"

Thelonious Monk is reported to have said, "Man, that cat is nuts!"

"He is an extension of Bird." That description is attributed to John Lewis; "the jazz of tomorrow" is attributed to Atlantic Records.

Comments on Ornette Coleman have ranged from conservative rejection to wild, enthusiastic support. But whatever the views expressed, it cannot be denied that there has been more talk, pro and con, about Coleman than anyone in jazz in the last decade.

Trombonist and composer Bob Brookmeyer had an experience with Coleman last summer, when Brookmeyer was on the faculty of the School of Jazz at

Lenox, Mass., and Coleman and Don Cherry were there as students. "I used to scream out of my window, 'Damn it, tune up!' as these cats would play evenings downstairs," Brookmeyer said. "The special interest in Ornette and Cherry, coupled with having to listen to their music constantly, was responsible for my leaving the faculty at Lenox." But Brookmeyer added: "Since they have been in New York, however, I have been going over to hear them at the Five Spot, and I've learned a lesson in tolerance. I'm sure that my rejection of this music was based simply on intolerance of (something) that I was not familiar with."

Bob is not the only one. I have learned a lesson in tolerance myself, in a less demonstrative way.

While working in Los Angeles with Miles Davis last summer, I was a guest at the home of Joe Castro, the pianist. One evening Castro was rehearsing his group for a record date. In the group were Leroy Vinnegar, Teddy Edwards, Don Cherry and Billy Higgins. The date was to include material composed by Don Cherry.

Don's thematic material was starkly fresh and flowing. But his improvisation seemed to have no connection with the theme. Bassist Vinnegar and drummer Higgins were really swinging, and urging Don on with little expressions such as "yeah, baby," which indicated that they really dug it.

Pianist Castro seemed confused.

This was only my second exposure to Don, who is Ornette's leading disciple and probably his most enthusiastic student. My first exposure had been a brief set at the Sundown Club, where he sat in with John Coltrane. At that time, I was amazed at the gall of an apparent amateur to play with a giant in jazz, for his performance was seemingly unintelligible and insincere. I frankly felt that he was joking.

Then, at this later date, Castro and I discussed this music with Cherry. Don spoke as a believer in complete freedom of expression, with occasional references to divine guidance, to Bird, and to Ornette.

I think the most interesting aspect of the conversation was his seriousness in explaining his music. I could not, however, help wondering, What kind of man is this Ornette Coleman? I couldn't at the time believe that they took this music seriously.

My first meeting with Ornette dispelled any such ideas.

When introduced to Ornette, I received praise and admiration to the point of embarrassment. I also received an invitation to his home to discuss music and the alto saxophone.

Even though this meeting never materialized in Los Angeles, shortly afterwards I purchased Coleman's only existing recording at the time, *Something Else.* I determined to give it exacting scrutiny and the most fundamental analysis. I was still confused by the music. The improvisation seemed inconsistent with both the implied chords of the melodic line and those played in accompaniment by the pianist.

The second recording, which did not include piano (*Tomorrow Is the Question*), seemed to be more logical in continuity.

Subsequently, I have become an Ornette Coleman booster. I am sure there is a place in jazz for an innovator of this type. I think my compassion for Ornette, coupled with his sincerity, is probably the prime motivating factor.

My analysis reveals consistency in some instances, such as a general sort of faithfulness to the blues. His intonation theories, however, disturb me. Dick Katz, an ardent Coleman supporter, explained, "Ornette does not use a tempered scale. Don apparently does, for they sometimes tend to clash." They both explain this phenomenon as the "human pitch" and suggest that this is also a freedom of expression.

I have also questioned their unfaithfulness to chords.

Ornette explains: "Chords are just names for sounds, which really need no names at all, as names are sometimes confusing."

For instance, F minor seventh is also A-flat major sixth. Coleman does play chords in improvisation, but does not play "changes," such as the standard II-minor seventh, to dominant seventh, to the I or III chords.

Ornette says he has discovered that the alto saxophone has 32 available natural pitches, from D-flat in the lower middle register to A-flat in the second upper middle register of the piano. He does not think in octaves. Each tone to him is a separate sound.

He respects Charlie Parker as the only musician, of those to play changes, who really exploited the sound of the instrument; and he has the unique idea that the alto voice should be thought of in the alto clef. Consequently, his E-flat alto C-natural concert is really B-flat in the alto clef. (My apologies to readers for using such musical terminology, but I am unable to find any

easier way to describe his category.)

There are many important musicians who are advocates of Ornette's freedom theory in improvisation. But there are fewer who would use his approach to sound and harmony. I would say that 75 percent of jazz musicians dismiss Ornette's whole thing. But he has caused more reflection and analysis than anyone since Bird, Diz and Thelonious.

But the so-called music of tomorrow theme, which accompanies his performances, is more harmful than good. For Ornette is a man to be reckoned with today. A Miles Davis is basically an impressionist, Charles Mingus a surrealist, John Lewis a neoclassicist. But how do you classify an Ornette Coleman?

His followers believe that his is the "shape of jazz to come." I feel that though Ornette may influence future jazz, so will George Russell's Lydian concept of tonal organization, Coltrane's sheets of sound, Miles' melodic lyricism and Gil Evans' clusters of sound in rhythm. Ornette Coleman is an innovator of the first water. But he is certainly no messiah.

Julian "Cannonball" Adderley.

May 26, 1960
. . . .

Another View of Coleman

by Charles Mingus

[Editor's Note: When bassist Charles Mingus took Leonard Feather's Blindfold Test recently, he volunteered a long afterthought on Ornette Coleman. It is included here to give a still different perspective on the controversial altoist.]

You didn't play anything by Ornette Coleman. I'll comment on him anyway. Now, I don't care if he doesn't like me, but anyway, one night Symphony [Sid] was playing a whole lot of stuff, and then he put on an Ornette Coleman record.

Now, he is really an old-fashioned

Ornette Coleman with his plaque for winning the 1960 DownBeat Critics Poll in the alto sax category.
(DownBeat Archive)

alto player. He's not as modern as Bird. He plays in C and F and G and B-flat only; he does not play in all the keys. Basically, you can hit a pedal-point C all the time, and it'll have some relationship to what he's playing.

Now aside from the fact that I doubt he can even play a C scale in whole notes— tied whole notes, a couple of bars apiece— in tune, the fact remains that his notes and lines are so fresh. So when Symphony Sid played his record, it made everything else he was playing, even my own record that he played, sound terrible.

I'm not saying everybody's going to

have to play like Coleman. But they're going to have to stop copying Bird. Nobody can play Bird right yet but him. Now, what would Fats Navarro and J.J. have played like if they'd never heard Bird? Or even Dizzy? Would he still play like Roy Eldridge? Anyway, when they put Coleman's record on, the only record they could have put on behind it would have been Bird.

It doesn't matter about the key he's playing in—he's got a percussional sound, like a cat with a whole lot of bongos. He's brought a thing in—it's not new. I won't say who started it, but whoever started it, people overlooked it. It's like not having

anything to do with what's around you, and being right in your own world. You can't put your finger on what he's doing.

It's like organized disorganization, or playing wrong right. And it gets to you emotionally, like a drummer. That's what Coleman means to me.

Sept. 15, 1960

Perils of Paul: A Portrait of Desperate Desmond

by Marian McPartland

A few months from now, the Dave Brubeck Quartet will celebrate its 10th anniversary as a unit. Few, if any, jazz groups now playing have endured that long, though the Modern Jazz Quartet is just about the same age. And few have achieved anything even approaching the broad acceptance that the group has found throughout the world.

Today, with a rhythm section comprising Joe Morello on drums and bassist Eugene Wright, the group is, in the opinion of many observers, playing better than ever before. It has not given in to apathy or the repetition of past successes that seem to rob almost all groups of their vitality when they have stayed together too long.

Why?

Undoubtedly a big reason is the tremendous mutual understanding and sympathy—both musical and personal—of Brubeck and his star soloist, alto saxophonist Paul Desmond.

Desmond's status in the group and, in fact, in the music business, is unique. With Brubeck, he has all the privileges of a leader, much of the acclaim and few, if any, of the headaches and responsibilities. It is, as Paul puts it, "a limited partnership." He and Dave consult on choice of tunes, tempos, choruses and so forth. He also takes a generous percentage of the group's earnings.

"In most groups," Paul says, "if they make it, the leader still goes on paying the same money to the sidemen. So eventually they split like amoebae all over the place. In this case, Dave and I worked out a pretty good arrangement some time ago, and that's the way it's been ever since."

One might assume, therefore, that Paul has a dream job. But on closer look, one is tempted to wonder if, for a man of Paul's talent—in many ways, untapped talent—it might be a gilded cage.

For Desmond has a mind that can only be called brilliant—incredibly quick, perceptive, sensitive. He is also remarkably articulate (his original goal in life was to be a writer, not a musician) and witty, with a skill at turning apt and hilarious phrases that leave his friends in hysterics. For example, when a drug company ran an ad for a tranquilizer that showed a bust of composer Richard Wagner (who suffered from splitting headaches) and said that if he'd lived long enough, the new product would have relieved his misery, Desmond promptly dubbed the product "post-Wagnerian anti-drag pills."

Some of his friends are even prone to collecting and quoting Desmondisms, the way in the classical world musicians cherish and repeat the wisecracks of Sir Thomas Beecham.

And his conversation ranges over a vast variety of subjects. Of Jack Kerouac, he said, "I hate the way he writes. I kind of like the way he lives, though."

Of *Vogue* fashion models, he said, "Sometimes they go around with guys who are scuffling—for a while. But usually they end up marrying some cat with a factory. This is the way the world ends, not with a whim but a banker!"

Of yogurt, he said, "I don't like it, but Dave is always trying things like that. He's a nutritional masochist. He'll eat anything as long as he figures it's good for him."

And he said (self-revealingly) of contact lenses: "Not for me. If I want to tune everybody out, I just take off my glasses and enjoy the haze."

And so it goes. Acute perception of life goes on incessantly within Paul and finds its way out in pithy expressions that are only one part of his eloquence. Given so great a versatility (he is also a skillful photographer), such enormous public acceptance and the respect of a heavy percentage of his fellow musicians, why should Paul not be perpetually blissful?

Alto player Lee Konitz, whose playing has been likened to Desmond's, said recently, "There's an area in Paul that he

Paul Desmond.
(Oscar Callender Jr, for DownBeat)

hasn't been able to realize yet. That's why he gets so depressed—he needs more time to know himself, so that he will get to like himself better. I don't think he has enough time for reflection and thought. I feel that Paul has experienced greatness, and once this feeling of playing what you really hear has been felt by a player, it's difficult to settle for less than this."

"I feel pretty close to Paul," he added, "as I've gone through these things myself, and I still haven't reached the point where I'm happy with what I'm doing."

Paul Ernil Breitenfeld ("I picked the name Desmond out of the phone book," he

says) was born in San Francisco in 1924. His father played organ for silent movies, wrote band arrangements (and still does) and played accompaniments for vaudeville acts.

As a boy, Paul found family life difficult. When he was five, his mother became ill and he was sent to live with relatives in New Rochelle, N.Y. In an odd way, his jazz career began there—in grammar school.

"They had a music period," Paul remembers. "Like a postgraduate kindergarten band, with psalteries and chimes and all.

"By the end of the term I was getting to be like the Terry Gibbs of Daniel Webster, so they put me down for a solo at one of the assemblies. I was supposed to play one of those grisly semiclassical things. Dance of the Bridge Trolls by Glinka, one of those kind of things. Ridiculous. I figured if I just went out and made up something as I went along, it couldn't be any worse. So that's what I did, and it was a gas.

"It was the first thing I'd enjoyed doing. (I was kind of a walking vegetable as a kid. Amiable but unfocused.) I didn't realize until about 15 years later that you could make a living doing this."

Paul returned home to San Francisco in 1936 and started going to Polytechnic High School. "I wanted to learn French," he said, "and I was kind of thinking of starting clarinet, but they were both at the same time. So I signed up for French and violin. Dad was very drug when I came home with the program. 'With the violin, you'll starve,' he said. 'Violin players are a dime a dozen. And French you don't need. Take clarinet.'"

So Paul started studying clarinet and Spanish. "Which was kind of a drag last year when we were in Paris," he said. "El bombo grande. Well, you can't win 'em all."

Paul played in the school band, edited the school newspaper and assiduously dodged all forms of exercise. "I discovered early in life that if you take gym first period, you can go into the wrestling room and sit in the corner and sleep."

But it was not until 1943 that Paul began to play alto. That year, he went into the Army. For three years he was stationed in San Francisco with the 253rd AGF band. "It was a great way to spend the war. We expected to get shipped out every month, but it never happened. Somewhere in Washington our file must still be on the floor under a desk somewhere."

There were some good local musicians in the band, notably Dave Van Kreidt, a tenor saxophonist and arranger who has been a great friend of Paul's ever since.

One day a friend of Van Kreidt's came through San Francisco. He was a piano player fresh off the ranch, en route overseas as a rifleman and eager to get into the band. His name was Dave Brubeck.

"We had a session in the band room," Paul recalled. "I remember the first tune we played was 'Rosetta.' I was really dazzled by his harmonic approach."

Then Paul said with that expression that tells you you'd better take him with a grain of salt for a moment, "I went up to him and said, 'Man, like Wigsville! You really grooved me with those nutty changes.' And Brubeck replied, 'White man speak with forked tongue.'"

Whatever Brubeck and Desmond actually did say to each other, they did not meet again until after the war, when Dave was working around San Francisco, mostly at the Geary Cellar with a group called the Three D's. It was led by a tenor player named Darryl Cutler, and the bass player was Norman Bates.

"I went down and sat in," Paul said, "and the musical rapport was very evident and kind of scary. A lot of the things we've done since, we did then, immediately—a lot of the counterpoint things, and it really impressed me. If you think Dave plays far out now, you should have heard him then. He made Cecil Taylor sound like Lester Lanin."

Shortly after that, Paul hired Cutler's group away from him—"at some risk of life and limb; Darryl Cutler was a pretty rugged cat"—to work a few months near Stanford.

"It was a 60-mile ride, and we were making about $50 a night. I was splitting it with the guys and paying for the gas, too. That's when I decided I really didn't want to be a leader. A lot of things we did later with the quartet began there.

"I've often wondered what would have happened if we'd been in New York at the time—whether it was really as good as I think it was. I have a memory of several nights that seemed fantastic, and I don't feel that way too often. I'd give anything for a tape of one of those nights now, just to see what was really going on.

"I know we were playing a lot of counterpoint on almost every tune, and the general level was a lot more loud, emotional and unsubtle then. I was always screaming away at the top of the horn, and Dave would be constructing something behind me in three keys. Sometimes I had to plead with him to play something more simple behind me.

"It seemed pretty wild at the time; it was one of those few jobs where you really hated to stop—we'd keep playing on the theme until they practically threw us off the stand.

"Anyway, that's where the empathy between Dave and me began, and it's survived a remarkable amount of pulling and pushing in the 11 or so years since.

"Then the Dave Brubeck Octet started, mainly as a Saturday afternoon rehearsal group for the guys studying composition with Milhaud (Brubeck, Van Kreidt, Bill Smith, Dick Collins and Jack Weeks). I was the only musical illiterate with that group—I wasn't studying with Milhaud.

"I was going to San Francisco State college, studying to be a writer. It was the only major where you could get credit for anything you felt like taking—playwriting, social dancing, basket-weaving, anything. I finally decided writing was like playing jazz—it can be learned, but not taught.

"The social dancing was kind of wild, though, a sort of Arthur Murray for misfits. The girls were all sort of thin and 6 feet tall, and the guys were mostly scrawny with glasses like ice cubes. We met twice a week in the basement of a Greek church near the school, and they had a hand-wound phonograph and about three records. I don't know how old they were, but on one of them, before the music started, you could hear a voice saying, 'What hath God wrought?'"

Time slipped by, and all of a sudden it was June 1950. "My only jobs that year had been two concerts with the octet and a Mexican wedding," Desmond said. So he decided to take a job with Jack Fina's band. The job got him to New York, with plans in his head to leave the band and go on from there. "But when I arrived in New York," he said, "all that happened was that all the guys I talked to wanted my job with Fina, which was pretty discouraging.

"Meantime, back at the ranch, Brubeck had started the trio with the advice and support of our patron saint, Jimmy Lyons (then a disc jockey, now manager of the Monterey Jazz Festival). Dave had also started his own record company, which was really a hurdle back in those pre-LP days. So I went back to San Francisco and stayed there for a while with my nose pressed firmly to the window, and in 1951 we started the quartet."

Even then, Paul had a kind of veneration for Brubeck, compounded of affection, admiration and respect. In answer to the oft-made observation that "Dave never would have made it without Paul Desmond," Paul says stoutly, "I never would have made it without Dave. He's amazing harmonically, and he can be a fantastic accompanist. You can play the wrongest note possible in any chord, and he can make it sound like the only right one.

"I still feel more kinship musically with Dave than with anyone else, although it may not always be evident. But when he's at his best, it's really something to hear. A lot of people don't know this, because in addition to the kind of fluctuating level of performance that most jazz musicians give, Dave has a real aversion to working things out, and a tendency to take the things he can do for granted and spend most of his time trying to do other things. This is OK for people who have heard him play at his best, but sometimes mystifying to those who haven't.

"However, once in a while somebody who had no use for Dave previously comes in and catches a really good set and leaves looking kind of dazed."

Because of his affection for Brubeck, Paul feels it sharply when his friend is criticized. And the Brubeck group has run into perhaps more than its fair share of criticism. "Yet Paul usually gets off unscathed. Ira Gitler recently wrote a stinging review of a new quartet record. Yet, he said, "Paul Desmond's playing is another proof that jazz has many shades of expression, that you can communicate deep emotion without histrionics: However, I'd like to hear him play a set with Al Cohn and Zoot Sims; I think it would prove stimulating."

And, though Desmond has characterized himself as the "disembodied saxophonist of the Brubeck group," John S. Wilson wrote after the group's performance this year at Newport, "Desmond seems to be the bellwether of the... quartet. When he is uninspired, the entire group is affected, largely because Brubeck seems to push harder, bringing out the worst side of his playing. But when Paul is at the top of his form, Dave really relaxes."

Desmond seems to command an enormous amount of respect among fellow musicians, though by no means all of them. Miles Davis, who has put down a good many of his fellow artists, has said loftily, "I just don't like the sound of an alto played that way."

More specific in his criticism was alto saxophonist Jackie McLean. "Desmond's playing is pleasant—progressive—but not particularly moving to me. As far as technique is concerned, he has wonderful control of his instrument. But then, so has Dick Stabile. I feel that his playing is sort of a launching pad for Dave's music. But it's very lyrical, he plays good ideas, and they are his own ideas."

But Julian Adderley—who is Paul's archcompetitor for top alto spot in the various polls, most of which Paul has won in recent years—said, "I believe that Paul Desmond shares with Benny Carter the title of most lyrical altoist. He is a profoundly beautiful player." Sonny Stitt, another of today's top altoists, said, "He plays good music. He's not on cloud nine all the time, like some of those guys. I like him very much."

And Dizzy Gillespie, a sort of father figure for a great many of today's jazzmen, said, "Paul and Dave sure do something for one another. The ideas that Paul gets are in the same groove as Dave's. They seem to have terrific rapport. It takes a lot to get such cohesion between two people in a unit."

Perhaps the best appraisal of Paul Desmond and his music comes from the man who knows both better than anyone else—Dave Brubeck.

"I've heard him play more than anyone else has," Dave said, "and even after all these years, he still surprises me. There are so many imitators of Charlie Parker, and to me Paul is one of the few true individuals on his instrument. Musicians will put one idol before them and think that everything should revolve around this person and that everyone should play his way—and this curbs individuality.

"Paul's big contribution is going to be that he didn't copy Charlie Parker.

"I believe that Paul and I make a good team. We've had many conflicts and we will probably have many more, but there are a lot of things we haven't done yet and can do if we can stick together and put up with each other."

Yet even though Paul finds his association with Dave so satisfying (and vice versa), there are constant, if subtle, pressures on the altoist to strike out on his own. Desmond has made notably few recordings with anyone but Brubeck, leading many musicians to wonder—like critic Gitler— how he would sound in another context.

Of those few discs Desmond has made with others (Gerry Mulligan, Don Elliott), his favorite is one made recently for the Warner Bros. label. Working with him were Percy Heath, Connie Kay and Jim Hall. Though suspicions are occasionally voiced that anyone who has been a sideman for 10 years would run into difficulty as leader, guitarist Hall's comments on the date would tend to indicate the contrary.

"I learned a lot about Paul," Hall said, "due to the fact that each of us had to give a high-level performance at the same time as the other fellow. I was very impressed with his musicianship, especially his ability to play a long melody line through a series of choruses. We made several takes, and every one of his takes was almost perfect; we were the ones who messed up.

"But aside from the music, he's such a charming guy, and though he may not be forceful in the same way some musicians are, I know that he knows what he wants from a group. He may not stomp and shout, but he gets things done just the same."

Paul continues to have the same lack of enthusiasm for leadership that he did when he hired the Darryl Cutler group away and tried the role for a while.

But the time may come when he will give in.

"I guess it's inevitable that I'll have my own group one of these days," he said, "if for no other reason than that Dave will probably wander off into other fields and not do as much playing as he's doing now.

"The problem then will be to find guys I can communicate with musically and get along with the rest of the time. The ideal, for me, is a group with a lot of cooperative playing going on, as opposed to a procession of virtuosi, if that's the word I want. Guys who can improve together in such a way that the whole turns out to be greater than the sum of all the parts. I have that feeling with Dave a lot, which is one reason I've hung around this long, also with Gerry Mulligan and Jim Hall.

"Finding the right guys, I think, is really the hardest part of being a leader. The rest gets to be largely routine and resigning yourself to being a bad guy part of the time. And a certain amount of patience, fortitude and delicate negotiation is necessary even for 'illustrious' sidemen like me."

Whether or not he does strike out as a leader, however, Paul has more than enough to keep him occupied or preoccupied, as the case may be. He is pursuing his own musical ideal, and his distinctive sound—light, liquid, at times mournful—will continue to be an important voice in jazz.

"I love the way Miles plays," he said. "I still think the hardest thing of all to do is to come up with things that are simple, melodic and yet new. Until fairly recently, most of the landmarks in jazz history could be written out and played by practically anybody after they had been done. It just took a long time for them to be thought of. There's a lot more going on now in terms of complexity, but it's still a long time between steps.

"Complexity can get to be a trap, too. I think it gets to be more fun to play than to listen to. You can have a ball developing a phrase, inverting it, playing it in different keys and times and all. But it's really more introspective than communicative. Like a crossword puzzle compared to a poem.

"What would kill me the most on the jazz scene these days would be for everybody to go off in a corner and sound like himself. Let a hundred flowers bloom. Diversitysville. There's enough conformity in the rest of this country without having it prevail in jazz, too.

"I should mention in connection with anything critical I say about anyone else that about 80 percent of the things I play, I hate to listen to afterwards. I kind of know what I'd like to be doing ultimately on the horn, but it's hard to make any progress while you're traveling. Hard enough even in one place, as far as that goes.

"But the things I'm after musically are clarity, emotional communication on a not-too-obvious level, the kind of form in a chorus that doesn't hit you over the head but is there if you look for it, humor and construction that sounds logical in an unexpected way.

"That and a good, dependable high F-sharp, and I'll be happy."

Desmondisms

Some off-the-cuff comments on a variety of subjects:

Playing funky. It's kind of a trap. It's easy to do, but the mental process involved is self-destructive. After a while it gets difficult to do anything else.

Brigitte Bardot. That was my favorite thing about playing England—all the girls looked like Brigitte Bardot, and all the guys looked like me.

Cocktail parties. Depends who's there.

Miltown. Depends who's there.

Bill Crow. Miltown.

Texas. No thanks.

One-nighters. It's a living.

Mantan. As Mort Sahl says, "If you can't believe in the sun, what can you believe in?"

Yoga. I could never cross my legs.

Ornette Coleman. One thing I'm really against is the tendency for everybody to play like everybody else. You'll hear someone developing and he'll have a definite style of his own, and then you hear him six months later and he sounds like whoever is currently fashionable. There's a lot of submerged individuality which will never appear, I think. That's one thing I like about Ornette. I'm glad he's such an individualist. I like the firmness of thought and purpose that goes into what he's doing, even though I don't always like to listen to

it. It's like living in a house where everything's painted red.

May 25, 1961

The Years with Yard

by Dizzy Gillespie

(with Gene Lees)

It's very hard for me to believe that Charlie Parker has been gone six years. To tell the truth, it doesn't seem to me that he is gone.

And in fact, he isn't gone. It sounds like a cliché to say that his music will be here forever, but that is the truth. And there are precedents for believing this.

The same thing could be said of Charlie Christian and Lester Young. They are not gone, either. These three men left a heritage; they set the rules. Therefore, they are still with us.

I haven't heard an alto player who wasn't close to Bird. Of course, the closest to him that I have heard is Sonny Stitt. When I hear a record sometimes, I won't be sure at first whether it's Sonny or Yard. Sonny gets down into all the little things of Charlie Parker's playing. The others just play his music; Sonny plays his life. If they ever make a movie about Charlie Parker, Sonny Stitt is the man to play the part.

It's hard, too, to remember when I first knew Bird. It seems to me that I always knew him, as far back as I can recall, though that isn't true, of course.

In South Carolina, we heard none of the Kansas City bands. They didn't come through that part of the country. We heard only the bands from the East Coast.

But I knew little Buddy Anderson, the trumpet player. Later, he developed tuberculosis and had to quit playing, but he was a fine trumpet player.

When I joined Cab Calloway's band, we went to Kansas City. This was in 1939. Now, Buddy Anderson was the only trumpet player I knew who had the idea of exploring the instrument through piano. I played piano, too, and sometimes we'd spend the day at the piano together, never touching a trumpet. And he kept telling me

about this Charlie Parker.

One day while we were in Kansas City with Cab, Buddy brought Charlie Parker over to the Booker T. Washington Hotel and introduced us. We understood each other right away.

Yard had brought his horn with him. The three of us played together, in the hotel room, all that day. Just the three of us. You didn't find many musicians who could show you on the piano what they were doing. But Charlie Parker could, even then. He was only a kid. We were both only kids.

I returned to New York, and then Charlie Parker joined Jay McShann's band and came to New York, too. In 1941, I left Cab. I played two weeks with Ella Fitzgerald and then with Benny Carter, at Kelly's Stable. In the band was Charlie Drayton on bass, Sonny White on piano (he's with Wilbur DeParis now), Kenny Clarke, drums, and Al Gibson on tenor. Nat Cole and Art Tatum were playing opposite us. Did we hear some piano playing!

After that, I went out with Charlie Barnet for three weeks in Toronto, then rejoined Benny, then went with Coleman Hawkins. This was getting on toward 1942 or 1943. I worked with Earl Hines and Billy Eckstine in 1943–'44, Then, in late 1944, Oscar Pettiford and I formed a group, as co-leaders. And we immediately sent Charlie Parker a telegram asking him to join us. By the time we heard from Yardbird, we'd been in there for several weeks, Don Byas had come in to work as a single and Oscar Pettiford and I had broken up the group. In fact, I was co-leader across the street from the Onyx with Budd Johnson, and Bird still hadn't showed up. Budd and I were there six weeks. By then, Charlie Parker was just getting into town… and I no longer had a group for him to work with!

But Yard was in New York, and that was the main thing, and a number of us were experimenting with a different way of playing jazz.

There has been a lot of talk about where and when so-called bebop started.

But a simple answer to the question is impossible. It depends on your viewpoint and on what you consider were the important contributing factors.

If you consider that Charlie Parker was the prime mover, then bebop started at Clark Monroe's Uptown House, because that was where Yard used to go to jam. If you consider that Thelonious Monk was the prime mover, then it was Minton's, where Monk was playing after hours with Joe Guy, Nick Fenton and Kermit Scott. I was in an odd position: I was jamming at both places, and ducking the union man at both places!

Bird used to come to Minton's to play, too, but he was jamming mostly at Monroe's.

Who do I consider was the prime mover in the bebop movement? I would answer that with another question: what is the most important ingredient in spaghetti sauce?

But this much I can say: it is true that we used to play unusual substitute chords and extensions of the chords to throw some of the other musicians who came up to sit in. That did have a lot to do with it.

I can remember when nobody except us played the chord progression A minor seventh to D seventh to D-flat. That was one of the chord progressions I showed Monk. But Monk was the first to use E minor seventh with a flatted fifth, or as some call it, an E half-diminished. Monk just called it a G minor sixth with an E in the bass.

By this time, Bird and I were very close friends.

He was a very sensitive person, in the way that many creative people are. Everything made a profound impression on him. He also was very loyal, and he had a terrific sense of humor.

I remember one incident that illustrated all these characteristics.

It was after the period of Minton's and Monroe's Uptown House. We were with the Earl Hines Band. I was sitting at the piano one night in Pine Bluff, Ark., and some white fellow came up and threw a quarter on the bandstand to me and said, "Hey, boy! Play 'Darktown Strutters Ball.'" I paid him no mind and kept playing.

When the dance was over, I went to the men's room. As I came out, this guy hit me on the side of the head with a bottle. Blood was spurting, and I grabbed for a bottle myself. Some people grabbed me, before I could crown him with a bottle of seltzer.

They took me off to the hospital. I remember as they were taking me out, Charlie Parker—he wasn't very big— was wagging his finger in the man's face. I'll always remember his words. He told the guy: "You cur! You took advantage of my friend!"

He was such a wonderful person, and I have seen so much written about him that is false or unimportant. I remember him as

a person as much as a great musician.

I was the first one to join Earl Hines, though Yard came with the band right after.

I had been with the Lucky Millinder Band. He fired me in Philadelphia, in 1942. I worked a club there for a while and then joined Hines in '43. We all started asking Earl to hire Bird. Unfortunately, there were already two alto players in the band. That didn't stop us. Billy Eckstine said, "Let's get him anyway—he can play tenor."

So Yard joined the band right after that, on tenor. He played superbly with that band. I remember Sarah Vaughan would sing "This Is My First Love," and Bird would play 16 bars on it; the whole band would be turned to look at him. Nobody was playing like that.

We stayed with Earl Hines until Billy left to form his own band. Sarah left, too. Yard and I joined Billy. Gale Brockman and Benny Harris were in the brass section with me, and Billy Frazier, Dexter Gordon, Lucky Thompson, John Jackson, Charlie Rouse and Gene Ammons were in the sax section at one time or another with Bird. That was a radical band. It was the fore-runner of all the big modern bands. But a lot of ballroom operators didn't dig it. They thought it was just weird. But it was a very fine band, very advanced.

I can't recall whether Charlie Parker and I left the band together. We must have, because from the band, we went into the Three Deuces. That was in early 1945. The group was in my name, and the members included Stan Levey, Al Haig, Curly Russell and Bird. We were there for several months. In December 1945, we went to Billy Berg's club on Vine Street in Hollywood. Ray Brown had replaced Curly Russell, and Milt Jackson had been added on vibes.

I wasn't always sure Bird would show up, and that's why I hired Bags. The contract was for only five men. With Bags we were sure to have at least five men on the stand whether Bird showed up or not. Later, Billy Berg said we needed more body! And he had us hire Lucky Thompson on tenor. That gave us up to seven pieces.

We stayed there eight weeks. Ah, it would be nice to work eight weeks in one club again. The musicians out there were all over us. We had a ball, but we didn't do too well as far as the public was concerned.

But by now, bebop was well established. Fats Navarro, Howard McGhee, Wardell Gray, Freddie Webster and, if memory serves me, Miles Davis were all on 52nd Street in New York when we

returned from California in 1946.

Bird had stayed on to gig on the coast. Bebop was getting lots of publicity, there had even been articles in *Life* magazine.

Clark Monroe, who owned the Uptown House, helped me put together a big band in 1946. When we got back to New York, the Three Deuces wanted us, and Clark wanted us for his new Spotlite club—he'd moved downtown, you see. He offered us a deal. If we didn't go into the Three Deuces, we could come into the Spotlite for eight weeks with a small band and then eight weeks with a big band. He said we could build it from his club.

At one time, for a one-week date in the Bronx, I had Yardbird, Miles and Freddie Webster in that band. That was only temporary, of course. While I had the big band, Bird had his quintet. He had such people as Miles, Max Roach and Duke Jordan with him.

I didn't know it, but the job in Hollywood had been the last time Bird and I were ever to work together in a permanent group.

Bird's contribution to all the jazz that came after it involved every phase of it. He sure wasn't the beginning, and he wasn't the end—but that middle was bulging! But even he had his influences.

You see, Charlie Parker had a Buster Smith background. And, of course, there was Old Yard—an old alto man—in Kansas City. He had that same feeling. Charlie came up under the aegis of Lester Young and Buster Smith. Regardless of what anyone says, there's so much music out there in the air, all you have to do is get a little bite of it. Nobody can get more than a little bit, but some guys get more than others. Charlie Parker bit off a big chunk— I'll tell you! Still he had influences—Lester and those others. But he added to it.

One thing he added was accent—the way of stressing certain notes. And a different way of building melodies. When he was playing a B chord, he was playing in the key of B.

Another thing was rapidity with sense—not rapidity just for the sake of rapidity, but melody rapidity. He was so versed in chord changes and substitute chords that he was never lost for melody. Regardless of what chord was being played, he never lost melody. He could play a blues and sound just like a blues singer, just like he was talking.

I saw something remarkable one time. He didn't show up for a dance he was supposed to play in Detroit. I was in town, and they asked me to play instead. I went up there, and we started playing. Then I heard this big roar, and Charlie Parker had come in and started playing. He'd play a phrase, and people might never have heard it before. But he'd start it, and the people would finish it with him, humming. It would be so lyrical and simple that it just seemed the most natural thing to play. That's another important thing about Charlie Parker—his simplicity.

And Charlie Parker was an accompanist. He could accompany singers like they never had been accompanied. He'd fill in behind them and make little runs. He could make a run and make it end right where it should. This is very hard to do. What a mathematical mind he had.

I remember one record date for Continental especially. It was with Rubberlegs Williams, a blues singer. Somebody had this date—Clyd Hart, I believe. He got Charlie Parker, me, Oscar Pettiford, Don Byas, Trummy Young and I don't remember the drummer's name. The music didn't work up quite right at first. Now, at that time we used to break inhalers open and put the stuff into coffee or Coca-Cola; it was a kick then. During a break at this record date, Charlie dropped some into Rubberlegs' coffee. Rubberlegs didn't drink or smoke or anything. So we went on with the record date. Rubberlegs began moaning and crying as he was singing. You should hear those records!

Yard used to come and play with my big band. He'd never heard the arrangements before, but you'd think he'd written them. The brass would play something and cut off, and bang! Charlie Parker was there, coming in right where he was supposed to. It's a shame that when he was making those records with strings that the music wasn't up to his standards. There should have been a whole symphony behind him.

I doubt, though, whether he knew everything he was playing. I'll bet that 75 percent of his playing he thought of, and the other 25 percent just fell in place, fell under his fingers. But what he did was enormous. You hear his music everywhere now. And yet it's still hard for me to talk about him—not because he's dead, because he's not really gone to me, but because it's hard for me to think where my life ends and his begins; they were so intertwined.

You hear so much about him that I don't like to hear—about his addiction and all sorts of irrelevant nonsense. What kind of man was Beethoven? Perhaps he wasn't a very admirable individual, but what has that to do with listening to his music?

Not that I didn't think Bird was admirable. He was. But people talk too much about the man—people who don't know—when the important thing is his music. The Negro people should put up a statue to him, to remind their grandchildren. This man contributed joy to the world, and it will last a thousand years.

July 20, 1961

Wes Montgomery

by Ralph J. Gleason

Few jazz musicians have had the rise to professional acclaim that John Leslie (Wes) Montgomery, the guitar-playing member of the Indiana Montgomery family, has had in the last two years.

Up until that time almost unknown to the jazz public outside his native Indianapolis, Montgomery was heralded by Cannonball Adderley, Gunther Schuller and other musicians who heard him and was brought by Adderley to the attention of Orrin Keepnews of Riverside Records, who promptly recorded him. Since that debut (his second, for he had toured with Lionel Hampton for two years in the early '40s), Montgomery has run away with the New Star Guitar category in *DownBeat*'s International Jazz Critics Poll and today seems a cinch to live up to his billing as the "best thing that has happened to the guitar since Charlie Christian."

For the last year, Wes has worked with his brothers, Buddy (vibes) and Monk (bass), as the Montgomery Brothers. The other two Montgomerys are half the original Mastersounds quartet, which a few years ago won the Critics Poll as Best New Small Group.

Pinned down recently between rehearsals and pool games (shooting pool is his only hobby), Wes discussed guitar players (including himself) with the ease and familiarity born of years of listening:

"I started in 1943, right after I got married. I bought an amplifier and a guitar around two or three months later. I used to play a tenor guitar, but it wasn't playing, you know. I didn't really get down to business until I got the six-string, which was just like starting all over to me.

"I got interested in playing the guitar because of Charlie Christian. Like all other guitar players! There's no way out. I never saw him in my life, but he said so much on the records that I don't care what instrument a cat played, if he didn't understand and didn't feel and really didn't get with the things that Charlie Christian was doing, he was a pretty poor musician—he was so far ahead.

"Before Charlie Christian I liked (Django) Reinhardt and Les Paul and those cats, but it wasn't what you'd call new. Just guitar. For the exciting new thing, they didn't impress me like that. But Charlie Christian did; I mean, he stood out above all of it to me.

"'Solo Flight' was the first record I heard. Boy, that was too much! I still hear it! He was it for me, and I didn't look at nobody else. I didn't hear nobody else for about a year or so. Couldn't even hear them.

"I'm not really musically inclined. It takes guts, you know! I was 19 and I liked music, but it didn't really inspire me to go into things. But there was a cat living in Indianapolis named Alex Stevens. He played guitar, and he was about the toughest cat I heard around our vicinity, and I tried to get him to show me a few things.

"So, eventually what I did was I took all of Charlie Christian's records, and I listened to them real good. I knew what he was doing on that guitar could be done on the one I had because I had a six-string. So I was just determined I'd do it. I didn't quit. It didn't quite come out like that, but I got pretty good at it, and I took all the solos off the records. I got a job playing just the solos, making money in a club. That's all I did—played Charlie Christian solos and then laid out! Mel Lee—he's the piano player with B.B. King—had the band, and he helped me a lot.

"Then I went on the road with the Brownskin Models and later with Snookum Russell. Ray Brown was on the band at that time. I didn't realize he was playing so much bass until I heard him with Diz!

"Hamp was the only big band I went with, 1948–'50. I didn't use any amplifier at all. He had a lot of things for the sextet, but he never got to record that group.

"I'm so limited. I have a lot of ideas—

well, a lot of thoughts—that I'd like to see done with the guitar. With the octaves, that was just a coincidence, going into octaves. It's such a challenge yet, you know, and there's a lot that can be done with it and with chord versions like block chords on piano. But each of these things has a feeling of its own, and it takes so much time to develop all your technique.

"I don't use a pick at all, and that's one of the downfalls, too. In order to get a certain amount of speed, you should use a pick, I think. You don't have to play fast, but being able to play fast can cause you to phrase better. If you had the technique you could phrase better, even if you don't play fast. I think you'd have more control of the instrument.

"I didn't like the sound of a pick. I tried it for, I guess, about two months. I didn't even use my thumb at all. But after two months time, I still couldn't use the pick. So I said, 'Well, which are you going to do?' I liked the tone better with thumb, but I liked the technique with the pick. I couldn't have them both, so I just have to cool.

"I think every instrument should have a certain amount of tone quality within the instrument, but I can't seem to get the right amplifiers and things to get this thing out. I like to hear good phrasing. I'd like to hear a guitar play parts like instead of playing melodic lines, leave that and play chord versions of lines. Now, that's an awful hard thing to do, but it would be different. But I think in those terms, or if a cat could use

octaves for a line instead of one note. Give you a double sound with a good tone to it. Should sound pretty good if you got another blending instrument with it.

"Other guitar players? Well, Barney Kessel. I've got to go for that. He's got a lot of feeling and a good conception of chords in a jazz manner. He's still trying to do a lot of things, and he's not just standing still with guitar, just settling for one particular level. He's still going all he can, and that's one thing I appreciate about him. He's trying to phrase, also. He's trying to get away from the guitar phrase and get into horn phrasing.

"And Tal Farlow. Tal Farlow strikes me as different altogether. He doesn't have as much feeling as Barney Kessel to me, but he's got more drive in his playing, and his technique along with that drive is pretty exciting. He makes it exciting. I think he's got a better conception of modern chords than the average guitar player.

"A lot of guitar players can play modern chords, they can take a solo of modern chords; but they're liable to leave it within the solo range that they're in. They're liable to get away from it and then come back to it, get away from it and come back to it. Tal Farlow usually stays right on it.

"Jimmy Raney is just the opposite from Tal Farlow. They seem like they have the same ideas in mind, the same changes, the same runs, the same kind of feeling. But Jimmy Raney is so smooth. He does it without a mistake, like some cats play piano they couldn't make a mistake if they wanted to. That's the way Jimmy Raney is. He gives it a real soft touch, but the ideas are just like Tal Farlow's to me.

"And then George Henry, a cat I heard in Chicago. He's a playing cat. He asked could he play a tune, and so he gets up there, and that's the first time I ever heard a guitar phrase like Charlie Parker. It was just the solos, the chords and things he used were just like any other cat, you know. And there's another guy from Houston who plays with his thumb.

"And naturally, Reinhardt, he's in a different thing altogether. And Charlie Byrd. You know, I like all guitar players. I like what they play. But to stand out like Charlie Christian. Well, I guess it's just one of those things.

"My aim, I think, is to be able to move from one vein to another without any trouble. If you were going to take a melody line or counterpoint or unison lines with another instrument, do that and then, maybe after a certain point, you drop out completely, and maybe the next time you'll play phrases and chords or something or maybe you'll take octaves. That way you have a lot of variations, if you can control each one of them and still keep feeling it. To me the biggest thing is to keep the feeling within your playing regardless of what you play. Keep a feeling there, and that's hard to do.

"You know, John Coltrane has been sort of a god to me. Seems like, in a way, he didn't get the inspiration out of other musicians. He had it. When you hear a cat do a thing like that, you got to go along with him. I think I heard Coltrane before I really got close to Miles. Miles had a tricky way of playing his horn that I didn't understand as much as I did Coltrane. I really didn't understand what Coltrane was doing, but

it was so exciting, the thing that he was doing. Then after I really began to understand Miles, then Miles came up on top.

"Now, this may sound pretty weird—the way I feel when I'm up there playing the way I play doesn't match—but it's like some cats are holding your hands. C'mon, you know, and they'll keep you in there. If you try to keep up to them, they'll lose you, you know. And I like that. I really like that.

"Sometimes I'll do nothing but listen to records. All kinds, over and over. Then, after a while, it breaks and I don't even want to hear them. Nothing. I think it's because at the times I don't want to hear, I've heard so much it's got me confused and I'm so far away from it on my instrument—from the things I've been hearing—that I've got to put it aside and go back to where I am. And try to get out of that hole!

"I was surprised to win the *DownBeat* thing. I think I was playing more in 1952 than I ever have."

April 12, 1962

John Coltrane and Eric Dolphy Answer the Jazz Critics

by Don DeMicheal

John Coltrane has been the center of critical controversy ever since he unfurled his sheets of sound in his days with Miles Davis. At first disparaged for his sometimes involved, multi-noted solos, Coltrane paid little heed and continued exploring music. In time, his harmonic approach—for the sheets were really rapid chord running, in the main—was accepted, even praised, by most jazz critics.

By the time critics had caught up with Coltrane, the tenor saxophonist had gone on to another way of playing. Coltrane II, if you will, was much concerned with linear theme development that seemed sculptured or torn from great blocks of granite. Little critical carping was heard of this sec-

ond, architectural, Coltrane.

But Coltrane, an inquisitive-minded, probing musician, seemingly has left architecture for less concrete, more abstract means of expression. This third and present Coltrane has encountered an ever-growing block of criticism, much of it marked by a holy-war fervor.

Criticism of Coltrane III is almost always tied in with Coltrane's cohort Eric Dolphy, a member of that group of musicians who play what has been dubbed the "new thing."

Dolphy's playing has been praised and damned since his national jazz-scene arrival about two years ago. Last summer Dolphy joined Coltrane's group for a tour. It was on this tour that Coltrane and Dolphy came under the withering fire of *DownBeat* associate editor John Tynan, the first critic to take a strong—and public—stand against what Coltrane and Dolphy were playing.

In the Nov. 23, 1961, *DownBeat*, Tynan wrote, "At Hollywood's Renaissance Club recently, I listened to a horrifying demonstration of what appears to be a growing anti-jazz trend exemplified by these foremost proponents [Coltrane and Dolphy] of what is termed avant-garde music.

"I heard a good rhythm section... go to waste behind the nihilistic exercises of the two horns.... Coltrane and Dolphy seem intent on deliberately destroying [swing].... They seem bent on pursuing an anarchistic course in their music that can but be termed anti-jazz."

The anti-jazz term was picked up by Leonard Feather and used as a basis for critical essays of Coltrane, Dolphy, Ornette Coleman and the "new thing" in general in *DownBeat* and *Show*.

The reaction from readers to both Tynan's and Feather's remarks was immediate, heated and about evenly divided.

Recently, Coltrane and Dolphy agreed to sit down and discuss their music and the criticism leveled at it.

One of the recurring charges is that their performances are stretched out over too long a time, that Coltrane and Dolphy play on and on, past inspiration and into monotony.

Coltrane answered, "They're long because all the soloists try to explore all the avenues that the tune offers. They try to use all their resources in their solos. Everybody has quite a bit to work on. Like when I'm playing, there are certain things I try to get done and so does Eric and McCoy Tyner [Coltrane's pianist]. By the time we finish, the song is spread out over a pretty long time.

"It's not planned that way; it just happens. The performances get longer and longer. It's sort of growing that way."

But, goes the criticism, there must be editing, just as a writer must edit his work so that it keeps to the point and does not ramble and become boring.

Coltrane agreed that editing must be done—but for essentially a different reason from what might be expected.

"There are times," he said, "when we play places opposite another group, and in order to play a certain number of sets a night, you can't play an hour-and-a-half at one time. You've got to play 45 or 55 minutes and rotate sets with the other band. And for those reasons, for a necessity such as that, I think it's quite in order that you edit and shorten things.

"But when your set is unlimited, time-wise, and everything is really together musically—if there's continuity—it really doesn't make any difference how long you play.

"On the other hand, if there're dead spots, then it's really not good to play anything too long."

One of the tunes that Coltrane's group plays at length is "My Favorite Things," a song, as played by the group, that can exert an intriguingly hypnotic effect, though sometimes it seems too long. Upon listening closely to him play "Things" on the night before the interview, it seemed that he actually played two solos. He finished one, went back to the theme a bit, and then went into another improvisation.

"That's the way the song is constructed," Coltrane said. "It's divided into parts. We play both parts. There's a minor and a major part. We improvise in the minor, and we improvise in the major modes."

Is there a certain length to the two modes?

"It's entirely up to the artist—his choice," he answered. "We were playing it at one time with minor, then major, then minor modes, but it was really getting too long—it was about the only tune we had time to play in an average-length set."

But in playing extended solos, isn't there ever present the risk of running out of ideas? What happens when you've played all your ideas?

"It's easy to stop then," Coltrane said, grinning. "If I feel like I'm just playing notes... maybe I don't feel the rhythm or I'm not in the best shape that I should be in when this happens. When I become aware

John Coltrane.
(Prestige Records)

Eric Dolphy.
(Prestige Records)

of it in the middle of a solo, I'll try to build things to the point where this inspiration is happening again, where things are spontaneous and not contrived. If it reaches that point again, I feel it can continue—it's alive again. But if it doesn't happen, I'll just quit, bow out."

Dolphy, who had been sitting pixie-like as Coltrane spoke, was in complete agreement about stopping when inspiration had flown.

Last fall at the Monterey Jazz Festival, the Coltrane-Dolphy group was featured opening night. In his playing that night Dolphy at times sounded as if he were imitating birds. On the night before the interview some of Dolphy's flute solos brought Monterey to mind. Did he do this on purpose?

Dolphy smiled and said it was purposeful and that he had always liked birds.

Is bird imitation valid in jazz?

"I don't know if it's valid in jazz," he said, "but I enjoy it. It somehow comes in as part of the development of what I'm doing. Sometimes I can't do it.

"At home [in California] I used to play, and the birds always used to whistle with me. I would stop what I was working on and play with the birds."

He described how bird calls had been recorded and then slowed down in playback; the bird calls had a timbre similar to that of a flute. Conversely, he said, a symphony flutist recorded these bird calls, and when the recording was played at a fast speed, it sounded like birds.

Having made his point about the connection of bird whistles and flute playing, Dolphy explained his use of quarter tones when playing flute. "That's the way birds do," he said. "Birds have notes in between our notes—you try to imitate something they do and, like, maybe it's between F and F-sharp, and you'll have to go up or come down on the pitch. It's really something! And so, when you get playing, this comes. You try to do some things on it. Indian music has something of the same quality—different scales and quarter tones. I don't know how you label it, but it's pretty."

The question in many critics' minds, though they don't often verbalize it, is: What are John Coltrane and Eric Dolphy trying to do? Or: What are they doing?

Following the question, a 30-second silence was unbroken except by Dolphy's, "That's a good question." Dolphy was first to try to voice his aims in music:

"What I'm trying to do I find enjoy-able. Inspiring—what it makes me do. It helps me play, this feel. It's like you have no idea what you're going to do next. You have an idea, but there's always that spontaneous thing that happens. This feeling, to me, leads the whole group. When John plays, it might lead into something you had no idea could be done. Or McCoy does something. Or the way Elvin [Jones, drummer with the group] or Jimmy [Garrison, the bassist] play; they solo, they do something. Or when the rhythm section is sitting on something a different way. I feel that is what it does for me."

Coltrane, who had sat in frowned contemplation while Dolphy elaborated, dug into the past for his answer: "Eric and I have been talking music for quite a few years, since about 1954. We've been close for quite a while. We watched music. We always talked about it, discussed what was being done down through the years, because we love music. What we're doing now was started a few years ago.

"A few months ago Eric was in New York, where the group was working, and he felt like playing, wanted to come down and sit in. So I told him to come on down and play, and he did—and turned us all around. I'd felt at ease with just a quartet till then, but he came in, and it was like having another member of the family. He'd found another way to express the same thing we had found one way to do.

"After he sat in, we decided to see what it would grow into. We began to play some of the things we had only talked about before. Since he's been in the band, he's had a broadening effect on us. There are a lot of things we try now that we never tried before. This helped me, because I've started to write—it's necessary that we have things written so that we can play together. We're playing things that are freer than before.

"I would like for him to feel at home in the group and find a place to develop what he wants to do as an individualist and as a soloist—just as I hope everybody in the band will. And while we are doing this, I would also like the listener to be able to receive some of these good things—some of this beauty."

Coltrane paused, deep in thought. No one said anything. Finally he went on:

"It's more than beauty that I feel in music—that I think musicians feel in music. What we know we feel we'd like to convey to the listener. We hope that this can be shared by all. I think, basically, that's about what it is we're trying to do. We never talked about just what we were trying to do. If you ask me that question, I might say this today and tomorrow say something entirely different, because there are many things to do in music.

"But, overall, I think the main thing a musician would like to do is to give a picture to the listener of the many wonderful things he knows of and senses in the universe. That's what music is to me—it's just another way of saying this is a big, beautiful universe we live in, that's been given to us, and here's an example of just how magnificent and encompassing it is. That's what I would like to do. I think that's one of the greatest things you can do in life, and we all try to do it in some way. The musician's is through his music."

This philosophy about music, life and the universe, Coltrane said, is "so important to music, and music is important. Some realize it young and early in their careers. I didn't realize it as early as I should have, as early as I wish I had. Sometimes you have to take a thing when it comes and be glad."

When did he first begin to feel this way?

"I guess I was on my way in '57, when I started to get myself together musically, although at the time I was working academically and technically. It's just recently that I've tried to become even more aware of this other side, the life side of music. I feel I'm just beginning again. Which goes back to the group and what we're trying to do. I'm fortunate to be in the company I'm in now, because anything I'd like to do, I have a place to try. They respond so well that it's very easy to try new things."

Dolphy broke in with, "Music is a reflection of everything. And it's universal. Like, you can hear somebody from across the world, another country. You don't even know them, but they're in your backyard, you know?"

"It's a reflection of the universe," Coltrane said. "Like having life in miniature. You just take a situation in life or an emotion you know and put it into music. You take a scene you've seen, for instance, and put it to music."

Had he ever succeeded in re-creating a situation or scene?

"I was getting into it," he said, "but I haven't made it yet. But I'm beginning to see how to do it. I know a lot of musicians who have done it. It's just happening to me now. Actually, while a guy is soloing, there

John Coltrane and
Eric Dolphy. (Herb Snutzer)

are many things that happen. Probably he himself doesn't know how many moods or themes he's created. But I think it really ends up with the listener. You know, you hear different people say, 'Man, I felt this while he was playing,' or, 'I thought about this.' There's no telling what people are thinking. They take in what they have experienced. It's a sharing process—playing—for people."

"You can feel vibrations from the people," Dolphy added.

"The people can give you something, too," Coltrane said. "If you play in a place where they really like you, like your group, they can make you play like you've never felt like playing before."

Anyone who has heard the Coltrane group in person in such a situation knows the almost hypnotic effect the group can have on the audience and the audience's almost surging involvement in the music.

But sometimes, it is said, the striving for excitement per se within the group leads to nonmusical effects. It was effects such as these that have led to the "anti-jazz" term.

Such a term is bound to arouse reaction in musicians like Coltrane and Dolphy. Without a smile—or rancor—Coltrane said he would like the critics who have used the term in connection with him to tell him exactly what they mean. Then, he said, he could answer them.

One of the charges is that what Coltrane and Dolphy play doesn't swing.

"I don't know what to say about that," Dolphy said.

"Maybe it doesn't swing," Coltrane offered.

"I can't say that they're wrong." Dolphy said. "But I'm still playing."

Well, don't you feel that it swings? he was asked.

"Of course I do," Dolphy answered.

"In fact, it swings so much I don't know what to do—it moves me so much. I'm with John; I'd like to know how they explain 'anti-jazz.' Maybe they can tell us something."

"There are various types of swing," Coltrane said. "There's straight 4/4, with heavy bass drum accents. Then there's the kind of thing that goes on in Count Basie's band. In fact, every group of individuals assembled has a different feeling—a different swing. It's the same with this band. It's a different feeling than in any other band. It's hard to answer a man who says it doesn't swing."

Later, when the first flush of defense had subsided, Coltrane allowed:

"Quite possibly a lot of things about the band need to be done. But everything has to be done in its own time. There are some things that you just grow into. Back to speaking about editing—things like that.

I've felt a need for this, and I've felt a need for ensemble work—throughout the songs, a little cement between this block, a pillar here, some more cement there, etc. But as yet I don't know just how I would like to do it. So rather than make a move just because I know it needs to be done, a move that I've not arrived at through work, from what I naturally feel, I won't do it.

"There may be a lot of things missing from the music that are coming, if we stay together that long. When they come, they'll be things that will be built out of just what the group is. They will be unique to the group and of the group."

Coltrane said he felt that what he had said still did not answer his critics adequately, that in order to do so he would have to meet them and discuss what has been said so that he could see just what they mean.

Dolphy interjected that the critic should consult the musician when there is something the critic does not fully understand. "It's kind of alarming to the musician," he said, "when someone has written something bad about what the musician plays but never asks the musician anything about it. At least, the musician feels bad. But he doesn't feel so bad that he quits playing. The critic influences a lot of people. If something new has happened, something nobody knows what the musician is doing, he should ask the musician about it. Because somebody may like it; they might want to know something about it. Sometimes it really hurts, because a musician not only loves his work but depends on it for a living. If somebody writes something bad about musicians, people stay away. Not because the guys don't sound good but because somebody said something that has influence over a lot of people. They say, 'I read this, and I don't think he's so hot because so-and-so said so.'"

Dolphy had brought up a point that bothers most jazz critics: readers sometime forget that criticism is what one man thinks. A critic is telling how he feels about, how he reacts to, what he hears in, a performance or a piece of music.

"The best thing a critic can do," Coltrane said, "is to thoroughly understand what he is writing about and then jump in. That's all he can do. I have even seen favorable criticism which revealed a lack of profound analysis, causing it to be little more than superficial.

"Understanding is what is needed. That is all you can do. Get all the under-standing for what you're speaking of that you can get. That way you have done your best. It's the same with a musician who is trying to understand music as well as he can. Undoubtedly, none of us are going to be 100 percent in either criticism or music. No percent near that, but we've all got to try.

"Understanding is the whole thing. In talking to a critic try to understand him, and he can try to understand the part of the game you are in. With this understanding, there's no telling what could be accomplished. Everybody would benefit."

Though he said he failed to answer his critics, John Coltrane perhaps had succeeded more than he thought.

Nov. 22, 1962

Inside the New Bill Evans Trio

by Gene Lees

Somebody said recently of Bill Evans, "It's as if a gray cloud followed him, haunting him."

There is a measure—but only a measure—of truth to this. Evans' fortunes this fall began to take a distinct turn for the better, but his career has been plagued by disappointments, ill health, financial problems, mishandling by some of the business people in jazz and outright tragedy.

Despite it all, he has left along his route a sprinkling of albums that constitute what may prove the most important body of jazz piano recordings since Art Tatum. Those recordings have spread his influence throughout the world.

It is an approach that, once heard, is as easy to identify as it is hard to describe. One can call it exquisitely lyrical, superbly thoughtful, highly imaginative, rhythmically unique… but these terms don't fix for examination a kind of jazz piano playing which, for its admirers, has the flavor and emotionality of a personal letter.

Martin Williams has said, in a *DownBeat* record review, that Evans seems to have a communication problem. And perhaps he has. But obviously he gets through to all those people who care enough about jazz to listen genuinely, including Williams, whose review was highly favorable. Recently, checking through Bill's scrapbook, I was astonished to discover that he also had received rave reviews from Nat Hentoff, Frank Kofsky, Ralph Gleason, John S. Wilson, Don DeMicheal and myself. I know of no other subject on which you could get all of us to agree.

Evans communicates equally well to musicians, one of whom is 23-year-old Chicago pianist Warren Bernhardt, who now lives in New York City. The young pianist offered this comment on Evans' playing:

"Everything he plays seems to be the distillation of the music. In 'How Deep Is the Ocean?' he never once states the melody. Yet his performance is the quintessence of it. On 'My Foolish Heart,' on the other hand, he plays nothing but the melody—and you still receive that essence of the thing.

"Pianistically, he's beautiful. He never seems to be hung up in any way in doing anything he wants to do—either technically or harmonically. You can voice a given chord many different ways, but he always seems to find the correct way. When he's confronted with a choice on the spur of the moment of improvisation, he doesn't have to wonder which voicing is best, he knows. And he is physically capable of executing it immediately. It's as if the line between his brain and his fingers were an unusually direct one.

"You see, a given voicing will have different effects in different registers, especially when you use semi-tones as much as he does. So he constantly shifts voicings, depending on the register. Yet he doesn't seem to have to think about it, because he's been thinking about it for years."

Evans' own comments corroborate and complement this view. Of chord voicings, he said recently:

"It's such an accumulated thing. The art lies in developing enough facility to voice well any new thought. It's taken me 20 years of hard work and playing experience to do as well with it as I can. There's no shortcut. It takes a lot of time and study."

Various observers have noted the apparent influence of certain classical composers in Evans' voicings, particularly Ravel, Debussy and Chopin. Was the influence absorbed directly and deliberately? "No more than from jazz," he said. "It's whatever I've liked the sound of. I've built it by my own study, never consciously looking at a voicing in a score and saying, 'Gee,

The Bill Evans Trio, from left, Evans, drummer Larry Bunker and bassist Chuck Israels.
(Ron Skeetz)

this would be nice to use.'"

However arrived at, Evans' voicings are an important part of his style. But there are other parts. For one thing, he has magnificent time. He thinks so far head of what he is doing that he phrases in whole choruses, and his phrases always come out right. His way of swinging is one of the most subtle in jazz. And the swing is so self-generated that he and guitarist Jim Hall, performing without rhythm section, were able to set upon an astonishingly powerful pulse on the "My Funny Valentine" track of the United Artists album *Undercurrents* a few months ago. Many New York musicians think the track is a classic of jazz.

Finally, there is his tone, one of the loveliest jazz piano has ever known. It can

be hard and muscular, as on the "Valentine" track. But usually it is soft and round, so soft in the ballads that a TV director, hearing him for the first time, exclaimed, "Good God, the man must have fur-tipped fingers!"

Whatever they're tipped with, they are remarkable fingers and lately they are conveying to those who know Evans' music a rising morale and improving health. A year ago, they were communicating the pianist's despair over the death of bassist Scott LaFaro. The death of LaFaro left Evans so broken in spirit that he didn't play publicly for six months.

To understand why, it is necessary to consider the history of the Bill Evans Trio. Paul Motian, Evans' drummer almost from the beginning, recalled: "After I got

out of the Navy late in 1954, I entered the Manhattan School of Music. I completed a semester and a half. But by then I was working gigs about six nights a week, and I was falling behind in my studies, so I left. I started playing with different people, including George Wallington. That summer—the summer of 1956—I worked in a sextet with Jerry Wald. The piano player was Bill Evans.

"After that, somehow, Bill and I seemed to work together in a lot of bands. We both worked for Tony Scott and Don Elliott. And we worked on a George Russell album together.

"Bill was living on 83rd Street at the time, and we used to play together a lot—almost every day, in fact. Then Bill went with Miles Davis, and I worked with various people, including Oscar Pettiford and Zoot Sims.

"After leaving Miles, Bill formed a trio. He had Kenny Dennis on drums and Jimmy Garrison on bass. That sort of petered out. In the latter part of 1959, he went into Basin Street East. He had a lot of trouble, and he changed rhythm sections several times.… On drums, he had Philly Joe Jones for a few nights and Kenny Dennis for a few more and me. He must have gone through about eight bass players.

"Scott LaFaro was working at a club around the corner. I'd first heard him some time previously, when Chet Baker was forming a group. Chet called me and Bill, and we worked out. I wasn't too impressed by Scott's playing at that time. Anyway, Scott used to come around to Basin Street East and sit in with Bill. And I was impressed.

"From Basin Street East, we went to the Showplace, with Scott. That was actually the beginning.

"It's hard to describe what Scott's death last year did to us. Bill telephoned me. I was sleeping. It seemed like a dream, what he told me, and I went back to sleep. When I woke up, I was convinced it was a dream. I called Bill back, and he told me it was true.

"When it began to sink in, we… we didn't know what to do. We didn't know if we'd still have a trio. We'd reached such a peak with Scott, such freedom. It seemed that everything was becoming possible.

"We didn't work for six months—between the last two weeks of June 1961 until Christmas. Then we went to Syracuse, N.Y., to work a gig. Chuck Israels went with us on bass.

"That must have been a difficult time for Chuck. It had taken us two years to get to the peak we had reached with Scott, and now we had to start all over."

Rapport between Israels and the other two members of the trio didn't happen overnight.

"Because everyone was looking at Chuck with Scott in mind," Evans said, "he was in a very sensitive position. He did admirably, but he had many things on his mind—things of a technical nature, concerning the musical means with which we work.

"I think that this, coupled with replacing a man of great talent who had taken part in the development of the group, was all happening during the engagement we

played earlier this year at the Hickory House. And though there were many encouraging aspects of it, I had slight apprehension about whether his self-consciousness would prevail for a long period, obstructing or misdirecting the natural way the group could develop.

"About the time we left the Hickory House, Chuck had a big overhauling job done on his bass, and we didn't have a chance to find out what effect it would have on the sound of the group. But obviously, during the month-long layoff, many of the problems, musical and otherwise, must have settled or resolved themselves for Chuck.

"Opening night at the Vanguard last July, we felt… well, it's difficult to describe the amount of difference that we all immediately felt as a result of his ability to play within the group with such a natural flow. Now I have no apprehension about the ability of the group to develop in its own direction and no hesitation about performing for anyone anywhere."

Recalling that Vanguard opening, Motian said: "It started to jell. We could feel it immediately. I thought, Oh, oh, we've reached that point again. I knew we could continue where we left off when Scott died."

To this Evans added: "Not that we're trying to duplicate the point of development we reached with Scott. Chuck is a strong, intelligent and accomplished talent in himself. It's a different trio now.

"And I'll say this. This is the first time I've been genuinely excited about the trio since Scott's death. Not only about the prospects, but what we've already arrived at."

In view of the rich textures Israels, Motian and Evans are capable of weaving, it is probably not without significance that all three of them had childhood groundings in non-jazz musical cultures. In Evans' case, it was a double background. Of Welsh and Russian descent, he was surrounded with the traditional Welsh love of vocal music, and with Russian Orthodox church music. Though his mother was born in this country, she speaks Russian and is steeped in the music of the church. One uncle was a choral director, and so is Bill's cousin, Peter Wilhausky, who was a choral director for Arturo Toscanini and is now head of the New York Secondary School of Music. "I think what I got from that environment," Bill said, "was a true and humble love of music!"

Israels' background is strikingly simi-

lar, though derived from another culture, Jewish. One of his uncles is a member of the music faculty at the University of California in Berkeley. His maternal grandfather was an amateur musician and an officer in the musicians union local in Yonkers. His stepfather, whom Israels said "had a monumental influence on the life of my family," is Mordecai Baumn, a cantor and an influential figure in music education.

In Motian's case, the childhood musical influence was Armenian. "I heard a lot of Armenian music at home," he said. "My parents had a lot of it on records, and I used to dance to the rhythms. I still like Armenian music very much. The rhythms are interesting and some of them swing along nicely. They have a lot of rhythms in 5/4 or 7/8 or 9/8."

It is interesting to speculate how much these "alien" musical influences may have contributed to the trio's musical freedom. Certainly the three men have shown a remarkable ease in handling material in time figures other than the traditional 4/4 of jazz. The group is notably able to dispense with forthright and heavy-handed statements of the underlying rhythmic pulse of a work, all three taking off in individual and yet beautifully interrelated directions without ever losing their bearings. The word "freedom" crops up constantly in their talk.

Israels, who has dedicated himself to music only for the last two years (he has been a photographer, sound-equipment salesman and repairman, recording engineer and an experimental engineer for a hi-fi components manufacturer), says that "only with Bill have I begun to realize my conception of music. It's a melancholy thing to say, but, in a way, if Scotty hadn't died, I'd be struggling still to find a situation in which I could play what I want to play. I like to make the bass sound good. If playing time in a deep and firm and flowing way sounds good, then that's the way I like to play. If playing more delicate counterlines and fill-ins sounds right in a situation, then I want the bass to sound light and clear."

"What's a groove about the trio is that there's never a hassle," Motian said. "It's never, 'Do this or do that.' It's just three people playing together."

Only once since Israels joined the trio—and this was immediately after he joined—has the trio held a formal rehearsal. New material is simply introduced and then allowed to evolve on the job. Consequently, the group is simply not a piano-accompanied-by-two-rhythm trio. Its music has a true conversational quality, each member contributing what he feels is appropriate. This is a remarkable thing, in view of the individuality of its leader's playing.

It is this newfound group strength, which dates back only to July, that is the main cause of Evans' brighter outlook.

"He seems like his old self again," Motian said, "as witty as he used to be. He can be a very funny guy, you know."

All of which leads us right back to the communication problem noted by Martin Williams.

"This isn't a problem I'd deal with directly," Evans said. "I find that when I'm feeling my best, spiritually and physically, I project. For example, I think the record on which I project most is the *Everybody Digs* album. I'd had hepatitis, and I went to stay with my parents in Florida to get over it. When I came back, I felt exceptionally rested and well. I made that album at that time. And I knew I was communicating the way I'd like to communicate.

"Right now, I'm starting to gain some weight that I'd lost, and I'm getting into a more secure financial period, and believe me, it's raising my morale 12,000 percent.

"I think it's making a real difference.

"Remember how Miles suddenly came out? The fact that musicians and critics had known about him for years didn't dispel the fact that he was saying, in effect, 'Here I am, I know what the quality of this work is, and if you want to know, you'll have to come and get it.' Yet eventually he succeeded in communicating.

"All of this is a social-personality question. It takes a profound personality evolution to affect it. I want to communicate, I want to give. But I'm not foolish enough to think I can go to a teacher to learn how to communicate."

With that, one can only ask if Evans has any advice for aspiring younger musicians.

"Well, there was a shipwreck, and the only man who survived was the bass player from the band. He floated on his bass for days, burned by the sun and half frozen at night, and at last he was sighted off Long Island. The press and TV people rushed down to the shore to interview him, and as he waded out of the water, dragging his waterlogged bass, they asked him, 'As the survivor of this terrible tragedy, do you have anything to say?' And the guy says, 'Ooooh, m-a-an, later for the music business.'"

June 6, 1963

Bringing Up "Fatha"

by Russ Wilson

Back now in the musical groove that he helped form, 57-year-old Earl (Fatha) Hines, one of the first great style-setters on jazz piano, is looking at a future flavored by memories of the past.

Heading a mainstream swing sextet, which is sailing high in the San Francisco Bay Area and may go on the road, and with a new big band album in the works at Capitol Records, Hines seems to be in position to move into the forefront of the current jazz scene. One factor that could steer him that way is the experience he gained for years as an orchestra leader—a period on which he looks back fondly, and longingly.

Sitting in the comfortable family room of his big, stylishly furnished home in a quiet Oakland, Calif., neighborhood, Hines let his memory roam through the years he headed one of the country's widely known orchestras.

The offer of leadership came to Hines while he was in New York in 1928 recording piano rolls for the QRS company.

"I'd just come out of a little Chicago club, the Apex, where I'd been working with Jimmy Noone," Hines related. "There was a guy named Percy Venable—he's living out on the coast now—who was producing shows at the Sunset Cafe in Chicago. After it closed, he was hired to open the Grand Terrace, and he was looking for a 'name' attraction. Well, there weren't any 'names' there at the time; Louis was in New York and so was Fletcher Henderson, and the only person that was living in Chicago then was me—though I was in New York making those piano rolls.

"Venable sent the offer to me in New York through Lucius Millinder, who was working for him (he didn't become Lucky Millinder till after he got in the band business some years later). Lucius said, 'Earl, we'd like you to come back and open a club,' and I said OK. He told me it would be called the Grand Terrace and asked if I had a band. As a matter of fact, I had been rehearsing a band back there for some time.

When I got back to Chicago, I got the guys together, and we started working on the first show. That's how I actually got started in the band business for the Grand Terrace."

In making his offer, Venable was aware of the fact that Hines had played with Louis Deppe's big band in Pittsburgh and had been music director of the former Carroll Dickerson Band, with which Hines and Louis Armstrong had been playing, after Armstrong had succeeded Dickerson as leader.

"That gave me the experience of directing a band and accompanying vocalists and all that, so when I got my own band I knew my way around," Hines said.

The orchestra made its debut on Dec. 28, 1928, a date Hines always will remember—it's his birthday anniversary. Hines identified its members as trumpeters Walter Fuller, George Dixon, who doubled alto and baritone saxophones, and Charlie Allen; trombonists Louis Taylor and Billy Franklin, who also sang; reed men Omer Simeon, who played alto and baritone saxophones as well as clarinet; Darnell Howard, clarinet, violin and alto saxophone; Cecil Irwin, clarinet and tenor saxophone; Lawrence Dixon, who doubled banjo and cello; Quinn Wilson, bass and tuba; and Wallace Bishop, drums, who utilized chimes, gongs, tympani and a variety of tom-toms in addition to the standard bass and snare drums.

As the years went on, there were additions to the orchestra as well as other changes of personnel. Many of its instrumentalists and singers who later became names were musical nonentities when they joined Hines, he said.

"I had to make my stars rather than buying them," he said. "I was working with a man that just wasn't going to put out too much money. So I just stayed with my guys, coached 'em and built the things for them I thought they could handle. Then they began to acquire greater ability and confidence.

"And I've always made mental pictures of my bands and vocalists. I just see my band onstage, and I hear them play certain things, and if it doesn't sound good to me, I know it doesn't sound good to the audience, and if they don't look good to me, they don't look good to the audience. I've pictured certain numbers for Billy Eckstine and Sarah Vaughan and Madeline Green and given them to them and then gone off to one side and watched them and realized that isn't the way they should look or sound. So those numbers went out.

"I've done the same way with my present group and with the Dixieland band I had before it. For instance, I'd show [trombonist] Jimmy Archey and [clarinetist] Darnell Howard what I wanted from them, the type of endings and so on. In doing this, I'd know how to direct it, how to sell that person because I knew what he was going to do."

Of his Grand Terrace band, Hines said:

"It never was a typed organization because I didn't want it to become such. That's why I used a variety of arrangers from all over the country—so there'd be no one certain style. And I'd exchange arrangements with Fred Waring, Tommy Dorsey and Jimmy Dorsey. The only time the listeners knew it was my band was when they heard my piano.

"We got a lot of different sounds, but we needed them for the shows we played. Why, the first section of the shows was an hour and a half long, so you know how much music we had to play.

"In those days we worked seven nights a week, and the hours were rather long— we'd start at 10 p.m. and go to 3:30 and 4 a.m. every day except Saturday. On Saturdays we went 'til 5. No matinees, though, thank goodness."

The band's first out-of-town trip, for an engagement at the Earl Theater in Philadelphia, is another of Hines' bright memories.

"We didn't know what it was all about," he said. "We went there because it was touring for us, and we were just a bunch of kids. Fox [theaters] gave us a dinner on the train, and we thought that was wonderful."

A little later, on a trip to Washington, D.C., Hines' path crossed that of Jimmy Mundy.

"Guys were telling me that Mundy was one of the best arrangers in the area. So he brought me five arrangements, at $5 apiece. I tried them out, and one of them was this tune 'Cavernisin.' He was working in a place in Washington called the Crystal Cavern, playing sax. We put the tune in our book and used it as a closing theme while we were broadcasting." Mundy, who later was to become famed as an arranger, joined the Hines band in 1929.

"At that time," Hines said, "Cecil Irwin—who was way ahead of his time— was doing all the arrangements for the band. Mundy worked with him, and what happened is that Jimmy got a lot of his ideas from Irwin. It was during this time

that Benny Goodman and a lot of other bandleaders used to come in and listen to the band, and the arrangements that Benny heard and thought were Mundy's tunes were Irwin's tunes, but Jimmy never did tell him anything different.

"When Jimmy went with the Goodman band (in 1936), why, naturally Mundy got the publicity and this other boy was never thought of; but actually this boy, Cecil Irwin, did an awful lot. When Cecil was killed in a bus accident, we had Mundy get all of the books that he, Irwin, was studying from Cecil's wife. But Mundy was a great arranger—he was always a good arranger—but there were some great ideas that this kid had."

Washington also was the city from which Hines obtained trombonist Trummy Young.

"Somebody told me about him, and I heard him play," Hines said. "But there was the problem of the size of my band. Trummy and his wife cried because they thought I wasn't going to take him. I finally put him in the bus and brought him into Chicago, and my manager at the Grand Terrace, the owner, said, 'What are you trying to do? You're going to have more men in the band than you've got coming in the club.' I had to pay part of Trummy's salary out of my own pocket—like I'd had to do with Mundy. But a little while later we were doing so much business the owner gave them a salary."

Hines said he was as adventurous with vocalists as he was instrumentalists. He singled out a few singers:

"So many people told me about Arthur Lee Simpkins, when he first came on, that I brought him from Augusta, Ga. I found Herb Jeffries in Detroit—they talked so much about him—that's how I got him. Ida James had just won an amateur contest in Philadelphia, and Madeline Green, she was supposed to go out with Benny Goodman, but they had some kind of hassle—I don't know what—and I took her with me."

The most famous male singer to work for Hines was Billy Eckstine, who joined in 1939 and later became known as something of an instrumentalist.

"I got Billy started as an instrumentalist because of a union hassle," Hines said. "In those days almost all the bands were coming out with vocalists and were actually taking advantage of some of the clubs that had singers. That is, some of these clubs wouldn't hire a singer if the band had a vocalist. The singers were under AGVA

[American Guild of Variety Artists], and it was getting left out of the picture. So AGVA decided that all vocalists with bands had to join the organization.

"The way I got around it, when Billy joined the band, I had him take a trumpet when we did "Jelly, Jelly" and play one note—B-flat—because he didn't have to push a finger down or anything, just blow. I brought the other trumpets out front and put Billy right in the middle of them, and when they played the last chorus, he just held that one note. When AGVA asked about that, I said, 'He's a musician with a card in the musicians union,' so they couldn't say more about it.

"The same way with Sarah Vaughan. I had her sitting at a piano, and she'd play it a little while I was out front directing the band on some things. Then when she got ready to sing, AGVA couldn't say anything."

Hines said Eckstine began to like the trumpet so much that he got Dizzy Gillespie and the other horn men in the band to coach him to play it. Later he shifted to valve trombone.

What about those stories that Gillespie and Charlie Parker were creating a ruckus while they were members of the Hines band in '43?

"No, no," Hines replied. "That's a lot of stories. They had fun, but they didn't do anything that any other person hadn't done. They were kids at the time so they didn't care."

The leader attributes the stories about these men to writers whose chief interest was sensationalism, not factual reporting.

It should be pointed out, however, that (1) jazz history, in regard to the innovations of Parker and Gillespie, does not bear Hines out, and (2) he, naturally, is biased in favor of his own musicians. Like all leaders, he had plenty of problems in this field. Or, as he puts it:

"You've got to study each man in the band, because each has a different disposition. Actually, you've got to use a lot of psychology because they all have different temperaments and habits. You have to holler at some guys—others you have to joke with. Another you may have to take across the street to the bar to get your point across. You must impress them that to be a musician you've got to do the things that are required of a musician—look the part, play your horn; also time-making."

Touching upon another phase of individual idiosyncrasies, Hines said:

"Some guys didn't aspire to be soloists;

others wanted to. Trummy Young was one of the latter. He was always venturing out, always wanting to play his horn. Everywhere he went he carried his horn with him. The same with Benny Green. These men later turned out to be outstanding. Like Walter Fuller, he was another, and there are several others I can name—Omer Simeon, Darnell Howard and, of course, Budd Johnson and Jimmy Mundy, though it finally turned out he didn't want to be a soloist—he wanted to arrange—but he played a good horn. In the trumpet section, Dizzy stood out so much.

"Other guys didn't want to be soloists; they got their kicks out of sitting up there and playing their horns and listening to the other guys playing solos."

As for the entire era, Hines summarized:

"Of course, the big band days then were more enjoyable because you found musicians were closer together. They all used to help each other, and it was a pleasure for them to go to rehearsal; they got such kicks out of rehearsing, getting new numbers and any idea at all could be brought up—playing different instruments, singing or whatnot. In anything pertaining to the band they all worked as one.

"It wasn't until years later, when the recording companies began to get involved, that all of them decided they wanted to be bandleaders; that's what caused quite a number of the big bands to break up. By the time you got numbers written for certain members, they were gone, and that group of tunes was lost."

The fun and pleasure must have evened up the headaches and heartaches, however, for Hines says he still would like to get back in the big band milieu.

"I think all of us who had big bands have that feeling," he said, "because there's more to work with; the sound is bigger, and it's more enjoyable. But in the early days we were young and wild and didn't care; if we worked, all right; if we didn't, so what? You're off a month or so; you laughed about it. You can't do that today, let's face it. I've got a family, and my expenses go on.

"So I like the big bands, and I want a big band, but if conditions won't allow it, I just can't have it, that's all."

The family to which Hines referred includes his wife, whom he met in California in the 1940s and who, as Janie Moses, sang for two years with his band, and their daughters, Janear, 12, and Tosca, 9.

As for his present happy musical state,

it began early this year, when Hines opened a three-month stay with his new sextet in the Churchill Room of Oakland's Hotel Claremont, which nestles in the hills overlooking San Francisco Bay.

Dancers and listeners alike were intrigued by the group's pulsating swing and persuasive solos. The mainstream format is far removed from the six years Hines put in as leader of a Dixieland combo, much of that time at the now-defunct Hangover Club in San Francisco.

"It's a relief," Hines said of his current group. "I can work out my own ideas, and I'm working with young musicians who are willing to learn."

Feb. 28, 1964

The Resurgence of Stan Getz

by Leonard Feather

As these words are written it is two years since Stan Getz stepped off the SS *Kungsholm* at New York City, ending his two-and-a-half-year self-imposed exile. During most of his absence he had been living in Helsingor, 25 miles north of Copenhagen, Denmark, with his pretty blond Swedish wife, Monica, and two daughters, all of whom came to New York with him while two sons, then 12 and 9, stayed in Switzerland to attend school.

Getz's often-rumored, long-delayed return led to speculation concerning the length of his visit. How soon would he go back to his adopted home in Denmark?

"I don't know," he told *DownBeat*, "but I hope to be here at least six months."

Although the months have stretched into years, and there is now no prospect of his returning to Helsingor for an indefinite period, the probability that things would work out this way seemed very remote during the first year of his renewed U.S. career.

What happened to Getz during that first year, and what has happened during the second, constitute not only a study in contrasts but also more significantly a reflection of the unpredictable, often cruel vagaries of the old art-versus-show-business, music-versus-commercialism conflict.

It was common knowledge in the music world that the return of Stan Getz was not accorded the treatment usually expected for a conquering hero returned from overseas battle.

Bill Coss, reviewing his Village Vanguard re-debut in the June 8, 1961, *DownBeat*, synthesized the problems that Getz had to face: "There were in attendance the haters, musical and otherwise, who came to find out whether the young white man, who had long ago lengthened the legendary and unorthodox Lester Young line into something of his own, could stand up against what is, in current jazz, at least a revolution from it (or a revulsion about it)."

While asserting that in his own view Getz could and did and seemed as if he always would measure up, Coss added that "the still broad-shouldered, blue-eyed, bland-faced young man met musicians backstage, and they tried him with words and with Indian-hold handshakes of questionable peace and unquestionable war. The young man out front was his arrogant best, holding his audiences with strong quotations from his past and much stronger assertions of his version of the newest (but much older) sound!"

Clearly implied were the facts of jazz life that had come into focus during Getz's absence: the cool sound and the cool attitude had given way, during those two or three years, to a concern for heavy, aggressive statement, to an atmosphere of racial hostility without precedent in jazz, to an accent on musical anger and disregard for fundamentals—characteristics that were not to be found in the light lyricism of a Stan Getz solo.

The writing was already on the ballot: because of these trends, aggravated by his absence from the scene, Getz had slipped in the 1960 Readers Poll from the tenor slot he had won every year since 1950.

The consequence of his fall from fashion was soon made clear. Not long after his return, his quartet (with Scott LaFaro on bass) played at a Hollywood club that Miles Davis packed the previous week. To put it mildly, he bombed. Business was so bad that the club owner persuaded him to change his engagement by stretching it over instead of attempting the hopeless task of bringing in business on weeknights.

Soon after, Getz played a San Francisco club at the same time that his successor in the jazz fans' esteem was working another spot in that city. The contrast was sharp and, for Getz, depressing. John

Stan Getz with Max
Roach on drums and
Ray Brown on bass.
(DownBeat Archive)

Coltrane played to packed houses while Getz died another death.

What did all this have to do with music? Very little. It was a matter of fads and foibles, not ability; Coltrane was a performer whose qualifications suited the jazz public's mood of the moment. It was not that one was "better" and the other inferior; it was more as if they played two different instruments, and this was not the time for the particular horn Getz played.

The tide did not turn until some time after Feb. 13, 1962. That was the day when, at Pierce Hall in All Souls Unitarian Church in Washington, D.C., Stan and Charlie Byrd recorded the *Jazz Samba* album.

"I didn't know anything about bossa nova," the saxophonist said. "Charlie Byrd came into the club one night and asked me if I'd like to stay with him. At his place I listened to the Joao Gilberto LP. He told me about the tour he'd just made for the State Department and about Brazil and all the other countries he'd visited.

"The idea developed of making an album of some of these tunes. I just thought it was pretty music. I never thought it would be a hit.

"The album that was released actually was a second try. We attempted it once in New York, but it didn't work out. Then we tried it again at the session in the church, and it was released and got a nice reaction, but I still didn't have any real idea just how big it was going to be."

What happened cannot be summed up in exact facts and figures; it depends which press agent you talk to. But Bernie Silverman of Verve Records confirms that the single records of "Desafinado" out of the album has passed 500,000 and that the LP itself has sold "several hundred thousand" and should also wind up close to 500,000.

Who were the purchasers of this vast quantity of records by the man who had come back to face white tablecloths and red accounting sheets? Were they the same people wooed back into the fold, or an entirely new audience attracted by the intrinsic charm of the music? Getz finds this hard to analyze, but how it happened doesn't worry him too much; he is happy enough that it did happen.

"I'm very pleased, too," he added, "that as a result of all the excitement about *Jazz Samba*, the *Focus* album is beginning to attract more attention. I think Eddie Sauter did a marvelous job with *Focus*, and incidentally, it won a German Jazz Federation Award as the album of the year.

I'd like very much to take it on tour, with Eddie conducting the orchestra. You know something—more people ask me about *Focus* than about *Jazz Samba*."

Silverman said the success of *Jazz Samba* "has definitely stimulated the sales of every Getz album we have in the catalog, though, of course, he always sold steadily. But what *Jazz Samba* did for him was get him on rock-and-roll stations, so that teenagers were listening to 'Desafinado.' It brought good music into unlikely areas, so it's been a healthy thing for music in general."

At this writing the album is in its 20th week on the bestseller charts in the trade press. In the stereo list it is still in second place, topped only by the *West Side Story* soundtrack and outselling Vaughn Meader, Allan Sherman, Ray Charles, Elvis Presley, Nat Cole and even Bent Fabric. Getz is the only jazz saxophonist on the charts. In a culminating irony, he returned to top place in the 1962 *DownBeat* Readers Poll.

As is the lot of a man with rivals who earns a resounding success in his field, Getz is now the object of much jealousy and resentment. All that matters to him is that he is now able to produce whatever music he likes and can be sure of an audience for it and that when he announces "Desafinado" (or "Dis Here Finado," as he calls it), he introduces it as "the tune that's going to put my children through college—all five of them." (Another son was added to the family a year ago. All the children are now in the United States with Stan and Monica.)

Creed Taylor, the A&R man behind the *Jazz Samba* album, naturally has further plans to record bossa nova with Getz. The first follow-up, the big-band set with Gary McFarland, has been on the charts for several weeks.

Getz and Taylor are aware that there is no need to throw all the eggs in a Brazilian bag. Plans are set for Getz to record albums with Luis Bonfa and Joao Gilberto (accompaniments by Lalo Schifrin and Oscar Castro-Neves); there will also be a *Jazz Samba #2* with Byrd. (Another irony is the fact that nowhere, in title, tunes or liner notes, did the words "bossa nova" appear in the LP that turned out to be the catalyst for the bossa nova mania in this country.) But there will be many non-bossa nova albums in the foreseeable future. As Getz says, "bossa nova is a bestseller at the moment, but jazz is going to be around for a long, long time."

Getz now can command a nightly four-figure salary, the royalties from his albums are expected to run ultimately into six figures, and he can count on the kind of lifelong security that only a year ago seemed hopelessly out of reach. A year ago, nevertheless, Stan Getz was playing as brilliantly, as soulfully, as swingingly and as sensitively as he does today. The difference is his success—and that's show business.

May 21, 1964

An Afternoon with Ben Webster

by Stanley Dance

Stride piano, the left hand fast and precise, filled the telephone receiver.

"Hello."

"Ben?"

"Yeah. Wait till I turn my waking-up music off."

The sound of James P. Johnson's piano was abruptly diminished.

"You downstairs? Come on up."

One of tenor saxophonist Ben Webster's afternoon musicales was in progress. A tape on which the Lion, the Lamb, James P., Fats Waller and Art Tatum strove mightily together—his waking-up music—was still on the Wollensak, but an album by Tatum was now placed on the phonograph. A facet of that pianist's genius was about to be demonstrated to Duke Ellington's bassist, Ernie Shepard, and drummer Sam Woodyard—who occupied nearby hotel rooms and had come in to discuss the previous night's activities.

Webster had sat in for a set with the Ellington band at its Basin Street East opening, and he was happy about the experience. Chuck Connors' arrival having been delayed that night, Webster had taken Connors' seat in the trombone section and been duly introduced to the audience by Ellington as an expert on claves in cha-cha-cha. When the saxophonist came down front later, Ellington had suggested he play "Cottontail," Webster's best-known recorded performance during his principal stay

with Ellington, 1939–'43. The performance ended with a chase between Webster and Ellington's regular tenor saxophonist, Paul Gonsalves. It had been a kick.

"If Duke likes you," Webster said, "you're home free." There were bottles of beer sitting on the windowsill outside, cold and ready to drink, and ale on the dressing table, but the main business this afternoon was music and reminiscence. A tape of a 1940 Ellington performance at the Crystal Ballroom in Fargo, N.D., was produced.

"It was so cold there that night," Webster remembered, "we played in our overcoats, and some of the guys kept their gloves on!"

The music coming from the tape had an exciting kind of abandon—the abandon, perhaps, of desperation.

"Sometimes," he added, "when you've traveled all day in the bus, and had no sleep and are dead tired—that's when you get the best playing out of a band. It just happens. And sometimes the opposite."

The material was inspiring. After "The Mooche" came "Ko-Ko," "Pussy Willow"…

"I learned a lot from Rab [Johnny Hodges], but you know what his only advice to me was when I came in the band? 'Learn your parts.'"

The tape continued rolling. "Chatterbox," "Harlem Airshaft," "Jack the Bear," "Rumpus in Richmond," "Sidewalks of New York," "The Flaming Sword," "Never No Lament"…

"That's why Duke leaves his mark on you, forever," Webster said.

"Clarinet Lament," "Slap Happy," "Sepia Panorama," "Rockin' in Rhythm," "Cottontail"…

"Sonny Greer, and he's swinging!" Webster exclaimed in admiration of the drummer who worked with Ellington from the '20s to the '50s.

"Conga Bravo," "Stardust," "Rose of the Rio Grande" and "Boy Meets Horn" preceded the finale, an uproarious version of "St. Louis Blues," on which trombonist Tricky Sam Nanton took over from Webster and carried through to the coda.

"We were drinking buddies," the saxophonist said, and laughed, "but you heard how he tore right in on me there."

After a few jokes, the conversation came back to piano, steered by the host, and the striding hands of yesterday stretched out again on tape and vinyl. Often they belonged to Fats Waller.

"All that fun but never a wrong note," Webster remarked. "If only he could have

Ben Webster.
(World Pacific Records)

lived until TV!"

Contemporaries were considered and Ralph Sutton commended as "a wonderful cat." Earl Hines, too: "Earl swings his head off."

A memory of the Beetle intervened, the diffident-seeming Beetle who took part in the piano battles uptown and seldom played anything less than an easy, rocking, medium tempo but who triumphed nevertheless. Another memory returned, of the Lamb—Donald Lambert—who came to the battlefield once or twice a year, astounded everyone, and then retired to

New Jersey again. From that point, it required little urging to get Webster to tell of his first experience with the Harlem piano school.

"I shall never forget the time when I met Count Basie," he began. "It was while he was in Kansas City with Gonzel White, and he used to stop the show. I always did like Basie, and I always did want to play the piano. He bore with me for a long time, and he told me that in the event I ever got to New York, I was to be sure to find the Lion—Willie Smith. He had already told me that the bosses were James P. Johnson

and the Lion, and that then came Duke, Fats and Willie Gant. I don't remember all the names, but there was a gang of great piano players in those days.

"Clyde Hart and I managed to get with Blanche Galloway. Clyde was a friend of mine, a piano player, and Edgar Battle sent for us in Kansas City. We played the Pearl Theater in Philly, at 22nd and Ridge, I think it was, and Clyde and I got on the train the first day we had off and came to New York.

"Basie had briefed me. 'Go to the Rhythm Club,' he said, 'and that's where you'll find the Lion. He knows all the piano players and all the good musicians. They hang out there, and the Lion will introduce you right. Naturally, I wanted to hear people like Benny Carter, Johnny Hodges and Coleman Hawkins too. Basie had also told us how to approach the Lion so that he would bear with us. Basie said he liked a little taste every now and then, that he loved cigars, and that maybe he would play a little for us.

"So we walked up to the Rhythm Club on 132nd Street and Seventh Avenue, and we met the Lion. There was a cigar store right on the corner, and in those days they had great big El Productos, three for a half-dollar.

"'Mr. Lion,' we said, 'would you care to have some cigars?'

"The Lion rounded on us and said, 'Say, you are pretty nice kids. Yes, I'll have a cigar or two.'

"So we walked with him to the corner and asked him how many could he smoke.

"'Oh, maybe two.'

"So we bought him half a dozen, and then he smiled and said, 'You kids are really nice kids!'

"Then we asked him, 'Would you care for a little drink, Mr. Lion?'

"'Yeah,' he said.

"Then we told him we would like to hear him play, and at that time there was a place right across from the Rhythm Club, and he took us over there, and he got in the mood with his cigar and a little taste in between.

"It was one of the greatest experiences of my life to hear a man play like this. Though I had heard James P. Johnson around 1925 in Kansas City, that was a little early, and I think I could understand more of what I was listening to when I got to the Lion.

"He played for us for three or four hours, and we kept buying him a little taste, and he kept saying we were nice kids. I had a beautiful day and I never will forget it."

Until about a year ago, Webster had resided for several years in Los Angeles, taking care of his mother and grandmother, but when they both died within a year's time, he had no family reason to stay in California, and he moved to New York City.

He has brought back to the ingrowing New York scene the good humor and expansive generosity of spirit that have been dwindling for some time among its hard-pressed musicians. Webster is big physically—broad-shouldered and straight-backed—and he is bigger than the rat race. One is soon aware that music occupies his mind far more than money—music as, above all, a means to enjoyment.

Ellington's wasn't the only band he sat in with during the winter. Gerry Mulligan's Concert Jazz Band found it had an impulsive new pianist one night in Birdland, and at the Metropole on another occasion, Webster took Marty Napoleon's place at the keyboard for a set.

The appearances with his own quartet at the Shalimar, Birdland and the Half Note have proved popular. His material, consisting mostly of the better standards and well-known Ellington numbers, is strong on melodic content. Just as he did 20 years ago, with men like pianists Marlowe Morris and Johnny Guarnieri and drummer Sid Catlett, he likes to open and close a performance with a statement of the theme. Good melody, well phrased, communicates as strongly in the jazz idiom as in any other, and there are distinct advantages from the audience's viewpoint to having the melody established in the mind when following the variations. Webster recognizes this, plus the importance of good tempos.

Stylistically, he illustrates the evolutionary process always at work within the music.

The jazz audience was probably first made aware of him in 1932 on the several explosive records that indicated the musical ferment in Kansas City—those made by Bennie Moten with Basie, trumpeter Oran (Hot Lips) Page, trombonist Eddie Durham and reed man Eddie Barefield, in addition to Webster—"Moten Swing," "Lafayette," etc.

In his subsequent recordings, there was uninterrupted development, but up until the time he joined Ellington, listeners generally recognized the influence of Coleman Hawkins rather than the personality of

Ben Webster. Yet, as Hugues Panassie perceptively noted, "The grace of his melodic line makes one think of Benny Carter." In fact, it is Carter whom Webster names first among saxophonists—then Hawkins, then Johnny Hodges ("the most feeling") and then Hilton Jefferson ("the prettiest").

Established stylistically in 1940, Webster himself became an important influence. Prominent among those to acknowledge it was Eddie (Lockjaw) Davis, at one time known as Little Ben.

When Paul Gonsalves took the tenor chair with Ellington, his ability to play solos in Webster's style profoundly surprised the leader, but in the 14 years that have followed, Gonsalves' musical personality has developed on strongly individual lines, a fact evident when he and his early mentor played "Cottontail" at Basin Street East. It was even more evident in a jam session at Count Basie's bar in Harlem, when Webster, Gonsalves and fellow tenor man Harold Ashby were together on the stand. Ashby is a close friend of Webster's who proudly proclaims his friend's influence, but all three were individually and instantly identifiable by tone and phrasing.

"He's improved so much he scares me," Webster said of Ashby's playing, using his most admiring epithet.

Gonsalves, too, he esteems highly. One of the records often played on his phonograph is "I've Just Seen Her," from Ellington's *All American* album, a Gonsalves performance that never fails to impress saxophone players.

At Webster's musicale, Gonsalves reminisced about the first time he heard Tatum. He had gone to a club with Webster, Basie and trumpeter Harry Edison to hear Tatum, but the master didn't feel like playing that night. So Webster sat down at the piano and played awhile. Then Edison played, and finally Basie. With that, Tatum decided to play—"Get Happy" at a very fast tempo. What astonished him, Webster said, was the way Tatum's left hand took care of business while the right reached for a drink.

Perhaps this anecdote passed through Webster's mind at the jam session at Basie's club. He called "Get Happy." They took off, lightning fast, and Gonsalves went into a furious and fantastically devised solo.

"Paul's getting so hot," Webster exclaimed with mock alarm, "I don't think I should have called this tune!"

Another afternoon visitor was tenorist

Budd Johnson, who had first shown Webster the scale on saxophone and how to play "Singin' the Blues." Webster had been taught violin, but had not liked the instrument. There were two pianos in the Webster house, his mother's and his cousin's ("I ruined my cousin's piano playing blues"), and when he should have been practicing violin, he was usually busy on one or the other of them. Pete Johnson, who lived across the street, taught him how to play the blues.

"If you lay the violin down a week, you're in trouble," Webster said, "but you can lay a horn down a year and be OK." So when he switched to piano, it was the end of the violin phase.

He was playing piano in a silent-movie house in Amarillo, Texas, when Gene Coy's band came to town, and he met Budd Johnson and his brother, trombonist Keg. The saxophone fascinated Webster, and in 1929, when he was 20, he heard that the Young family band needed another saxophone player; he went to see Lester's father.

"I can't read," he said.

Mr. Young was amused.

"I haven't got a horn," he added.

Mr. Young was then even more amused, but he provided Webster with an alto saxophone and taught him to read.

"Lester's father mostly played trumpet, but he could play anything, and, what's more, he was a master teacher," Webster recalled.

Lester played tenor, and Webster insists he was playing wonderfully even then. Lee Young and his sister, Irma, were also members of the band and played saxophones at that time, too.

The group went to Albuquerque, N.M., for some months, and it was there that Webster, a strong swimmer, helped save the lives of both Lester and Lee. Lester got into difficulties in the Rio Grande and was carried away, tumbling over and over in the water until Webster and guitarist Ted Brinson rescued him. On another occasion, Lee stepped off the bank into a deep sand hole, and Webster managed to haul him out.

"Lee dived right in again," Webster remembered, "but Lester didn't want to think about swimming for a long time after that."

Some months later, after Budd and Keg Johnson had left it, Webster got a call to join Gene Coy's band ("about nine or 10 pieces") in which Harold Coleman was playing tenor. That was really the begin-

Dizzy Gillespie takes the oath of office flanked by (from left) Kenny Barron, James Moody, Rudy Collins, Chris White and Shelly Manne. (Ron Skeetz)

ning of the professional career as a saxophonist that brought him, experienced and mature, into New York City, 1964.

"I think I'm playing better than ever right now," he said. Then he repeated, "I think."

Nov. 5, 1964
. . . .

The Candidate Meets the Press

Presidential Candidate John Birks Gillespie Views Affairs of State with Jaundiced— and Jolly—Eye

As the hustle on the hustings continues up

to Election Day, with Democrat and Republican decrying one another's policies and impugning one another's honor and worse, John Birks (Dizzy) Gillespie plows his own political way in his race for the presidency of the United States. The 47-year-old trumpeter from Cheraw, N.C., is pursuing his political campaign, offering several solid planks: intelligence and humor about the whole business of running for office, sincere dedication to the principles of Negro rights and the fight to win them fully, and lots of the best jazz there is.

Following are excerpts from a recent press conference held in Los Angeles.

Q. In your campaign, do you have any specific criticisms of the platforms of the two major parties? If so, what are they?

A. First things come first. First, civil rights. I think that some of the major civil rights groups are on the wrong track. The real issue of civil rights is not the idea of discrimination in itself, but the system that led to the discrimination. Such as the schools—the teaching in the schools. They

don't teach the kids about the dignity of all men everywhere. They say that there should be education. OK. I say education, yes, but the white people are the ones who should be educated into how to treat every man. And the system of discrimination started during slavery time—with the slaves—it's an economic thing. Of course we don't have that slave system at the moment, but we do have something in its place, such as discrimination against people economically.

Economics is the key to the whole thing. For example, if all of my followers said that we weren't going to buy one single product for three days, think of what would happen to the stock on that one product on the stock market in one day. If it would drop drastically—boom! They would hurry up to protect their investors; they would hurry up to rectify a gross injustice.

Q. How many people do you think would be involved in this, in terms of purchasing power—20 million... 30 million?

A. There are millions and millions of right-thinking people in this country.

Q. Not just Negro people?

A. Not just Negro people. No, no.

Q. Then you'd probably get 60 million to go along with you?

A. I'd like to see that… 60 million people wouldn't buy a product for three days…. There would be bedlam on the stock market. And they would hurry up and do something about this… thing [discrimination].

The other thing is about the income tax situation. There are certain elements in our society that have better breaks on the income tax situation than others. I say we should make "numbers" legal. A national lottery for the whole country. And everybody—little grocery stores, gasoline stations—would sell books of tickets. All that money would go to the government. Do you realize that millions and millions of dollars a day are taken in "numbers" (which is illegal). Everybody is a gambler. When you come here on earth, you gamble [on] whether you want to live to see tomorrow. So they should channel those virtues in the right direction.

Q. What about accusations that "numbers" bleed the poor and that only the rich people can back the "numbers"?

A. That's who's [the rich] getting all the loot, that's who's getting all the money now. But the government would get that money.

Q. Wouldn't you lose a lot of supporters from the church and from church-going people?

A. I notice in some of the churches they have bingo nights. People go to bingo night better than they would come to see me in a club where they have whisky. Of course, you would have to get the clergy behind you. And then if you hit the "numbers," if you hit for a dollar, you get $600.

Q. We've been hearing so much for the last six months or so about the so-called white backlash. Do you have any comment on that?

A. Yes. In the first place, the people who are affected by the white backlash, we haven't had them anyway. See? If we are going to judge how to treat a human being by a bunch of hoodlums' riots in certain places, well, we don't need them anyway. I have that much confidence in the integrity of the American people that we have enough people to really do something about the situation. So the ones who are affected by the backlash—shame on 'em. We never had 'em anyway.

Q. In the interim period—while the school system is being settled and minority groups are getting equal opportunities—what do you suggest to raise the economic level of Negroes and other minority groups until they have the opportunity to have the same education and, therefore, get the same types of jobs as whites?

A. I would suggest that when an applicant for any employment… when an applicant comes in to take his… to decide on his qualifications for a job, it should be behind a screen. This system of discrimination against us is so strong that the moment a black face walks in, we know that we're going to have to do a little more than the white person to get the job. But when an applicant comes in, and he's behind a screen, his aptitudes for a job are on paper and you ask him questions or something and you won't know what you've hired until he has either flunked it or made it.

Q. Could we have your comments on the two candidates of the major parties and their programs? First, Sen. Barry Goldwater.

A. I think his program stinks. I think the senator's program is ultraconservative; I think that Sen. Goldwater wants to take us back to the horse-and-buggy days when we are in the space age. And we are looking forward, not backward. President Johnson? He's done a magnificent job.

Q. In what area?

A. In the area of civil rights—for what he has done and with the backing he has. But I'm sure that if I don't get to be president—which I hope I shall—then I think that President Johnson would make a much, much, much better president than Mr. Goldwater.

Q. We're in an era in which we are told only a millionaire can be president. Are you a millionaire? [laughter]

A. Not by any stretch of your imagination. I remember some years ago when I was in Paris, I saw a headline on one of the tabloids—the *New York Mirror*—which is presently defunct, and it said in the headline: "Bebop Millionaire in Trouble." There are certain spheres of our media of communication, there are certain newspapers that I don't believe anything I read in them. This one was preposterous because at the time I didn't know one bebop musician who had two quarters to rub up against one another.

Q. Seriously, how important do you consider a lot of money is in political campaigning?

A. I understand Gov. Rockefeller…. There will be a moment of silence when I mention that name. I understand that he spent in the primaries alone almost $2 million or something like that.

But I look at it this way: suppose I were a millionaire. (That's a very far-fetched idea.) And suppose there was a guy in trouble someplace, and I say here's $10,000—with the television camera on me, and the radio—$10,000 clear. [Then] if I were a poor man, say, making $75 a week, and I see a guy who's ragged and doesn't have any shoes on and his clothes are in tatters and I walk up to him and I say, "Come here." And I go to a secondhand store and buy him $6.79 worth of clothes. My idea of that is, I've done more by giving this guy this little gift. I call it having respect for, and having a big heart for, the little guy.

Q. What do you think of Hubert Humphrey?

A. When we toured for the State Department the first time, in 1956, we were invited to play for the White House Correspondents' Ball. I had the good fortune to meet Sen. Humphrey. I walked up to Sen. Humphrey without an introduction. I said, "Do you know one thing? I don't particularly care for politicians." He looked at me. I said, "But you are my favorite politician." He came right back and said, "If you ever come to Minneapolis, I want you to look me up." So maybe I might get some backing from Sen. Humphrey.

Q. What about the residue from the New Frontier, the men who surrounded President Kennedy and are still in Washington?

A. I can't say that I blame President Johnson about that because when he repudiated all the men that surrounded the late President Kennedy…. You see, President Johnson has a problem. We loved the late President Kennedy, as did most Americans; we were madly in love with him. My wife cried for weeks and weeks and weeks after his death. But you see Johnson had to do that because in history he wants to he judged by what he did, not for what President Kennedy started. He wants to identify himself with his ideas about social problems that have to be faced. He wants to live and die with his philosophy. I'll go along with that.

Q. If you were to pick a vice-presidential running mate, who would it be? Or have you done so already?

A. I was thinking of asking Phyllis Diller. She seems to have that sua-a-a-a-ve manner; she looks far into the future. She's looking into the future. So I'm a future man, I said to her.

Q. Have you approached her?

A. I sent one of my emissaries. I sent one of my emissaries to sound her on that. I understand that she is for it. She was going to vote for me, anyway, so she'd just as well get in there and work.

Q. What about your cabinet? Who would you select for cabinet officers?

A. In the first place I want to eliminate secretaries.

Q. Why?

A. In French that would be feminine gender, and we don't want anyone effeminate in our form of government. I'm going to make them all ministers.

Minister of foreign affairs: Duke Ellington.

Minister of peace: Charlie Mingus. Anybody have any objections to that? I think it would get through the Senate. Right through.

Minister of agriculture: Louis Armstrong.

Q. Why?

A. Well, you know, he's from New Orleans; he knows all about growing things.

Ministress of labor: Peggy Lee. She's very nice to her musicians, so… labor-management harmony. It's harmony between labor and management.

Minister of justice: Malcolm X. Who would be more adept at meting out justice to people who flaunted it than Malcolm? Can you give me another name? Whenever I mention this name, people say, "Hawo-o-o-o." But I am sure that if we were to channel his genius—he's a genius—in the right direction, such as minister of justice, we would have some peaceful times here. Understand?

Ministress of finance: Jeannie Gleason. Ralph Gleason's wife. When she can put the salary of a newspaperman—you know it's not too great, you have to pinch here and there—when she can keep that money together, she's a genius. So I'm sure that she would be able to run our fiscal policy.

My executive assistant would be Ramona Swettschurt Crowell, the one who makes my sweatshirts.

Minister of defense: Max Roach.

Head of the CIA: Miles Davis.

Q. Why?

A. O-o-ooh, honey, you know his schtick. He's ready for that position. He'd know just what to do in that position.

All my ambassadors: Jazz musicians. The cream.

Gov. George C. Wallace: Chief information officer in the Congo…. Under

Tshombe.

We would resume relations with Communist Cuba.

Q. Why?

A. Well, I've been reading the newspapermen who were invited to Cuba to look at the revolution there…. It seems Premier Castro wants to talk about reparations. But he wants to talk about it on a diplomatic level, which means respect. I am a man to respect, to respect a country, Cuba, regardless of their political affiliations; they are there, and there's no doubt about it.

And I was reading in the articles that they'll be there a while. So I would recognize that we send an ambassador, in an exchange of ambassadors, to Cuba to see if we can work out this problem of indemnity for the factories and things that they have expropriated. I think that any government has that privilege of nationalizing their wealth. It's theirs; it's just theirs. So, if they want to pay for it…. Of course, we built it up, we were out there; it wasn't our country in the first place. But since they built it up and Mr. Castro wants to pay you for it, I think we should accept the money with grace.

Q. What about Communist China?

A. I think we should recognize them.

Q. Why?

A. Can you imagine us thinking that 700 million people are no people? How much percent is that of the world's population? I think we should recognize them. Besides, we need that business. We're about to run out of markets, you know. All of a sudden you wake up and there's 700 million more people to sell something to. And jazz festivals. Can you imagine: we could go to China with a jazz festival and spend 10 years there at jazz festivals. We'd forget all about you over here. We'd send back records.

Q. We're very deeply involved in Vietnam; what would be your policy on this situation?

A. We're not deeply involved enough in Vietnam. I think we should either recognize the fight or take a chance on World War—is it three? There's been so many. Either do it, or get out of there. Because every day American soldiers are walking around and—boom!—out, finished, kaput. They're being killed, and they don't even know hardly that they're even at war. We haven't declared war. So I think we should really either straighten it out—and we have the means to do that—or get out of there. I think we should do it or don't do it. But if

I were president, I'd get out of there. I'd say, look, y'all got it, baby. Yeah, good luck. I'd get American soldiers out of there.

Q. As one of our most prominent musicians, you are aware that automation has played the devil with musicians' livelihoods. What would your policy be on automation?

A. Automation will never replace the musician himself. We would have to set up some kind of a thing to protect the musician from that. There's a bill in Congress now—oh, it's been up for a long time; I get letters from ASCAP and my Society for the Protection of Songwriters; writing letters to senators to get them to vote for this bill—to make them give us part of that money that's going into jukeboxes. As soon as the jukebox operators find out that you have to pay some money out there, a nice little taste of money, they'll start hiring live musicians again, I think. Instead of having the jukeboxes there, they'd hire some musicians.

Q. What do you think the role of the musicians' union should be in this regard?

A. Aw, the musicians' union! Why did you bring that up? Is this for publication? It is? Ah, the role of the musicians' union—it has been very lax in this space age. They have wallowed in the age of the horse and buggy and the cotton gin. I don't think they're doing a very good job. All they're doing is taking the money.

Q. In a recent interview, Duke Ellington said that from his personal standpoint he didn't agree with subsidies for his music. What should your attitude as president be toward federal subsidies for the arts, particularly music?

A. We need subsidies for the arts. I'm a firm believer in that. Since jazz is our prime art, that should be the first thing we should subsidize.

Q. How would you go about that?

A. I'd have to work it out with someone who is familiar with it.

Q. How about a civil-service nightclub?

A. Now, that's a good idea. A civil-service nightclub. That'd be nice. I've been speaking to Max Roach about an organization composed of jazz musicians to perpetuate our own music. This year at Newport we had a jazz festival. Also they had a folk festival, which was marvelous. I mean, it just got down at the bottom of everything.

Y'see, jazz musicians—they're so busy being jealous of one another that they can't get together, so they need some rallying point. Max told me, "You're the only one that could do it. You should call a summit meeting and have all the guys. Send them a letter; say, 'Be there!' And they would be there." So we were speaking about this. So we're probably going to get together....

But musicians should be on the production end of jazz. Like Shelly Manne is here in Hollywood. He's a musician who's on the production end of it, and I'm sure that the atmosphere in his club is different from any club in the country because he thinks like a musician. Just think of an organization of musicians who would dictate the policies of clubs where you play: "Say, look, you've got to have a piano that's in tune—that's 440—and lights and maybe little stairs going here and going there." Musicians got some ideas. I imagine if you'd turn them loose on ideas of what kind of people they should have in the clubs and how best they could present that music to people, then all of us would benefit by it because all of us would be doing it. So the musician, with his fantastic ideas about music, if you could channel them into the production end of music, how best we could serve the public—which we are in it to do—I imagine there would be a big rejuvenation of jazz. We could put on four mammoth concerts in one year—one in New York, one in L.A., one in Chicago and one in the Midwest. They would be in the biggest ball parks, and we'd have people who love jazz, such as Frank Sinatra, Nat Cole (a jazz musician himself), Marlon Brando, Phyllis Diller, Harry Belafonte, all of those people have been helped by jazz. All of them have been helped by it, and I'm sure they would go all out to put a little thing into it. So they would help us with these things.

And we would get an administrator to run it—and pay him, pay him to run it. And let it be run on a business-like basis, like U.S. Steel is run; we'd have an executive board, a chairman of the board, directors, president and all that jive.

Q. On a personal level, what is your own opinion of Cassias Clay, or Muhammad Ali, as he is now known?

A. My personal opinion of him? I don't know him that well to pass a personal opinion of him. I would have to know a person very well before I would pass an opinion.... I'm a firm believer that if you can't say something good about somebody, don't say anything at all.

Q. If your opponents in the presidential race start any mud-slinging...?

A. Oh, that's different. A campaign is something altogether different. And then afterward you kiss and make up.

Q. Goldwater, too?

A. I don't think we would be on too good terms, not on kissing terms anyway.

June 3, 1965

Monk on Monk

by Valerie Wilmer

Now it's Monk's time. Times have been bad for the eccentric genius and the work all but nonexistent.

But he's famous now. He appears in the slicks, he wears $150 suits and stays at the best hotels. But as his wife, Nellie, says, "He's no more impressed with himself than he was in the dark days."

Music is his life, and he appears to be concerned with little else outside of it, himself and his family. If he ever thinks of the way of the world, he rarely shows it. Speaking of Monk the composer, Quincy Jones summed it up: "Thelonious is one of the main influences in modern jazz composition, but he is not familiar with many classical works, or with much life outside himself, and I think because of this he did not create on a contrived or inhibited basis."

An interview with Monk takes patience, but while he was on a European tour recently, he had more time than usual to relax. In London, there was opportunity to find out the way he feels about his music and other subjects.

"I started to take up trumpet as a kid, but I didn't play it," he began tentatively. "I always wanted to play the piano, and jazz appealed to me. I just like every aspect of it. You can try so many things with jazz. I was about 11 or something like that when I started, and I used to play with all the different side bands when I was a teenager."

Did he ever think he might become a world-famous jazz pianist?

"Well, that's what I was aiming at."

Although he received classical training, Monk plays "incorrectly," with his hands held parallel to the keyboard. He doesn't stab at the keys the way some imagine. It's a flowing thing.

Was he ever taught to hold his hands in the formal manner?

"That's how you're supposed to?" he asked, wide-eyed. "I hold them any way I feel like holding them. I hit the piano with my elbow sometimes because of a certain sound I want to hear, certain chords. You can't hit that many notes with your hands. Sometimes people laugh when I'm doing that. Yeah, let 'em laugh! They need something to laugh at."

Monk lived with his parents off and on until his marriage, an unusual pattern for a jazz musician, although he claims, "I don't know what other people are doing— I just know about me. I cut out from home when I was a teenager and went on the road for about two years."

His mother, who was particularly proud of her well-behaved son, sang in the choir at the local Baptist church in New York City, where the family lived; whenever she had a leading part, Thelonious would accompany her on piano. And she would visit the dives where he worked.

"My mother never figured I should do anything else," Monk said. "She was with me. If I wanted to play music, it was all right with her, and Nellie is the same way.

"Yeah, I played in the Baptist church, and I'll tell you something else—I worked with the evangelists for some time, too. The music I played with them seems to be coming out today. They're playing a lot of it now. I did two years all over the States; playing in the churches was a lot of fun. When I got through, I'd had enough of church, though. I was in there practically every night. But I always did play jazz. In the churches I was playing music the same way. I wouldn't say I'm religious, but I haven't been around the churches in a good while so I don't know what they're putting down in there now."

Of Minton's, the Harlem club long held the incubator of bop, Monk, like others of his fellow iconoclasts of the time who played there, declared that the music "just happened. I was working there, so the others just used to come down and play with me. I guess they dug what I was doing. It was always crowded there, people enjoying themselves all the time. What I was doing was just the way I was thinking. I wasn't thinking about trying to change the course of jazz. I was just trying to play something that sounded good. I never used to talk about it with other people, but I believe the other musicians did. It just happened."

For a long time the pianist found it difficult to obtain work, but he says with typical Monkish nonchalance, "I didn't notice it too much. I had certain things to do. I wasn't starving."

Thelonious Monk, center, with singer Jimmy Rushing and Japan Air Lines hostess Kumiko Kasuya from 1963.
(Japain Airlines publicity photo)

Nellie, whom he married in 1947, was a great help and comfort through the lean years. She worked at a variety of clerical jobs and when she was pregnant with their first child, Thelonious Jr., used to take in sewing.

"Music to him is work," she said. "When he wasn't working regularly, he'd be working at home, writing and rehearsing bands that didn't have the prospects of a dog. He just did it to know what it'd sound like. In the 'un' years, as I call them, as far as he was concerned, he felt just as confident as he does now that what he was doing musically could appeal to other people if only they took the opportunity to listen.

"We live music every day. Thelonious has never attempted to do anything else except play music. He's always been optimistic."

Her husband confirmed this: "How can I be anything other than what I am?"

A couple of years ago soprano saxophonist Steve Lacy declared his intention to limit his repertoire to Monk tunes, of which there were almost 60 then.

"Yeah, I heard he was doing that," Monk said. "But I haven't heard him yet. I guess if anybody wants to do that, it's OK."

He says he has no particular favorites among his many compositions and that the unusual names for many of them "just come to me." He composes at the piano sometimes, though more often than not he has a melody running around in his head. Although he said, "You have to stay home and relax to write the music," his wife commented, "He thinks about music all the time when he's not talking. He may be able to compose in a room full of people, just standing there. I don't know anybody else who can just withdraw like that. He has a marvelous capacity for withdrawal."

This withdrawal includes not speaking to his wife for days on end, "unless he wants me to fetch something," and she will only break the silence if she has something urgent to tell him.

"Even then he might not reply or show that he's heard," she said, "but in emergencies his reactions are very fast. He's more contained than most people and, therefore, more helpful than someone who falls apart and goes to pieces."

When he is writing, Monk said he does not think of the actual notes or the effect his finished work will have on his audience.

"I'm just thinking about the music," he added. "You think about everything else automatically. I think about what anyone else does."

And what does he think of the public?

"I think very highly of the public. I think they're capable of knowing if something sounds all right. I figure that if it sounds all right to me, it sounds all right to them."

The pianist has lived in the same place for 30 years. It's a small, undistinguished apartment on New York's West 63rd Street, and he is very attached to it.

"There's nothing special about it," he said, "but I guess I'll always keep it."

He once remarked that if he couldn't live in New York, he'd rather be on the moon, but he denies this tongue-in-cheek statement:

"Did I say that? Can't remember it. I

don't know what's happening on the moon, but I know what's happening in New York. I like New York City. I haven't been anywhere that tops it yet.

"I have to listen to New York; I live there. I wasn't born there, but I've been living there all my life. [Monk was born in Rocky Mount, N.C.] You can't shut the sound out too easily; you always hear some kind of noise going on. I guess all sort of things have an effect on what you're writing. But I was raised in New York, and it's home to me. That's what I dig about it. You want to know what sound I put into my music—well, you have to go to New York and listen for yourself. I can't describe them. How do you expect me to describe to you right here how New York sounds? How does London sound? Can you tell me how it sounds—huh?"

Onstage, Monk often will rise from the piano stool and stand listening intently to the other soloists, swaying slightly in what has been termed Monk's dance. He gets exasperated over comments on such aspects of his behavior.

"What's that I'm supposed to be doing?" he demanded. "I get tired sitting down at the piano! That way I can dig the rhythm better. Somebody's got something to say about everything you do!

"I miss a lot of things that are written about me. I don't read papers. I don't read magazines. Of course, I'm interested in what's going on in music, but I'm not interested in what somebody else is writing or anything like that. I don't let that bug me. In fact, I don't see those 'columns' or whatever you call 'em. People write all kinds of jive.

"I've got a wife and two kids to take care of, and I have to make some money and see that they eat and sleep, and me, too—you dig? What happens 'round the corner, what happens to his family is none of my business. I have to take care of my family. But I'll help a lot of people, and I have.... But I don't go around... [asking]: 'What's the matter with you?' No! I'm not interested in what's happening nowhere. Are you worried about what's happening to everybody? Why do you ask me that? Why should I be worried? You're not! Why do you ask me a stupid question like that? Something you don't dig yourself? I don't be around the corner, looking into everybody's house, looking to see what's happening. I'm not a policeman or a social worker—that's for your social workers to do. I'm not in power. I'm not worrying about politics. You worry about the poli-

tics. Let the statesmen do that—that's their job. They get paid for it. If you're worried about it, stop doing what you're doing!"

And Monk does not concern himself with the racial scene in any way.

"I hardly know anything about it," he said. "I never was interested in those Muslims. If you want to know, you should ask Art Blakey. I didn't have to change my name—it's always been weird enough! I haven't done one of these 'freedom' suites, and I don't intend to. I mean, I don't see the point. I'm not thinking that race thing now; it's not on my mind. Everybody's trying to get me to think it, though, but it doesn't bother me. It only bugs the people who're trying to get me to think it."

Monk is a self-willed person. Rarely does he do anything that does not interest him. He seldom goes to parties, and when he is neither working nor walking around New York City, he is at home with Nellie and their two children, Thelonious Jr., who is 15, and 11-year-old Barbara. Now, at 45, he seems hardly aware of the substantial increase in his income in recent years and says money makes no difference to his way of life.

"If I feel like it, I'll spend it," he said, "but I spend it on what anybody else spends it on—clothes and food. My wife and kids spend a lot of money, but I really don't know how much I make. I'd go stupid collecting and counting my money. I worked at $17 a week when I was a kid—make thousands now. At 14, 15 years old, I could do anything I wanted with that money. It wasn't bad for that age.

"I really don't want to do anything else other than what I'm doing. I like playing music. Everything's all right. I don't look like I'm worrying about anything, do I? I don't talk much because you can't tell everybody what you're thinking. Sometimes you don't know what you're thinking yourself."

A perceptive wife, Nellie added, "You wouldn't know whether he was happy or not at any time. He's always been very agreeable. Even in the direst situations you can't see if he's worried from looking at his face. Maybe you can tell from a chance remark, but he isn't a worrier. We have a theory that worry creates a mental block and prevents you from being creative. So worry is a waste of time."

When he is not working, the pianist likes to walk. And when he walks, he says, he walks in a daze. And he and his wife are television addicts.

"I haven't been to the movies in a long time," he said. "I look at TV, see everything there just laying in the bed. You have to get up and go to the movies, where you fall asleep in your chair. That way you're in bed already. But I never get enough sleep. I haven't slept eight hours through in a long time."

Monk is noncommittal about his favorite composers and musicians.

"I listen to 'em all," he says.

But it is hard to believe that he ever goes out of his way to listen to the music of other people. One evidence of this could be that his own work is so self-contained, so very personal. Today, however, he finds little time to write. His most recent composition, "Oska T," was written more than a year ago, and he continually records the same tunes. Why?

"So somebody will hear 'em!" he replied.

For the last 10 years or so, Monk's music has become easier to listen to, though it is not necessarily any simpler. What he is doing is as engaging and profound as ever, though seeming to be less provocative than when he was upsetting the rules.

"If you think my playing is more simple, maybe that's because you can dig it better," Monk said, and laughed. "It takes that long for somebody to hear it, I guess. I mean, for them to understand it or for you to get to them for them to hear it, because you might be changing and then stop playing, and they'd not get a chance to hear it.

"But I never be noticing these things. I just be trying to play."

Nov. 18, 1965

Ella Today (and Yesterday Too)

by Leonard Feather

"I don't know what we're going to talk about," Ella Fitzgerald said a little testily as she closed the front door and walked me into her living room. "All I see is people putting each other down, and I sure don't want to get into anything like that."

Even when the interviewer is an old friend who met her when she was a gawky

Ella Fitzgerald.
(DownBeat Archive)

teenaged vocalist with Chick Webb's band, Ella Fitzgerald is scared of talking for publication. The possibility that conversation may become controversy is as unnatural and terrifying to her as the eruption of a flashbulb during the tenderest moment of a ballad. Demons like these have pursued her through a 30-year professional life, and she can never reconcile herself to such supposedly necessary accoutrements of fame, any more than she can adjust completely to fame itself.

To put the afternoon on an informal basis, we forgot the interview and talked about her house. A handsome, lawn-fronted Beverly Hills home, with another broad grassy area in the back and a pool beyond it, it offers a variety of creature comforts to which Ella has added a few special touches from time to time, among them some exquisite furniture imported from Denmark, the country she considered her second home for a couple of years. The paneled living room has a bar. On a wall facing us, directly above the stereo set, was a large color picture of Norman Granz; beneath it was a photograph of a good friend and admirer of Ella's, the late Marilyn Monroe. On either side were photos of Ella at a recording session.

She brought out an acetate of a newly recorded album, for which Marty Paich had written and conducted the music.

"You want to hear the way I messed up your song?" she asked. As we listened to "Whisper Not," I knew that Benny Golson would feel about her treatment of his composition—the tempo, the mood, the slight variations—just as I felt abut my lyrics.

A few years ago I had learned, the lucky way, that a total understanding of what the Fitzgerald finesse can do for a tune is more easily reached if, like her, you are professionally involved in the writing and/or interpretation of songs. You realize instantly that she knew just what you meant by a certain phrase, that she dug your chord changes or sensed what lyrical point you were to make. You know at once that your few hours of effort have been sublimated by the touch of genius.

As the record played on, she sat with eyes closed most of the time, nodding gently, exhorting the musicians ("Yeah, Lou! Get 'em, Shelly!") and turning to me with an occasional comment. After "Thanks for the Memory": "I did this on *The [Ed] Sullivan Show*, and afterwards I got the cutest note from Bing Crosby." After one of the up-tempo tracks: "This album gets a little

bit back to the jazz thing. It probably won't sell very well; there are too many tunes in it that I like." The remark, made without a trace of rancor, nevertheless had in it a touch of kidding-on-the-square.

"Some arrangements," she said as the conversation veered to Marty Paich, "can really push a singer and make a big difference in the quality of the performance. They can make you sound better than you really are, yet the arrangers very seldom get credit for it. Maybe I feel this way because I started out as a band singer.

"And you can tell whether a singer really likes a song or not—no matter how hard they try with something they do for commercial reasons, if it's a song they are enthusiastic about you can just feel them putting that little something into the performance."

During the "Lover Man" track she said, "Ram Ramirez, who wrote it, was in the room one night in New York, so I did it for him—I didn't even really know the words. I always felt that there was only one person this song belonged to, and I didn't want to follow Lady Day. But the audience response made me keep it in, so now finally, after 20 years, I've recorded it."

During another tune, one with an unusual harmonic shape, she smiled and commented, "I still like songs with changes, songs that present some kind of a challenge and make you say to yourself, 'What are you gonna do with this?'"

One of the tunes was a number I had heard sung by Ethel Ennis. Mention of her name brought a warm endorsement: "Yes, she did a fine job on this. Ethel has a lovely sound and phrases well; she's really one of the best singers coming up.

"You know who else I like? That girl that did 'Somewhere in the Night.' Teri Thornton. Why haven't I head much about her lately?

"There's another singer I liked from the first time I heard her, but not enough people appreciate how much she can do—little Joanie Sommers. She's cute as a button, anyway, and aside from those novelty songs, I heard her sing some ballads somewhere, and I dug the feeling that she gets.

"Barbra Streisand I've never heard in person—I only saw her on the TV special, and that show was just something else. They need more of that kind of thing on television."

Though her own television exposure appears to concentrate on the type of mass-appeal vaudeville show in which she does not always seem entirely at ease, Ella has-

tened to point out the challenge presented:

"I've been fortunate that I was gifted with something whereby I could sing more than one type of thing. Now, the *Bell Telephone Hour* was like a *Song Book* type of appearance; that was one side of Ella. The *Song Book* material is beautiful, but with these show tunes you have to stick to a certain type of material and a main approach, and sometimes you can't do too much with these numbers before you get away from the essence of the tune.

"*The Dean Martin Show* was a ball, Les Brown has the band on it, and they had picked out a couple of things for me, but I always have to say to myself, 'What's it got that's gonna make me feel like I want to sing?' And so Les said, 'Just sing whatever you feel like singing,' so we wound up doing things like 'Mean to Me' and 'Time After Time.'

"Then on *The Andy Williams Show* I did 'Sweet Georgia Brown.' I had a long way to go out on that, really felt I could work with it, and got a happy feeling going. Being around Andy was a gas; he's a marvelous singer with fantastic breath control.

"On each of these shows I did something of a different type; yet each time I probably reached certain people who said, 'Now that's the way I dig her; that's the real Ella.' On another show I might do a little bopping and someone else will make the same kind of remark. Yet I don't want to feel that everything must be in any one of those grooves or that any one is the real Ella."

As we sat quietly chatting in the Beverly Hills setting, I thought of the real Ella Fitzgerald as I had met her 30 years earlier one Wednesday night at the noisy, stomping, crowded Savoy Ballroom at 140th and Lenox in New York.

Edgar Sampson, the Chick Webb band arranger, had introduced me to the orchestra's recently acquired 17-year-old interpreter of rhythm songs. (Webb, for the first year or two, felt she was not ready to sing ballads. Once, when a song she liked had been arranged for her but was reassigned by Webb to the male singer, Ella burst into tears on the bandstand.)

The clarion brilliance of the orchestra was interrupted now and then by the typically pompous male ballad singer, then one of Webb's proudest assets, but now long forgotten. At similar intervals there would be a number that included a vocal by Ella, her voice higher and thinner in texture but not greatly dissimilar in style to the Ella of today.

At that stage, the path of her progress had reached its second major way station. Only a year or so had passed since the traumatic moment when she was booed off the stage during an amateur hour at the Lafayette Theater in Harlem—one of the few minor chords in the affirmatively orchestrated chart of her career.

The Hollywood producer, looking for a story in Ella Fitzgerald, will find nothing downbeat enough or neurotic enough to keep his scriptwriter's pen filled with bitter blue ink.

True, she never knew her father nor her hometown of Newport News, Va., but she had pleasant memories of her childhood in Yonkers, N.Y., where her mother and stepfather raised her. Though she looked a little undernourished and constantly had to be prevailed on to drink more milk, she was a healthy youngster whose idea of a good time was dancing, singing, sneaking off during lunch hour at junior high to catch singer Dolly Dawn at the local theater with George Hall's orchestra, or listening to the radio for a show featuring the Boswell Sisters, one of whom, Connee, was to become her favorite and decisive vocal influence.

"Everybody in Yonkers thought I was a good dancer," she recalled. "I really wanted to be a dancer. One day, two girl friends and I drew straws to decide which of us would go on the amateur hour. I drew the short straw, and that's how I got started winning all those shows."

Though dancing was still her first love, she sang on that initial appearance, and won. In the Apollo audience was Benny Carter, who with John Hammond took her to Fletcher Henderson's house. ("I guess Fletcher wasn't too impressed. He said, 'Don't call me; I'll call you!'")

Soon after, somebody at CBS heard the word, and contracts were drawn up for a show with Arthur Tracy, the "Street Singer," which at that stage of broadcasting history was equivalent to an opportunity today for an unknown youngster to make her debut on Andy Williams' show. At the critical moment the plan collapsed with the death of Ella's mother. Orphaned, a minor, she had nobody to take the legal responsibility of signing a contract for her, and a week later she returned to the amateur-hour circuit.

It was during that brief period of gloom that she scored her one miss. Looking slightly forlorn in a black dress, she walked nervously onstage and sang "Lost in a Fog." ("The pianist didn't know the chords, and I really was lost.") She ran offstage to the accompaniment of catcalls. But it was not long until she worked her first professional week, for $50, at the Harlem Opera House.

Tiny Bradshaw's band was in the show. "Everyone had their coats on," she said, "and was ready to leave when Tiny introduced me. He said, 'Ladies and gentlemen, here's the young girl that's been winning all the contests,' and they all came back and took off their coats and sat down again."

The band due to follow Bradshaw at the theater was Chick Webb's. Despite warm endorsements from Benny Carter and Bardu Ali, the showman who fronted Chick's band, the drummer refused to entertain the thought of supplementing his vocal department; he was happy with the since-forgotten male crooner.

"He just didn't want a girl singer, so finally they hid me in his dressing room and forced him to listen," Ella said. "I only knew three songs, all the things I'd heard Connee Boswell do: 'Judy,' 'The Object of My Affection' and 'Believe It, Beloved.' Chick didn't seem sold, but he agreed to take me on a one-nighter to Yale the next day. Tiny and the chorus girls had all kicked in to buy me a gown. The following week we opened at the Savoy, and I guess you know the rest."

The only pauses in the steady upward graph from that point were the death in 1939 of Webb, who had become her guardian and mentor (Ella then took over leadership of the band herself for two years), and two marriages that failed to work out. Yet a conversation with Ella today would seem to indicate that of all the nights she can remember—and they include thousands of triumphs in clubs, theaters, and at festivals and concert halls around the world—the one that remains strongest in her memory is the night at the Lafayette. It would be melodramatic to claim she has a fear that it could happen again; yet her sensitivity to criticism, and to anything less than complete audience acceptance, has been a constant source of tension for her and for those around her.

A few months ago, working a typical European concert tour on a characteristically grueling schedule, the insecurities mounted to a point without precedent.

"We were running from one town to another, and I began to feel I just couldn't take it," she said. "One night I thought I was about ready to faint onstage. Gus Johnson [the drummer in her accompanying group] had to lead me off, and I was almost literally trying to climb the backstage walls."

A doctor, warning that she was on the verge of a nervous breakdown, advised Granz to cancel most of her engagements. For a while the word was around that she would not work for the rest of the year. Only a few weeks elapsed, though, before she was tired of resting at home and ready to take on a few television shows. It is doubtful, though, that she will ever again invite the emotional chaos that was brought on by the one-nighter rat race.

Ironically, the European scene basically was a morale booster. "With the trend like it is now," she said, "the teenage sounds and everything, it's almost like you're afraid. There's nothing worse in life for a performer than to go out there and do nothing with an audience. I'm very self-conscious about people not liking me. I had gotten in a rut for three or four months at home, and I just began to feel like, well, I don't have it, you know when you don't have a big hit record going for you. It took Gus and a lot of people to convince me that those things aren't everything."

Despite the depressing overall trend in U.S. popular music as she diagnoses it from the Top 40 charts, Ella hears a hopeful note in the increased musical sophistication of the college audiences:

"I think we're building a bigger and better audience for the concert-type show at colleges and universities. There is a more mature crowd ready to show that they feel something has been missing. Look at the concert we did last spring in Los Angeles with Count Basie's band and Tony Bennett: we had a packed house, and the audience was not only college age but people in their 30s and 40s.

"The audience really listened, too. Back in the early days of the tours with Norman, everything was just hollering. They didn't really listen to what you were doing; they just hollered. But today it's a pleasure when you do one of those concerts. With stereo and everything, people have become more music-conscious instead of just looking for noise and excitement.

"I would like to see Norman bring back Jazz at the Philharmonic in this country, with the kind of show these audiences would go for today. I think this is the right time for it."

Her relationship with Granz has been

the most durably fruitful of her career. When the band that Ella had inherited from Webb hit Los Angeles 25 years ago, some of the men earned an occasional extra $6 a night for playing at jam sessions run by the youthful Granz in a small local club.

"Sure, he used my musicians, but he didn't want me—he didn't dig me," Ella recalled with a smile.

A few years later, when Granz had moved from the clubs to concert halls and had bassist Ray Brown as a member of his road company, Ella came to a concert to see Brown. Spotted in the audience, she was asked to do a number. Granz grudgingly agreed, and Ella proceeded to gas the entire assemblage, including Granz. He offered her a contract, and she has remained the staple of his entourage from that day in 1948 until now.

During the early 1950s, Granz moved closer and closer into the picture. Despite the fact that she was with a booking agency and had another manager, he was instrumental in helping her to attain many goals that seemed beyond reach. For several years, with mortifying reluctance, he had to cut all her parts out of the series of JATP concert albums, because she was still contracted to Decca (and was still recording, for the most part, conventional pop songs with conventional backgrounds that did little to advance her musically). Not until 1955, when he finally negotiated a release for her, was Granz at last able to place her on his own label, Verve.

Not too long afterward, on a handshake basis, a personal management setup was established. For the last few years, though he now lives in Switzerland, Granz has continued to do a magisterial job, much of it by long-distance telephone, of guiding Ella's career. He still flies to this country every time she has a record date.

Granz and Ella fight as much as most artists and managers, perhaps more than most. The disagreements, often as not, concern choice of material.

"One time in Milan," Granz recalled, "she wouldn't sing 'April in Paris,' even though it was her big record at the time; she let the audience shout her into 'Lady, Be Good.' When she came offstage she yelled at me, and I yelled louder at her, and we didn't speak to one another for three days. Some night I may tell her to do six songs, but she feels good and goes out there and stays on for an hour and a half. It's part of her whole approach to life—the desire to sing and to please people by singing."

Her desire to stay as long as she is wanted can easily be understood. Onstage, in command of an audience, she reveals little of the inner tensions that have wracked her so deeply. Offstage she can relapse too easily into a self-concern for which there is rarely, if ever, any artistic justification.

A typical incident that shook her fragile composure was the *Life* magazine story on Frank Sinatra a few months ago, in which he assessed some of his contemporaries, including Ella, whom he had known and admired apparently without qualification for 25 years.

"Frank said I didn't know how to breathe right, and my phrasing was all wrong," she said. "I was so upset about that, I really couldn't sing for a week."

It was not enough for anyone to assure her that similar criticism made of Sinatra by a fellow singer would roll off his back like Jack Daniels, and that his criticism of her, according to a heavy majority opinion, is not supported by the facts. But Ella's thin skin made it hard for her to take this one little sprinkle of negative comment, from a place she looks up to as the peak of the mountain despite the thunderstorms of praise that have fallen on her since long before Sinatra's name was ever heard of in music. To her, the Sinatra put-down was just another reminder of the uncertainties of her profession and of a situation that accords her a mere 99.99 percent of universal acceptance.

"The music business is funny," she said, "You hear somebody this year, and next year nothing happens. If you don't know anything else in life... well, when you start out it's a pleasure, but later on it becomes your livelihood. For anyone who loves music as much as I do, it's a part of you, and you don't want to ever feel defeated."

Told that her worldwide public image over the last three decades was more important than one man's opinion or her current position in the charts and polls, she replied, "Yes, you can keep telling yourself that, but you can't always believe it deep down. I needed that boost overseas, because I felt like nothing was happening here. And it was great, until the overwork caught up with me. Paris was wonderful. Dublin this year was just unbelievable. I just stood there onstage and cried; the audience was just too much. We played Hamburg, and they wouldn't let me off; of course, they are very, very music-conscious there."

The shifting areas of music-consciousness in her native land and the musical leanings of the younger generation give rise to mixed feelings in Ella, who has watched the problem impinge slowly on her own family life.

"Raymond is 16," she said, indicating the strapping young man, an inch over six feet tall, who had just arrived home from Beverly Hills High School. "I've got a little problem trying to make up my mind what to do about his music. He had a fine teacher, Bill Douglass, who said he has a good feeling for drums. He's got that edge, and I would like him to take advantage of it, not just play the Ringo beat, which is what I call it because that's where it all started. But he does these little weekend gigs for a few dollars, and it's very exciting to him; but I'd like for him to concentrate on learning to read music so that he can do more with his ability. It's a good thing that his father [Ray Brown, who was married to Ella from 1948 to 1952] is coming to Los Angeles to live. He'll probably stay behind him and make him realize he's got to do more. I don't think Ray is in favor of his playing with these types of groups."

For all her reservations about the premature career of Ray Jr., Ella will not invoke a blanket put-down of rock and roll. She recorded a Beatles song, "Can't Buy Me Love," wrote one of her own called "Ringo" ("but the disc jockeys just wouldn't play it") and retains too much of a sense of humor to be unduly bugged by the musical and personal eccentricities she sees on television.

The Ella Fitzgerald who came home from Europe in a state of semi-collapse is yesterday's child. Today, though still easily bruised, she is more relaxed, seems to have a firmer sense of her own direction and looks forward with enthusiasm to a greater measure of spare time.

"I've got music stacked six feet high over in that other room—songs people have sent me that I never got a chance to look at," she said. "Thousands of them. I want to really go through them and find some fresh, unused, good quality tunes. I've been running so fast for so long that I never got a chance before.

"I want to catch up on my music studies, too. Sure, I can read music, but not as well as I'd like to.

"I've always wanted to play vibes and guitar. Well, you see that guitar case over there? That's my guitar, and I really want to learn. Herb Ellis may be coming out with me on some dates, and I'd like to take lessons from him. I've got the chord books and everything."

Did she plan to play jazz guitar, bossa nova or just simple chord accompaniments?

"I could never play bossa nova style," she answered. "Not that I wouldn't love to. I love some of the things that Antonio Carlos Jobim does. He gave me a tune one day that nobody's done vocally, at least not in English, I don't think." She hummed a few bars of "So Danco Samba (Jazz 'n' Samba)." "You know it? It's a real swinger the way he does it in the album. Yeah, I dig that! But I would just like to learn guitar because there are a lot of folk tunes, and other kinds of beautiful songs, where maybe I could just help out by adding a few chords of my own.

"We haven't arranged a starting date yet for my lessons, because I'm all tied up now getting ready for a new album with Duke Ellington. By the time this article is printed, it'll be finished. Jimmy Jones— now there's a great underrated talent— Jimmy is coming out to get my keys and work on some of the music for Duke. This ought to help smooth things out a little, because the last time, it was a panic scene, with Duke almost making up the arrangements as we went along. Duke is a genius. I admire him as much as anyone in the world; but doing it that way, even though it was a lot of fun at times, got to be kind of nerve wracking."

As we made plans to meet again at one of the Ellington dates, Ella came to the door, stopping for a moment to show me the autographed photograph of her with President Lyndon Johnson, which he had signed when she made a recent appearance to aid the campaign against school dropouts. The pride and humility with which she talked about the meeting reflected the persistent paradox of her life. Catapulted into a world that demands more and more work, often intense egocentricity and bitter rivalry in the fight for the gold-plated plaque at the end of the rainbow, she has remained one of the few singers for whom the typical American goals remain normal. Because it has always been the singing itself that means most to her, and because her modesty and musical honesty remain deeply ingrained, there never was any danger that Ella would go the wrong route— the route taken by those who, hell-bent for financial gain, become artistic dropouts.

As she stood at the door, she smiled broadly. Her parting remark seemed to be made almost to herself:

"Well, it wasn't such an ordeal after all, was it?"

Blindfold Test

Harry Carney and Gerry Mulligan

by Leonard Feather

The Battle of the Baritones came about purely by chance. Harry Carney was in town; I had never conducted a Blindfold Test with him and made a solo appointment. Then Gerry Mulligan, who has visited this page three times before (but not in the last five years), became available on the same day. As any student of the saxophone should know, Carney is to the baritone what Coleman Hawkins is to the tenor. In addition to his role as founding father, he has the unique distinction of being the sideman of longest duration in any jazz group now extant, having recently started his 40th year as a member of the Duke Ellington Orchestra.

Mulligan, though only 38, may seem to younger jazz fans like a senior citizen, almost two decades having passed since he went to New York from Philadelphia and joined Gene Krupa's big band.

1. Donald Byrd. "6 M's" (from *Royal Flush*, Blue Note). Byrd, trumpet, composer; Pepper Adams, baritone saxophone.

H.C.: They all got in a very good blues mood there. It had a nice feeling all the way. I don't know who the baritone player was, but he got a good, big sound.

G.M.: It was interesting to me in that this is essentially a very basic, three-chord blues thing, and under these circumstances, sometimes it's difficult for a soloist to keep his conception on a very elementary level harmonically. It seems to me that the trumpet player did this more completely than the baritone, who tended to become little more complicated.

H.C.: I'd say it's worth four stars.

G.M.: I'll go along with that.

2. Woody Herman. "I Remember Duke" (from *Road Band*, Capitol). Herman, clarinet, composer; Nat Pierce, piano; Jack Nimitz, baritone saxophone. Recorded in 1955.

G.M.: Yeah! Woody!

H.C.: Right—you can't mistake that sound. It was a hard-swinging band, too. There was a little Ellington touch when they used the plungers in that first chorus…. I liked the stride piano effect, but he didn't keep it going.

G.M.: I'm trying to figure out which Herman band this is. It could be from the early period. There was one passage that sounded like an awkward splice, but I wonder whether it wasn't made before they started using tape. Anyhow, the solo work was good. The baritone was effective toward the end, but he used some questionable changes. As far as his sound is concerned, he sounded like me; from the period this comes from, and the uncertainty about changes, it could be Serge Chaloff.

H.C.: I liked it three-and-a-half stars' worth. Baritone was nice on the whole.

G.M.: I'd say about three.

3. John Coltrane. "Chim Chim Cheree" (from *John Coltrane Plays…*, Impulse). Coltrane, soprano saxophone; McCoy Tyner, piano; Jimmy Garrison, bass; Elvin Jones, drums.

H.C.: The tune itself is all right; we played it in the Ellington album of *Mary Poppins* tunes. I liked the part in front where they played the melody. Then it started going into those Eastern sounds, almost like an Oriental-type instrument, instead of a saxophone. I've heard things like that played in the Middle East. It gets kind of monotonous after a while. The rhythm section was good. I'd give it maybe two to three stars.

G.M.: You're right, it did get to sound like a double-reed instrument. It wasn't exactly my favorite record. I'd agree with your rating.

4. Maynard Ferguson. "The Lady's in Love with You" (from *Color Him Wild*, Mainstream). Ferguson, trumpet; Ronnie Cuber, baritone saxophone; Don Rader, arranger.

H.C.: There seemed to be some difference between the balance on the saxophone passages and the sound on the rest of it—it didn't match. But the trumpet player was good, and the arrangement built up well enough.

G.M.: The baritone player sounded like he had a hell of a lot to say, but…

H.C.: But he was trying to say it all at once.

G.M.: Right. And between the big sound and everything he was blowing, it

Harry Carney and
Gerry Mulligan.
(Ted Williams)

got to be a bit overpowering. You can get a sound like that just by getting right on top of the microphone. He eased up a little later in the solo. I'd say three stars.

H.C.: Make mine three and a half.

5. Elvin Jones. "Elvin Elpus" (from *And Then Again*, Atlantic). Charles Davis, baritone saxophone; Jones, drums; Melba Liston, composer.

G.M.: Boy, that just had to be a date where the drummer was the leader. There was no mistaking that. There sure was an awful lot going on, but it didn't jell too well. It just wouldn't be fair to judge the baritone player by what he does here.

H.C.: I think that what they were attempting here had some possibilities, but perhaps they should have devoted more time to it. Three stars.

G.M.: He gives it three stars because he's nicer than I am. I'll give it two. Incidentally, they didn't do very well with the 5/4 meter; it sounded more like an unswinging job of 3/4.

6. Gerry Mulligan and Ben Webster.

"Chelsea Bridge" (from *Mulligan Meets Webster*, Verve). Webster, tenor saxophone; Mulligan, baritone saxophone; Billy Strayhorn, composer.

G.M.: Ten stars! Anything Benjie plays on automatically gets 10.

H.C.: Of course, Ben can do no wrong, and here he's playing this beautiful opening solo; yet you're forced also to listen to Gerry's obbligato. This commands immediate attention right at the beginning of the record, and all the way through there's something to keep listening for and you always know it's going to come off. Gerry does just about everything good that can be done on the baritone; in terms of mood, quality, taste, control, ideas, it was perfect; and the tune itself, of course, is beautiful.

G.M.: God, I love to play with Ben.

H.C.: I'm sure, by the same token, he had a ball.

G.M.: It's very hard for me to select one album as the best of all I ever made, but this really does rate as my favorite.

H.C.: I'll go the limit on that one. Five and then five more!

7. Duke Ellington. "Rhapsody in Blue" (from *Will Big Bands Ever Come Back?*, Reprise). Jimmy Hamilton, clarinet; Paul Gonsalves, tenor saxophone; Harry Carney, baritone saxophone; Sam Woodyard, drums; George Gershwin, composer; Billy Strayhorn, arranger.

G.M.: What a wonderful opening. I'll give it five stars on its own and another five for Harry. I also love the beautiful, gentle tenor solo that Paul plays. Jimmy Hamilton's solo was fine, and the arrangement was great.

The only passage I wasn't too crazy about was where it got into the use of the kettle-drum effects, making it a very percussive thing. It was a little in the style of the way Whiteman played it when Ferde Grofe orchestrated it. I know what the intent was, but it's a really haunting melody, and I prefer not to hear that done to it. I never did like the Whiteman version.

On second thought, I don't even mind that part; I like the whole arrangement. Nothing associated with the Ellington sound ever needs any justification.

H.C.: The arranger was beautiful.

The arranger is beautiful. And, of course, it comes out in this.

G.M.: That Swee'pea?

H.C.: Yes.

G.M.: It was gorgeous.

Afterthoughts by H.C., G.M.

G.M.: Baritone players tend to have an inconsistency of sound between different parts of their register. Some baritone men can't work up a consistent sound because they use it as a secondary instrument.

H.C.: This session has been most enlightening and enjoyable. I've heard some fine baritone players.

G.M.: Yes, I heard some interesting things and some wonderful playing, but I still have only one favorite baritone player—even if he does happen to be sitting here.

H.C.: You must be getting into ESP—you just beat me to the punch, vice versa!

Oct. 20, 1966

Art Tatum

Genius in Retrospect

by Rex Stewart

At every dance that Fletcher Henderson's band played, there'd be someone boasting about hometown talent. Usually, the local talent was pretty bad, and we were reluctant to take the word of anyone but a darngood musician, such as alto saxophonist Milton Senior of MiKinney's Cotton Pickers, who was touting a piano player.

"Out of this world," Milton said. We were persuaded to go to the club where this pianist was working.

The setting was not impressive; it was in an alley, in the middle of Toledo's Bohemian section. I'm not sure if the year was 1926 or 1927, but I am sure that my first impression of Art Tatum was a lasting one. As a matter of fact, the experience was almost traumatic for me, and for a brief spell afterward, I toyed with the idea of giving up my horn and returning to school.

Looking back, I can see why Tatum had this effect on me. Not only did he play all that piano, but, by doing so, he also reminded me of how inadequately I was filling Louis Armstrong's chair with the Henderson band.

To a man, we were astonished, gassed, and just couldn't believe our eyes and ears. How could this nearly blind young fellow extract so much beauty out of an old beat-up upright piano that looked like a relic from the Civil War? Our drummer, Kaiser Marshall, turned to Henderson and said it for all of us:

"Well, it just goes to show you can't judge a book by its cover. There's a beat-up old piano, and that kid makes it sound like a Steinway. Go ahead, Smack, let's see you sit down to that box. I bet it won't come out the same."

Fletcher just shrugged his shoulders and answered philosophically, "I am pretty sure that we are in the presence of one of the greatest talents that you or I will ever hear. So don't try to be funny."

Coleman Hawkins was so taken by Tatum's playing that he immediately started creating another style for himself, based on what he'd heard Tatum play that night—and forever after dropped his slap-tongue style.

To our surprise, this talented youngster was quite insecure and asked us humbly, "Do you think I can make it in the big city [meaning New York]?" We assured him that he would make it, that the entire world would be at his feet once he put Toledo behind him. Turning away, he sadly shook his head, saying, kind of to himself, "I ain't ready yet."

However, as far as we were concerned, he was half-past ready! I can see now that Tatum really thought he was too green and unequipped for the Apple, because he spent the next few years in another alley in another Ohio city—Cleveland—at a place called Val's.

It was probably at Val's that Paul Whiteman "discovered" him a year or so later, when Art was 19, and took him to New York to be featured with the Whiteman band. But insecurity and homesickness combined to make him miserable, and after a short time, he fled back to Toledo. This is a good example of a man being at the crossroads and taking the wrong turn.

After returning home, Tatum gradually became confident that he could hold his own. When Don Redman was passing through Toledo a year or so later, Art told him, "Tell them New York cats to look out. Here comes Tatum! And I mean every living 'tub' with the exception of Fats Waller and Willie the Lion."

At that time, Art had never heard of Donald (the Beetle) Lambert, a famous

young piano player around New York in the '20s, and he came into the picture too late to have heard Seminole, an American Indian guitar and piano player whose left hand was actually faster than most pianists' right hands. In any case, to Tatum, Fats was Mr. Piano.

The admiration was reciprocated. The story goes that Fats, the cheerful little earful, was in great form while appearing in the Panther Room of the Sherman Hotel in Chicago. Fats was in orbit that night, slaying the crowd, singing and wiggling his behind to his hit "Honeysuckle Rose."

Suddenly he jumped up like he'd been stung by a bee and, in one of those rapid changes of character for which he was famous, announced in stentorian tones: "Ladies and gentlemen, God is in the house tonight. May I introduce the one and only Art Tatum."

I did not witness this scene, but so many people have related the incident that I am inclined to believe it. At any rate, before Tatum did much playing in New York, he spent a period of time with vocalist Adelaide Hall as part of a two-piano team, the other accompanist being Joe Turner (the pianist). Miss Hall, then big in the profession, took them with her on a European tour.

In appearance, Tatum was not especially noteworthy. His was not a face that one would pick out of a crowd. He was about 5 feet, 7 inches tall and of average build when he was young but grew somewhat portly over the years. Art was not only a rather heavy drinker but was also fond of home cooking and savored good food. As he became affluent, his favorite restaurant was Mike Lyman's in Hollywood, which used to be one of Los Angeles' best.

An only child, Tatum was born in Toledo on Oct. 13, 1910. He came into the world with milk cataracts in both eyes, which impaired his sight to the point of almost total blindness. After 13 operations, the doctors were able to restore a considerable amount of vision in one eye. Then Tatum had a great misfortune; he was assaulted by a holdup man, who, in the scuffle, hit Tatum in the good eye with a blackjack. The carefully restored vision was gone forever, and Tatum was left with the ability to see only large objects or smaller ones held very close to his "good" eye.

Art had several fancy stories to explain his blindness, and a favorite was to tell in great detail how a football injury caused his lack of sight. I've heard him go into the routine: he was playing halfback for his high school team on this rainy day; they were in the huddle; then lined up; the ball was snapped… wait a minute—there's a fumble! Tatum recovers… he's at the 45-yard line, the 35, the 25! Sprinting like mad, he is heading for a touchdown! Then, out of nowhere, a mountain falls on him and just before oblivion descends, Tatum realized he has been tackled by Two-Ton Tony, the biggest fellow on either team. He is carried off the field, a hero, but has had trouble with his eyes ever since.

The real stories about Art are so unusual that one could drag out the cliché about fact being stranger than fiction. When Art was three, his mother took him along to choir practice. After they returned home, she went into the kitchen to prepare dinner and heard someone fumbling with a hymn on the piano. Assuming that a member of the church had dropped by and was waiting for her come out of the kitchen, she called out, "Who's there?" No one answered, so she entered the parlor, and there sat three-year-old Art, absorbed in playing the hymn.

He continued playing piano by ear, and he could play anything he heard. Curiously, there was once a counterpart of Tatum in a slave known as Blind Tom. Tom earned a fortune for his master, performing before amazed audiences the most difficult music of his time after a single hearing. But Tom couldn't improvise; he lacked the added gift that was Tatum's.

Tatum played piano several years before starting formal training. He learned to read notes in Braille. He would touch the Braille manuscript, play a few bars on the piano, touch the notation, play… until he completed a tune. After that, he never "read" the song again; he knew it forever. He could play any music he had ever heard. One time, at a recording session, the singer asked if he knew a certain tune. Art answered, "Hum a few bars." As the singer hummed, Art was not more than a half-second behind, playing the song with chords and embellishments as if he had always known it, instead of hearing it then for the first time.

His mother, recognizing that he had an unusual ear, gave him four years of formal training in the classics. Then the day came when the teacher called a halt to the studies, saying, "That's as far as I can teach you. Now, you teach me."

Tatum carried his perception to the nth degree. Eddie Beal, one of Art's devoted disciples, recalls their first meeting,

Art Tatum, publicity photo.

which happened at the old Breakfast Club on Los Angeles' Central Avenue at about 4 a.m. The news had spread that Tatum was in town and could be expected to make the scene that morning. Just as Tatum entered the room, as Beal tells it, "Whoever was playing the piano jumped up from the stool, causing an empty beer can to fall off the piano. Tatum greeted the cats all around, then said, 'Drop that can again. It's a Pabst can, and the note it sounded was a B-flat.'" Rozelle Gayle, one of Tatum's closest friends, tops this story by saying that Tatum could tell the key of any sound, including a flushing toilet.

Genius is an overworked word in this era of thunderous hyperbolic press agentry.

Still, when one considers Arthur Tatum, there is no other proper descriptive adjective for referring to his talents. I have purposely pluralized them, for Tatum possessed several gifts—most of which remained unknown to all but a few of his best friends—his prodigious memory, his grasp of all sports statistics and his skill at playing cards.

Art was a formidable opponent in all types of card games, although bid whist was his favorite. There are a few bridge champions still around who recall the fun they had when Tatum played with them. According to one's reminiscence, Art would pick up his cards as dealt, hold them about one inch from the good eye, adjust them into suits and from then on, never looked at his hand again. He could actually recall every card that was played, when, and by whom. Furthermore, he played his own cards like a master.

He had an incredible memory not only for cards but also for voices as well. One account of his aptitude in catching voices has been told and retold. It seems that while playing London with Adelaide Hall back in the late '30s, he was introduced to a certain person and immediately swept along the receiving line. Six years later, when he was playing in Hollywood, the person came to see Tatum. He greeted him with, "Hello, Art. How are you? I'll bet you don't remember me." Tatum replied, "Sure I remember you. Gee, you're looking good. I'm sorry I didn't get a chance to talk to you at that party in London. Your name is Lord So and So."

I realize that nature has a way of compensating for any inaccuracy, but Tatum's abilities transcended ordinary compensation. With only a high school education, he was a storehouse of information. His favorite sports were baseball and football, followed by horseracing. Tatum could quote baseball pitchers' records, batting averages for almost all players in both big leagues, names and positions for almost all players, the game records any year, and so forth. Rozelle Gayle, one of Tatum's closest friends, recalls back in Art's Chicago days (the '30s) that all the musicians frequented the drugstore on the corner of 47th Street and South Park. Art became so respected as an authority on any subject (and that included population statistics) that the fellows would have him settle their arguments, instead of telephoning a newspaper.

Despite impaired vision, he was a very independent man. He had little methods to avoid being helped. For example, he always asked the bank to give all his money in new $5 bills, which he put in a certain pocket. When he had to pay for something, he gave a 5 and then counted his change by fingering the $1 bills and feeling the coins. The 1s then went into a certain pocket and the coins into another. He had a mind like an adding machine and always knew exactly how much money he had.

One of the most significant aspects of Tatum's artistry stemmed from his constant self-change.

At the piano, Art seemingly delighted in creating impossible problems from the standpoint of harmonies and chord progressions. Then he would gleefully improvise sequence upon sequence until the phrase emerged as a complete entity within the structure of whatever composition he happened to be playing. Many is the time I have heard him speed blithely into what I feared was a musical cul-de-sac, only to hear the tying resolution come shining through. This required great knowledge, dexterity and daring. Tatum achieved much of this through constant practice, working hours every day on the exercises to keep his fingers nimble enough to obey that quick, creative mind. He did not run through variations of songs or work on new inventions to dazzle his audiences. Rather, he ran scales and ordinary practice exercises, and if one didn't know who was doing the laborious, monotonous piano routines, he would never guess that it was a jazzman working out.

Another form of practice was unique with Tatum. He constantly manipulated a filbert nut through his fingers, so quickly that if you tried to watch him, the vision blurred. He worked with one nut until it became sleek and shiny from handling. When it came time to replace it, he would go to the market and feel nut after nut—a whole bin full, until he found one just the right size and shape for his exercises. Art's hands were of unusual formation, though just the normal size for a man of his height and build. But when he wanted to, he somehow could make his fingers span a 12th on the keyboard. The average male hand spans nine or 10 of the white notes, 11 is considered wizard, but 12 is out of this world. Perhaps the spread developed from that seeming complete relaxation of the fingers—they never rose far above the keyboard and looked almost double-jointed as he ran phenomenally rapid, complex runs. His lightning execution was the result of all that practice, along with the instant communication between his fingers and brain. His touch produced a sound no other pianist has been able to capture. The method he used was his secret, which he never revealed. The Steinway was his favorite piano, but sometimes he played in a club that had a miserable piano with broken ivories and sour notes. He would run his fingers over the keyboard to detect these. Then he would play that night in keys that would avoid as much as possible the bad notes. Anything he could play, he could play in any key.

With all that talent, perhaps it is not strange the effect that Art had on other pianists. When he went where they were playing, his presence made them uncomfortable. Some would hunt for excuses to keep from playing in front of the master. Others would make all kinds of errors on things that, under other circumstances, they could play without even thinking about it. There was the case of the young fellow who played a great solo, not being aware that Tatum was in the house. When Art congratulated him later, he fainted.

This sort of adulation did not turn Tatum's head, and he continually sought reassurance after a performance. Any friend who was present would be asked, "How was it?" One couldn't ask for more humility from a king of his instrument.

A little-known fact is that Art also played the accordion. Back in Ohio, before he had gained success, he was offered a year's contract in a nightclub if he would double on accordion. He quickly mastered the instrument and fulfilled the engagement, but he never liked the accordion and after that gig, he never played it again.

Tatum always liked to hear other piano players, young or old, male or female. He could find something kind to say even about quite bad performers. Sometimes his companion would suggest leaving a club where the pianist could only play some clunky blues in one key. But Art would say, "No, I want to hear his story. Every piano player has a story to tell."

His intimates (two of whom—Eddie Beal and Rozelle Gayle—I thank for much of this information) agree that Tatum's favorites on the piano were Fats Waller, Willie (the Lion) Smith and Earl Hines. He also liked lots of the youngsters, including Nat Cole, Billy Taylor and Hank Jones.

In the days when most musicians enjoyed hanging out with each other, Art and Meade Lux Lewis palled around; Two more dissimilar chums could hardly be imagined. Tatum was a rather brooding, bearlike figure of a man, and Meade Lux was a plumper, jolly little fellow. They kept a running joke going between themselves, Meade Lux cracking that Art was cheap, even if Tatum was paying the tab.

Tatum's leisure hours began when almost everyone else was asleep, at 4 a.m. or so. He liked to sit and talk, drink and play, after he finished work.

There was a serious and well-hidden side to the man. His secret ambition was to become known as a classical composer, and somewhere there exist fragments of compositions he put on tape for orchestration at some later date.

Tatum also wanted, very definitely, to be featured as a soloist accompanied by the Boston or New York symphony orchestras, which he considered among the world's best. As a matter of record, this admiration for the longer-haired musical forms was mirrored; he had numerous fans among classical players, who were astonished at his skill, technique and imagination. To them, his gifts were supernatural. Vladimir Horowitz, who frequently came to hear Art play, said that if Tatum had taken up classical piano, he'd have been outstanding in the field.

It's been said that Tatum forced today's one-hand style of piano into being because after he'd finished playing all over the instrument with both hands, the only way for the piano to go was back, until the people forgot how much Tatum played.

Another of Art's ambitions, also unrealized, was to be a blues singer! He loved to relax by playing and singing the blues. He knew he didn't have much of a voice, but when he was offstage, he'd sing the blues. He had a feeling for the form but kept that side of himself well hidden from the public. He really adored Blind Lemon Jefferson, Bessie Smith and, especially, Big Joe Turner.

Most musicians could never guess what Art was going to play from one moment to the next, which made the group he had with guitarist Tiny Grimes and bassist Slam Stewart unquestionably the best combo he ever had. The trio played on New York's 52nd Street around 1945. These three communicated, anticipated and embellished each other as if one person were playing all three instruments. It was uncanny when it's considered that they never played it safe, never put in hours of rehearsal with each sequence pinpointed. On the contrary, every tune was an adventure, since nobody could predict where Art's mind would take them.

Tatum loved to go from one key to another without his left hand ever breaking the rhythm of his stride. Even in this, he was unpredictable, since he never went to the obvious transpositions, like a third above. No, Art would jump from B-flat to E-natural and make the listener love it.

While Art was alive, and as great as he was, there were still a few detractors. One such critic had been trained as a classical pianist but was trying desperately to apply his academic training to jazz. This fellow said, during one of Tatum's superb performances, "Sure, Art's great, but he fingers the keys the wrong way."

How sour can grapes get?

Another compatriot who used to haunt every place that Art played, night after night, made the public statement: "Good God! This Tatum is the greatest! Thank God he's black—otherwise nobody's job would be safe." I suspect there was a lot of truth in that remark.

Art never seemed to let the inequities of his situation bother him. Still, in the early morning when he had consumed a few cans of beer and was surrounded by his personal camp followers, he would unburden himself, asking, "Did you hear so-and-so's latest record? What a waste of wax, for Christ's sake! There must be over 2,000 fellows who can play more than this cat. But you see who he's recording for? It will probably sell half a million copies while Willie the Lion just sits back smoking his cigar, without a gig. When will it end?"

Tatum was a great crusader against discrimination, but in his own quiet way. He used to cancel engagements if he found that the club excluded colored persons. Loyalty to his friends, even when it was not advantageous to his career, was another strong point. (I recall the time I went to catch him at a club called the Streets of Paris, in Los Angeles. After a period of superlative enjoyment, I went to the piano to pay my respects and leave. But just as Art said, "Hello, how long have you been in the joint?" Cesar Romero and Loretta Young walked up. So I stepped back to let Art converse with the movie royalty. Art said, "Come on back here. I want to introduce you. Cesar, Loretta, I want you to meet Rex Stewart," and went on to build me up, undeservedly, till they asked for my autograph!)

Art was no glad-hander. He was polite, reserved, affable but not particularly communicative unless the conversation was about one of his hobbies. A more self-effacing person would be hard to find, and he was generous to a fault with his friends. Yet he could summon up a tremendous amount of outraged dignity when it was called for.

Perhaps Art Tatum would have been assured a firmer place in musical history if he had not alienated too many of the self-righteous aficionados who preferred their piano sounds less embroidered, less imaginative and more orthodox. Therefore, it follows that Tatum would never be their favorite pianist. Posterity tends to prove that Art requires neither champion nor defense, since the proof of his genius remains intact and unblemished. The

beauty within the framework of his music transcends the opinions of critics, aficionados, fans and musicians themselves. History is the arbiter. For the truly great, fame is not fleeting but everlasting.

Dec. 1, 1966

On the Boardwalk with Johnny Hodges

by Stanley Dance

"Will my bodyguard be ready at 7?" Johnny Hodges was preparing for his daily march from the Hotel Dennis to the ballroom at the end of the Steel Pier in Atlantic City, N.J., where Duke Ellington's band was playing a week last August. It may not have been a mile, but it seemed like it that hot, humid evening, because holidaymakers jammed the Boardwalk. Although he had been playing with organist Wild Bill Davis until nearly daybreak, Hodges looked surprisingly fit as he sauntered along.

"I don't sleep long at a time," he said. "I gave up cigarettes six years ago, and I haven't had a drink since April 26, when the doctor said it would be best for me to quit. Now… you see that shape?"

A girl was moving down the Boardwalk ahead with an undulating walk. Hodges was silent but observant.

It was barely 8 p.m. when he reached the dressing room behind the ballroom stage. The band didn't hit until 8:30, and, as he leisurely changed, he began to reminisce:

"We were in Antibes this summer, the town where Sidney Bechet was married, where they had the parade and everything. They have a square named after him there and a bust in the park. It's about three feet tall, I'd say, and mounted on a pedestal. They took my picture looking at it, and it brought back some memories. It's kind of odd that it's where it is, but he was very well known and lived in France for years. There isn't anything similar in this country that I know of, but there ought to be. He ought to be in the *DownBeat* Hall of Fame, too, and I hope he will be.

"I met him in Boston years and years ago, when he was playing in burlesque, in Jimmy Cooper's Black and White Show. I had a lot of nerve when I went backstage to see him, with my little curved soprano wrapped up under my arm. But my sister knew him, and I made myself known. 'What's that under your arm?' he asked me.

"'A soprano.'

"'Can you play it?'

"'Sure,' I said, although I had only had it about two days.

"'Well, play something,' he said.

"So I played 'My Honey's Lovin' Arms.'

"He encouraged me.

"'That's nice,' he said.

"I think sopranos were played more in those days, but I just liked mine because it looked so pretty. Later, I changed to alto, for so many people told me where it fitted in the family of saxophones, although at the time a lot of musicians were playing C-melody, and some bass saxophone, besides the others. I took to alto, but later I ran into Bechet again. I had taken a liking to his playing, and to Louis Armstrong's, which I heard on the Clarence Williams Blue Five records.

"I didn't have any tuition, and I didn't buy any books. A friend, Abe Strong, came back and showed me the scale just after I bought the horn, and I took it up from there by myself, for my own enjoyment, and had a lot of fun. So far as reading went, I took a lesson here and there, and then experience taught me a lot, sitting beside guys like Otto Hardwicke and Barney Bigard. They were very helpful to me."

Before Hodges had got the saxophone, he played drums, but not professionally. He also played "house hop" piano. (Hodges' family, from his mother to his son and daughter, play piano for enjoyment.) He remembers playing house parties for $8 a night and that once, when Count Basie was in town with a show, he took over as Hodges' relief man.

"After we had moved from Cambridge to Hammond Street in Boston," Hodges said, "there were several other young musicians nearby. Howard Johnson used to live around the corner from me on Shumant Avenue. His was a very musical family. He played saxophone, his brother Bobby played banjo, his mother, his sister, his other brother and his uncle—they all played piano. Charlie Holmes lived on Tremont Street, and I think he took up saxophone in the high school band. Harry Carney lived just a couple of blocks away

on Cunard Street."

Hodges went back to soprano when he joined Sidney Bechet at his club, the Club Bechet, on 145th Street and Seventh Avenue in New York. Bechet had another soprano, a straight one, that he gave to Hodges and would teach him different tunes to play as duets. Hodges learned the introductions and solos, and if Bechet was late, would take over until he got there. This was in 1923 or 1924, before he joined either Chick Webb or Ellington. The latter used to come to Boston every summer and ask Hodges to join him, the altoist said.

"Neither the straight nor curved soprano is easy to play," he continued, "and both are just as hard to keep in tune. But there is an advantage to the curved one— you can cheat more on it. There are a lot of ways of cheating, though many saxophone players might not approve of them. I think you can get the same tone on the curved one as you can on the straight, but you've got to practice every day. You can't just pick it up and play one chorus tonight, and then play it again two nights later. I gave it up when Cootie Williams left the band in 1940. The last thing we played was 'That's the Blues, Old Man.'"

There was no special reason that he gave it up, but he was getting a lot of alto solos to play and figured they were responsibility enough.

"Duke had been writing a whole lot of arrangements with soprano on top," Hodges said, "and the responsibility of playing lead and then jumping up and playing solos, too, was a heavy one. So I just laid it away. I know the soprano has come back into popularity, and someday I hope to get mine out again. I'd like to get it together and then make a record."

Before Antibes, the Ellington band had been to Dakar for the first World Festival of Negro Arts. Hodges seemed to have taken Africa in stride.

"There was the city, of course, and the people," he said. "The drummers were Sam Woodyard's stick, but I've been listening to drummers for years, and I heard a lot when my daughter was dancing in the African Village at the New York World's fair. I used to go out there regularly. The Watusis had that terrific rhythm. They'd put those big drums on top of their heads—a hand at one end, and then take the sticks with the other and rattle them. I don't think Sam Woodyard ever heard them, but he's been doing that rhythm for years. He just fell right in there. Every night he does it, but I don't

think more than two or three guys in the band know what it is.

"It was a funny thing, but when they were out at the fair and you got within two or three blocks, it was as though those drums would draw you. I was talking to a clarinet player yesterday who worked out there with Olatunji, and he was telling me that after you put those drums on top of your head, you could imagine you could hear a whole arrangement with violins, harps, flutes, piccolos and everything— through the drums and the beat. I guess it's something like when a bass player puts his head down on the strings."

The night before the foregoing conversation, there had been a live recording session at Grace's Little Belmont on North Kentucky Avenue. The room is small, but the producer and engineer had managed to get all the recording equipment into a window alcove. Wild Bill Davis and his organ; Dickey Thompson, guitar; Bob Brown, tenor saxophone, flute; and Bobby Durham, drums, normally had minimal working space in the middle of the oval bar, but now Hodges and trombonist Lawrence Brown were added to their number and accommodated by a slight extension of the stand into one of the bar gangways.

Although it was very hot, the atmosphere was happy and full of anticipation. Across the street, the doors of the Club Harlem were wide open, and the loud sounds of the alternating Willis Jackson and Jimmy Tyler bands were wafted in between numbers.

There were numerous jazzmen working the Atlantic City clubs that week, and the Ellington musicians, Duke among them, came by to size up the situation. Buster Cooper and Chuck Connors, of the trombone section, were there all the time.

"We have to support our leader," Cooper said with a grin, nodding in Lawrence Brown's direction.

Paul Gonsalves arrived from another club where he had been jamming.

"It's how it is sometimes in the band," he said, appreciatively. "When Rab [Hodges] feels like blowing, he stirs us all. He's got a heart, believe me, and he'd give you the shirt off his back."

Brown was causing a lot of excitement, too, playing with unusual fire and energy. The word got around among young local musicians, who soon came to listen.

"They don't often get a chance to hear trombone playing like that down here,"

Hodges said as he sipped a Coke at the bar during intermission. "They nearly all play saxophone, because that's what they hear most of with the organ groups, and they go around like gunfighters trying to cut each other down. You can tell by the way they look that Lawrence got to 'em."

Then everything was shaking on the stand again. Fellow Ellington altoist Russell Procope was celebrating his birthday, and he, his wife, Cue Hodges (Johnny's wife) and Cooper were dancing like a chorus line in the aisle.

The tempo changed, and the group went into a standard Hodges had thought of as he walked by the sea to the club.

"Let's do it again," he called to the A&R man. They did it three times, and then it wasn't the famous standard any longer.

"You see what I mean?" Brown asked when he came off. "He's been doing that all his life. He gets an idea, thinks up a countermelody, and you end up with a whole new song. Yet nobody seems to recognize him as the composer he is."

Hodges was happy with what had happened.

"I think that will be enough for tonight," he said.

Later, in the hotel, he looked up from his tea and lemon and asked, "You remember when Duke went to England with Ray Nance and Kay Davis in 1948, after his operation? Well, while we were laying off, Russell Procope and I came to Atlantic City with our wives for a little vacation. One night, we decided to go to the Belmont and hear Wild Bill. He invited us to a jam session, so we took our horns and jammed until 7 or 8 in the morning.

"Our jamming drew most of the people over from the Club Harlem, and a couple of club owners from New York heard us. One of them had the Apollo Bar on 125th Street, and when we got back, he approached me about getting a little band together. So Billy Strayhorn, Tyree Glenn, Jimmy Hamilton, Sonny Greer, Al Hibbler and I went in there, and we got very lucky and started putting 125th Street on the map again. Later on, we added Junior Raglin on bass, and we stayed there for seven weeks, until Duke came back. He got right off the boat and came to the Apollo Bar to find out what was going on and whether we were going to continue with this little band. But we were loyal, and we broke the band up and came back."

A few days after the most recent session at the Little Belmont, Hodges was into

Johnny Hodges.
(Skippy Adelman)

something else again, this time in Rudy Van Gelder's Englewood, N.J., studio. The band consisted of Snooky Young and Ernie Royal, trumpets; Tony Studd, trombone; Frank Wess, Jerome Richardson, Jimmy Hamilton and Don Ashworth, reeds, woodwinds; Hank Jones, piano; Kenny Burrell, guitar; Bob Cranshaw, bass; and Grady Tate, drums. Jimmy Jones wrote the scores and conducted.

"I tried to give Johnny a new framework," Jones said. It was certainly unlike any in which the altoist previously had been recorded. The musicians soon were creating an agreeably smooth ensemble sound, but Jones detected imperfections and began to wrestle with them. Hodges, as

soloist, stepped away from the debate.

"That's why," he said, taking off his hat, "I still have all my hair!"

When the problem had been ironed out and a clean take of "Blue Notes" made, he came over to where Tom Whaley, an arranger-copyist who has been associated with Ellington for several years, was sitting. Whaley, also from Boston, is close to Hodges, and his seniority in age permits him to act as the voice of dissent.

"You ought to record with some gutbucket musicians," Whaley said.

This was somewhat unexpected, to say the least, because Whaley never hesitates to declaim against sloppy playing that may occur on Ellington recording dates.

"There's a difference between 'inside' and 'outside' musicians," Hodges countered. "Studio musicians play more exact."

Whaley, meanwhile, was paying close attention to Jimmy Jones' writing.

"You know," he said suddenly, "I think I'll go and take one of these modern courses in arranging. There's always something new to learn."

At the next session, Hodges recorded another original, 'Broad Walk,' with Royal using the plunger effectively in a big, shouting climax.

"Now where did you get that from?" Whaley asked.

Hodges smiled and said, "Remember the Boardwalk in Atlantic City, young man?"

April 20, 1967

The Nouveau Rich

by Harvey Siders

"Who's leaving now?" That's supposed to be a joke, the standard response of bandleaders whenever their road managers ask to speak with them. On good authority, the line is meant to be funny and not a defense mechanism designed to soften the blow of some internal hassle. The authority is Buddy Rich. Last month, he was extolling the virtues of Jo Jones when his road manager, Jim Trimble, came into the dressing room of the Chez, in Hollywood, Calif., and asked to see him.

Until the interruption, Rich had been talking about how great Jones was with the hi-hat, with brushes and just plain keeping time. Rich was talking and sweating with equal profusion, having just completed an exhausting set.

It was Saturday night. And Saturday night in Hollywood is no different than Saturday night in Dubuque. Everybody was out, and it seemed they all had come to the Chez to hear the drummer's band. It also seemed that Rich and the band were pushing themselves beyond their usual, hard-driving threshold, inspired by the deafening audience response and the standing ovation led by Judy Garland.

The contrast between the human dynamo generating white heat among his sidemen and the slouched figure trying to cool off in his underwear in the dressing room was the kind that made me feel guilty for trying to interview him between sets—like asking for his autograph during an eight-bar rest.

Perhaps the interview might continue after the last show?

"Hell no!" he growled. "When 2 a.m. comes, I'm through. No more music, no more musicians, no hippies, no interviews, no nothing. I go right back to my hotel and take it easy. Call me tomorrow—but don't you dare call me before 2 in the afternoon. Is that clear?"

One could hardly misinterpret.

During the last set in the split-level main room of the club, the crowd was electrified by the amazing display of raw energy. The carefully planned program built in intensity, broken up by a couple of well-spaced trio numbers (pianist Ray Starling, bassist Jim Gannon and Rich) but never diminishing in excitement.

Occasionally, he would come out to the mike and talk about a particular number or introduce some celebrities at ringside. His out-of-breath banter was welcome, pithy and often sarcastic, never dull. Then he'd make his way back to the drums and plunge into the next number with a long, mood-setting cadenza.

At the end of the set, he gave his fans what they'd been clamoring for all evening—the medley from *West Side Story*, arranger Bill Reddie's 11-minute kaleidoscope of Leonard Bernstein's themes, with constantly shifting tempos and a climactic extended drum solo that inevitably leaves Rich and his audience limp.

What made the whole scene incredible was the knowledge that Rich, who is twice as old as most of his sidemen (he'll be 50 in June), was the source of energy: he was the one urging them on, exhorting soloists and sections to the point where his young players could hardly take their eyes off him.

Rich sticks to his after-hours embargo and makes no exceptions. And during those precious minutes between sets, competition for Rich's attention is prohibitive. The best time for an interview was his day off. It was quite a compromise on his part, as he made plain:

"These 24 hours belong to me. I like to stay as far away from the scene as possible. I may choose to stay in bed and watch TV—daytime TV, you know, soap operas.

I may go to a movie. Or else I'll jump in the car and go for a ride to the beach or out to some golf course."

His room at the Continental Hotel had a commanding view of Los Angeles. Rich, however, was engrossed in a science-fiction thriller flickering across the television screen. But instead of watching it until the end, he turned a few dials on his video-tape recorder, lowered the sound and began to talk about big bands. He would watch the rest of the program later.

Why did he leave the security of being probably the highest paid sideman in the business for the headaches of fronting his own band?

"What is security?" he asked. "What are headaches? Is there security in crossing a street? Don't you think a guy who operates his own gas station has headaches? And when he gets home at night he still smells of gas, right?"

But why did he leave the Harry James Band?

The answer was terse: "'Cause we needed some good music in the business."

Then he added, "Sure, I had a good-paying job—four and a half years. It was beautiful. But for four and a half years, I didn't play a goddamned thing. I sat up there; I went through the motions. Night after night, I knew what tunes I was going to play. I even knew what time we were going to play them. I had two solos in the band, and what the hell—that wasn't for me.

"It was security, all right. But what good is security if you're not happy, and especially if you know you can do better, be more creative, and let your personality come out? But if you're being held down, so to speak, in somebody else's band, what good is it taking home a heavy check every week? So when the opportunity presented itself, I jumped at it."

The opportunity came a year ago. Is he still happy about his decision?

"Happy? I couldn't be happier. Let me repeat that. I couldn't be happier for anything on this earth. The results are beautiful. The band is excellent, and it's a contemporary band. The kids in it are beautiful to work with. They enjoy what we're doing because we're playing young music, and they project their youth through what they're playing. It certainly latches on to the youth wherever we play. Our young audiences understand it, and as you can see, the spenders come out, too!"

That reminded him of what he had said about the need for good music in the

Buddy Rich.
(Joseph L. Johnson)

band business, and he launched into an analysis of the business today.

According to Rich, the attempt to bring back the old bands is self-defeating. His advice is to forget about the old days and the old ways and concentrate on today's sounds.

"You can't fool the public," he said. "You can't go on saying, 'This is the original Glenn Miller Band,' or 'This is the original Tommy Dorsey Band!' You just can't continue putting people on like that.

"The Glenn Miller sound was an insipid sound in 1942. It certainly wouldn't be good enough for 1967. It was contrived and mechanical and had no more feeling to it than if you were hypnotized. You knew every night the arrangements were going to sound the same, the tempos would be the same, even the solos were the same. There was no emotional involvement!"

He conceded that "it must have been popular, though, since so many people turned out to see the Miller band." That

concession served as a bridge to his own popularity 25 years later. He said his band has not met with the slightest resistance since its inception. He has been invited back to every club he's played.

"We played Lennie's-on-the-Turn-pike [just north of Boston], and even before we got there, all seven nights and the matinee had been sold out," he said. "Lennie couldn't squeeze in an extra person. We're going back there in July after the Newport Festival.

"That's the way the reception has been all the way. GAC is handling the band now, and I've got the best arrangers writing for me [he listed Bill Holman, Oliver Nelson, Bob Florence and Shorty Rogers] and the best producer in the business—Dick Bock [of Pacific Jazz]. In fact, you can't get no better."

Everything seems to be groovy for Rich, but it wasn't that way 21 years ago. When he organized his first band in 1946 (following a stint with Tommy Dorsey's

band and a hitch in the Marine Corps), he had a modern-jazz outfit, with such side-men as tenorists Al Cohn and Alien Eager and the Swope Brothers (trombonists Earl and Rob). It was a bad time to form a hard-driving band. The trend towards combos was beginning then, accompanied by the postwar decline in dancing. When ball-room operators asked Rich to tone down the jazz, he got cocky and insisted he would do things his way ("This is what I play; take it or leave it"). The big band venture didn't last long.

The following year he began his association with Jazz at the Philharmonic. Then, between leading his own small groups, he rejoined Dorsey for a while, and was in and out of the James band a few times.

Going out on his own again provoked criticism from skeptics who predicted the band wouldn't last. In Las Vegas, especially, odds were figuratively posted not on whether but how soon Rich would be back with James, drawing his "heavy check every week."

Did this give rise to Rich's wanting to "show" his detractors?

"Certainly not," he answered. "I couldn't care less about them. And if you know anything about me, you know I don't give a damn about anybody's opinion. I do exactly what I think is right for me. That shows how much jealousy and envy exists on the part of other people who have led bands or have tried to start bands but were not as successful as I've been with this band. Sour apples, that's all it is—sour apples.

"Actually, it's a compliment to me. Maybe they don't realize it, but every time they knock my band, they're complimenting me, because—against all their great minds, great brains and business sense—my band is a success."

No doubt about it, as the band's reception at Basin Street East will attest. And regardless of how big one makes it in Las Vegas or on the West Coast, New York is still the nut to crack. If the band was such a great success, it must have been a happy band. Why then the noticeable change in personnel between his first and second engagements at the Chez?

"John Bunch, my piano player, quit to work with Tony Bennett," he said. "John's not a youngster anymore, and working with Tony would mean less traveling, and that appealed to him. But I fired a half dozen others."

(Naturally, there are two sides to the firing story. Rumors around Los Angeles indicate that the dissatisfaction was mutual in many cases, and a check with two of those who were allegedly fired revealed some confusion as to whether or not the half dozen were fired or quit. Whatever the full story is, the dissension within the band seems to have come to a quick end.)

"If I hire you in the beginning," Rich said, "it's because I dig what you're doing, dig how you play and dig your personality—and for me to have to fire somebody is a big drag. But it's another way of saying, 'You're a detriment to what I'm trying to produce.'" Then, as if to justify his actions, he said he believes that the band is a better-sounding unit now.

Singers, Rich feels, have no place with his band. They are merely "a throwback to the '40s." Furthermore, he's convinced they just slow down the pacing of the entire set—unless "they happen to be a Sinatra, a Torme or a Joe Williams." In seeming contradiction, while he was recording his second live album at the Chez, his 12-year-old

daughter, Cathy, sang with the band. They were trying out a new arrangement of the current rock favorite, "The Beat Goes On."

"My daughter knows the song," Rich said. "She got up on the stage—first time in front of an audience—and she recorded it. When I went over to Liberty to start editing the tapes, I heard it, and it was a gas."

From rock 'n' roll, the conversation swung to the other extreme: the avant-garde.

Rich made no bones about his impatience with "know-nothing hipsters who can't even find '1.' They just decide to smash a cymbal here, add a rim shot there. Then other hipsters think that's the thing to do and they follow suit. And that's the story of 'hipdom.'"

He recounted what he calls the funniest contact he's ever had with the avant-garde. It happened at the Pacific Jazz Festival last October in Costa Mesa, Calif. His band had been scheduled to follow the Charles Lloyd Quartet, and Rich was waiting on the platform behind the canvas that covered the outdoor stage on three sides. Peering through the peepholes used by photographers, he found himself directly behind Lloyd's pianist, who was plucking the piano strings, gesticulating wildly as he reached over the keyboard.

"That had to be the craziest thing I ever saw," Rich said. "I was nearly hysterical. I don't think I've ever laughed that much in my life. I just couldn't conceive that they thought they were playing music. And that drummer—he had no idea of what the other guys were doing. That must have been the greatest put-on since the Four Stooges."

He began talking about the music and musicians that were meaningful to him, and the first and only band that fit that category was Count Basie's. Rich said that some of the best big band drummers have worked for Basie: Shadow Wilson, Gus Johnson, Sonny Payne, Louie Bellson—but he named Jo Jones as the best:

"He fit the band in the way Freddie Green does. Jones, Green and Basie and Walter Page on bass—that's the 'all-American rhythm section' for you."

From Basie's drummers to big band drummers in general was a natural transition. Among Rich's favorites were Gene Krupa, Alvin Stoller, Sol Gubin, Jack Sperling, Mel Lewis, and Don Lamond—all of whom, he said, could play anything required of them in a big band.

He takes a dim view of what he calls

"specialization." As he put it, "In the old day, when a drummer was hired in a band, he was expected to do anything that was called for: if the arrangements required the power of a marching band, that's the way you played; if it called for the drummer to be as gentle as a mouse, that's the way you played; and if there was a combo within the band, if you had to play with a sextet—you know, like Gene Krupa with Benny Goodman's band—you just did it. I can't see a guy with a big band make the announcement, 'Now we're going to do some combo numbers, so now I'd like to present my combo drummer.' Man, what the hell is that—the two-platoon system?"

The two-platoon idea brought up the subject of the two-books concept used by some bands—a book for dancing and a book for listening. Does his band use this method?

"Well, first of all, we play very few dances as such," he said. "We have toured a number of colleges and played what you might call a dance, but actually we played what we play at the Chez or Basin Street East. The big difference today—and another reason why we're so successful—is the big beat. The young crowd has changed their style of dancing so that they can dance to what we play."

Rich will soon find out how European youngsters react to his brand of big band jazz. This month the band is touring England, Switzerland and Italy—the kind of traveling the drummer likes.

"That's the beauty of this business," he said. "You get paid to see the world—and I love it. I hate to spend too much time in one place, anyhow. Besides, it'll be great for my family. Marie [his wife] and Cathy will be with me, and it should be quite an education."

But there are many musicians who wonder just how long Buddy Rich can hold up under his present rigorous routine—not in terms of popularity, but in terms of physical endurance. Rich claims he doesn't look back at what happened seven years ago (the first, and most serious, of three heart attacks).

"I can't worry about that," he said. "I just take care of myself—I got no bad habits—and keep right on working. Any doctor will tell you that if you got a heart condition, you should keep active."

But why does he drive himself to the point of exhaustion? His answer had the direct honesty that cancels any rebuttal:

"Man, 'cause I love it."

June 29, 1967

George Benson
Guitar in the Ascendancy
by Stanley Dance

George Benson.
(DownBeat Archive)

"I was about six," George Benson said, "when my stepfather came around with the first electric guitar I ever heard. It amazed me. I couldn't imagine how the guitar sound got through the wire into the amplifier. Although it was very pleasant to my ear, I never thought I would be able to play it."

The stepfather, Thomas Collier, was a Charlie Christian fan. He taught George the fundamentals of the guitar, until the youngster's inclination for running the streets and playing ball caused him to give up in disgust.

"He figured I wasn't going to learn," Benson said, "and for five years we didn't have a guitar at home, but I used to go to other guys' houses—wherever there was a guitar—and play all day. I used to sing and pick up the guitar and try to figure out chords to play behind myself. Finally, when I was 15, my stepfather made me a little electric guitar.

"Around this time, a guitarist named Chuck Edwards suddenly appeared in Pittsburgh, my hometown, and everybody liked him right away. They still do. He's a heck of an entertainer, and he can really create a lot of excitement. He sang rhythm and blues, but he brought a different sound, and he was always coming up with unorthodox tunes, some of them in a flamenco vein. He had one number called 'The Bullfight.' It was completely rhythmic, because he wasn't concerned with harmonic intricacies. It got so you had to play something like that there then, or the people would say you couldn't play. So I arranged something along those lines, and they gave it the same title. Although the melody was a little different, and I used to improvise more, the two numbers were basically similar. I recorded mine on my first Columbia album.

"Although he's not a practicing musician anymore, my stepfather is a very good musician, and even now he will show me things I don't know. He just didn't realize how I'd learned to play songs by myself until almost 10 years after he had given me

up. He would have liked to have been a professional musician, but when he met my mother, that was the end of that.

"He liked some of the guitarists who came up after Charlie Christian, but they didn't play the swing type of music he had ears for. I'm a great Christian fan myself, and I think he was a very great man, but I like the modern guys, too. It was when I

heard a Hank Garland album that I realized all the possibilities of the guitar. I thought of things then further than I've yet reached, but I started practicing single-line things that I didn't have the chance to use at that time."

Born March 22, 1943, in Pittsburgh, Pa., Benson left school when he was 17 and formed a little rock 'n' roll group in which his singing was the main feature. He did a good deal of playing in jam sessions, but apart from what his stepfather had taught him, he picked up the rest of his musical knowledge himself.

"When guitar players came to town," Benson said, "I'd go find them and ask them questions. I'd wake 'em up out of bed, worry 'em to death. I particularly remember Thornel Schwartz, Eddie McFadden and the guitarist Chico Hamilton had in 1958. They really helped me. I used to go to see Jack McDuff's guitarist, Eddie Diehl, too. I loved his playing. He's on a few recordings, but he never stretched out and played any long solos. The last time I saw him, he was working with Miriam Makeba, and he told me he was going to South America.

"I never thought I'd leave Pittsburgh, because I always loved it there—and the little towns around. I was 18 when Jack McDuff came through and hired me. Then I found out how far behind I was, but I hoped he would let me hang on until I caught up. In the rock 'n' roll band I hadn't played what I needed to play to improve, but now I got the chance to play some of the lines I used to practice. The McDuff group gave me a different conception, but I think the greatest thing was that it gave me the chance to hear what everyone else was doing from coast to coast.

"Grant Green made the greatest impression on me. Before he went out on his own, he got his first recognition with McDuff, too. It was his lyricism I liked. He could play very melodically, and still swing, and never lose the groove. That's the main thing I liked about his playing, and I still do.

"I'd heard Wes Montgomery before I left home, and he'd made a different kind of impression. He's a wonderful musician, a kind of virtuoso, but that wasn't the groove I wanted to get into. As a matter of fact, I felt I could never get that far! So I reached for something I felt I could get closer to in my lifetime. Now I'm hearing so many different things, and they're influencing me as I go."

Benson was with McDuff for three and a half years, and during that time the personnel of the group remained the same; Red Holloway was the tenor saxophonist and Joe Dukes the drummer. The quartet's development was traced in a series of Prestige albums.

"Although the group swung more than those I'd been in before," Benson observed, "I found the organ limited me in some ways. You can't get too intricate in a combo like that, and what you do in a record studio is quite different from what you do in a club when business is slow. Then you try things you would not dare when you're recording. But I was able to concentrate and grow with McDuff because I was playing guitar day in and day out. I didn't want to become any kind of virtuoso then. I just wanted to swing. I still like to do that, but I get bored with myself if there's nothing else happening. Now I want to play things that have never been done before, and that's easier said than done."

In 1964, the quartet played at the jazz festival at Antibes, France, and then went on to the Golden Circle Club in Stockholm, where it broke all records.

It was in Sweden that Benson encountered Jean-Luc Ponty, a French violinist who exerted an important influence on his musical thinking.

"I worked with him on a TV show," the guitarist said, "and he hipped me to a lot of things that can be done with modes. When I heard him play, I said I would be happy if I could play even a couple of bars on the violin, so he made me go out and buy one. I'd love to have some of his records, because when I tell people about him, they don't believe me. It was the first time I realized the potential of that instrument. I'd heard classical music on it, but it bored me, because after a while the sound became like a monotone in my ear. I'd never heard anyone improvise and swing like Jean-Luc did. I've heard Stuff Smith, and I like him, too, but Jean-Luc is more modern. I haven't had time to really work on the violin yet, but I intend to, and I'm going to get a teacher this time because I know it's a hard instrument."

Benson said that the drawing power of organ groups does not appear to have been fully recognized by European bookers. His own has been invited to this summer's Antibes festival, but unless other bookings materialize, he said it would be impractical to make the trip for just two performances.

"When we were in France last time," he recalled, "I think there were about two organists within 500 miles, and if a man can't play on his own instrument, he at least wants to play on the same model."

Although the McDuff years were happy ones, after a time Benson began to feel the need for the greater personal expression that would be possible only if he led his own group.

"McDuff," he admitted, "was playing some beautiful things that hadn't been done by any other organ group, but I had different ideas. I wanted to try my own organ quartet and play some tricky 'heads.' So I went back to Pittsburgh for three months and played in the Rendezvous Lounge with just drums and upright bass. Where I'd been limited to a few choruses, I was now able to play as much as I liked, and I learned to play a lot of things I didn't think I could do. With that kind of accompaniment, I had the major responsibility, but it released me from staying with the one particular chord being played behind me. I could hear just what was possible, and it gave me a lot of confidence."

After returning to McDuff for three months, he set about forming his own group. He remembered organist Lonnie Smith, who came from Buffalo, N.Y., and had once sat in with the McDuff quartet.

"When I thought about organ players," Benson said, "he came into my mind, because he can swing. When I called him, he was working with a rhythm-and-blues group, but he decided to take a chance with me, although I had nothing lined up. I took him on a gig with me at the same Rendezvous Lounge, and we rehearsed for a couple of days, but when we came to New York, I think we had only about three tunes that we could play. Philip Terrell, from my hometown, was on drums. My manager decided to put us on a rhythm-and-blues kick, because we were unknown in New York, and we did that for six or eight weeks. Then I ran into John Hammond.

"We were working at the Palm Cafe on 125th Street. I spotted him right away, because people had told me how he liked guitarists, and I could tell him from the way he was acting. John had us in the Columbia studio a week later, and that was when we got our baritone saxophonist, Ronnie Cuber.

"I had worked opposite him at Birdland in 1964, when I was with McDuff and he was with Maynard Ferguson. We got to know one another, and he used to come and sit in with us when we were on rock-'n'-roll gigs. He can play, and he inspires me.

"After Terrell had to go back to Pittsburgh, we used Charlie Crosby on drums. Right now, we have Marion Booker from Atlanta, Ga., and he fits very well. The drummer is very important in a small group, because he is really its backbone. Jimmy Lovelace was with Wes Montgomery at one time, and he was freelancing in New York when he recorded with us.

"Our second album outsold the first one. We used trombonist Bennie Green on a couple of numbers, and I think John was impressed by him. I know I was. I never realized before how smooth the trombone could be. Of course, I love J.J. Johnson, too, but Bennie Green is not much interested in tricky things. He plays right down the road.

"Our third album will be a little different. Ed Bland has written some arrangements on rhythmic, bluesy numbers, which we hope will sell a few records for us. We'll add Blue Mitchell on trumpet, and a tenor player, and use a pianist on a couple of tunes. I'd love to have King Curtis if we can get him. He made an album with Lonnie Smith recently; I was on the date, too."

Benson really began his public career while still a child, as a singer. Both his mother and stepfather liked to sing, and they encouraged him. Although there were two vocals ("Summertime" and "A Foggy Day") on his first Columbia album, he has done relatively little singing recently, because he has "been trying to get the guitar across." At Minton's in New York, where he was again appearing when this was written, performances are entirely instrumental, but out of town, in clubs with "a mixed clientele, where rhythm-and-blues fans come in," vocals are a necessity. This conflicts not at all with the doctrine of flexibility to which he subscribes.

"I'm not interested in becoming typed," he insisted. "I think it's to a guy's advantage to be able to play a variety of music. You never know when things are going to change, anyway. I quite like the pop field, but I also like to improvise. I don't see why all the pop hits have to be played as commercially as they are. They used to play them and improvise on them years ago. I like to hear really good musicians play pop tunes, because their versions are usually so rich and strange. And when you're making records, a hit with a standard or a pop tune may help pull your originals up.

"A lot of people liked our 'Jaguar.' We had two versions of that. The one they didn't use was more down to earth, because we used a rhythm-and-blues drummer, and his beat fit the melody. I hoped they'd put it out as a single, because everywhere we go people ask for that and 'The Bullfight.'"

Asked about tone and amplification, Benson replied with a series of interesting observations:

"It takes years to develop a tone on guitar. All the guys I've ever talked to say the same thing, and I know it to be a fact in my case. When I listened to some of the older records I made with McDuff, I noticed—although it didn't really bother me at the time—that my notes were much shorter. I couldn't make them last as long as I wanted to, and I used to wonder why. You hear a guitarist like Johnny Smith, and he'd hit a note and it would ring for it seemed as long as he liked. I wondered why he could do it and I couldn't. It has to do with the way you hold the pick, precisely at a certain place on the strings, so as to cause the vibrations to be stronger. It has to do with the angle of the pick, the pressure you apply with your left hand, and so on.

"The amplifier is important, too. In some cases, the amplifiers and the speakers are designed to give a mellow tone. That's good in one respect, if you don't play hard. I've learned to pick hard. That's a bad habit in some things, but good when you're trying to create excitement, because you can punctuate better. If you like to play pretty, like Kenny Burrell, then you want a mellow amplifier, something that will eliminate the highs. But it isn't too good with an organ group, because it doesn't cut through. On records, it's different, because the engineers can amplify their own way, but in a club you've got to have an amplifier that gives you a spontaneous response. With mine, I'm used to hearing the note exactly as I hit it.

"There are electronic problems, too, when the organ and the guitar are both amplified. If you use the amplifier away from the guitar, you have to play louder, because otherwise the organ will overshadow you. If you play with the speaker directly behind you, as I do, you can play with a better groove, because you're not striving so hard to hear. Normally, I have mine about a couple of feet behind. Lonnie Smith is not a loud organist, which is one of the things I like about him, because a lot of organ players will drown the guitar out. He uses the foot bass in unison with his left hand, but he only uses it to accentuate and punctuate certain parts. It never gets in the way or bothers me. I like a guy to play what he feels, but I prefer the finger bass, because it is much smoother. I don't like the growl of the foot bass, and I think Lonnie knows it. Sometimes I think the depth of the note goes beyond the speaker range. Before McDuff played organ, he played piano and bass, so the two really came together in his case.

"Lonnie uses vibrato, but a lot of organ players don't. Jimmy Smith, for instance, does a lot of intricate things where vibrato could get in the way and confuse. He has good tone and doesn't need vibrato on those fast single lines. But I also like to hear guys like Wild Bill Davis play those chords. He is really a chord man!"

Benson's admiration for other guitarists could be expressed in catalog form, but he summarized his views as follows:

"I love the guitar, period. I love to hear the blues on it, flamenco, the classics, the semi-classics, the bossa nova.... I've heard a lot of Django Reinhardt's records, and he was a real virtuoso. Even if anyone could copy him, I don't think they could get the feeling, because he was strictly Django. Oscar Moore, who used to be with Nat Cole, had a conception like Kenny Burrell's. They both loved to play pretty. I don't think anybody could have fit better with Nat than Oscar, because they both had the same conception. I've heard a lot of blues guitarists, and I love B.B. King. I met T-Bone Walker out in California about four years ago, and he impressed me very much. Then there's Lightnin' Hopkins.... The finger system they use in bossa nova is beautiful, but I've never gotten into that. I feel if I started now I would lose something in the single-line thing. I'd like to explore it as much as possible, but one thing at a time!

"Then, you know, there are a lot of remarkable guitar players who have maybe never been heard of outside their own towns. They do things I've never heard anyone else do, and they've shown me things I couldn't do. Sometimes they've lucked up on something that took them into a groove, which they investigated thoroughly, until they came up with something entirely different. That's why Wes Montgomery made such a good guitar player, because everything was strictly from him. So far as its being unorthodox, it really wasn't unorthodox to him."

At 24, George Benson is a calm, self-possessed young man whose future seems assured. Early this year, at Carnegie Hall, his group got the Spirituals to Swing Concert off to a swinging start. In October, he will tour Europe and play the Berlin Jazz Festival with a guitar workshop in which Elmer Snowden, Buddy Guy, Jim Hall, Barney Kessel and Larry Coryell will also participate.

"I'm looking forward to that," he said simply.

Audiences should be, too.

Nina Simone.
(Joseph L. Johnson)

Jan. 11, 1968

. . . .

The Real Nina Simone

by Michael Zwerin

I heard Nina Simone for the first time in person in October at the Village Gate. Impressed, I readily agreed to the suggestion of an interview by a press representative of the company for which she records. We met at noon in her manager's carpeted and well-appointed Fifth Avenue office. In addition to being bugged, as always in midtown Manhattan during the working day, I had a dandy hangover. But my spirits were soaring compared to Miss Simone's.

M.Z.: You are going to Las Vegas next week. I understood there is a reason you never worked there before.

N.S.: Same reason I haven't worked a lot of places, I guess.

M.Z.: Has it changed out there?

N.S.: I don't know what you mean.

M.Z.: I understand it's a segregated town.

N.S.: Lots of towns are segregated where I've worked. I don't know if that has anything to do with it or not.

There was a long pause here, ended by her manager, who is also her husband. "What kind of thing are you doing? We're not interested in the race issue," he said. I explained what I do and who invited me. I asked what they were interested in.

N.S.: What do you mean, "What am I interested in"? You're the writer.

I almost got up to leave. I wasn't in any mood to cope with this kind of thing. I have always hated formal interviews, anyway. Why had I come? I'll never learn, I thought.

N.S.: It makes no difference to me. I'm not the one who wanted the interview.

M.Z.: [Losing his cool fast.] Well, you told me what you are not interested in. I'm asking you what is it you would like to talk to me about.

N.S.: That's up to you.... Can I bum one of your cigarettes?

I gave her one. We lit up. There was another long pause. We were both resisting.

N.S.: You must have a line of questioning that you've already planned.... Oh, you don't?

More silence. I sank further into my chair. I asked her what pop groups or singers she likes to listen to. Not much of a question, but better than nothing.

N.S.: Which ones in particular, you mean? I don't know. Well, in general, I like what's happening in pop music. It's taking on some standards—I'm glad to say—that it should have had years ago. I believe the time will come when the whole definition of pop music will change. It will get to the point where a song will not be a good song until it has a high level of creativity in writing and performance. In other words, in order to be popular, songs will have to meet these high standards.

There were a few interruptions here. The phone, a secretary walking through, etc. Miss Simone told me she had given a concert tour in Europe recently. We agreed about what a good city Amsterdam is. We both relaxed a little. I became aware of her stunning, natural black beauty and the intelligence in her eyes.

N.S.: And because of the better quality in pop music, I find that the gap between my audience and what I am trying to say is closing. I still have the old audience I had before, but it's growing now. However, it is difficult to retain your standards with the pressure of trying to make money, which always has its rules.... It's hard to walk the tightrope of doing what you think is your best and making money at it. The pressure of show business is on all the time, and show business is a fickle business. Whatever is popular now—that's all that counts. I have to constantly re-identify myself to myself, reactivate my own standards, my own convictions about what I'm doing and why.

M.Z.: That's why the Beatles are so amazing. They don't have to grow or change, but they seem to have a need to...

N.S.: The Beatles are lucky, very lucky. But what has happened to them has nothing to do with them, in a sense. They came along at the right time. Attention was focused on them. They've had the chance to grow in almost any direction they wanted. Very lucky. They are not exceptionally talented. Uh-uh. They may be. But they are just starting to create. They have just discovered that they have talent, friend. Fate was good enough to give them time to think about their talent, to develop it as they please, without fighting everybody around them.

M.Z.: I was listening to some old Joao Gilberto records the other night, and I thought about how bossa nova came into the spotlight around the same time as rock. It was eclipsed. I think it could have been much bigger had the timing been different.

N.S.: Could be. I have been using what might be called a rock beat for years and years. It doesn't matter to me what is going on today because my music encompasses every kind of mood that exists in human beings. That's my stick. I know 700 songs—just like that. So out of them, there is bound to be almost any kind of "style" you could imagine. You know Bobbie Gentry's "Ode to Billie Joe"? I do a tune, "When I Was a Young Girl," I've been doing it for years—same type of thing.

M.Z.: You talked about walking the tightrope between compromise and integrity. What if you didn't have this limitation?

N.S.: Exactly what the Beatles have done. Except I would have done it before now. There are all kinds of things that can be done. You can change rhythms, you can change chords, you can change whole concepts. But it will only work, on a record or in a performance, if you can make the people buy it. If there were no restrictions, the first thing I would have done—six years ago—don't print this, please…. That's what I would lave liked to have done. Would still like to do.

I'm sorry not to be able to tell you exactly what she would have done. I don't think, however, she would mind my saying that, in general, it had something to do with extended works.

M.Z.: Jazz has been moving more and more in that direction…. What jazz musicians do you like?

N.S.: As far as piano players are concerned, Oscar Peterson is my very favorite. I also like McCoy Tyner. I think that the big jazz stars, both now and in the past… how shall I say it? These guys are as great as Bach, Beethoven, all of them. People don't know it yet. If jazz survives and is put on a pedestal as an art form, the same as classical music has been through the years, a hundred years from now the kids will know who they were, with that kind of respect. This may or may not happen. In the meantime, unfortunately, as they get older, some

of them get bitter. Music is an art, and art has its own rules. And one of them is that you must pay more attention to it than anything else in the world, if you are going to be true to yourself. And if you don't do it—and you are an artist—it punishes you. It's true! Like when I leave you…. You'll have to forgive me if I'm a little brash today. But I have a rehearsal this afternoon. That's mostly on my mind. That music—it's something else. It really gets you.

We talked about her group, and I told her how much I liked it, her piano playing and the fact that her bass player was properly amplified. My pet peeve has long been the inaudibility of basses in jazz. (I noticed my hangover was gone.)

N.S.: I know exactly what you mean. Me too. Sweetheart, I have asked 50 guys over the last 10 years: Don't you realize we can't hear you? Does it make any difference that we can't hear you? That doesn't make any sense. I don't know—it's weird.

M.Z.: I think that is symbolic of what is wrong with jazz. There is a lack of simple planning, a…

N.S.: I agree with that. That's true, love, that part is true. It's unfortunate. It is assumed, for instance, that pianos are never tuned in jazz clubs. It's part of the sound. Half of the broken-down sound—in the old days, anyway—was the broken-down conditions that the music was played in. Then, when the music began to change, the musicians still didn't give a damn because the owners didn't give a damn. When you think about things as simple as cleaning a men's room—the musicians really have nothing to do with that—but it affects them. And when you start screaming about having a decent mike, the guy looks at you as if you are crazy. He thinks you are egotistic because you want a simple thing to do your best. That's the way it goes. By the time the musicians do get a decent place to play in, and the conditions they have been screaming for, by that time they seem not to care anymore. So it goes.

M.Z.: It's different, though—better—in Europe. Why, do you suppose?

N.S.: You know why. You know why… the people. We're in trouble over here, bad trouble. And I mean a lot more than with jazz.

M.Z.: Have you ever thought about moving to Europe?

N.S.: I think of it a lot. I'm just riding with the wind. You know, I was born here, and nobody really wants to move from where their roots are. Whichever way it

goes, though, I'll go. In a way, the fact that we are in trouble is a good sign. We recognize it now, at least. In order to make things better, you've got to clean up all the crap. You can't do that until you realize that—you—are—in—the—midst—of it. We got so much crap here. Wow! It tends to be obscured, though. We bury it with intellectualism, with confusion. So much talk going on that it is hard to think clearly. And we hide, avoid the unpleasant things going on. I saw something yesterday. I was going to church on 54th and Lexington. There were some kids in the street playing football right on Lexington Avenue. I'll tell you what hit me. What amazed me was the order of things—the fact that we wear clothes, that an office has to look a certain way, the whole bit. It's amazing how accustomed we have become to a certain order. And you become more aware of that order when you see someone change it. Everybody turns around and stares. But why, really? Rules, orders. We have ordered things so long in a certain way, we are numb. Nobody dares question it. This is what is wrong, symbolically, with my country.

We had been at it for over an hour by this time. It was time to wind things up. "Where is the rehearsal?" I asked.

N.S.: At my home.

M.Z.: Where's that?

N.S.: In Westchester. Mt. Vernon.

M.Z.: You came all the way in from there to see me? Thanks. Yow. I'd better let you get back to music. No more public relations today.

N.S.: It's all right. I have to do it all the time. It's funny about music… music is like… music is one of the ways by which you can know everything which is going on in the world. You can feel… through music… Whew… you can feel the vibrations of everybody in the world at any given moment. Through music you can become sad, joyful, loving, you can learn. You can learn mathematics, touch, pacing… Oh my god! Ooh… Wow… You can see colors through music. Anything! Anything human can be felt through music, which means that there is no limit to the creating that can be done with music. You can take the same phrase from any song and cut it up so many different ways—it's infinite. It's like God… you know?

Afterwards, despite the shoving, fumes and noise of Fifth Avenue in the afternoon, I felt that interviewing people wasn't so bad after all.

Jimi Hendrix Experience, from left, Mitch Mitchell, Hendrix and Noel Redding. (MCA Music)

April 4, 1968

Jimi Hendrix

An Experience

by Valerie Wilmer

There is no experience that compares to the first time the blues get to you. The hairs on your neck stand up and an uncanny churning sets up between your heart and your stomach. It's the universal experience that unites the blues world.

Today that world is wide open. The fences are down. The boundaries have been extended to take in the music's love child, rock 'n' roll, and through the disciples of Muddy Waters and B.B. King, Chuck Berry and Bo Diddley, the experience continues, though with the accent on a battering-ram intensity of sound, not nearly as convincingly as it might. But the important thing is that it keeps on happening.

Right now, across the Atlantic, a unique blues experience is taking place—the Jimi Hendrix Experience, a marriage

between a couple of British rock merchants and an American Negro.

Although he has been adopted by the British faction of the flower-power syndrome as a kind of high priest, guitarist Hendrix, through the screaming bravado of his music, belongs to the other side of the love generation coin. Violence is, for him, an integral part of the blues of today, and so he feels free to play the guitar with his teeth, set his instrument on fire, hurl it against an amplifier.

"Our music is getting uglier," he has said, and it rages like an angry torrent, almost overpowering at times because of the amplification. But unlike so many of the loudness-is-synonymous-with-excitement groups, Hendrix's sound is not only highly electrified but electrifying, too.

From out of the musical maelstrom, the howl of the leader's guitar comes leaping like a thing possessed, lashing with the anguish of a stricken giant. In contrast to a fair proportion of rock guitarists, whose lack of an individual conception is shown up by the aimlessness of their playing, Hendrix is in firm control of his direction. In his use of feedback, for example, he stretches the notes over several bars, occasionally accompanying the harmonics emanating

from this device with a highly developed melodic line.

He claims to have soaked up influences from "everyone from Buddy Holly to Muddy Waters and through Chuck Berry way back to Eddie Cochrane," and one can hear just about everything from sitar-like riffs to crying Delta blues from his screaming strings.

"Cats I like now are Albert King and Elmore James," he said, "but if you try to copy them, want to play something note for note—especially a solo or a certain run that lasts over three seconds—your mind starts wandering. Therefore, you dig them and then do your own thing."

When the thin, stooped, sad-eyed young guitarist came gangling into London in September 1966, he gave the floundering local scene a much-needed injection and with his unkempt mane of bushy hair started a fashion unprecedented since the heyday of the Presley sideburn. His hairstyle had already made him an outcast in Harlem, and when Chas Chandler, former bass guitarist with the Animals, and the group's manager, Mike Jeffery, first heard him, he had taken refuge from the uptown jibes in Greenwich Village. As Jimmy James, he was playing with his own combo of two months' standing, the Blue Flame.

"We just didn't feel like trying to get into anything because we weren't ready," recalled Hendrix (his real name, incidentally), but for the two Britishers, he was saying something.

They foresaw a place for the shy young man with the despair-drenched voice and the reverberating electric guitar on the London scene and persuaded him to try his luck there.

"I said I might as well go because nothing much was happening," recalled the guitarist. "We were making something near $3 a night, and you know we were starving."

Hendrix was born 22 years ago on the wrong side of the tracks in Seattle, Wash. He brought with him to England an aura of mystery concerning his origins and musical experience and a tailor-made line of hard-times-and-poverty stories. His colonial version of how he traded the life of an itinerant guitarist for a place in the Isley Brothers' backing group was widely quoted in the British musical press: "Yeah, I'll gig. May as well, man, sleepin' outside between them tall tenements was hell. Rats runnin' all across your chest, cockroaches stealin' your last candy bar from your very pockets." (On his current U.S. tour, he was given a gala reception in his hometown and presented with the keys to the city by none other than the mayor himself.)

After a spell with the Isleys, the guitarist wandered to Nashville, Tenn., where he joined a package show starring B.B. King, Sam Cooke, Solomon Burke and Chuck Jackson and paid his gigging dues until one day he missed the band bus and found himself stranded in Kansas City, Mo.

"When you're running around starving on the road, you'll play almost anything," said Hendrix ruefully. "I was more or less forced into like a Top 40 bag. Playing the things that I'm doing now would have been very difficult in that area."

In Atlanta, Ga., he found a job with the Little Richard tour, and on the West Coast he played with Ike and Tina Turner. Then Richard's show took Hendrix to New York, where he played with people like King Curtis and Joey Dee's Starliters.

"Oh man!" Hendrix exclaimed. "I don't think I could have stood another year of playing behind people. I'm glad Chas rescued me!'

The guitarist has the restless nature of the itinerant bluesman. "I get very bored on the road," he admitted, "and I get bored with myself and the music sometimes. I

mean, I love blues, but I wouldn't want to play it all night. It's just like although I like Howlin' Wolf and Otis Rush, there are some blues that just makes me sick. I feel nothing from it."

The chance to improvise is, he said, of prime importance in his playing. "I love to listen to organized Top 40 R&B, but I'd hate to play it," he said. "I'd hate to be in a limited bag; I'd rather starve."

When the Experience was formed on Oct. 12, 1966, three very different personalities were more or less thrown together. Hendrix was united with rock guitarist Noel Redding, who switched to bass guitar, and the explosive drummer Mitch Mitchell. Said the drummer, a devotee of Elvin Jones, "I wasn't at all interested in blues. I was more interested in a sort of pseudo-jazz thing. Noel was very interested in the rock 'n' roll scene of two or three years ago, and so it could have clashed like mad. Instead, we all threw in our ideas, and now we play individually to make one sound."

The first thing that struck Hendrix on his arrival in Britain was the high quality of many of the local musicians and their awareness of "soul."

"One of the first people I ever heard was Eric Clapton with the Cream," he recalled. "I had a couple of his records, but in person he really knocked me out. I didn't know quite what to think, but I guess that if they can dig a cat like Ray Charles, who's one of the all-time greats when you're talking of soul, it isn't too surprising if they come up with that soulful feeling. It just shows that they're listening."

It is obvious from Hendrix's eclectic guitar style that he has not only been influenced by people like Waters, James, King and, in particular, Buddy Guy, but has done a complete turnaround in Britain, listening to the local synthesizers of blues guitar—people like Clapton, Peter Green and Jeff Beck.

"I really don't know about that!" he said smiling. "I listen to everybody, you know, and a lot of the people now are British. But whatever you do, you have an open mind. You don't necessarily take things, you just listen and accept."

Declared Londoner Mitchell, "I don't think this country has anything to teach Jimi, because basically he hasn't changed since he came over. Maybe his outlook has changed a little bit and he's got more scope, but what he is doing is just an extension of his original ideas."

From his viewpoint, Hendrix said,

"When you have people to work with who will work with you, quite naturally you're going to start moving. If you're really interested and really involved in music, well, then you can be very hungry. The more you contribute, the more you want to make. It makes you hungrier, regardless of how many times you eat a day."

Hendrix has slipped fairly easily into the British rock scene, and his attitudes are, at times, surprisingly un-American. Nevertheless, at such times he also seems to be rather uncomfortably straddling the fence between his own blues tradition and the Beatles heritage. It seems safe to assume that had he stayed in the United States, he might have been forced to cut his hair and dress less outrageously than he does in Europe.

As for smashing up instruments onstage, the group has been criticized for following the path of the Who, the first pop group to introduce auto-destruction to the music. To this, Mitchell has a reply:

"Some nights, we can be really bad. If we smash something up, then it's because that instrument, which is something you dearly love, just isn't working that night. It's not responding, and so you want to kill it."

Hendrix further likened the process to the love-hate relationship. "It's just like maybe you feel at times when your girlfriend starts messing around. You might feel that you wanted to do that but you couldn't but with music you do, because an instrument can't fight back."

The Experience has an enviable reputation for the comparative ease with which it records, one of its singles having made the grade on the second take, something almost unheard of in contemporary rock. This stems largely from group rapport. Hendrix is such a magnetic figure that the two sidemen are stimulated by him, and they, in turn, free him from the restrictions that less intelligent musicians would impose.

"You've got to be musically one jump ahead to completely interpret what Jimi wants and put yourself into it." Mitchell said. "Certain times you might feel his equal, and then he comes out with something that stimulates your mind just a bit.

"I don't know if the public realizes this, but we could make a damn site more money by going out doing one-nighters than by recording. When we record, we pay for the studio ourselves and waste a lot of time finding out the different sounds and things. It's easy to go into a 12-bar nothing and put it on a record, but we spend so many hours trying to get new effects, it should be obvious that we're not trying to con the public."

At a recent rehearsal, where proceedings were held up for a couple of hours, the restless Hendrix sat down at the drum kit and tried his hand with the sticks.

"Gotta keep it moving," he commented. "You don't care what people say so much—you just go on and do what you want to do. You never do it quite—I always try to get better and better—but as long as I'm playing, I don't think I'll ever reach the point where I'm satisfied."

In spite of the fact that Hendrix has no particular wish to be hailed as the new king of the blues, he is a unique contemporary interpreter of the genre and a musician whose impact on various areas of the scene has been considerable. The blues, in spite of that intrinsic resignation of much of its subject matter, has, as a musical force, an enduring optimism.

"The blues will never die," the bluesmen repeat with reassuring regularity, and it's probably true. In their own peculiar ways, people like Hendrix are carrying on the tradition.

June 13, 1968

Sun Ra's Space Probe

by J.C. Thomas

Sun Ra and Buddha seem to have things in common.

Both have their own metaphysics and philosophies; complete conceptions of the universe.

Each is a teacher, not a preacher; each has his own ideas to express, and others are free to accept or reject them as they choose.

And the gentle Sun Ra—polite, soft-spoken—has a Buddha-like confidence that he is traveling the particular path that will take him to his destiny.

Buddha, of course, has a few more followers. Yet Sun Ra's disciples seem totally devoted to their leader; they apparently absorb his music through a sort of osmosis, with an intuitive feeling for the complex sound cycles he creates and the spatial vibrations in which he specializes.

Who is Sun Ra? What is his Solar Arkestra?

Sun Ra can be compared to playwright Harold Pinter in his reticence to talk about himself. Like Pinter, the information he deliberately withholds is probably more pertinent than the little he lets out. Unlike Pinter, whose plays are almost specific in their ambiguities, Sun Ra's music is concrete and complete, strong and surging, yet chilling in its complexities and startling in its sonorities.

"Ra means god in Egyptian," he explained. "I always called myself Sun Ra. I can't remember ever having any other name."

His origin he keeps purposely vague. He is a short, rotund, genial man who looks to be 40 or so, but all he will admit to is that he was born "in the month of May, arrival zone U.S.A." When he says that, his round face crinkles into an enigmatic smile; he knows; we have yet to discover.

Some aspects of his early history, however, are verifiable. He grew up in Gary, Ind., Washington, D.C., and Chicago, where he became known before moving to New York in 1961. In Chicago, he wrote the music for the shows at the Club De Lisa, then a showcase for such jazz luminaries as Earl Hines and Billy Eckstine (the place was reopened a few years ago as simply the Club). In the late 1940s Fletcher Henderson was one of the leaders in residence there, and Sun Ra played piano in his band. (Then, strangely enough, he was Le Sony'r Ra to all others, but Sun Ra to himself.)

"I was playing my own inversions of the chords the way I felt them," he once said. "It disturbed the band but it didn't bother Fletcher."

Later, in Chicago—sometime in the 1950s—he organized his own band and played around the city wherever he could get a gig. The music was called by many names—Solar, Solar-Nature, Space—but orchestra was spelled "arkestra," then as today. And today in New York—where the band is now based, and from which location it has played dates around the country—the musicians and their conceptions are known collectively as The Space Music of Sun Ra and His Space Arkestra.

The nucleus of the band is roughly a baker's dozen, although the ensemble has varied from a low of eight to a high of 22. More a family than an orchestra—most of the members left Chicago to make the move to New York with their leader, and

several have been with him for 10 years or longer—they congregate around the Sun Studio in New York's East Village, a combination residence, rehearsal hall, studio and space station where the master and his disciples "work things out."

As thickly congested with clothing and accessories as a jumble shop, the studio is spray-painted with such cheerful colors as bright orange, sparkling silver and solid gold. Nailed to one wall is an interesting piece of legal paper—a charter of incorporation issued by the state of Illinois on April 10, 1967, for Ihnfinity Inc.

"The idea of Ihnfinity Inc. is that everybody on this planet should have a share in the universe," Sun Ra explained. "We had to make it a profit-making corporation to get it stamped, and we wanted to make it profitable in a humanitarian way. So we did, and the state stamped it and gave us our charter. No one else has a charter to own space.

"Churches are always talking about immortality," he continued. "But for righteous people only. I want everybody to have immortality. It's too big for one nation, one people or even one planet."

Immortality might just be too large a subject to be successfully handled by anybody. However, it is to Sun Ra's credit that he is at least making the attempt.

When Sun Ra discusses the more introspective aspects of his metaphysics, his eyes gaze benignly as his facial expression becomes serious, almost stately; his voice is muted and subdued, yet clear and articulate as the words march out in measured cadence and assemble themselves like his musicians for the enlightenment of your mind and the entertainment of your ears.

"I'm in tune with nature and nature's vibrations," he said. "But most people are not. They're getting all kinds of other vibrations from outer space, bad vibrations. The purpose of my music is to counter these bad vibrations. If any force from outer space were to attack this planet, they'd do it with vibrations. My music counteracts these vibrations.

"The planet is in confusion, and so are the musicians. Music is part of some great source, yet most musicians are just tapping in on the line. Early jazz was happy music, and today it's anything but that. There's no more brotherhood; everyone's gotten so mercenary. Now, all the musicians talk about is doing their own thing."

Ironically, Sun Ra too is doing "his own thing." To add a further note of paradox, it has been essentially a "new thing" that he's been doing for the past two decades, yet his music is really never put in that particular bag. Artists like Archie Shepp, Pharoah Sanders, Roswell Rudd, Ornette Coleman—and perhaps John Coltrane just before he died—are known as New Thingers, yet few include Sun Ra in this category.

To some ears at least, his music is strange. His space music, with its emphasis on extraterrestrial vibrations, seems more than music; spiritual, almost religious in feeling, as if something more than waves from a pulsar star, many light-years removed from us in the outermost boundaries of immeasurable space, is turning him into a cosmic consciousness.

Some of this music is available on record from the labels of Saturn, ESP and Delmark. But it is in New York that the sounds of Space Music are most frequently heard—in Central Park and Carnegie Hall, to name two settings for concerts he has conducted recently. (His two-nighter at Carnegie Hall last April saw the band backed up by a full-fledged light show—a perfect setting. But attendance was disappointing.)

The steadiest gig of all—and the place where he has been most consistently heard—is Slugs' Saloon, just a few blocks away from the Sun Studio. A dark, murky, wood-paneled pub, probably dating back from the days of Maxwell Bodenheim, Slugs' has a casual easygoing informality in its atmosphere that affords Sun Ra the maximum of musical freedom and "feelin' good" that he misses so much from the early days of jazz. Here, as he has for almost every Monday night for the past 18 months, Sun Ra and his musicians "tune in, turn on and take over."

The men shamble onstage, almost single file, dressed in the wildest dreams of any Upper East Side boutique—fur hats, flowing robes, African print shirts, beads and bells. The instruments and cases spill out into the drinking area, so small is the bandstand. Sun Ra, who perhaps is the most unobtrusive leader in jazz, since he always is found at the rear of the band rather than in front, sits astride his instrumental trio of piano, clavinette and something he calls the spacmaster—an organ specially manufactured for him by the Chicago Musical Instrument Co. that sounds like a cross between a theremin and bagpipes. Occasionally, he will play a one-stringed instrument he says is a Chinese violin.

Sun Ra.
(Thomas Hunter)

His men tune up their instruments, which represent a veritable United Nations of sources. Chinese bamboo flute, bass clarinet and bassoon, Japanese koto, African koru, oboe and English horn, Sun Harp (a small harp designed like the golden rays of the sun that gives off beautifully resonant tones)—to name a few. Percussion, too, as every man doubles on at least one drum, and two or three are not uncommon—bongos, claves, maracas, conga, gongs, bells and enough authentic African drums to equip a tribe.

The audience, as heterogeneous as the music that they'll soon hear, is quiet, respectful and attentive. They may, however, become slightly restless during the next three hours—for that's the usual length of a set at Slugs', as the sounds of Sun Ra segue from one composition into another without stopping. His Space Music makes almost as many demands on his audience as it does on his musicians, and it's sometimes hard to ascertain who's the more exhausted after a night of six solid hours of music.

If Sun Ra speaks to the crowd, he will probably say: "I believe in beauty, and my music is happiness."

His music is also a "Happening," in the more positive sense of that much-misused word. Like the best of jazz, it goes all the way back to the earliest blues, and moves forward through time as well as space to pick up multiple time signatures, tight ensemble voicings (especially in the reed section), brass fugues, constantly changing harmonic variations and time signatures, atonal dissonances and astringent melodies that splash upon the ears like vast tidal waves of sound, shifting and shading in volume and sonority; a sort of controlled chaos.

Through compositions titled "Angels and Demons at Play," "Rocket No. 9 Takes Off for the Planet Venus," "Spontaneous Simplicity," "We Travel the Spaceways" (which seems to be the band's theme, for the musicians flavor the tune with a cheerful vocal chorus about the delights of space travel) and a surrealistic setting of "King Porter Stomp," the sounds are evocative, introspective, intuitive and expressive; played with power, drive, precision and joy. And with plenty of percussion.

There are such outstanding soloists as Marshall Allen, the man on alto sax, oboe and bamboo flute; the bursting baritone of Pat Patrick; trombonist Dick Griffin; and boss tenor John Gilmore. Bassist Bill Davis and drummer Clifford Jarvis drive the rhythm section right into outer space.

Judging by audience response, the music travels the inner spaceways, too.

Dec. 12, 1968
. . . .

Creativity and Change

by Wayne Shorter

ED NOTE—Tenor saxophonist-composer Wayne Shorter first came to prominence with Art Blakey, with whom he played from 1959 to 1963. Since 1964, he has been a member of Miles Davis' group. His most recent recordings under his own name are *The All-Seeing Eye* (Blue Note 4219) and *Adam's Apple* (Blue Note 4232). He won the 1962 *DownBeat* Critics Poll New Star Award as a tenor saxophonist and the 1968 Critics Poll Talent Deserving of Wider Recognition Award as a composer.

Art. Art as a competitive thing among artists. I've been wondering how it has come about that art is, in fact, a competitive thing among artists. I wonder if artists choose to compete among themselves, or are they goaded, pushed or lured into it as a result of the makeup of this particular society? I wonder if a young musician, hearing another musician, has an instinctive desire to compete with this other musician or instead to join forces and compare notes? I wonder if the two of them were to get together and compare notes, and their notes were appraised by a third party, the critic, would these two artists be so influenced by what the third party says that they would strive to compete with one another to please the critic? In addition, the critic speaks to a fourth party, the public, and in pleasing the critic do you please the public?

I wonder if a poll or a contest is valid to give artists an incentive to create, to go on, or to run the mile in less than a minute. Is art an art or a sport? I think polls, awards and Oscars come right out of the school system—the star you get on your paper, the A B C D mark. If we could get rid of the stigma that grading over such a long period of time has produced, I think we might have a clearer idea of what a person does when he is creating something. For instance, if a person wins first place in a category in the arts through a voting system, and he feels good about it, is he actually going to create or merely perpetuate the poll system?

It's hard to get away from voting or polls all the way, because, if you're going to play for an audience, the applause is the same thing in miniature size. Some people even consider applause as greater than a citation or trophy. Applause is gratifying to me and a lot of other musicians. Some musicians would deny it, but I know how they feel inside. I cannot say truthfully that lack of applause is not gratifying for me, because I can't say that lack of applause means lack of recognition. That has happened to me quite a bit, especially when I first started out. Even now it happens sometimes, but then when I come down from the bandstand, someone will come up and say something profound about the whole set, not just about me. This one person sounds like he's speaking for the whole audience, and he

might say, "That was a deep set—a lot of thought going on." I think in that sense he was trying to say that there was no room for applause—they didn't want to disturb the essence of the moment.

Does a person create because of recognition by a large body, and, if he is recognized, does he stop creating? I wonder if any artist can grade himself, using himself as his own ruler? Maybe that has to be taught. I've rarely had a teacher who said, "I'm going to teach you to grade yourself against yourself, use yourself as your own incentive force." You can draw power, drive, from yourself, from nature and not necessarily from another person. It's hard to do, but once you know what it is and you start to reach for it, it's really something. If anyone has seen *2001*, it's like reaching for that black monolith, that symbol of Why and What and Where. If you're curious enough about yourself, you don't have too much time to be curious about what the next person is doing. You don't try to compete with something superficial and exterior, a "keeping up with the Joneses" idea. I think that if artists learned to use themselves as their own ruler, then audiences would have to learn to do this, too. When they go to see Broadway plays they won't have to read what the critic says.

Who decides what is good art? It's a highly individual thing, with or without a body of people calling themselves critics or an audience calling themselves critics. A lot of people do not want to be individual thinkers and analyze something by themselves, so they turn to polls and awards to make up their minds. If enough people make up their minds that way, they might miss a lot of creative people who have something to give, without asking for something in return. When an artist creates he can feed the soul, heal the soul, make the soul well, but a lot of people in an audience listen not with their souls but with computerized minds, assembled and conditioned by the system, which includes polls and awards.

I wonder if those who believe in polls and awards believe that they are building a bridge across a body of water for someone who can't swim? The polls may be like water wings, but there'll come a time when you have to take those water wings off. What I'm worried about is the perpetuation of water wings and bridges. I don't believe that the designer, the critic, really perpetuates it, although he has an advantageous perch. The only one who can perpetuate it is the person who needs it. As I write now, I'm trying not to sit in judgment, because everything is en route, everything is in the interim. If I were to judge, I might as well try to get a great big pencil about the size of the sun, and put a period on this earth. That would be supreme judgment.

If a critic has the job of criticizing and rating records, and he is torn between giving record A a high rating and giving record B a lower rating, and the reason he is torn is that the musicians on record B, while not as good, are trying very hard, and he doesn't want to step on the toes of the musicians on record A, that's a hard thing to be confronted with, especially if that's your job. His job and his conscience... his conscience is a job, too. If he made up his mind to give record A a higher rating and record B a lower rating, and the musicians on record B were very honest, I think that, though they may be hurt, along with honesty comes a kind of strength. But would their efforts to get a higher rating bypass real creativity? I suppose it's up to the musicians to rely on their strength to know which way to go, no matter what who says.

Is creativity good, in the sense of originality? How can you be so original, when you walk a little bit like your mother or father, or have the color of your father's eyes, or you make a gesture and someone says, "You did that just like your father used to do." Charlie Parker, for example, said that when he was young, his idols on the alto saxophone were Rudy Vallee and Jimmy Dorsey. If you've heard Bird, and if you've heard Rudy Vallee and Jimmy Dorsey, I think you'd have to dig very deep, tear off many layers of wallpaper before you could find any similarity in sound, approach or technique. I would say that the only thing which would confirm what Bird said about his admiration would be the sophistication of his approach. It's the sophistication of Westernized music, Western scales. But let's go back even further. Western scales came from around Greece, Jerusalem and Arabia. They're world scales, really. People are taught music history this way, separating Western music from Eastern music, but I think it's one big circle. It's hard to keep from using labels. For instance, when I said that Bird idolized Rudy Vallee and Dorsey, some people's minds would stop and they'd say, "Ooo, that's who he dug!" But I tend to use those names as a springboard into history, going all the way back to the great explosion that started this planet. You can't just go on what Mr. X said, you've got to do a little

Wayne Shorter.
(DownBeat Archive)

thinking of your own.

We hear a lot of the word "freedom," and if you're going to have freedom, a critic has to have freedom, too. A lot of critics don't consider criticism a job. With some, it's a very esthetic thing. When they put their thoughts on paper about something they've seen or heard, they've more than seen or heard it. They get involved in it. I'm not saying that they get so involved that they're "swayed," because a great critic can retain a helluva sense of balance.

When reading his words on paper you can feel that, actually, he's not criticizing something—his words turn into a poetic thing, become an extension of the art experience. At the same time he's not putting anyone or anything up on a pedestal. Art comes first—the Baby, save the Baby!

I'd like to return to the other side of competition—the joining, the getting together, comparing notes. When I was 16, I used to get a copy of a magazine that had articles about a musician who was playing a new music called bebop, and I heard Charlie Parker and Bud Powell on the radio. I had to get to New York... because of reading about how things had started at Minton's, where a lot of getting together and comparing of notes had been going on. A number of musicians then were thrown together out of poverty. They lived together, cooked together... they even helped bury each other. Today, the ones out of the '40s who have made it, the ones who have their own groups now, I'll always remember the togetherness they had then, but through their fame they have to travel their separate roads. There's some resurgence of that now among the younger musicians—the wanting to get together. They want to get together in large numbers—the big band thing, the studio thing. A few musicians have studios where they can teach students and at the same time get together, but the jam session thing is gone. That was the other way of getting together... just jamming.

I hear all across the country, "Where can I go to play, where can I go to be heard, what is it like in New York?" It's the same old question, but New York is... the same old New York, as far as being the center of almost anything. When I finally did go to New York in the days when I was commuting from New Jersey with my horn, I remember just before I was drafted into the Army, I went to a place called Cafe Bohemia. Charlie Parker had just died, and I walked in with my horn. There was a drummer there who now lives in Europe; there was an organ player who just got in town (he's very big today), and an alto saxophone player who's very big today had just arrived. They were all on the bandstand with Oscar Pettiford. I had a chance to sit in with them. Everyone was together, liking each other. When we got down from the bandstand we were shaking hands and talking, and you could see the light in all these people's eyes as if they were making plans for getting groups together out of the people who were there. I was feeling kind of bad because I was going into the Army and I didn't know whether I was going to be included in those plans. When I went into the Army, I felt, "That's the last of the jam session thing," but when I got out it was still perpetuating a little bit. There were enough jam sessions going on so that well-known musicians could get around to know people and see who they would like to hire.

Getting started means getting confidence, putting yourself in a context. Being around musicians who are playing, meeting them, talking to them, you're getting conditioned. You're watching how a musician walks up to the microphone and plays, or how another one may shy away from the spotlight. You make up your mind how you want to be, because the way you are does affect what comes out of the horn. You produce barriers of shyness, barriers of lack of confidence or barriers of overconfidence. You have to get your own balance together.

I guess I was pretty lucky, because even when I was in the Army, I had a chance to work with one of the well-known groups. I was stationed in the East, Fort Dix, so I was not far from the Blue Note in Philadelphia, and not far from New York and Washington, D.C. I was there one night when I really heard Coltrane (I had heard him before in New York but I really heard him this night. He was breaking away from something.) I would be in New York on a weekend pass, playing, and Coltrane would come out of nowhere and we'd talk. As a result, when I got out of the Army, 'Trane and I spent a lot of time together in his apartment in New York. We spent a lot of time at the piano, and he was telling me what he was doing, which way he was going, and what he was trying to work on. We'd stay all day and all night. I would play the piano and he would play his horn, then he would play the piano and I would play my horn. That kind of getting together is not going on too much now. Maybe in certain areas of New York, musicians who live in the Village who have lofts can get together. I'd like to see more of it. I'd like to branch out and help this get going. On my next record date I'd like to do a large thing, maybe 19 or 22 pieces, and call on those musicians to help perform this work. While recording, I'd like to create the atmosphere that we're not just at a recording session. I've written something down but we'll have a jam session spirit.

The term "musician" can become a hard shell. You can become callous and impersonal, but there's still a human thing there. For example, two musicians will meet in Europe (it always happens in a way out place somewhere), and they belong to two different schools of music, but they will be glad to see each other, shaking hands and talking. I had a long talk with a very well-known saxophonist in Switzerland— some people call him the father of the jazz saxophone. We were just sitting there and I asked him how he was doing, and before he said he was doing all right, he started talk- ing about economics. It was as if I were at home talking to an uncle. In the back of my mind I was thinking of people who admire people; a young fan of 17, for instance. If he could see a young musician that he knows and an older musician, he would feel, "Wow, there they are together." I used to feel the same way.

In Paris in 1961 (I went to Paris with a well-known group), the bandleader walked into my room along with Bud Powell. We all sat around and then everyone left except Bud Powell. He looked at me, my horn was on the bed, and he said, "Can you play something for me?" I said OK, and I was thinking about when I was 17 and had to sneak into Birdland and sit way in the back and watch Bud play. I picked up my horn and tried to play one of the things he wrote named after his daughter, "Celia," and then I tried something else of his, just playing the melody. When I finished he looked at me and smiled, didn't say anything else, got up, kept smiling and walked out.

At this point in my life, when I see people who are famous and great, I don't want to ever lose the memory of the awe I had when I was younger. I don't want to become so sophisticated and confident that I can say, "We're all in this together"—a sort of smug "thing." Now, when I am in the company of a large number of great musicians, I feel very comfortable and I can see them as human beings, see myself as a human being among them, and respect and dig whatever they have produced through the years.

Where is the new music going? I don't know if that's as important as where did it come from, because if you know where it came from, it's going anyway. I don't like labels, but I'll say "new music" anyway— total involvement. When you're playing, the music is not just you and the horn—the music is the microphone, the chair, the door opening, the spotlight, something rattling. From soul to universe.

I saw something on television where they had total involvement. Two men were discussing what was about to happen. Then there was a little ballet. It started and the camera went from the dancers to the two men talking, and they were a part of the ballet, still talking about it. I liked that, as a start.

I think this is a very exciting time to live in. Some people are concerned with an end of things. Then, all of a sudden you hear a small voice say, "This is a renaissance." Things are happening now that have never happened in history, and art will reflect this. Everything is speeded up so you can see the change and feel yourself changing. Those who don't change, who refuse to change, can feel themselves not changing, and some of them don't like it.

Every time we go to California, I always make it a point to go to Berkeley. I've visited the homes of students out there. Some of them are 14 years younger than I am, and everything was very communicative. I found it easy just to be me, not to be young. We were all together. No one asked me my age. They want change.

About certain people being reluctant to change for the betterment of all concerned—I find that the people who find it easiest to change and keep evolving, who don't want a status quo, are able to move around. A person who is stationary finds it difficult to change. In the business I'm in, we move around and travel like troubadours. We are not bound to any city government or neighborhood government. The students I met out in California live in Berkeley and go to school there, but I noticed that they kept moving around. They'd go to San Francisco, then to L.A. and up to Seattle, then all the way to New York, and then back to school.

I saw evidence of a great change when we played two concerts at Berkeley. One change was this—the concert was given by a 21-year old Chinese girl, a jazz impresario. She told me she had been listening to jazz since she was 8. She put on the concert with a lot of opposition from the school staff about allotting money and other things, but she worked and did it. She had some of the most well-known names in jazz. At the last concert she gave, there were over 20,000 people at the Greek Theater in Berkeley. The audience was rock 'n' roll–oriented and most of the people had never seen these artists before and had rarely heard them. I saw them turning their ears to jazz, something they had never really heard. They focused their attention and they listened with a lot of respect and at one point they kind of went wild with applause.

When I hear a jazz musician say, "Well, the young people—rock 'n' roll is their thing—they're not going to even listen to jazz"—I think that they'll change and grow up. Rock 'n' roll is changing with them. I'm hearing a whole lot of things from them. The "labels" are being taken off the bottles. As I said about the different scales, Western and Greek, it's all one big thing. I saw kids with long hair, beards and sandals, sitting right

down in front of the bandstand and they were part of a thing called jazz. The same thing happened in New York at the Village Gate. I met a lot of young people there, and I spoke to one person who had long hair and everything. I'll describe the way the person looked and then you'll have to piece together how he looked and what he does. He had long hair, beard and mustache, and he had on beads, a buckskin jacket, and an Apache head wrapping. He writes opera! He came to listen to the music labeled jazz, and he's meshing and welding what he knows about sound with what he hears everywhere. He said, "I have to be here. It's part of the thing."

East and west I saw evidence of a meeting of minds. The change I like is always that getting together. The person who has been labeled "hippie and rock" is breaking out and taking his own label off. The younger people will tend to look at the artists who are really doing something and use them as guides, so there's nothing really to worry about. I'm saying all these things because I myself don't like to stand still. Art Blakey told me once, "Music is like a river. It must flow." When someone would ask, "Why does it have to flow?" he would say, "If a body of water has no inlet or outlet, it's bound to get stagnant!" I doubt if you'd find anything living in it. He who drinks from it will have an awful stomachache—or start digging six feet. Any person knows when he's stagnant. If he doesn't know, there's a whole lot of "camouflage" going on. You can be taught to know things, and you can be taught not to know things. If you think you're not stagnant, check yourself out.

When we played at Berkeley with a 19-piece orchestra, I looked out in the audience, I looked at Miles, I looked at Gil Evans, I looked at a 19-year-old girl who was playing the harp, then in the French horn section there was an elderly man whose hair was stone white, there was a middle-aged lady playing French horn next to him, then I looked at Howard Johnson on tuba, and I said, "All ages, all ages here, and we're having a ball with sound." No one questioned, "What is this—it's not normal." The young female harpist would only ask a few technical questions and that was all. That's what goes on in music, the interplay between ages. I saw life come to life that night. I'd like to see that with young people and the elders throughout the world. The youth can't get their hands on the tanks, they can't get their hands on the plans at the Pentagon and the Kremlin,

they can't get their hands on the buttons, they don't have access to the material power, but if the elders are so nervous about the youngsters and they aren't getting nervous about the power they have in their hands, evidently the youngsters' mental power is upsetting someone.

Just recently I've been looking at clothes, and I found one place in New York where a lot of young people hang out. One thing caught me as soon as I walked in— they were playing records in the store. Everybody was looking at clothes and some people were kind of swinging and swaying to the music. I went back to the store another time—no one was buying, everyone was dancing, and the owner was dancing, too. He said, "Well, the main thing is to have some fun, as long as I can survive." He's not afraid if someone comes in the store and doesn't buy. They'll buy or trade something eventually and at the same time they're trading a little happiness. I like that approach. The same spirit—breaking up something that's stiff—happens on the bandstand sometimes. When there is an obviously straight up and down audience, sometimes I know that the musicians feel compelled to throw themselves into the music and break up the ice.

Life to me is like an art, because life has been created by an artist, the Chief Architect. Some people can only relate their soul to God. It seems as if they can only do it when it's time to go to church, or when times are hard. They think that the soul in relation to the universe has to do with religion all the time. I think part of the stiffness we see is due to that, because they cannot relate their soul to a table, for example. They can't see any practical use in relating their soul to a table, to a bug on a windowsill, to musicians on a bandstand, or a picture hanging on a wall, or salt and pepper. You can say that's going from the sublime to the ridiculous, but is it? It's like saying, "A bird does not fly because it has wings. It has wings because it flies!"

People who are hung up in stiffness think in issues, broad issues, the issue of making a living, the issue of crime in the streets. The issue turns out to be a hangup—the issue of asking someone over to your house to have dinner. What is an attitude and how can you change an attitude? They say how can you legislate attitudes, but when you get down to the nitty-gritty, you say, "Come over to my house and have dinner." Some people say, "I don't want to associate with 'outside' music, I don't want anything to do with it." What I hear from younger people is who needs that hang-up, everything is everything, let it be, let's do it whenever, if I can't get you tomorrow, whenever....

Among these young people there's no room for jealousy as a force, jealousy between men and women, jealousy about things. I like to call jealousy an emotional rage, and it exists very much among the older age bracket. In the last few years I haven't heard the word "jealousy" used among the young people. When I look at some of the soap operas, I see in their conflicts that they're still perpetuating those things that the young people have almost completely eliminated.

I can't talk about music at this stage of my life without putting it in a wider context. I can't talk about social ills or goods without trying to sneak in something about art. Many musicians who came up about my time are taking care of business when they're not performing, taking care of paperwork, legal things. For a long time I used to hear, "All you've got to do is play your horn and the business will take care of itself, you'll have people to take care of business for you." I think musicians today should try to read about business and copyright laws, etc. They should know what certain words mean when they're confronted with a contract and not just look at the number of zeros attached to a digit and a dollar sign. I wonder how many musicians today have thought of drawing up wills.

Music has always played a great part in inventions. I think there may be something coming along that would be an extension of the TV set, and I believe that music will play a part in it. Along with these inventions there comes a new amendment in your business mind. I've written to Washington to get the jukebox bill passed, and I know Stan Kenton's working on it. That, and royalties for the way an artist interprets a certain piece of music. No one's getting any royalties from jukeboxes. The copyright law says that royalties should be distributed to the artists in the event of any mechanical reproduction of musical sound. If they can't get the jukebox bill passed, anyone who invents something to reproduce music may look at the jukebox as a loophole, since it would be advantageous for him not pay the people whose music is being reproduced.

I mentioned the idea of "total involvement." Everything I've said about art, about youth, about business, indicates that

the music and musician of tomorrow will be totally involved. Neither he nor his art will be confined to the stage.

Aug. 7, 1969

Father and Son

An Interview with Muddy Waters and Paul Butterfield

by Don DeMicheal

There's only one way for a young man to learn true blues: from older men—black men. This sort of teacher-student relationship is rather common today, or at least it has been since the blues gained such popularity with the seemingly ever-fickle young white audience. One of the most popular of the young blues men is Paul Butterfield. But Butterfield is an old hand at the blues, having drunk from the deep well on Chicago's South Side several years ago. This spring, he and guitarist Michael Bloomfield were reunited with two of their main teachers—singer/guitarist Muddy Waters and pianist Otis Spann (Waters' half-brother and longtime sideman). The reunion took place in the Ter-Mar Recording Studio at Chess Records, and for three nights a rather remarkable recording session rolled from one artistic peak to another. Following the last night, Butterfield, Waters and, later, Spann discussed the session and the ways they learned the blues. What follows is an edited version of the conversation.

DeMicheal: Paul, when was the first time you sat in with Muddy?

Butterfield: About 1957.

DeM.: How old were you?

P.B.: About 18. The stuff I play now... my band's got horns and things, and we do a lot of different stuff, 'cause I got guys in my band who can really play—but they can't play that old stuff. It's just a certain thing I came up in, that I learned, and what I was really listening to—and I mean live; I ain't talking about listening to records—was Muddy. Muddy had a real good band then. You had Pat Hare on guitar....

Waters: Willie on drums.

P.B.: No, it wasn't Willie.

M.W.: Then it had to be [Francis] Clay.

P.B.: No.

M.W.: Was it S.P. [Leary]?

PB: No.

M.W.: Then it got to be Clay.

P.B.: Then it was Clay. And Little Walter used to come in and sit in.

M.W.: Magic Sam, Otis Rush all those boys used to come and sit in. They all sat in because I'm not the kind of guy who'll hold the bandstand for myself. I'm not like a lot of the older guys who've been in the business for a long time, 'cause I'm not jealous of nobody—you play what you play and I'll put you on my bandstand.

DeM.: How did you get turned on to the blues, Paul?

P.B.: I'll tell you the truth, man. My brother, my family used to play a lot of blues records. Old 78s. They used to listen to people like Muddy, Gene Ammons, Charlie Parker.... It was more jazz than blues, but the feeling I got was from blues. So I got it early. There used to be WGES, and they used to play from 11 to 12 o'clock at night nothing but blues. And Nashville, Tenn., John R. used to play nothing but blues. We used to hear it when I was 10 years old. My brother started buying blues singles when I was out playing baseball. I don't know what turned me on, but I just liked that kind of music better than any other kind of music. I like lots of kinds of music. I like Roland Kirk, Stanley Turrentine, Gene Ammons... a whole lot of people. But that was the music that really got me interested in playing.

DeM.: Interested in playing harp?

P.B.: Naw, I never thought about playing the harp. I just started playing the harp. I just enjoyed playing it. I didn't have no plan or say, "I'm gonna learn how to play the harp like so and so or learn how to do this or that," y'know. I just started playing it. I mess around with any instrument I can get next to. It wasn't, "I want to learn like Little Walter or Sonny Boy Williamson." I just wanted to learn how to play.

M.W.: In music of this kind everybody got to be influenced by somebody.

P.B.: I was influenced a lot by Little Walter, and when I got to play some more, by Sonny Boy, the second. Then a little after that I started getting influenced by Gene Ammons, Stanley Turrentine...

M.W.: After you've mastered your instrument, you can go the way you want to go at that particular time. When I began I was influenced by Son House and Robert Johnson. That doesn't mean you have to be

Muddy Waters and
Paul Butterfield.
(James Powell)

exactly like them, 'cause when you get out there, you learn other people's work and you put more of your own material in it and then you're on your own.

P.B.: There ain't no musician in the whole world that isn't influenced by a whole lot of people. They're influenced by anybody they hear that's good.

M.W.: That's right. What makes me happy is to see how many kids been influenced by me.

P.B.: There was a scene in Chicago, Detroit, St. Louis—the Midwest—where guys would say, "I'm gonna get up there and burn this cat." A lot of underneath stuff.

DeM.: Cutting contest.

P.B.: Yeah. That mostly came from Chicago. Isn't that true, Muddy?

M.W.: Yeah. Years ago—I'd say back in '47 or '8—Little Walter, Jimmy Rodgers and myself, we would go around looking for bands that were playing. We called ourselves the Headcutters, 'cause we'd go in and if we got a chance we were gonna burn

'em. Today, people's not like that. You just get up and play. I'm not like that no more. Just play what you can play, and if the people like it, fine; if they don't, try again next time. But today, Paul, we have some people—I won't call no names—that still got that feeling: want to be the best. You can't be the best; you can just be a good'un.

P.B.: Just be you.

M.W.: And that's it. Whatever you do, try to do it good.

P.B.: I played this place in California, man, that all these kids came down and the only thing in their minds was to wipe me out. So I said go ahead and play, and I'll play what I play. Musicians are supposed to be loving each other...

M.W.: Together.

P.B.:... and giving stuff to each other and making each other feel good. What I'm talking about is music, not just blues. I'm ready to do something that maybe somebody's not gonna dig at all, but if it's music I'm supposed to be sharing it, learning

about it. That's the only way you can do it. One of the main reasons why I never really tried to play Little Walter's solos or Sonny Boy's or any other cat's exactly the way it was is that, in the first place, I couldn't.

M.W.: Paul, in this field today, if you pick up a harmonica, you got to go through John Lee Williamson [Sonny Boy No. 1], Rice Miller [Sonny Boy No. 2] or Walter Jacobs [Little Walter].

P.B.: Right.

M.W.: Because they set a pattern out here, and there's nobody been born yet that can do too much more stuff to go with it. So if you say I try to play like Son House— sure, I'm glad of that 'cause Son was a great man. Robert Johnson was one of the greatest there's ever been. So that makes me feel proud, 'cause I got my pattern from them. I can't go around it too far because I got to come back around to something in that particular field. Between the three of us, I'm doing Muddy Waters, but because I use a slide, I can't get away from the sound of those two people 'cause they made it popular years and years ago. This sound is 200 or 500 years standing.

DeM.: I'm curious to find out if the learning process was similar for the two of you. When you went into playing blues, Muddy, how did you go about learning?

M.W.: I was first blowing harmonica, like Paul here. I had a young boy by the name of Scott Bowhandle playing guitar, and he learned me the little he knowed. One night we went to one of these Saturday night fish frys, and Son House was there playing. I was using the bottleneck because most of the Delta people used this bottleneck-style thing. When I heard Son House, I should have broke my bottleneck because this other cat hadn't learned me nothing. Son House played this place for about four weeks in a row, and I was there every night, closer to him than I am to your microphone. You couldn't get me out of that corner, listening to him, what he's doing. Years later, down around 1937, I was very good then, but I hadn't been exposed to the public—I heard this Robert Johnson come out, and he got his teaching from Son House. He had a different thing. Where we'd play it slow, Robert Johnson had it up-tempo. The young idea of it, y'know what I mean? I didn't know Johnson much; I saw him one time in Friars Point, Miss. I knew Son House very, very good.

DeM.: Paul, was your experience similar, only 20–30 years later?

P.B.: The people I most listened to were Muddy, Spann, people who were around—Robert Nighthawk was playing, and Wolf was playing, and Magic Sam… like, Magic Sam is pretty close to my age, and Otis Rush is—but I listened to anybody I could listen to. I used to go out and play with Muddy when I couldn't play nothing, but he'd let me come up.

DeM.: When I first met you and Mike Bloomfield in 1962 or so, you were both living on Chicago's South Side…

P.B.: Naw, Michael never lived on the South Side. Michael was in rock-and-roll bands when he was 16, 17 years old. He was from a whole different area, the North Side. I never even worked out of the North Side until I started working at Big John's. Michael really got interested in blues like Muddy and those cats, after he'd been playing in rock-and-roll show bands. He was never down on the South Side before then. I never saw that cat on the South Side.

I never practiced the harp in my life. Never. I would just blow in it. I was blow-ing some lousy stuff. Just blowing it, drinking wine, getting high and enjoying myself. Nick Gravenites was the first cat to take me down to see you, Muddy, about 1957. We were more interested in getting high, dancing and having ourselves some good times than anything else. I never sat down and tried to figure out what he's doing with this stuff. I just played it. Muddy knows that I used to come down to him and play some nothing stuff but nobody ever said, "Well, man, you're not playing too well.'

M.W.: But you always had this particular thing, this something that everybody don't have, this thing you're born with, this touch. 'Cause you used to sing a little song and have the joint going pretty good. As soon as you'd walk in, I'd say, "You're on next, man."

DeM.: Now after all these years, you two finally have made a record together.

M.W.: It sure was an enjoyable time for me.

DeM.: How did the record come about?

M.W.: The idea came from my "grandson," Marshall Chess.

Chess: Michael was at my house, and he said he'd like to do a record with Muddy and Paul. The title, *Fathers and Sons*, was his idea.

M.W.: Is that the name of it? That's a very good title, 'cause I am the daddy, and all these kids are my sons. I feel there are so many kids tracing in my tracks that I'm the father out here.

DeM.: How do you think the session went?

M.W.: I think it was one of the greatest sessions we did since Little Walter's time and Jimmy Rodgers'. We was close to the old sound.

P.B.: I tell you, man, I think some good things came out of this.

DeM.: When was the last time you two played together?

M.W.: In California. I was playing in a club out there, and Paul was off this particular time, and he came in and sat in with us. It was a beautiful night, but it was nothing like the session. At the session, we was right down to it.

DeM.: You did mostly old things?

M.W.: We did a lot of the things over we did with Little Walter and Jimmy Rodgers and [Edward] Elgin on drums. We tried to get ready for that particular thing, as close as possible. It's about as close as I've been to it since I first recorded it.

P.B.: Duck Dunn, the bass player, came in from Memphis. I came in from New York. Michael came in from San Francisco. Muddy came up from Texas. Now, I don't have any time off, none, but it was an honor for me to get together with Muddy and have a good time and play some music.

M.W.: One thing, I hope it's not the last time we get together.

P.B.: Duck Dunn had never played this kind of music, really. And most of the cats haven't been playing this type of music for a long while. It really made me feel good to get back and really be playing some stuff on the harp that was what I came from, the thing that really turned me on to be playing in the first place. Now I'm playing different things, different changes. It made me feel so good to be playing something that wasn't just, "Well, we'll get together and do this recording." We've been enjoying ourselves. Really felt good…. A lot of it had to do with Muddy's singing. Muddy might not be a young cat anymore, but he's doing it. He still gets an awful good feeling for me for playing. He's the main cat; we're playing with Muddy. It's his feeling, and the way he's doing the stuff is making us feel really good. Feeling is 99 percent of it. If you're not feeling the music, how can you expect the other cats who are playing to really feel it? You doing an article or what?

DeM.: I'm gathering material for some articles.

P.B.: This may be jive, man, so tell me if I'm wrong. If you write an article I hope you write something about human beings 'cause I love Muddy, and I'm tired of hearing about this black-and-white bullshit. I want to hear some stuff about human beings. If you want to write an article, man, and getting back into that separation bit, then forget about me. Don't even mention my name, 'cause I don't want to have anything to do with it.

DeM.: This is a conversation, isn't it?

P.B.: I'm trying to tell you…

DeM.: I'm answering your question right there. You're both sitting here talking, right?

P.B.: That's just the way I feel about it, y'know? I feel people are trying in this country right now, they're trying to get together, and there's going to be some heavy shit going down. There's some bad stuff with the black people and there's some bad stuff with the white people. A lot of separation; there's a lot of understanding that's got to come down. But I'm just talking about what we're talking about—

music, human beings. I love Muddy the way I love my father, my brother. And he's no black cat or white cat or anything; he's just a human being, man. The cat plays some music I respect, and I dig playing with him. These papers come out and say this is black over here and white over there, I don't want nothing to do with it. I'm proud of being a human being and where I'm at. I am what I am, and Muddy is what he is. And the whole thing is to get some people to love each other and really be able to give something to each other. I'm playing the music I love, and I'm not black; I am just what I am. They put that stuff on Muddy. He goes to New York and they start rapping on him about some bullshit.

M.W.: I think about the white group the way I think about the black group: if you're good, you're good.

P.B.: Right.

M.W.: If you're trying, you're trying.

P.B.: Sincere…

M.W.: And that's the way it is. They've come to me thousands of times: "Do you think a white boy can play the blues?" I tell them they can play the blues better than me, but they'll never be able to sing them as good as me. I'm just telling the truth about it. White boy can run a ring around me playing the blues.

P.B.: Nobody can run a ring around nobody.

M.W.: It comes down to I play my way, my style. That's it.

P.B.: Music has got to do with love, human beings digging each other. That's the only way you can play music; you can't play music with somebody you hate. Every writer who ever writes something on the blues writes some jive. Every article I've ever seen on the blues is from such a narrow viewpoint that it never gets down to what the music is, never gets down to the feeling that's going down. Maybe I shouldn't even be talking about it, but I'm disgusted with all this separation stuff. Every time they do a write-up on me, Muddy, they're talking about my father was a lawyer. Man, my parents never had any money. My parents got put out of business for $1,000 from the income tax people. Which has got nothing to do with nothing. If Muddy is the richest man in the world, he's still got the feeling, he's still the man. I wish I was rich. I never had any money, but if I get some, I sure am not going to feel bad about it. I'm sure gonna groove. I'd go buy me a fast car, some good food, get high and enjoy myself and play music…. I'm only talking about

the only person who can mess you around is yourself. Little Walter, man, I had the greatest respect for that cat. He always treated me good. But he messed himself around by juicing too much. He was a great cat, a great musician, but he messed himself around. That's sad, y'know?

M.W.: You're saying the truth, but I got to say he was one of the greatest harmonica players that ever lived.

P.B.: You got it, man.

M.W.: You got to take advantage of anything you start and not let it take advantage of you. I used to be a good liquor drinker, but when the doctor told me to come off the liquor, I said this is it, no more whisky.

(Spann enters.)

DeM.: Otis, how do you feel about the session?

Spann: I feel the same way my brother feels about it. It was a beautiful session.

M.W.: I think it was one of the closest sessions that we had since Little Walter and Jimmy Rodgers' time and your time, Otis. 'Cause we did those numbers over again and everybody tried to get close to 'em. It wasn't just playing or just blowing.

O.S.: It did remind me of old times. I had more feeling in the session than I've had in a long time. It's a funny thing, the people say the white kids can't play blues, but that's wrong.

M.W.: I'll say this: we got to bring a boy child into the world who can sing the blues like a black man. 'Specially my age, that came up through this scene that one day I eat, the next day I don't. Ain't got them kind of blues today. The colored ain't. The black people ain't got it today. Eat every day. Eat good. If you don't give it to 'em, they take it. I was afraid of taking something, afraid of going to jail, but the black man ain't scared to go to jail no more. That's why I say he can't have the blues I had 35 or 40 years ago.

DeM.: Otis, what do you think of the title of the album, *Fathers and Sons*?

O.S.: Let me be the son.

M.W.: A lot of people want to know how Otis got to play the blues so good. They never knowed this particular thing: he used to come to my house and park in front of the door with a bottle of whisky, and I'd sit there and teach this man, tell him exactly what to do.

O.S.: That's the truth. Ride around, be daybreak before we got home. Sit there talking.

M.W.: Telling him what to with the

piano when I was singing the blues.

O.S.: I don't believe there'll be another musician, up to date, that can follow my brother Muddy singing, because he's a "late" singer. If you don't wait for him, he's not there. He sings behind the beat.

M.W.: This is the wonderful thing about the white kids that played on this session, they got that understanding.

O.S.: They lay right there and did it. Paul came up on us, and I used to teach Paul. He got it. He knows. He used to be like me. When Muddy taught me, I didn't think nothing about no timing. Pat my feet faster than I play.

M.W.: Watch his feet, you will not play nothing.

O.S.: That's the truth.

P.B.: The first record we put out—*Butterfield's Blues Band*—everything was fast as a mother, man. Just pushing everything. We weren't ready to wait for anything, just go. Remember that thing we did for Chess, Muddy? "Walkin' Blues?" The same thing.

M.W.: Taking all the feeling out of it.

P.B.: Yeah, making it real fast. We couldn't help it, I was so energetic.

M.W.: I want you to know one thing, he did one blues tonight that was a real killer, man, that blues we did with all the relaxing, take your time and do it. "Mean Disposition." It's a stone killer. It may not sell five records, but, me, I'd buy as much as 10 myself, and I ain't bought a record in years. But what you cats were putting in behind me just can't be beat.

DeM.: Otis, you were saying in the old days you and Paul used to get together. What'd you do?

P.B.: Drink wine. Play and get high. That's when you were living in that basement.

DeM.: Does the same sort of thing still go on, guys hanging around wanting to learn the blues?

M.W.: Sure, I could have a hotel room full at all times.

P.B.: I'm learning from people right now. I hear stuff I'll be learning for the rest of my life. And I bet Muddy's listening to some people.

M.W.: You can look in your 'cyclopedia and history books, but you never finish that music. You can hear somebody playing and make one particular thing and you say I dig that. Then you say I'm going home and get my old guitar and gonna see can I lick this note. If you miss it, then you go back tomorrow night. I used to say to

Son House, "Would you play so and so and so?" 'Cause I was trying to get that touch on that thing he did. Bukka White got a thing I been trying to learn for five years, and I ain't learnt it yet.

Dec. 11, 1969

"And in This Corner, the Sidewalk Kid..."

by Don DeMicheal

A little man scurries down the dark staircase of the dingy old building on Chicago's 63rd Street.

"Is this Johnny Coulon's Physical Training Club upstairs?" I ask him.

"Third floor," he pipes.

"Miles Davis up there?"

"Oh yes. You just missed seeing him box. Knocked a fellow down twice."

On the third floor, Miles Davis the boxer is busy skipping rope before a full-length mirror... Dittle-e-dop, dittle-e-dop, dittle-e-dop. His feet dance lightly over the rope and across the floor. There isn't an ounce of fat on him.

"Hey, Don," he says, not missing a skip. "You should have seen me box."

Dittle-e-dop...

"A man just told me you knocked a guy down twice."

Dittle-e-dop...

"Naw, man"... dittle-e... "We"... dop... "just sparred a little."

He drops the rope and goes over to a punching bag suspended at head height by ropes connected to the ceiling and floor.

He tries some combinations and jabs on the bag, dodging it as it bounces toward him. A heavy-set man comes up to him and starts sparring lightly, giving advice as Miles tries unsuccessfully to land a light blow. Miles stops and listens to the man, who is Kid Carson, a trainer. He tries what Carson tells him, finds it works and smiles.

Miles introduces me to Carson; Johnny Coulon (the little man on the stairs); and his eldest son, Gregory, up from East St. Louis, Ill., Davis' home town, for a visit.

"Greg won three titles while he was in the Army," says the young man's obviously proud father. "Plays drums, too."

"Can you beat your old man?" I ask, but the son is noncommittal, and the father chuckles.

"Hey, try to lift Johnny," Miles says with an impish glint in his eye.

This didn't seem to be a problem, since Johnny Coulon, who was bantamweight champion many, many years ago, weighs about 90 pounds. So I lifted him.

"Now try it again," Miles says, suppressing a laugh.

Coulon cannot be budged.

"Ain't nobody ever lifted him when he didn't want 'em to," Davis says. "Show him your pictures, Johnny."

Coulon conducts his standard visitor's tour among fading photos of such boxers as Braddock, Dempsey, Carnera, Tunney, Louis, Clay—all trying to lift the little man. In the middle of Coulon's reminiscences, Miles walks up in a white terry-cloth robe.

"Hey, man," he whispers gleefully, "keep your cool, but dig when I turn around." There in that cloth script one has seen on hundreds of boxers' robes is inscribed "Miles Davis." Miles looks over his shoulder and flashes that beautiful smile of his. Miles Davis, boxer, seems a happier man than Miles Davis, musician.

After Miles had dressed, we climbed into his Volkswagen bus (used to haul his quintet's electric piano) and headed for Floogie's Restaurant, one of his favorite eating places in Chicago.

"Turn on your recorder," he said. "We can talk while I drive." And we did, while Miles dodged the traffic.

The obvious question was first:

DON DeMICHEAL: Why do you box?

MILES DAVIS: It gives you a lot of strength. It's good for your wind. I mean, when I go to play something that I know is kind of impossible to play, I have that strength, that wind. And it blows the smoke out of your lungs from last night.

D.D.M.: Do you work out every day?

M.D.: Uh-huh. Like today I did about seven rounds, boxed four and worked out about three.

D.D.M.: Did you ever think about boxing a bout somewhere?

M.D.: It didn't go that way with me 'cause I always could box, you know? Anybody'd I'd box as a kid I could beat. It's just a natural thing. But I like to go up against trainers like Carson to find out what they know. Carson trains Eddie Perkins. Eddie's the welterweight champ. I boxed Eddie yesterday, four rounds. He's so slick, can't even touch him.

D.D.M.: How long have you been doing it?

M.D.: All my life.

D.D.M.: I mean working out in a gym.

M.D.: I started about 10 years ago.

D.D.M.: Anybody ever try to start some trouble with you? Say, in the club where you're playing?

M.D.: I'd kill a man in the club.

D.D.M.: I mean, does it ever happen?

M.D.: Uh-huh. If they start it, I just tell 'em, you know? I just say point blank, "Y'wanna fight?" or "What's happening?" A man in the street is no contest against what I can drop on him. Even if he hits me three or four times, he'll be tired. I don't get tired. I just tell him, "Go on down and enjoy yourself." A guy who doesn't know how to fight is the one who always wants to fight. They think it's a big deal to fight, but it's the easiest thing in the world to whip somebody like that. Can scratch their eyes out, kick 'em in the groin, and then they say that's not fighting fair. But a fight is a fight. Ain't nobody gonna stand up to me and say watch the Marquis of Queensbury's rules. If I get in a fight, I'm choking the mother. I just box on account it makes you graceful, and it shapes the body nice.

D.D.M.: To play music you have to be in good physical shape.

M.D.: You can say that again. And the way I play... I play from my legs. You ever notice?

D.D.M.: Yeah, I've noticed how you bend your knees.

M.D.: That's to keep from breaking the embouchure.

D.D.M.: How does that keep you from breaking your embouchure?

M.D.: You see, when I play... You notice guys when they play—and this is some corny stuff—they play and they breathe in the regular spots; so, therefore, they play the regular thing.

D.D.M.: You're talking about two- and four-bar phrases, things like that?

M.D.: Yeah. But if you keep your embouchure up there and breathe out of your nose—or whatever comes natural—you can play different things. But don't drop your hands. (*Sings broken-rhythm phrases to show what can be done by not dropping hands.*) See, it'll fall in different spots. (*Sings short, jerky phrases.*)

D.D.M.: You break the flow.

M.D.: You break the flow, and it's the same thing. You're playing in a pattern. Especially if the time is getting mucked up, and you're playing in a pattern, it's going to get more mucked up 'cause you're going to start dropping the time when you drop your horn down, 'cause whoever is playing behind you will say, "Well, he's resting." You never let a guy know when you're gonna rest. Like in boxing, if I jab a guy, I won't relax, 'cause if I jab him, that's a point for me. If I jab him, then I'm gonna do something else. I mean, you've got to keep something going on all the time.

D.D.M.: If when you move, you break your embouchure, why move at all?

M.D.: You keep getting your balance. You keep getting your balance back. Certain things jerk you. Say, like last night I was playing triplets against a fast 4/4. Jack [DeJohnette, his drummer] was playing (*Miles taps his fingers at a fast tempo against the dashboard*), and I'm playing like (*sings quarter-note triplets as he moves slowly up and down*); it's got to break....

D.D.M.: You mean different muscles, different pressures, to get the notes?

M.D.: Yeah. So you got to keep getting your balance and... I mean you just got to keep in time [with the body] so it'll swing, or so it'll sort of stay connected. It's according to how you think. When you box, you gotta watch a guy. You understand? You gotta watch him, anticipate him... you gotta say if he jabs, I'm gonna stop it with my left hand. All this stuff has to be like this (*snaps fingers*).

D.D.M.: Then you're saying the same thing's true in music.

M.D.: The things of music you just finish. When you play, you carry them through till you think they're finished or until the rhythm dictates that it's finished, and then you do something else. But you also connect what you finished with what you're going to do next. So it don't sound like a pattern. So when you learn that, you got a good band, and when your band learns that, it's a good band.

D.D.M.: A lot of times you'll let, say, eight bars go by during a solo without playing anything.

M.D.: Yeah.

D.D.M.: Doesn't that break the flow you talked about?

M.D.: It doesn't break the flow because the rhythm section is doing the same thing they were doing before.

D.D.M.: In other words, you're letting

Miles Davis.
(DownBeat Archive).

the tension grow in there.

M.D.: No, I'm letting it go off. Whatever's been happening has been happening too long; if it dies out, you can start a whole different thing.

D.D.M.: As a listener, though, I feel there is another kind of tension in those places, of anticipation of when you're going to come back in, of what's going to happen. So that in that space, I feel a tension growing...

M.D.: Yeah.

D.D.M.:... So when you come in, then

the release comes.

M.D.: Sometimes if you do the same thing, it hits the spot.

D.D.M.: You mean: Do the same thing you ended with.

M.D.: Yeah. It'd be mellow, you know? (*He turns to go into the parking lot.*) You're not going to believe this... (*drives up the sidewalk and turns into a parking place*)... screw it.

D.D.M.: Say, you came driving out on the sidewalk the other day.

M.D.: Right... the Sidewalk Kid.

Cannonball the Communicator

by Chris Albertson

Ten years ago, as we entered the '60s, teenagers were wearing out the treads of their factory-dirtied sneakers to the rather basic tunes of such items as "Kookie Kookie (Lend Me Your Comb)," "Lipstick on Your Collar" and "Itsy Bitsy Teenie Weenie Yellow Polkadot Bikini," while the middle-of-the-road themesters were sipping cocktails to "Mr. Lucky," "Peter Gum" or "Exodus" and the don't-mention-rock-and-roll-to-me jazz followers were discovering a new Cannonball Adderley Quintet through its first hit record, a churchy tune by Bobby Timmons called "This Here."

There existed at that time a rather wide gap between jazz and rock. As much rock music has gained musical sophistication, and a great deal of experimentation goes on in both musics, that gap has now narrowed considerably.

The secret of Cannonball's success 10 years ago was partly his quintet's use of highly melodic material imbued with more than a hint of gospel and blues flavoring,

resulting in a sound that was both traditional and thoroughly modern. The success was probably also due to the fact that Cannonball communicated verbally as well as musically with his audience—something that many of that period's jazz groups avoided.

All this was, of course, not anything new (Horace Silver and others had been doing it for some time), but Julian Adderley has a very special gift for personal communication, and the verbal improvisations with which he introduces each number create a rare intimacy. Critic John S. Wilson summed it up in a 1961 issue of *DownBeat*: "His unique ability to talk to an audience with intelligence, civility and wit does a great deal toward establishing a warm, receptive atmosphere for his group."

The new Adderley Quintet was born on the Riverside label, whose driving force was the late Bill Grauer, an enterprising man who greeted the sounds of King Oliver's Creole Jazz Band and a new Quincy

From left, Cannonball Adderley,
Carmen McRae and Shelly Manne.
(Patricia Willard)

Jones Orchestra with equal, boyish enthusiasm. In Cannonball's music, Grauer saw earthy elements that were missing in the so-called cool jazz and the free-form music that Ornette Coleman was pioneering—Cannonball's music had soul.

Just how the term "soul jazz" came about is uncertain. Cannonball believes it was coined by Grauer, and it might well have been. Certainly, Grauer did a great deal to promote the use of the term, to the point where its application became so widespread that it lost any meaning it might have had.

Today the term "soul" has a different connotation, having become a synonym for "black." Today's soul music is that performed by the Temptations, James Brown or Gladys Knight and the Pips. "Let's say that soul has developed the way it should have, according to Bill Grauer's concept and the way I thought it was going to be," says Cannonball. "It has developed along the lines of the old things, utilizing elements of contemporary beats and stuff like that... now the blues, the same old blues that we loved 25 or 30 years ago. It's a big thing and it's called 'soul' music instead of the blues... B.B. King is a lion after so many years of being just B.B. King, and I think it's beautiful."

With the tremendous impact of rock music in recent years, and its wide popularity among "intellectuals," including many jazz followers, performers and critics, there are those who believe that jazz is dead or, at least, dying. Cannonball does not subscribe to those theories, although he does see jazz taking a backseat to rock. "There's no question about it," he says, "but everything else is, not just jazz. We found that we get more bookings these days on the same program with a symphony orchestra, simply because they need the help—they've been dying on the vine. The Cleveland, Boston, New York and Philadelphia orchestras are OK, but the San Francisco Orchestra, for example, is in trouble. It doesn't draw the way it should. They go on the road, they make college tours and they go to the boondocks during their six-month off-season. The people in Butte, Montana, won't come out to hear the San Francisco Orchestra, but they will come out to see it with Ramsey Lewis, and that is weird, but that's the kind of thing that's going on."

As for jazz, Cannonball feels that it will survive, but that attempts are being made on its life. "I am chauvinistic enough to want to see jazz protected institutional-ly," he notes. "I think that it has been assaulted by the people who claim they love it, by creating the idea in the minds of the world that jazz is a dying institution. I think it is a terrible thing to see an article with a byline by a major jazz writer saying, 'Why Is Jazz Dying?' That is a most negative concept. People will say, 'All the jazz clubs are closing... when Birdland closed, man, something really went out the window, blah, blah, blah.' That is true, except that they don't put it the way it really is... nightclubs are dying, not jazz clubs. Latin nightclubs are dying, the old-fashioned supper club concept is dying... the local concept of a nightclub, that's becoming history. Night life is being hurt for various reasons... why should anyone go out and spend 55 or 60 dollars for him and his wife to have dinner and see a show with Sammy Davis Jr., when he can sit down and watch it on television and have a TV dinner and not have to put his shoes on. You see, it is not the jazz club that is dying."

The blame, Cannonball feels, is not just competition from television but also, in part, lack of exposure and promotion of jazz. "Kids don't know anything about jazz because a whole generation hasn't heard it. We've got a decade of people who have been constantly exposed to rock, you know, all their life," he says. "They're 20 or 25 years old, and, since they were 15, they've been listening to radio and television, and in that length of time they never heard of Thelonious Monk... they don't know what it means at all.

"An example of what I mean by promotion and exposure is this sudden popularity of the blues. That's because it's being exposed... they got endorsed by the lions of rock. All of a sudden the Rolling Stones said, 'B.B. King is the greatest'—B.B. King, Chuck Berry, they run these names down and so the kids say, 'Well, who is that?' And when they hear it, they love it."

Cannonball's quintet has recently been booked into some of the country's rock palaces, such as San Francisco's Fillmore West and Chicago's Kinetic Playground. The result was interesting. "The kids really enjoyed our music," he recalls, "and the more far-out we played, the better they like it. If we played a traditional Monk-type tune, it would go over like a rock but if we really got into other things, expressionism, they called it 'doing your thing' and they dug it. Today, John Coltrane would probably be bigger than bubble gum; he'd probably be a big man in the business.

"I'll tell you something about this business," Cannonball continued. "If we got strongly endorsed by Blood, Sweat and Tears or Sly and the Family Stone, and an interview in two or three of the major pop publications, our records would sail—they would just sail... kids would want to know, 'Who is this Cannonball? If Blood, Sweat and Tears dig him, he must be beautiful.' I don't particularly care for an artificial endorsement, you know; I'm not looking for the money, but I would like to have all the kids hear what we have to say and make up their own minds as to whether it has some validity."

As previously noted, many jazz performers are now digging rock, and Cannonball is no exception. His favorite groups are Sly and the Family Stone and Blood, Sweat and Tears, two groups that are generally considered to be strongly jazz-influenced. Cannonball disagrees. "You know," he said, "I have never felt that, although I often hear it said. I look at Blood, Sweat and Tears as another institution, another music altogether. I don't feel that they bridge any gap. I think that they utilize jazz and rock elements in their presentation, but it comes out as something altogether different because they don't have the spontaneity that jazz players have... they have it all figured out, and worked out, and written out. I don't mean that it's over-arranged, but it's another musical concept that I think is a great one."

Of his own current group (brother Nat, cornet; Joe Zawinul, keyboards; Walter Booker, bass; Roy McCurdy, drums), Cannonball says: "It's the finest group I've ever had. The whole concept of the group is much more unitized—we all think alike musically and we're beginning to really get a groove that is... it's fantastic."

Cannonball also feels that his own playing has changed. "Frankly, years ago. I never dismissed the avant-garde," he notes. "I was confused by some of the elements of it, the first Ornette Coleman record I ever heard, but I've always liked advanced music and never knew how to apply it. Now I play everything more freely than before. This is, I don't have the concept of, 'Well, I'm going to play this tune, so I'm going to have to play it this way.' I'm going to play the same tune differently the next night; I don't mean different notes, because that's automatic; I mean a different concept. I might apply my information about how to play the old way, approaching it like

Ben Webster or Johnny Hodges or Charlie Parker, because that's an old way. You might ask, 'What's your own way?' and that is a collection of all the knowledge that I've ever had, the same way that everybody else's way is, except that when I directly try to emulate somebody, it takes a great amount of summoning information that I have accumulated."

About a year ago, Cannonball took up the soprano saxophone. "It's a total new experience for me," he says, "because it is not like the alto sax or the tenor sax; it takes another kind of technique to play it well. I have much more admiration for Sidney Bechet now than I ever did, although I always loved him musically... the technical aspects of being a good soprano saxophone player are frightening. You have to use what we call a tempered intonation concept because you can't find an instrument that is really built in tune. Consequently, as you play, you have to make adjustments for the intonation in order to maintain a sound. Of course, John Coltrane was the outstanding modern soprano sax player, so it is difficult to find some way to play this instrument, which only has the major Sidney Bechet and John Coltrane influences to go on." So far, Cannonball has recorded one album using the soprano sax, *Accent on Africa* on the Capitol label.

Back in 1961, Cannonball Adderley, who had spent eight years as a music teacher, tangentially re-entered the field of education by narrating a Riverside album entitled *A Child's Introduction to Jazz.* "Ten years ago," he recalls, "we were secure enough to think that kids who listened to rock would grow into jazz." He still believes that an initial interest in rock can lead to jazz, but he realizes that this is generally not happening today, simply because the younger generation is not given the opportunity to hear it in a proper perspective. A couple of years ago, he had an experience that made him decide to again become a serious jazz educator, this time on the college level.

"We went to Georgia," he explains, "and spent a week in residence at Albany State College, during Black Heritage Week. We found out that the kids there, all black, had no concept of what jazz represented. They knew who we were because we had a record called 'Mercy, Mercy, Mercy,' and they identified us as 'Cannonball Adderley, Mercy, Mercy, Mercy'... and that was the limit. So I did a little inquiring and discovered that not only did they not

know anything about jazz but they didn't know anything about any of the music that they danced to or sang. They take for granted that there is going to be a new James Brown record, that there is going to be a good choir at the church that will provoke certain things for them or that B.B. King is going to come out with a new record and it's all going to be beautiful. They take it all for granted, but why? What is it all about? They're all wearing dashikis and natural hairdos and saying, 'I'm black and I'm proud,' but proud of what? Are you proud because your skin is black? Is that the reason you're proud? I don't think that skin color is any reason to be proud or sorry. I think that a person should be proud of himself—for whatever he is, if he has reason to be proud of himself. By the same token, he should not be ashamed of himself unless he has reason to be ashamed of himself. So, you walk around and say that you're black and proud, but do you know anything about black? Yes, they run down things to you, like Malcolm X or Stokely Carmichael or anything that's recent and they even get into something about Africa, 'Well, we know that the slaves came over here, and so forth,' generalities.

"And I say, 'Well, you have a lot of things that are a part of your everyday existence that you have reason to be proud of— you should be proud of this music that is black-oriented, that was begun, nurtured and developed by black people, in essence. And you don't know anything about it. Why don't you? If you're really proud of being black, why don't you know something about it—you should.' You see, we have been told in print and over the air that, by and large, the music is dying... jazz is dead or dying... and I resent it because there's really a lot happening. We have become alarmed about this thing and, fearing that the rumors might become reality, we decided to do something about it."

What Cannonball did was to devise a program of jazz education which, conducted by all the members of the quintet, is offered gratis to any institution that books the group for a regular concert appearance. "Our seminar workshops," explains Cannonball, "consist of lecture demonstrations on jazz, styles in jazz and why jazz is a little bit different. We also go into the sociological aspects of jazz and why we talk black. We don't talk black about militancy or any such things... we never suggest that there is anything wrong with any other music. It's ironic that one of our teachers

and members is Joe Zawinul, who is white and has a great concept of expressing this black-oriented music—anybody can do it if they love it and get involved in it.

"Racial orientation has nothing to do with the performance of the music. We talk about its origins and development on the basis of its blackness simply because that's the way that it has to be, but we don't say that this is something which is peculiar to black people, because that is ridiculous."

So far, the quintet has been performing all the musical demonstrations, but they hope to be able to prepare some special tapes of recorded illustrations in the near future. Last year, Cannonball played 40 college concerts, and he already has over 60 bookings for the current academic year. Mailings are sent out to schools, offering the free seminars along with paid-for concert bookings, and a syllabus, developed by Cannonball and his touring faculty, will be in print by early 1970.

Several institutions of learning now feature courses in black music, such as the jazz history course taught by Ernest Dyson, a faculty member at Federal City College in Washington, D.C., and tenor saxophonist Joe McPhee's course, which is part of Vassar's Black Studies program.

Today, when the step from rock to jazz is shorter than it ever was, Cannonball Adderley's group and individual jazz educators around the country stand a very good chance of dispelling those death rumors that have been circulating. As Cannonball says, "You'll find very few young people interested in anything old, unless it's new. Jazz is still new."

Amen.

April 30, 1970

Straight Ahead with Ike and Tina

by Harvey Siders

Did you ever have a neighbor whose political views were so complicated you didn't know what to burn on his lawn? Well, I

Ike and Tina Turner, center, surrounded by the Ikettes.
(Liberty Records)

know a couple whose musical neighbors are doubly frustrated: they not only can't figure them out—they wouldn't dare trespass on their lawn! But that's getting slightly ahead of our story.

The couple in question is Ike and Tina Turner. Those who have seen their revue, or heard their records, or simply know about them, would never separate the names. No one ever says "Ike Turner" or "Tina Turner." The collective professional name has achieved that enviable status of household expression. "Ike and Tina Turner"—like "Simon and Garfunkel," or "Rimski and Korsakov." Inseparable. And—despite the facetiousness—just as diverse in their musical presentation as the "teams" cited. Paradoxically, the mixed bag that is their repertoire may be a source of admiration to their fans, but it creates a semantic smog for the Turners.

According to Ike and Tina, there is no one category large enough to contain them. Their recordings and their shows run the complete gamut from blues and rhythm and blues through soul and gospel to rock and jazz. Yet critics continue to search for

a convenient label, which makes Tina smile sympathetically, but drives Ike right up the wall. I made the mistake of asking how he would classify himself. Ka-pow! We had been sitting in the living room at the time. (At least I think it was a living room. In the adjoining room that also looked like a living room, there was a dance rehearsal going on for a couple of new Ikettes.) But suddenly Ike jumped up and said, "C'mon—it's too noisy here. I want to play some records for you."

An hour later, it became evident that what had begun as an interview with the Turners had evolved into Ike Turner giving me a "blindfold test." The Turners have a large console in their master bedroom, which is partially obscured by a huge pile of EPs and 45s. Ike kept throwing on records (and when I say "throw," let me explain there isn't a disc in that collection that doesn't sound as if it's been wiped with sandpaper), and asking, "Now what style is that?" or, "What would you label that?"

The point was made. There isn't a "sound" or category that hasn't been exploited by Ike and Tina. And Ike is as

familiar with all the other sounds as his own. (He does all the charts and assists Tina in the choreography for their revues.)

"I study and study all these records," he said. "I never stop listening. I've got a lot of expensive equipment in this house and it's in use all the time." Then he proceeded to play certain recordings for me by Sly and the Family Stone and James Brown to illustrate the difference in how guitars should be recorded. "James doesn't have it yet. He's getting there—but listen to Sly again. Hear what he did? Plugged himself right into the console in the booth. He wasn't in the studio. That's the way to record a guitar."

From his self-imposed "homework" Ike is convinced that very few groups know how to record properly. "The Beatles, the Beach Boys and some artists at Motown know what to do. The rest depend on luck."

The playing of a Bobbie Gentry record led to a discussion of Tina's style. If critics are confused about pigeonholing Ike and Tina, there is universal agreement on the distaff half. Tina is sex personified when she performs, which makes watching her almost as important as listening to her.

And which also makes finding a category for her rather uncomplicated. Sex is sex, and when it's projected through the medium of music, only the degree varies—from subtle to blatant.

"I predict," Ike said, gouging a few grooves as he gently yanked the arm off a seriously wounded 45, "within the next six months, Tina will be the biggest attraction in the market. I'm certain of that." Considering the fact that Ike and Tina are supposed to be the Siamese twins of show business, I asked how he could cut the corporate name in half and just speak of Tina. "Well, I plan eventually to phase myself out and just stay in the background," he answered.

Speaking of background, the past for the Turners amounts to a decade of paying dues. They met in East St. Louis in 1956. Tina had come there from Ripley, Tenn.; Ike's home was in Clarksdale, Miss. Three years after they met, they merged: professionally and domestically. Her specialty was singing; his was guitar and piano. Together they made beautiful music the first order of business—and their ages (reading from then to now) are 11, 10, 9, 8 and 13 months.

The idea of a revue, as opposed to a husband-and-wife team, gradually took shape and from it emerged the present entourage of eight musicians (trumpet, trombone, tenor sax, baritone sax, guitar, piano, bass and drums), four Ikettes (girls who sing and dance), a sound man, a light man, a bus driver and a car driver.

That kind of overhead might have been the thing that discouraged the Rolling Stones from following through on their initial offer to Ike and Tina in 1964. The Turners had been reaching a limited audience and had enjoyed modest success, but with the nut that the revue represented, even the faint scent of success meant scuffling.

The main reason their message wasn't getting across in a louder voice was strictly racial. As Ike commented: "Black artists are always branded as R&B, and therefore there's little or no chance of breaking into the Top 40 market. That's the reason I broke my first contract with Liberty Records. They wanted to build us as R&B. Yet in clubs we were drawing white audiences over black at about a 30-to-1 ratio."

Getting back to the Stones, the Britons were familiar with Ike and Tina and made it known that they dug the duo. They asked the Turners to tour with them for the specific purpose of allowing them to ride on the Stones' coattails. It was tempting, but Ike and Tina turned down the free

ride, holding out for the entire revue.

Two more years of scuffling and trying to break down a stereotype followed. Finally, in 1966, the idea of the whole package was bought—proving that Rolling Stones, while gathering no moss, apparently gather some bread.

For Ike and Tina, that tour was the turning point. It's been a fast uphill climb ever since. They'll soon be on Ed Sullivan's show for a second guest spot; another tour with the Stones is in the works—a worldwide tour; and they'll host their own TV show, which is scheduled to debut locally in California this summer in hopes of being picked up for syndication.

"Just one year ago, our asking price was $850 to $1,200 per night," Ike pointed out. "Today it's $30,000 a week. And we've only just begun. You ought to see the new five-year contract we just negotiated with Liberty. Wait, I'll have Ann bring it in to you." Ike jumped across to the other side of the huge circular bed and attacked the phone—which must have as many buttons as the Pentagon switchboard. During our conversation, any time Ike had a question, or forgot a name, or wanted a cup of tea, he'd lunge for the phone and call Ann. (Frankly, if I had a secretary as stunning as Ann, I'd do the very same thing—only more often.)

When the contract arrived, Ike couldn't contain himself. He was bubbling over with enthusiasm. He made me read certain sections—with the proviso that I not divulge any of the financial data—and I must admit, after scanning the document, that the Turners have every justification for being ecstatic. It stipulates every aspect of promotion, which is probably the sorest of all sore points between musicians and record executives. The Turners are guaranteed advertising in specific newspapers, trade papers, magazines, college papers and underground press to coincide with each new release. There will be literature in the clubs they play; buttons, streamers, even bumper stickers. Above all, key radio stations are named by call letters for promotion.

The Turners must approve all album covers (and Ike proceeded to show me some artwork for a new album that he was sending back with suggestions), and Ike will produce his own albums.

What particularly pleases Ike is the emphasis on promotion. "If you light a fire under a record company, they'll promote your product," he claims. But he's still not pleased with the reception that black artists

in general get from radio stations. "I remember a record we cut for Phil Spector (on the Philles label)," he said. "It cost us $18,000 just to record one side, but we knew what we wanted. That was 'River Deep, Mountain High.' Well, you know that record shot up to number one on the charts in England and stayed there for 15 weeks! But it had no home in America. The black stations kept telling me, 'It's too pop'; the white stations claimed that 'it was too R&B.' That experience caused Phil Spector to temporarily quit the record business."

And it apparently caused Ike to negotiate hard for the promotion clause in his new Liberty contract. Not that Ike didn't always have a good business head. He runs his own management and booking agency—with a name as far removed from "down-home" as you can get: Sputnick. As for practicalities, Ike explained the reason a rehearsal was going on in the house at the time.

"You gotta keep spare girls on hand. Once they perfect their specialties, they tend to go on their own. Also, psychologically, it's good for us if they know someone is waiting to replace them. So we always have two or three standing by.

"You never even know when you're going to lose a girl—wrongfully," he continued. "Just before we closed in Las Vegas (they had worked the new International Hotel just before the brief strike that shut down the gambling casinos along the glittering Strip), one of my girls was picked up for prostitution. But it was nothing more than harassment by the sheriff's deputies. We got off the stand at 4 a.m.; she was picked up at 4:05. Now really! And on top of that, she was handcuffed. When they finally bothered to verify her identification, she was released. I don't know what I plan to do about it. We open in Miami in two days."

One thing is certain: he'll have greater peace of mind because of the fuzz—but that's a different set of circumstances. In April of 1969, three armed robbers broke into the Turner house, tied up the secretary and the housekeeper and stole $80,000 worth of furs and jewelry. If they had known the Turners had a Great Dane (roughly the size of a dinosaur), they might not have attempted the crime. Onyx, the dog, happened to be locked in the children's room at the time. While the robbers were methodically going from room to room, they opened the door to the kids' room. Onyx leaped at them. One of the robbers fired a shot and fortunately missed. The robbers were eventually caught and the loot recovered.

But Ike never quite recovered. He now has one of the most elaborate security systems I've ever seen installed in any home. Panic buttons and lights on every wall to warn of trespassers; alarms on every door and window and direct contact with a nearby security force; plus guns— one for Ike, one for Tina and one for the secretary. And don't forget Onyx! Ike accidentally tested the security setup recently. He still doesn't know what he stepped on or tripped, but he had no sooner walked out onto his patio than he found himself looking directly into the business end of a double-barreled shotgun, and had to identify himself to a very skeptical guard. Such is the price of success. A $100,000 home in the View Park section of Los Angeles, right near Nancy Wilson and Ray Charles.

But there's one thing no one can steal: the formula that Ike and Tina have, not only for success but happiness. "You know, we work together and live together—that's a 24-hour operation, and it's not easy, but we got a beautiful thing going."

"What about all the astrology books in the house?" I asked.

"Oh, that's Tina's. She reads all that crap. I don't dig any of that superstition."

"Well, what about the Jewish star you wear around your neck?"

"Oh, well, someone gave it to me years ago when I was working for a booking agency. It's just a good luck piece."

That's the first requisite for getting "a beautiful thing going." You have to have a lot in common.

Oct. 1, 1970

Rahsaan Roland Kirk: Heavy Vibrations

by Michael Bourne

Rahsaan Roland Kirk: Why are you so uptight when you ask me these questions?

Michael Bourne: I don't know.

Rahsaan: Why don't you know?

The music of the Vibration Society is as compelling as its leader: eclectic, frenetic, providing that elemental compulsion to tap the foot. Thus it is strange that Rahsaan Roland Kirk has so consistently escaped frantic adoration, for the frenzied theater of his performance is the stuff of pop idolatry. And he does complain of such lack of notice: of Top 40 blindness to jazz, or rock stars stealing jazz techniques without the talent to work them, of people not accepting his art as it is. Consequently, the Vibration Society, a come-together of kindred souls, becomes for Rahsaan the compatible element within a sadly deaf pop culture, a union of those who exist in and for the music.

Bourne: Why is the group the Vibration Society?

Rahsaan: I'm not talking about my group, not necessarily. I'm not talking about the group that you see. The group we're talking about includes this group and a whole lot of other people.

Bourne: Musicians?

Rahsaan: No, just people! I got a whole big book of people all through this land in the Vibration Society. See, that's what I'm saying: you're prejudging everything and you don't know.

Bourne: What prejudging?

Rahsaan: You said, why did I pick my group? But you don't know all these people here inside this book are part of the Vibration Society. And there'll be more.

Bourne: Then what is the Vibration Society?

Rahsaan: Why do you want to know?

Bourne: Because I want to know, why do you want to create a Vibration Society?

Rahsaan: I don't have to create a Vibration Society. The Vibration Society created us.

Bourne: How does your music represent the Society?

Rahsaan: Our music is the vibrations that hold the Society together.

Bourne: Then there are vibrations that are not necessarily only musical; they're human, also.

Rahsaan: What do you mean?

Bourne: The vibrations among human beings that can be expressed in music.

Rahsaan: It's brought about through the music. The Vibration Society we're talking about is brought about through the music.

Somewhere in each set by the group, a

sermon of sorts is preached: either percussionist Joe Texidor cutting those in the audience who chatter rather than listen, or Rahsaan bad-rapping whatever evil has lately struck him (disrespect to blind people, jive record companies, etc.). Sometimes serious, sometimes comic ("The police take your pot and they smoke it theyself"), such happenings are stylistically integral to the spirit of their performance, for the expression of the Vibration Society is sensual beyond merely sound. Thus arrangements he so forcefully directs with the movement of his body, from the immediate shock of bizarre instruments to his riotous clarinet march through the crowd on "Little Liza Jane." And of all the elements in his creations, it is this synthesis of rousing foolery and often grotesquely powerful wit, which, after the music, most emphatically distresses or most passionately fascinates his audience.

Bourne: You call it a music of surprise.

Rahsaan: I said people like to be surprised.

Bourne: How do you surprise them?

Rahsaan: I surprise a lot of people. I surprised you. How did I surprise you? It don't matter what way it was. People will be surprised by some of the things we do, and I know this. I don't have a set way of how to surprise them. I just know that something on the set will surprise somebody in the house. I know that to be a fact.

Bourne: Do you want to shock people? Do you want people to become more aware of something?

Rahsaan: I don't want people to feel nothing, just what they want to do. But through our music.

Bourne: Like the people that giggle when you play nose flute, that's surprise.

Rahsaan: Well, maybe they're gigglin' because they don't know. That's all the further that they have been able to look... is past the giggle. Maybe they ain't let their ears in for the impact.

Occasionally, a recorded laugh box emits a savage cackle above Rahsaan's remarks, an alienation effect that at first seems almost antagonistic mockery, but eventually, by distorting the sense of rhetoric, does affectively focus Rahsaan's message. As he shouts in one of his musical rages: "Hang it up, take it down! Hang it up, take it down! Don't misinterpret it for no clown! 'Cause it's the straight-ahead truth goin' around!" And this registration of the artist beyond the jester has always been the one paramount perspective to apply to Rahsaan's art.

Bourne: Your music seems both joy and anger: the response evoked in the audience. Is this what you mean by brain-sucking?

Rahsaan: No… to be brainwashed you have to dig it 'cause there's no other choice. Like when you see all the television channels taken up with the moon shot, you bein' brainwashed. But if you were bein' brainsucked, maybe one of the channels would have it and be something so interesting it would keep your attention. Maybe they would have all kinds of different aspects to show you about why you should look at this moon shot. I mean, you would have a choice. And after your brain has been sucked thoroughly, if you dug it, then your brain is completely together, put back to how your brain should feel.

Bourne: You seem to constantly bring to people what you know as the truth. Musical truth, like your complaint against jazz-rock and cats who don't know their changes. Or in your monologues, like when you bitched at the TV cat trying to teach blind people how to dial a telephone. Is this part of brainsucking?

Rahsaan: Look, I don't say that this truth I feel has to be true in the whole world. I'm just talking about the way I live. This doesn't have to mean that it's right for you. I'm just talking about me.

Bourne: You talk about musicians not looking to their roots.

Rahsaan: Today, people don't know their roots. Black people don't know the roots of where they came from and where their music comes from. And if they know them, they tend to laugh at them. They tend to not really look back at Louis and these different people and see that Louis and them were doing the same flexible things in their day but in a different context.

Bourne: Do you hope to change people through your Society?

Rahsaan: I'm not going to say our Society is going to change that thing, because people are people. Maybe we'll be able to get a few more people together. But I don't plan to change nobody's religion and what they see about music. We just sort of let our music be part of them.

Bourne: And through that they get closer to themselves?

Rahsaan: If they let the music sink in them, yes.

Bourne: Is that your message for the seventies: let the music sink into you?

Rahsaan: No, I'm not gonna just aim that for the seventies. I mean that for now!

Rahsaan Roland Kirk. (Jon Randolph)

As Rahsaan confesses some nights at the clubs: "We hope you enjoyed yourself… or not. We hope this was either the best or the most beautiful thing… or the worst, most miserable experience in your life. No in-between!" And thus the response to the Vibration Society is quintessentially subjective, in the head of the beholder and how he can touch where the art of Rahsaan hits: the art of joyfully wailing to rattle our cultural chains.

In any commentary, what must become the ultimate conclusion is Rahsaan's own statement from the liner notes of *The Inflated Tear:* "When I die I want them to play 'The Black and Crazy Blues,' I want to be cremated, put in a bag of pot and I want beautiful people to smoke me and hope they get something out of it."

After witnessing the power of Rahsaan Roland Kirk, I can only dream upon the wondrous flash that experience could create.

Jan. 21, 1971

Herbie Hancock: Into His Own Thing

by Brooks Johnson

Herbie Hancock had been doing SRO business all week at the Cellar Door in Washington, D.C., and it seemed inconceivable that things could get any better. The crowds were receptive and the group—consisting of Eddie Henderson, trumpet, fluegelhorn; Julian Priester, trombone; Benny Maupin, tenor sax, flute; Hancock, keyboards; Buster Williams, bass; Billy Hart, drums—really swung. It was Saturday night and the Cellar Door was as jammed as I had ever seen it, but there were two people present in the audience who probably helped to inspire the group to even greater heights than usual: Dizzy Gillespie, seated in a chair on the aisle, and Bill Cosby, seated on the front stairs. It was just that crowded.

As expected, the group really let it all hang out on "Fat Albert Rotunda." There are magic moments in a jazz listener's life when a certain combination of factors produces a truly memorable experience. It was after this performance, the last set of an exceptionally fine week, that I interviewed Herbie Hancock. I had been particularly impressed with the way in which the rhythm section seemed to work, and the thought struck me that they played so well together and got so much out of three pieces that there did not appear to be that much need for anything else. I was curious why Herbie wanted the sextet sound and feeling; thus my first question to him and the start of a rather revealing interview.

Brooks Johnson: One of the first questions that comes to mind, particularly when I heard the trio work, and the way it was swinging, is what are your basic motivations for performing with a group consisting of six pieces?

Herbie Hancock: Well, when I did the sextet album, I liked the sound of that particular combination of instruments. So right then and there, I decided that if I got a group together, it would have to be that. In

using this instrumentation, I've got the same flexibility a small group has and yet I have a vehicle for getting orchestral colors the way a large group might. I've got three horns—that's almost like a lower limit for making what we call harmony. You can do it with two instruments, but three is the least comfortable number of instruments for getting harmonic colors. Let me explain on that just a little bit: The three instruments being trombone, fluegelhorn and alto flute for the ensemble, I can use, I get a chance to experiment with woodwind color, which a saxophone will not give you. And then the fluegelhorn has enough of a trumpet quality, yet enough of a more blending quality because of its mellowness so I can use it with the alto flute. It sort of overlaps in sound, and then the trombone gives it a little brassiness. This way, I get a chance to really use different kinds of colors, not just because of the harmony I can use, but because of the instruments that I have.

B.J.: Now, assuming that you had a concept in mind, or a type of sound you wanted, I'd like to know when you started to choose your personnel, and let's review them individually, by what criteria; what were you looking for, what did you hear? Let's start with Billy Hart—what attracted you to him?

H.H.: Well, actually, I'd heard him with Wes Montgomery and Jimmy Smith. That alone didn't convince me that he would be the right drummer for my band. It was just that I had to have a substitute drummer one day, and Buster Williams told me to call Billy Hart—he said he's out of sight. I said OK. I really didn't know he was going to work out.

When he swings, when we're doing a thing that's supposed to swing, he swings hard. And when we're doing things that are... well, I guess I can break it down by saying the scope of the band is very broad. We do things from finger popping, swinging things through things that are more like rock or rhythm and blues, on through impressionistic-type things, and then on up to very far out things. So we cover a very wide area, and I want to have somebody who can do all of that—just play music for the sound of the music, not a guy that can play a bossa nova, and he can play a rock beat, and he can play this or that, not that, but a guy who has a style that encompasses everything. Now that applies to all the guys in my band.

B.J.: What particular quality do you hear and feel most from Buster Williams?

H.H.: His walking style. When he

walks on the bass, he places the notes in exactly the right place in the beat so that he really swings. His musical conception is what really knocks me out.

B.J.: How about Julian Priester—he's a recent addition to the group, right?

H.H.: Right. Julian is probably more steeped in tradition, I think, than the other guys in the group. He worked with Max Roach quite a few years ago, and with Lionel Hampton and Duke Ellington. But he knows the trombone. He just brought up, a couple of days ago, his bass trombone, and he's going to bring an alto trombone in addition to a tenor trombone, so he's going to play all of those on the gig. It was funny, the first few days he worked with us, I didn't know whether he was going to give me what I needed.

B.J.: And Eddie Henderson?

H.H.: Well, there's a certain lyrical quality about Eddie's playing that is the kind of thing I was looking for. He doesn't just play the changes and run chords off the changes. He constructs melodies that stand alone without the changes, and builds them a lot on composition.

B.J.: We talked earlier about the particular use of the fluegelhorn. Do you want to elaborate on that and how it brings in the certain tone quality and texture that you're looking for?

H.H.: The fluegelhorn has a sound that to me is somewhat between a trumpet and possibly a French horn. It's sort of a mellow trumpet because of the construction of the horn itself. It blends better with the alto flute and the trombone—better than the trumpet does. We use the trumpet when we need a lot of pure power. But on the other things, we use the fluegelhorn because it blends better with the other instruments.

B.J.: The saxophone player is Benny Maupin. What is it that particularly recommends him, or his playing, to you?

H.H.: Well, Benny plays pure sound. He gets inside of the music that's going around and grabs out the core. You know, he uses the chord changes only as a point of reference in most cases, and I mean a point. You hit that point and he goes off someplace else and comes back and hits that point and goes off someplace else. In addition to that, his style—all the guys' styles broaden the scope of the band.

B.J.: OK, now you have five talented musicians and yourself, which makes six. Now you've had it both ways—as a sideman, part of a rhythm section, you had a studio thing, and now you have your own group. Can you point out the things that you dig, the things that are special and peculiar about having a group?

H.H.: I get a chance to play my music and, as a group, we get a chance to evolve the music. You can't do that at a recording session that is a one-time thing—you have to play tunes over and over in different settings on different occasions. Subsequently, the tune will change shape depending on the individual feelings of the musicians who are playing it.

B.J.: What are some of the problems about being a leader?

H.H.: Well, I'm responsible for paying the guys and making sure that they work so I can keep a band. That's one rough thing, because I have to worry not only about my family, I have to worry about six families— I have to be aware they're there, and if I'm going to keep a band, I have to make sure that we're working so that they can feed their families as well as I feed mine. Secondly, I guess the leader, depending on the guys in the group, can run into problems with personality, and I guess it's up to the leader to really keep the situation open enough so that personality conflicts don't erupt, keep some kind of harmony in the band. It's kind of rough.

Also—well, this isn't much of a problem with this band—a bandleader could run into the problem of not allowing enough of the personality of the individual players to be present in the music. They have to all feel that they are responsible for doing the best they can. If they don't feel the responsibility, if they don't feel that they're really contributing, then they may feel that they're sort of dead weight in the band—just holding an instrument and not serving a real function. So their personality has to be present in the music.

B.J.: What about the experience or the influence that your stay with Miles Davis might have had? For example, what things about Miles, as a sort of group leader, do you yourself think were worthwhile salvaging in terms of your bringing together your own group?

H.H.: One thing I just mentioned—the openness of the music. With Miles' band we were all allowed to play what we wanted to play and shaped the music according to the group effort and not the dictates of Miles, because he really never dictated what he wanted. I try to do the same thing with my group. I think it serves this function that I just mentioned—that everybody feels that they're part of the product, you know, and

not just contributing something to somebody else's music. They may be my tunes, but the music belongs to the guys in the band. They make the music—it's not just my thing—that's one thing.

Miles showed me some other things, even the construction of the music. I used to bring tunes to Miles and he would take things out and put different bass notes on certain chords and extend certain phrases, and put spaces in there that I hadn't even conceived of. It's kind of hard for me to describe exactly what he does, but he uses certain devices in order to make the tune more meaningful and make it—actually, make it slicker. Miles really knows how to make a tune slick, and I learned a lot about that from watching how he goes about making a tune. He doesn't put too much in it or too little, you know, and none of his stuff is commonplace.

B.J.: There seems to be a trend in music, probably exemplified by your band, toward playing music that a lot of people can relate to. It's not so far removed that the listener can't get into it. Would you care to address some remarks to that—what do you think the trend is and the feeling is in terms of, say, just as a music, and in terms of the audience returning to the clubs?

H.H.: Well, let's start with my group. I personally have always been involved with a variety of music from things that I did with Miles to the things I did with Wes Montgomery to the things that Mongo Santamaria got involved with, and so I've had a chance to experience firsthand a broad scope of things. One thing I wanted the group to be involved with is the whole, total picture of music. I think everybody in the group enjoys that as well as I do. This keeps the group interesting to its members and keeps the music interesting to the audience. Now that's just part of the picture.

Another part is that when we play, we're not playing for ourselves, purely. We are conscious of the fact that there are people out there. It has nothing to do with the people who are paying to hear us or whatever it is. It's just the fact that the people are there and they are part of the surroundings that produce the music. We're just a vehicle that the music comes through, so the audience plays a definite part—we don't try to shut them out of the musical situation.

B.J.: They're part of the whole catalytic process then, and the creation on any given night to some degree reflects whatever is coming from the audience itself?

H.H.: Right. To get into the other more

general question you were asking about the direction of jazz today. There was a time when you could say that there was a direction in jazz, and the people who didn't follow that direction usually stood alone, you know. But there was a general direction that everybody went in. Not so much today. I think there are many directions happening in jazz, and you can't pin it down to one. There is what's called the avant-garde; there's what's called the jazz-rock idiom; there's what's called I guess you'd have to say a post-bebop flavor to music. Then there are some groups that are involved with total theater—involving not just music but some visual things too. Right now, I'm thinking of the AACM in Chicago, the Association for the Advancement of Creative Musicians, and it's really hard to pin it down.

There are certain people like, for example, Miles Davis, Tony Williams, Cannonball Adderley and myself who have gotten into using electronic instruments— you know, electric bass, electric piano and exciting instruments like the bass clarinet in my band, and in Miles' band, he's got Airto Moreira, he's a Brazilian, playing all kinds of Brazilian instruments. And in Cannonball's band, he's got the electric bass and sometimes they even play guitar. The bass player, Walter Booker, plays guitar sometimes, and Joe Zawinul plays the electric piano.

But these groups are influenced by things that are happening in rock, and we've found ways to use some of the things we've heard in more commercial aspects of black music that can be employed to expand our horizons. But that's not the only direction that the groups that I've mentioned are going in. Miles is still as far out as he's ever been—farther out, if anything. The same thing with my band, and Cannonball's too. In addition to that, there are also the more lyrical-type things that we also do that may be linked with impressionistic flavor, if anything.

B.J.: My feeling is that the thrust or partial thrust of some of the music is going to bring a lot of the people back in—people like myself, who are used to hearing changes and things like that. Do you think this is going to continue to be the case?

H.H.: Well, we don't play changes the way we used to anymore. But we are, in most cases, aware of the changes. In most cases, we're not just playing a melody and then just going off and playing whatever we feel at the moment. There usually is a chordal basis that underlies whatever direction that we go in.

B.J.: There is a common denominator that has some substance and some form that runs through all music, and I think the audience eventually picks it up. There's got to be a certain common denominator of familiarity. But too often the avant-garde went beyond the range of familiarity for listeners and even in some instances, musicians as well.

H.H.: Could be. On the other hand, I think that since our involvement in the avant-garde, the music in that particular direction is really beginning to take shape. It's not amorphous anymore. I mean, the sound is not totally unfamiliar to the musician anymore, so that certain things have been established, even in the avant-garde. There are certain things that are part of it. One thing seems to me to be the energy that comes out of the rhythm section. You take a guy like McCoy Tyner, and Elvin Jones or Freddie Waits or whoever he uses on drums. Even though they may start out with a song, and after the song is played, they leave the changes and just play what you might call a through-composed piece—it just goes straight ahead—the energy level sustains the interest of the audience. There are ways of using dynamics in playing your melodies no matter how jagged or how weird they'll be that can stimulate some inner feelings within yourself as a listener that, even though you may not be able to relate to the notes or the chords or the sounds that are being played in a way that you're used to relating to them, you still react because that emotional element is there. It can be quite a shock to walk into a club and hear some music that you've never heard before, but you are totally stimulated by.

B.J.: So the person should listen for and feel for, not the familiarity of the changes, but look to the energy, the dynamics as a source of familiarity as opposed to looking for the progressions and things like that?

H.H.: Actually, the person shouldn't listen for anything. The person should just go in there and listen to whatever is going on and then make his decision. He should try not to walk in with criteria in his arms, but just walk in empty-handed and listen to whatever's going on. If it feels good, he digs it—doesn't deny it—but if it doesn't feel good, familiar or unfamiliar, nobody should object if he is not able to accept it. But so much of what's happening today in the most modern aspects of jazz does feel good—I think even more so than in the past.

B.J.: Let me ask you this then, in some

note of closing. What—either primary or secondary, defined or undefined—goals or objectives do you envision for your group? What is it you want to accomplish?

H.H.: Well, I'd like to bring more people into listening to my music, so that whatever direction we might take in the future, they might have an easier time following that direction. I think that the material we're using now should help that situation. In other words, part of what I want to do is find that part of my musical being that relates to the most people because I'm a "people" too, you know, so part of me is part of them, and there must be some part of me that they understand just as there is a part of them that I understand. You know, we're all really the same, and I'm searching for that part of my musical experience that relates to them. If they can grasp that, then as the group takes further musical steps, that can be a reference point. As has happened in the past with any performer, Miles started out playing a certain way and he evolved, but he gathered his audience in the beginning, and as he evolved, the reference point was the first point. It's just like arithmetic: you learn the first lesson, then you learn the second one, then the third. You might have a hard time jumping in there on the ninth lesson to begin with, without knowing the first lesson. That's not always the case, but once you can grab on to the moving train, you're on the train.

B.J.: Is there anything you want to say in closing? Anything you want to make sure we get in?

H.H.: Well, I guess the main thing is that jazz is not dead. The music has continued to evolve. I think it's better now than it's ever been—I really do.

Feb. 18, 1971
. . . .

Me and Beefheart at Manteno

by Michael Bourne

The Manteno Festival may be the only festival not covered by the usual media

overblow—mainly, of course, because Cincinnati is hardly your basic cultural Mecca. Also, no film was made, no records were cut, no one was killed or over-stoned or rioted—only music happened, albeit quite theatrical music, and a good but not revolutionary time was had by all.

Well met at the Ludlow Garage on Nov. 20–21, local entrepreneur Jim Tarbell by beneficent accident had simply assembled a jumble of freaky bands for two evenings of hot licks: the hometown Balderdash, two Georgia gangs (the Avenue of Happiness and the Hampton Grease Band) and the Screaming Gypsy Bandits from Indiana (for whom I drum)—all of whom journeyed to play for mere expenses to share the program with head artists Captain Beefheart and the Magic Band (who had never performed east of Denver). Ultimately, the experience was eminently satisfying.

Mostly electric ensembles, except for the Avenue, who specialized in musical burlesques and the like. The crowd seemed appreciative and not the usual boppers demanding a "heavy" din. (A few weeks earlier, when the Bandits soloed there, we had followed Brownsville Station and a month-long parade of such hard-style groups, so that the crowd was not well prepared for complex charts, long collective improvisations or especially bizarre theater pieces.) So luckily for all at Manteno, those types prone to boo and scream "when ya gonna play some rock and roll?" were blissfully absent; except for one dude one night who kept shouting, "You're a sham!"—but then he was splotcho from the start.

Naturally it would appear fairly pretentious of me to criticize our own playing, so as to the Screaming Gypsy Bandits. I will conclude the self-reportage at: fun and sound seemed prevalent. And as to the other relative unknowns, each was at least unique, and certainly joyous.

Balderdash offered an intense organ-bass-drums fury that never sounded too derivative, but somewhat lacked a good balance of musical elements. Often the three played as if accenting to each other without directing enough definite melodic thrust, a state they improve the more I witness their energetic style. As I have already noted, the Avenue of Happiness featured mostly off-key parodies, with ruinations of "See Me, Feel Me" and "I Can't Turn You Loose" particularly hilarious—yet never did they prove capably straight, notably the lead singer who eventually appeared actually more half

baked than pretending. So should they continue, I hope they better synthesize their rather perverse charm with more evidence of expertise than is now present.

Finally, all that may be noted about the Hampton Grease Band (who are recording for Columbia, I am informed) is that their basic instrumental excellence and the fine vocals of Bruce Hampton became pointless when too loud. Listening to them, I was for the first time truly conscious of the potential physical damage of high volume, so painful was the P.A. power—for not only could the music be no longer appreciated, but the end result was a rather hurting skull throb and the sense that my bones were shattering. And fortunately, after numerous complaints, on the second night the decibels were severely restrained.

But we had all come so far for free to share the stage with the Captain, surely the best testament to our respect for him, and I am content that most of us considered the varied road and rack hassles worth suffering to witness the Magic Band alive and beautiful.

Bizarre in their music, the six players additionally embellish their antic performing by assuming stage personalities—for percussionist Artie Tripp a monocle, a long brimmed golfing cap, a green mustache and the name Ed Marimba.

Captain Beefheart himself is Don Van Vliet and wears a quasi-stovepipe hat that narrows toward the top, with the brim cut away until only two points jut from each side, and capped by an upside-down badminton bird. And thus the Captain may by such whimsy offer his audience "a chance to, without any set pattern, use their imagination. Obviously, someone's told them not to. Somebody all along the way tells them not to, which is weird. School is weird. A school of fish is nice."

As jovial as they are so curious, the atmosphere created by the Magic Band is simply that: magic, fun—and Beefheart considers no other description:

Captain Beefheart: I don't like music. I don't really play music. I like people.

Michael Bourne: So what is it you do up there on the stage?

Beefheart: I don't know. I've never watched. Seriously, sitting here on my cat's paw heels, I really don't know. I'm just living my life up there.

Of course, what appears to be happening is a constant bursting energy: frenetic, yet controlled by a strange logic, mostly

urged by Drumbo, who is surely the most atomic (in the sense of fission) drummer I have ever witnessed. Often in duet with other drummer and marimbist Ed Marimba, the two create not so much syncopation as a propulsive percussive momentum, not so much an explosive as an exploding music, and indeed become the leaders of a kind. For Ed, "this is basically a rhythm band. It's all in the drums. Every player has to be a drummer."

And really, such an ideal seems evident in the Magic Band as both guitarists, Zoot Horn Rollo and the Winged-Eel Fingerling, do essentially accompany the rhythm section. Consequently with the motion ever quick and unpredictable, the music assumes a crisis pitch at all times—as if one were anticipating loud firecrackers: first popping orderly, then suddenly disjointed into new tempers.

Bourne: Do you write what you do? Is it planned?

Beefheart: I don't know if it is or not. It's put on tape. A lot of the time everybody in the group, other than arrangements, they just play what they want to play. It's hard for me to talk about it. I really don't think that it's music. The way music is exploited and used as an alibi and a pocket comb and whatever they use it for, I prefer to think it's just all of the people in this group up there doing what they're doing.

Perhaps even more ironic than this facet of the Magic Band is the status of bassist Rockette Morton, who received as

much if not more audience adulation than the Captain—for his playing maintains an eminence not afforded too often to his instrument. Always warm and peaceful (and a rampant vegetarian), with his mustache and goatee twisted to string-like points and even two small horns of hair above, Rockette's manic a cappella features prove an instrumental capacity (even sounds) I would have never expected from the bass—like the force of electricity itself.

And to all this the Captain offers tough blues harmonica or a never less than fiery soprano sax, with his voice like a benevolent meat grinder. Often incomprehensible amid the P.A. ultra-potency, his vocals are otherwise more an additive to the ensemble than a vehicle for the lyrics, many of which he reads from a folio—for to him "words aren't important. That's why I carry that thing. I occasionally refer to words."

In what is certainly the most amusing interview I've ever conducted (how indeed may one play question/answer with one who speaks in delightful and often striking imagery?), the Captain and I spoke after I had just played an exhausting set—and I report these excerpts as much from our pleasure as for whatever enlightenment:

Beefheart: I refused to train myself in school. At anything. I suppose that's why I stand out. I mean, people come around and ask me things, and I suppose that's why. I don't know any other reason why they would. I know nobody else has time. A lot of people think they have time, you see, and they put on a little circle on their wrists, which is really amusing: keeping time. Like one time a fellow I was on a label with recently, who starved my group for a year and a half, told me I didn't have a proper time concept, and then not too long ago told me I had a selfish viewpoint of the universe. And the thing is, where do you get a viewpoint of the universe? I mean, there's no point. If that were true, stars would cut your eyes out, right? I laughed at him… For a fact, I'm being absolutely down to earth, I have no idea what I do up there.

Bourne: Some sort of theater?

Beefheart: Well, they call it theater. They don't have any theater anymore, you know, with swank Egyptians sand ashtrays, pomade and powder puffs and things. I long for a lady's compact, you know what I mean? I put them in a lot of poems I do. They call them poems, right?… It's fun for me to go up there. It's fun for me to go and play anywhere. I don't know how to call it, though. I don't know if it's playing or not. I've never been able to understand why, say, I picked up a Pepsi cup and another person picked up a Coca-Cola cup—well, what about the people who were watching them pick those things up? Wouldn't that get a little boring? I'm talking about business. All roads lead to Coca-Cola, and I don't believe that, you see. I don't believe in road maps or deemed names. I believe in divas. But I don't believe in deviations.

Bourne: Are you anti the authority that would have trained you?

Beefheart: No, not at all. I'm not a cop to that. If you are anti something, you're getting irritated. The revolution's been over for 10 years. The beatniks did it, and that was it, right? It's still very dramatic.

Bourne: What did they do?

Beefheart: They did the beatniks. The hippies did the hippies. Do you think that the hippies call themselves the hippies? Do the beatniks call themselves the beatniks? Why would they want to label themselves? I say, "Lick My Decals Off, Baby!" I'm not interested in making any new mustard or ketchup. I make very good mustard.

Bourne: What are you interested in besides mustard?

Beefheart: I love to say aaaaahhh. That's all I do is say aaaaahhh.

Bourne: Do you prefer anything?

Beefheart: I prefer life to death. I think everybody just does what they want to do, don't you?

Bourne: If you couldn't play music, would you die?

Beefheart: Of course not.

Bourne: Will money ruin you?

Beefheart: No, it'll probably get me more vegetables. I'll give it away. I'll give it to people who require it. What can you do with money? I mean, you can only eat what you can hold in your hand. After that, it's abuse.

Bourne: How can you avoid having what you do exploited?

Beefheart: Well, I'm sure… I want people to hear it. What I mean is: it's not held to religious standards. Nobody made the rules. People just try to impress other people. Like Grauman's Chinese, right? Go put your feet in the cement.

Bourne: You don't want to put your trout mask in cement and have the people stick their face in it?

Beefheart: Well, I don't care what they do as long as they enjoy themselves.

Bourne: You just want people to have fun?

Beefheart: Well, of course, what else?

Bourne: You're not offering a message of "peace and love"?

Beefheart: No, I'm just offering whatever we're doing at the time. If they get peace and love out of it, that's great. But I refrain from the words "peace and love" because people use that as a shock of value. There's always been love. Why is it so prevalent right now?

Bourne: Because it's a saleable item.

Beefheart: I wish everybody'd quit backtracking. Archie Shepp said it: "Mama Too Tight." I think he meant you can't go back up your mama. Just let her be a friend, and if she won't be a friend, just let her be. The same with the father. In all nature, when animals leave their father and mother, they leave. They don't bother each other. What about human beings? They're animals.

Bourne: Come out and go into the world and live?

Beefheart: Right.

Bourne: And do what you want?

Beefheart: Right, what else?

* * *

To me, Captain Beefheart rises as one, indeed the only one true genius I have met—and not by intellect or artistry or any capacity, and not by the medals or the scars of accomplishment, but by the simple vibration of a whole natural human: indefinable, confusing at times, communable on that intangible, perhaps esthetic plane.

His music was wondrous, and to most of us playing at the Manteno Festival even inspirational—surely to me at least, for I played better than ever after hearing the first-night Magic Band sets.

Of course, not enough people came to hear, and likely no one else will journalize the Manteno experience—but that is life, or (to Captain Beefheart and me and other festives) living.

And P.S.: For those who have yet to hear Captain Beefheart, his fifth album was released in November: *Lick My Decals Off, Baby* (Straight/Reprise 6420), and well contains what the Magic Band makes in concert. As to the rest of us, we will record when it happens, although I am particularly anxious to experience rating stars up the other end.

Music Annual 1972

There Won't Be Any More Music

by John B. Litweiler

"You know, someday soon there won't be any more music. Oh, there'll still be musicians, but they'll only be playing in their homes, in their living rooms, for their families and other friends. Money! That's what it's all about." —Roscoe Mitchell, Oct. 1, 1971

The Art Ensemble of Chicago began in fall of 1968, when the Roscoe Mitchell Ensemble (Lester Bowie, trumpet; Mitchell, alto sax, woodwinds; Malachi Favors, bass; all, percussion) added altoist-woodwind soloist Joseph Jarman.

Since late 1961, Jarman and Mitchell had performed frequently together in several Chicago groups and had realized that their destinies paralleled. Over the years Jarman had sought a poised, lyrical, dramatic art. Mitchell, no less dramatic, consciously seated a more melodic, expressive and complexly internally structured music with various partners—Favors, Bowie, trombonist Lester Lashley, tenorist Maurice McIntyre, drummer Philip Wilson—who shared his ideals.

The parallel concepts of drama, the

The Art Ensemble Of Chicago. From left, Roscoe Mitchell, Malachi Favors, Joseph Jarman, Don Moye and Lester Bowie.
(ECM Records)

common philosophies of what jazz is and ought to be, and the years of rehearsing and sometimes performing together brought about the union of Jarman and the Mitchell group. Also known as "Joseph Jarman and Company" and "The Lester Bowie Quartet" on occasion, the Art Ensemble of Chicago performed usually in their hometown for small fees at concerts they set up themselves. In June 1969 they and their array of instruments sailed to France (Jarman: "On the S.S. *United States*—Zoom!"). Bowie and his family found a country estate near Paris, and for nearly two years the Art Ensemble lived there. In that time they recorded 11 LPs, three movie soundtracks, and performed in hundreds of concerts throughout France, Germany, Holland, Italy, Scandinavia.

Along the way Mitchell, Jarman, Bowie and Favors added a young drummer, Don Moye (who came from Detroit). The Art Ensemble of Chicago established its reputation once and for all in Europe,

winning a handful of awards from European societies and magazines, and from America's *DownBeat*. In order to return home in April of 1971, the Art Ensemble had to peddle masters of material they had recorded on their own initiative.

Joseph Jarman: (Born Sept. 14, 1937, in Pine Bluff, Ark.; moved to Chicago at an early age.) I had always been interested in music, because my uncle was a jazz fan—Illinois Jacquet, Lester Young, Nat Cole, Basie, Ellington. World War II—they came out of the Army and brought all of that music. They were even into Charlie Parker in 1946. I went to DuSable (high school) about 1954 and started to study drums with (Captain) Walter Dyett. And then I didn't study them again. Then I went off into space. I went into the Army, and I had to get out of the line, so I bought a saxophone and got me a saxophone teacher and learned the fundamentals and auditioned for the Army band. I stayed there for about

a year and a half. I started to study clarinet because they had too many saxophones.

Then I got out of the Army and wandered around for a couple of years. I went to discover America. I had an alto saxophone, but I wasn't playing it. I went all over the United States and hung out in the Sierra mountains in northern Mexico. I sat in with jazz bands and blues bands as I went around. There's nothing but blues bands in the Southwest—it was Southwestern, Ornette Coleman blues, all rural—backbeat, simple structures. But I was going through a whole lot of changes, so I wasn't really dealing with my music.

I didn't start doing my music until I came back to Chicago and started school. That's where I met Mitchell and Favors and (Anthony) Braxton; Wilson Junior College. I used to be into the Student Peace Union, that kind of thing, during those times. I've always been interested in politics, but now I'm more toward the left in a nationalistic way, black nationalism. But we, the Art

Ensemble, we're not about politics.

John Litweiler: (To Roscoe Mitchell.) Were you a good singer at the age of eight?

Roscoe Mitchell: (Born Aug. 3, 1940, Chicago.) Certainly. I used to imitate all the dudes, Nat King Cole, Billy Eckstine, Louis Armstrong—I even imitated Mario Lanza.

Jarman: You can hear him singing in *A Jackson in Your House* (BYG 529. 302, a French LP).

Mitchell: I always wanted to be a musician, and I didn't want to be a singer. It wasn't rare to see jazz records and artists and stuff in the house when I was growing up. I was very young when I first heard Billie Holiday. My mother and uncle were into that kind of bag.

I played baritone sax in the high school dance band, and I didn't really get into the alto until my senior year. Then I played baritone and alto in an Army band. There were a couple of places in Germany where we could play. I played a rock gig during the Fasching season—it's like Halloween, except it goes a week or two. Everybody is drinking and partying in the streets. When I got out of the Army, in July of 1961, me and Joseph and (tenorist Henry) Threadgill and this fellow Richard Smith playing drums, Louis Hall, piano, we had a group for a long time. We were into Art Blakey charts and things like that. Wayne Shorter was my man—Joseph and them used to dig 'Trane, but I used to dig Wayne Shorter.

Litweiler: Joseph Jarman, what were you playing like then?

Jarman: Well, I was just trying to play changes. (Considerable laughter from Mitchell, Jarman and Malachi Favors.)

Mitchell: People didn't really listen to us much. Threadgill stopped playing for a while—oh, he played, but he was just playing in church. He was going through some changes. Favors and I were going to school together. I don't remember playing with another bass player, other than Maurice Chappelle and somebody else.

Favors: When I first heard you, you were sounding like Bird.

Jarman: Favors didn't even speak to us, because he was in the union.

Brother Malachi Favors: (Born Aug. 22, 1937.) Into being in this universe some 43,000 years ago. Moved around and then was ordered to this planet Earth by the higher forces, Allah De Lawd Thank You Jesus Good God a Mighty, through the Precious Channels of Brother Isaac and Sister Maggie Mayfield Favors; of 10.

Landed in Chicago by way of Lexing-

ton, Miss., Aug. 22—5:30 a.m. for the purpose of serving my duty as a Music Messenger… ALL PRAISE.

That announcement just sums everything up, and anyone who wants to do an article on me, that's it. I started playing music just after I finished high school. My people were very religious people, and they kept me in church most of the time. They were very strict. (Favors' father is a pastor.) I considered that a form of brainwashing, because they had been taught that certain great black music was evil, wrong. I never had any aspirations of becoming a musician. I remember once at church, I was about 15, I went up and touched a bass, and it was so hard to pull the strings down, I said, "Ohh, I'll never do this."

Music was just something that grabbed me all of a sudden. I started right off in music—I was playing professionally a month after I got my bass. When it grabbed me, I wasn't sincere—it was a thing to be seen; then it was, how much prestige can I get from the music? But then I got hooked, which was the primary object of the forces that grabbed me in the first place. Now I'm not up there playing for the girls.

I initially was inspired by the bebops—Charlie Parker, Oscar Pettiford, all those people. I got to know Wilbur Ware after I got started; he was my main man. He had it, it was just inspirational. The first time I went to his house, he had a drummer down there and he asked me to play with this drummer. This was a very good drummer, and I got up and I just was not into it at all. Those were very depressing days. I guess it's like that with every musician, you know, coming up, he doesn't think he ever will play.

(In 1958, Favors recorded an album with pianist Andrew Hill; they played together about two years. Favors supported himself by playing with popular Chicago pianists and organists over the years; he met Roscoe Mitchell in the autumn of 1961, and AACM mentor Richard Abrams shortly thereafter. Throughout the early 1960s, Abrams' big Experimental Band, the source of the AACM by 1965, regularly included Jarman, Mitchell and Favors. By then Mitchell, with Favors and Jarman, had begun work with their own groups, and a "dust-biting" trumpeter, Lester Bowie from St. Louis, had settled on Chicago's North Side.)

Lester Bowie: (Born Oct. 11, 1941, Frederick, Md.) I first heard "Ambassador Satch" (Columbia CL-840, now out of

print), I guess I was about 13. I read the story of how Louis Armstrong got with King Oliver, so I used to practice with my horn aiming out the window, hoping that Louis Armstrong would ride by and hear me and hire me to play with him. I turned professional when I was about 15. I had a band; it was a combination of maybe Dixieland and boogie-woogie and rhythm-and-blues types; the instrumentation was trumpet, alto, piano, sousaphone and an occasional drummer. We played a kind of square music there compared to bebop; a lot of real hepcats didn't dig us. I started hanging around this trumpet player named Bobby Danzier, who was big in St. Louis—he and Miles came up together, and he had the same kind of approach. But I still didn't want to be a musician—I'd say, I'm doing this because I'm young; when I'm older I'm going to be a lawyer or something.

I was playing all through school, all through service (with the Air Force Police), with bands, blues bands. The thing that really sent me out there was Kenny Dorham and Hank Mobley, the Jazz Messengers record with "Soft Wind," "Prince Albert," "Minor's Holiday." Kenny Dorham sounded so hip, and Bobby Danzier years before had been telling me about having context in your playing, and being soulful. I decided then that when I got out I wouldn't do anything but just play.

[After the service, I] played around in St. Louis for another minute or so, and then went to school. Once I decided to deal music, that's about all I did. I don't think I ever bought a book. (Bowie spent a year at North Texas State, mostly performing throughout Texas with tenorists Fathead Newman, James Clay and roommate Billy Harper.) They play it up because it's the great institute of jazz, or some business. I ended up flunking out. After that, I figured, enough—the only good school for a musician is the road.

(Bowie traveled the Midwest with a blues backup band.) We ended up getting stranded in Denver. We were supposed to work for Solomon Burke—anyway, we worked two weeks at this club, and then the union man came. You know how the unions are, like gangsters. Our cards weren't that straight, so we had to give him some money. Then he said, 'Be out of town by the time sunrise comes,' so I went to California. Me and altoist Oliver Lake and drummer Philip Wilson (both St. Louis contemporaries of Bowie) hung out for a long time in Los Angeles.

I met Fonty (popular singer Fontella Bass, now Mrs. Bowie) while I was with Oliver Sain, a St. Louis bandleader-producer. I started directing her music, I think it must have been late '65, then we moved to Chicago. (A friend took him to an Abrams rehearsal in June 1966.) I felt right immediately. Kind of like being at home. Richard had me take a solo, and as soon as we finished everybody came over, Roscoe and Joseph gave me their phone numbers right away, and then that same night Roscoe called and wanted me to do a concert with him. We started rehearsing the next day.

The years 1966 and '67 were crucial to these players. By fall 1966 Bowie's partner, Philip Wilson, had joined the Roscoe Mitchell Art Ensemble and proved to be the catalyst in the development of a highly sophisticated group identity. Mitchell had been experimenting with bells, whistles, harmonicas and gourds as rhythmic and primarily sonoric effects in his music. Wilson's dynamic and rhythmic sensitivity, his graceful skill and volatility, made him the perfect accompanist; during that period he was surely the leading drummer in the New Music. Bowie and Favors were inspired to add "little instruments" to their collections. The astonishing variations of themes, structures, sounds and contexts conceived by Mitchell in this period remain a landmark achievement.

Wilson participated in the Mitchell group's visuals. For example, one concert opened with a player, accompanied by Favors' banjo, fox-trotting with a huge Raggedy Ann doll, followed by an angry, shotgun-toting Wilson. Another found a Wilson mallet applied to cymbals, snares and Favors' head, until the bassist collapsed in a mock faint.

Two LPs made a year apart without Wilson demonstrate how the Mitchell group's music grew during Wilson's nine-month tenure. The exploratory, intense *Sound* (Delmark 9408) is a bit cautious with the unconventional instruments, while *Lester Bowie—Numbers 1 & 2* (Nessa 1) from August 1967 was confident in its highly detailed group improvisation structures and by now beautifully conceived flow of sound. But a month earlier Wilson had abandoned jazz almost completely; since then he has had a successful career in rock 'n' roll.

Bowie: When you take an important part out, the music has to make compensa-

tions. It was more of a challenge without him. In the next concert we had a bit where the telephone rang and we answered and said, "Philip's not here." It was a drag to lose him, but things still go on. We added a lot; the instruments started building up. We used to have just a little bit, and now we have a whole houseful.

Mitchell: I felt that the music was in a very sensitive period, and most of the drummers I was digging just weren't melodic enough to be dealing what we were dealing.

(There were no limitations to the group's scope. One performance might present free ensemble improvisation, shifting within subtly structured areas, such as "Number 1"; the next might include a series of songs, usually Mitchell's: vaguely Mingus-like lines, a rock piece, a samba, a bop line, a Favors banjo piece, "Muskrat Ramble.")

Bowie: With Roscoe, there was no limitation about what you could deal from. You wouldn't have to play something melodic all the time, or something fast all the time. It was a combination of any kind of way you could do it. It was the only group I had seen that I could do anything I wanted without feeling self-conscious.

Jarman had acquired a youthful quartet (Christopher Gaddy, piano; Charles Clark, bass; Thurman Barker, drums) which had achieved a range of conscious romanticism quite unique and marvelous in free jazz, based in large degree on Gaddy's original harmonic relationships. Jarman's personal accomplishments were twofold: as composer he scored successfully, brilliantly in an extended-work idiom (most notably in *Causes II* and *Winter Playground 1965* with a large group—among free jazzmen only Ornette Coleman has approached Jarman's success within near-classical forms), and as alto saxophonist he offered an idealized style of astonishing virtuosity, lyric sensitivity and often expressive wit. Like Mitchell, Jarman had acquired "little instruments," though Jarman's presentation was simpler and more formularized. Throughout the years there were flamboyant multi-media Jarman works, with dancers, poets, actors, even films.

In summer 1967 Gaddy was hospitalized for a heart ailment, and a doctor warned him against "music and other strenuous exercise." Gaddy died the following March. The prodigious Charles Clark was a near virtuoso, basically bearing Min-

gus' principles of creation into free jazz; as Terry Martin wrote: "His solos… can also attain an almost unequalled emotional intensity for this instrument." My own introduction to the variety and wonder of Chicago Civic Symphony immediately recall that awe. He left Jarman in late 1968 to work with Chicago's Civic Symphony. His April 1969 death was a shocking blow. Clark was only 24. The Chicago Civic Symphony immediately inaugurated a Charles Clark Memorial Scholarship for young musicians.

By autumn 1968 the Roscoe Mitchell Art Ensemble was in a state of musical and professional flux. Jarman joined at this time.

Jarman: When Christopher and Charles vanished, I went through a very emotional thing. It really wiped me away, and it was a very heavy emotional thing. I mean, I felt and they felt that many of our tenets were common about what music is; they were the only musicians around. Although Thurman (Barker) was still on the scene, we weren't strong enough to make a thing, because of what we emotionally and psychologically put into the music with Christopher and Charles. So Lester and Malachi and Roscoe saw the state I was in, and they knew I was going to just flip on out, so they hit on me to play a concert. I played it, and it was very good, so then there was another concert and a couple other concerts. Finally we realized that we all had this vital thing in common.

Litweiler: Why did the musicians move to France?

Mitchell: We always felt we wanted to spread the music out. I mean, me myself; I don't want to sit in one place all the time. You can call it a missionary thing, if you want.

Favors: I went because the group went. I really didn't want to go, but I wanted to stay with the Art Ensemble. I was overruled. I felt that it might have been a little more difficult but that we could have made it here. Going to Europe still is not a gas to me.

Bowie: We were always interested in reaching out to more and more people, getting the AACM's name out there. For years before, we had traveled more than anyone else here (in their Chicago years they worked briefly in New York, San Francisco, Detroit, Toronto, St. Louis). The only other place to go was to Europe. We had to live, and we wanted to live by playing music. We weren't working that much around here.

We just left. We worked maybe the second day we were there, at a place called the Lucienaire, a small theater. Immediately we got a lot of attention—like, *L'Express*, that's like *Time* magazine, and *Paris-Match*, all the papers were immediately interested. The next week we did a recording. We used the Lucienaire for a base about three weeks, maybe, and the people would come from all over. Some would say, "Come to here and do a concert," and we'd go there and return to the Lucienaire. We dealt from there.

We did 35 concerts in 1970 for the French Ministry of Culture. Every little town, could be a town of 50,000 people, they've got a big opera house somewhere where they bring in different arts, and they were interested in our music, along with symphony orchestras, ballets, anything. And black music, too. France is just about the most advanced country for the music that I can think of.

Jarman: One of the important things the European experience did was to open my eyes up to a broader world. Being exposed to and in the midst of other cultures and other thoughts and other musics allowed a perspective on myself and my society that I never would have realized before. Meeting, for example, African musicians and their attitudes about music.

Bowie: We played all over Europe. Our situation in Europe was completely unique among groups; the way we carried ourselves, the way we conducted our business. Most cats were in the regular jazz thing: you come, get a hotel room, and blah blah blah. But we had children, a dog; we lived in the country. It was unusual because most of the jazz cats were sitting around Paris, and we had a nice big estate, cherry trees and apple trees, ha... I was leading up to how we traveled: we had equipment; as we traveled, instead of squandering our money, we would collectively get together and buy things that the group needed—instruments and equipment. We had a Volkswagen, and we bought two more trucks over there, and this let us be mobile. No other group over there had any kind of mobility. We could travel anywhere, and this is mostly, I think, the reason we were so successful. We could be hired for Germany; all we had to do was pack and come over, whereas to a lot of groups it would have meant trains and planes. We spent the whole summer of 1970 just traveling. We did radio and TV concerts all over.

Radio and TV over there is all state-owned, so there was always somebody who worked on the station and could get us a job doing a program. In France alone we did about six TV shows and about six or eight radio concerts. Some were live, like from Chateauvallon; it was an arts festival, but the show was just us. They take the music much more seriously than they do over here.

Jarman: Of course, you know how Don Moye got with the group.

Favors: One Saturday night we were doing a gig at the American Center for Students in Arts in Paris. I saw this cat with two conga drums, and I said, "This cat's from Africa"—the African cats were on opposite us, you know. So he came over and just set his drums up. I said, "Somebody bring me a soda"—he said, "Yeah, bring me one, too." Then we heard him play, and we said, "Hey, this cat's bad, ain't he." Then he was playing with Steve Lacy, and I went down and saw him playing trap drums.

Don Moye: (Born May 23, 1946, Rochester, N.Y.) I was going to Wayne State University in Detroit, '66, '65. I was playing with Detroit Free Jazz; we were just young guys. I took some percussion classes, but I wasn't a music major. Those music schools, whew. I used to go over there, and nobody even looked like they were into anything. I couldn't even find anybody to play with, hardly, in that music department. But there were plenty musicians around Detroit.

I used to go over to (trumpeter) Charles Moore's house, he used to show me a whole lot of stuff. Everybody used to go over there to see what was happening. I met Jarman in Detroit, at the Artists' Workshop. I also worked on *Guerilla* (published by Artist Workshop Affiliates)—I was circulation manager on that. That was a good magazine. (Moye was in the Artists' Workshop the evening of the famous mass arrests.) Everybody who got took in spent their little time in jail. Just a plumb outrageous number, 54 or 60. They just wanted to put John Sinclair out of the picture... I was kind of disillusioned with the Detroit situation, because the whole musical direction was changing. They were going more heavily into the rock thing. By that time Charles Moore and all the cats had disappeared, so there really wasn't anybody on the scene for inspiration.

We (Detroit Free Jazz, a quartet) just went out to Europe—we got it together when we got there. We went to Copenhagen first; we got our first gig in Switzerland. We arrived in May '68, and by June we were playing all over... A gig fell through in Milano, Italy, so we went to

Yugoslavia to see what was happening. We were musicians, so they probably figured we were pretty harmless. But we knew they were following us the whole time. At the end, the sequence of events was, I recognized this cat on numerous occasions.

Litweiler: He never spoke to you?

Moye: Naw, there wasn't too much to say. If his job is to follow you, he's going to follow you. They watch Americans. Plus, it was the ninth Annual Communist Convention or something—all these big wheels in town. There were all these police and soldiers around everywhere. (This was in the winter of 1968–'69.) It was in Tangiers that we got tired of cops, again. Randy Weston got us out of the country. The Moroccan cats, they're mean ones, and if they want to hold you, they'll just hold you. We were all on the boat when they picked one of the cats and said, "No, you can't go." They put him right back on shore. Randy Weston went to these heads of, ah, they were high up in the structure, and had them put him back on the boat. It was weird.

(Before meeting the Art Ensemble in Paris, Moye worked with Steve Lacy in Rome.)

Moye: He's one of those prolific cats. When he was in Italy, he was doing a lot of writing—and a lot of starving, I imagine. We didn't work but three concerts in four months, and he was there two years before that... I was over there two years and 11 months.

Bowie: We had one session where we called in the strings from the Paris Opera. Roscoe had written the string music. They were used to playing the regular whole notes and stuff. They got there and could not play it. We had to cancel that session. Then we got the string players from the Paris Conservatory. Well, they didn't smoke it, but they played it. They were younger; the avant-garde string players, you know. That was really a funny day when those cats couldn't play that music.

(The December 1969 Baden-Baden Free Jazz Meeting found Bowie, Jarman, Mitchell and Chicago drummer Steve McCall joining a selected group of expatriate and European musicians to record new music for television.)

Jarman: Both Mitchell and I took compositions to the Baden-Baden recording. They required the musicians to use some musical skills, you know—like reading notes off the page. And these great European musicians, they say, "Oh, that's difficult," so we couldn't deal our compositions. We tried to rehearse, and they were not capable of reading the music. We just put it in our briefcases until we could get to Chicago and struggle through it with the AACM big band.

There ain't no European jazz musicians, unfortunately. If you check their music and check them, you'll find their roots are right here. You'll find they're copying the best black styles they can. They can get to certain levels of things, as far as mechanics are concerned, but the innate core is beyond them, and they never will be able to grasp it. Unfortunately. They may be able to get the meat, but not the bone the meat is on. Black music just contains properties that their heritage and culture does not have!

Favors: People over there beat us out of all our money; they haven't paid us yet for what we've done. Why do you think we're poor now? If you make movies and records, you should have money. These people haven't even paid us our royalties. We're members of this organization called SACEM—it handles all the affairs of artists, period. It's supposed to be much better than BMI; in fact, Johnny Griffin swears by it. SACEM tells us, "Well, you'll get your money here," then they say, "Well, the money is here," but we never get it. There's always a later date. It's a world-wide organization; they have a branch here, but this branch tells us that we have to collect from Paris. We had a contract with BYG, they were supposed to buy us a Volkswagen bus. We never got that.

Jarman: Racism in Europe is just as bad as it is here.

Bowie: Oh, yes, yes, yes, yes. That is the home; the original racists came from Europe. My personal feeling is that the reason more Europeans are open to black music is that they don't have that large black population to contend with. Art is enlightenment for people. In the States, you have millions of blacks, so the Man isn't too interested in promoting black art because he's got that lower-class population that may learn something. In Europe they don't have any fear of anything like that.

Favors: In France they don't have black people to worry about like they do here. Consequently they go all out. They sent me a statement—I'm not even a citizen—asking me if I needed any assistance. That statement would have given me the right to go to a doctor and everything else—that's right! And over here they're just killing people about this little money

they're giving them; it's a big thing because you're getting a few pennies from the government, and it's only because you're black. If they didn't have black people, they wouldn't even think about the relief.

Jarman: The music doesn't have any association with the interpretations some writers put on it. What's the spirit of that to you when you see us painting our faces? A lot of people like to suggest this has to do with a militant attitude, when in fact it's a tribal attitude. The mask, in African culture, functions to alleviate human beings so the spiritual aspects of things can come through. When people check this out, they have a real warm feeling. Then this other person comes and tells them. "Well, it's about war paint, it's not a love feeling," and they get these contradictory vibrations.

Litweiler: Do the musicians feel better about playing back home?

Mitchell: We're still not getting our asking price. I mean, we might get one gig, but that means we turned down about six. So on the average, we're really not getting anything. We don't produce concerts ourselves any more, except with the AACM. We want money, and we're willing to negotiate. We want you to print: A fair amount of money for the Art Ensemble, you dig? Stop fooling yourself, get us some money.

Favors: I mean, what did they have coming down to Bloomington, Ind., after us? Nitty Gritty Dirt Band—$3,000, or more than that, you know.

Jarman: We got that award from *DownBeat*, and somebody told us we'd get a lot of gigs that way. We had to laugh about that.

Bowie: We've just received a grant from the Missouri Arts Council to perform a series of concerts in Missouri, along with other groups from BAG (the St. Louis Black Artists Group). They come five concerts in a series, and we're attempting to be funded for about three more series. Illinois has something like that here, but this is a much bigger place, and you've got much more happening, more graft and things. The Art Ensemble is the outside element of BAG.

BAG was formed by cats who grew up together, Oliver Lake, (drummer) Jerome Harris Jr., (altoist) Julius Hemphill. We're kind of proud of that, because we've got our own building, all that business, and the bebop cats never achieved that; they have to play in taverns and what have you. BAG's inspiration was the AACM; they've achieved some things that the AACM hasn't achieved merely because it's a smaller

place; it's easier to break through.

Jarman: There's a magazine that the AACM is going to publish. This is just my opinion, you know—for what I see as part of my contribution to the Art Ensemble of Chicago is that we are becoming interested in speaking of the depths of the music, the conditions of our lives—I mean, we are hungry, poor, we need money to survive, all this, and people should know that instead of trying to politicize our work, instead of trying to construct moralistic or movement values off of what we're dealing, that it should be looked at from an internal perspective.

Litweiler: Would something like a Ministry of Culture and the French Culture Houses work here?

Mitchell: They have them, but it's not for black people. A lot of rich communities in America have the facilities for people in the community—you see them all the time. The thing about Lincoln Center was that was in the black community. I remember Lincoln Center from back when I was going to high school.

(Now razed, Lincoln Center was the drafty old settlement house where the AACM gave concerts throughout the 1960s.)

Litweiler: Do you feel that the center, if it were French, would have been government-supported?

Mitchell: Oh, yes. But it wouldn't be like that, it would be a brand-new building. Don't think for a minute that the States are a slouch and don't have anything happening. I think they do a bit more in St. Louis than they do in Chicago. The Missouri Council of the Arts, yeah. The experience I've had with that is that the Council will start off doing like this here [raises his hand], and then it goes right on downhill. But they do give them something. They paid for this building BAG has for a year or so. A lot of things are more available there that the musicians here have to seek for themselves.

Jarman: The writers had a great deal to do with destroying the reality of the music when they started giving it labels and titles. A lot of musicians think that free jazz means you just... OK, somebody gave me this instrument, but I'm a free-jazz player, see, so it's true and proper that this is the music [he strums a lute at random]. That kind of view is prevalent, there's lots of people who think that even in 1971.

Exhausted from the wars of getting their music before the public, the Art Ensemble has settled down for the time being. Bowie and his family live in a suburb in St. Louis; the other four live in an 1892 townhouse, one of Chicago's first, with a basement full of trunks and equipment and a whole floor, the kitchen excepted, set up with musical instruments. In back sit two German Ford trucks, both out of commission; parts are unavailable here. In its homeland, the Art Ensemble, since April 1971, has presented concerts in Lenox, Mass.; Bloomington, Ind.; and Chicago. That's all.

As individuals, the five have performed throughout the summer and fall with the BAG band in St. Louis (including a television show) and the AACM big band in Chicago. The situation is sorrowful. Judging from recordings, the early potential of a Jarman-Mitchell-Bowie-Favors union has recurringly been fulfilled. *People in Sorrow* (Nessa 3), their 1969 French prize-winning work, and *Les Stances a Sophie* (Nessa 4), a French film soundtrack, are now available in the U.S.; certain specialty stores import the somewhat excellent BYG recordings; one American LP, *Phase One*, has been issued in France.

It is redundant to point out that these men are among the small handful of seminal musicians to appear in the post–Ornette Coleman era of jazz. Their music, based on full use of as much sonoric variation as possible within essentially melodic and usually complex structures, still seems the way of the future. The Art Ensemble is an entity of five diverse minds directed toward realizing, in instrumental interplay, the only true ensemble music in many years, and perhaps the most challenging ensemble music in all of jazz.

The Art Ensemble needs to perform, on the same basis that other jazz groups perform; its requests are not unreasonable. The fact that they are not able to do so is a crime.

Sept. 12, 1974

Boy Wonder Grows Up

by Lee Underwood

At age 24, Stevie Wonder has reached a height of popular and critical success that few recording artists attain in an entire lifetime.

At his recent birthday party held at L.A.'s Speakeasy Club, Motown's president Ewart Abner presented him with a gold pendant and still another gold single. "Higher Ground" brings the complete total to 13 gold singles, two gold albums (*Innervisions*, *Music of My Mind*) and two platinum records (*Talking Book* and *Superstition*).

At this year's Grammys, Stevie won four awards, including Best Album of the Year for *Innervisions*, Best Male Pop Vocal Performance for "You Are the Sunshine of My Life" and Best R&B Vocal for "Superstition."

In *DownBeat*'s 38th Annual Readers Poll (Dec. 20, 1973), Stevie Wonder placed in no less than five categories. He won the Pop Musician of the Year honor, had two albums in the Pop Album of the Year section (*Talking Book* and *Innervisions*), placed third in the Best Male Singer slot and was also recognized for both his Wonderlove backup group and his talents as a composer. Most recently, Stevie tied for first place in the *DownBeat* International Critics Poll in the Those Deserving Wider Recognition Male Vocalist category.

Sitting behind his desk at Motown Records, Stevie Wonder, blind since birth, danced his fingertips across the control board of the massive Sony TC 850 tape recorder. He punched the rewind buttons, and the old tape spun down. Stevie removed it, took a new 10-inch reel out of a box and threaded it up. We were about to listen to his new album, *Fulfillingness' First Finale*, the final mix completed only the night before. This was the first hearing outside of the studio.

"It's very important that you concentrate on the lyrics," he said. "I feel very peaceful inside for the first time."

He leaned forward and smiled. The scars from his car accident a year ago were smooth. Only a bump remained above his right eyebrow, with a few smaller scars on his right cheek.

"Things change when you meet someone that is very positive and gives you peace and understanding far better than any relationship in the past."

Finale burst from the speakers and swirled throughout the room with joy, anger, compassion, new love, new dreams, new hope and a lot of downright filthy funk.

Earlier, Stevie's friend, confidant and publicist, Ira Tucker, said, "*Fulfillingness' First Finale* is almost an anthology of *Music of My Mind*, *Talking Book* and *Innervisions*. But the new material since

the accident takes you to that other level no one thinks he can reach after Innervisions. But he has. You can feel the difference. That's his genius."

The accident, before and after. The pivot point, the reference point, an inescapable landmark in the life of Stevie Wonder.

Aug. 6, 1973: While traveling north from Greenville, S.C., to Raleigh, N.C., on a two-lane road, driver John Harris, Stevie's cousin, tried to pass the logging truck that was weaving from lane to lane in front of them. The trucker suddenly slammed his brakes and stopped right in front of John. The logs from the truck fell off and crashed through the windshield on Stevie's side of the car.

Stevie was in a coma for three days, a semi-coma for seven more.

"My outlook on life has gotten a little deeper—closer to me," Stevie said, his voice almost a whisper. "I learned who loved me—like Abner, president of Motown, stuck with me all the way. And I learned about those who just said, 'Is he gonna be able to work again?'

"I also see that God was telling me to slow down, to take it easy. I still feel I'm here to do something for Him, to please people, to turn my world into music for Him, to make it possible for people to communicate with each other better. And that's what I'll do. If you go by your feelings, your first impressions, they'll almost never lead you wrong. That's what I didn't do before."

Born May 13, 1950, in Saginaw, Mich., he is the third of six children. Stevie's uncle gave him a four-hole key-chain harmonica at age five, and Stevie was off and running. He began piano lessons at six and started playing drums at eight. He was just about ready.

When Ronnie White of the Miracles introduced him to Brian Holland of the Holland-Dozier-Holland Motown writing team, Holland took him to Berry Gordon Jr., top gun at Motown. Gordy signed him, changed his name to Wonder, and a superstar was born.

Because he was a 10-year-old minor, Stevie could not have a writer's contract. He had an artist's contract in which Jobete Publishing (Motown's main house) got 100 percent of the royalties. This condition changed dramatically when Stevie re-negotiated at age 21.

Stevie praises the excellent job Motown did in setting up his legal guardian, a Detroit lawyer, and establish-

Dizzy Gillespie and Stevie Wonder recording at Wonderland Studios in Los Angeles in 1982. Dizzy was a guest on the tune "Do I Do," which appeared on *Original Musiquarium 1*, a compilation of Wonder's greatest hits from the 1970s with four additional tracks. (Michael Jones for Black Bull Music)

ing his trust fund. When he turned 21, he went through the courts and the judges, and was completely satisfied with the accuracy and honesty with which that trust fund was handled.

There were no alterations or bendings of the Michigan statutes regarding minors performing in public places. "The laws protected him," Tucker explained. "First of all, he did not play clubs. He played large halls. That's where his first hit, 'Fingertips, Part 2,' was recorded. When he turned 18, he could play some places where alcohol was served—New York, Detroit, etc.

"And by law, Stevie had to have a teacher—not a tutor, but a teacher. He had to put in a certain number of hours every day with that teacher, even if he was traveling and working, like with the Motortown Review (a Detroit-based show). He would do one or two shows at night and then have to go to school on the bus or the airplane afterwards. But he went to school."

When Stevie was 13, Motown suggested he attend the Michigan School for the Blind in Lansing, from which he graduat-ed. "They taught me all the usual things," Stevie says, "but what I liked was the swimming pool and the wrestling team. They had a music department, too, and that exposed me to all those classical dudes, like Bach and Chopin. You can hear some of that on 'They Won't Go When I Go' on the new album."

When Stevie turned 21, he battled for months with that patriarchal giant, Motown Records: the formula sound, the iron-fist controller of royalties, publications, production, publicity and direction.

Stevie slashed loose and established an unprecedented Motown deal. He emerged with his own publishing company, Black Bull Music; his own production company, Taurus Productions; 50 percent of the royalties; the right to record whenever and however he chooses; and, just recently, the power to decide which album cuts will be released as singles.

"He had enough insight to see what he needed to sustain Stevie Wonder as an individual, not just as a product of a record company," Ira explains. "It's kind of awesome. I tend to think he had it all figured out from the time he was 14. Basically, God manages Stevie, and Stevie manages himself."

"That's right," Stevie says, toying with the gold pendant Abner gave him. "'Uptight' was the first thing I wrote, along with Silvia Moy and Henry Cosby, but the first thing I recorded was 'Mother Thank You,' originally called, 'You Made a Vow.' Nothin' really happened, though, until 'Fingertips.' I was 13," he said, leaning across the desk, smiling slyly. "I was 13, but they said I was jus' 12. Ha!

"And the first released thing I produced was 'Signed, Sealed, Delivered.' My mother helped me write it. So did Lee Garrett, another blind cat. He's recording for Warner Brothers now.

"I also produced the Spinners' 'It's a Shame,' and the follow-up, 'We'll Have It Made.' I did an unreleased thing with Martha, 'Hey Look at Me,' and a David Ruffin piece, 'Lovin' You's Been So Wonderful.' Oh, lots of people. Now my ex-wife Syreeta's second album just came out. I produced both of her albums, too, and wrote a lot of the stuff."

Lee Underwood: How long were you married?

Stevie Wonder: A year and a half.

Underwood: Was one problem a clash of artistic wills?

Wonder: No, man. We're just better as friends. We still write things together.

Underwood: Were you runnin' around, Stevie?

Wonder: (Laughs.) I wasn't runnin' around. (Laughs again.) No, she's a Leo, and I'm a Taurus. They're two fixed signs, and I'm awful stubborn.

Underwood: What are your sleeping dreams like?

Wonder: My dreams are my life. It's the same feeling. I've been blind since birth, so there's no difference in my dreams. You're used to seeing things and hearing things. But do you ever experience smell in dreams? I do. And touch and sound—everything except sight, and for me that's everything.

Underwood: When you were 17, there was a lull between *Where I'm Comin' From* and *Music of My Mind*. How come?

Wonder: I just needed some time away from recording. But I was working—playing, writing, playing, writing all the time.

Underwood: Even though you're only 24, you've been a pro for 14 years. That's a long time. You ever worry about burning out?

Wonder: Well, it's something I think about. You have to always keep putting wood in the fire, you know. *Fulfillingness' First Finale* was going to be a double album, but instead we're going to release it in two parts, and I might wait a long time, maybe more than a year after the second record, before I release another album. The title indicates that this is the last of this kind of stuff that I'll be doing—different songs and essentially the same instrumentations. I think my next thing might be a large orchestral thing. A long piece.

Underwood: In "Bird of Beauty," on *Finale*, you speak of resting and of letting your mind find the answers to things you always wanted to know, of taking a furlough, of recreation, having fun, of mind excursions and traveling. Are you finally going to take that trip to Africa you've been talking about for so long?

Wonder: Yeah, in September. There's gonna be a festival for the Ali-Foreman fight in Zaire, Africa. I'm going to do one show there. Through Taurus Productions, I'm also contracting other acts for the festival, and we're going to film it all for a TV

special. We're gonna donate all the money to the African drought areas.

Underwood: Sounds like work to me. Fun work, but work.

Wonder: Well, yeah. But after that, we're going to tour—Ghana, Nigeria, Tanzania, all over. It's not only that. I was to start a foundation to find a way to restore the eyes of people blinded by a fungus carried by flies that goes to the cornea of the eye at eats it away. Some 40 percent of the people in Ethiopia are blind because of that fly.

Underwood: What kind of fly?

Wonder: I don't know the exact name of it.

Underwood: What do people think of your going to Africa?

Wonder: It hurts me that a lot of American blacks think I'm turning my back on this country. It's not that I dislike America. It's that I want to experience Africa and help out as much as I can.

Underwood: Do you feel your roots are there?

Wonder: As a culture, as a motherland, I've always hoped to go there. And the culture of America has also given a lot. But in Africa there's not really a conception of time. Things are slowed down, and you have a chance to let your mind grow. To just think and to observe... the outdoors, insects, living off the land. "Feeding off the love of the land," like in a song I wrote.

Underwood: Someplace you said you wanted to go to Africa to feel the oppression and the pain, and to bring it into your music.

Wonder: Well, I think that there has been a great deal of oppression in this country, but definitely not as much as has been, and is being, experienced in Africa.

Underwood: The SLA might take issue with that, not to mention the thousands of less radical militants. There's so much oppression here to experience, how could you want to go anywhere else?

Wonder: African people feel we're living a great deal better. The massacres there are just not happening here. The oppression a junkie feels here is only artificial and superficial—it's not real. He's lost, and his mind is not working properly.

Underwood: And after Africa?

Wonder: I learn off of life—knowledge is my firewood, you know? So I'll read, travel, listen to the music of different cultures and different people from far away and near.

In "Bird of Beauty," I say life is gonna be what it is. "Cause what is / is gonna stay / till the heart of time / decides to

change." And I really believe that. You have to do something with the time Father is giving you.

Sometimes I feel when I write lyrics that the Supreme Being is speaking to me. And I'd like to feel He is speaking through me. It's a very special thing to me to write a word, to express how I feel.

Underwood: In many of your songs you tell people to live up to the best in themselves—that's a hard demand, almost a cruel demand to make, isn't it?

Wonder: If you're angry inside, why not turn it around the other way, do things to make it go away? I can't control what you do, but I can control what I do.

Underwood: Turn negative energy into positive energy?

Wonder: Let God's love shine within to save our evil souls.

Underwood: When you were a little kid, a junior deacon in the Whitestone Baptist Church, why did they throw you out, man?

Wonder: 'Cause I was singin' rock 'n' roll! (Laughs.)

Underwood: You've been influenced by a lot of white musicians, haven't you?

Wonder: I like a lot of people. I've liked Bacharach since Chuck Jackson's recording of "I Wake Up Crying." Dylan, Simon and Garfunkel, Crosby, Stills, Nash and Young. I like the way the Beatles used their voices and echo on "For the Benefit of Mr. Kite."

Underwood: Who else?

Wonder: Well, I like Roberta Flack, and I've always liked Jesse Belvin. He's dead now, but he recorded for RCA. He's a very, very warm person. I like the sound of his voice. Listening to his singing, I felt if I ever met him, his character would be the same as mine. Not the lyric exactly, but the spirit of his music.

Underwood: Did you ever do any formal vocal studying?

Wonder: With an L.A. teacher, Seth Riggs, for about three months. He taught me how to sing without straining my throat.

Underwood: What have you done since the accident besides the record?

Wonder: Mostly cooled out. But I've also done four shows since then, three of them benefits. We did Madison Square Garden and donated the money to Mini-Sink Town House, an organization to send the children of Harlem to summer camp. We also did two shows at the Rainbow Theater in London, and a benefit for Shaw University, a black school in North Carolina.

Underwood: Was the Stones tour a rough one for you?

Wonder: Not as rough as everybody thinks. I mean, I used to do gigs, ride 500 or 1,000 miles in a bus, play another gig, then do it all over again. But the Stones tour was a good one because it was instrumental in exposing my music to a huge audience, and they loved it. When you write this, you let the public know I really love them back, won't you?

Underwood: You just expressed it. But one of the major criticisms is that your music is rock 'n' roll.

Wonder: That's by people who hear only the singles, who never really get into the albums, and who don't really know that my music is a progression of my being. It grows the way I grow. I not only play the ARP and the Moog synthesizers, which a lot of people attack as being white, but I turn right around and put 'em in "Superstition" and just kill 'em!

Underwood: And the clavinet, the string bass, the drums, the piano—everything. Is *Fulfillingness' First Finale* all yours?

Wonder: I wrote all the lyrics except for "They Won't Go When I Go"—Yvonne Wright did those. I had the idea in my head, but she put it all together.

Underwood: And the music?

Wonder: Yes, the music. And I arranged all the horns and the voices and I played almost all the instruments.

Underwood: Who are the other voices?

Wonder: I used the Jackson 5 on "You Haven't Done Nothin'," and the Persuasions on "Please Don't Go."

Underwood: Which songs were written before the accident?

Wonder: I wrote the music for "Heaven Is Ten Zillion Light Years Away" before the accident and the words after. Did the music for "They Won't Go When I Go" before, and did all of "Boogie on Reggae Woman" before. Everything else came after. I did "Bird of Beauty" and "You Haven't Done Nothin'" just a few weeks ago.

Underwood: What about drugs?

Wonder: I smoked grass once, but I don't need that. Before the accident, I drank wine and beer, but now I only have a beer once in a while. I eat a lot of cookies! (Laughs.) Really! A lot of cookies.

Underwood: I notice that your blindness doesn't seem to hamper you.

Wonder: I do almost everything you do. I watch TV, read, go to the airport—I even flew an airplane once, a Cessna some-

thing. I shop for clothes, use a cassette for my telephone book—I do everything except drive a car. Bein' blind ain't no big problem for me.

Underwood: What about the remark Miles Davis recently made about you in *Downbeat* (July 18) regarding your old bass player, Michael Henderson?

Wonder: What remark was that?

Underwood: Well, Miles refused to see Mick Jagger, and when he was asked why Jagger wanted to see him in the first place, Miles said, "One of his friends was trying to impress him by saying he knew me. Stevie Wonder, now there's a sad motherfucker. He thinks I stole Michael Henderson from him, but Michael came to me. I never did anybody like that in my life."

Wonder: Oh, really? Did he say that? He shouldn't have said that.

Underwood: So, what happened?

Wonder: Michael went and did a session with him… for Miles to say that… I think for Michael to go with him was an expansion.

Underwood: So you don't think that Miles did steal him.

Wonder: No. Maybe Miles did, I can't really say. But never did I feel that Miles stole my bass player. I didn't know he said that… I don't even have any reply. I think it's ignorant, really. Why would he fix his mouth to even say that?

Underwood: Were you trying to impress Mick Jagger that you know Miles?

Wonder: That's really… that's… I mean, I'm somewhat shocked at what he said. I've always admired Miles' music and his talent, but you can dilute your talent by having a character like that…. That's really horrible, man. "A sad motherfucker." (Hurt laughter.) Wow! You know? How can he even do that? Just hold the tape just one second, I have to regroup…. I'll say one thing: Miles is smart enough to get young musicians, 'cause he lost it. It's cruel for him to say that. Why would I want to tell Mick Jagger I know Miles? I mean, I'm not into gossip. I prefer being alone.

Underwood: You once said you didn't think you'd paid a lot of dues. You still feel that way?

Wonder: I have not paid as many dues as, say, some of the musicians with Duke Ellington or Count Basie. I've been on the bus and rode for 14 hours and had to change out back somewhere and had to sing through mikes made of cardboard. But I'm very, very lucky and have to thank everyone my success has come early. I

thank God and all the people who've made it possible… I… I don't see how Miles could say that, man.

Underwood: Well, you answered him. You covered it. Do you listen to jazz much?

Wonder: I've been listening a great deal lately to Chick Corea's *Return to Forever* album.

Underwood: How about John McLaughlin?

Wonder: Not that much.

Underwood: What would you say is your most lasting song?

Wonder: "Visions" will always last. I hope that will be the song I'm remembered by.

Underwood: And what song do you like the least?

Wonder: "Hey, Harmonica Man." Yeah… But, hey, listen. I gotta mention this. James Jameson. He was one of the bass players on all the early Motown records. When you mention Miles, just say this: how could he have stolen Michael from me, when actually a great deal of Michael's style was from James Jameson? And that's the truth. Nothing belongs to me, nothing belongs to him. We just extend by adding our own. We play the same music, but we have our own call letters, like radio stations. It will go on even after we're gone, and the best we can do is to continue to complete it.

Underwood: Your soul is beautiful, Stevie…. One last question: do you listen to electronic music composers, people like Berio, Subotnik, Xenakis, to help you learn more about the synthesizer?

Wonder: Some. The great thing about electronic music is you can make things larger than life. You can choose colors, and you can make the sounds of an instrument that does not exist.

But I feel you have to stay on the ground, that you can go too far and you lose the people—for me, anyway.

You listen to "They Won't Go When I Go." That'll tell you where I'm going—away from sorrow and hate, up to joy and laughter.

I feel everyone should be able to grasp what you're doing. I shouldn't be so complicated that it's beyond everyone's capabilities, nor should it be so simple that you cannot use your mind to think about it.

I would like to feel that as my albums change my people—meaning all people—will come with me, that we will grow together. Everything that I experience is in the songs that I write. You see, my music is my way of giving back love.

Feb. 27, 1975

There's a Mingus Among Us

by John B. Litweiler

The music of Charles Mingus played a vital role in my first discovery of the wonders and mysteries of jazz. His Atlantic records were new, and already creating something of a sensation back then. The very first Mingus I heard, in fact, was the tempo-less bass solo that opens the Atlantic "Haitian Fight Song," with those brilliantly struck notes—so different from anything any other bassist has played—and that fearsome bass melody announcing apocalypse. The ensemble playing that followed this introduction was equally thrilling, with shots, shouts and cries crashing within the theme, and all sorts of multiple and stop-time ideas from the rhythm section. The piece rides on waves of turbulence.

I quickly uncovered the Mingus-McLean-Montrose "Pithecanthropus Erectus." Mingus still considers it a major milestone, and that particular performance, with its tonal perfection, still seems one of the most challenging and perfectly realized of modern performances. That it combined tonal, modal and atonal sections in a flowing manner—several years before the explorations of Coleman, Miles and Coltrane—remains less important than the agonized unity of perception and execution by the reeds, and the beautiful, amazing theme. After these early excavations, there were more to come for me: the astonishing debut of Eric Dolphy, the daring of big band works, the freshness of new compositions, and eventually the increasing reassessment of tradition.

The day Mingus and I met to talk was impossibly warm and bright for late-autumn Chicago. The streets were overflowing with human bodies and, as we walked along Lake Michigan, salmon were evident everywhere, scurrying to their winter grounds. By and large, Mingus' mood did not fit the day.

Two years ago, the last Mingus inter-view *DownBeat* printed included the remark that he couldn't say much: because he was working on a book. This time he again prefaced by saying, "I'm doing another book right now—that's why it's difficult to talk to you. A whole lot of *Beneath the Underdog* was edited out—a lot of stories in there weren't used. I wrote a thousand pages, and they only used 300. The rest of it's lost, and so I'm dictating it again."

Dictations notwithstanding, I began to search out some background. Leonard Feather asserts that Mingus once played with the bands of Louis Armstrong and Kid Ory; I reckoned that Mingus must have been pretty young at the time. "Yeah, I was pretty young. Armstrong had a big band when I was with him. I was with him just a little while, about two or three months. We went north, to Port Angeles, Washington, then to Canada, across the river. It was on the ferry boat going to Canada that somebody said we were going to the South, and I gave them my views. I wasn't going to take any shit from anybody in the South. So Louis decided that it was best that I leave the band. I could have stayed longer; he figured I wouldn't come back.

"I was with Louis after John Simmons and Sid Catlett left. Playing with Kid Ory came much later. I played in Barney Bigard's band, and Kid Ory was in that band. Bigard brought Kid Ory up out of the mothballs, and then Kid Ory got a band after that, after Barney Bigard left California. I was never in Kid Ory's band.

"I hardly played one year with Lionel Hampton. I wrote a lot of arrangements for him, but I took them back when I left; he never paid me. That's why he's a millionaire. I had a copyright on 'Mingus Fingers' myself, I copyrighted it in California, but his wife said they wouldn't record it unless I assigned it to their publishing firm. A lot of people do that.

"I only played in small groups with Fats Navarro in Lionel Hampton's small band. When we played onstage, he brought a small band out. Me and Fats used to go jamming after we got off the job, though. He knew where they had jam sessions. He used to go to some Puerto Rican places, some Cuban clubs, too, and sit in with the Cuban bands. He knew all the Cuban tunes, he enjoyed that. He could play anything he wanted to play. He had a big soul, a fat soul. I know Fats and Miles and Dizzy used to love each other, they used to kiss each other." Fats emerges as probably the most vigorous of Mingus' portraits in *Beneath the Underdog.* "I got him," Mingus says. "I captured him there."

By the '50s, Mingus was dividing his time between playing primarily with the unique vibes-piano-bass trio of Red Norvo, composing on his own and working on original material with similarly minded, daring young musicians. "The Jazz Composers Workshop was a whole group of guys who wrote music, and a big band to play it. Teo Macero was playing more avant-garde then than musicians do now. The record was just a small group out of that big band. I liked the way John LaPorta played clarinet better than his alto playing." LaPorta, Macero and George Barrow appear on the Mingus sextet side of the Jazz Composers Workshop record. "I had (trombonist) Eddie Bert and George Barrow in my first band; George Barrow was a good tenor player."

A conflict with Red Norvo led to another early '50s venture, the unexpected founding of Debut Records. During its brief existence, Debut kept a remarkably high standard of musical quality. The Parker-Gillespie-etc. Massey Hall concert was the label's most famous release, but there was an unusual series of Parker nightclub performances as well. Miles Davis and Max Roach were among the Debut artists, and Thad Jones made his first (some argue his best) dates as a leader for the label. There were also strong Mingus group recordings; and he and Roach—the label's partners for a while—managed to appear on the greater number of Debut sessions.

"It began on a claim of $500 I got from Red Norvo; from that I made my first record." Debut was not a large-scale operation (20 or 30 records), not even on the scale of its then-budding LP competitors: Blue Note, Prestige, Savoy and Riverside. Eventually, money problems caused its failure. Discussion of Debut is difficult for Mingus, partly because of the label's disposal. "I gave the tapes to my wife because I couldn't afford it sticking in my side. I wasn't working every day. She married the guy who took over Fantasy Records, then. Jimmy Knepper had a whole suitcase full of Charlie Parker tapes: they only used one-tenth of them. They have a lot of other good music that they should put out."

The conversation turned to the many musicians who have toiled under the Mingus baton over the years, some—and one in particular—radically innovative. "I knew Eric Dolphy in California, before he played with me. He was quiet. Didn't say anything, hardly. Very sensitive. Very alert—his eyes were very alert. Very kind, very thoughtful of other people. I don't think he thought he was great; I don't think he was aware of how good he was. He talked about God—that seemed to be his only subject. I remember when we were in Europe. He and John Coltrane were eating honey, I think it was a vegetarian diet, and trying to find the Lord." Was this when he and Coltrane were working together? "No, this is when Dolphy was in my band."

A remark about the influence of Ornette Coleman and Eric Dolphy on today's jazz found an angry response: "How can you talk about Ornette Coleman and Eric Dolphy? Eric Dolphy was a master musician. Ornette Coleman can only play in the key of C. Ornette Coleman doesn't have any color in his music. Jazz is supposed to have a tradition. I don't hear any tradition in Ornette. I don't hear any Parker in his playing. Now, I like the songs he writes—he writes good songs. But he never could be the player Eric Dolphy was."

We talked about others who'd helped realize Mingus' music over the years. "I was working in a club, and the drummer we had, Willie Jones, couldn't play the fast tempos. In between shows, Lou Donaldson told me there was a drummer standing outside who could play anything. It was Dannie Richmond; I had him play the next set, and that parted it." Richmond remained with Mingus for nearly all of the following 17 years, to provide one of the most musically stimulating and long-lasting associations in jazz, with the alternating fire and humor of each man perfectly complementing the other.

"Jaki Byard is a great piano player—he can do anything. Charles McPherson was with me quite a while, off and on. Bobby Jones was never in my band. Bobby Jones came up and told me all he needed was a dollar a day, something like that, and he said he just wanted to play in my band. I would never have hired Bobby, he's not my style of tenor player. I told him I could only get enough money for five pieces, but he said he wanted to go in the band, and he would work cheap. He read good, so I took him. Then after he stayed in the band awhile, he got to Europe and started talking about how I was underpaying him—and I could barely make the transportation.

"I haven't worked with Jimmy Knepper in 10 years. I think Jimmy Knepper is probably the greatest trombone player who ever lived. He's very underrated. I know

Charles Mingus.
(Atlantic Records)

what he can do, man. He can conform to any kind of music. He can play classical music, he can read it exactly the way it's written; he's the greatest reader I know on trombone."

One particular collaboration outside Mingus' own bands stands out. The Ellington-Mingus-Roach *Money Jungle* was one of Duke's very few dates without horns, and was widely applauded when it first appeared. "Duke just wanted to do a date with us. I got a call from the record company, and then we went by to meet with Duke at his office and discussed what we wanted to do. That date, incidentally, is what ruined my date at Town Hall. I was busy writing for Town Hall, and the same company I was recording it for set the Duke

date up just in time to interrupt my writing and set me back.

"The music wasn't copied. I had plenty of music, man, but I was writing new music. It was the promoter's fault, the A&R man, whatever his name is. He begged me to do Duke's date; I told him I couldn't do it, I'd be behind in my music for my own date. They ought to have done just the big band date." That Town Hall concert, by one of the largest groups Mingus has ever directed, was widely billed to be one of the most important events of 1962. It ended up as an open rehearsal, with copyists busy onstage while the orchestra played for a surprised audience, to say the least.

Our personnel dialogue turned to a

discussion of brass:

Charles Mingus: I don't find that many great trumpet players, man. Most trumpet players can't play, at least the ones I can afford. They don't move, they're not flexible, they don't have enough range, they're not all Jon Faddises or Dizzy Gillespies.

John Litweiler: The time I met Gene Shaw, he said he'd have enjoyed playing with you again.

Mingus: Oh, yeah, man, I wish I could have got him. I dig trumpet like that. All the good trumpet players, like Marcus Belgrave, they won't travel. I can't get good trumpet players. If I had Marcus Belgrave, I'd have the greatest band going. I saw him in Detroit, but I can't afford him, the kind of money I make.

Litweiler: Was Jon Faddis with you regularly?

Mingus: No. He made some records, the ones at Philharmonic Hall, with Jug. Then he went to Europe with me. The company didn't get a good balance on that, man. That would have been a great record. The concert was very successful.

Litweiler: Had you played with Ammons before that?

Mingus: No, only jamming. Fats used to go around where he was playing; that's how I first met Gene.

Litweiler: What do you look for in a musician who plays in your band?

Mingus: Well, nowadays I don't care how a guy solos, because I can't get blamed for the solos. If they get a good tone and can read... 'cause the approach to solos is so different, now. Most of the kids think they're playing avant-garde. I don't compare the bands I've had: they're all different. This band now plays different kind of solos—or they think they do. I don't listen to music in clubs. I don't even own a record player right now. All these young musicians think they're playing avant-garde, when I was playing one-chord 20, 25 years ago. There's a tenor player I like very much, Sam Rivers. I haven't heard his band, I heard him: he played in my band one time, and I liked his playing. I haven't heard him since then. I used to play avant-garde bass when nobody else did; now I play 4/4 because none of the other bass players do.

Litweiler: Do you think the economic situation for jazz musicians has improved or worsened since you started leading groups?

Mingus: I don't know, man. I notice that Thad Jones takes a band on the road, has a valet and all that, to set the music stands up. I can't get enough money to have a valet to help carry the musicians' instruments around. Me and Dannie do all that work. Unless I pay my sidemen more—maybe his sidemen work cheaper. I fly everywhere I go: it cost me a thousand dollars to come out here, over a thousand dollars worth of tickets, with the whole tour from Madison, Wis., to here to Pittsburgh, then back to New York.

I worked in Madison four nights. They do very good business there—packed every night. Better than Chicago. We did very well here last time. Maybe the customers are worried about money. It's a depression, isn't it?

I'm making a lot of gigs now, because Dannie Richmond wants to make money. But I love to compose, I love to write music. I got to play music. I'd like to add a trumpet to this band. If I worked with a large band, I'd have a small band in it, as I have done on my records. I wouldn't enjoy a large band—I like to solo a little bit. I'd like to have a bigger band than I got, though, to play my arrangements. I could make it with four, three or four horns. Did you hear any of the new things the band is doing, any of my new compositions? I did one for Ellington.

Litweiler: I heard that, "Duke Ellington's Sound of Love," and several pieces from the recent Atlantic album. Is "Opus 3" a deliberate update of "Pithecanthropus Erectus?"

Mingus: Yes. I rewrote it because my life has changed since then."

Litweiler: Can the soloist play as long as he chooses in each sequence?

Mingus: He has a musical cue, like a conductor does it. The drummer does it; on the record, piano does it. I have a new Atlantic record coming out—it's a concert at Carnegie Hall, last year. The first half of the concert I did some new music with Jon Faddis and my band, but they didn't record that. The second half was just jamming, I was calling it a "Battle of Saxes." John Handy, Charlie McPherson, Roland Kirk, George Adams, [Hamiet] Bunny Bluiett and Jon Faddis. We did Ellington's tunes, "Perdido" and "C-Jam Blues."

Mingus' current group—Adams, tenor; Bluiett, baritone and clarinet; Pullen, piano; Richmond, drums—plays with a fire that has occasionally been absent from some other recent Mingus bands. The music is a mixture of new and recent works, including the Ellington dedication (on which Mingus plays a lovely ballad solo) and an Adams piece, and familiar Mingus works, mostly requests from the audience. Adams is a wild player, within the post-Coltrane context but an original. Bluiett's baritone, while more boppish, has an unusually strong sound, exhibiting a rare control in the higher registers (Note: Bluiett is no longer with the group; he has been replaced by Jack Walrath's trumpet.) Pullen has lived, and creates, seven lifetimes of jazz piano; he is the most rewarding of these three. Richmond is consistently amazing, perhaps even more volatile than Mingus, and his art is the element that binds the group into a unity. A totally involved performer, Danny keeps a verbal commentary running throughout his performances that, while inaudible to the audience, sometime cracks up his mates on the stage.

Mingus' playing is as exciting as expected. There are the personal set pieces with tempo variation and bass line variation, and during Richmond's "Opus 3" solo he may suddenly interrupt with a strong bass phrase, a challenge to duel. A nutty series of exchanges between the two may follow, culminating in Mingus playing a particularly insulting phrase and Richmond catcalling obscenely. Despite the fire and seriousness in most of the shows, Mingus' dominant musical impression is usually optimistic and expansive.

It's true, as Mingus says, that his art to a large extent—perhaps as much as Miles'—predicted the course of jazz for the last decade and a half. His music is as volatile ever, and Mingus the man is as strong-willed and fully individualistic as he was in his youthful prime. Hearing him is nothing like rediscovering a legend. The music is alive, as much a reflection and assessment of the present as one man's statement can ever hope to be.

May 8, 1975

Blindfold Test

Wayne Shorter and Joe Zawinul

by Leonard Feather

The fusion of talents represented by Weather Report's co-leaders actually had its beginning when both men were members of the Maynard Ferguson Orchestra, in the summer of 1959. Their paths crossed again when Miles Davis used them both on the *Bitches Brew* album.

Neither Shorter nor Zawinul attached much significance to the contrast in their backgrounds. What they have in common, they feel, is far more significant: their openness, a continual refusal to recognize idiomatic or stylistic barriers.

Weather Report was launched in 1971 with unprecedented brouhaha, even including a liner note encomium by Clive Davis on the initial LP. There have been many successes since then, such as the triumphant tour of Japan in 1972, Album of the Year, and Combo of the Year awards in several countries and in *DownBeat*, and artistic accomplishments that have given the group its own imprimatur from the start.

Though Shorter and Zawinul no longer have any of their original sidemen (Airto, Miroslav Vitous and Alphonse Mouzon having gone on to do their own things), the Report remains what it was then: fair and sunny. As this Blindfold was conducted (Wayne's first, Joe's third), they were looking for a new drummer and preparing to go on the road after a long stay in Los Angeles, where they both now live.

They were given no info about the records played.

1. Thad Jones and Mel Lewis. "The Groove Merchant" (from *Central Park North*, Solid State). Jones, fluegelhorn, arranger. Mel Lewis Drums, others.

Shorter: Sounded like Thad Jones…

Zawinul: Bad Jones!

Shorter: Thad Jones–Mel Lewis. Thad has a way of treating the reed section, inner voices, that sort of spiral around. I like the way he does that. They go around chromatically or something. Not too many other bands even touch that. Except Dizzy Gillespie's old band—they did it another way. And Stan Kenton's reed section. But even that was different. Thad has almost a funnel of sound… just swirls and spirals around.

The music just gave me a certain picture of New York City, or Chicago… definitely city-like.

Zawinul: I think it was Thad Jones' band, and I liked it very much.

Shorter: As far as a rating is concerned, originality is coming into my mind, so I think two and a half.

Zawinul: You're cold, Wayne! I'd say four. Just to be able to play… you know,

Wayne Shorter and Joe Zawinul. (Steve Morley)

this is some pretty old kind of music, but it's really beautiful.

2. Turiya Alice Coltrane and Devadip Carlos Santana. "Illuminations" (from *Illuminations*, Columbia). Coltrane, harp, arranger (strings); Santana, guitar, composer; Tom Coster, acoustic piano, composer.

Zawinul: It's a little strange. I don't really know who it was. It sounded to me like it could have been Carlos Santana… those few guitar notes. It was kind of unnatural-sounding to me, the way the strings were written. Kinda between Eastern European and French—Bartok and Ravel clashing. Sounded like a background

to a movie about animals, a documentary.

I think it is a great effort for somebody to write that many notes.

Shorter: That was the first word that came into my mind—effort. There was a reaching out… I think it's Carlos Santana… he's reaching out, but the way you reach, maybe he has to discover this. It lacks feeling…

Zawinul:… and he can really feel—if it was Carlos. But this was a bad mix, I feel, bad chemistry.

Shorter: I think there's a lot of woodshedding needs to be done. I'll give it four for effort, because if only one person from that kind of success can try to do something and he's gonna be all alone, then he's got to have four stars.

3. Walter Norris and George Mraz. "Rose Waltz" (from *Drifting*, Enja). Norris, composer, piano; Mraz, bass.

Shorter: Reminds me a lot of... someone plays something like that at the Village Vanguard, had more than 88 keys on the piano. Reminds me of Don Shirley, something funny about the touch, about the choice of composition. This is what sticks in my mind. I don't think Don Shirley would choose that composition to record. But this man's a protégé—or woman!

Zawinul: I like the way the piano is recorded, but all those arpeggios in the left hand... it sounds a little strange to me.

Shorter: It's been a long time since I heard Marian McPartland play that slowly...

Zawinul: I think that's Marian McPartland... I'll rate the recording, the engineer five. I didn't like the way the bass player played.

Shorter: Another person it might be is Barbara Carroll... she has a sound something like that.

Zawinul: I felt the bass player was out of tune when they played those low notes together; it's bothering me.

Shorter: Yes. The long bass notes must complement the piano chords.

4. Louis Hayes. "Breath of Life" (from *Breath of Life*, Muse). Hayes, drums; David Williams, bass: Charles Davis, composer.

Shorter: It's been a long time since I heard something like this. I used to hear something like it a lot when Charlie Mingus was playing with Danny Richmond . .. the early '60s. I spotted a little of that Mingus drive with bass.

Zawinul: I think that intonation on top of the bass, Mingus would not do that. It was very strange there. I agree, though, with Wayne that there are some ingredients of that certain era. It could have been Danny Richmond playing drums. I don't think it was Mingus playing bass. I didn't like the composition. I liked when he started playing and something was happening emotionally with the composition. To me the introduction was like just covering some time.

Shorter: I got another picture... of a man setting off in Birdland or somewhere like that writing for his band, and the composition they have is half done, and they decided to complete it on the bandstand. I

noticed that the horns were always kind of back... never really out there. I would give it four stars for consistency and drive.

Zawinul: About two stars.

5. Woody Herman. "Corazon" (from *Thundering Herd*, Fantasy). Carole King, composer; Bill Stapleton, arranger; Herman, soprano sax.

Zawinul: Anonymous. I don't like this kind of music at all.

Shorter: Sounds like somebody preparing it for a prom, high school prom... they got a name big band and said, "OK, lets put this and this in the repertoire, because the kids need it."

Zawinul: Maynard used to do that a lot of times.

Shorter: The horn going diddle-de, diddle-de, diddle-de... I used to hear Woody Herman do that a long time ago... on soprano sax.

Zawinul: Sounded beautiful, the soprano sax... I really like the soprano. It could actually be Woody Herman's band. They play a lot like that. No rating.

Shorter: If it's not Woody, then it's somebody who knows Woody. No rating.

6. Dave Brubeck. "Circadian Dysrhythmia" (from *Two Generations of Brubeck*, Atlantic). Brubeck, composer, acoustic piano; Darius Brubeck, electric piano; Chris Brubeck, trombone; Danny Brubeck, drums; Jerry Bergonzi, saxophone; Perry Robinson, clarinet; David Dutemple, bass; Randie Powell, percussion.

Shorter: That was some kind of Dave Brubeck...

Zawinul: Dave Brubeck blood was in there...

Shorter: That sounded like some kind of gathering to make the date... not the regular quartet.

Zawinul: I feel like that was one or two of the Brubecks... they're very talented. But I forgot the composition already; I was hoping it comes back... just at the end of it, it sounded like a composition by Dave.

Shorter: I think that as a composition it's a long way off from "In Your Own Sweet Way."

Feather: How do you feel about Brubeck in general; do you think he has made a contribution?

Shorter: Yes, in the sense that he plays definitely on the beat. If someone wants to learn how not to play on the beat, listen to Dave Brubeck. That's not putting him down; you've got to have different people

doing different things. And he digs playing that way...

Zawinul: I heard him once play ballads alone, solo piano; it was a fantastic experience. Dave Brubeck is a heck of a musician; I'd rate this record two and a half.

Shorter: I'll just go with it as a composition, so I think about two stars.

Zawinul: Two and a quarter!

June 17, 1976

Bitin' the Green Shiboda with Tom Waits

by Marv Hohman

He looks as if he might have stumbled onstage by accident, this refugee from some chump change cafe, decked out in tattered sport coat and weather-beaten tweed cap. His white shirt soiled by who knows how many gas-forming bowls of chili. He barely glances up at the audience before launching into a torrid finger-snapping motion. When he tugs the ever-present cigarette from his mouth and starts to deliver the first monologue of the evening, he sounds every bit as deadly as he looks, his menacing rasp testifying to tales of chugged six packs and chain-consumed cartons.

Raconteur extraordinaire, poet laureate of the luncheonette, strip-show aficionado, voyeur of the great American down-beaten—all these terms serve to describe the 25-year-old songwriter, vocalist, sometime keyboardist and yarn-spinner known as Tom Waits. Jive talkin', speed rappin', equipped with an encyclopedic hunk of poetic street slang culled from panoramic flirtation with the cavalcade of Great American Losers, Waits glories in the seamy world of after hours bars, all night cafes, rundown bus terminals, seedy tattoo parlors. Name the place you'd least like to spend the next week and chances are Waits not only knows about it but he plans to immortalize it in some still half-formed monologue of the future.

Rhythm is his forte, the manic finger-snapping serving as the backdrop to an

Tom Waits.
(Asylum Records)

incessant collage of fantastic characters and bizarre events. It's not an easy brand of music to peg; it owes more to the era of beatnik jazz than it does to rock, with a healthy dose of Tin Pan Alley more than occasionally making its presence felt. The songs never come across the same way twice, as Tom's rambling palaver mutates the arrangements as well as the general aura surrounding them. One night, "Semi-Suite" emerges as the sentimental lament of a truck drivin' widow. On the next, it will somehow be invested with an air of humor and whimsicality. "The Heart of Saturday Night" can amaze with the sheer power of its imagery one night, and come in the next on the back of an uproarious monologue detailing the weekend antics of a group of drag strip rowdies.

New images and occurrences are constantly popping up in the songs, phrases Waits hews from the conversations he is eavesdroppingly addicted to—the cliché-ridden, daily-burdened, color-frocked jargon of the working class, a language that runs the gamut of human emotion, lauding the mundane at the expense of the maudlin.

Waits first appeared on the recording scene back in 1973, via a debut album called *Closing Time*. Although few copies of the disc were sold, somebody was evidently listening. The album's opening cut was "Ol' 55," a song dedicated to a steel Pegasus, well-worn but sturdy, and its highway adventures. Subsequently recorded by Ian Mathews and the Eagles, the tune has already achieved mini-standard status. Other *Closing Time* goodies such as "Rosie"

and "Midnight Lullaby" marked Waits as a composer of promise, one who dared to fuse coherent lyrics with inventive melody.

As encouraging as this debut was, it failed to hint at the astonishing accomplishment that emerged on the follow-up LP, *The Heart of Saturday Night*. Each of the 11 cuts is a small gem, Tom's musical maturity having been perfectly wedded with his private vision of Americana, circa 1970. Many of the songs sounded strangely out of place (much in the sense that the best Randy Newman material does), the tunes evidencing distinct ancestral connections, canvassing the spectrum of American pop-dom throughout the last century.

"New Coat of Paint" and "Depot, Depot" both possess a lighthearted cama-raderie, a bluesy-ness that genuflects back toward a simpler, less high-strung era. "Drunk on the Moon" and "Fumblin' with the Blues" conjure up the image of a citified Hank Williams, a late-night *loup garou* aimlessly cruising the porno book stores and raunch-laden swap shops. "Semi-Suite" and "Please Call Me Baby" show Waits' compassionate side, the latter featuring one of the more poignant phrases in recent lyricdom: "If I exorcise my devils / my angels may leave, too." "Diamonds on My Windshield" hints at what was to come on the third Waits album, *Nighthawks at the Diner*. Accompanied only by throbbing bass and drums, Tom delivers an amphetaminic rap that conveys the feel of flying down an interstate during a driving rainstorm, metal-encased jockeys vying for the express lanes, the wind howling like a banshee. A modern-day "Hellhound on My Trail," if you will.

It is the adventurous, speed-spoken "Windshield" cut that prepares the listener for the radical experience of *Nighthawks*. A double album recorded "live" in July of last year, Waits broke new artistic ground on the outing, eliminating the restrictions heretofore imposed on him by studio recording. The entire set pulsates with urban verve, Waits skillfully stitching songs like "Better Off Without a Wife," "Eggs and Sausage" and "Big Joe and Phantom 309" together with convoluted and many-faceted monologues that are themselves small works of art.

The following conversation took place on a blustery and bleak Chicago day, in the shadow of an overhanging elevated train platform and a world-famous tattoo parlor, and over interminable cups of coffee in a dingy round-the-clock cafe. Obviously, Tom found these surroundings to his liking.

Hohman: Let's start off by talking about *Nighthawks at the Diner*. Your previous two albums didn't really capture the ambience of your stage act. *Nighthawks* was a giant step forward in that it seemed to portray the real, live, onstage Tom Waits.

Waits: Yeah, I'm proud of it. Pete Christlieb played tenor sax on it, he's with the NBC Doc Severinsen orchestra. He also drives the Ontario Motor Speedway; he just plays with Severinsen as more or less as a sideline. Jim Hughart, the bassist, he's got a pedigree all his own. He does studio work in Los Angeles, he's done a lot of road work with Ella Fitzgerald. Bill Goodwin is on drums. He lives in Pocono, Pennsylvania, so he flew out for the date. I'd

seen him before with Mose Allison in New York. Hughart lives in L.A. So does Mike Melvoin (the keyboardist on the album) and Christlieb. I was just trying to find a band that could naturally play what I wanted and not have to teach or tell 'em what to do. I wanted them to stretch out on their own.

Hohman: The first time I saw you perform was back in St. Louis a few years ago, when you were playing Kiel Auditorium as a solo warm-up act for Zappa and the Mothers. Not only were you swamped by the sheer immensity of the hall, with your vocals almost totally inaudible, but the crowd was obviously a rock-oriented set. They were far from being into a lone guy up there singing tales of broken-down autos and barroom troubles. That was a bad scene.

Waits: Aw, man… the worst. I bit the green shiboda on that tour with Frank. That wasn't even the worst night, though; if I remember correctly, St. Louis was a snap. I had some real bitches on that tour. We played a lot in the South and ended up on Mothers Day at midnight in the Philharmonic Hall in New York. That tour was my own decision, though. I wasn't doing anything at the time and Frank's original opening act had quit. So he was stuck and I volunteered my services. It was like mercy killing, you know—an experience that turned into a real catastrophe. The cats in his band were easy to get along with, it wasn't their fault. Tom Fowler was in Frank's band at the time, Bruce Fowler on trombone, Napoleon Murphy Brock, George Duke, Ruth Underwood. I went out every evening and proceeded to ruin my evening, and the audience's too, I guess.

Hohman: Your songs all seem to have a rootless, wandering spirit to them. Where are you from?

Waits: I grew up in Whittier, California, lived in Hollywood, went to high school in San Diego, moved back to L.A. after high school. I've been on the road doing clubs for about four years now.

Hohman: Did you start out working in a combo, or were you a solo act right from the beginning?

Waits: I did a few rock things; I was in a group called the Systems. I was rhythm guitar and lead vocalist. We did Link Wray stuff.

Hohman: Link Wray—that's the guy who made all those killer rock instrumentals back in the late '50s, "Rumble," "Rawhide," "Comanche" "The Swag."

Waits: Yeah, "Rumble" was his first hit. I've been trying to pin down Frank Zappa's guitar style for a long time, and I think Link Wray is the closest I can get. I think Frank is trying to be Link Wray. We did stuff by the Ventures, too, a lot of instrumentals. I finally quit that band; we had a drummer with a harelip and a lead guitar player with a homemade guitar. Actually, there were only three of us, so in a sense we were sort of like pioneers.

Hohman: An early power trio, huh?

Waits: Yeah, that's it. Anyway, then I started writing my own stuff, and that meant going out and getting a lot of different kinds of jobs.

Hohman: What kind of jobs do you mean, music or otherwise? Your songs mention a slew of gigs, everything from pumping gas to flopping pizzas.

Waits: I had a lot of jobs. I worked as a cook and dishwasher and waiter and janitor. I worked in a jewelry store, a hardware sore, a cleaners. I drove a delivery truck, and ice cream truck, a cab for a while…

Hohman: Did you ever have any formal musical training?

Waits: No, nothin', I never had any real academic stuff, which I think becomes sort of obvious when you notice my pedestrian style.

Hohman: There's an entire persona to your stage act that must cause some people to wonder whether you're really for real, whether you are the same guy offstage as on. Are you really you?

Waits: Well, the last time I checked I was. You see, there has to be a certain amount of exaggeration in order for a performance to be educational as well as entertaining. I mean, I don't normally wear Bermuda shorts and white socks and wingtips and read Kahlil Gibran, you know. I'm the closest thing to myself that I know. Does that make any sense?

Hohman: That's surprising; I had you pegged for a *Prophet* freak. If you don't read Gibran, what are some of the things you do read? What literary influences have affected your style?

Waits: Oh, you know, I read a little, not passionately or nothing. I like John D. McDonald, Damon Runyon, Carson McCullers. I like Charles Bukowski, Hubert Selby Jr., John Rechy.

Hohman: All the Grove Press gang?

Waits: Yeah, I like all those guys. I like Gregory Corso and Ed Sanders and Allen Ginsberg and Jack Kerouac, Larry McMurtry some of the time.

Hohman: How about Richard Brautigan?

Waits: No, no thank you, uh-uh.

Hohman: When you look at the inside jacket of *Nighthawks* and see the amount of lyrics and monologues, it's almost overwhelming. How do you get all of your stuff down pat—the rapid-fire delivery, the rhythmic sense, the one-liners?

Waits: I don't just sit down at a typewriter and write. I pick up stuff from conversations in bars and cafes and cabs and clubs. The monologue generally comes out of stuff I experiment with onstage.

Hohman: Some guy sitting in front of me during your set the other night said, "Where does he get all those one-liners?" It seems to me I've heard some of them before, yet others seem like they might be your own.

Waits: Yeah, I steal a lot of them from somebody else. There are a lot of tired, old one-liners hangin' around that aren't being used, it all depends on whether you can make 'em palatable for what you're performing and who you're performing for. I like to get a chortle or two from the crowd on occasion.

Hohman: Do you think you'll always rely on the same sources for inspiration? Can you keep hanging around greasy spoons and Greyhound terminals and turning what you see and hear into fresh, vital material?

Waits: What you essentially do is just look around you, take the raw material and forge it into something meaningful. It's as much the way you deal with what you're dealing with as what you choose to write about.

Nighthawks was a result of spending eight months on the road; it's just a lot of travelogues strung together. When you're on the road doing clubs, it's hard to stay out of the bars in the afternoons. You got time to kill before the show. Then you hang around the club all night and you're up till dawn, so you hang around coffee shops. It stops being somethin' you do—it becomes somethin' you are.

Hohman: Ken Nordine made a series of recordings in the late '50s, something called *Word Jazz*. Are you acquainted with it?

Waits: Oh yeah, I used to listen to that. I was listening to Lord Buckley and Lenny Bruce too.

Hohman: You obviously didn't hear those guys on the radio. What did you listen to when you were growing up?

Waits: It was mostly the hit parade, that kind of stuff. There are a lot of composers I like: George and Ira Gershwin, Jerome Kern, Johnny Mercer, bless his soul, Cole Porter.

Hohman: That stamps you as somewhat of a throwback these days, more than a little out of sync with the mainstream of the American music scene.

Waits: Well, I do like some of the current people. I like Martin Mull, Randy Newman.

Hohman: That's one element that sets you apart from the majority of contemporary music. Both you and Newman write songs, tunes with readily comprehensible lyric, and a discernible and ofttimes hummable melody. Certain songs of yours, especially "New Coat of Paint" and "Drunk on the Moon," somehow remind me of Hoagy Carmichael, and in a strange way, Hank Williams, and a lot of other '30s and '40s composers as well.

Waits: Another composer I like is Bob Dorough. He wrote "Baltimore Oriole" back in the '50s; nowadays he writes mostly for kid shows. The first time I got hip to him was on an album called *Poetry and Jazz*, John Carradine was on it reading some Dylan Thomas stuff. Dorough did a Ferlinghetti poem, something called "A Dog," I think.

Hohman: Speaking of contemporary songwriters, one of last year's more depressing events was the unexpected death of Tim Buckley. In many ways, both of you guys work with the same subject matter.

Waits: Yeah, that was a real shock. Yeah, old Tim—I think you'll probably never go broke underestimating the collective taste and attention span of the American public. When it comes down to the hit parade, things are so tight-assed and exclusive that the stuff people have to base their own musical frame of reference on is limited, all except for the people that are curious enough to go out and do their own research. If all you do is listen to the hit parade, man.

Hohman: That's one thing about *Nighthawks*, I can't imagine how the record guys can ever pull a three-minute single out of that album.

Waits: Myself, I like "Eggs and Sausage" and "Spare Parts." I'd like to hear those as singles.

Hohman: I notice you're always carrying a small notebook around with you.

Waits: Yeah, I'm constantly jottin' things down. I keep the notebook in my pocket. That's why I'm so anxious to get home after a few months on the road, I just dump out all my suitcase full of things I've written. I take down people's conversations in cafes, then I make music over the notes.

Hohman: You can write your own music then. Where did you learn to do it?

Waits: I taught myself, primarily so that I could understand what I was trying to do technically on the piano. Usually you write within a framework, however limited you are, then that's as far as you'll go. Instead of learning theory and then learning how to play the piano, I learned theory through writing.

Hohman: You pick out your melody on piano rather than guitar?

Waits: Yeah, I don't play much on guitar. Piano's my main instrument.

Hohman: Your voice seems to have grown steadily coarser over the progression of the last three years.

Waits: Yeah, that's due to a certain amount of self-abuse, I guess... the beer, the greasy spoons, Old Gold filters.

Hohman: Where do you live in L.A.?

Waits: I live in a little apartment in Silver Lake. It's almost to downtown L.A., a Mexican-Oriental neighborhood. I hang out in the Food House and the Casino Club, the Mohawk. I play a lot of craps. In fact there's this club in D.C. where I did a week. After the place closed up one night, all the waiters, the bartenders, and the manager, we all hit this place down the corner and threw craps until dawn. I made a little more than chump change and somehow one cat had turned on the tape and got the whole thing down, taped a real serious crap game, the yelling, everything. That gave me an idea for something to do on an album: I'm going to take a trio in the studio and set 'em up in the corner, hunker down and roll craps and tape the whole thing.

Hohman: Let's go back to *Nighthawks* again. How long did it take to record?

Waits: Two nights. I spent two weeks rehearsing for it. It was done like a club date, nonstop. We invited 200 people and had booze, tables, chairs. A stripper named Dewanna opened the show. The band played "The Pink Panther" and "Night Train."

Hohman: How much of your audience do you think is hip to all the slang terminology you use? It seems you've made an exhaustive study of American pop culture, especially the underside of it. There are terms I know that I'm sure most people don't, things like Thunderbird, Stacy

Adams, names like Texas Guinan.

Waits: Yeah. Kerouac made a record back in '59 on Hanover Records with Steve Allen and he talked about her. Her famous line was, "Hello, sucker." I use stuff that's an integral part of an American conversation, things we don't even realize until they're broken down. Like restaurant calls, you know, like, "Adam and Eve on a log and sink 'em," "shit on a shingle," "eggs blindfolded," "eggs overwhelming," "chicken catastrophe."

Hohman: What do you have planned for the next album?

Waits: It's gonna be called *Pasties and a G-String* and it'll dig deeper, even farther into the bowels of I don't know. We got ideas… but it's hard to really talk about it until I get home and work with the concept.

Hohman: What would have happened to your head if *Nighthawks* would have started selling fantastically, like Springsteen's *Born to Run*? Would your outlook have been altered?

Waits: I don't know, man. I can't make no predictions on anything like that, no. I think I'm my own handicap. So I don't know. I never really expected that to happen.

Hohman: *Nighthawks* did make it to 166 with a bullet on the *Billboard* charts, I think, that ought to be good enough to keep it out of the cutout racks for a while.

Waits: Yeah, the bargain bin… that's where I might find an album I've been trying to get my hands on, it's called *Blues Haikus*, by Al Cohn and Zoot Sims. Al Cohn used to play strip joints with Lord Buckley. He's an amazing player.

Hohman: Do you think you could ever be really comfortable with anything other than the California lifestyle?

Waits: It's OK, I grew up there, so at least I'm familiar with it.

Hohman: California has often been tagged the home of American crackpot culture, what with the various religious and social phenomena that dot the landscape. That's one thing—though you shoot lots of barbs at the various aspects of America, you seldom make reference to religion.

Waits: What're you talkin' about, religious sects or religious sex?

Hohman: I mean the guru stuff.

Waits: Well, I do consult my guru before I do an interview.

Hohman: Who's that, Herb Cohen or Joe Smith?

Waits: "I don't know who the guy in the robe with the towel on his head is, but that guy next to him is Joe Smith." That's the punch line to an old story, one that's so old that I think it might even be a Damon Runyon story.

Hey, did you ever read that Kerouac novel—it's out in Grove—called *Pic*? It was written about '56, published after he died, it was written like a Mark Twain story, all in phonetic black jargon.

Hohman: What about *Mexico City Blues*? Do you know that?

Waits: Yeah, Kerouac had Charlie Parker in there, The Wheel of the Quivering Meat Conception, a lot of real strange ones. I liked that a lot.

Hohman: Have you ever seen any of Lou Reed's poetry? Some of it is very fine, a lot better than the stuff he has put to music.

Waits: No, I haven't. Real good, huh? What do you think of Patti Smith? Her band buries her, on record and onstage, too. She's a merchandisable commodity and she's being marketed as a poet and it just seems that under those circumstances that she should be a lot more concerned about her storytelling and the way she comes across lyrically. A lot of it is just lost.

Hohman: What do you think about that whole genre in music, the deco-rock brigade; Patti Smith, Reed, the Blue Oyster Cult, the Tubes?

Waits: Well, you know, cosmic debris…

Hohman: Do you know who Frank Zappa wrote that song ["Cosmik Debris"] about?

Waits: Yeah, well, I think it was about this little 15-year-old boy wonder from Denver, the little perfect master. He's got a Mercedes and a Maserati and lives in a castle. He's been 15 for about 10 years now.

Hohman: I haven't seen you in front of a hostile audience, not since that fiasco with Zappa. Do you get heckled much nowadays? What's the worst club scene you've ever had?

Waits: Heckling, hell, that happens all the time. It's usually affectionate hostility, you know, somebody who really likes what I'm doing wants to be a part of it, wants to ask me something or yell something at me.

Hohman: As far as pianists go, who do you listen to and admire?

Waits: I like Al Red Tyler, Huey Piano Smith, all of Art Tatum, Professor Longhair. I like Mose Allison a lot; we did a Soundstage show together awhile back.

What's Thelonious Monk doing now? The best thing he had out was called "The Man I Love." The last time I saw him in San Diego, his son was playing drums. I certainly admire him. I love his private solo version of "'Round Midnight," the way it drags and pulls at your heartstrings. Al Cohn and Steve Gilmore played that one night in a storeroom of some club in New York, it just killed me, man. It's such a low, moanin' lonesome, real tragic style.

As far as other musicians go, I like Charles Mingus, Tampa Red, Bo Carter, Memphis Minnie… I saw Count Basie, Ella Fitzgerald and Frank Sinatra at the Spectrum in Philadelphia awhile back. Ella was amazing. That's the worst place to hear anything, but it's a great place for hockey.

Hohman: One more thing, Tom. Let's say you're putting together an anti–Michelin Guide to cheap diners. How would you decide whether or not a greasy spoon is a five star joint?

Waits: Anyplace I can come out of with enough gas to open a Mobil station is all right by me.

Right before this article was scheduled to be sent off to the printer, Tom swung back into Chicago with his new trio, a group featuring Frank Vicari (formerly of Maynard Ferguson's and Woody Herman's bands) on tenor sax, Dr. Fitzgerald Hunnington Jenkins III on upright bass and Chip White on drums. Tom explained that he had been performing with the trio for a while, and that even though it was costing him money every night they stayed together, he had already lined up a European tour for midsummer, the highlight of which would be a two-week stopover at Ronnie Scott's in London.

The addition of the trio has finally allowed Waits the freedom to really stretch out onstage, lending an added dimension to his already powerful ramble. He sat down to the keyboards for a brief "New Coat of Paint," unveiled the title song of the upcoming *Pasties and a G-String* album, delivered a slam-bang "Depot Depot" and kept the overflow audience in the palm of his grubby hand throughout.

Waits is indefinite as to how long the present trio will stay with him. Although he claims that he and his sidemen are "thick as thieves," financial worries may dictate the future course of Tom's ensemble plans. Regardless, Waits is on his way to Europe, in his first attempt to see whether he can communicate his individual vision of America to music buffs on the other side. Odds are that he will succeed. For Waits defies classification, remaining a true original in a world of exploding imitations. He is one performer you can't afford to miss.

Feb. 10, 1977

Dexter Gordon: Making His Great Leap Forward

by Chuck Berg

The October return of Dexter Gordon was one of the events of 1976. SRO crowds greeted him with thunderous applause at George Wein's Storyville. Music biz insiders packed an RCA studio control room to savor each passage as Dex and a cast of all-stars set down tracks for Don Schlitten's Xanadu label. Long lines of fans snaked up the stairs of Max Gordon's Village Vanguard waiting their chance to share Dexter's musical magic. The reaction to the master saxophonist's New York stopover was nothing short of phenomenal.

There was also an avalanche of newsprint, spearheaded by Gary Giddins' perceptive piece for the *Village Voice* and Bob Palmer's appreciative overview in the *New York Times*. More significant, perhaps, was the genuine enthusiasm in the street. The standard conversational opener was, "Have you seen Dex?" The reviews corroborated these ebullient responses and certified Dex's return as one of the great musical triumphs of recent times.

At 53 Dexter Gordon is one of the legitimate giants on the scene. His credits include tours of duty with Lionel Hampton, Fletcher Henderson, Louis Armstrong, Billy Eckstine, Charlie Parker and a wide range of small groups under his own leadership. Influenced by Lester Young, Gordon in turn became an important model for tenor greats Sonny Rollins and John Coltrane. Today, he stands as a beacon of musical integrity and excellence.

I met Dexter at his suite of rooms at the South Gate Towers near Madison Square Garden. During our three-hour conversation, Dexter revealed the warmth, encyclopedic memory and playfulness that have emerged as major facets of his music. The recollections and stories, intoned by his

Dexter Gordon.
(Jan Persson)

smoky basso voice and punctuated with a broad spectrum of laughs, rolled out effortlessly over the coffee and cigarette smoke.

Berg: On your album *The Apartment* (Inner City 1025), you quote the opening phrase of "Santa Claus Is Coming to Town." Last night at the Village Vanguard there were more borrowings from "Santa Claus." Do you celebrate Christmas all around the year?

Gordon: Just call me Kris Kringle. You know, things like that just happen. But I dig the tune. It sits nice. Actually, when those quotes pop out I'm usually not thinking about them. Of course if it's Christmas time, I'm more apt to be thinking about something like that. Usually it's just something that happens. It's kind of built in, built into the subconscious.

Berg: Dex, how does it feel to be back in the Apple with the kind of reception that you've been getting?

Gordon: It's great to be back. Of course I've been going out to the West Coast for years, which has been very nice. But I had forgotten how fantastic and exciting New York is. There's no place like this in the world. This is it, you know. It's always been that way. This time, for me, it's been overwhelming because from the minute we got off the plane everything has been fantastic, unbelievable. I really wasn't prepared for this kind of a reaction, "the return of the conquering hero" and all that.

Berg: The crowds have been absolutely ecstatic. Last night, for example, there were a couple of phrases in "Wee Dot" where you started at the bottom of the horn. Then, as you went up and up, one could feel the audience going right up there with you to the high F and beyond. It was a collective sharing that was quite unusual.

Gordon: It's been like that from the first note. The opening night at the Vanguard on Tuesday was sold out. And when I walked into the room from the kitchen, working my way around to the bandstand, I got an ovation.

Berg: I noticed the same thing last night. It was beautiful.

Gordon: I hadn't played a note. I just walked into the room, you know, and they applauded.

Berg: Well, you are a commanding presence. And the people appreciate the opportunity to hear your music.

Gordon: It was really something.

Berg: Let me ask you about the recording for Don Schlitten's Xanadu label. I caught two hours of the session and it sounded great. Barry Harris, Sam Jones, Louis Hayes, Al Cohn, Blue Mitchell, Sam Noto and Dexter Gordon… that's quite a lineup.

Gordon: Yeah. That was an all-star date. It was all beautiful. All the cats, you know, are just beautiful.

Berg: When can we expect that on the street?

Gordon: I don't know. I haven't really talked to Don about it. But this week we'll probably have dinner or lunch and talk about it. He's an old friend of mine, you know. An old tenor freak.

Berg: He is?

Gordon: Yeah. For Don, bebop's the greatest. We've done a lot of things together. He was my man at Prestige when I signed.

Berg: Dex, let me ask you about a rumor that's been running around town involving you recording for Columbia. The story has it that a group of Columbia executives were so impressed by performance at Storyville last week that they've set up a record date with you, Woody Shaw, Louis Hayes, Ronnie Matthews and Stafford James. Is that correct?

Gordon: Apparently so.

Berg: Will it be a live date?

Gordon: Yeah. It should be something else. It will be the second week in December at the Village Vanguard. That's a good time because I'll have the first week of December free. I'll be able to get to a piano to work some things out so we can do something new, something fresh. We have a whole week at the Vanguard: The first couple of days we'll put it together, iron it out, and then the rest of the week we'll record.

Berg: Dexter Gordon with the Woody Shaw–Louis Hayes Band… that should be a landmark!… In view of the tremendous welcome you've received, have you had second thoughts about moving back to the States? Are you tempted to set up a base of operation here and commute between Copenhagen and, say, New York?

Gordon: Well, all those things have occurred to me. But basically Copenhagen is home. We have a nice house and a garden. It's ideal, really. Nothing special, but very comfortable. Of course, if I'm going to be commuting as much as it seems, maybe a place here is necessary. But, as I said, basically Copenhagen is home. So I don't visualize moving permanently to the States. Of course, you never know.

Berg: Let me ask a question for all the saxophone freaks out there. You play a Selmer Mark VI with an Otto Link metal mouthpiece. For all of us who have tried getting that big, full-bodied Dexter Gordon sound, what kind of setup do you use?

Gordon: A #8 facing and a #3 Rico reed.

Berg: I'll try it.… There are a lot of younger musicians who don't know that much about your background. Therefore, I'd like to ask you about some of your early influences, who they were and what, specifically, you picked up from them.

Gordon: Well, I started listening at a very early age, before I even started playing, in my hometown, Los Angeles. We're talking about the '30s now because I was born in 1923. When I was nine and 10 years old I was listening the bands on the radio on my own. Prior to that my father used to take me to the theaters in town to dig the bands and the artists. He was a doctor and knew a lot of them: Duke, Lionel Hampton, Marshall Royal, Ethel Waters. They'd come by for dinner. And I'd go see them backstage, things like that. It was just part of my cultural upbringing. On the radio I was picking up the late night shots, air shots from the East: Chicago's Grand Terrace, Roseland Ballroom, you know, and people like "Fatha" Hines, Fletcher Henderson and Roy Eldridge. So when my father gave me a clarinet when I was 13, I had done a lot of listening.

Berg: Clarinet, then, was your first instrument.

Gordon: Oh, yeah. Benny Goodman, Buster Bailey, Barney Bigard… I used to dig them all. My first teacher was a clarinetist from New Orleans, John Sturdevant. He was one of the local guys in L.A. and a very nice cat who had that big fat clarinet sound like Bigard's. I remember asking him about that, which knocked him out. I said, "How ya get that sound, man?" Almost all of those New Orleans clarinet players—Irving Fazola, Albert Nicholas, Bigard—have that.

When I started playing I had some kind of idea about music, about jazz, because I was into everybody. I used to make money cutting lawns in the neighborhood, which I spent on secondhand records from jukebox companies because a lot of the jazz things they'd never used. I'd get them for 15 cents. I had quite a nice collection when I was 12, 13 years old.

So I was listening to people like Benny Carter, Roy Eldridge, who is one of my all-time favorites, and Scoops Carry, who played alto with Roy's little band. I also like Pete Brown. Of course I heard Chu Berry, and Dick Wilson, who played tenor with Andy Kirk, and Ben Webster. I first heard Ben on a record he made with Duke called "Truckin'." He was shoutin' on that. But then I got my first Basie record and that was it. I fell in love with that band—Lester, Herschel Evans, the whole band. Duke was just fantastic, but the Basie band really hit me.

After a couple of years I got an alto and started playing it with the school band and in a dance band with a lot of the neighborhood kids. Before that, though, we had what you'd call a jug band where the kids had homemade instruments.

Berg: What were you playing then?

Gordon: Well, I was the only one with an instrument.

Berg: You were the legitimate player.

Gordon: Yeah. The other kids were all trying to play something. The guy playing drums had a drum made out of a washtub, and pie pans for cymbals and something else for a snare.

Berg: Did you guys ever record? That would be a treasure.

Gordon: I don't know about that, man. Some of the cats had kazoos. Someone even stuck a trumpet mouthpiece into a kazoo. We played some amateur shows around the neighborhood, but then when I got the alto I started playing with different young browns around town. I started gigging, too. Playing weekends in sailor joints for a dollar and a half a night and the kitty. So I started like that and kept going to better, more organized bands. Then when I was 17 I got the tenor.

Berg: When you got the tenor was it love at first sight, or rather love at first breath?

Gordon: Yeah.

Berg: Did you instinctively know that the tenor was it?

Gordon: It was really after hearing Lester that I knew. And Herschel Evans and, like I said, Dick Wilson. Wilson's playing with Andy Kirk was beautiful. He was lead tenorist with the Kirk band when Mary Lou Williams was there. Mary Lou used to write lead parts for Wilson. She was about the first one I ever heard using the tenor to lead the section. They had a big hit called "Until the Real Thing Comes Along" and Wilson played lead on that. Just beautiful.

I listened to everybody. There were also some cats around town who had a lot of influence on me. Another teacher, a man named Lloyd Reese, was a multi-instrumentalist who was best known for his trumpet playing. He used to work with Les Hite. He was very popular in the neighborhood, a very good teacher. Many of the cats studied with him: Mingus, Buddy Collette, me. We also had a rehearsal band that met on Sunday mornings at the old colored local, Local 767.

Berg: Was that something that Reese organized?

Gordon: Yeah, for his students, plus other cats who were just beginning to write charts.

In the high school I went to we had a swing band plus the regular orchestra and marching band. There were a lot of people that came out of that band: Chico Hamilton, Melba Liston, Bill Douglass, Jackie Kelso, a very fine clarinetist, Vernon Slater, Lammar Wright Jr., Vi Redd, Ernie Royal. At another school in the neighborhood there was Mingus and Buddy Collette. So there was a lot of activity. Then when I was just getting ready to finish school, I joined Hampton's band.

Berg: That must have been quite a transition.

Gordon: Yeah, it was. Hamp had just left Benny Goodman, which was one of the bands, you know. His association with the Goodman band, quartet and trio made him very popular. So he left Benny and formed his big band out on the coast.

Berg: That was the first big-time gig for you?

Gordon: Oh, yeah. That was really my first professional gig. The other things were just more or less on a school level. When I joined the band the musicians in town said: "Dexter who? Dexter Gordon? Who's that?" I used to go around all over the place and talk to all the cats, you know, but they didn't know who I was. I was just another young player.

I started making the rounds when I was 15 because I've been this tall since that time. I could usually get into places without anybody saying anything. I had a baby face, of course, but being so big, people didn't bother me. I also used to get into dances because I'd talk to the cats. There would always be somebody who would let me carry his instrument case in. So I'd walk in with the band. It was a funny thing because later on I'd let the young cats walk in with me, you know, people like Jackie McLean and Sonny Rollins.

So anytime there was music in Los Angeles I was there. I even went by some of the places I couldn't go in. I'd just have to go stand outside and when the door would open I'd hear a little bit. There were some good musicians in Los Angeles, most of them from the Southwest.

I remember a good band led by Floyd Ray that was like a territory band. They had a lot of good young cats that I used to hang out with. One of the alto players, Shirley Green, used to show me some shit. They were good guys. But when I joined Hamp that was really a great leap forward.

Berg: How did the gig come about?

Gordon: Marshall Royal had called me one afternoon after school and said, "This is Marshall." I didn't believe him. I thought it was one of the cats playing a trick. Finally he made me believe him and he asked me about joining the band. I still don't know why he called me. I'll have to ask him next time we get together. Why the hell did he call me? I don't understand. Anyway, we went down to Hamp's house for a little session. There was Sir Charles Thompson, Irving Ashby on guitar, Lee Young on drums, Marshall and Hamp. We just jammed two or three tunes and Hamp said, "Would you like to come into the band?" I said yeah.

Berg: That was your audition.

Gordon: Right. So three days later we were on the bus. Before that, though, I went home and told Mom and she said, "Well, what about school?" I said, "Mom, I can do it later." She knew there was no point in saying no or trying to put up a barricade. So on December 23 during Christmas vacation we set out for our first date at Fort Worth, Texas, in a rickety old bus that was all right for California. When we got to New Mexico, though, the weather changed. It started getting winter and this was strictly a California bus.

Berg: A Southern California bus.

Gordon: Yeah, a Southern California bus. So by the time we got to El Paso there was a revolution on the bus: "We're not going no further!" We had one of those band managers who was cutting all the corners. But he straightened things out so that we got a real bus in El Paso. We finally got to the Fort Worth Hotel the day after Christmas. I'd had no rehearsal or anything. In fact I didn't even have a uniform. They gave me a jacket with sleeves that stopped at the elbows.

The first couple of gigs, I didn't play a right note all night because I wasn't ready or used to his arrangements. I expected him to send me home every night. Fortunately, about three days later in Dallas we had a rehearsal, my first. So I kinda got it together. It started happening then, you know. But I still felt the cats were going to send me home or something. But they stayed with me, so in a month or so it was all right. I was very lucky because the band was on its way to New York.

We then opened at the Grand Terrace in Chicago around the end of January. The band hit instantly. We went in there for two weeks and stayed six months. Hamp was with Joe Glaser and Joe was connected with the Chicago scene. I think this was the gangster scene, you know, Capone and all that shit. They had all the joints. The Grand Terrace was the home of Fletcher Henderson and Earl Hines. The club was in trouble, but when we came, bang, it happened. And we sat there for six months. I think we worked every night playing shows for acts, chorus lines, everything.

Berg: So you got a heavy dose of showbiz right from the start.

Gordon: Right, man. The whole thing. I don't know why, but my timing has been just fantastic at each stage of my career. I've been in the right place at the right time. I've been lucky. Anyway, the Grand Terrace was fantastic. In six months the band put it all together. We made a couple of replacements, Shadow Wilson on drums and Joe Newman on trumpet. Joe was going to school at Alabama State and we heard him on the way to New York. I kept bugging Hamp, "Get that cat." So first chance we got, we sent for him. It was a fantastic band. All the first men were unbelievable—Marshall Royal playing lead alto, a cat named Fred Beckett playing lead trombone, who we called Black Dorsey, and a first trumpet player named Carl George, who later played with Kenton and who had a crystal-clear sound like Charlie Spivak. So the first chairs were all perfect. For saxophones we had Marshall Royal, Illinois Jacquet and Ray Perry on alto and electric violin. He played violin like Stuff Smith but never really got the recognition because he died too early. Ernie Royal, Joe Newman and Carl George were the trumpets. All the cats were great.

It was really my school. I learned so much. Marshall stayed on my ass all the time. He'd say, "Hold that note down, hold that note down." It was something else, you know, because we were holding phrases of four, five, six bars and breathing in specific places together. Marshall forced me to learn about crescendo, decrescendo, piano,

forte and all those things I didn't know anything about when I was in high school.

Berg: So, Marshall was the section leader.

Gordon: Yeah. He thought he was the concert master for the band, too, but he was my immediate supervisor. I used to get so mad because it seemed like it would never be right, but later I told him thanks a mil. He taught me so much. Unbelievable. And, yeah, I learned a lot of shit from Jacquet, too. He was also young, a few years older than me, but he was already playing, already a soloist, with his shit together. A lot of people don't seem to understand that Jacquet's a hell of a tenor player. We used to sit next to each other, which was great, and we used to do a two-tenor number called "Porkchops." It wasn't extensive, you know, but we played a few choruses together. I forget what the format was but it was nice.

Berg: Did you and Illinois ever sit down together and play or talk about improvisation?

Gordon: Constantly. Every day, man. On the bus, off the bus, in the hotel, on the stand. We talked about what we wanted to do, who we liked. And he showed me a lot of shit like altissimo fingerings, playing over the high F.

Berg: How long were you with Hamp?

Gordon: I was with him until 1943, about three years.

Berg: Where did you go from there?

Gordon: Back to L.A. to gig around town. I worked in a band that Lee Young had at a place called Club A La Grand. There was a place around the corner called the Ritz that was an afterhours joint where we used to jam. This was when I ran into Art Pepper. He used to come around and we used to jam together. I then got him a gig in Lee's band working at A La Grand. I also worked with Jessie Price, the drummer from Kansas City who had been with Basie. Oh yeah, Fletcher Henderson came out with a nucleus of a big band and picked up four or five cats in L.A. to fill it out. I worked with him for about a month.

Berg: How was that?

Gordon: Great, man. His brother Horace was with the band and we worked in a nightclub called The Plantation. There's even a record on it that we did for the Armed Forces Jubilee show that was originally recorded on one of those big V-discs. I'm featured in the band with Fletcher. Can you believe that? I grew up listening to those cats. Fletcher used to write in

the sharp keys, you know, to give the band a more brilliant sound. But I don't really like playing in the sharp keys. I like flat keys. For instance, I've always dug D-flat because that's a beautiful key for tenor. It puts you in the key of E-flat and your 5th is on the bottom.

Berg: Speaking of the bottom of the horn, I noticed a couple of low A's last night.

Gordon: Yeah. I grew up with this guy named James Nelson, and he lived right around the corner from me. He was a couple of years older, so naturally when he moved into the neighborhood I was right on him. His brother played the piano, so I was there all the time. Anyway, James is the one that showed me that low A with the knee covering the bell. He used to take me around a lot, too. When you speak of influences, there are so many people that I've been fortunate enough to learn from.

Berg: What came after Fletcher?

Gordon: All during this time Nat Cole had his trio out at a place called the 331 Club. It was very popular for quite some time. On Mondays, our off-nights, they'd have sessions, and the guy promoting the sessions was Norman Granz, who was a student at one of the city colleges. So I used to go out there and play with Nat. During this time we also made some records. We played "I Found a New Baby" and "Rosetta." I was very Lester-ish at the time.

Berg: In *Jazz Masters of The Forties*, Ira Gitler talks about your role as one of the first players to adapt Charlie Parker's innovations to the tenor saxophone. When did you start listening to Bird?

Gordon: Well, the first time I heard Bird was in 1941. When I was with Hamp's band, Parker was with Jay McShann. It was here in New York at the Savoy when they would have two or three bands. We played at the Savoy opposite McShann. They had that Kansas City sound, and the alto player was playing his ass off. Beautiful. That's when I first met Bird. I had heard the recordings he made with McShann with Walter Brown singing "Moody Blues" and "Jumping the Blues." It was a rough band but the ingredients were there. Bird was just singing through all that shit. The other alto player was beautiful, too, a cat named John Jackson who I later worked with in Eckstine's band. Anyway, the next year Bird went with Earl Hines. Then when Eckstine left Earl's band he took half the guys with him, including Bird. So during that time I often ran into Bird in Boston or New York.

Bird and Lester both come from Kansas City, and Bird was very influenced by Lester. So the Lester influence is part of the natural evolution for him and for me. Because I heard him right away, there were similar feelings, you know. Also, Bird had other influences. There was a cat called Prof. Smith, an alto player around Kansas City who was important. Then Jimmy Dorsey. A lot of cats don't know that, but Bird loved Jimmy Dorsey. I loved him, too. He was a helluva saxophonist, a lot of feeling. Bird dug Pete Brown, too. When Lester came out he played very melodic. Everything he played you could sing. He was always telling a story, and Bird did the same thing. That kind of musical philosophy is what I try to do because telling a story is, I think, where it's at.

In the '30s, cats were playing harmonically, basically straight tonic chords and 7th chords. Lester was the first one I heard that played 6th chords. He was playing the 6th and the 9th. He stretched it a little by using the same color tones used by Debussy and Ravel, those real soft tones. Lester was doing all that. Then Bird extended that to 11ths and 13ths, like Diz, and to altered notes like the flat 5th and flat 9th. So this was harmonically some of what had happened.

Like I said, I was just lucky. I was already in that direction, so when I heard Bird it was just a natural evolution. Fortunately, I worked with him and we used to hang out together and jam together around New York. It just happened for me that it was the correct path.

Berg: What was your gig with Louis Armstrong like?

Gordon: I joined Louis in Los Angeles. I was working at the time with Jessie Price, and one night after the set somebody says to me, "Hey, cat, sure like that tone you're getting." I looked up and it was Pops. The next night Teddy McRae, the tenor player who was the straw boss in Pop's band, came in. I had met Teddy before when he was with Chick Webb. Also, I think he took my chair in Hamp's band. Anyway, he asked me if I'd like to join the band. I'd been in Los Angeles long enough and I wanted to check Louis out, so I joined the band.

The band was part of several major feature films: *Atlantic City* (1944) and *Pillow to Post* (1945) with Ida Lupino. It was also nice because I was the major soloist in the band then, other than Pops, I mean.

Berg: How was it working with Louis?

Gordon: Oh, great. Love, love, love. Just beautiful. Always beautiful. It was just a gas being with him. He let me play all the time. He dug me.

Berg: How long were you with Louis?

Gordon: About seven or eight months. Actually, it was a mediocre band. They were just playing Luis Russell arrangements from the '30s, "Ain't Misbehavin'," all those things. So nothing was happening. When we got to Chicago I knew that Eckstine had formed a band. In fact, I had heard some of their records and it was happening, it was the new sound. So, anyway, when we got to Chicago at the Regal Theatre, Eckstine's good friend and buddy, a guy named Bob Redcross who Bird later named a tune for ("Redcross"), came backstage and said that Eckstine needed a tenor player. He had heard me on the air with Pops and wanted to know if I'd join the band. I said yeah. So two weeks later I joined the band. It was fantastic. It was a hell of a jump, the difference between night and day.

Berg: Who was in Eckstine's band at that time?

Gordon: They were all young and unknown at the time, but later it proved to be a million-dollar band. The arrangers were Jerry Valentine, a trombone player from Hines' band, and Tadd Dameron. Diz also had a couple of things in the book. For reeds we had John Jackson on lead, Sonny Stitt on third alto, Gene Amnions and myself on tenor and Leo Parker on baritone. The trombones were Jerry Valentine, Taswell Baird and Chips Outcalt. The trumpets were Dizzy, Shorty McConnel, Gail Brockman and Boonie Hazel. John Malachi played piano, Connie Wainwright, guitar, Tommy Potter, bass, and Art Blakey, drums. And our vocalist was Sarah Vaughan. Unbelievable, huh?

I joined the band in Washington, D.C., at the Howard Theatre in 1944, and was with the band for the next couple of years except for a couple of months off at one point. But it was a fantastic band in a fantastic period, you know. This is when I met Tadd, my favorite arranger and composer. I did some things with him later.

Berg: After Eckstine came New York and 52nd Street. What was that period like?

Gordon: Ahhhhh... every day there was something happening. This new music thing, bebop, was taking shape and becoming recognized, so it was a very exciting period. Every day there was something exciting, something ecstatic, something. And all the cats loved each other and practiced together at Tadd's house, Monk's house, at sessions. Then the street started opening up for the cats. So, it was happening. I worked on the street a lot with Bird and Miles. Miles was just coming up then. He was still eating jelly beans at that time. Do you believe that? Malted milks and jelly beans. I worked with Bird at a place called the Spotlight with my sextet, with Miles and Bird, Stan Levey, Bud Powell, Curly Russell and Baby Lawrence, the dancer. Lawrence was the show, but really he was part of the band.

Berg: How did playing with a dancer work out?

Gordon: Good. He danced bebop. The way those cats danced, man, was just like a drummer. He was doing everything that the other cats were doing and maybe more. Blowing eights, fours and trading off. He just answered to the music. There were several cats on that level, but he was the boss. Baby Lawrence. Fantastic. He used to do some unbelievable things.

Dancing in those days was a big part of the musical environment, you know. Everybody was dancing to the music, to whatever they wanted, different dances and everything. Just as music was growing, dancing was growing. Like I said, we used to play with all those shows, chorus lines and all that. To me it was great. I loved it.

Berg: That's quite interesting because I've gotten the feeling that musicians have generally resented backing up dancers, singers, whatever.

Gordon: No. I never have. Especially if it's good.

Berg: Many people have mentioned your influence on 'Trane. Did you know 'Trane?

Gordon: Not really. I knew him, but not well. He was from Philly. He was younger, of course, but I had met him here and there. Philly Joe reminded me recently, a few months ago when we were on tour together in Europe, of the time that Miles' band came out to Hollywood. 'Trane was playing his shit, but it wasn't projecting, he didn't have the sound. So one day we were talking and I said, "Man, you play fantastic, but you have to develop that sound, get that projection." I gave him a mouthpiece I had that I wasn't using. I laid that on him and that was it. That made the difference.

Berg: That's incredible because there are many things in 'Trane's sound that are reminiscent of your sound.

Gordon: He was playing my mouthpiece, man! Again, it's the same line— Lester to Bird to Dexter to 'Trane. There was evolution, of course, but really the same line.

Berg: Let me ask you about Sonny Rollins. I talked to Sonny about a month ago and your name came up as an important influence. He speaks of you with great warmth. What was your relationship like?

Gordon: Well, Sonny and Jackie McLean were the young cats coming up in the late '40s, early '50s, you know. I wasn't really around them too much because as they were beginning to mature I was out on the coast. But again, it's the same story. They came up in the same line. Of course, they have their own things, which is natural because we all learn and are influenced by different people and situations.

Berg: There's one thing that especially impressed Sonny and which has always intrigued me. That is the way you lay back on the melody or phrase just a bit behind the beat. Instead of being right on top of the beat with a metrical approach like Sonny Stitt and a lot of the great white tenor players, you just pull back. In the process there are interesting tensions that develop in your music. How did that come about?

Gordon: Yeah. I've been told that I do that. I'm not really that conscious of it. I think I more or less got it from Lester because I didn't play right on top. He was always a little back, I think. That's the way I felt it, you know, and so it just happened that way. These things are not really thought out. It's what you hear and the way you hear it.

Berg: What happened after 52nd Street? I know you moved to Denmark in 1962, but my knowledge of your activities during the '50s is sketchy.

Gordon: Well, during the '50s things got a little tough because like everybody else I had a habit. I was paying the dues. So my career was very spasmodic. Thankfully, I was one of the lucky ones who got pulled out and started putting it back together again. I did do a few things during that time but not a great amount of work. There were some nice recordings with Bethlehem. And in the early '50s Wardell Gray and I were doing our thing, you know, the chase with a quintet.

Berg: When you moved to Denmark, what was in your mind? Why did you make that decision?

Gordon: There wasn't any decision. In 1960 I started commuting to New York because I had signed with Blue Note. So I was coming here to record. Then, in 1962 I moved to New York and was here for six or

seven months. I met Ronnie Scott at a musician's bar called Charlie's, and he introduced himself and asked if I'd come to London. I said, "Yeah, sure." So I gave him my address and he said he'd be in touch. A couple of months later he offered me a month's work in his club and a couple weeks touring around England. He said maybe he could get me a few things on the Continent. So after I left London I went to Copenhagen to the Montmartre. It developed into a love affair and before I knew it I'd been over there a couple of years.

I was reading *DownBeat* one day back then, and Ira Gitler referred to me as an expatriate. That's true, you know, but at the time I hadn't really made up my mind to live there, so I came back here in 1965 for about six months, mostly out on the coast. But with all the political and social strife during that time and the Beatles thing, I didn't really dig it. So I went back and lived in Paris for a couple of years. But the last nine or 10 years I've lived steadily in Copenhagen.

Copenhagen's like my home base. So I more or less became Danish. I think it's been very good for me. I've learned a lot, of course. Another way of life, another culture, language. I enjoyed it. I still do. Of course, there was no racial discrimination or anything like that. And the fact that you're an artist in Europe means something. They treat you with a lot of respect. In America, you know, they say, "Do you make any money?" If you're in the dollars, you're OK, you're all right. But over there, it's an entirely different mentality.

Berg: What does the future hold for Dexter Gordon at this point?

Gordon: Well, it looks like I'm about to take a great leap forward.

Berg: Here, here!

Gordon: So, you know, it's moving. I'm very optimistic. About the future, and about music. These last five years, I think, have been good. All over Europe and here there has been a renaissance in music, and jazz in particular. And that's what we're talking about, jazz. I like the word "jazz." That word has been my whole life. I understand the cats when they take exception to the name, you know. But to me that's my life.

***

Fortunately, we will be able to hear more of Dex in 1977. On wax, there will be the all-star date on Xanadu. There will also be the live session at the Village Vanguard

with Woody Shaw, Louis Hayes, Ronnie Matthews and Stafford James on Columbia. And in May, Dex will be returning for an extended tour of the States under the auspices of Ms. Management in New York. All this represents a new plateau in Dex's career and, for us, the opportunity to share in the workings of one of the great hearts and minds in contemporary music.

May 5, 1977

Ray Charles: Senior Diplomat of Soul

by Pete Welding

"When I was a youngster, in my teens, I wanted to do things like make a record one day. I wanted to do things like play in New York, at Carnegie Hall, have a big band, have a million-seller or a gold record, win a Grammy. I wanted to make a movie and star in it. And I've done all these things.

"I've even gone to the White House, which I must tell you, and I don't want to overdramatize it, but I come from a little small town in Florida, in the South, blind, and in those years although I felt that I was accustomed to the situation, still I never would have thought as a youngster in this little town that I would ever set foot in the White House! I mean, really, I got to be honest. I tell you! And to talk to the president of the United States! I mean, shit, that's heavy. But I've done that, too. I've gotten keys to cities, had mayors honor me with this and that. So, I've had these honors and I treasure them. You can never take those memories away from me. I've been a very blessed man."

Ray Charles was reflecting on his life in music, which by any yardstick has been formidable. One entire wall in his spacious office was filled, from floor to ceiling, with plaques, awards, framed certificates and other honors he had garnered in his nearly three decades of performing. And were he to display all the gold and platinum records he's won in that time it would probably take all the remaining wall space.

Ray Charles.
(Jan Persson)

Charles is, let's face it, one of the major performers of our time, a brilliant, compelling singer whose distinctive, emotion-drenched delivery and thrilling dark-hued voice are capable of energizing virtually any type of song. In his long career he's had hits, and many of them, too, with blues, R&B, the modern soul music he almost singlehandedly created, country-and-western material, popular ballad standards, novelty tunes and contemporary songs (just last year he won a Grammy for his deeply affecting version of Stevie Wonder's "Living in the City"). Nor is there

apparently any end to his ability to remake any kind of song material into pure Ray Charles. Simply, he is one of the master song stylists of our age who, through the deep power and strong personality of his singing, can transform anything that marvelous voice touches into pure gold, distilling from it all the best it possesses.

The major accomplishments of his career are too well known to warrant retelling here. Suffice it to say that from the middle 1950s, when he electrified popular music with his brilliant fusion of R&B and gospel music, later extending the basic style

to incorporate such diverse elements as country music and standard ballads, Charles has been one of the most widely successful and broadly accomplished performers in all of popular music. Nor has his appeal been limited by national or linguistic boundaries, for he is now (and has been for some time) one of the leading concert attractions in world music, his greatly successful tours taking him and his show through Europe, South America and Asia, where he remains one of the favorite of all-American musical attractions to perform annually.

While he is what is referred to as an

"established" artist, Charles is not content to rest on past laurels. He continues to record and to perform with tremendous enthusiasm, with the same fervor, passion and painstaking attention to detail he always has lavished on his music, driving his associates no less than himself to perform at peak expressiveness. He will settle for nothing less. For all his success, Charles appears to be a driven man constantly trying to prove himself. In his mind, the reason is simple.

"See, you don't know whether or not what you do is going to be a success. You don't know that: nobody does. What you do know is that you put your all into it. And as long as you do that, if you really be honest with yourself—of course be sure you're putting your all into it—long as you do that, I don't give a shit what happens. You can't do no more! So there ain't no point in worrying about trying to keep up with what you did last year."

An interesting point, that. Given the old showbiz adage, "If they liked it once, they'll love it twice," aren't there tremendous pressures placed on a performer who achieves great success, pressures to continue with what has proven so successful? To keep on producing basically the same kind of things so as not to jeopardize that success?

"The pressures are ones that you will get yourself," Charles observed. "You got to be sure that you don't allow that to happen. You can't stop some of it from happening to you because it's going to happen. I mean, what can you do? You're going to feel it, you got to feel it. You can minimize it, however. The point is not to let it control you. You must control it. How do you do that? You control it by saying to yourself, 'Everything that I do, at the time I do it, I'll give it my all.' And then, after that you just walk away from it. I mean, don't get no hang-ups in trying to outdo yourself. What you do, when you do it, is give it all you got then.

"You see, the thing about creating anything—the next day or the next week, whenever it is, you always can hear or see something in what you have done that, now that it's out, you wish you had done before it came out. You will always see that and you will always feel that. But you can't let it mess you up. You've got to say to yourself, 'When I do this today and I put my seal on it, I know that from what I felt at the end of that day I gave it all I had.' Now, once the song is out on the street, next week I might feel that I wish I had done such and such on it. Well, if it's really some-

thing good that was not on the record, that's OK, too, because when I perform I can make it up there, make the performance of the song better than the record was. So I have that opportunity.

"Now, these things are not errors; I don't mean that. It's what you feel on a given day. That's the thing about creating, and thank God for it. I'm glad that life lets you not just stay with the rub-board all the time. I mean, thank heaven there was somebody to say, 'Wait a minute. The rub-board's fine, but I got a feeling that if we make this thing do this, and go like this, we won't have to use that rub-board. We can use something else.' That's what you're doing when you sing, when you perform, when you make a record: to know that you've given it all you got and at the time that record was to your mind as good as you could make it. Besides that, many times what worries you about a given thing, the public may never notice it, 'cause you're looking at it through a microscope."

Does he feel his singing has changed in any way over the years he's been performing?

"I think my voice has leveled out more, in the sense that it's not as light as it was in my 20s. My voice was very light then. I think it has taken on more of a seasoned sound over the years, but that's about it. And also some of that, I'm sure, is due to the fact that I know how to control it better. I do think, however, that there is an honest difference in the sound of my voice than, say, at 21 or 23 than what it is now at 46. It is a little heavier, gotten a little more weight to it. Now, that's the voice itself. But what I think has happened more so, though, is the fact that I have learned from doing a lot of singing, and singing under adverse conditions. I mean, singing many times when the mike's bad or singing many times when you don't feel good, you're sick—and you learn how to take your voice and get the most out of it. You learn what it will do at the time and what it won't do at the time. You study yourself, I think, the same as you study an instrument, your voice is an instrument. I know I do. If I happen to be hoarse, I pretty well know what I can do. I'll test it when I'm singing on a gig. I'll find out, I'll run it through its paces in a song to find out what it's going to allow me to do on that night. And I'll adjust to that.

"While it's true that your satisfactions become different as you learn more about your voice and what it's capable of, as you

grow as performer, it's also fair to say that you are more critical of yourself because you know what you're capable of. That's why I really understand what people mean when they talk out the difference between a guy who is a thrower and one who is a pitcher. It's the same in music. In my case, I've already set a philosophy for me, I've already set my guidelines. My guideline is that on any given night, the minute I hit that stage, you can be sure if it's 500 or 5,000—if anything, more so if it's 500—I'm going to give it all I got. The reason for that is, if there's 500 people in the audience, I want those people to walk out and tell their friends, 'Well, honey, there wasn't too many of us there but he put on a bitch of a show. You really missed it.' I prefer that to, say, 'Hey, man, wasn't too many of us there, and I'm sorry I went 'cause the show was a drag.' I'm just that way. That's for openers. I believe this is the attitude one should direct his attention to. But above all, and I really and truly mean above all, I have to be good to me. I must please me, and I'm a hard sonofabitch to please. And that's the truth."

That tells us much about Charles' philosophy as an entertainer, how he views himself and his approach to music. But where is he now? Where does he stand in reference to contemporary music and contemporary musical thought? What does he think about the music of today? Does he listen to much of it and, if so, what sorts of things does he find himself attracted to? How does he view himself within the context of the current music scene or is he, in a sense, above and beyond it? Where, for example, does his career stand now?

"I think my career has been very steady, very level for some time now. I guess one could always say one could do better, have better things happening to them, but then one could have a hell of a lot worse things happening to them, too. So what I'm really saying is that my personal feeling about my career is this: it has been very even in the sense that the public has genuinely supported me. You know, every time you add on a year in this business, to my mind, you're really doing something. Most artists can come out and make a couple of hit records and they may stay out three, four, five, maybe six years, and that's usually about tops. So when you think that over the last 10 years I'm still able to go places and play and fill the house—certainly, you know, 80 percent—well, that's gratifying.

"I wish I had a command of language

sufficient to really describe how it makes you feel inside to know that you have people who really love what you do, people all over this world, and I mean they are very loyal to you. I mean, we can play in a little town in Japan—I don't mean Tokyo 'cause Tokyo's a big town and a lot of people speak English there—but I'm talking about the little towns in Japan. The auditoriums are packed and three-fourths of the people don't speak any English. And yet they're there, and you know they love you 'cause they can't say anything to you except they want your 'autogram' or something, meaning an autograph, and just touch you, shake hands with you. I don't know of any word that can do justice to describing how that makes you feel, especially as long as I've been in this. So you know it's not an overnight thing that's going to fade. And the people are very, very genuine in their reactions. And that's beautiful. It's like my listening to Spanish singing; I don't understand the words but I can understand the feeling.

"My audiences are made up, I think, of my old fans and new listeners. Both of them. Little kids that I run into at airports, in hotels and places, they run and get their parents, their mothers, and say, 'That's Ray Charles.' And of course when kids can come to places where youngsters are allowed, they're there.

"I still record, too, different ways. I mean, I still record my bluesy thing or my rhythm-y thing or soul thing or whatever the right name is—I don't know; they got so many, I lose track. And I still will do a song like, say, 'Country Roads,' which the people really love, or 'You Are the Sunshine of My Life.' I still sing 'Georgia on My Mind,' and the people still love it. I don't do medleys of my hits, although I know I should do at least one.

"My feeling is that what we try to do is to take the songs that we know have proven themselves—not only at the time they were recorded but even over the years—songs that people still love to hear, and we try to get about 65 or 70 percent of the songs that we know people have spent their money to come to hear. The programs may change. For instance, I might do 'Born to Lose' one night; at another show instead of doing 'Born to Lose' I may do 'You Don't Know Me' or 'Take These Chains,' which were very big songs, too. One may change the position of songs and also, me, I'm very spontaneous. I don't sing written notes. I sing whatever I feel on that night.

So 'Georgia' is never the same, not because I'm trying to make it different but just because that's how I sing.

"We have quite a big band book, that's true. And, of course, you're always changing things. There are new things we're recording all the time and we add them. And arrangers bring me things, instrumental things for my band to play. See, I'm a great lover of big bands. I love to hear a band really shout. I have great admiration for bands like Duke's and Basie's and Woody Herman's. Woody Herman, he's one of my true favorites. He always comes up with some hell of a sounding cats.

"As for listening, I listen to jazz a lot today. I guess I'm probably like everyone else—I mean, you listen to the people you really like. I don't really know who all is out there today, and that's why I mentioned Woody Herman's band. I listen to the radio; you always listen to what's going on around you—if you love music. So I listen to the jazz stations, the so-called pop stations, to the soul stations. I always listen 'cause, first of all, I want to know what's happening in my world. That's for openers. But secondly, like anybody else, it depends on my mood and what kind of music I think I would like to hear, providing I'm not going to play records, my own tapes or whatever.

"My own favorites, I'd start off with Charlie Parker or Art Tatum, guys like Clark Terry, Dizzy Gillespie, Lockjaw Davis and Johnny Griffin. Stan Getz can play his ass off, too, I'll tell you. A lot of people don't realize that, but he plays! Of course that's just a few. There's a guy I love to hear play—he hasn't been around all that long—Niels (Henning Orsted) Pedersen. I think he's from Denmark. He reminds me of Ray Brown, only I think he has really gotten more deeply into it. Just like if you think of a guy like Jimmy Blanton, and then along came Ray Brown; it's the same type of thing with Pedersen. He's taken it along from Ray Brown.

"I still listen to Artie Shaw; I'm a great lover of his. I got to tell you that even during the era when everybody was saying the King of Swing was Benny Goodman—you know, that's the way he was considered—then and even now I still feel that Artie Shaw played as much as him but with more feeling. That's my honest opinion. To me there was a guy that really and truly was a bitch of a musician. He had a great band.

"As far as popular music goes, I like Aretha. I like Stevie. I feel he's going to develop, in my mind, into one of the Duke

Ellingtons of this century. I mean, he's young now, but then Duke was young, too, when he got started. But you can see it there, it's there now and as he gets older and, of course, if he's dedicated—see, that's one thing about what Duke was, God rest his soul—you got to be dedicated with this stuff. And if he's really dedicated to it, he's going to be tremendous, because he's got youth on his side.

"Why I say Stevie is more like Duke, or would be the coming Duke Ellington of our time, is because he is a composer, and that's what I mean. And Stevie, even in addition to that, where he has some pluses, too, is that he does a couple of other things exceptionally well. Forget for a moment the records—I ain't talking about his records. He really and truly is a bitch of a harmonica player. I have to say that. I think he is next to Toots Thielemans. Now that's kind of heavy, ain't it? But I believe it. I think he understands the harmonica quite well. And he plays piano, synthesizer and so on, and I think somebody told me he plays drums as well. So he can obviously be a great entertainer onstage, to start off with, not to mention his singing, performing and producing on records.

"I think what sets him apart, however, is his writing. He's a good writer now, which means that he cannot do anything but improve if he's dedicated and works at it. Look how his writing has improved over the years. I think that if he doesn't have anybody to hassle his mind, that kind of improvement will continue; the main thing is if people will leave him alone and let him do that. Because that's important, too, to many artists. Some artists don't have as much strength as others when it comes to how much hassling they can take, and I don't know for sure whether Stevie is strong that way or whether he's one of these kinds of people who one day may just say, 'Oh, fuck it, why should I have to go through such... ?'

"I also like Chaka Khan; I think she's a nice singer. I have a fellow here called Darrell Fletcher who records for my company [Crossover Records]. He's a young boy and he's really going to be very good. There are many others. Billy Preston's out there. I think Earth, Wind and Fire is a very decent group. See, these are all singers that are in what I would call the soul field.

"Well, that's what I do when I'm home. I listen to people like that. I don't listen to much rock music because I don't know too much about it. But for me, what I do is just do me, whatever comes out, that's it. But there isn't any point in my getting into nothing like, say, the Rolling Stones' music. It's not that I can't get into it; that has nothing to do with it. I know exactly what's happening and going on there, obviously, because I think I'm a halfway decent musician, and so I know what's being done there. But my point is that it's not my kind of thing and, for me, I prefer to stay more in my little feelings. I don't care whether I'm singing a country and western song or whatever, I prefer to stay in my feelings. Now, I use certain things that are used today in contemporary music, like I'll use a synthesizer, an ARP, or a wah-wah or a phase shifter. You got to keep up with things, after all, but I'm still me.

"As for selecting material to record, I select it the way I've always done. If I hear something I like, I do it. I have a little file of things I've heard and liked, and sometimes I come down here [to the office] at one o'clock, two o'clock in the morning when it's quiet and I play a lot of demos and tapes that people send me—not only from publishing companies but from ordinary people who think they got a song. I have been known to do songs that people send me that way. It's a matter of what I like. I don't have no producer. I do what I want to do, so if I feel the song, if it turns out I like the song, really like it, I'll record it. That's all there is to it.

"I think there are certain things that happen when you have groups that are really good recording groups. That's a field of its own, in a certain sense. See, some people you say, well, they're good performers but they don't record good, and some people are good at recording but don't perform well, and so forth. But I think the name of the game is within the artists themselves. How limited are the people who are doing what they're doing? That's what it boils down to being. I think the better you improve your musicianship, the easier you're going to find it is to communicate. Just like you perfect anything. I used to hear people say, 'Oh, Willie Mays made a spectacular catch. It looked so easy, like he wasn't doing anything!' That's the way it's supposed to be, supposed to look. So, I think that's the key to singing or playing an instrument or whatever it is you want to do—you got to really work at it. And of course you've got to have some natural talent, too.

"I feel that the kids of today, and this is not a put-down, I just think it's an hon-est statement, I think the sad thing is that far too many youngsters don't take the time to really learn their instruments like musicians used to. So, as a result, there's not that much creativity in music nowadays. I'm not talking about a guy who goes and makes a record and has a hit; I mean, that has nothing to do with how well you play. See, I think that what's helpful, and what cats had to do in earlier years is that they did have to try to expand their musical ability. Just because it was a matter of survival, so that was the motive for their doing that. Probably now, with the affluent situation being what it is—I mean, there ain't nobody really that hungry, when you get right down it—it means there is no motivation unless a kid just happens to care and really wants to see what he can really do with his instrument. Instead of saying, 'Hey, man, I can play two chords like Bob Dylan,' or, 'I can play a lick like B.B. King'—and that's it.

"Musicianship is de-emphasized. I think what a guy should want to do is to really go and learn his instrument and find out what the hell is going on with it. Actually learn it inside out, 'cause I'll tell you something: You can take some of the older guys and set them in a one-on-one situation with a young musician—you know, like you play basketball one-on-one—and the kid, you know, he gets smothered. This goes for young listeners, too, because, for whatever reasons, I think they are not exposed to enough of what instruments can do, and what musicians ought to be able to do with these particular instruments. This is not saying that if you know a certain trend is in for making a record you can't do that. You can do that and a lot more besides. Studying the instrument thoroughly is not going to hamper you as far as that goes. You will be able to do it all. After all, there are many, many guys who, whatever situation you put them in, they can take care of business.

"That's what I see as the pity of it now. I'm not saying this is true of all rock musicians, but I am saying that it is for far too many. Because, you see, you got certain guys who came along and did a lot of creating, particularly in jazz. You take a guy like Louis Armstrong; well, he's gone now. Duke Ellington is gone. Charlie Parker is gone. Art Tatum is gone. Charlie Christian is gone. Coleman Hawkins is gone. So, basically what you have left is, say, you got Dizzy Gillespie left, you got Oscar Peterson, you got Milt Jackson. But most of these guys are getting up in age. There ain't nobody coming along; well, I shouldn't say there ain't nobody. But if there is, it's like one or two people maybe coming along. But for the most part, with the youngsters and the availability that kids have now for so many things and opportunities that a lot of us didn't have when we were coming along, it's sad that there aren't more people to come along and pick up that slack.

"As to playing rock and contemporary music, if you're a good jazz musician you can go right ahead and go on and do that. Say, look, if that's what they call for, I can do it, man. You just put your mind to it and really go out and go ahead and do it. 'Cause, you see, you got to feel it and you got to know how to do it. You can't go the other way. That's what I am talking about. See, I could take Milt Jackson under any conditions and say, 'Look, man, this is the kind of shit we're going to play, some low-down filthy blues, or we gonna play what they call rock.' Here he is, he's got it. It ain't necessarily his thing; that ain't what he likes to do to make himself happy and comfortable, 'cause he likes jazz and that's the world he wants to be in. But he can sit right there and play the shit out of it. No problem. I'm telling you, I've seen him do it. Play the hell out of some blues.

"And that's the thing I'm talking about. Out of that you take what you particularly like to do and you do that. Because that's what makes you happy, and you're cool and you're saying to yourself, 'Well, hell, I could make more money doing such and such kind of music, but I like this. It makes me happy and I'm comfortable and I dig it, so I'm going to do that and make less money.' But your choices have not been limited by your lack of knowledge because you know more, you can choose more wisely. That's what I mean."

There can be no doubting the sincerity of the singer's concern over what he feels are serious deficiencies in the musicianship of many young performers today. Given the painful difficulty with which he acquired his own musical education, Charles appreciates, as do the performers, the value of a solid grounding in the fundamental principles of music and a thorough mastery of the full potentialities of whatever instrument is studied. He is genuinely saddened, and perhaps even nonplussed, at the present devaluation of what are, to his mind, proven, time-honored principles. He views them as critically valuable, necessary aids to genuine and, what's more important, sustained creativity, qualities he finds were fully absent in much of contemporary music, a lack that stems in large part from the incomplete knowledge that far too many young performers bring to their musical productions.

This, it seems to me, is not so much the "sour grapes" thinking of one on the down slope of the so-called generation gap—and Charles is, after all, 46 years old—or an inability on his part to come to grips with a new musical conception that is in many ways radically different from his own or that of his generation, as it is a matter of his recognizing real and serious shortcomings in a great deal of contemporary music, particularly rock and related forms. If he pays little attention to them, as appears to be the case, it is undoubtedly the result of their simplism, the narrow compass of their forms and devices and concerns, and the limited range of their potentialities for creative expression and continued growth. Rock is not expansive enough for Charles, one feels, and this is the major reason he largely is indifferent to it. The level of its musical thought is too low, and this the singer feels is the direct result of the general lack of real musicianship among younger musicians. Coupled with and compounding this problem is the related factor of present-day radio programming practices, a subject Charles views with some concern.

"I think radio as it is today," he observes, "is too sterile in the sense that there ain't nearly enough variety available to the listener. That is, on our radio, here in America. When I travel around the world, visit different places, Asia, Europe, South America, wherever I go, everywhere except in America the people have a chance to hear some other kinds of music, even if they listen to just one station all the time. If you like to listen to that station, what they do for you, they're going to play you some of the things you like but they're also going to play some other kinds of music, too. So, at least you know what else is happening besides the same shit you hear hour after hour.

"You turn on a station here, though, and what you're going to hear all day is basically the playlist. That's it. Somehow that's sick; I think it's crazy. You see, what's bad about it is the effect it has on people. It makes the people, the listeners, limited, too. I think radio could do a hell of a thing by expanding its programming. Because, you see, if you turn on your favorite station and you like basically what they play, that gives them the opportunity to let you know, say, what the number-one song is in France. That's what they do in Europe, for example. I don't mean that they give you a steady diet of it, but at least you get to know what the top songs are in France, in England or in Italy. And that's good. Or they will also let you hear, say, one short minute or something like that. And that's good for people. Because you can't blame the people for not knowing or liking a certain thing if they don't get to hear it. See, I can't tell you that I don't like olives if I'm not exposed to them. It's the same thing with music: I got to have it, got to hear it a couple of times.

"What I mean by that—take, for example, a certain type of music you're familiar with, the first time you heard it you didn't necessarily like it. Right? Haven't you heard songs and said to yourself, 'Well, I didn't like that thing when it first came out but the more I hear it, it kind of grows on you, doesn't it?' That's what I'm talking about. You got to give people the chance to find out if they like something, and what you do is integrate it with other things you know they like. I don't think you need to stuff things down people's throats. That's not it. I think the trouble with a lot of programming today is that what they try to do is go all out in just one direction—in other words, they're going to give you all of it at one time, or nothing.

"I think what you have to do is to kind of wean people into something, just like you wean a baby off a bottle. And radio can do that, just like television can do that.

"In fairness I should say that I think that, if anything, there probably is a little more variety in the music on radio now than there was in the 1940s. Certainly at least in the sense that for the most part soul music, as we call it nowadays, was very minute on radio in those days. I mean, you might have one specialized station that might have done it, but for the most part you wouldn't hear any 'race music' on the radio as such. Chances are you wouldn't catch a WNEW playing anything like that then. Now in the '40s, I was only 10, 12, 14 years old, and I was raised in an area of the South. But I don't believe, at least not from the stories I've heard from people in other parts of the country who were listening to radio in those days, that it was that much different in other places. As regards 'race music,' that is.

"See, that's what it was called then— 'race music.' We would say 'soul music' now, which is in essence the same kind of music it always was. I mean, people who were singing the blues and everything else they sung, they sung with some feeling, either if they liked it from a bluesy or a spiritual feeling. I was raised up with that. I've watched that kind of music come up with at least four or five different names, starting out with 'race music.' It's still the same thing. I can get you some old records and, of course, you won't have the Fender bass and you won't have the electric guitar, but the shit, it's the same. You understand what I'm saying? I mean, it's what it is, and that's it!"

After having recorded for a number of large record firms in the past, notably Atlantic Records and ABC Records, Charles currently releases his recordings on his own label, Crossover Records, an outgrowth of his earlier ABC-distributed Tangerine Records operation.

"When I got with ABC," he recalled, "I had a dual purpose with them. I was an artist and a producer. See, I didn't produce anybody else; I only produced myself, but I was the producer because my contract called for that. In other words, in this contract I was paid so much on a record as a producer besides being a performer. And I mean it was very substantial, I must say. It was a hell of a contract, perhaps the first of its kind, to be honest.

"But then around '61 I wanted this record company and ABC allowed me to have my own record label. Which means, at the time, in '61, I couldn't record for it, but I could have other people record for it and ABC would distribute it. We had Percy Mayfield, Louis Jordan, Terrell Prude, John Anderson's big band and mine, too. We also had a group called the Vocals, which eventually became the Fifth Dimension. Those were the main artists. It wasn't a big company. Even my company now [Crossover Records] is not a big company. Except the difference now is that I record for it. Well, I started Tangerine in '61, as I say, and that went on until '65, so this was about five years of that. And, then, I started recording for myself in 1965, and ABC continued to distribute it for me up until about 1973. That's when Crossover was started.

"We release, I would say, about four singles and two or three albums in the course of a year, something like that. The roster consists of myself, the Raelets, Joel Webster, Darrell Fletcher and the Sims Twins. And that's about it, five artists. As a producer, I'm involved with some of these, with myself, naturally, and the Raelets. And whenever I'm asked, because many times the kids will come to me and ask if I'll help them out. Like, many times Darrell seems to get inspiration, he says, from me and he'll ask me to do something or to help him with something. But mainly I'm involved only with my recordings and the Raelets', and that's it.

"For the last 12 or 14 years I've been working pretty much the same way. I take the first three months of the year off from performing and touring. This serves a dual purpose. It gives me a chance to be at home for a while, that's for one. It also gives me a chance to devote a continuous amount of time to recording, like every day, so whatever your ideas are you don't have to put them off. It gives me a chance to do a little television, some interviews, and do a little producing, things like that.

"Besides, to my mind, this time of year is kind of rough. I have worked in this time of the year and I've found that, for the most part, it's a little rough in the sense that it's wintertime and the first three months till about the end of March the weather's bad. And people have just had Thanksgiving and Christmas and New Year's. Which means that by the time they've gone through all that buying and giving and such, everybody's for the most part a little broke. So I don't want to hurt the concert promoters. I like for the cat to be able to make some money. So I figure I'll cool it for three months and kind of let the pocketbooks fill up a little.

"As to my goals, I've pretty much done everything I've wanted to do. I would like to be more involved, or spend more time working with young talent—you know, with young performers where the talent is there, maybe it's just kind of raw but it's there—and producing, helping them to come along. I'd like to spend more time actually doing that.

"I got to say this again, and I really mean this from the bottom of my heart, I'm very thankful to the public for all this. Because they've seen to it—without them, obviously, I feel that I couldn't have done these things. They're responsible for it. I think one of the most marvelous things to have happen to you is to have people in small towns, most of them don't speak no English, come and hear you. I had an incident happen to me one time when I was in Jamaica. It was raining cats and dogs, and we were playing in an outdoor place, and the people were there and sat in that rain

through the whole concert. The band had a little shed, so it wasn't raining on us, but in getting to the bandstand, two of the people literally had to carry me on their shoulders—that's how much mud they had in this place. I will never forget that as long as I live. Because, anybody who will do that... I don't know if I would sit through the rain and walk in the mud if Christ came. I mean, He'd have to do a little talking to get me to do that!

"My music is all me. I give the world my soul, my insides. That's the way I characterize my music, 'cause whatever I'm playing, whatever branch of music it is—if it's country and western or if it's a blues or if it's a love song or if it's a fun song like 'Smile with Me' or if it's jazz—whatever it is, I give the public all. They get all of it. They get all of me. So that would be the only way I know, sincerely, to characterize my music."

May 18, 1978

Frank Zappa: Garni du Jour, Lizard King Poetry and Slime

by Tim Schneckloth

In the last 15 years, the boundaries between various musical genres have all but dissolved. And somewhere along the line, people began realizing that serious music doesn't have to be dealt with as a sacred entity—it can be approached with a sense of fun and irreverence; it can be juxtaposed with other, less valid kinds of music to create startlingly original statements.

Frank Zappa seems to have had this kind of vision all along. From the early days of the Mothers of Invention in the mid-'60s, Zappa's composing, arranging and performing have embraced any number of styles. And the question of the legiti-

macy or illegitimacy of the sources doesn't seem to apply in Zappa's case. Everything fits into his unique artistic perspective.

After a long spell between releases, Zappa recently presented his public with *Zappa in New York*. Recorded live late '76, the album features a number of instrumental works that show off the talents of Randy and Mike Brecker, Ronnie Cuber, Tom Malone, Lou Marini and David Samuels, as well as Zappa's '76 touring unit.

For his most recent road trips, Zappa's band has consisted of Zappa and Adrian Belew on guitars, percussionists Terry Bozzio and Ed Mann, bassist Patrick O'Hearn, and Peter Wolf and Tommy Mars on keyboards. As might be expected from the presence of two keyboardists in the band, synthesizers have a lot to do with defining Zappa's current sound. The following interview focuses on that instrument, as well as observations on the state of contemporary music.

Schneckloth: What are you up to now?
Zappa: I've been in the studio doing overdubs on some live material. I like that process because you can get rhythm tracks with live excitement. Then you can go in and add orchestration to them.

Schneckloth: It seems like you've done a lot of live albums over the years.

Zappa: Some of them have been totally live, some have had orchestration added on. Fillmore East was about 90 percent pure live; *Just Another Band from L.A.* was 100 percent. That was a four-track recording right off the P.A. *Roxy and Elsewhere* had some things that were live, some were overdubbed.

Schneckloth: In the last few years, it seems you've been going away from larger orchestrated things back to a fairly basic rock-band format. Is there a conscious reason for that?

Zappa: No, I do whatever I feel like doing. See, all you know about what I've done is what's been released on records. And all you know about that is what you've listened to. Right now, I think there are about 45 albums out that I've made over the last 14 years. Chances are you haven't heard all of that, and that's maybe 50 percent of what's actually available to be released. I've got orchestra stuff that's been recorded, more elaborate compositions that haven't been released yet. They're just sitting around waiting for a home.

Schneckloth: Do you anticipate releasing it all someday?

Frank Zappa and the
Mothers of Invention.
(Bizarre Records)

Zappa: Oh yeah, I hope so. It's very difficult to do because record companies, in order to protect their investment, try to avoid putting out more than two albums per year on an artist because they want to milk the sales on each release as thoroughly as possible. I think that's a fantasy in my case because we sell so much in catalog. Whether the album becomes a hit when it's first released is irrelevant, because the stuff just keeps selling. People hear about it by word of mouth.

Schneckloth: That's true. Looking through record stores, I notice most of your stuff is still there, even going back to the Verve things. That's unusual.

Zappa: Maybe it's because some of the things that were said on those early albums are things that still remain true today, and there are young people who want to hear that stuff being said. I don't need to repeat myself. If I've already done it once on an album, I don't need to go back and do it again.

Schneckloth: There's a lot of talk about the mellowed-out '70s—how the world's falling asleep. Do you miss anything about the '60s? Was there an urgency to making music then that doesn't exist now?

Zappa: I don't miss the '60s at all. I don't miss anything.

Schneckloth: Things haven't changed that much?

Zappa: Well, they do change, but I feel those changes are external to the way I do things.

Schneckloth: What about your audiences?

Zappa: Oh, they change. They change every season.

Schneckloth: What about your audiences now? Are they more jaded? Do they demand more in the way of entertainment?

Zappa: They're more enthusiastic. They're more alert because there's less acid being used—which is not to say they don't use other things. But the type of drug that is popular with the audience has some bearing on the way in which they perceive things. There was so much acid during the '60s that it was very easy for large numbers of people to think they had seen God as soon as the Beatles went boom, boom, boom, you know? So that particular chemical made a lot of really peculiar things possible in terms of musical sales. And since the status of that drug has been wearing off, and other things are taking its place—notably wine and beer—you have a different kind of audience mentality.

Schneckloth: I would think you've kept a lot of your original audience—people who are around 30 now.

Zappa: Some of them still come to the concerts. But usually they don't, because now that they have wives, kids, mortgages, day jobs and all the rest of that stuff, they don't want to stand around in a hockey rink and be puked on by some 16-year-old who's full of reds. So consequently, our audience gets younger and younger. We've picked up a larger number of female audience participants, and there's been an increase in black attendance.

Schneckloth: How do European audiences react to your music?

Zappa: The audience in London is very similar to the audience in L.A.—which is to say, singularly boring and jaded. The audiences in some of the smaller places in Germany are more like East Coast or Midwest audiences—they have a good sense of humor, they like to make a lot of noise, but they're not obnoxious. And then you have your pseudo-intellectual audiences like in Denmark. Paris is a pretty good audience; I'd have to give Paris like a San Francisco rating.

Schneckloth: Maybe one of these days the State Department will ask you to go to the Soviet Union or something.

Zappa: I don't think the State Department is ever going to seek my services. And if I go to the Soviet Union, it won't be for a long time, I'll tell you. I'm not a communist enthusiast.

Schneckloth: As a rock musician, it seems you're carrying on a tradition that you don't hear that much of any more—the long, blues-based guitar solo. Nowadays you don't hear much that's over three minutes.

Zappa: Well, a reason for that is because you only have a certain number of minutes to deal with on an album side, and it's a big risk to fill up album grooves with a lengthy solo because they don't all sustain interest.

Schneckloth: It may be getting progressively harder to sustain interest with long things. Maybe it's all caught up in the disco thing—people have to hear things that are concise.

Zappa: I don't care about that stuff. I figure that a person that's buying my record is interested in what I'm doing, OK? And I do him a favor by doing what I feel like doing, because then he hears who I am at that moment in time. If they don't like it, fine. If they don't, they can go out and buy another record, I don't care. I don't claim to be a universal entertainer, a man for all seasons... I don't want to run the entire show.

Schneckloth: What are the ramifications of disco-mania?

Zappa: Disco music makes it possible to have disco entertainment centers. Disco entertainment centers make it possible for mellow, laid-back, boring kinds of people to meet each other and reproduce.

Schneckloth: Driving around Los Angeles listening to the AM radio, everything somehow seems more appropriate; it seems to fit better than in other places—disco, Tom Scott, sax solos, country-rock...

Zappa: Tragic, isn't it? I'm not too much for that laid-back syndrome. That's the kind of music that, if you had to have something piddling away in the background while you did you job, country-rock would be better than clarinet and an accordion and a trombone playing "Anniversary Waltz." It's superior to that kind of music for that function. But as a musical statement, it doesn't get me too much.

Schneckloth: You're well known as a satirist of many facets of pop music—things like long, overwritten rock poetry. You used to call it Lizard King poetry. Does that kind of comedy writing come easy for you?

Zappa: Oh yeah, you can crank it out by the yards, man. There's so much negative stimuli to make it happen.

Schneckloth: Do you think you'd make a good gag writer for somebody like Johnny Carson?

Zappa: Gee, do you think he'd stay on TV if I was writing gags for him? Only let's face it, there are a lot of things to laugh at. I mean, Lizard King poetry is only scratching the surface. And there are plenty of proponents of pseudo-Lizard King poetry today. I've always felt that poets who decided to pick up a musical instrument and get into the world of rock were really not good. There's hardly anybody around that qualifies for the title poet anyway. And when they take it to the extreme of playing an instrument badly and having simplified monotone background so they can recite their dreck over it—I think it's too fake for my taste.

But if hearing that kind of music or Lizard King poetry reaffirms your belief in life itself, well, then you're entitled to hear it. I'm glad that it's available for all the people in the world who need it.

Schneckloth: Speaking of humor, I saw you on *Saturday Night Live* a while back. How did you get Don Pardo to debase himself like that? (NBC announcer Pardo had assumed the title role in a spirited rendition of Zappa's "I'm the Slime.")

Zappa: Debase himself? That's not right. That's really not right. First of all, he has a good sense of humor. Second, he really enjoyed doing that. And thirdly, he actually came to the concerts we played in New York after the show and performed with us live on stage. See, Pardo's never been on screen on that show. He's never been seen. The man has been working there for 30 years and nobody knows what he looks like. So I thought, fantastic, let's bring Don Pardo live out onstage and let the world see him. We got him a white tuxedo; he did some narration for some of the songs we were doing; we brought him out to sing "I'm the Slime." And the audience loved him… the highlight of his career. He's a nice guy; I really like him. And I don't think it was debasing at all. It was giving him an opportunity to expand in other realms.

Schneckloth: I was using the term…

Zappa: Facetiously? Facetiousness hardly ever translates onto print.

Schneckloth: How do your bands come together? Is there an element of accident?

Zappa: Well, I found a lot of people just by going into bars and seeing bar bands. I'll find one guy out of a band that sounds good to me, get his name and address, and when I have an opening for that instrument, I'll get in touch with him, bring him to California and have him audition. Sometimes they make it, sometimes they don't.

Schneckloth: What kinds of things do you look for?

Zappa: A combination of skill and attitude.

Schneckloth: Does a person have to know how to read to be in your band?

Zappa: It always helps. The main thing a person has to have is very fast pattern recognition and information storage capability. That's because we play like a two, two-and-a-half-hour show nonstop with everything organized. There are solos, and those are improvised. But the sequence of events is planned out so that the show is tight and the audience doesn't have to sit around and wait for something to happen. So it requires a lot of memorization—fast memorization. You can't spend a year teaching somebody a show. With the band that I've had on the road for the past two tours, we spent three months, five days a week, six hours a day memorizing it and getting it just right. Now that's a very

expensive investment, because it's $13,250 a week for rehearsals—we rehearse with full equipment, full crew and a soundstage. So I prefer people who learn fast.

Schneckloth: There was a time when you had to adjust your writing to the capabilities of your players.

Zappa: I still do.

Schneckloth: You mean, there are times when you'd like to write some things that are so complex that you can't get anybody to play them on tour?

Zappa: Every day. I'll tell you, the kind of musicians I need for the bands that I have doesn't exist. I need somebody who understands polyrhythms, has good enough execution on the instrument to play all kinds of styles, understands staging, understands rhythm and blues, and understands how a lot of different composition techniques function. When I give him a part, he should know how it works in the mix with all the other parts. You'd be surprised how many people who have chops in one department are completely deficient in others.

Schneckloth: Maybe one of the difficulties with performing your music is the surprise factor—different sound, different instrumentations, different rhythms come at the listener in abrupt shifts.

Zappa: See, that's only unusual if you're accustomed to music that's boring and bland and all the same color. That's not the way music should be, I feel. What to you is an abrupt shift is functional orchestration to me. If you change the color of the instrumentation that's playing a certain part of a line, it changes the emotional value of the line; it changes its relative importance.

Schneckloth: Leading into the subject of synthesizers, does it get harder to find sounds that will surprise, sounds that aren't bland?

Zappa: Absolutely not. That surface hasn't even been scratched yet. Without even touching a synthesizer, there are so many things you can make with normal instruments, and in a diatonic context. There are so many people who are dashing away from diatonic music in order to give the appearance of being modern—which I think is a waste of time.

Schneckloth: Do you write specifically with synthesizers in mind?

Zappa: I have. I've developed different types of notation that accommodate the different things that synthesizers can do—like parallel chord tracking and things like that. There are ways of indicating what kind of parallel chord the thing is going to

track. Then you can just add a little inscription at the head of the bar, kind of like a key signature. Next, you write a single line, and, if the guy sets his synthesizer up right, that single line will yield parallel chords tracking around. So it saves you a lot of writing on paper.

Schneckloth: How do you arrive at the synthesizer sounds you want?

Zappa: Well, obviously the best way to deal with music is according to your own ear and your own personal taste. And since most synthesizers that people work with are production models off the assembly line, and there are slight differences in the way the settings of the knobs respond, if you're a composer and you're writing out a complete description of what all the knobs are supposed to be set at, chances are that you won't get the exact same result each time from instrument to instrument. It's just because of different things about the parts.

So the first thing you have to know is how to talk to the synthesizer player. If you're a composer or arranger and you want to use the synthesizer, you have to know all the basic language of what the instrument is dealing with. You have to know what an oscillator is; you have to know what a filter is; you have to know what an envelope is; and all the rest of that stuff. So when you tell the guy, "No, that's wrong, I want more of this," you're not telling him in romantic terms, you're saying, "Give me more frequency modulation" or "Open your filter up to make it brighter." Just so you can communicate with the people who play the instruments.

The way I learned was by buying an ARP 2600, getting the manual, and just sitting around and piddling with it. Then I got a mini-Moog and a lot of other kinds of synthesizers and got my own hands on them, even though I'm not a keyboard player. I was just familiarizing myself with them.

Schneckloth: I understand the percussionists in your band are using drum synthesizers?

Zappa: That's very true. Not only do we use them as drums, we use them as synthesizers. We started doing something on the last tour that I think Pollard [manufacturer of the Syndrum] is going to be pretty thrilled about when he hears it. Terry Bozzio got to be very good with the Syndrum—he can control them fantastically well and still be playing his set. He can reach over and change the setting and still keep time.

For some of the things we were doing,

if you put the sustain on the Syndrum up to a very long time, you can hit it and get like a constant pitch coming out. And if you move the little knob, you can play tunes on it. So I had chorales between the two keyboard players and the two Syndrums and the bass. All I did was conduct a downbeat, and anybody could hit any note they wanted on that downbeat. And every time I'd conduct a beat, they'd pick another note. The results were fantastic.

Schneckloth: How about the guitar synthesizers? Have you tried those?

Zappa: Yeah. The problem with guitar synthesizers, versus me, is the way I play. There's so much left hand business going on, and the synthesizer is more interested in what's happening with the pick. In order for the synthesizer to track what you're playing, it prefers to see one string, with nothing else being held or rattling, neatly picked so that the note just comes right out. Then the synthesizer can make up its mind and play the note for you. But the faster you play, and the more pull-off, hammer-on stuff you do with the left hand, the harder it is for the synthesizer to track you.... It requires a more legitimate guitar technique.

I'm not adverse to guitar synthesizers. I think the idea is good, but, to me, it's not going to be a practical musical thing to deal with until the synthesizer will play exactly what you're playing and not just give you a hint of it—so that the synthesizer won't get in the way of your style. Right now, it's kind of like the tail wagging the dog, because you have to slow yourself down and play in a different way in order to make the thing talk.

Schneckloth: Have you ever used a really large synthesizer setup in the studio?

Zappa: I've got one, but I've never used it in the studio. It's an Eu, and it's about a $50,000 system. It's got a computer and all that stuff. I don't have it set up; it's in storage. Stevie Wonder called the office the other day wanting to rent it.

Schneckloth: How much work is involved in setting it up?

Zappa: It requires a technician. It's fairly easy to set it up and put it all together. It's portable; it was designed to be taken on the road. But there's so many modules and stuff built into it that I prefer to have someone who is conversant with the electronic ins and outs of it set it up for me and tell the keyboard player what to do with it. I have enough to worry about with the console without having to worry about the synthesizer. It's got 14 oscillators or something like that.

Schneckloth: What other kinds of keyboard synthesizers do you tour with?

Zappa: For the last U.S. tour we had a very elaborate setup. We had two players and each had about eight instruments. Peter Wolf was playing a Rhodes, and Electrocomp, a mini-Moog, the Eu, a Clavinet, an ARP 2600, and a Yamaha Electric Grand. Tommy Mars had a Hammond, a Yamaha Electric Grand, an Electrocomp, an ARP String Synthesizer, a Clavinet and a Roland.

Schneckloth: When you get all that stuff together, it seems like the arranging problems would be really complex.

Zappa: It doesn't make the problems complex, no. It gives you more latitude. But it makes the performance a little bit more difficult. The more things there are to stick your hands on, the more wires there are to get out of whack when you set it up every day.

Schneckloth: There are those who take a somewhat snobbish view of synthesizer playing. They feel that a person really has to know exactly what's happening electronically with the instrument in order to be a truly good synthesizer player.

Zappa: A guy's got to start somewhere. You've got to mess around with it. Even if you think you know how they work, there's always a chance that you'll come up with something new just by doing a dumb experiment. Remember: dumbness is the American way. Dumbness has created more progress for this country—just from people saying, "Well, I really don't know what's going on here, but let's try this." And then they come up with something great. The best example of that is Thomas Edison. You know about the filament in the electric light bulb, don't you? He'd tried everything until he finally said, "I'd be willing to try a piece of dental floss with some cheese on it if I thought it would work."

Schneckloth: What about those who feel that synthesizer, and electric instruments in general, somehow detract from the humanity of the music being played?

Zappa: Let me tell you something about that kind of thinking. People who worry about that are worried about their own image as a person performing on the instrument. In other words, the instrument is merely a subterfuge in order for the musician to communicate his own personal, succulent grandeur to the audience—which to me is a disservice to the music as an art form. It's the ego of the performer transcending the instrument.

Now when you start talking about humanity—who cares about that? If you're going to play music, I think the music is important. And I think the guys that say this makes it less human aren't really talking about the feel of the music, they're talking about something that's going to get in the way of the audience understanding how swell they are. You've seen soloists get up there—they're not playing music, they're playing their egos out. And there are whole bands of people who get together to do nothing but explain to the audience through their instruments how fabulous they are. Well, who gives a shit?

I don't want to go and see somebody's deep inner hurt in a live performance. I don't want to hear their personal turmoil on a record, either. I like music.

Schneckloth: Can't it be a moving thing to hear somebody express his soul through, say, a very sad-sounding trumpet solo?

Zappa: I don't care about souls; that's the Maharishi's department. See, I take a real cold view about that stuff. I think that music works because of psycho-acoustical things—like the way in which a line will interact with the harmonic climate that's backing it up. And all the rest of it is subjective on behalf of the listener. Maybe you wanted to hear a sad trumpet solo, but it wouldn't be sad unless the notes he was playing were interacting in a certain way against the background. The best test is: if it was a 24-track recording, take the same trumpet solo, change the chord progression behind it, and see if it sounds sad anymore. People see and hear what they want to see and hear. If you're in the mood, or have a deep, personal need for sad music or soul-searching or sensitivity in that stuff, you'll find it wherever it is. You'll go into an art gallery and be totally amazed by the things you see, whereas I might go into the gallery and go, "Hah?"

This is a gross example, but say a person buys a Kiss album and listens to it and has a moving experience from it. I mean, are they wrong?

Schneckloth: Well, people go crazy at their concerts, and that may be understandable.

Zappa: I'm not talking about their concerts. Take the fire bombs away, take the blood capsules and the rest of that stuff away. Just listen to the record. There are people who listen to the records and get off on them.

Schneckloth: Speaking of that band, you once said, "Americans hate music, but they love entertainment."

Zappa: You want me to explain that to you?

Schneckloth: Yeah, if you would.

Zappa: Sure. The reason they hate music is that they've never stopped to listen to what the musical content is because they're so befuddled by the packaging and merchandising that surround the musical material they've been induced to buy. There's so much peripheral stuff that helps them make their analysis of what the music is.

Here's the simplest example: Take any record, stick it in a white jacket and hand it to somebody and let him listen to it. The next day, hand him the same record with a real album cover—with a picture and some type on the back that gives him some key to what the music is. The results are completely different.

The way in which the material is presented is equally important as what's on the record. It's the garni du jour way of life.

You go buy a hamburger. If somebody gives you a hamburger on a dish, it means one thing. If somebody gives you a hamburger on a dish with a piece of green stuff and a wrinkled carrot and a radish—even though you don't eat that stuff—it's a Deluxe Hamburger. It's the same piece of dog meat on the inside, but one's got the garni du jour. Americans have become accustomed to having a garni du jour on everything.

Maybe the world is moving too fast for this now, but in the old days, you used to be able to go to a record store and listen to the record before you bought it. You can't do that now, and that's been one of the major factors in the type of merchandising we have in music today.

Schneckloth: Over the years you've managed to turn the system to your advantage. To what do you attribute you longevity in the music business?

Zappa: What do you attribute Stravinsky's longevity in the music business to? He didn't want to stop composing. I'm just using that as an example; I'm not comparing myself to Stravinsky in any other way. I'm just saying that if a person wants to write music, he's going to do it whether he's getting performances or not, and that's the attitude I take. I started off putting a band together because I wrote music and I wanted to hear it and nobody else would play it.

Schneckloth: On the subject of performing, you've always been underrated as a rock guitar player. I guess you'd call it a blues-based style, but it's very original and distinctive.

Zappa: The basis of that kind of music is derived just as much from Eastern music as it is from the blues.

Schneckloth: Where does it come from?

Zappa: I think it's just natural to me. Part of the Eastern influence is like Greek, Turkish, Bulgarian kinds of sounds as well as Indian sounds.

Schneckloth: Have the various composers who have influenced your writing had any effect on your guitar style?

Zappa: Well, I think that if there's anything from the composers I like that's incorporated in my guitar playing, it's Stravinsky's idea of economy of means, because I'll take just a few notes and change the rhythm. If you want to look at it in purely scientific terms, you have a chord that tells you where your harmonic climate is—where the event is taking place. The chord is like the establishing shot in a movie—where you see the exterior of the building, or the alley with the garbage cans. It tells you where it's happening. Then the action takes place.

So you have a chord, and you have three notes that provide certain types of emotional activity versus the chord. And that emotional activity is redefined every time you change the order of the notes and the space in between the notes. That's the kind of stuff I'm dealing with.

When you listen to the thing in continuity, it sounds like there's a line going on and there's something happening. But what's really happening in the solo is this: for each harmonic climate that's presented, there are experiments being conducted, in real time, with different notes and weights and measures of those different notes, versus the climate. And every time you change the position of the note, it has a different impact. That's especially true of bent notes.

Schneckloth: Do you still get an exhilaration from playing live? Does it make the whole thing worthwhile?

Zappa: It's the greatest thing there is. As a matter of fact, it is the only thing that makes it worthwhile. Some of the drudgery you have to go through on the road is so boring. And once you get a chance to do that… I wouldn't even care if there wasn't an audience there. It's just that you've got all the equipment set up, the musicians are

there and paid for, the lights are on, it's just the right temperature, the stage is the right color, it's the right mood. And then you play, and you can create things right there. And fortunately, there are cassettes of it so you have a chance to hear it back later and see if your experiments were successful or what. That's one of the prime reasons for me going out on the road and touring.

Schneckloth: Do you think of yourself primarily as a guitar player then?

Zappa: No, I think of myself as a composer who happens to have the guitar as his main instrument. Most composers used to play the piano. Well, I'm not a piano player, so, obviously, because of the technical limitations of the guitar versus the piano—in terms of multiple notes and so on—the stuff I write is determined by my interest in the guitar.

And consequently, it provides difficulties for other instruments. If I hear something in my head that's guitar-based—bends, and stuff like that—a lot of times, those things can't be executed on other instruments. So it provides a slight element of frustration when you hear your lines played on instruments other than what they were intended to be played on.

Schneckloth: As far as the technical limitations of the guitar are concerned, with the electric guitar today, it seems you can do almost anything—legato stuff and so on.

Zappa: With feedback and sustain you can do some really beautiful legato stuff that wasn't possible before heavy amplification. In the earliest days of electric guitar playing, first you had the advantage of being heard at the same volume as the saxophone player. Then came fuzz, which gave you a chance to add a different emotional slant to your notes. In other words, a C note played clean is different from a C note played with fuzztone. It means two different things. One of them is wearing little white gloves and the other one has brass knuckles on.

Schneckloth: When you visualize it, it's the difference between a thin straight line and a thick, jagged one.

Zappa: Yes, it occupies more space. And when you get right down to it, what is music, really? Did you ever stop to think about what's really going on?

Here's my theory. First of all, music functions in the time domain—there's decor and the time domain. That's the canvas you paint on when you're working with music.

Another distinction: written music is to real music what a recipe is to real food. You can't listen to music on a piece of paper and you can't eat a recipe, so I put them both into the same category.

And once the music comes off the paper and goes into the air, what you're literally doing is making a sculpture with the air, because your ear is detecting the perturbations in the air. It's decoding the way the air has been shaken by the different instruments.

So the duration of your piece occupies a space of time—that's your canvas. And the medium you're working in is the air. So no matter what you play, you have to be consciously aware that it is not just a note. It is an impulse which is going to alter the shape of the air space, which in turn is going to be detected by the human ear.

Now, you compound the misery when you start dealing with recorded material, because usually the material, if you're doing it in a studio, is being recorded in a very unimpressive air space. It's blank, dead, uninteresting. All the reverberation is being added electronically. Furthermore, the person who finally listens to the piece is going to be listening to it on equipment that is not quite as spectacular as the stuff in the studio. So you have to rely on the efficiency of the home speaker to create your air sculpture live in person for the listener.

Schneckloth: That must get frustrating.

Zappa: Well, you know that the guy sitting in his house is never going to hear the sculpture the way it was designed, because most home units can't reproduce the top and bottom end the way they're supposed to be. All you're giving them is the mid-range. And there are also problems with disc recording. Discs can't reproduce everything you can get on a tape. And neither disc nor tape can give the listener the dynamic range you get in a live performance. I mean, you can turn the record up so it's loud, turn the bass up so it's beating on your chest, but it's not the same thing as sitting in a hockey rink and listening to an immense mass of air being shaped and moved around by heavy amplification. So what if there's a lot of echo? I like to play in hockey rinks.

Schneckloth: Don't they present a lot of problems?

Zappa: The problem about playing hockey rinks is that sometimes it's hard to hear the words. If you're word-oriented, OK, that's tough. But that air space you have in there is such a great thing to work with—it's this huge tonnage of air. And when you go "wham" and hit a big chord, you've taken all that and spewed it over 15,000 people.

Schneckloth: That must be quite a feeling of power.

Zappa: It's not just a feeling of power. If you want to play really soft, think how soft one note is diluted in the air space of a 15,000 seat hockey rink. That's really soft. And one note played really loud is really loud. So the dynamic range in a place like that—softest note versus the loudest note, the top to bottom of your sculpture—with the right equipment, gives you a chance to do a more interesting and complicated sound event. Forget about whether it's a song or a drum beat or a scream on the microphone or whatever it is—those are sounds that are moving air around. Taken in the purest abstract sense, the opportunities in a large, enclosed, resonant place like that are very interesting.

Schneckloth: People still complain about those places, though. I don't know if they're looking for intimacy, or what.

Zappa: That's because people have different desires when they go to a concert. The prime desire of the concertgoer is to see the person that they bought the ticket for reproduce the record they have at home. In other words, they want a human jukebox; they want that replica. And they're never going to get it, not in a place like that, anyhow.

Schneckloth: Do you think the high-amplification thing can be overdone?

Zappa: No, I think it's necessary, it really is. It's not just because it makes it louder, but if you have all that wattage, you don't have to run the thing at full blast, which gives you more head room and you get cleaner sound.

Schneckloth: How much work is involved in moving all that sound-reinforcement equipment around?

Zappa: In the U.S. we use two 45-foot trucks and a 22. In Europe we were using two 40s. For every person onstage playing an instrument, there are two other guys in the crew. There's seven people in the band, 21 total traveling. And they all work. There are no traveling hangers-on. It's not like the Grateful Dead tour or something like that.

Schneckloth: I've seen you take your sound checks right up to the performance. The audience is already seated, and you're still working away at getting the sound right.

Zappa: Sometimes the trucks get held up and you can't have it all set up and waiting when the audience gets there. So you have to make a choice—are you going to be a star or are you going to play music? Some groups don't even do a sound check. We do one every day.

Schneckloth: Getting back to performing, how conscious are you of the outrageousness factor in your music?

Zappa: Wait a minute, let's examine what outrageous is. That means something deviates so far from the normal contemporary accepted standard that it appears outrageous. Well, after Watergate—finding out that the president of the United States may be a crook... I mean, what's outrageous? Is it outrageous to go onstage in a funny costume and spit foaming blood capsules all over the stage? Well, that's what people think is outrageous.

Schneckloth: It's all entertainment, anyway.

Zappa: So, you have to assume that Watergate was the finest entertainment America had to offer.

I think the president we have now is not exactly of Watergate stature but will ultimately provide a certain amount of entertainment for the history books. The thing that marketed him in was the more-wholesome-than-thou attitude, and I don't believe people like that exist.... You have this desire among the American people to find something nice. So anybody that is personally clean-looking and smiles a lot can get away with murder. It's the garni du jour.

It's equally true of the jazz world. The whole jazz syndrome is smothered in garni du jour. People who really have very little to say on their instrument and have built their reputation on one or two albums have wound up forming and reforming into supergroups to produce jam session albums of little merit other than very fast pentatonic performance.

Schneckloth: The whole "fusion" thing—is that a dead end?

Zappa: Well, first of all, in order to be "fusion," in order to match that marketing concept of what people think of as fusion—it has to sound "fusion." This has little to do with whether of not it's actually fusing anything together. It just means that the keyboard player has to sound like Jan Hammer, the guitar player, drummer and bass player all have to play in a certain vein. And after each guy has molded himself into that certain syndrome, then the whole musical event that they perform has to be further molded into the syndrome. So, what have you got? Nothing. It's whank music.

The problem is that people then start looking down their noses at three-chord music or one-chord music or two-chord music. And with fusion music, what do you have? Some of it is three-chord music, it's just that the chords have more partials in them. Instead of being I, VI, V, they're playing I, II flat-seven or some other simple progression that allows them to run a series of easily recognizable patterns over it. It's all mechanical.

See, part of the problem is the way in which consumers use music to reinforce their idea of what their lifestyle is. People who think of themselves as young moderns, upwardly mobile, go for the fusion or disco—that slick, cleaned-up, precise, mechanical kind of music. And they tend to dislike everything else because it doesn't have its hair combed. Three-chord fuzztone music is not exactly the kind of thing that you'd expect a young executive to be interested in. He wants something that sounds like it might be really good to listen to riding around in a Maserati.

So ultimately, that cheapens the music and whatever the musicians have done.... But like I said, it's a good thing that all that music is there for all those people. Because without it, their lifestyle would lack something.

Jan. 25, 1979

Milt Hinton: The Judge Holds Court

by Larry Birnbaum

"Bass means bottom. It means foundation, and bass players realize that their first job is to support the musicians and the ensemble. Bass players know more about sharing and appreciating one another than any other musicians. In all my years I have never heard a bass player put another bass player down; they have great love for each other and they learn from one another and they share experiences and even jobs. That's why the art of bass playing has made more progress in the last 40 years than the art of any other instrument."

Milt Hinton should know. At 68, the dean of American bassists stands at the summit of a half-century career that has taken him from the speakeasies of Chicago to the pinnacle of the big-band era with Cab Calloway to the jam sessions at Minton's in the early days of bop. He has worked behind jazzmen as diverse as Freddie Keppard and Dizzy Gillespie and has known and played with many of the greatest names in music, from Armstrong, Basie and Goodman to such popular luminaries as Bing Crosby, Barbra Streisand and Aretha Franklin.

An exponent of the revolutionary stylistic innovations of Jimmy Blanton, Hinton has himself been an influence on other masters, including Oscar Pettiford. As one who has seen the bassman's art evolve from the even-tempered quarter-note rhythms of New Orleans jazz to the electrified styles of today, Milt waxes enthusiastic about the current generation of bassists, citing Eddie Gomez, Stanley Clarke, Ray Brown, Richard Davis, George Duvivier, Major Holley and Ron Carter as personal favorites. He attributes the "fantastically improved" techniques of contemporary bass players to the superior and scholarly dedication of today's young musicians and to such technological input as higher-quality strings and adjustable bridges.

Insisting that the vogue for electricity has not cost him any work, Hinton notes that certain tones can only be obtained on the acoustic instrument, adding that he's "never seen anyone bow a Fender," although he has no hostility towards the electric model, and has even dabbled on it himself. His own big, thumping tone was developed in pre-amplification days when a strong right hand was necessary if one was to be heard—the powerful plucking earned him the nickname "Fump" during his tenure with the Calloway band.

Since then the sagacious Hinton has become known as "the Judge." A member of his church board, Milt is a clean liver who admits to having smoked but a single stick of reefer in his lifetime. But as Cab Calloway relates in his autobiography, Hinton was a disastrous gambler until his wife-to-be cured him of the habit 40 years ago. Mona still controls the purse strings to this day: "I owe everything to her, my entire career," he says. "If it hadn't been for Mona, I'd have ended up in the gutter."

Far from the gutter, Milt Hinton today is a teacher at Hunter College, a jazz historian and collector of memorabilia, a contributor to the oral history project of the Smithsonian Institution, and a co-chairman of the National Endowment for the Arts. He remains active in the studio, as the house bassist at Michael's Pub in New York, and as a touring musician. He had recently returned from an engagement at Disney World with Hank Jones when I spoke to him in his hotel room above Rick's Cafe Americain in Chicago, where he was appearing with Carl Fontana, Bobby Rosengarden and John Bunch. The set I caught was a mainstreamer's delight, as mellow and robust as vintage wine, and the familiar surroundings of his old hometown seemed to bring a rush of memories as Milt spoke for an hour virtually without pause.

"Well, my name is Milt Hinton, and I'm a pretty old bass player—I've been around a terribly long time. I was born June 23, 1910, in Vicksburg, Miss., but I came to Chicago very early, at about seven or eight years old. My whole background has been in Chicago. I came up and went to school here; in the '20s, Chicago was just a hotbed of jazz.

"My mother was a music teacher, just a home-style teacher. I received my first lesson from her and then I studied violin at Wendell Phillips High School. An awful lot of musicians came out of there; but I was there before Captain Walter Dyett. When I was there a man named Major N. Clark Smith was the bandmaster, and the music teacher was Dr. Mildred Bryant Jones. I graduated in 1929 or '30 from Phillips.

"In high school I wanted to get into the band because they got to go to all the football games free and on trips with the team. First I took up the pick horn, which is an alto horn something like a French horn. On the pick horn you play the second part—oom pah pah pah, oom pah, oom pah—and then you learn to count, going one and two and three and four. It's a very good academic instrument, but it wasn't very glamorous to me. If it wasn't big, it wasn't for me. I went from that to the bass sax—about that time the great Brown Brothers were here in Chicago and had all of those saxophones—so I played that in the band for a while until I saw that tuba back there, which was just glamorous.

"It was the thing in those days amongst families, especially in the black community, for girls to take up piano and boys to take violin. It wouldn't seem like in the black society that you would have so many violin players, but in the '20s there was work for them. In Chicago, many theaters had orchestra pits and each theater had a band.

"There were loads of violin players working in the theaters, and it worked out just great. The boys who had potential and who were into music typically took up the violin or the trumpet. Later they got into the trombone and things like that, but it was chic to study violin. Most of the girls would take up piano, which was the thing.

"Then in 1929 Al Jolson made that picture *The Jazz Singer*, which was the first sound movie—I can remember it quite well. Shortly after that, all theaters began to drop the pit orchestras because there was no need to have a show before the movie. Every theater had a trio that played music to the movie and then after the movie they had a big stage production, so they had bands and they had singers. Now that they had sound on the screen there was no necessity for that, and in the black community, which was the only one I knew about, they just dismissed all the orchestras.

"So we had all these black violin players with no place to go. There I was, all ready to play violin, but I didn't know what the heck to do. Then Al Capone opened the Cotton Club over in Cicero and hired Walter Barnes' band, a black orchestra, and all the guys in my age bracket that were playing all these instruments got a chance to go into that band. One of the kids that I called my half-brother—he was really my play brother—Ed Burke, a trombone player, got a job in that band and I'm still delivering newspapers because I'm playing violin. I knew the music and I could read well, but they weren't using any violin players. I remember how terrible I felt—at 4:30 a.m., I would be getting up to deliver newspapers and these fellows would be getting off from Cicero and coming down South Parkway or Grand Boulevard as we called it then. (I might note that Martin Luther King Drive has had three names in my lifetime. It was Grand Boulevard when all those big mansions were there that were owned by the Armours and the Swifts. Then when the black community began to move in there, I guess it was no longer grand enough to be called Grand Boulevard, so the name was changed to South Parkway.) Anyway, I felt terrible about letting them see me with my newspapers, so I would kind of hide in the corners and let them go by. This is when I really took seri-

ously to studying bass.

"I had a tough time around here trying to get into playing because there was only one big band on the South Side of any stature and potential, Earl Hines' band at the Grand Terrace. And Earl Hines already had a bass player, Quinn Wilson. Before that he had Hayes Alvis, who had converted from drums.

"At this time they were beginning to stop using the tuba, although Hayes Alvis was a tuba player and he doubled. Certain bass players—like John Lindsay from New Orleans—were former trombone players. When the bands began to split up into small combinations, they wouldn't have but one trombone, so the lesser trombone players didn't have work. That's why a guy like John Lindsay converted to string bass; he was already in the bass clef with the trombone. He was one of the bass players I looked up to, and there was Bill Johnson, also from New Orleans. There was a big New Orleans settlement here.

"The first time I came on the job with a bass violin, some of the guys said, 'Oh no, here comes a guy with that bass fiddle,' because the drummers had been accustomed to having that big percussive sound—they still hadn't really converted. The drummers included Big Sid (Catlett)—he was around—and a fellow named Richard Barnet, with whom I worked when I was with Erskine Tate and who was one of my dearest friends.

"I later played with Jimmy Bertrand in Eddie South's orchestra—one of my customers on my newspaper route was Eddie South's mother. She paid 20 cents a week for the *Chicago Herald Examiner*; she was a very pretty lady and she had all these pictures on the wall of Eddie South. She said, 'That's my son, Eddie South,' and I said, 'Yeah, I know his name very well, I'm studying violin and playing bass in school.' So she said, 'I hope one day you'll have a chance to meet my son; maybe someday you'll play with him.' Her son was in Europe at the time making a tour with a small group; when he returned I was in his band.

"I got the chance to play in Eddie South's band about 1930 or '31. Eddie was the darling of Europe—he had been playing for the Rothschild family at their private dinner parties and all of that. While Eddie was in Europe, he wrote to a violin player named Charles Elgar, who was quite an historian and a fine violinist himself. Eddie asked Elgar to organize a band.

We rehearsed with five or six violins, Ed Burke on trombone, Bob Shoffner on trumpet, I think Jimmy McEndry was the drummer, and I was on bass. We had all these beautiful dance songs like 'Dancing on the Ceiling' and 'Stardust,' and when Eddie came back we rehearsed with him, guitarist Stanley Wilson and clarinetist Cliff King. But nobody wanted Eddie in hotels like the Palmer House or the Edgewater Beach. It wasn't the time for a black orchestra to play that kind of music in those places.

"But this contractor, Sam Skolnick, had signed up each of us to a contract, each for $75 a week for 48 weeks a year, which was pretty good in the '30s. Eddie had to buy the contracts back from the musicians, for $300 a piece. When they got to me, Sam Skolnick told Eddie, 'Look, you're going to need a bass player—so don't give him the $300. Just keep him and when we get a job we'll use him.'

"Immediately we went to work on the North Side of Chicago at the Club Rubia. It was owned by the powers that be at the time—the mob—and was a very chic club, seating about 80 people. We went in with Spaulding on piano, Stanley Wilson on guitar, Cliff King on clarinet, I'm playing bass, and Eddie South is playing violin—we had no drums—and it became the big in-spot for people to come after hours to hear music.

"Ben Bernie was at the College Inn—I remember quite well because Dick Biele, the great saxophone player who now lives in New Orleans, was the top saxophone player with Ben Bernie's band. Biele's father was a violinist, so after hours Dick would bring his dad over to hear Eddie South. There was a big nightclub over on the North Side that had a band led by Ben Pollack. Jack Teagarden and Gene Krupa and all those guys were in that band, and on their intermission they used to come over to hear us. We were really continental—we played everything from 'Rhapsody in Blue' and 'An American in Paris' to Eddie South's jazz solos. They gave me a chance to slap the bass; because we didn't have a drummer, I kept this rhythmic thing going where I did quite a bit of slapping the bass and it was very effective.

"We worked there quite awhile, until 1932. The Democratic National Convention met at the Congress Hotel, and nominated Franklin Delano Roosevelt for president; somebody got us the gig in the Congress' lobby. It had a big fountain, and we

Milt Hinton.
(Veryl Oakland)

played music as the delegates came in from all over the country. Chicago was really the center of the universe at that time—anyone going between New York and California had to stop in Chicago to change trains. All business conventions were held in Chicago, where people from both coasts could meet centrally. The hotels were buzzing, salesmen were here, and it was some place to work. I worked there with Eddie South and then we left thinking what to do.

"In 1933 Eddie and I went to Hollywood and we stayed a few months at a place called the Club Ballyhoo. By this time we had changed personnel—Anthony Spaulding on piano and Everett Barksdale on guitar. We played California and did some little transcriptions for radio commercials for hand lotion—we did a one-day-a-week, 15-minute spot, so we were getting into the commercial end of it. At that time a team that later became known as Amos 'n' Andy was beginning to get very, very popular, but at first they were called Sam and Henry at WGN. I remember seeing and hearing them, and they were quite the thing—you could walk down the street in summertime and hear every word of the program, because without air-conditioning everybody had their windows open and everybody was tuned to hear this great comedy team.

"After playing California we came back to Chicago. Eddie was a dear friend of Joe Venuti, the great violinist who died last August. Venuti was with Paul Whiteman at the College Inn. Whiteman had a great singer, Bea Palmer, who was accustomed to singing to violin accompaniment. At this time Eddie South was at the Vendome Theater with Erskine Tate. Joe Venuti had decided to leave Whiteman and go out on his own, and this lady was distraught. Joe, who to my knowledge never had a prejudiced bone in his body, had always admired this young kid Eddie South, and so he recommended Eddie. She wanted him, but Whiteman couldn't have that in his band—it just wasn't the time. So they put her on the stage and put up a screen, and Eddie South stood behind the screen and played the accompaniment for her. It was nothing really, it was the usual thing for that time, but it struck up a great friendship and love between Eddie South and Joe Venuti.

"When Joe Venuti went out on his own, he began to play all these different country clubs around the Midwest. Every time he would play—the dining rooms of these country clubs became known as violin rooms—they would ask Joe who else they could get and he'd always recommend Eddie South. Consequently we got a little circuit going. Joe would do four weeks in a country club and then we would go in and do four weeks.

"Joe always left little notes for Eddie South in the piano or somewhere. Years later I got to meet him, and in the last 10 years I really got to know Joe Venuti and work with him after all of those years of seeing those notes and knowing that he had recommended us for those jobs that had never been open to blacks before.

"Eddie finally saw the jobs begin to fade out for violin players as jazz began to catch on. Earl Hines began to go over, and Louis Armstrong became just fantastically famous. Louis got a chance to make his first big tour and go to New York with his own band in 1934 or '35.

"So they were looking for a substitute for Louis Armstrong to put in a club on Lake Street, and they got Jabbo Smith to do it. That was my first shot to get into an organized band. I had been floating around and people began to call me when another bass player died or if there was nobody left on Saturday night or New Year's Eve, so I finally began to make good. I even played a couple of gigs for Freddie Keppard on 35th and State at the Binga Bank Building, and I played with Huey Swift, one of the first black trumpet players, who had a band at the Jeffrey Tavern. I also played with Bill Samuels, one of the officials of our union here in Chicago—I'm still a member here with a gold card.

"Jabbo Smith had a good band—Cassino Simpson was the piano player; Floyd Campbell was on drums; Jerome Pascal and Scoville Brown on saxophone; Tic Grey was one of the trumpet players; and Ed Burke played trombone—that was Jabbo's first band.

"This club was in the basement; during the day it was a bookie joint, and at night it was a nightclub. Well, Jabbo Smith was a handsome man and the girls just loved him. I don't blame them because he was very handsome and was the most magnificent trumpet player I ever heard in my life. I can still hear the sound of the greatness of Jabbo Smith. He was so fluid, he was like a combination of Charlie Shavers, Roy Eldridge and Louis Armstrong all wrapped into one. He played fast, he played soft, he ran changes, he played anything with a cup on it, trombone, tuba, anything. He was out of the Jenkins Orphan Home. The kids there would have this little band that used to go around playing and begging for money for this orphanage. A great many black trumpeters came out of that same orphanage—Cat Anderson, and I think Punch Miller, too.

"Jabbo couldn't make the gig on time. We didn't start until 11 p.m. but we had to go until four or five in the morning. The band would be there ready to play, and no Jabbo. He was living next door to a girlfriend of mine, and I asked her if she would go over, knock on the door, wake Jabbo up and tell him that he had to go downtown to work. We caught him at 11 o'clock, still in bed, and we didn't have all those expressways like now so you can imagine that by the time he got downtown it was 1 o'clock. While we were waiting we jammed, and Cas Simpson, being the piano player, would write out the arrangements and have the band swinging by the time Jabbo got there. The guys and everybody at the club finally got kind of sick of that, so the next season they told Cas, 'You got the band.' That's how Cassino Simpson took over the band; you've seen the pictures. I don't remember ever recording with this band, though.

"I did record with Tiny Parham in 1930—I worked at the Mirror Garden Ballroom with him. I recorded with Eddie in 1933, I think, and I have some of those tapes and records. I did a vocal on one song that I recorded—'Old Man Harlem'—and it turned out to be the record of the month.

"Around 1933, Teddy Wilson was in town. We were gigging and playing little clubs around town, and then Benny Carter sent for Teddy Wilson to come to New York and work in his band. When Teddy left, it just broke my heart because nobody sent for me. Then Ked Johnson, the trombone player, joined Benny Carter's band—about '34—and then I was really alone; my friends were all making it and nobody sent for me.

"By the end of '34 Keg Johnson got with Cab Calloway, who was doing great and was going to Hollywood. Cab started in Chicago, too, at the Sunset.

"A lot of drummers in those days would sing. There were a lot of guys that were like pimps—they didn't really play good drums, but they were good-looking guys and they wanted to hang around clubs where they could meet all of these chicks and do their business with them. They would sing a song and snap a little on their drums and they would look all sharp and pretty, and they'd get to meet all the ladies that way. So Cab became one of those kind of guys—he was good-looking and his sister was a star, so that's how he got in there.

"But to get back, in '35 Cab went to California to do a movie with Al Jolson called *The Singing Kid*. His bass player, Al Morgan, was a fantastic visual player. He was really my idol; I used to watch him just to see how a great bass player acted, and that's what I figured I would be like when I grew up—of course I'm nothing like that at all. When they made this movie, the cameras would be grinding away and every time Cab looked around, instead of the camera being on him it would be on Al Morgan, because he was a tall, black, handsome guy and he smiled and twirled his bass as he played. This got under Cab's skin because it was a little too competitive for him. But nothing happened about it until one of the producers said to Al Morgan, 'Look, you're so very photogenic that if you were going to be around here, every time we made a picture with a band scene in it you would get the job.' So this guy quit Cab in California and joined Les Hite's band with Lionel Hampton and all those guys who were established in Hollywood, and he stayed there.

"Cab started back east without a bass player, and my friend Johnson told Cab that if he was going through Chicago he should stop at the Three Deuces and dig Milt Hinton. By this time Simpson's band had broke up and the owner had opened a Three Deuces at State and Lake. Zutty Singleton was the bandleader and Art Tatum was the relief piano player there. When Art played, it was my responsibility to stand by and come in for his finale. He played solo piano, but for his last tune, which would be something up-tempo, I was supposed to join him and take it out and then come on with Zutty's band. Of course, Art Tatum was so fabulous that I don't think I ever caught up to him; his changes were too fast for me and he left me standing at the post. But it was such a joy to see him, and he was a very nice person. He could see slightly if you put a very bright light behind his eye, so during intermissions we played pinochle together.

"Zutty had the band, mostly New Orleans guys. It was Zutty playing drums, Lee Collins, a great trumpet player whose wife recently put out a book about him; there was a kid from New Jersey, Cozy Cole's brother, who played piano, and

Everett Barksdale was the guitar player. We worked for months at the Three Deuces and my acceptance as a musician was established, because Chicago was a New Orleans town—all the jazz was New Orleans jazz—and Zutty Singleton was the drummer. There was Baby Dodds and Tubby Hall, but Zutty was really the guy. He had been with the Louis Armstrong Hot Five, with Earl Hines and Lil and Preston Jackson, who is now living in New Orleans. Zutty finally decided to take me into his rhythm section. Now I was with the king and now I was established as a top bass player in Chicago.

"And now Cab comes down and he listens to me play. He never said a word to me, he just sat there—I saw him in the room—and a guy said, 'Cab is in.' He came in with a big coonskin coat and a derby and, man, he was sharp, people were like applauding. He sat at a table and listened to us play, and on the intermission he invited Zutty over to the table to have a drink with him—not me, but Zutty. He said, 'Hey, I'd like that bass player, I heard he's pretty good.' Zutty was most beautiful and kind to me and he was only too happy to have me make some progress, and he said, 'You can have him,' in that long drawl, New Orleans accent he had. So Cab said, 'Well, thanks man, and if you ever get to New York and there's anything I can ever do for you, you just let me know,' and they shook hands. Then Zutty came upstairs—I'm playing pinochle with Art Tatum—and said, 'Well, kid, you're gone.' 'Where am I going, Zutty?' 'Cab just asked me for you and I told him he could have you.' I said, 'Don't I have to give you some kind of a two-week notice or something?' and Zutty said, 'If you don't get your black ass out of here this evening, I'll shoot you.'

"Cab finally comes up and sings a song with us, he hi-de-ho's and breaks up the house—and as he's leaving he says to me, 'Kid, the train leaves from LaSalle Street Station at 9 o'clock in the morning. Be on it.' That's all he said to me, no discussion of salary or anything. I dashed to the phone, called my mom, and told her to pack that other suit I had and my extra shirt. I got my stuff—of course, there was no time to sleep—and I met the band at the station. It was quite an experience, because I had never been on a train except coming from Mississippi to Chicago, and you know I didn't come on a Pullman or any first-class train—we were right next to the engine. I'd never seen a Pullman in my life,

and here all of these big-time musicians were on this train, on their own Pullman.

"There were these fabulous musicians: Doc Cheatham, the trumpet player; Mouse Randolph, another trumpet player; Foots Thomas, the straw boss, the assistant leader of the band, a saxophone player; Andy Brown, a saxophone player; and the drummer, Leroy Maxey. These guys had been working in the Cotton Club in New York and they were really professional: Lammar Wright was another great trumpet player in the band; Claude Jones, a great friend of Tommy Dorsey's, was the trombone player; and there was my old friend Keg Johnson who had recommended me.

"I must have looked pretty bad. I had the seedy suit on, a little green gabardine jacket with vents in the sleeves—we called them bi-swings in those days. Keg was introducing me around, and the great Ben Webster was in the band. He and Cab had been out drinking that night and they missed the train at LaSalle Street, but you could catch the train at the 63rd Street station. They were out on the South Side balling away with some chicks and they didn't have time to come downtown. So they picked up the train at 63rd Street and got on just terribly drunk. I was sitting there and Keg was trying to introduce me to the guys, and Ben Webster walks in terribly stoned and he looked at me—I must have weighed 115 pounds soaking wet—and said, 'What is this?' and Cab said, 'This is the new bass player,' and Ben said, 'The new what!?' I remember thinking I would never like Ben, and he turned out to be one of my dearest friends.

"I hadn't asked anybody about the price, but I was making $35 a week with Zutty at the Three Deuces and that was one of the best jobs in town. Fletcher Henderson was at the Grand Terrace at that time with Roy Eldridge, Coleman Hawkins and Chu Berry and they were making 35 bucks a week. I didn't know how to approach anybody about money with Cab, so finally I told Keg that Cab hadn't said anything to me about money. Keg said, 'Oh, everybody here makes $100 a week.' Well, I almost fainted—$100 I had never heard of; it was a fantastic amount of money. This is before Social Security—they only took out $1 for union dues and you got $99, and $99 in those days was like $9,000 today. Honestly, you could get a good room for $7 a week; you could get a fantastic meal for 50 cents and cigarettes for 10 or 15 cents a pack; bread was five cents a loaf; so you can imagine what the thing was like.

"Cab told me after we started making one-night stands that he was only hiring me until he got to New York and got a good bass player. I was quite happy even to do that for 100 bucks a week. We made one-nighters for three months before we hit New York, all through Iowa—Des Moines, Sioux City, everyplace, and I got a chance to really get set and all the guys liked me.

"Well, Al Morgan was not a reading man. He had been in the band so long he had memorized the book, so there was no bass book. And here I was quite academic—I'd studied violin and I'd studied bass legitimately with a bass player from the Chicago Civic Opera and I never had a problem with reading—I was playing Mendelssohn's Concerto in E-minor so there was no problem. I said, 'Where's the music?' and there was no music, so Benny Payne, the piano player, said, 'You just cock your ear and listen, and I'll call off the changes to you.'

"Benny was most kind and we've had many laughs about this later; I'm about 5'7" and Al Morgan was a tall man, he must have been 6'3". There was no time to get new uniforms so I had to wear his clothes, and when I put on his coat I was just drowning in it. His arms were much longer than mine so that you couldn't see my hands because they didn't come out through the sleeves. The guys said I looked like Ichabod Crane or somebody—I'm playing bass through the coat-sleeves and they were laughing.

"I had never really played with a big band of that caliber, and when they hit it that first night it almost frightened me to death. The black guys in those days used to wear their hair in a pompadour—it was long in front and we would plaster it down with grease and comb it back and it would stay down. Of course, when it got hot that grease melted and our hair would stand straight up. I had this big coat on and I got to playing and the grease ran all out of my hair and my hair was standing up all over my head and Benny Payne is calling out these chords to me—'B-flat! C! F!' The guys in the band told me later that they were just rolling with laughter, they could hardly contain themselves, because I was really playing good but I looked so ungodly funny.

"Finally Cab saw that the guys liked

me and we were having so much fun that he said, 'We'll give him a blood test.' There was a special tune that Al Morgan did, featuring a bass solo, called 'The Reefer Man.' Cab said, 'OK—"The Reefer Man,"' and my eyes got big as saucers because I didn't know anything about this new music. I said, 'How does it go?' Benny Payne said, 'You start it,' and I said, 'What!?' He said, 'We'll give you the tempo but it just starts with the bass—just get into the key of F.' I tell you, I started playing F, I chromaticized F, I squared F, I cubed F, I played F every conceivable way, and they just let me go on for five or 10 minutes, alone, playing this bass, slapping the bass, and doing all this on this F chord. Finally Cab brought the band in with a 'two... three... four' and they played the arrangement. Benny's calling off the chords to me, and after three or four minutes the whole band lays out and Benny says, 'Now you've got it alone again,' and here I go back into this F. I must have played five or 10 minutes, and Benny comes over and says, 'Now you just act like you've fainted and just fall right back and I'll catch you,' and I did it and it was quite a sensation as far as the public was concerned, and the musicians were just out of their skulls they were laughing so.

"By the time we got to New York, Ben Webster liked me and Claude Jones liked me and the guys all said, 'This guy's going to make it,' so I was in. I stayed with the band 16 years, until 1951.

"Now, the Cotton Club was coming down to 48th and Broadway. They opened in 1936 where the Latin Quarter was and where the Palais Royale, where Paul Whiteman played, used to be, and the name is now the Cotton Club Downtown. It was opening and the first show was Cab Calloway with Bill 'Bojangles' Robinson the featured attraction. We didn't worry, we were going to rehearse for two or three nights, then they found out that I didn't belong to the New York union, so they wouldn't allow me to work. Cab's going to send me back to Chicago—of course I don't want to go—but the guys in the band now like me and they told Cab that he was a big man and he could make some connections and keep me in the band, which he did. He hired another bass player, Elmer James, to work while I worked out my transfer with the union.

"It was a very beautiful time, 1936—I was at the Cotton Club and Benny Goodman, who was very popular, was at the

Pennsylvania Hotel, and I was seeing my old friends like Lionel Hampton and Teddy Wilson. Teddy got the contract to do some recordings for Columbia and later to record with Billie Holiday, and since I was an old friend he used me so I got to make some of the early recordings with Billie Holiday. Lionel Hampton got a contract on RCA, so Hamp began to use me a little bit to record with him and Charlie Christian and Cozy Cole and Clyde Hart. That's how I got into that New York society and into recording.

"As I said, I stayed in Cab's band 16 years—I didn't quit, the band just disintegrated. It broke up around 1948 and we continued as seven pieces with Jonah Jones on trumpet, Sam 'the Man' Taylor on tenor, Hilton Jefferson on alto, Keg Johnson on trombone, Dave Rivera on piano and Panama Francis on drums, and we traveled around the country playing small clubs for several years. Then things got a little rough and we went down to a quartet with just Jonah Jones, Dave Rivera, Panama Francis, me, and of course Cab was singing. We played Milwaukee and ran into great jazz musicians there, and then we played Cuba and worked all the nightclubs in Cuba. In 1951 we organized a big band again and went to South America, to Montevideo, and we did carnivals for a month or two. When we came back the band fell apart, and that's when I was left without a job, because there was just no work for us.

"I finally ran into my old friend Jackie Gleason and he gave me a job recording with him. I got to make all those records with Bobby Hackett, like *Music for Lovers Only*, and I got to do *The Honeymooners* and my name was being kicked around. At this time in New York we were like the Jackie Robinsons of the music business because they didn't have any black guys in the studios recording. I began to get work, from one band to the other. Then Joe Bushkin saw me and I went into the Embers with him, Buck Clayton and Jo Jones and we stayed for a couple of years.

"Gleason liked us and took us on tour with him. We toured in the summer after his show was over in places like the Chicago Theater. He took *The Honeymooners* cast, he took the DeMarco sisters and Zano Cunningham, and Art Carney went along, and Steve Allen's wife, Audrey Meadows, and the Joe Bushkin Quartet; we toured every major city in the Midwest. I did the music for the whole *Honeymooners* series, with Sammy Spear conducting. I began to get known in the recording business and it got very lucky for me. I got to make recordings with every big artist in New York. In the beginning I made the first records with Johnny Mathis, the first records with Aretha Franklin, the first records with Barbra Streisand, and I recorded with Hugo Winterhalter, Andre Kostelanitz and Percy Faith.

"It was a great challenge to do all these different things, because at that time I was a studio guy on call during the day and at night I worked in a club and played jazz. I was making lots of bread, man; I might be making 300 or 400 bucks a week, which was fantastic. I got to do a Saturday morning radio show with Bernie Leighton called *Gil Hendricks, The Housewives Protective League*. Also on Saturday I did the *Woolworth's Hour* with Percy Faith, who had a big orchestra with 50 or so men, and on Wednesdays I did *The Big Record* with Patti Page on CBS.

"I'm in all of these bands, and these were the same bands that were doing all of the recording sessions. I got to know all of the really good players and naturally improved because I played all the time. We formed a combo with the rhythm section—Hank Jones, Barry Galbraith, the late Ossie Johnson, and myself—everybody wanted us and we did so many records together that we became known as the New York Rhythm Section. For years we went from one studio to another recording with all different artists, Dinah Washington and just everybody and it was quite a thing.

"That's been going on right up to now. We went out to Vegas with Barbra Streisand when she made her first appearance at the International Hotel, and I've been touring with Pearl Bailey recently. I made the very last tour with Bing Crosby—I was with him just before he died. We finished at Brighton on Monday, I left Tuesday, he went to Spain to play some golf and that Friday he was gone. I was working with Bobby Rosengarden on *The Dick Cavett Show*—George Duvivier, who is a friend of mine, alternated with me. I'm teaching at Hunter College now and I've been doing quite a bit of work at Michael's Pub in New York with people like the late Joe Venuti and Red Norvo and Matt Dennis, and I'm going back soon with Sylvia Sims. That brings us up to this December 1978."

Feb. 8, 1979

Weather Report Answers Its Critics

by Larry Birnbaum

"This is an all-star band, man, and by its own virtue, not by putting it together. Usually they put all-star bands together—they say OK, get me this guy, that guy. But with us, three out of four regular members had first places in the Readers Poll, also in the Critics Poll, also in the European polls, also in the Japanese polls. And Peter is going to be up there, too."

Josef Zawinul has never been accused of excessive modesty, but no one can gainsay the phenomenal success Weather Report has enjoyed among critics, musicians and listeners alike since its inception in 1970. Their latest album, *Mr. Gone*, is currently near the top of the jazz charts after a mixed critical reception ranging from ecstatic raves to dismal pans, including a one-star drubbing in *DownBeat* that caused Zawinul no end of consternation.

"We really care, you know? Hey, man, *DownBeat* is my favorite magazine. You know why? Because I grew up on it, it was my connection to America and it brought me into jazz music.

"But there is no way in the world that a record like this could get a one-star review. I have seen many reviews of this record. People like Conrad Silvert, Len Lyons, Robert Palmer, Ken Anderson, Bob Blumenthal, all thought it was a great album. You know what one star means? It means this is a poor record. This band has never put out a record that we didn't believe in, and there's no way in the world that anybody was ever involved in a one-star album. This is a heavy thing, man. I mean, even if somebody didn't like the record, just for the compositions alone it's got to be five stars. We played it very well; we worked hard on this record. Anybody who gives this record one star has got to be insane."

Zawinul's meteoric career has been extensively documented, as has that of his renowned collaborator Wayne Shorter, one

of the giants of modern saxophone. The unlikely coupling of the brash, fast-talking Austrian keyboardist and the humble, soft-spoken American reedman has proved to be a most fruitful and long-lived partnership. The duo became a solid triumvirate in 1976 with the acquisition of electric bassist Jaco Pastorius, the "Florida flash," whose extraordinary technique and flamboyant showmanship catapulted him swiftly into the ranks of stardom. The latest addition to the group is former Kenton drummer Peter Erskine, who, like Zawinul and Shorter, is also an alumnus of the Maynard Ferguson band. In the past, Weather Report has always included a percussionist, but with Erskine they have rounded down to a sleek quartet, yielding a less cluttered sound that spotlights Zawinul's synthesized polyphony with superior clarity.

Through eight albums, Weather Report has developed from a loose improvisational ensemble whose interwoven counterpoint lines had a spontaneous, searching quality into a tightly integrated programmatic unit given over largely to extended written arrangements. Although the material remains complex and challenging, their music has evolved from the moody gropings of their early outings through an eclectic middle period featuring funk and ethnic effects and finally to its present tuneful incarnation. With highly wrought but catchy melodies soaring buoyantly over heavy bass ostinatos, Weather Report's current style is joyously celebratory to its admirers, slick and cynical to its detractors. In the process of becoming more accessible, their music has attracted adherents even as it has alienated some critics, and their sales figures have climbed to new peaks.

Despite progressive refinement in the direction of more elaborate orchestration, the underlying conceptual structure of the music has remained remarkably unchanged. Weather Report's original conglomeration of electronic and acoustic voicings over a shifting matrix of strong, regular syncopations remains unmistakably its own. Characteristic use of counterpoint to develop thematic material, as opposed to sequential soloing, brands the music with an indelible signature stamp unique in contemporary music. For all their public disavowal of rock and fusion influences, the group's sound is clearly rooted in the early electric experiments of Miles Davis, where virtually all of the prominent names in the modern fusion school won prominence.

Zawinul's "In a Silent Way" and Shorter's "Nefertiti," each the title track from an influential Miles album, were two of the seminal compositions of the new genre, and both men contributed to such important recordings as *Bitches Brew*.

As of this writing the group is just completing an extended world tour that has taken them to Europe, Japan and South America before culminating in a sweep of the U.S. In a November performance at Chicago's Park West, all delicacy of nuance gave way to a strident, heavily percussive mix amplified to rock-concert intensity.

Shorter has been playing more tenor lately and his pungent, earthy solo was easily the highpoint of the set, contrasting markedly with the haunting soprano airs for which he has become known in recent years and demonstrating that he remains a nonpareil exponent of the big horn. Pastorius perambulated all over the stage, plucking resonant bass lines with the sustained energy that has led some album reviewers to confuse his thick tones with Zawinul's synthesizer. Jaco's solo spot combined histrionics with electronics as the bassist generated amazing feedback effects that lingered in the air until he finally quelled the throbbing instrument by leaping down on it from atop an amplifier.

In addition to these antics, the act featured a smoke machine and a fancy lighting backdrop, but music had the last word as Zawinul performed an extended electric piano encore with all of the fluid facility he once displayed with Cannonball Adderley's band.

I spoke to the band over Mexican food between shows as they prepared to head west on the last leg of their tour. Blunt and outspoken as usual, Zawinul did most of the talking, evincing not a little testiness as he fumed again at the thought of the offending review.

"There's got to be a certain professionalism," he protested. "You don't give Horowitz one star or two. You just don't do it, because it's beyond. Certain things are beyond and what this band is doing is beyond anybody. If we tried to make a one-star album, we couldn't do it, because it's just not in us. We are goddamn sincere with what we are doing."

I queried the band about changes in their music:

Joe Zawinul: Well, it's developed and it's grown, but a human being is a human being and you really can't change that much.

Jaco Pastorius: Your personality doesn't change, it just grows.

Wayne Shorter: Your name was the same when you were a baby, too.

Larry Birnbaum: Well, there have been different personnel in the band also.

Shorter: We have a different president of the U.S.

Zawinul: But it's the same Constitution.

Birnbaum: On the new album I hear big-band voicings but onstage it sounds more like a rock band. Do you try to get a different feeling in live performance than in the studio?

Zawinul: We don't try nothing, man. We're just human beings and we're just doing what we do, and it's very good. We have the best composing on this record ever, the best composing of anybody, not just of ours. Some of the tunes are incredible.

Birnbaum: What kind of music do you listen to?

Zawinul: I listen to my music.

Birnbaum: You seem to use quite a bit of different ethnic music. Do you listen to say, Brazilian or Middle Eastern music...

Zawinul: No.

Birnbaum:... or does that just come out naturally?

Zawinul: Yeah. I'm an international person and I've always traveled. I come from a Hungarian-Czechoslovakian family background, and, you know, it's just whatever comes out. I play now like I played when I was still in Austria. Stylistically, idea-wise, composition-wise, I did pretty much the same thing 20 years ago.

Birnbaum: When you were in Vienna did you listen to Gypsy music or anything like that?

Zawinul: Well, this is just something that's there and it's a part of the atmosphere. You just go out there and you play with the people and just hang out with them. I always learned more from the people than from their music. Anyway, I never heard that stuff in the group at all. All of the guys that played percussion with us, for instance, even if they were from Brazil or wherever, they were really jazz musicians, jazz drummers.

Birnbaum: Hearing the band live last night I was really struck by the heavy rock feel, especially in the bass and drums.

Pastorius: Well, then you got a total misconception of the music...

Zawinul: I think so.

Pastorius:... because if there's a heavy feel, it's R&B, not rock. There's a differ-

ence between rhythm and blues and rock 'n' roll. I grew up playing nothing but colored music all my life, and that's it.

Zawinul: That's the difference, we don't play no white music, because rock 'n' roll is a white music.

Birnbaum: What about Chuck Berry?

Zawinul: That ain't no rock 'n' roll, Chuck Berry, that's R&B.

Pastorius: I don't play nothing but R&B. It ain't no rock 'n' roll.

Zawinul: English music is rock 'n' roll.

Pastorius: Yeah, if we did an album with "Penny Lane" on it, you could say we were playing rock 'n' roll.

Zawinul: But even the themes we're playing are different. Maybe on one tune we play something that might sound like R&B, but all our rhythms are totally different. No R&B group plays rhythms the way we do. It has the power of R&B, but there's a difference, man.

Pastorius: We have the drive of a soul group.

Zawinul: It has that strength and power, but the rhythms we play are unique. I don't know if most people can identify what we play in the first place, but we've had some of the best copyists in the business trying to transcribe our music for publication and they cannot chart down what we're playing—it's totally different, man. I mean, if you analyze the rhythms we play on the new record alone... have you ever heard a rhythm like "The Pursuit of the Woman with the Feathered Hat"? I know you haven't. Check out the "River People" rhythm—it's a totally different approach, man.

Birnbaum: I find the rhythmic concept similar through the whole series of Weather Report albums, but it is unique, really. It gives the band a very distinctive sound.

Zawinul: Yeah, because it's similar people playing.

Birnbaum: You've gone through quite a few different percussionists. When you get someone new, do you tell them what to play?

Zawinul: Oh, yeah. You have to, man.

Birnbaum: Now with Peter in the group, will you still use different drummers in the studio?

Zawinul: The reason we used Peter on only one tune is because we met him when the record was already done.

Pastorius: We finished the record back in May and then we had to go out on tour in June, so we got Peter to go out with us to Japan to start the world tour. But he was playing so good we said let's get Peter on the record. He just happened to come in on the tail end.

Birnbaum: Do you feel comfortable now as a quartet without the additional percussion? It sounds very clean that way.

Pastorius: Fantastic.

Zawinul: It's a little more focused. It helps the bass player.

Pastorius: There's a certain timbre in some of the percussion instruments that takes away a lot of the mid-range, mid-range and below. Joe and I might be playing and we can take more space and not have to force our way through.

Birnbaum: [to Shorter] You're playing more tenor now.

Shorter: Yeah, because we're getting a much better mix for it now.

Birnbaum: It's a different style than your soprano work. It reminds me more of the way you used to play with Art Blakey.

Shorter: That's not surprising. It's like two different people—it's a schizoid kind of thing. One thing is that when you hold a soprano you feel more like a trumpet player. With the tenor it's down on your chest somewhere, so it's like changing roles.

Birnbaum: You've done some things on your own with the soprano—*Native Dancer*, the album with Milton Nascimento.

Shorter: And on the tenor. My new album will be a combination of both but with some big surprises and some little ones, too.

Birnbaum: Do you ever feel confined at all in the context of Weather Report?

Shorter: You mean like locked into an R&B thing or something? No, I don't feel confined in a rock thing or anything like that. But I'm very careful about thinking about something that's going to do something to me. I'm slowly just finding out that what happens to a person is that person's own doing. It's me, you know? I'm very careful about placing fault or blame outside myself. If you place fault on something outside of yourself you can't change anything because you're always just the object of another subject. But if you have the right attitude you can work with everything, you can work with the whole world. A question like "Do you feel confined?" or something like that gives me the knowledge that most people are having the experience of being confined by things themselves, therefore they question about that energy. That question is limited.

Birnbaum: Do you feel that you're under any commercial pressure?

Zawinul: No.

Pastorius: Nobody at CBS even hears the record until it's mastered. There's no pressure at all.

Birnbaum: Do you plan for a hit like "Birdland," where a single breaks out of the album?

Zawinul: We don't plan that, but when it comes along it's great. It would be great to sell a million records, you know, of some real music.

Birnbaum: But you don't sit down with the idea of writing a single.

Zawinul: Nah, you can't do that, man.

Pastorius: There's no way.

Birnbaum: What about the stage show? Do you feel that you're playing to the audience with the smoke machine and the light show?

Zawinul: I like that stuff. But we're definitely playing to the audience. There's an audience out there and you've got to play to them—goddamn, you'd better believe it.

Birnbaum: Are you playing down to them? Is that a concession?

Zawinul: There's no concession—it's fun. It fits the piece of music.

Birnbaum: Then it's just something you feel?

Zawinul: Of course.

Shorter: If you don't feel it, you've got to quit the business.

Birnbaum: [to Zawinul] You get a very distinctive sound on the synthesizer. It's often said that everybody sounds alike on electronic keyboards, but that's not true in your case.

Zawinul: I know it ain't true.

Birnbaum: But you do program the synthesizers in a particular way to get that sound. I mean, even when you only play one note it still sounds like you.

Zawinul: Well, goddamn, it's me playing. What reason would there be to play if you didn't sound like yourself? But I could always hear different sounds than electric piano, so I do set it up in a certain way, but it sounds like me no matter how I set it up.

Birnbaum: [to Pastorius] What kind of bass were you playing?

Pastorius: I made my bass myself. It's just an old Fender bass, standard bass, but I took the frets out. It's a Jazz Bass, the only bass, 1962—it's the bass of doom. I had to put wood filler in it to fill in the holes where the frets used to be and that's why it looks like the frets are still there.

Erskine: That's the original wood filler and everything.

Pastorius: It's original, man. I have not touched that thing in seven or eight years. I keep sanding it down every year and I put boat epoxy on it. I still ain't through with it.

Birnbaum: When you get those feedback effects, do you set the amps in a certain way? Could you do that with any amp, or have you got some special equipment rigged up?

Pastorius: I could do it with any Acoustic 360—that's the same amp I've been playing through for eight and a half years now. It's just got a little fuzz tone—you put it on and go. Most of what I'm doing to make that sound is just fundamental harmonics through that fuzz tone.

Birnbaum: Your next album will be a live LP. Were you recording last night?

Zawinul: No. We couldn't do a sound check last night. The recording will be done in California at the end of the tour. We could have recorded now, but it's a matter of equipment and all of that. It's less expensive to do it out there, and you get better people.

Birnbaum: Weather Report was one of the first fusion bands…

Zawinul: What does that mean?

Birnbaum: Well, you use electronics and…

Zawinul: So electronics means fusion, eh? I've never been sure what fusion means.

Birnbaum: I thought the band had sort of a rock conception when it first came out. It had electronics and a strong beat. Even the name of the group—it was the first jazz group to have a name like a rock band. It appeals to many people who are primarily into rock music rather than jazz. But what I was getting at is that for the most part the fusion school has gone down the drain in the past few years and Weather Report keeps going strong.

Zawinul: It's because we're saying what we're saying and it goes on strong because it's real and it's genuine and there's nothing false about it. It was always real, good or bad, but it's real, man. The compositions were always great and the playing was always great and that's it.

Birnbaum: I heard Jack DeJohnette's new group with Lester Bowie, and in a certain way it reminded me slightly of Weather Report.

Zawinul: Yeah? Well, that's what slowly lots of people are going to remind you of.

Birnbaum: They're also coming out of that Miles bag, more or less.

Zawinul: We ain't coming out of that.

Birnbaum: Originally I think it was Miles who first got into that electronic, percussive sort of sound.

Zawinul: I'll tell you something, man. Do you know who was the first guy to play and record on electric piano, outside of Ray Charles in 1959? It was me, man. Miles came to see me and checked it out, and then he got an electric piano for Herbie Hancock. But we were already playing new things with Cannon's band. We played "*In a Silent Way*" two years before I gave it to Miles to record.

Birnbaum: That was really the album that started it all.

Zawinul: Well, then you know what I'm saying.

Birnbaum: To me it all seemed to take off from what Miles was doing at that time. All of the heaviest names in so-called fusion music, people like Chick Corea and John McLaughlin, come out of the Miles band.

Zawinul: Sure, but that doesn't necessarily mean that Miles was the sole father of all that.

Birnbaum: What about the rhythms? The rhythms of Weather Report are similar to the rhythms that Miles was using then, the things that Tony Williams and Jack DeJohnette were playing.

Zawinul: But you see, man, we are all into this for a long time. Like, I was involved in Haight-Ashbury when it was really at its height, checking out Jimi Hendrix. I mean, it's a long time that we are all involved in this.

Shorter: Since I was born, man.

Zawinul: Yeah, and in general, Art Blakey's band was actually a modern R&B band, when you really think about it, and so was Cannonball's band.

Birnbaum: But Miles was breaking away from the Blakey concept.

Zawinul: Well, Miles was doing something different, but you've got to consider one thing, man. On this first album, *In a Silent Way*, he had a lot of bass lines added on and they were my bass lines. I put them on there, to give it a certain feeling. On *Bitches Brew*, Miles wasn't even playing much—Miles was inside the booth with Teo Macero and he just came steppin' out here and there and played a couple of notes, but mostly he just let us play. It was Chick and me playing and Wayne was back there with Bennie Maupin. We had this music, man, and we played and we rehearsed and we put things together. I mean, I, too, think that Miles was... let's

say he was where everything centered toward because he was the most forward-looking and creative musician of the '60s.

Birnbaum: What about Ornette and Ayler and all those people?

Zawinul: Of course, there were other directions going on, too. There were a whole lot of things going on. But I dug all that from the very beginning. I dug Ornette and I dug Archie Shepp a lot and I heard Cecil Taylor. I dug those people more than I did Coltrane for some kind of reason. But I'm an old jazz fan.

Birnbaum: It seems to me that there's really a division between the people who follow Miles and...

Shorter: A division? Is that what you're really talking about, how things divide?

Birnbaum: I was trying to say that there are two different schools, one represented by Miles' approach incorporating electronics and rock effects and...

Shorter: I tell you, it's a lot of fun.

Zawinul: Everything is a lot of fun.

Shorter: It's just as much fun as watching cell division.

Zawinul: Right.

Shorter: I mean, we're so used to talking about things separately in this hemisphere. We break things up, you know? But there's a whole thing that we're dealing with. The whole universe is fission and fusion, but if I'm gonna look at something that's breaking up it's going to take me that much longer to really deal with the things that I want to do.

Zawinul: There's got to be more education from the writers. The writers have got to learn about all these things so that we don't have to talk about the same shit all the time.

Pastorius: Every writer asks the same questions.

Zawinul: What I'm saying is that the things are already known by you all. But we could talk about something much more interesting—life itself. Because we've done a lot of cover stories and we talk about the same shit we always talk about and it's getting boring, because people don't know what to write about. I mean, who gives a shit, man—that Miles Davis thing is gone, his stuff is gone and he's totally somewhere else, man. There is not even a connection, absolutely none, not even close, and there's never been, man. You listen to our album, man, and then you listen to Miles' music. You listen to our first album—there's no connection. The only connection is that Miles recorded a tune we did on the second

album, a tune called "Directions," and that became a sort of theme song for him. This is the only thing remotely like Miles, I think, because we didn't record *In a Silent Way*.

The way things come out in these articles is not right. One time I said something like, "I'm going to be the next great innovator," but it was printed in such a way that it sounded like I was saying that nobody else could, that I'm the only one that could do it. I still believe in what I said, because I know what I'm gonna do.

But we don't want to hurt nobody, man, and we don't want to be put higher than what we are—we just want to get the truth out and let the people decide. We don't want someone to just go out and take a picture of us while we're onstage and put it on the cover. We don't make a whole lot of money; our only take is to get our... I don't want to call it dignity, but there's a certain respect we have for what we are doing.

Al Green: Soul Reborn but Sales Waste Away

by David Less

It is the second anniversary of Al Green's Full Gospel Tabernacle Church. A film crew from France's national television network is present with lights, microphones and cameras. The choir, wearing firehouse red gowns, sits elevated in the corner under a huge banner that reads, "Let God Be Magnified." A band is cooking while gospel shouter Ruby Wilson, her hair perfectly coiffed, wearing a three-quarter-length fur coat despite the heat from the television lights, sings "Precious Lord."

A young girl in the choir stands clapping and dancing and suddenly falls to the floor with a violent jerking motion. Another choir member quite routinely goes over to check on her and once convinced of the younger girl's safety, retakes her seat. The audience is a sea of hands with scattered women leaping to dance, trance-like, up and down the aisles. In the middle of all this is Reverend Al Green. Tall and muscular, wearing a white three-piece suit and waving a handkerchief, it seems inconceivable that this bespectacled young man who looks like an accountant will within a matter of minutes take complete control of the congregation. To this spectator the service is like a roller-coaster ride. The Frenchmen appear totally befuddled.

By the time Reverend Green approaches the podium, the congregation seems out of control. All eyes are on Green as he takes charge: "Praise Jesus. Can I get a witness?" Hands raise as the hypnotic speech patterns of Green's sermon begin to take effect.

Green's service is not unique. In a number of black (and a few white) churches across the country, rapid-fire sing-song phrases, facial contortions, a dancer's moves from the pulpit, and intense involvement and interaction of the congregation are all commonplace. But the Full Gospel Tabernacle Church is different—its pastor, Al Green, is an internationally popular recording star.

The skills of the successful gospel preacher are those of an effective entertainer. Insistent, compelling rhythms of speech and song, along with an ability to sense and control the shifting moods of the audience, make for smooth transitions between preaching and entertaining.

Many blues singers, popular as recording artists in the 1920s and 1930s, went on to preach. Former bluesmen Rev. Robert Wilkins and Ishman Bracey, for example, devoted their time to their congregations and gave up blues and any other form of secular music.

Reverend Clay Evans of the Fellowship Baptist Church on Chicago's South Side is just one modern-day example of the skills common to preacher and performer. Mr. Evans makes records leading his church's 200-voice choir, and can be expected to break into song during his sermon as he struts and holds a microphone that has at least a 50-foot cord.

As Green's latest album, *Truth N' Time*, testifies, popular music is still a part of the preacher's life. What do tunes like his disco version of Lulu's '60s hit "To Sir with Love" have to do with the Lord?

Al Green Enterprises is housed in a modern brick office building set back from Winchester Road in Memphis, Tenn. It is situated behind an older house with a neon sign in front reading "Al Green Hair Port." Al Green Enterprises includes the Al Green International Fan Club, Al Green Hair Products, promotional facilities, Green's offices and a recently upgraded 16-track recording studio worth at least half a million dollars.

From outside, it looks like any other office building. In the foyer is a large photograph of Reverend Green in his white suit sitting on a throne-like chair and smiling. The hustle and bustle of this busy office soon make it obvious that everyone on Al Green's staff is not only efficient but committed.

"Everyone here has concluded that this man is serious about what he's doing," Green explains in his office. Talking with Al Green can be a bit confusing, at least until one realizes that he may refer to himself in the third person ("this man," "Al Green"), or the royal "we," or even the first person "I."

"Now, either I'm with it or I'm not. So if it's all about going to church, then let's go to church. If that's where it's at, then that's where it's at. If it's not, then let us know. But we are willing to do and follow."

At 32, Green seems to have made it. He is the pastor of a large, apparently prosperous church. In 1972 he was voted Best Pop and Rhythm and Blues Vocalist by *Cashbox*, *Billboard* and *Record World* magazines. Then, too, *Rolling Stone* voted him Rock 'n' Roll Pop Star of the Year. His tune "Call Me" was a Grammy nominee in 1973, and in 1975 he received another nomination for "L-o-v-e." Green's most recent major award was for Best Vocalist at the Tokyo Music Festival in June 1978. Many albums and singles have gone gold, and Green's overall record sales top 30 million units.

In 1977, Green became his own producer, and also wrote all the material for *The Belle Album*. Green's songwriting abilities have been recognized by other artists, and his "Take Me to the River" was recorded in 1978 by New Wave rock band Talking Heads on their album *More Songs About Buildings and Food*, by ex-Band drummer and singer Levon Helm on *Levon Helm*, and by the idiosyncratic crooner Bryan Ferry on his latest opus, *The Bride Stripped Bare*.

Al Green's success story begins in a familiar way.

"I was from Forrest City, Arkansas, and I came up being interested in how cotton was planted, how soybeans is picked and how vegetables grow. And listening to Sam Cooke sing spirituals on the radio," Green says while relaxing in the conference room at Al Green Enterprises.

The son of religious parents, Green was forbidden to listen to popular music as a child. "My father says, 'No pop music in the house,'" Green reflects. "That gives me a greater desire for pop music. Because of the longing for it, the idea that I know I can do that. I have this something inside that says that I can do it, and that enhanced it more than anything else."

Al Green formed his first pop group, the Creations, when he was 16. Basically a vocal group, the Creations worked in Grand Rapids, Mich., and the surrounding area with a backup band that later became Jr. Walker and the All Stars.

In 1967, at 21, Green recorded his first single, "Backup Train," written by fellow Creation Palmer James. Released by Bell Records, "Backup Train" was successful enough to put Green the on chitlin circuit.

"When you have one record people have a tendency to put a limit on you. That's all you can do," Green says. "Getting from Bell Records to Hi Records took two years. Doing that, you lose grip on your recording; you kind of go down the drain for a while. And you get used to the drain. It educated me tremendously so that when I did become hooked up with Hi Records and Willie Mitchell, I was well educated in the field."

At Hi Records, Green became part of a hit-making production package that achieved a miraculous degree of success. Working mainly with producer/musician Willie Mitchell and the late Al Jackson Jr., legendary drummer for Booker T. and the MGs, Green had two platinum albums, *I'm Still in Love with You* and *Let's Stay Together*, in 1972, two gold albums, *Living for You* and *Call Me*, in 1973, and another goldie, *Al Green Explores Your Mind*, in 1974. It was back to platinum in 1975 with *Al Green Is Love* and *Greatest Hits II*.

The "Hi sound" of the early '70s was characterized by heavily accented, rudimentary drumming, a muddy bass, crisp, clear high ends and fundamental soul horn riffs played by the Memphis Horns.

Although he is not credited, Al Jackson played drums on Al Green's records in unison with Howard Grimes. "Al Jackson was the most influential drummer that I have ever known. He played things that wouldn't normally be played," Green continues as he picks up his guitar. "It was a

Al Green.
(Rick Ivy)

good package. Al Jackson did the rhythms. Like, [strumming emphatically and singing] 'Let's, let's stay together.' Willie Mitchell would create the music and Al Green would come up with, [singing] 'Let's stay together / Lovin' you forever.' Now Al Jackson's sitting there beating on tables all day but he's got no words. Willie Mitchell was playing on a piano but he had no words. Al Green came along with the words—and boom.

"And so when we had the misfortune of losing Al Jackson [murdered in his home in Memphis], it kind of dampened my spirits as far as the package was concerned because I rode on the rhythmic patterns that he played."

In 1977, armed with a new contract and newly reorganized Hi Records (after its sale to Los Angeles–based Cream Records), Al Green went into his own eight-track studio to produce an album without his former co-producers. The result was *The Belle Album*, which is considered a classic by some critics and fans. The sound was distinct from earlier Al

Green records, but the powerful, gutsy, natural tenor vocal still made the characteristic octave jumps into the contrasting falsetto. The drums were more disco but still ballsy, and the new group pushed the music while at the same time laying back enough to spotlight Green.

By this time Green had been ordained as a preacher and purchased the building that soon became the Full Gospel Tabernacle Church. He wanted to change his sound—certainly not because of lack of commercial success, but for artistic reasons.

Before Green assumed the role of producer, he says, "The music, although it changed, stayed the same in a lot of contexts. And the production pattern remained the same because the drummer is on pot nine, the guitar player is on pot five and it never did change. Once you found that formula, you kept it. Well, that formula was good for seven years, but after that I think it was good to experiment with the fresh, the new, the unknown."

Although Al Green's last two albums, *The Belle Album* and *Truth N' Time*, have been (for him, moderately) commercially successful, they also carry an underlying message. These are not gospel records, but many of the lyrics are designed to preach Christian doctrine.

"The album is gospel," Green asserts. "If you listen to 'Happy Days' and ask yourself, 'Why?' it says, 'I've found myself a brand-new friend.' It says, 'I've found a new way of living / I've found a new way of giving.' And what is that? Well, just keep looking up.

"'Wait Here' is actually taken out of the Book of Job. When Job was sick and so on and so forth, he said, 'I believe I'll wait until my change comes.' Well, what does 'Wait Here' say? 'I believe I'll wait here 'til my change comes.' But if you didn't know that, it would slip right by you. The lines are taken from the concept: 'All things in time.'"

Al Green seems supremely confident; unquestionably, he has been extremely successful and is unusually talented. On the nationally broadcasted public television show *Soundstage*, Green was filmed both in interview and performance in Chicago. The audiences for these performances, typical of television studio crowds, are generally distant and restrained. Even blues superstars Bobby Bland and B.B. King received only polite applause in their *Soundstage* appearances.

By the end of Green's filming, the crowd was dancing in the aisles, clapping and swaying in rhythm to his infectious beat. When he approached the edge of the stage, they clamored to touch him while he threw scarves out to the audience a la Elvis Presley. How does Green feel about performing?

"I'd be so scared before I'd go out onstage to do a concert. I've never talked about this before with people, I don't know, these things—I just don't talk about them. But I'd be so scared. I'm talking about my flesh trembled, right?

"I'd say my prayers before every show, standing there backstage behind the curtain." Green mimics an emcee's voice: "Now, ladies and gentlemen…

"Well, I'm praying because I'm scared. And I want to do a good job. And some people assume, 'Well, Al Green, he's gonna do a good job. He's been doing this for 10, 12 years.' But I have the possibility of failing as well as succeeding. So I always pray for the success of things. I'd be so scared before going on the stage I'd actually be trembling—until I'd sing the first song and then I'd be OK."

Green has taken prayer much further in the last two years. When talking about his metamorphosis from soul superstar to religious leader, he always speaks of himself in the third person.

Asked to explain the shift in lifestyle, Green responds, "It's called the new Al Green. You had the first Al Green and that Al Green lived from point one to point 30. The first Al Green wants to grow and come up to a point where he attains success and the exposure and the records and the great opera houses and so on. He does that. The gold records are in the office on the wall.

"But the Al Green on the inside—not the one that you see on the outside—wants something else. I've already done the theaters, the opera houses. The new Al Green is first of all quickened, converted, which means to be turned around about face, if you will. He's converted, and what has he converted? He's converted his ways. To be anything new, you have to be something different."

Putting away his guitar and speaking deliberately, Reverend Green continues. "There are things done by the old Al Green that the new Al Green most certainly cannot do or hesitated to do. You can't spoil the new Al Green. You got to give him a chance to grow. Give him a chance to wean hisself from the bottle. He's just got here. He's fresh; he's brand-new. He don't know anything. Really, he's just a kid.

"The new Al Green is a different Al Green. The new Al Green is a free expression Al Green, the believer. Al Green, the guy that wants to go by Mama and Daddy's rules, not by what I had thought of previously to go by—do my own thing, play with women and Cadillac cars. No. The new Al Green says it's not what you have. It's what's in your head. It's not in material things; we must build our hopes on things that's gonna last a little longer."

Al Green is part of a tiny group of religious leaders who have international name recognition. Popular recording stars often lend their names and talents to worthy causes, but few devote their position of power totally towards a specific, personal, humanitarian purpose.

"My ministry has been given to me to preach the gospel of Jesus Christ. Music speaks louder than words. I can reach many more people by singing what I want to say than talking. So I just sing what I want to say.

"The idea is to reach as many people as possible. Just gobble up nations and nations of people. We all have a responsibility to reach as many people as we possibly can. And then when you reach those people, don't shove anything down their throats. Just say, 'Here it is. Listen to it for yourself.' Let every man be persuaded by his own opinion."

Al Green is smug about his business abilities. "They say that I'm one of the best businessmen in the world," he boasts. "I think that has to do with the last contract that I negotiated while my lawyer was out of town. I think it's a good contract. I think it's a fair contract. I think it was overwhelmingly successful in reference to us, what we have to do, what was asked of us. And I think the price was fair."

But confident as he may be in his business abilities, the fact remains that his last platinum record was *Al Green Is Love*, in 1975. The promotional people associated with Green are not forthcoming with explanations for the drastic drop in record sales. Although the self-produced *The Belle Album* was the subject of many rave reviews, the buying public did not share those critics' views. Turning the precious-metal trick was formerly easy for Al Green; between 1972 and 1975 he had seven gold albums, four of which went platinum through Green's alchemy. But at press time, *Truth N' Time* was mired at number 57 on *Billboard*'s Soul chart.

Maybe his hair products are doing well, but Green's music is taking a commercial beating. One might yield to the temptation to say that only the hairdresser knows for sure, but if that's the case here, the hairdresser isn't talking. Perhaps it's a combination of poor distribution and lack of promotion, or maybe the singer has just traded his pop audience for a congregation. The old Al Green reached a phenomenal peak during those four years, '72–'75. But anyone associated with the new Al Green must agree that the Reverend has a new mountain in front of him.

Maynard Ferguson.
(Columbia Records)

July 1980

Maynard Ferguson: Rocky Road to Fame and Fortune

by Lee Underwood

Maynard "Double-High C" Ferguson, who considers himself to be a "multi-directional" trumpet player and bandleader/composer/producer, has entertained international audiences for more than three decades.

Today's parents and grandparents thrilled to his screaming, *DownBeat* poll–winning high and double-high C's in the famous 1950-'52 Stan Kenton band. They remember Maynard's 1956 Birdland Dream Band (featuring Al Cohn, Clark Terry, Clifford Brown and Ray Brown), as well as his 1957–'59 13-piece "jazz farm," which included Don Ellis, Don Sebesky, Joe Zawinul, Bill Holman and Chuck Mangione. That band recorded *A Message from Newport* and won second place (behind Count Basie) in the 1959 *DownBeat* Readers Poll.

Today's generation of high schoolers and collegians knows Ferguson and his 13-piece band for his Grammy-nominated version of Bill Conti's "Gonna Fly Now" (the theme from *Rocky*). They know him for his follow-up disco hit "Rocky II" (highlighted by Sylvester Stallone's spastic pummeling of a real punching bag in the background). They know him for his flamboyant extravaganzas of still other themes from film, TV and classical music: *Summer of '42*, *Battlestar Galactica*, *Star Wars*, *Star Trek*, "Maria" from *West Side Story*, "Scheherazade," and, of course, his famous "Pagliacci," which he played live at the closing ceremonies of the 1976 Montreal Olympic Games.

Ferguson is quick to point out that he has also recorded Sonny Rollins' fast-paced "Airegin," John Coltrane's "Naima" and Thelonious Monk's "'Round Midnight."

Careful not to offend those who don't care for movie themes or vintage jazz, Maynard has also recorded pop tunes by James Taylor and the Beatles, and rock tunes by Stevie Wonder, Paul McCartney and Stanley Clarke. Multi-directional, indeed.

Born in Verdun, Quebec, on May 4, 1928, Ferguson, now 52, studied piano and violin at age four; enrolled at the French Conservatory of Music at age 9; studied all reed and brass instruments; settled on trumpet, and began leading his own jazz band at age 15.

After playing with Boyd Raeburn, Charlie Barnet and Jimmy Dorsey in the late '40s, he joined Kenton and attained international fame. During the late '60s, he lived in England and India, signed with CBS in 1969, returned to the States in 1973, and has been popular ever since with such albums as *MF Horn*, (which included "MacArthur Park" and led to *MF Horn II* and *III*), *Chameleon*, *Primal Scream*, *Conquistador* (with Jay Chattaway's arrangement of the "Rocky" theme), and two recent albums he produced himself, *Carnival and Hot*.

Maynard has long been interested in music education and in designing new musical instruments. For years, he has conducted clinics in high schools and colleges. He has also designed the MF Horn series of instruments for Holton-LeBlanc, including the Firebird (combination of valve/slide trumpet) and the Superbone (combination valve/slide trombone).

Fame, the most unstable drug there is, makes peculiar demands. On the one hand, people listen to what the celebrity wants to say. On the other hand, the celebrity who takes a strong stand risks offending those who do not agree. Commercially successful and politically astute, musical celebrity and veteran of a thousand interviews, Maynard Ferguson knows all of the pitfalls, which is perhaps one of the reasons he is affectionately known by some as "the Fox."

The position which Maynard has attained, and for which he deserves all due credit, raises several serious questions among those musicians the world over who wrestle in their souls with what they see as a conflict between art and commerce—often feeling, as trombonist Glenn Ferris once explained, that the dictates of commerce can be antithetical to the dictates of art.

"A lot of musicians," said Ferris, "are racking their brains out, feeling that their music is not worth pursuing because there aren't any money people hanging around saying, 'This is where it's at. This is hip.' Doubt sets in; and the musician winds up putting down the true flowering of himself and his music. The expression of his awareness of life through music becomes sidetracked into being what the system demands and applauds and pays for.... This economic trip has nothing to do with music. It's business, and business has to do only with who you know and who likes you and which of their 'bags' you fit into—they've got a 'bag' for everything." ("Profile," *DB, Dec. 15, 1977*)

Ferguson: I always have that fun thing with composers and arrangers. I say, 'Are you sure what my thing is?' As soon as they say, 'Yeah, I know what your thing is,' I say, 'Great. Now do something different.' That is, something which is me, but which I don't impose on other people.

Basie, for example, has sounded the same for many years, and yet I can still sit in front of that band and thrill to it. The same thing with Ellington, even with his great creativity. The same thing with the Beatles. I refer only to their validity. I have no interest in talking about the things that don't enhance me. Their music is their right, their privilege, their art.

DownBeat: At the same time, from the age of four to the present, you have plunged into all kinds of music, and your key word has been "change." To refuse to comment on music you don't like is, of course, politically tactful. That way, you don't offend somebody such as Basie, who has not changed. Nor have Oscar Peterson, Bill

Evans, Dizzy Gillespie and numerous others. They find their sound, stick with it, and do not evolve conceptually. That kind of a remark is not necessarily a criticism. It can be a simple, legitimate observation.

Ferguson: I can't sit there and listen to Oscar Peterson play his buns off and then say, "Boy, that was really boring." If I heard Oscar right now, I know I would love it.

DownBeat: The question is not whether Oscar is great or not. We know he is. The question involves whether or not you as a musician feel free enough to articulate what you truly feel about the work of other artists, thereby giving the readers insight into both you and those other works.

Ferguson: A few years ago, I went to hear Oscar after not hearing him for seven years. I was thrilled. I have no preconception about whether I'm going to be bored or entertained. It's a great pleasure not to be bored.

DownBeat: In 1978, your version of Bill Conti's "Rocky" theme was nominated for a Grammy. You've been playing it virtually every night since you recorded it in 1977. How do you keep from getting bored with it?

Ferguson: Duke Ellington played "Take the A Train" for a zillion years. And for many years, nobody looked at Maynard Ferguson. Now they do. I love that independence.

DownBeat: Independence?

Ferguson: I love the independence of if I never have another hit single, we're still gonna burn it out every night and we know we'll have good albums. I enjoy doing my own thing and being contemporary, and doing it honestly. I really enjoy playing "Rocky," and if you listen to it, you'll see that, in person, my solos are not the same, and the drummer doesn't play it the same way.

DownBeat: When you were 15 and forming your first band, what was your original vision of yourself? Have you become what you wanted to be? What did you aspire to?

Ferguson: I felt it was amazing that people applauded me more than the other guys in the band, because a lot of the other guys were over 30 then, and I was busy learning from them. People liked what I played, and musicians were either dazzled or offended. It's been that way almost my whole career.

If you listen to some of my earlier things, like "All the Things You Are," I started doing things that I stopped doing. I

felt inhibited. I was afraid the guys wouldn't like me. I've always wanted the guys to like me, and that includes people like critic Leonard Feather and all the guys who are a lot older than me.

Also, I'm a great believer in change. I don't know what I said in my last *DownBeat* interview, but I reserve the right to say the opposite today, if that's what I feel.

DownBeat: How would you describe those changes?

Ferguson: When you say you didn't have an idol when you were a kid, it sounds politically evasive, but that's really the truth, in that I had so many of them, not just one.

Certainly Dizzy was an influence, Roy Eldridge, Louis Armstrong, and all of Duke's players. I hate to say that, because it leaves out so many others. I've played free music with John Surman in England, and I love classical improvisation, a bag of mine on fluegelhorn.

On "Pagliacci," for example, I don't play a single phrase from the jazz bag. I do my Enrico Caruso thing. Sometimes I walk in the audience, sometimes I walk over by the piano and play acoustically beside David Ramsey. We never play it the same way twice. If you picked up your guitar there, and you played in the Segovia bag, I would stay with you harmonically, but without playing anything from the jazz bag.

DownBeat: Does "Rocky" give you the identity you really want?

Ferguson: When you say "want"—Peter Philbin of Columbia heard my band, then caught a sneak preview of a movie called *Rocky*. He and others thought the picture was going to be a hit. Arranger Jay Chattaway and pianist Bob James and about seven other heavyweights thought it would be really hip if my band did it. So we did it, and it took off. Of course, if the film had flopped, then our single wouldn't have had time to sustain itself.

DownBeat: In relation to "Pagliacci," Leonard Feather discussed what he called excesses, the flamboyant big sound, the expansiveness. Have these elements not become a kind of standard Maynard Ferguson formula for commercial success?

Ferguson: No more than it was a formula for Enrico Caruso. Surely, as much as I may try, I'm probably not as flamboyant as Enrico. I mean, his white gloves, his walking among the people, his singing.

Besides, opera is not as formulated as we may think it is. We don't understand the words. We are moved by the vocal music, the pure music of it, without the words. When I listen to opera, I'm not spending my time with a dictionary. I'm more interested in the music itself, the music of the voice.

DownBeat: The question was not directed toward a discussion of opera, but toward you and the concept of commercial formulas. To what extent can you maintain your allegiance to artistic change and growth, while at the same time complying with the commercial requirements of giving people more "Rocky," more "Battlestar Galactica"?

Ferguson: I think it has to do with the advancement of young people. They are really interested in artistry, and I find it really important to base everything on enjoyment. So I go my own way, changing my mind freely, delighted whenever I discover something new.

DownBeat: The suggestion of the question was that perhaps for some time you have not changed your mind.

Ferguson: If I haven't changed, my mind has nevertheless been open to it. You mentioned "Pagliacci." I'd love to know the formula we played that in.

DownBeat: That was my word. Your music and Leonard Feather's comments in the *L.A. Times* prompted me to ask that question about formulas. He said, "The florid, fulsome adaptation of the 84-year-old aria from *I Pagliacci* is the kind of vehicle Harry James might have been expected to use in 1941. As long as the public exists to eat up excesses of this kind, there will always be performers to minister to its hunger."

Ferguson: That's all right. Leonard was a man in 1941 when I was a young boy. To me, there's nothing wrong with 1941, or else he wouldn't have loved Harry James [Feather was 26 in '41].

DownBeat: I don't think he was saying he loved Harry James. I think he was suggesting that possibly your "Pagliacci" was calculated commercialism, derivative, excessive, and dated.

Ferguson: Leonard and I go out to dinner with our wives and have a good time. I love one of his lines. He said, "As long as we agree to disagree, Maynard." I said, "I don't agree." I don't go out to dinner with Leonard because I agree to disagree. I do it because he came up to Ojai where I live, and he's talking about his kids, and I'm talking about mine.

Anything other that that, unless he plays my trumpet for me, is kind of silly.

I'm certainly not going to write his articles for him. He's got to do his gig, and I've got to do mine.

DownBeat: Again that nicely evades the essence of the question, which is not about critics in general or about Leonard in particular, but about a specific issue regarding your music.

Ferguson: My gig has to please me. If I sound like a 1941 Harry James to Leonard, well, it's not my job to give a rebuttal. His job is to get paid so many dollars per word. My job is to enjoy myself playing the trumpet.

Romanticism is still a part of music. I also reserve the right to snake out. I don't think I sound very romantic when I'm playing a fast tempo "Airegin."

DownBeat: There are many musicians coming out of schools and clinics now. Besides your band and a few others, where can they work? Are we over-producing musicians?

Ferguson: No, I don't think we can ever over-produce musicians. Many of them are not only musicians. They are doctors and lawyers who also love playing the piano or the tenor sax.

DownBeat: Do you still use live auditions?

Ferguson: No, because too many good musicians don't play well at auditions, so I listen to cassette tapes of their work and go by that.

DownBeat: You are well known as a clinician. How might today's clinics be improved?

Ferguson: I used to do a lot more than I'm doing now, and I miss doing them, but when you're playing seven nights a week in halls or universities, colleges, junior high schools, which is what I love, that's when you know that really young people are into your thing. We've been doing this success thing enough now, and we're suddenly getting probes from Las Vegas and places like that, where, for a while, we were Death Valley in those places, because if you're a kid's favorite, as you know, the main disease in Las Vegas is children. If you really want to bore, show up in Las Vegas with seven children like I did at the Tropicana once, and they go "Yeeeech." I mean definitely, you know, your children, I mean… Number one, they can't go across the lounge, because they have to cut through the gambling casino; they have so many like no-no's, unbelievable. All my kids used to play the slot machines. I think that that's a Ferguson trait right there. As soon as

you're told you can't do something, you know. They all got busted. Every one of them got busted in the lounge at least once when we were playing the Tropicana years ago. You know, like looking around, then slapping a quarter in and pulling the thing, and then the nice man says, "What room is your daddy in?" "Oh my daddy's conducting the show right now." [Laughter.]

DownBeat: So much for clinics. What will you be doing on your new as-yet-untitled album that you might consider to be a step forward?

Ferguson: It's a little early to answer that one, because the album is not yet completed. One of the things I enjoy is the work of that great Indian violinist Subramaniam, who is a good friend of mine, so I got together with trombonist/arranger Nick Lane, and I think we'll do something in the Indian bag. It's a difficult piece of music, so I don't know yet whether it will go on the album, but I hope we can include it.

Clark Terry: Big B-A-D Brassman

by Larry Birnbaum

"Nobody wants to give me my just due," says Clark Terry. "I've always been a boy and never a man." With that, he leans back in his chair and emits a hearty laugh. No, Clark Terry is not a bitter man. After all, he is one of the most successful, renowned, and certainly busiest of jazz musicians today—maintaining an incredibly hectic schedule of concert tours, record dates, and school clinics that keeps him in all but perpetual motion. Still, he remains better known for his burlesque scat singing and for his 14-year tenure with Doc Severinsen's *Tonight Show* band than for the brilliant and distinctive trumpet technique that first brought him to prominence in the bands of Count Basie and Duke Ellington.

"I used to do all of Quincy Jones' contracting," Clark relates, "and then a friend of mine began to do it. He stopped calling

Clark Terry, left, and pianist Hubie Blake share a laugh at the Molde Jazz Festival in Norway, 1973. (Randi Hultin)

me for Quincy's dates, so I called him up and asked him why. He told me, 'When you're in the section, even though you might not play the lead, your sound is too individual—it sticks out too much.' That's the kind of left-handed compliment I've been getting all my life."

Terry's dazzlingly bright and fluid attack may be instantly recognizable, but his style is not so easily pigeonholed. Inspired by Louis Armstrong and Roy Eldridge, he embraced the bebop innovations of Dizzy Gillespie, though never to the point of imitation. An amazingly versatile player, he has been labeled a progressive and a mainstreamer, but perhaps it is more appropriate to categorize him simply as a St. Louis trumpeter.

From the days of riverboat legend Charlie Creath—the "king of the cornet"—to Terry's early admirer Miles Davis and the exuberantly contemporary Lester Bowie, St. Louis has been home to an extraordinary succession of fine trumpeters. "New Orleans was the cradle of

jazz," Clark says, "and many of the New Orleans musicians played on the riverboats that came up the Mississippi. A lot of those cats got off the boats in St. Louis, so this is why St. Louis became one of the big spots."

As a youth, Terry heard local trumpet players like Sleepy Tomlin, Mouse Randolph and Dewey Jackson. "One of the musicians who influenced me the most," he asserts, "was Dud Bascomb. Not too many people even know who he was, but he played all those beautiful trumpet solos with the Erskine Hawkins band, the Tuxedo Junction band. He was a beautiful player with a unique harmonic approach, much more original than most of the trumpet players on the scene at that time.

"There was also a lot of good blues singing and playing around St. Louis," he adds. "I even played with a little blues band called Dollar Bill and the Small Change." Clark drew on his memories of old bluesmen to create his biggest hit, "Mumbles," a hilariously unintelligible scatted parody of 12-bar inebriation. "That was on an album

called *Oscar Peterson Trio Plus One*. We had finished the session and I asked Oscar to let me do this thing as a favor, and he liked it so it ended up on the record."

The blues left its mark on Terry's instrumental approach as well. "When a kid came out to play for the first time, one of the prime prerequisites was to be able to bend a note and moan. You couldn't come out and play the blues with a straight pure tone." Clark's superlatively controlled embouchure—he often performs mouthpiece solos—produces a rich palette of smears and blue notes, and has produced some critical confusion as well.

Rex Stewart, his predecessor in the Ellington band, introduced the novel effect of partially depressing the pistons of his horn to alter its pitch. The technique is generally attributed to Terry as well, but he adamantly denies the connection. "I had never even heard Rex Stewart. Leonard Feather told that fib, and it's been sticking to me like a leech ever since. He said I play half-valves, and the only time I ever play half-valves is when the damn valves stick. I can't even play 'Boy Meets Horn.'"

More clearly established is that "C.T." is almost single-handedly responsible for the revival of the fluegelhorn, which by the mid-'50s had become a pawnshop relic. "I was always hearing saxophone players get that more intimate sound, and that's probably why I fell in love with the fluegelhorn. The very first note I ever played on fluegelhorn was on a record called *Taylor Made Jazz* by Billy Taylor. They didn't make fluegelhorns then, and there were very few on the scene; the only cats I knew of that had fluegelhorns were Shorty Rogers, Emmett Berry, and Miles. I had been working with this technical adviser down at Selmer; I asked him if they could reconstruct it, and he said, 'Yeah, I think we can.'"

Having brought the buttery-toned fluegel back into production, Terry championed its acceptance in the recording studios. "They used to put trumpet, cornet, and fluegelhorn in the same category, so we told them about the saxophone players. Tenor sax, alto, and flute are all different instruments, and each time a saxophone player has to switch horns on a date, he gets extra money. They refer to those as doubles, and we had to fight hard with the union to make the fluegelhorn a legitimate double, but we finally succeeded."

The consummate master of the instrument, Terry uses the fluegel not just for mellow ballad colors, but on up-tempo blues as well—and with the full speed and mobility of the trumpet. He can play acrobatic triple-tongued runs or delicate legato passages with equal facility and in nearly any context. Critically neglected in recent years, he remains a popular favorite, as much for his personal warmth and unflagging good humor as for his broad-ranging virtuosity.

Born in St. Louis in 1920, Clark was smitten by the trumpet early on, but was too poor to afford one. "I wanted a trumpet so badly when I was a kid that I concocted a little gadget out of a coiled-up piece of garden hose, with a kerosene funnel stuck in it to look like a bell and a piece of gas pipe on the other end to look like a mouthpiece. It wasn't too musical at all, but it had a trumpet-type sound, just a blatant noisy sound.

"When I got to high school, there were no more trumpets available. The only thing left was an old ragged valve trombone, so the trumpet teacher, Clarence Wilson, said, 'Take this and get out of here. It has the same fingering and you can make more noise with it anyway.' So I took it.

"That was at Vashon High School in St. Louis, and my friend Ernie Wilkins was attending a rival high school, Sumner. When we started our own little jazz band, I used to walk all the way out to the west end of town to have our rehearsals, about nine or 10 miles. We played Ernie's first arrangement, 'Forrest Fire,' which he wrote in honor of Jimmy Forrest, who was a class ahead of me in school."

Terry was a high school boxer, "Until I found out that boxing and trumpet playing don't mix. You can't play with a fat lip." Instead he developed his musical prowess. "I always enjoyed practicing. A lot of kids like to swim and roller skate, but I found that practicing was fun for me. Later, in the Navy, I used to practice out of a clarinet book, because I always wanted to play fast passages, and I noticed that the clarinet books had faster things to play."

Times were hard when Clark moved in with his older sister. "I needed to earn my board and keep, so I used to haul ashes. Years ago they used to have mills, fractions of a penny, that you'd get in change. They were round paper things, and I used to advertise on the back of the mills, 'Let the Terry Brothers do your hauling.'"

After high school he traveled through the South with the Rueben and Cherry Carnival. "That was a biggie, a railroad show, and then in the winter we got on a smaller show. One time in Mississippi, the merry-go-round broke down—it actually did—and we had to get back to St. Louis. The guy who ran the carnival had a monkey show with a ride and about 15 monkeys, and Willie Austin, the band director, conned him into letting us ride back with him in this truck. Willie rode in the cab with the driver, and the rest of us were all in the back with the monkeys for 750 miles."

Terry hit the road again with blues singer Ida Cox's "Darktown Scandals" show. "Ida Cox was a great experience. We used to travel in an old broken-down bus, and every time we'd get to a hill, everybody had to get out and push. There was a midget named Prince on the show, and he just sat in the bus, so one day Ida Cox asked him what he was doing there. 'I'm too small,' he said, so she said, 'We got a tiny little place for you to push.' I'll never forget that."

Back in St. Louis, he worked with Fate Marable, whose celebrated (though unrecorded) riverboat bands bred talents from Louis Armstrong to Jimmy Blanton. "Fate was quite a character—changed his

name from Marble to Marable. Whenever Fate was going to fire a person, he'd take one of the fire axes from off the wall of the boat and put it in the cat's seat. He would call the rest of the band in early, and when the guy came on board, they'd start to play. Naturally the cat would figure he was late, and as he ran up the band would be playing 'There'll Be Some Changes Made.' But we all believe that that's how the term 'getting the ax' got started."

In 1942, Terry enlisted in the Navy, and for the next three years he played in an all-star band at Chicago's Great Lakes base with Ernie Wilkins and Gerald Wilson, under the leadership of altoist Willie Smith of the Jimmy Lunceford band. On leave, he journeyed to New York's 52nd Street, where he saw "Bird and Diz, Ben Webster, Coleman Hawkins and Don Byas. We got there just when George Shearing got off the boat from England."

Upon his discharge, he briefly joined Lionel Hampton, then spent 18 months as straw boss and lead trumpeter with the George Hudson band. "George Hudson is a skinny little trumpet player out of St. Louis," Clark explains. "He built a reputation with the house band at the Club Plantation, because he had musicians like Singleton Palmer, Weasel Parker, and myself, conscientious cats who really loved to play things right. When acts would come in, we would rehearse their music like it was our own, and they never heard their music played so beautifully. The word got around, and we had a reputation even before we got to New York. When we did get there, we made history. Our little tenor player, Willie 'Weasel' Parker, had such a fantastic solo on 'Body and Soul' that Illinois Jacquet, who was a big star at the time, ran backstage and protested, 'Take it out! Take that number off!'

"Then I went to Los Angeles to join Charlie Barnet. He had an integrated band, and it worked because Charlie was a millionaire, and he didn't care about anything. He called me up, and I took the train to California and went to Gerald Wilson's home, then over to Hermosa Beach where the band was playing. They were on the air when I walked up, and in the middle of a coast-to-coast radio broadcast, Charlie Barnet signals that I should get my horn out. The announcer says, 'And now our new trumpet player,' and I had to go right into the number. I don't remember the tune, but luckily I was familiar with the changes."

His 10 months with Barnet were followed by stints with Charlie Ventura and Eddie "Mr. Cleanhead" Vinson. "The first commercial records I ever made were with Eddie Vinson and his big band," he says, "and two of the tunes we did were 'Railroad Porter Blues' and 'Kidney Stew.'" Terry and Vinson have been reunited on Clark's latest Pablo album, *Yes, the Blues*, performing those and other bluesy chestnuts.

Count Basie beckoned him to join his faltering organization in 1948. "I joined Basie with the big band at first, and then he encountered some financial problems, and his office instructed him to break it down to a small group. I went back to St. Louis, and Basie told me to look around for a tenor player, so I brought Bob Graff to Chicago and we opened at a place downtown called the Brass Rail with Buddy DeFranco, Bob Graff, myself, Freddy Green, Gus Johnson and Jimmy Lewis on bass. Bob Graff went with Woody Herman, and we got Wardell Gray and then Charlie Rouse, and we recorded with Charlie Rouse, Serge Chaloff and Buddy.

"Shortly after that, Basie went back with the big band and he needed an alto player. I told him I knew somebody in St. Louis and he said, 'Call him up!'—he was in the steam cabinet at the Strand Theater with his head sticking out. I went to his phone and called Ernie Wilkins, who had never played alto in his life, and very quietly I said, 'Can you get an alto? Do you want to come and join Basie?' So he borrowed one of those silver-colored student saxophone—we called them 'gray ghosts'—and I brought him up to see Basie the next day. The band was still skunked, so I suggested that Ernie might write some material. He wrote all those great tunes for Joe Williams, and from that point the band skyrocketed, all because of that whispered phone call."

Basie still had a few combo engagements to fulfill, and in 1951 Duke Ellington dropped in on one of these and discreetly hired Clark away. "Duke said he would put me on salary and that I should go home to St. Louis and wait until the band came through, and I would just happen to join them there. So I gave my notice to Basie—he took back the raise he had just given me—and I went back to St. Louis and joined Duke. And for the next nine years I attended what I call the University of Ellingtonia, because I learned an awful lot through osmosis, just being there with him."

Terry's reputation spread rapidly among musicians, and he began to record—as a sideman and under his own name—with many of the top names in jazz, from Art Blakey and Horace Silver to Johnny Griffin and even Thelonious Monk. Monk was so impressed with Clark's work as a last-minute replacement for Ernie Henry on *Brilliant Corners* that he agreed to accompany him on Terry's own *In Orbit* LP.

Clark left Ellington in 1959 to join Quincy Jones in Europe in the Harold Arlen blues opera, *Free and Easy*, returning to New York and a job with the NBC staff a year later. He became a *Tonight Show* regular, supplementing his income with commercial studio work, until the networks dissolved their staffs and *Tonight* moved to the West Coast. "It would be difficult to categorize that band," says Terry. "You had to swing, you had to be legit, you had to play any kind of music that came along. It was just a unique band."

His television exposure led to an ongoing involvement in education. "People started requesting different members of the *Tonight Show* band to appear at public schools and colleges. The instrument companies came in as sponsors, and soon I was into the clinic circuit full blast. It's fun—it keeps you alert, it keeps you abreast of things, and it keeps your mind young and fertile."

Through the mid-'60s, Terry co-led a highly successful combo with trombonist Bob Brookmeyer, and by the end of the decade the enterprising trumpeter had incorporated his own recording and publishing company, Etoile, with Phil Woods and Melba Liston. In 1970, his newly formed Big B-A-D Band played Carnegie Hall, going on to tour Europe in 1973. "Phil Woods wrote the original book, and we've had a lot of good players in the band, cats like Jimmy Nottingham, Ray Copeland, Frank Wess, Jimmy Heath, Duke Jordan, and of course Ernie Wilkins and Chris Woods, who became more-or-less regulars."

Memphis-born Chris Woods, a St. Louis transplant, is the only remaining veteran in the band's current incarnation, which comprises students and young professionals recruited through notices posted at colleges around the country. The group's original material was similarly solicited. The 18-piece ensemble packs a brassy, swinging punch with solid section work and agile bop-oriented solos. Altoist Woods, who played alongside Terry in George Hudson's band, doubles as road manager and featured soloist, but inevitably Clark steals the show with his timelessly modern style and glorious chops.

The indefatigable Terry divides his time between the road, studio and the campus, touring Europe several times a year with his big band or with stellar combos like Oscar Peterson's. He has recorded prolifically for Norman Granz's Pablo label in the past few years, in settings that range from swing-era tributes to Third Stream concert works by composer Charles Schwartz.

Terry is one of the few jazz artists who have achieved broad popularity without sacrificing integrity. "I played commercial dates to subsidize what I believed in, but I stuck to what I believed in. I found that to be the easier route, to stay involved and to stay out of the controversial categorizing thing. You just stay yourself and play things that people can recognize, and you do it your way."

November 1981

Freddie Hubbard: Money Talks, Bebop Walks

by Steve Bloom

"Give me five minutes, Bloom. You know we're gonna do it."

With that, Freddie Hubbard ducks back into his dressing room—which is more like a hall closet for two at the New York club Fat Tuesday's. It is five minutes before two in the morning, and though the music has stopped, the procession of Hubbard's long-time-no-see friends and other reasonably good-looking well-wishers marches on. Actually, there was one point this evening when I almost got my interview. Between sets, Freddie moved upstairs to the restaurant for a quick steak platter. But then, at the exact moment I was pumping my first question, a smallish gentleman with a strong resemblance to Truman Capote

Freddie Hubbard and singer Nina Simone together in Boston in 1987. (Herb Snitzer)

materialized. It was Creed Taylor, the former president of CTI Records, for whom Hubbard recorded what are arguably his best dates of the late '60s. Later for me, it was hastily determined.

I should have been annoyed, but I wasn't. Hubbard and his New York–assembled quartet—pianist Kenny Barron, bassist Buster Williams, drummer Al Foster and saxman David Schnitter—had just offered two wonderful sets of sho' nuff jazz, from Hubbard's "Little Sunflower" to "Body and Soul," that had the joint jumpin'. And Freddie was burnin'. He soared from one octave to the next with the ease of a Concorde's trans-Atlantic flight. He'd reach out and grab the high C and hold on to it for what seemed the equivalent of a 40-hour work week and, after he dropped back down, faces in the audience appeared to quiver in awe. Hubbard, who seemed on a mission of sorts, pulled out all his once familiar stops. He still has the chops.

"People been sayin' 'Freddie lost his chops,'" Hubbard tells me when we finally sat down for a chat at half-past two. "I went into fusion. It didn't work. I just can't fit in. I wanna play too much. I've been through so many different styles—Slide Hampton, J.J. Johnson, Sonny [Rollins], Art [Blakey], 'Trane, Gunther Schuller, Ornette [Coleman]. I had to make up my mind who Freddie Hubbard was. I have my own identity now. But there was a point when I wondered if people really liked me.

"Everyone thought I was going after the money," Freddie rambles on. "I'm the type of cat that likes to venture into all kinds of music. So what if I play on Billy Joel's record? I know McCoy [Tyner] and Cecil [Taylor] have stuck straight on out with their thing, but my lifestyle is different. I wanna live good. When Columbia gave me money, I moved to L.A., bought my house, cars, a pool. But then I started acting weird, like telling jokes at concerts. I

ain't Flip Wilson."

Suddenly, we notice all but one light in the now nearly deserted club has been extinguished. We get the message. On our way upstairs and out onto the New York street, Freddie explains that this week at Fat Tuesday's has been a "spiritual one" for him. "Things are too relaxed in L.A.," the 43-year-old trumpeter complains as we search for an empty cab. "People are constantly asking me, 'Why are you here?' I think I'm gonna move back to New York for a while. You know of any apartments for rent?"

Two months later I dial Hubbard long-distance, New York to Berkeley. Freddie's in the Bay Area adding some final touches to his Fantasy debut album, *Splash*. Earlier in the year, Columbia gave Hubbard his walking papers after eight albums. Freddie strolled right over to Fantasy, his sixth record label, which he says had been itching to sign him ever since he came to terms with Columbia back in 1974. "I'm producing it," he quickly brags. "I doubt if you'll know any of the cats on it, though—they don't have no names. Studio guys. Hey, are you the guy that interviewed me back in New York?"

I explain who I am and that this publication has assigned me the task of examining his musical career in print, "*DownBeat*?" he asks incredulously. "No shit. I haven't read *DownBeat* in a long time. Aren't they a rock & roll magazine now?… Hey, when's Miles playing?" The Kool/Newport Festival is scheduled to commence later in the week, with Davis and his newest quintet slotted for an appearance some 10 days into the program. Of course, everyone's talking.

"He's playin' again, huh?" Hubbard asks. "That's great, man, 'cause he can play. Only thing is when you lay off the trumpet for a long time it gets kinda weird. You know who else I'm looking forward to hearing? This cat Wynton Marsalis — I've been hearing a lot about him."

Totally impromptu, Hubbard begins a discourse on the art of jazz trumpeting. "See, when you're 19 [which Marsalis is], it's very hard to swing. It takes time to learn how to swing. You can play all the notes, but, like, Lee [Morgan] was the best mutha I knew in terms of being able to swing at a young age. He had the most feeling of the young cats. I was like Clifford Brown. I was copying him right off the record. The trumpet takes time. Not too many trumpet players who can swing anyway.

"I heard him [Marsalis] in Holland," he says, once again shifting topics in his none-too-discreet way. "I was walking around the place [Northsea Jazz Festival] and I hear someone and I say, 'Who the hell is that? It's not Woody [Shaw].…' I couldn't think of anybody else who can play. But I haven't really heard him. Well, when he gets through with that [his summer tour with Herbie Hancock, Ron Carter and Tony Williams], he'll be something 'cause Tony'll take him on a trip. He's kind of heavy back there. He'll get his chops together anyway."

I wonder if he would have liked to again accompany Hancock (who is producing Marsalis' debut album on Columbia) and company like he did three years ago in the V.S.O.P. tour? "I had to get out of that," Freddie says, "'cause I felt like they were trying to get me to take Miles' place—I don't know. I'm not playing that anymore. Anyway, I've been busy. I've

been running around the world. I did one date in Germany, five record dates in Italy—y'know, they just recorded each night. It was pretty good, it got me out of the hole. I went to Texas—where else did I go? A bunch of places.

"Know what I miss most about New York? The drummers. You can't find any decent drummers but in New York—most of the cats are there. Al Foster knocked me out. In a small place like that [Fat Tuesday's] you have to be very conscious about stuff like low ceilings—it was the first time I heard a drummer play with those kinds of dynamics in a long time. Billy Higgins could probably do it. And Tony. The drummers I like really actually change the way I play. They make me sound different. Like, I always loved Elvin [Jones]—that style of playing. But in California, they don't have that concept—that consistency and drive I'm accustomed to—so when I'm playing, there are a lot of things I'd like to go ahead and try that doesn't make sense trying 'cause it's not gonna sound right 'cause they're not hitting.

"It's so competitive in New York," Hubbard continues. "When I first came there [from Indianapolis in 1960], it took me six weeks before I had the courage to play at a jam session. I went up to Count Basie's every Monday night. I'd just sit there scared stiff. There were so many musicians—good ones—who wanted to get up there and show they could play. The sixth week I finally took my horn out and busted in. Yeah, I wanna get back to New York. Get me a good drummer. You say the weather's not too hot, huh?"

Three days later Hubbard's back in the Apple, courtesy of George Wein. He's among the special guests who've been assembled for the "Blakey Legacy" concert, a Kool Jazz tribute to the granddaddy of hard bop drumming. Past and present Messengers such as Donald Byrd, Jackie McLean, Curtis Fuller, Bill Hardman, Billy Harper, Cedar Walton, Walter Davis, Bobby Watson, Bill Pierce, and Johnny Griffin, are all on hand for this Carnegie Hall extravaganza. I arrive at Hubbard's Sheraton suite only moments after he has risen from a brief morning's sleep. Five hours ago he touched tarmac and then was swiftly limo-ed into town. Despite this, he's in particularly good spirits and further brightens when I show him the morning's paper, which includes an article about the concert and a photo of, among others,

Frederick Dewayne Hubbard.

I inquire as to whether Freddie might like to talk about some of his experiences at Columbia Records over the past eight years. "Uh-oh," he feigns. Though Hubbard suggests that he doesn't want to "get too far into it," it's not long before he finds himself knee-deep in "it." It seems obvious that he does want to talk.

"I think Columbia relied too much on Bob James to produce jazz artists," Hubbard begins, leaning forward on the couch. "He wasn't really a jazz producer. He was trying to get me away from jazz, which he did. Bob would just come in and lay down the tracks. I had to fit into what he had laid out. That was a mistake 'cause there was no looseness. Even so. *Windjammer* [1976] was a pretty good album.

"When I first went there in '73, this is what they told me: 'We're gonna make you the No. 1 trumpet player at Columbia because Miles isn't playing.' [Bruce] Lundvall [then a Columbia executive] said, 'Look, Freddie, I want you to just play.' So I felt pretty good. But then, it always ended up later on—'What's the material gonna be like?' And then when it came time for me to talk to Bruce one to one, he always put me over to Bob. So it ended up Bob saying, 'Let's do this, let's do that.' He was producing everybody.

"It's a funny thing. Some jazz dates I've done—even though some of them haven't been that great—I thought should've received much more airplay. *Super Blue* [1978] for sure. Those were some of my favorite musicians—Hancock, [George] Benson, Joe Henderson, [Jack] Dejohnette, Hubert Laws, [Ron] Carter—I had on that record. And what'd they do with it? *Love Connection* [1979] was a whole different thing. That album was overproduced. Where would you market that record? I mean, who's gonna play it? So I was stuck. [George] Butler [executive producer] was out there with it. He couldn't get any promotion money. Still, Bruce was taking me to the 21 Club, coming to all my gigs, bringing me Beaujolais and taking pictures—all that. Then, all of a sudden, I can't find him. I said, 'Uh-oh, something's happening.' Then they bring in Butler. He says, 'Yeah, Freddie, you my man.' And I helped him get the gig!"

[For the record, Butler is completely apologetic about Hubbard being dropped, explaining: "He was a victim of circumstances—of radio, the times, what can I tell you? He's one of the great ones."]

So Hubbard, who is unquestionably one of the finest trumpet stylists in modern jazz, and who once told an interviewer that "all of the music I've done before in my life and all the practicing and studying I've done will be in vain if I have to try to play the type of music that would sell," is going to use this opportunity—the label switch— to lay down some sho' nuff jazz like he did at Fat Tuesday's, right? Dead wrong.

"*Splash* is the most commercial thing I've ever done," Freddie reports. "It's the first time I've done something with some vocals. Ever hear of Jeanie Tracy? She's with Sylvester. I'm still bebopping on top of it. It's not to the point that it's so far away that I sound ridiculous. I'm still blowing. There's just not as many weird chord changes or stretching out. See what I'm saying? I think the whole movement," he adds with a knowing smile, "is getting into that fusion thing."

I can't believe what I'm hearing. Eight weeks ago, Hubbard testified the fusion blues to me in the afterglow of a very special jazz occasion in a nightclub in Manhattan. Now, with that experience neatly tucked away, Freddie is acting out his latest fantasy: he wants to be Tom Browne. "I can play 'Funkin' for Jamaica,'" he says proudly. Then, suddenly, Freddie cackles: "I was funkin' in Jamaica [the one in Queens, New York]."

Acting as his conscience, I press on with another quotation from his tumultuous past: "I switched from hardcore jazz to rock with rock cats, and they smothered me. It didn't come off 'cause I never had the feeling for the thing. I'm not gonna make that mistake again."

"This record ain't gonna be no mistake," he rises to his own defense. "They're gonna like this. I like it. A lot of other shit I was doing just to fulfill a contract. This record is playing. I spent time choosing material. It's hot."

We were just a bunch of white kids sittin' around jivin'. Eleventh grade, afterschool, just starting our marijuana habits. It was '69 and we were heavy into Chicago, Blood, Sweat and Tears, Traffic and Carole King. And protesting against "the war." I don't remember who bought it or much anything else about how it actually happened, but one day we really started to jam. We were all snappin' our fingers, tappin' our toes, bangin' our hands furiously down on any level surface. See, there were these 10 notes on the electric piano that a guy named

Herbie Hancock kept running over and over. The drummer, bassist, and conga player were right with him. And in what seemed very organized intervals, one instrument at a time would take solos over this incredible beat. First, we heard a trumpet that sounded mad, climbing one glorious hurdle after the next—then a sax, followed by guitar. But we kept on skipping back to the trumpet part. How could any instrument drive so swiftly into the psyche, we wondered? It was awesome. It was Freddie Hubbard. The song was "Straight Life."

Freddie dragged our pants down and strung them up a flagpole like the traditional fraternity initiation. And when we woke the next morning, we still didn't know what had hit us. For us it was *Straight Life*, for others *Red Clay* (including Kareem Abdul-Jabbar, who shortly after telling Hubbard that *Red Clay* was among his favorite records, found himself the subject of a track, "Theme for Kareem," on *Super Blue*). Little did we know that from those sweet moments on, we'd be hooked on jazz forever.

When Hubbard moved on to Columbia in '74, his sound began to change. Record companies had suddenly started to toe the line with jazz musicians, demanding they concern themselves with a growing commercial audience that enjoyed jazz, though not necessarily in its purest form. First, he tried rock (*Liquid Love*), then crossover pop (*Windjammer*, *Bundle of Love*). While Freddie was selling his share of albums, he found himself distraught: born and raised in the jazz tradition, he no longer felt a part of that. So when Herbie Hancock invited him to join the V.S.O.P. tour in 1977, Hubbard jumped at the offer. Afterwards, he went straight into the studio and recorded one of his finest albums ever—*Super Blue*.

Still, Hubbard wasn't satisfied. Two days before his Lincoln Center concert in November '78, I called him coast to coast for a brief interview. Our conversation began like this: "You want a story? Tell them I'm not coming to New York for my concert. Now you called Freddie Hubbard and you got the story."

Welcome to the world of Freddie Hubbard. He bitched and moaned about Columbia, audiences, recording contracts and, most of all, money ("I ain't makin' enough money, and I wanna live good. And the money's out here, and I want it. I mean, I want to play, too. Tell them that.") Hubbard did show for the concert, though obvi-

ously begrudgingly; he played only 45 minutes. Said a Columbia official then, "Freddie's digging his own grave."

At the time Hubbard also was telling every interviewer, including *DownBeat*'s, that his ideal band was Joe Henderson, McCoy Tyner, Cecil McBee and Elvin Jones (not keyboardist Billy Childs, bassist Larry Klein and drummer Carl Burnett, who were his touring trio, and still are), and that he would not be satisfied until he assembled it. The fact that he joined Tyner, McBee and Al Foster earlier in the year to record one-fourth of McCoy's last Milestone date, *4X4*, hasn't diminished Hubbard's desire to realize this project, he says, though I'm not sure what to believe any longer—especially after listening to *Splash*.

Unlike Tyner, whose use of vocals on *Inner Voices* [1977] was thoroughly innovative, Hubbard has fallen into the same trap every other jazz musician seeking crossover votes has before him. Vocalist Jeanie Tracy does not distinguish herself, plus the material is not first-rate (Hubbard co-writes only three of the seven tracks), and whereas the trumpeter may think he is effectively "bebopping on top of it," this is hardly the case. *Splash* is a poolful of chlorinated funk-jazz.

It saddens me to think that *Splash* is an indication of where Freddie Hubbard and the music business have evolved in 12 short years. Indeed, I can't imagine (rather, I don't want to imagine) uninitiated teenagers grooving to it as we did to *Straight Life*. Nor can I imagine my life without *Straight Life* and all the other enormous pleasures Freddie Hubbard has provided me.

Now, about that apartment in New York....

February 1982

"Play or Die"
Anthony Braxton Interview
by Peter Rothbart

Anthony Braxton's career has been marked by controversy ever since he joined the Association for the Advancement of Creative Musicians (AACM) in 1966. In the 16 years since, Braxton has continued to shake the musical world with his precedent-breaking solo saxophone explorations (e.g., *For Alto*), novel instrumental combinations (such as his works for five tubas), and his unique structural concerns. Equally adept at composition, his *For Four Orchestras* is a colossal work, longer than any of Gustav Mahler's symphonies and larger in instrumentation than most of Richard Wagner's operas. His current "experiments" (as he calls them) in multimedia production call for such collaborations as four slide projectors coordinated with a symphony orchestra (see "Caught," *DB,* Oct. '81).

Braxton has elevated the art of woodwind doubling (he calls it "multi-instrumentalism") to new heights, in the process giving new life to instruments that had long since fallen into disregard: the bass, contrabass, and sopranino saxophones, and the E♭ clarinet. Despite Braxton's commitment to music's cutting edge, he places a strong emphasis on tradition. His teaching method is firmly rooted in the classics. His two records entitled *In the Tradition* pay homage to the heritage of bebop.

Although he has won numerous polls—including a dozen *DB* polls on three different instruments, while the '77 critics chose *Creative Music Orchestra* (Arista) best LP—Braxton continues to struggle. Though his music is relatively well documented on record, it has never really reached the mass market. He remains uncompromising, despite the economic difficulties and critical rebuffs he has learned to expect.

Peter Rothbart: What about the accessibility of your music? What would you tell people to listen to in your music?

Anthony Braxton: First of all, in many quarters, my work is viewed as a violation of black creativity because of my emphasis on methodology, my interest in science, my insistence on saying I'm influenced by white or Asian musicians, and the racial makeup of my various groups. The fact that I would pay homage to Caucasian creative people has put me in a very strange position—not only with black musicians, but also with white musicians. Finally, it comes down to the fact that my music doesn't correspond to what jazz is supposed to be. In 1967, my group didn't have bass and drums. At the time we had that group, it was against the law to have an ensemble without bass and drums. Then the nature of the music, the kind of forms we used, the

kinds of languages, was perceived as a violation of the music. When I recorded *For Alto*, which was a two-record set of solo saxophone music, I was put down because that violated the music in the eyes of many of the people who defined terms in that period. The understanding was that you just don't play solo music on the saxophone, especially if the music is pointillistic, and not observing the structure of what jazz is supposed to be. Throughout all these various periods, I did have people who said positive things. I had support, too. But they called it a woodwind stunt when I moved into multi-instrumentalism. Now it's an accepted part of the scene. We're talking about a 16-year involvement with the music during which I've been challenged as to my right to do it. In every case the verdict has been that the music is not in the spirit of what jazz is supposed to be. In fact, at every junction, what motivates me transcends the present-day definitions.

Rothbart: Isn't art for art's sake a very romantic notion?

Braxton: In this culture we've come to look at creativity as entertainment. Of course, a given manifestation can be entertaining, but there's another whole reality that's attached to creativity, that being creativity as it relates to a spiritual and information dynamics of a culture; creativity as it relates to positive transformation; as it intertwines with science, spiritualism and philosophy. That's where I come in. That's the aspect of creativity I was always attracted to.

Rothbart: What do you mean by "information dynamics"?

Braxton: The best example would be the concept of "swing" and how it's written about in this period. We've come to view "swing" as when you have a certain kind of empirical rhythm. If it's done right, it has "swing." That's how it's been defined in the annals of jazz commentary. But I disagree with what's really happening with that, because there's nothing that happens that doesn't swing. Everybody has a rhythm and the reality of every rhythm cannot be seated in only its empirical dynamics. You have post–[Anton] Webern creativity that swings. There's no music that doesn't meet the criteria of "swing" if its rhythmic pulse is really understood.

Rothbart: How about the person who is playing it? Can he or she not swing?

Braxton: There's no person who plays, who, when he or she taps their inner reality or real affinity dynamics or real

affinity nature, doesn't swing.

Rothbart: So it's the person who's in touch with certain qualities within...

Braxton: Swings. And I'm saying that that alternative information dynamic would have to be taken into account, when they talk about swing. I'm saying that information dynamics is related to the philosophical hierarchy that it observes. The information dynamics surrounding the essence of post–[Albert] Ayler continuance was significant for what it posed to the black community and for the creative community. But that's never been commented on. It's only been talked about as a musician emotionally rejecting the system. There are reasons why people are in the emotional state that they're in. I don't see that music as only being a rejection. John Coltrane was written about during that period as playing nihilistic [or "hate"] music. He survived the storm of the '60s because of the obvious importance of his music.

Rothbart: Do you think in retrospect that it's still viewed that way?

Braxton: I think in retrospect, it's not even being viewed. Not only has post-Ayler creativity and post-Webern creativity been cast aside, but it's been redocumented in a way that it doesn't have to be dealt with anymore.

Rothbart: You refer to post-Ayler or post-Webern periods often. Why do you choose those as significant milestones? Why not post-Coltrane?

Braxton: I could go back and say post-Parker. That solidification which we now call bebop was important on a lot of different levels. In this conversation, I was referring to post-Ayler because by the time we get to post-Ayler and move into the AACM, we're really coming into another whole chapter in the music. Coltrane wasn't the only restructuralist in that period. We can't talk about Coltrane without talking about the significance of Sun Ra or Cecil Taylor or Ornette Coleman. Those four musicians solidify a very important step in the music. The significance of that music transcends any one aspect of their work. I go to post-Ayler because when Ayler came on the scene, it had been set up by the four musicians. His work represented a first composite of what these four musicians did...

Rothbart: A first distillation...

Braxton: Yes, so I generally talk of post-Webern in the same sense, because [Arnold] Schönberg set him up. Webern kind of crystallized the fact that something different was happening.

Rothbart: Webern is obviously an influence on you. His approach was that a single note could be the entire phrase—a pointillistic approach. You seem to go to the opposite extent, especially in your piece "For Four Orchestras." You've created a work that is longer than any of Mahler's—which brings up the idea of structural levels. With Webern, one note was crucial. In a work such as the four-orchestra piece, are you looking for the micro- or macro-structures?

Braxton: It was directional music, sound masses moving. Musicians playing on chairs with the directions choreographed...

Rothbart: With the music affected by the acoustical space...

Braxton: Yeah, spatial music. The actual note structure of the music does produce a kind of *klangfarben* [sound colors]. But that's not what I was really looking at. I'm not really interested in duplicating Webern or [Karlheinz] Stockhausen. I was attracted to pointillism in the same way I was attracted to Ornette Coleman's music.

Rothbart: To explore a different direction, what are some of your recent experiments?

Braxton: I'm working on a series of analyses. I just finished three books on aesthetics. My problem now is that I haven't got the money to put them out.

Rothbart: Analyses of what?

Braxton: My compositions, talking about what I was planning to do, what I was working with.

Rothbart: How are the volumes organized?

Braxton: The first three books — the ones on aesthetics — are along the lines of the philosophical basis that determines how we deal with creativity, as it relates to world culture, Western art music, and trans-African music. They're structured on three different levels. The first level is the philosophical basis. Level two is a composite, looking at all of world music, and the third level is questions and answers. The next book is the transition from Africa to Beethoven to Schönberg.

Rothbart: From a historical approach?

Braxton: Looking at the philosophical implications of the music and how all of that solidified. What we're dealing with now in this period, from, say, the post-Coleman junction of music to the post-Ayler junction, and later from the post-Webern to the post-LaMont Young junction. The third section of the first book is the post-Ayler continuum dealing with the New York School and the events which took

place in the middle '60s.

Rothbart: It sounds as if you don't make a distinction between the Webern school and Ayler.

Braxton: I look at all these continuums with respect to the individual particulars and with respect to their composite relationship to the total theater. I have always been attracted to the post-Webern continuum and its related projections as trans-African music—so-called jazz.

Rothbart: Trans-African?

Braxton: I use the word "trans-African" in this period to get away from the word "jazz." I've never understood what people are talking about when they say jazz, because they've frozen the music and applied definitions to the music in a way that never really satisfied the composite reality of the music. And in doing so, I feel that there are profound distortions surrounding our understanding of what we call jazz.

Rothbart: But why "trans-African"?

Braxton: I believe that one of the most important factors that determine the reality of a projection has to do with its vibrational and spiritual significance—what that projection poses to what I call "affinity dynamics." Affinity dynamics has to do with the reality of postulation; the nature of the being who postulates. From that context, I look at the continuance of a projection, of a total thrust as opposed to isolating one style. For example, bebop is swing music and if you have a C Major seventh, you have to play on top of a C Major seventh, and you have to use Charlie Parker's language. If you don't play this language, then it's not correct. I don't think that from what I'm looking at, there's such a thing as bebop, or the kind of projection we're talking about, because we've isolated it too much. Even though Charlie Parker introduced a dynamic language criteria to the music, it was not that foreign to the music. I mean, Lester Young, Don Byas and Coleman Hawkins had solidified the whole foundation. That music is as important for what it proposed to the transition of the music as Charlie Parker. I disagree with the idea of taking one person and saying this person started this—"He's the god of bebop."

Rothbart: But nevertheless there are certain basic characteristics along this continuum that show why a bebop tune will differ from a Dixieland tune.

Braxton: Yes, but those dictates aren't necessarily empirical. The interesting thing about so-called jazz is that Charlie Parker

wasn't trying to play Charlie Parker licks. He was playing his music. There's a big difference there. Everything I've ever read about Parker says that he was more impressed with creative musicians who didn't try to imitate him, as opposed to someone who could play every lick he had solidified for himself. Yet I don't mean to be disrespectful to the different aspects of the music. Look at restructuralism. We have stylism, and traditionalism. Look at what has happened in this period for instance, when people talk of what they call the blues, when present-day commentary interprets a given postulation. When it's supposed to be the blues, they talk in terms of minor thirds or sevenths. If you play a given sequence correctly, this is supposed to be the blues.

Rothbart: They're looking for specific traits, empirical information. This can be the pitfall of all theoreticians, their search for basic characteristics. For example, theorists talk of sonata form, yet few sonatas, especially by the master of sonata, Beethoven, fit the form exactly.

Braxton: That's right.

Rothbart: Nevertheless, there are general traits that you can look for, recognizing that there will be a certain amount of deviation.

Braxton: That's the same with blues, but it goes down even more than that. In my understanding of blues, we're talking about a vibrational continuum. There's no one kind of blues. There are four-bar blues, eight-bar blues, whatever kind of blues you want to play.

Rothbart: So you're more concerned with how it's being played than what is being played.

Braxton: I'm more concerned with what is being played than how it's being analyzed. I'm saying that some of the lower structures which have been imposed on the music run contrary to the vibrational and spiritual dictates of the music.

Rothbart: Let me try an example. While transcribing some Yusef Lateef oboe solos, I found that the harmony hits a dominant seventh chord, yet he always plays a Major seventh which is one of the "cardinal sins."

Braxton: Paul Desmond does that a lot.

Rothbart: But it works because of the way he plays it.

Braxton: Because of what he really understands. In other words, he's really playing the blues. That's also true for a musician like Albert Ayler. I disagree with our frozen interpretations—for what those interpretations have done to the essence of the music. The present-day commentary has gotten to the point where not only is it interfering with the music, but it's defining terms for the next generation of musicians. Many of the people who talk about themselves as so-called jazz musicians now are very far away from the spirit of what that music is.

Rothbart: Everybody's a jazz musician.

Braxton: I really don't understand the terms anymore. As a result I've backed away from it, because one of the problems I've had for the past 16 years has been that I have constantly been challenged as to whether I'm a jazz musician, or does my music swing, or meet the dictates of what the music of the day is supposed to be. But in fact, I never really was functioning with respect to those definitions. I view my activity as a logical extension of my involvement and concern about world creativity.

Rothbart: Can you explain world creativity?

Braxton: Projections we don't normally talk about, whether it's African music or Asian music, Japanese music, music of the American Indian, music from Sardinia.... So I've found in the past three or four years that many of the criticisms that I've read about my work don't even consider where I'm coming from. I'm being judged in the context of, "Is he playing a ii-V-I change like Charlie Parker would play it?"

Rothbart: That's more the fault of the analyst.

Braxton: Based on the articles I've been reading in the past two or three years, I've been noticing that the post-Ayler creativity is now being talked of as "Those angry niggers got really angry in the '60s and they screamed and hollered, but now they're coming home. The music's coming back. Everyone's getting back to what's really jazz. It's not about hate anymore." That kind of commentary permeates...

Rothbart: Are they talking about hate or alienation?

Braxton: Whatever they're talking about, they're not talking about the music, because the essence of that music transcended one context, first of all. I think it would be terribly disrespectful... no, not disrespectful... terribly untrue to paraphrase all of the music which has taken place as being only a rejection, or only hate, or only emotionalism.

Rothbart: But isn't music merely a reflection of the status of society, or does it lead society?

Braxton: I think there's definitely a relationship between music and society....

Rothbart: So wouldn't Ayler mirror society? Wouldn't Ayler's music reflect the discord that was occurring in our society?

Braxton: There's a difference between the discord that was happening in white America as it was defined by white writers, and the nature of what was taking place in the black community and what that posed for the black community. For instance, the problem of alien definitions. I most certainly can accept—even if I don't agree with the *New York Times* or the *Village Voice*—their commenting about the particulars of our intellectual community, or just the social reality as it is perceived by white Americans for white Americans. But when we talk about the reality of post-Ayler continuance, we can talk about it from the context of how the journalists wrote about it, or we can talk about it from the context of what that music philosophically posed, vibrationally posed, and spiritually posed for the people who were doing it, for its related information dynamics. I see the dynamics of post-Ayler continuance as being directly related to the progression or thrust of re-information dynamics, as those dynamics would relate to alternative functionalism. This is not only for the black community in America, because I'm not talking from only that perspective. I'm talking about alternative information dynamics, alternative functionalism as it relates to humanity—as it relates to the possibility for new ways of living, as it relates to political order, information dynamics, postulation. The continuum that we refer to as post-Ayler music is related to that. It represented a significant move for re-establishing information dynamics, especially in the black community.

Rothbart: Anthony, you've succeeded where other people have failed. You've survived for 16 years and have even prospered. What clues do you give to other people? There are a lot of people who would love to play the music that is true to them, but they're hungry.

Braxton: It's a hard decision. I have a family now, with two kids. It's not like when I was by myself and just living in the park playing chess for a living. My motto since I was 11 years old was, "Play or Die." If I wasn't able to achieve what I wanted in my life as far as my creativity and my life's

growth is concerned, I would feel bad, but not too bad. But I would find it hard to forgive not trying and not giving everything to the struggle. I've always admired those individuals who put their life on the line, whether we're talking about Harry Partch, Fats Waller, or Charlie Parker.

December 1982
· ·

Interview: Wynton and Branford Marsalis
A Common Understanding
by A. James Liska

Nineteen eighty-two was the year of Wynton Marsalis—*DownBeat* readers crowned him Jazz Musician of the Year; his debut LP copped Jazz Album of the Year honors; and he was named No. 1 Trumpet (handily defeating Miles in each category). In 1980, the New Orleans–bred brassman first stirred waves of critical praise with Art Blakey's Jazz Messengers; by the summer of '81 (with a CBS contract under his arm), he was honing his chops with the V.S.O.P. of Herbie Hancock, Ron Carter and Tony Williams. By early '82 Wynton Marsalis was topping the jazz charts: "Fathers and Sons"—one side featuring Wynton, brother Branford on sax and father Ellis on piano—soon followed (both remain charted to this day), as did whistle-stop tours with his own quintet (Wynton, Branford, pianist Kenny Kirkland, bassist Phil Bowler, drummer Jeff Watts). Now at only age 21, Wynton is on top, and rapidly rising 22-year-old Branford has been signed by Columbia on his own.

A. James Liska: Let's start by talking about the quintet—the Wynton Marsalis Quintet.

Branford: That's what they call it.

Wynton: When he gets his band, it'll be called the Branford Marsalis Quartet.

Branford and Wynton
Marsalis. (Skip Brown)

Liska: Are you going to play in his band?

Wynton: No-o-o-o.

Branford: He's barred. Let's face it, when you get a personality as strong as his in a band, particularly playing trumpet and with all this coverage, it would become the Wynton Marsalis Quintet.

Liska: Even though it would be your band?

Branford: That's what it would be.

Liska: Is that a reflection on your leadership abilities as well as your personality?

Branford: We're talking from a visual standpoint. When people come to see the band, the whole image would be like if Miles started playing with somebody else's band. You can't picture Miles as a sideman at any time.

Wynton: Co-op music very seldom works—the type of music in which everybody has an equal position in deciding the musical direction of the band. I mean, somebody has to be the leader.

Branford: Everybody else has to follow.

Wynton: The thing is, though, when you lead a band, you don't lead a band by telling everybody what to do. That's a distortion that I think a lot of people get by watching bands. Nobody has ever had a great band in which they had to tell all the guys what to do. What you do is hire the cats who can play well enough to tell you what to do. But you have to make it seem like you're telling them. It's psychological: you have to be in charge of it, but you don't want to be in charge of it.

Liska: Then the role of the leader is…

Wynton: What I'm saying is that the direction of the band is formed by the band, but it goes through one person: the leader. If you're a leader, you lead naturally, automatically.

Liska: From the co-op perspective then, don't all-star sessions generally work?

Wynton: They don't work as well as an organized band. Sometimes, something exciting can come about. But that's rare because jazz—I hate to use that word—group improvisation is something that has to be developed over years of playing

together or, at least, from a common understanding. The reason that these all-star things can work so well is that everybody has a common ground. It's when you lump people from all different forms of music together that it sounds like total shit.

Branford: Nowadays, sometimes the ego thing is so strong it's like, well, I've actually seen jam sessions where cats would say, "I'm not going on the stage first. You play the first solo." As soon as that starts, the music is over. I sat and watched, for over two hours, a battle of egos like that. It was the worst musical experience I ever had. The people were going crazy because there were all these great jazz musicians on the stage. If they only knew what they were listening to and what was really going on. It hurt me, man. I think that's the major problem with all-star things because when you have a group, you have one leader and some followers who maybe can lead but they're followers nonetheless. The position of the follower is always underrated. A band has to have great followers; you can't have five great leaders.

Liska: The too-many-chiefs, not-enough-Indians syndrome?

Branford: No Indians.

Wynton: The thing that makes it most intricate is that you have to realize that when you lead a band, you're leading a group of cats that know more about everything they do than you know. That's the one great thing I learned from Art Blakey. He's one of the greatest leaders in the world, and the reason is that he doesn't try to pretend that he knows stuff that he doesn't know. But he's the leader of the band, and when you are in his band, you never get the impression that you're leading it. I knew all the time that he was the leader. He didn't have to tell me that. He's that kind of man.

Liska: And that wasn't ego-inspired?

Wynton: His stuff has nothing whatsoever to do with ego, man. He's just a great leader. Of course, he's been doing it for so long. But that's true with a lot of different people. When Miles had the band with Herbie and them, do you think he told them what to do? He was struggling to figure out what they were doing. He had never had cats play like that, but he was wise enough to let them decide what was going to happen. He didn't make them play just what he could play. But they always knew he was the leader, and you can listen to the records and know he's the leader.

Liska: Is there a like situation in your own quintet? Are the guys telling you what to do?

Wynton: There are certain things that they do that I don't know what it is, that I have to ask about. You know, like, what was that you played? What is that? What chord is that? What voicing? What's the best choice of this? That's what you have to do to learn. The hardest thing about being a leader is that you have to lead a group of cats who might know more than you know.

Liska: Then why are you the leader if you know so little?

Branford: (Laughing.) He must know enough.

Liska: Are you a great follower?

Branford: I'm a great follower.

Liska: Do you think you'll be a great leader?

Branford: Great leaders were usually great followers. You have to be a follower before you can lead. That's what I've always thought. I'm learning a lot now, particularly economically, you know, business. He's setting the path for me, and I'm not going to have to make the same mistakes and go through the same crap that he's going through. While he's going through it, I'm sitting back observing, watching everything that they're trying to do to him.

Liska: Who are they?

Branford: Record companies, agents, managers, the whole works. The hassles with the music, the gigs, riders in additions to contracts.

Liska: So Wynton deals with it and you have the benefit…

Branford: Sitting around and learning. It's a drag that it had to be like that because all that pressure was thrown on him. People are always asking the classic dumb question: How does it feel to have a brother getting all that attention and blah, blah, blah? They obviously have no idea what all that shit entails. I sit down and watch him doing all of this and say, "Yeah, great… somebody's gotta be in the hot seat. Better him than me."

Liska: Is Wynton more able to deal with pressures than you?

Branford: He thrives better under pressure than I do. If I had to deal with it, I'd deal with it. But he functions best under pressure. I function best when people leave me the hell alone and I don't have to deal with a lot of crap. If I have to deal with it, I'll deal with it. But, like, he went to the hardest high school to go to.

Liska: By Choice?

Branford: By choice. He could have gone to the middle-of-the-road one like I did. I went to that one which meant I didn't have to study. He went to the hardest one. I'll admit it—I'm the classic lazy cat. I didn't want to be bothered; I didn't want to practice. I just wanted to exist. So I didn't practice. I played in a funk band and had a great time. When it was time to go to college, I went to the easiest one I could go to with the best teacher for music. But I really wasn't serious about music.

But back to the original subject; Wynton played classical music because someone told him black cats couldn't play classical music. The first time he went out there every one of the oboe players played the notes kind of out of tune, just to throw him off. He thrives best under that kind of stuff. If it were all relaxed and they just said, "Anything you want, man," I think he'd be kind of shaky. When people tell him "No," that's when he's at his best. So all the pressure's on him. Good. When I come around and get my band, there shouldn't be that much pressure.

Liska: Coming from the same family, being close brothers, how did you end up so different?

Wynton: My mother. My mother's a great woman. She treats everybody the same, so we're all different. When you treat everybody the same way and don't tamper with the way you treat them in accordance to their personality, then they act differently. They develop into their own person. Like Branford and me, we're totally different.

Branford: Radically different.

Liska: Yet you appear to be best of friends.

Wynton: Well, we have our things.

Branford: Appearances can be deceiving.

Wynton: All my brothers… we grew up living in the same room, you know? He was always my boy, though. Like, I could always talk to him.

Liska: You two are the closest in age?

Branford: We're 13 months apart.

Wynton: I always took my other brothers for granted. When Branford went away to college and I was still in high school, that's when I missed him. But we used to argue all the time. We think totally different. Anything I would say, he'd say just the opposite.

Liska: Just to be obstinate?

Wynton: Just to say it.

Branford: It wasn't just to say it. It was because I didn't agree.

Wynton: Nothing I say he agrees with.

Branford: Some things I agree with.

Liska: Musically, did you agree?

Branford: No.

Liska: Still?

Wynton: No.

Branford: Know what we agree on? I've thought about this a lot. I think we agree on the final objective. I think the common goal is there, but the route to achieve the common goal is totally different.

Wynton: Totally.

Branford: It's like catching the E and the F train. They both come from Queens to New York, and they both meet at West 4th Street, but one comes down Sixth Avenue and one comes down Eighth Avenue.

Wynton: The way I think the shit should be done, he doesn't.

Liska: How do you work so well together?

Branford: It's simple: he's the leader.

Wynton: Everybody thinks it's hard because he's my older brother. If we weren't brothers, if he was just another cat, nobody'd think anything of it. People are always going to try to put us together as brothers, and I don't want that. I tell people all the time that the reason Branford's in my band is because I can't find anybody that plays better than him.

Liska: Are you looking?

Wynton: No. (Laughs.) But if they come…

Branford: Bye-bye me.

Wynton: I don't have him in the band because he's my brother. I use him because I like the way he plays. Shit is very cut and dried with me: either you can play, or you can't; either you know what you're doing, or you don't. I use him because he's bad. Period.

Branford: I've always believed that when you're dealing with certain things, there are businesses and friendships. The two should never meet. The reason we get along so well is that when we play music, it's the Wynton Marsalis Quintet, and I'm in the band. When we're in this house, it's my brother, Wynton.

Wynton: What you have to realize is that everybody in the band is bad. That's what nobody wants to admit. They'll say, "Branford can play" or "Wynton's alright." Everybody in the band is bad. Jeff Watts knows as much as anybody about the music. Kenny Kirkland. Phil Bowler. These cats know about the music. It's not like one cat can play and he towers over everybody else in the band. People think that's how bands run. In this band, all of the cats have the capabilities. And when they do interviews…. What about Kenny? Why doesn't he get the publicity? What about Phil? Why doesn't Jeff get interviewed? It's because nobody's said that he's good yet.

Liska: Where did you find Jeff Watts, the drummer?

Wynton: Branford knew him from Boston.

Branford: I knew he was bad because nobody liked him. When I heard that, I couldn't wait to hear him.

Liska: Did you first hear him with a group?

Branford: No. It's hard to get a group in Boston, but we had the privilege of having ensemble rooms; we'd just sit around and have jam sessions, and every time he'd play, everybody would get lost. They couldn't tell where "one" was, and then they'd say, "He's sad. I can't hear 'one.'"

Wynton: He's conceptually bad.

Branford: Then we started hanging out and talking.

Wynton: He knows a lot of shit, man. He has a concept about the music.

Liska: What about Phil Bowler, the bassist?

Wynton: He played with Rahsaan [Roland Kirk] a long time.

Liska: How did you find him?

Wynton: I was playing everybody. Jamil Nasser recommended him. We had tried a lot of different cats. Phil's got great time, and that allows Jeff to play what he wants. Plus, he has a good knowledge of harmony and rhythmic-derivational things. He plays interesting ostinatos.

Liska: Where did you find Kenny Kirkland?

Wynton: Everybody knows him. He's one of the baddest cats playing piano today. You just know about him.

Liska: What's the most difficult thing about keeping your group together?

Wynton: Getting gigs. I worked three gigs in May with the band, and those were like one-hour gigs. You've got to gig all of the time, but you can't make money working in the clubs.

Liska: What about the concert hall situation?

Wynton: It hasn't hurt the music because the music in the clubs was dying anyway. It might be picking up now, but it was dying for a long time because the music changed.

Liska: How so?

Wynton: The music was different in the '50s and '60s than it is now. Then you could play popular tunes in the jazz setting and make them sound hip.

Liska: And now?

Wynton: You can't do that now because all of the popular tunes are sad pieces of one-chord shit. Today's pop tunes are sad. Turn on the radio and try to find a pop tune to play with your band. You can't do it. The melodies are static, the chord changes are just the same senseless stuff repeated over and over again. Back then you could get a pop tune, and people were more willing to come out and see the music because it had more popular elements in it. They could more easily identify with it.

Liska: Have the pop tunes of back then lost their meaning today?

Wynton: They haven't lost their meaning, but they're old. You've heard them played so many times by great performers that you don't want to play them again.

Liska: Any suggestions or solutions?

Wynton: I think one of the biggest problems is that nobody wants to do some-

body else's song. Everybody thinks that they can write great tunes, and all the public wants is that it sounds different. Music has to be played before it gets old. The music that Ornette Coleman played, that Miles and 'Trane played in the '60s, some of the stuff that Mingus and Booker Little and Charlie Rouse and these cats were starting to do… that music isn't old because nobody else has ever played it.

Liska: What happens, what is the reaction, if you do play it?

Wynton: People say, "Man, you sound like you're imitating Miles in the '60s," or else, "He sounds like he's imitating Elvin Jones." So what? You just don't come up with something new. You have to play through something. The problem with some of the stuff that all the critics think is innovative is that it sounds like European music—European, avant-garde, classical 20th century static rhythm music with blues licks in it. And all these cats can say for themselves is, "We don't sound like anybody else." That doesn't mean shit. The key is to sound like somebody else, to take what is already there and sound like an extension of that. It's not to not sound like that. Music has a tradition that you have to understand before you can move to the next step. But that doesn't mean you have to be a historian.

Liska: Earlier you expressed an aversion to the word "jazz." Why?

Wynton: I don't like it because it's now taken on the context of being everything. Anything is jazz; everything is jazz. Quincy Jones' shit is jazz, David Sanborn… that's not to cut down Quincy or David. I love funk, it's hip. No problem to it. The thing is, if it'll sell records to call that stuff jazz, they'll call it jazz. They call Miles' stuff jazz. That stuff is not jazz, man. Just because somebody played jazz at one time, that doesn't mean they're still playing it. Branford will agree with me.

Branford: (Laughs.) No. I don't agree.

Wynton: The thing is, we all get together, and we know that this shit is sad, but we're gonna say it's good, then everybody agrees. Nobody is strong enough to stand up and say, "Wait, this stuff is bullshit." Everybody is afraid to peek out from behind the door and say, "C'mon man." Everybody wants to say everything is cool.

Liska: Do you have as strong a feeling to maintain the standards?

Branford: Yes. Even stronger in some ways. I just don't talk about it as much. A lot of the music he doesn't like, I like.

Liska: Like what?

Branford: Like everything.

Wynton: Like what?

Branford: Like Mahavishnu. A lot of the fusion stuff.

Wynton: I don't dislike that.

Branford: It's not that you dislike it, it's that you prefer not to listen to it.

Wynton: That's true.

Liska: Do you think you're more open?

Branford: I don't consider it being more open; it's just that he's kind of set in his ways. What I feel strongly about is the way the business has come into the music. Everything has become Los Angeles—everything is great and everything is beautiful. It's kind of tired. Cats come up to and say: "What do you think of Spyro Gyra?" And I say: "I don't." That's not an insult to Spyro Gyra. I just don't like it when people call it jazz when it's not.

Liska: Any advice for young players?

Wynton: Avoid roots.

Branford: I think the basis of the whole thing is the bass player. The rhythm section is very important. If I've got a sad rhythm section, I'm in trouble.

Wynton: Listen to the music. High schools all over the country should have programs where the kids can listen to the music. Schools should have the records, and the students should be required to listen to them all, not just Buddy Rich and Maynard Ferguson. They should listen to Parker and Coltrane and some of the more creative cats. That should be a required thing. Jazz shouldn't be taught like a course. The students should know more than a couple of bebop licks and some progressions.

Branford: Never play what you practice; never write down your own solos—a classic waste of time unless you're practicing ear training.

Wynton: You should learn a solo off a record, but don't transcribe it. It doesn't make sense to transcribe a solo.

Branford: You're not learning it then, you're reading it.

Wynton: And learn a solo to get to what you want to GO. You don't learn a solo to play that solo.

Branford: What people don't realize is that what a soloist plays is a direct result of what's happening on the bandstand.

Wynton: You should learn all of the parts—the bass, the piano, the drums—everything.

Branford: Right.

Wynton: Music goes forward. Music doesn't go backwards. Whatever the cats couldn't play before you, you're supposed to play.

Branford: There's a huge movement for the perpetuation of ignorance in jazz. Play, that's all.

June 1983

Eno: Excursions in the Electronic Environment

by Bill Milkowski

"The things I think about mostly when I'm recording now don't seem to be musical considerations at all… more like descriptive thoughts… an aural picture." — Brian Eno

First, a few random facts about the enigmatic Eno:

• He does not read music, and for years has insisted he is not a musician at all, preferring to think of himself as a systems manipulator.

• He doesn't have a band, never tours and his albums on the independently distributed Editions EG label sell in modest figures (positively anemic by major label standards).

• His most recent album, *On Land*, was inspired by such diverse elements as Fredrico Fellini's *Amarcord*, Teo Macero's sparse production on Miles Davis' "He Loved Him Madly" and the sound of croaking frogs on Lantern Marsh, a place only a few miles from where he was born 35 years ago in East Anglia, England.

• He is leery of grants and collaborations, after being bombarded by bogus requests from artists and musicians all over the world.

• His current musical projects include soundtracks for a film about the opium trade in Burma, a documentary about the NASA Apollo moon missions, and an Australian film about a valley in the Himalayas that has more species of flowers per acre than any other place on the planet.

• His current video project is an upcoming exhibit in Japan, sponsored by Sony, which involves 35 TV decks and monitors.

• His full name is Brian Peter George St. John Le Baptiste De La Salle Eno (really).

BY THE TIME Beatle-mania swept England, carrying off a whole generation of susceptible adolescents in its tide, Brian Eno was safely tucked away in the cerebral solitude of the Ipswich Art School. It was there, at the age of 16, that he came under the spell of something far more intoxicating to him than John, Paul, George and Ringo. At Ipswich, Brian Eno discovered the tape recorder. It was perhaps the single most important find of his life, launching an ongoing journey of sound experimentation, which continues to this day.

Eno was encouraged to use the school sound taping facilities by the Ipswich faculty, a group of artistic revolutionaries bent on upsetting the preconceived notions about art that more conventional teachers espouse. They too played no small part in shaping Eno's view of the world. He thrived in this environment of "We're not going to tell you what is possible or isn't," as he continued to entertain all kinds of possibilities for both sound and visuals. At the Winchester School of Art, where he earned his degree in fine arts between 1966 and 1969, he became president of the student union and spent the union funds on having prestigious avant-garde musicians such as Cornelius Cardew, Christian Wolff, John Tilbury and Morton Feldman come to lecture.

Influenced by Cardew's "School-Time Composition," by John Cage's book *Silence* and by the notions of other systems artists ("Their emphasis is on the procedure, rather than the end product," Eno explains), he was brought to Reading University by Andy Mackay to lecture the students there. Years later, when Mackay and Bryan Ferry were forming the art-rock group Roxy Music, Eno was invited to join, playing Mackay's VCS3 synthesizer and mixing their sound.

It was the glitter era in England. Marc Bolan and T. Rex were big. David Bowie was in his Ziggy Stardust phase. Elton John had just released Honky Chateau to critical acclaim, and Roxy Music was opening for groups like Alice Cooper and Gary Glitter. With his own flair for visuals, Eno jumped into the movement with enthusiasm, sporting pancake makeup, eye shadow, rouge and lip gloss onstage. It was 1972, and Eno had become a full-fledged rock star.

But to balance these pop pretensions,

he maintained a sort of Jekyll and Hyde outlet for his "serious stuff." As early as 1972, he began conducting sound experiments in his home studio with King Crimson guitarist Robert Fripp, resulting in two LPs—*No Pussyfooting* and *Evening Star*. From the beginning, these collaborations explored a Zen-like flow of sound, combining Fripp's tone clusters and unremitting sustains on guitar with Eno's seemingly infinite capacity for programming tape loops via synthesizer. This risk-taking approach was clearly at odds with Eno's standing as a pop star, and his management objected vigorously. Yet, the experiments continued.

With his celebrated split from Roxy Music in 1973, Eno began producing his own solo albums, beginning with *Here Come the Warm Jets*, followed by *Taking Tiger Mountain (by Strategy)* in 1974. These were both ambitious, clever and dynamic pop projects, featuring Eno's vocals on all tracks. They are generally considered to be among the most adventurous and compelling statements '70s rock produced, though Eno now considers them a bit naïve. His third solo album, *Another Green World*, marked a significant transition in his career. On this icy, evocative album (which features few vocals), Eno the Pop Star and Eno the Artist were beginning to merge. Eno would make one more pop-oriented album, *Before and After Science*, in 1977, before discarding his pop persona altogether. Some of his comments about the rock star syndrome have since been quite critical.

Over the years he has been investigating sounds that encourage a dynamic relationship between people and their surroundings—music that responds to and enhances ambience. Functioning as an alternative to the bland pop arrangements of Muzak, this ambient music is intended to induce calm and create a space in which to think. "The idea of making music that in some way related to a sense of place—landscape or environment—had occurred to me many times over the last 12 years," he says in his notes to *On Land*. "My conscious exploration of this way of thinking about music probably began with *Another Green World* in 1975. Since then, I have become interested in exaggerating and inventing rather than replicating spaces, and experimenting with various techniques of time distortion."

When not occupied with his own ambient music projects, Eno has found time to produce a number of albums—three by David Bowie, three by Talking

Brian Eno.
(E.G. Records)

Heads, a funk/found-rap tape collage collaboration with Head-man David Byrne, a pair with minimalist composer/pianist Harold Budd, one with the Third World–inspired trumpeter Jon Hassell and albums by several new wave bands, including Television, Devo, Ultravox and the Lower East Side (Manhattan) bands featured on the *Antilles No New York* compilation. His most recent production credit is an album by Edikanfo, a group of African musicians from Ghana.

Bill Milkowski: You've made some anti-synthesizer statements over the years, yet you're often associated with them.

Brian Eno: People are always trying to sell me complicated synthesizers, or they write letters asking me what I think are the best synthesizers on the market... all this junk that people seem to think I know

about. I haven't a bloody clue what the best synthesizer is to the others. I'm just not excited by them at all. I'm not thrilled by something that does exactly the same thing over and over. Why people are is beyond me. I mean, they're not excited by assembly lines. If that's the kind of thing you want, go to the Ford motor factory and watch the car shells come off the assembly line.

To me, synthesizers are a little bit like Formica. If you see it from a distance, it looks great—this big panel of blue or pink or whatever that fits in well with your designer home. But when you get close to the surface of Formica and start looking at it, it's not interesting; nothing's going on there. Contrast this with a natural material like wood, which looks good from a distance but also is still interesting at any level of microscopic inspection; its atomic structure is even strangely interesting as opposed to Formica, which is regular and crystalline. Think of the forest, for instance. You look at it from the air and it's rich, complex and diverse. You come in closer and look at one tree and it's still rich, complex and diverse. You look at one leaf, it's rich and complicated. You look at one molecule, it's different from every other molecule. The thing permits you any level of scrutiny. And more and more, I want to make things that have that same quality... things that allow you to enter them as far as you could imagine going, yet don't suddenly reveal themselves to be composed of paper-thin, synthetic materials.

Milkowski: So you aren't interested in the high-technology hardware like the Fairlight or the Synclavier?

Eno: Not at the moment. I've been moving more in the direction of very low technology—found objects and other things that have some kind of interesting inherent sound to them—just anything lying around, really. I spend a lot of time around Canal Street [a long stretch of junk shops and flea markets located in the NYC Bowery] hitting things and listening to what this little bolt might sound like or this metal pot or whatever. As for high technology, all of the work I've heard from those machines is so unbelievably awful to me. Boring things like yet another synthesizer version of Vivaldi's Four Seasons... who needs it?

Milkowski: What synthesizer are you currently using?

Eno: One of my favorite instruments is the Yamaha CS-80, one of the first polyphonic synthesizers ever made. It's so simple—doesn't do anything like sequence or hasn't got any digital apparatus. It was actually a development from the organ, so it's very much like an electric organ with a sort of synthesizer panel, capable of really lovely sounds. It's perfect for me. I'd rather have six beautiful sounds from a synthesizer than a possible infinity of mediocre sounds.

Milkowski: You mentioned that you've gotten very suspicious of records lately. Can you elaborate?

Eno: I don't like the form very much anymore. I've become more and more interested in music that has a location of some kind, like gospel music—you go somewhere and you become part of something in order to experience the music. You enter a whole different social and acoustic setting. There's a whole context that goes with the music. Just sitting in your living room and sticking on some record is a whole other thing.

I think one of the things we have to do now is realize that the products of recording studios are another form of art. That's not music. There's been a break between the traditional idea of music—which still continues in many forms—and what we do now on records. That's something different. It's just like... at the birth of photography in the middle of the 19th century, what people started off doing was to try to make cheap portraits; it was a way of replacing a portrait painter by getting similar results, but much more cheaply. And, in fact, to this end they used canvas-textured paper, and they would tint the things and arrange everything to make it look as much like a portrait as they could. Similarly with film—the first films were just recordings of theater pieces. So film was really nothing more than the traveling version of a play. And the same thing happened when records were invented. They were invented to give everyone a chance to be at a Caruso performance, or something like that. Or to sell Caruso in a wider way than he had ever been sold before. Well, with each of those forms, a point was reached where it became realized that this medium had its own strengths and limitations, and therefore could become a different form through its own rules.

I think that's true of records as well. They've got nothing to do now with performances. It's now possible to make records that have music that was never performed or never could be performed and in fact doesn't exist outside of that record. And if that's the area you work in, then I think you really have to consider that as part of your working philosophy. So for quite a while now I've been thinking that if I make records, I want to think not in terms of evoking a memory of a performance, which never existed in fact, but to think in terms of making a piece of sound which is going to be heard in a type of location, usually someone's house. So I think, "This is going to be played in a house, not on a stage, not on the radio."

Milkowski: So with your recent works, particularly the Ambient series, you are more or less providing a stimulus for listeners to project into.

Eno: Yes, it's a different approach. It's an understanding that the record is only one part of the whole process, that actually what we're dealing with is the recording studio, this black thing in the middle called a record, and someone's hi-fi system. Of course, the assumptions you can make about how someone sits down and listens are a bit limited. In my case, I assume they're sitting very comfortably and not expecting to dance.

The way most producers work is like this: they say, "Here's the listener sitting here, so we'll have a guitar here, bass there, drums over there, horns there, vocals over here..." and so on. They're seeing it in two-dimensional terms, like a cinema screen. But I've been trying to get rid of the screen altogether. Forget about having this nice logical arrangement of things. I've become more interested in transferring a visual sense to music. What I want to do is create a field of sound that the listener is plopped inside of, and, within which, he isn't given any particular sense of values about things. It's much more like being in a real environment, where your choices are what determine the priority at a given time.

Milkowski: The first time I listened to *Discreet Music*, I was at work, the day had ended, all the people had gone home and the place was completely empty. During the day the atmosphere was generally hectic, with phones ringing and people rushing about, arguing, typing, talking. But this night it was so quiet I could even hear the fluorescent lights humming. I was sitting comfortably in a reclining chair, and I put on your record, not having any idea about what kind of music it was. It not only put me into a state of total relaxation, but it also sparked the most vivid memories of a special friend I hadn't seen in years—places we had been together, the smell of the air, the colors of the sunset.

Eno: You know, a lot of people have said the same thing that you're saying now about *On Land* as well, which was definitely the impetus for that record for me. When I was working in the studio, I always found that a piece would begin to come to life at the point where it would put me in that kind of mood, where I suddenly was in some way connecting with another place or another time. And as the piece developed, I'd get a stronger and stronger sense of the geography of that place and the time of day, the temperature, whether it was a windy or wet place or whatever. I was developing the pieces almost entirely in terms of a set of feelings that one normally wouldn't consider to be musical, not in terms of "Is this a nice tune? Is this a catchy rhythm?" Instead, I was always trying to develop this sense of the place of the music. It was and still is very hard to articulate because it's not part of the normal musical vocabulary.

I'm working on a piece now about an evening that I remember from a very long time ago in which nothing in particular happened, actually. For some reason this evening just stuck in my mind. I went for a walk—I was about 14—and where I lived, in Woodbridge, there's a dike that dams up the river. And there's a narrow path on top of it that goes for miles, just wide enough for one person to walk along. One night I went for a walk on it, and there was a low fog hanging over the marshes, just about at the level of this pathway so the effect was exactly like walking on top of this cloud. But above, the air was absolutely clear. And it was one of those deep blue nights with a lot of stars. So I started working on a piece of music, and something about it kept taking me back to that night. I don't think I had ever remembered it before. It was as though the piece suddenly reminded me of that. And the problem all the time was I had to get those stars in there somewhere. I kept thinking, "How do you make in music the feeling of a lot of stars?" You know, there's no sense in just having some cliché twinkling sounds or whatever...

Milkowski: Cue the star machine...

Eno: Right, so that was a problem. I worked on that for four or five days, experimenting with different things, and I had no idea where to start. There's no sort of tradition for making star sounds in music. Anyway, I came up with something that I like quite a lot. To me, it certainly gives that feeling of a huge space with lots of remote bodies that sort of cluster in apparently meaningful ways with one another. So that's the kind of thing that I think about mostly when I'm recording now. They don't seem to be musical considerations at all. They're more like descriptive thoughts. I think of it as figurative music in a certain way, where I'm actually trying to paint a picture of something. Well, people have said that for years. But I mean that in a fairly accurate way... an aural picture of some type.

Milkowski: Could you explain how you developed your so-called hologram theory of music?

Eno: I think two things started it. There was a book by Samuel Beckett that came out two years ago called *Company*. It's about a 90-page book with very big type, so in ordinary novel-size type it would probably be about 30 pages long or less. And for me, it's a great book. It's almost the same few phrases being permutated, the same things being said over and over again in slightly different ways. Almost all the material that appears in the book is there within the first two pages. Once you've seen the first two pages, you've effectively read the entire book. But he keeps putting them together in different ways. And one of the things that struck me about the book was you could take half a sentence from it, and first of all know instantly that it was Beckett, just something about the way the words were strung together. Also, from that half-sentence you would have a foggy impression of the feeling of the whole book. And that, in turn, reminded me of two things:

When I was in school—I went to a Catholic school—we were told that the host—the thing you get at Holy Communion—could be broken into any number of minute parts and that each part was still the complete body of Jesus Christ, even if it was only a tiny fragment. This always puzzled me. I thought about that a lot as a fine theological point. And then when I was about 18, I went to a lecture by Dennis Gabor, who invented the hologram; he said that one of the things that's interesting about the hologram is that if you shatter it and you take a fragment from the whole, you will still see the complete image from that piece, only it will be a much less distinct and fuzzier version. It's not like a photograph, you see, where if you tear off one corner, all you see is that corner. The whole of the image is encoded over the whole of the surface, so the tiniest part will still be the whole of that image. And I thought this was such a fantastically grand idea, and for the first time it gave me some understanding of the Catholic idea of the host; there was some scientific parallel to it.

So, those two ideas stuck in my mind for a long time. And when I started looking at this series of Cezanne paintings, I got the same feeling. You could take a square inch of one of those Cezanne paintings and somehow there was the same intensity and feeling and style within that one piece as there was within the whole picture. It's as if you saw the whole painting in that one piece because every brush stroke was charged just like the whole painting was charged—similarly with the Beckett book.

So I thought, "This is really how I want to work from now on. I don't want to just fill in spaces anymore." You know, a lot of the hard-edged paintings from the mid-'60s had to do with geometry and clarity of shape and so on, and the thing that made it

disappointing as a movement for me was the fact that a lot of what those guys were doing was purely mechanical, just filling in colors, almost like following a blueprint or a paint-by-numbers. It seemed to me they were cheating themselves because I think every stage of the procedure should be as vital as every other stage. There shouldn't be one stage where you just fill in, where it's too predetermined. At that point, it's just hack work. You can farm it out to assistants, which is what a lot of them did. In fact, I was an assistant to a painter for a while. I painted his pictures for him, and it was a similar-type thing, where he just had color areas sketched out that had to be filled in. It's done, but that's not what I want to do. I want to be alive every stage of doing any project.

Milkowski: Besides the obvious influence of painters on your work, you've mentioned such names as Philip Glass, Steve Reich, Terry Riley...

Eno: And LaMonte Young. He was sort of the conceptual father of that whole minimalist school, I suppose. At least in music. It's interesting, though, because that movement actually happened in painting before it did in music... this idea of a kind of continuum. Jackson Pollock and Barnett Newman are two good examples. But in music, LaMonte Young began experimenting with very long drones and continuous musical environments in the early '60s. He had a thing called Dream House, which was a series of generators that repeated single notes. These were very carefully built generators, so they didn't waver at all. The notes were as constant as possible for... months. This contraption was actually running for months and months. It was an idea that I'm very sympathetic to now. It was a piece of music that you walked into and you stayed for a while and you left it again. That was what *Music for Airports* was meant to be.

Milkowski: That idea of a continuum has been a running theme in your music since your first collaboration with Robert Fripp back in 1972 on *No Pussyfooting*. Using the analogy of painting, how would you say your own brush stroke has changed from that early work to your most recent ambient album, *On Land*?

Eno: Well, I think the palette is much broader now. There's a wider choice of colors, if you will. *Pussyfooting* is very much an album of musical types of sound—discernable guitar, electric instruments, mutable harmonies, chord clusters, and so on.

What's happened, then… with *On Land*, a lot of that has been broken down. There are far more types of sounds that aren't musical in a traditional sense. They're not sounds that you connect with any particular instrument or with any particular object. As an aside to this, whenever I release an album, it has to be copyrighted, so someone has to try to score this stuff. I saw a bit of the score for *On Land*, and the poor guy obviously had a real problem with it. You can't express it in notation; it doesn't work. So it rather came out as a kind of painting—a red spot here and a sort of blue stripe going across here and a roughly green area. So the difference is that at the time of *Pussyfooting*, I actually thought I was making music. Now with this new stuff, I feel that the connection has more to do with the experience of paintings or films or even non-cultural artifacts, like places. I'm quite inarticulate about it because I don't quite know what it is. There isn't any tradition for it.

With *Pussyfooting*, it's almost like being in some sort of tunnel. You don't have many choices about your direction within that. You sort of move forward as the piece streams along, and you can go a bit to the side as you're going. But with this landscape stuff, your direction can be really quite different on each listening. Maybe the first time you listen to it, you find it interesting but strange; you are disoriented within it. As you listen to it more and more, you attach yourself to certain little clusters that happen that you may recognize. You can then start making the choice about which journey you take through that music. The problem is always calling it music. I wish there were another word for it.

Milkowski: Do you feel that musicians are too preoccupied with technique and results?

Eno: I think it's more a case of… whenever you get into a spot, you can make yourself feel better by doing something clever. It's almost a sort of symptom of nervousness. I've seen musicians stuck for an idea, and what they'll do between takes is just diddle around, playing the blues or whatever, just to reassure themselves that, "Hey, I'm not useless. Look, I can do this." But I believe that to have that to fall back on is an illusion. It's better to say, "I'm useless," and start from that position. I think the way technique gets in the way is by fooling you into thinking that you are doing something when you actually are not.

Milkowski: As you strip down your process from album to album, has it become more difficult for you to work in the studio with other musicians?

Eno: I think it's getting harder for me to work with musicians who don't understand recording studios. Most musicians have their own idea about what the ingredients of a piece of music are. And one of the things that most of them think is that it's got to have a few tricky licks in it—something skillful—so they sit down and get all their ingredients together and sort of stick them all into a pot, thinking a piece of music will come out of it. It's like the recipe book without the procedure, where you just get the list of ingredients, but you don't bother to read about how to put them together or how to prepare them. You just bung them all into the pot and hope that you'll get lemon soufflé out of it in the end. Sure, you can work with the same set of ingredients all the time, but if you are going to keep yourself interested in it, then the procedure is where you have to direct your attention. So I don't like this ingredient way of working. It's like the formula disco style where it has to have this or that and it has to have the girls doing a refrain. You hear so much of this junk coming out all the time.

The difficult thing about working with skillful musicians is that sometimes I just can't explain to them the potential of something. Sometimes I know when I hear something that there are a series of operations that I can perform on it that will make it fabulous. This involves studio manipulation. And those kinds of manipulations, since they are in themselves ways of generating complexity out of sound, seem to work best on sounds that are initially quite simple. If the sound is musically complex to begin with, it's already a restrictive form to work with. So the problem with musicians is always telling them to have confidence in a simple and beautiful thing, to know that there's a whole world that can be extracted from a simple sound. And if they're not familiar with studios, they come in and give you some complex mess to work with, and then you have to spend two or three hours erasing all of that just to be left with this simple, beautiful thing. But to tell a musician, who is confident of his abilities and knows he can do lots of better things… sometimes people feel a bit insulted; they think you don't trust their intelligence. I think you can do the simplest thing well or badly. It's not that because it's simple, any idiot can do it.

There's sensitivity in the way you can strike just one note. Funk bass players know this very well.

Milkowski: How does that relate to your work with Talking Heads?

Eno: Well, I did this a lot with Talking Heads, extracting from simple things. For instance, I would take just the snare drum and use it to trigger one of my synthesizers, and then I'd put that output on a complicated delay. This allowed me to make cross-rhythms by using only that snare, just taking something that was there and shifting it in time, really, and putting it back into the mix again. And you weren't muddying the picture with these cross-rhythms, because as long as that snare drum stayed in time, this other fabricated rhythm stayed in relative time—it couldn't shift—so a lot of the cross-rhythms you hear on Talking Heads records are actually from the original instruments, but are being delayed or treated in various ways. Sometimes we would run the tape backwards and delay the sound backwards so you hear the echo before the beat, that kind of thing.

Milkowski: Did working with Edikanfo in Ghana have any effect on your ideas about working with Talking Heads?

Eno: Yes, but after the event. Watching those guys playing and seeing the relationship they had with rhythm was so totally disheartening for me. After seeing Edikanfo, I thought, "There just isn't a chance of ever even approaching this." They were good musicians, but not great musicians. But just seeing how they worked with rhythm made me want to give up right away. All the interactions between players and all the kind of funny things going on with the rhythm… there's a lot of humor in it. And then when I started listening to the stuff that we did with Talking Heads, it was just so wooden by comparison. I couldn't get very excited by it anymore. I could still get excited about it in other terms, but not in rhythmic terms anymore. It seemed to be really naïve.

It's like the same way I feel about the African sense of melody. Take King Sunny Ade, whom everyone is making a real big thing about lately. He has a great band, I must say, but I find him melodically quite uninteresting. I find his slide player, whom everyone is impressed by, quite boring. I've heard nine-year-old slide players who play better than that. It's like, if I want to hear great slide guitar, there are 150 bluegrass players who can really play that thing and play it with a kind of feeling for the instrument that the guy in Sunny Ade's band is never gonna have. Just like they play their drums with a feeling that I'm never gonna have, that I'm only beginning to understand. My friend Robert Wyatt once said: "You commit yourself to what you're left with." It's very true. After all the trial and error, you realize that you end up with one or two things you think you can do. So I'm not terribly thrilled by all the trans-cultural things going on at the moment. They seem to be well-intentioned, but…

Milkowski: Like mixing wood grains and Formica.

Eno: Yeah, it's a bit like that, you know. It seems that too often you get the worst of both worlds rather than the best.

November 1983

Tony Williams: Two Decades of Drum Innovation

by Paul de Barros

Tony Williams erupted onto the jazz scene in 1963, a 17-year-old prodigy with a full-blown, volcanic style of drumming that would blow hard-bop tastiness out the door. Williams' arrival was hailed with a great deal of fanfare. The week he came with Miles Davis to San Francisco's Jazz Workshop, the club temporarily relinquished its liquor license so the underage genius could play. I remember, because it was the first time I was allowed in as well. Williams played the drums that week at a level of energy and activity—not to mention volume—that was not only exciting, but liberating. Whirling from crash to ride to slack hi-hat, now pummeling, now ticking, now coaxing, he machine-gunned the bass drum, pulled low-pitched "pows" from the toms and jagged bursts from the snare as if his legs and arms were connected to four separate torsos. His complex, distinct style, which owed a lot to the floating time of Roy Haynes and thrust of Elvin Jones

(Sunny Murray's unbridled freestyle was a simultaneous development rather than an influence), suggested that jazz drumming might exist as an adjunct to, as well as a support for, the rest of the band.

Williams stayed with Davis five years. In 1968, like Herbie Hancock and Ron Carter before him, Williams left Miles, smelling rock & roll in the air. Joining forces with keyboard man Larry Young and British guitarist John McLaughlin (whom Tony discovered, but Miles snatched into the recording studio first, for *In a Silent Way*), the drummer recorded a groundbreaking jazz-fusion trio album, *Emergency*, for Polydor (recently reissued as *Once In a Lifetime*, Verve), of psychedelic fervor and volume. For a while it looked as if Tony Williams was going to take the electric '70s by storm, as he had the acoustic '60s.

But it didn't turn out that way. At Polydor he suffered poor management, poor promotion and poor sales. Fans who had exhaled "far out" for *Emergency* dumped *Turn It Over* and *Ego* into the used-record bins. The critics lambasted him, crying, "Sellout." Williams, for all his bravado a vulnerable fellow, retreated, confused. From 1973 to '75 and again from 1976 to '79, he vanished as a leader. When he did come back, with Columbia, it was with the crisp, straight-ahead rock of *Believe It*, pumped full of hot air by a discoing promotional department. Jazz fans shook their heads, wondering what had happened to their young hero. After an exhibitionist tour de force, *Joy of Flying*, in 1979, on which he amassed everyone from Cecil Taylor to Tom Scott, Columbia dropped Williams in the middle of a seven-record contract. More than ever, he began to look like the Orson Welles of jazz, bursting into the world with creative energy only to make a long, agonizing finish. One critic, Valerie Wilmer, even went so far as to dismiss him as a showman.

But Wilmer, and others, weren't really paying attention. While it was true that Tony Williams hadn't come up with any project matching the creative vision of *Emergency* or the late-'60s Miles quintet (hard acts to follow), he had certainly held his ground, which is considerable. He is every bit as good a jazz drummer as he was 20 years ago, as his recent performance in Seattle with V.S.O.P. II attested. Besides, none of the other great jazz drummers— Max Roach, Art Blakey, Elvin Jones—has altered his style after its initial break-

through. Williams' work in rock has been a mighty influence, right down to the current work of Journey's Steve Smith.

As for integrity, Williams has this to say to his critics: "People have this thing that if you like pop music, it's because of the money. My career will tell you I've never done anything for the money. Writers and critics and people in the jazz world think you cannot possibly like the Police because of the music, which is absurd. I do the things I do because they excite me, and the rest is a load of rubbish."

Williams continues to tour both in rock and jazz situations. In 1980, he played Europe with young Portland, Ore., fusion keyboardist Tom Grant and Missing Persons bassist Pat O'Hearn; in 1981 and '83 he toured with V.S.O.P. He plays on one track of Grant's Columbia album *You Hardly Know Me*, and on several with Wynton Marsalis, who replaced Freddie Hubbard in V.S.O.P.

In 1977, the drummer moved from New York to Marin County, north of San Francisco, where he lives in a country home with his girlfriend. Three days a week he drives to UC Berkeley, where he is studying classical composition with Robert Greenberg. When he is not composing fugues or studying counterpoint ("It's a mountain of work," says Williams), he is in the studio in San Francisco or busy catching up on some of the things he missed growing up a superstar: playing tennis, swimming, learning German and driving his Ferrari. Williams says the move to California has revitalized his creative life and helped him to get past the tangled 1970s.

Paul de Barros: You completely changed jazz drumming in the 1960s. Were you consciously aware at any certain point that you were doing something new?

Tony Williams: Not really. I guess I was aware that I was playing differently, but it was more of a thing that I was aware of a need, like if you see a hole, you think you can fill it. There were certain things that guys were not playing that I said, "Why not? Why can't you do this?"

de Barros: How important was Alan Dawson, your teacher in Boston, in your development of independence in all four limbs?

Williams: What I got basically from Alan was clarity. He had a lot of independence, but so did other people. I get this question about independence a lot, even from drummers, but they can't even be

Tony Williams.
(Ron Delaney)

clear about their ideas. I mean, you hear them play something, and you say, "What was it that he played?" Or if they hear themselves back on tape, they say they thought they played good, but that it didn't sound like that. So the idea is that when you play something for it to sound like what you intended, not to have a "maybe" kind of sound. So that's what I got from Alan, the idea that you have to play clearly.

de Barros: Were you thrilled to be part of the Miles band in the '60s?

Williams: Well, when you're doing things it's hard to say, "Oh gee, this is going to be real historical sometime." I mean, you don't do that; you just go to the sessions, and 10 or 20 years later people are telling you that it was important. When you're doing it, you can't really feel that way.

de Barros: What is your relationship with Miles now?

Williams: Very friendly. I saw him this summer. I haven't heard the new albums, but when we played opposite him, I heard bits and pieces of the band, and Miles was sounding good. He's been practicing. I liked Al Foster [Miles' drummer] years ago, when I was with Miles.

de Barros: You've played with a lot of illustrious musicians. Being a drummer, you have to adapt to each one differently. Let's talk about some of them, say, beginning with Sonny Rollins and McCoy Tyner.

Williams: Sonny has a very loose attitude about things—the time, the whole situation. With McCoy I always felt like I was getting in his way, or that it never jelled. I felt inadequate. Actually, with both Sonny and McCoy, it's like you're playing this thing, and they're going to be on top of it.

de Barros: How about John McLaughlin and Alan Holdsworth?

Williams: Completely different. John is more rhythm oriented. He plays right with you, on the beat. He'll play accents with you. Even while he's soloing, he'll

drop back and play things that are in the rhythm. Alan is less help. With Alan it's like he's standing somewhere and he's just playing, no matter what the rhythm is.

de Barros: Wynton Marsalis and Freddie Hubbard?

Williams: Freddie plays the same kind of solo all the time. I get the feeling that if Freddie doesn't get to a climax in his solos, and people really hear it, he gets disappointed. With Wynton it's always different. I don't know what he's going to play. It's always stimulating.

de Barros: I gather you think Wynton Marsalis' manifesto about only playing jazz—and not funk or rock—is not that important?

Williams: He thinks it's an important attitude. That's what counts.

de Barros: A lot of fans and critics still find a contradiction in your playing what they see as oversimplified rock as well as the kind of complex jazz you played with

Miles and you play now with V.S.O.P. What's your reaction to that?

Williams: Well, first of all, just because it's jazz, doesn't mean it's going to be more complex. I've played with different people in jazz where it was just what you'd call very sweet music. No type of music, just because it's a certain kind of music, is all good. A lot of rock 'n' roll is not happening. And a lot of so-called jazz, and the people who play it, are not happening. Complexity is not the attraction for me, anyway—it's the feeling of the music, the feeling generated on the bandstand. So playing in a heavy rock situation can be as satisfying as anything else. If I'm playing just a backbeat with an electric bass and a guitar, when it comes together, it's really a great feeling.

de Barros: You were quoted in *Rolling Stone* praising the drummer in the Ramones. Were you serious?

Williams: I don't remember the occasion, but I do like that kind of drumming, like Keith Moon, any drumming where you have to hit the drum hard; that's why I like rock 'n' roll drumming.

de Barros: Sometimes so much of that music seems very insensitive.

Williams: It depends on what you're saying the Ramones are supposed to be sensitive to. Just because it's jazz doesn't mean it's going to be sensitive to. You're trying to evoke a whole other type of feeling with the Ramones. When I drive through different cities and I look up in the Airport Hilton and I see the sign that says, "Tonight in the lounge, 'live jazz'"—I mean, what the hell does that mean? I'm not saying everybody's like this, but I can see a tinge of people saying, "This is the only way it was in 1950, and we're going to keep it that way, whether the music is vital or not, whether or not what we end up playing sounds filled with cobwebs." When John Coltrane was alive, there were all kinds of people who put him down. But these same people will now raise his name as some sort of banner to wave in people's faces to say, "How come you're not like this?" These same people. That's the hypocrisy, and I find it very tedious.

de Barros: How important is technique?

Williams: You've got to learn to play the instrument before you can have your own style. You have to practice. The rudiments are very important. Before I left home, I tried to play exactly like Max Roach, exactly like Art Blakey, exactly like

Philly Joe Jones, and exactly like Roy Haynes. That's the way to learn the instrument. A lot of people don't do that. There are guys who have a drum set for two years and say they've got their own "style."

de Barros: How can we prevent those kinds of guys from taking up more room than they deserve?

Williams: (Laughing.) Well, we could pass a law.

de Barros: The Bad Drummer Ordinance?

Williams: Exactly. Anyone who does not study is shot! Seriously, though, it's a big responsibility when you play the drums, and a lot of guys don't want the responsibility, but they want to play the drums. The drummer is playing all the time. You can have a terrible band and a great drummer, and you've got a good band; but you could have great horn players, and if the drummer and the bass player aren't happening, you've got a terrible band.

de Barros: Is tuning important?

Williams: Yes. I hear drummers that have maybe 12 drums that all sound the same. If you closed your eyes, you wouldn't know where they were on the set. Or else you'll have guys where each drum sounds like it's from a different set. It's important that the drum set sounds like one instrument. Like, if you have a piano, you wouldn't want the C to sound like a Rhodes, the D to sound like a Farfisa, the E to sound like a Prophet. A keyboard is a uniform system; a trumpet is a uniform system… drummers are out to lunch. On some of my drums, the bottom head is tighter than the top head. On other drums they're about the same. And on the bass drum the front head is looser than the batter side.

de Barros: Have you tried electronic drums?

Williams: Yeah! I tried the Simmons. The separation you get on tape is great. The programmability, the sound, the sequencing… it's another thing to do that seems very interesting. I have a DMX [electronic, programmable drum machine by Oberheim] at home.

de Barros: Will electronic drums be part of what you're doing in the studio?

Williams: Oh yeah, they already are.

de Barros: Can you say anything more about what direction your music is going?

Williams: The popular direction. I like MTV. I like the Police, Missing Persons, Laurie Anderson. I performed with her on a San Francisco date. It was great. I love the new Bowie album. Prince. I like the

idea of writing lyrics, of putting images with words that evoke a scene on top of the music. I like Herbie's new album. It's really happening.

de Barros: Are you interested in making a video yourself?

Williams: Sure. Growing up in this country, watching TV and movies, everyone would like to make a movie. It's a new thing to do. You know writers want to be painters; screenwriters want to be directors. Musicians want to make movies. Doing a project and having a lot of people like it and maybe listen to it on the radio, that appeals to me. What I'm trying to do is something that captures a lot of people's imaginations. If the result is I'm more famous, fine. But it's not like I'm after being a pop star.

de Barros: You've said in the past that jazz should be popular, not an elitist art form. But isn't it about time Americans claimed jazz as their art form and started recognizing it with the kind of respect they give to European music?

Williams: That's a fine thought, but how much is that really going to do for musicians? I don't think society really recognizes classical music, anyway. It's all patronage, and grants, a certain class of people. Jazz was originally the music of the people in the streets and not in concert halls, so when you lose that, you suffer the consequences. There's nothing wrong with jazz being an art form, but it has a certain roughness and vitality and unexpectedness that's important. I guess I'm old-fashioned.

June 1984

The Keith Jarrett Interview

by Art Lange

Ladies and gentlemen, meet Keith Jarrett. You say you already know all there is to know about the pianist/composer/improviser? You've followed him through his reputation-building term with Charles Lloyd in the late-'60s heyday of flower

Keith Jarrett.
(Teri Bloom)

rett the mystic, Jarrett the romantic, Jarrett the poseur, Jarrett the Platonist?

You may know all that, but I humbly submit that if you know Keith Jarrett through his music, you know him not at all, for music is sound, solely, and sounds can be deceiving. A note reveals nothing about the intent behind it—to discern that, you've got to open yourself. If nothing else, the encyclopedic list of activities above suggests a musician of more than a single mind; in fact, Jarrett is a man of contradictions. Some small sense of this can be heard in the range of emotions within his music— from the ruthless, slashing, Ornette-ish abandon of the American quartet to the simple, solitary, sweet, and sentimental ballad moments solo; from the gotta testify gospel chord changes to the meditational abstractions focusing on the beauty behind a single sound...

But contradiction goes beyond sound. Though identified closest with spontaneously conceived solo piano concerts, where he seems to go one-on-one with the muse, Jarrett's still concerned with the well-being of his audience. For the supposed egoist, he's insecure about his technique—so that his switch from solo concerts to classical concertos is a test not only for his audience but for himself as well.

"Do I contradict myself? / Very well then, I contradict myself / (I am large, I contain multitudes)," Walt Whitman wrote, suggesting that life is based on contradictions. Contradiction inspires concern and abandon—both necessary for a creative artist. Contradiction implies change and growth, not stasis. Contradiction allows for failures and successes. And contradiction acknowledged admits a struggle with forces possibly larger and more important than we casually care to recognize. Keith Jarrett, in his music and philosophies, is a contradiction. Good for him. Good for us.

Art Lange: I understand that you are concentrating on performing classical concertos these days, though you've been involved with classical music all your life...

Keith Jarrett: In the beginning I was trained to become a classical pianist, but it's just now becoming a public focus— actually it's not all that public yet. To develop repertoire takes a lot of years, and I'm mostly working on that now.

Lange: Why have you decided to start performing concertos at this time?

Jarrett: It's a complex question. It's

power; his subsequent electric excursions into Fillmore rock psychedelia alongside Miles Davis; his trend-setting solo piano extravaganzas stretching back over a decade; his two distinct yet decisive quartets, one American (Dewey Redman, Charlie Haden, Paul Motian), one Scandinavian (Jan Garbarek, Palle Danielsson, John Christensen); his chamber music experiments from *In the Light*; his spontaneous hymns coaxed from a baroque organ; his composed "concertos" for (variously) piano, flute, saxophone, bass plus orchestra; even his recent return to a stripped-down trio (Jack DeJohnette, Gary Peacock)—and you know just how to categorize him: Jar-not a decision as much as a pulling back from a kind of expectancy of freedom in what I've been doing up to now—and I don't mean my own expectancy, I mean the audience's. Their definition of freedom is becoming as limited as it was when, let's say, a solo concert would have been a revolutionary thing to do. So now the audience is thinking that unless it's an improvised solo concert, it isn't as much music making as it is in, say, a Mozart piano concerto. I would like to direct them slightly away from that focus—including the fact that solo improvised concerts can go on forever. There's no reason for them to stop, which is a good reason to stop.

In order to hear the recent solo concerts, a listener has had to hear how I'm playing the piano, much more than they did during the *Köln Concert* years. Then it was a flurry of ideas coming up within a limited dynamic range; now the dynamic range and how to play the instrument is so much more important in order to hear the concert. So maybe I can direct a classical audience to improvising and direct a jazz audience to trying to gain a little bit of interest, let's say, to come to grips with what that person is doing with his instrument.

Lange: How do you prepare for a notated classical piece? Is it different from the way you prepare for your own music?

Jarrett: It's exactly the same as if I were performing my own written music. But if I were going to improvise, then the preparation is reversed. Whatever you know about how to prepare for a written piece, you would have to reverse all the instructions for solo concerts. So you can understand why I cannot do both at the same time for very long periods of time. I'd go insane. "What am I doing tonight? Do I have the music? Do I have to have the music?" I have to sit down, for example, in order to play Mozart. Playing Mozart standing up is a contradiction in language. Also, it's important for any player to know a lot about that composer, not just look at the notes. That's another parallel to knowing your instrument: knowing about the composer. "We don't want to worry about the composer, let's just play these notes." Well, that doesn't work.

At any rate, the way I prepare for a concerto is the way any concerto player prepares; I think perhaps I'm more fanatical than most because I have much more to lose by not succeeding. No matter what I do, it will probably get written up, whereas in a debut of someone in New York, no

one's going to get all upset if he has a bad concert. If I have a bad concert, it's known all over the world.

Lange: So, technically, you practice, whereas in getting set for improvising, you don't want to practice because you don't want preconceived things going in.

Jarrett: Well, when improvising, you don't know what language you might have to use, or what language might come out that you'd have to be involved with. In other words, you shouldn't even hear pianos or be near pianos for a while. It should all be, again, a new sound, from almost a primitive beginning. But with, let's just take Mozart for an example, to even get past what is banal about Mozart's music means you have to understand the language he speaks. To understand that language means you have to know about fortepianos and harpsichords to hear the sound he heard. Once you get into all these things, you start to realize how few people play Mozart, you know? Most people play themselves playing Mozart, and the more they ignore that side of things, the more they would be playing their own natural tendencies rather than Mozart's music.

Lange: You're actually talking about another contradiction, because you're immersing yourself—or at least becoming comfortable—with certain aspects of Mozart's style, and "style" is a word that you want to avoid when you improvise.

Jarrett: That's right. Well, many improvisers might not think that way. The way I relate to it is that improvisation is really the deepest way to deal with moment-to-moment reality in music. There is no deeper way, personally deeper. But there is no less depth in working with someone else's music—having found his depth becomes exactly the same. And the people who think the two things are different are going to lose out when they come to listen to one or the other.

Lange: Of the concertos you've played so far, Mozart is the only non-20th century composer. Is that because it's harder to get close to Mozart's style because you're chronologically so far removed from it?

Jarrett: This choice of how to start the ball rolling was more to do with the audience being able to accept my playing Bartók first, rather than my wanting to play Bartók first. I would have wanted to play Bach, Beethoven first. If it was just like, "What do you want to play today?" I wouldn't say, "Hey, Bartók, man." I would say, "Well, in the situation I'm in what would be the way

to open this door?" Number one, the concerto I chose of Bartók's [Concerto #2] is one of the hardest piano concertos there is, so from the technical point of view, if I succeed at that, no one's going to fret anymore about whether I can play such and such a piece or not—including me. I mean, I have to prove to myself that I can do it. Secondly, from the point of view of the material and how it relates to what I've done up to that time, the shock is less great for the audience. I mean, to go straight into Mozart would have been very difficult.

Lange: Bartók, Barber, Stravinsky, who you've played, all have rhythmic elements that are closer to what a jazz audience is used to hearing than Mozart or Beethoven.

Jarrett: That's right; they can be digested. Their language is not that distant from what a jazz listener has heard. In fact, in Stravinsky's case, in Barber's case, they were influenced by a lot of jazz, wrote a lot of seemingly jazz-oriented things. Although in one of his interviews, Stravinsky—of all the people to choose as an example of an influential jazz player—chose Shorty Rogers: "If you listen to Shorty Rogers' phrasing you would find such-and-such a thing."

Lange: If left to your own devices, your own choice, you would have wanted to initially play Bach, Mozart, Beethoven…

Jarrett: Well, I only say that because I don't play or think about Bartók very often. However, I always find it healthy to listen to Bach, and often to Beethoven.

Lange: Do you think you'd like to play those pieces in public because they're so far divorced from jazz, so you'd personally want to go as far as you can in the other direction?

Jarrett: Good question. Right, except I have no intention of divorcing myself from jazz, and that's an interesting way of putting that question. I have absolutely no strings that have been untied from anything I have done; I'm just adding maybe a thicker rope, in a way, to all music that I consider, through certain subjective and objective processes, to be important to me. So the question about would I play Bach or Beethoven because of the difference—it's really the opposite. I feel that Bach and what I do myself are much closer than Bartók is to what I do in the solo concerts. It's the way the music sounds to the listener that makes it seem different. When it gets down to the nitty-gritty, Bach and I are friends, Beethoven and I are friends,

Mozart and I are friends sometimes, Bartók and I are friends because we're Hungarian, you know? And on and on. But I know if I went to jail and was allowed to take only one composer's music, I would probably take Bach's music.

Art Lange: Do you think you feel an affinity for the three you mentioned—Bach, Beethoven, and to a degree, Mozart...

Jarrett: I should add Handel in there too...

Lange:... because they were the improvising keyboard artists of their time?

Jarrett: I think the music is better because their relationship to improvising was so strong. I wouldn't say that I like their music because they were all improvisers, but there was something in the music, and I would say it is the ecstatic knowledge that comes through in Bach's music and in Beethoven's music. It's the knowledge of the ecstatic state—which means that's why their music conveys so much. [With Bach] almost every time and no matter what state you're in—at least I should speak for myself—there is something coming through, whereas with almost every other composer's music, I need to be in a certain mood to listen to it. So, to me, that means there's less being communicated. I know that when you're an improviser, a true improviser, you have to be familiar with ecstasy, otherwise you can't connect with music. When you're a composer, you can wait for those moments, you know, whenever. They might not be here today. But when you're an improviser, at 8 o'clock tonight, for example, you have to be so familiar with that state that you can almost bring it on.

Lange: So you do that—you bring the state on, but you don't bring on the music that that state leads to.

Jarrett: And this is what I can give back to all the composers I play, who I believe were familiar with that state. Within their own language I might be able to give them just a little gift of having understood how tremendous their struggle was with a particular note. Classical players are aware of this process because they're usually studious about everything they do—if they're good—but that doesn't mean they're aware of the state as much as, "Oh yes, this phrase means this." If you don't have a relationship with the state that produced the phrase, you can't be as good a player of the music. That's what I hope I can bring.

Lange: So far you've only performed concertos in public. Do you see yourself doing solo classical recitals?

Jarrett: Yes I do, but I'm not sure when.

Lange: Do you have any idea yet what music?

Jarrett: Not really. I've been working on the Beethoven sonatas for about 13 years now, fairly regularly. I didn't have this studio until several years ago, and before that I didn't practice a hell of a lot because improvising and practicing don't work together.

Lange: I take it you wouldn't consider doing a program of a Bach toccata, a Beethoven sonata, and a Jarrett improvisation.

Jarrett: No, probably not. That subject has come up, as you can imagine. An orchestra says, "Would you do this concerto with us and would you improvise in the second half?" No. I feel that is using my music merely as a means of filling out the program.

Lange: You don't feel that it might highlight some of those connections to the audience—you've played Bach and then you play your music so that they could hear some of the things you hear?

Jarrett: It certainly would be possible, but it would be too easy. For them and for me. Already we're at the point where they want to hear rich ideas related to their favorite solo recordings. They do not want to see that next step, and they won't accept that next step within the context of a solo improvised concert.

I had an interesting interview with the Japanese composer, Toru Takemitsu, recently. He decided he wanted to interview me for their classical music magazine. He was asking why my solo concerts were slowing down and stopping, and he said something about, "Is it because you don't want to possess the music anymore?" And that was precisely right. The only reason I bring this up is because I don't feel like a composer at this moment at all. And I talk to people about my stopping the solo concerts, and they say, "Oh my god," or, "Well, maybe you'll be writing something soon." And I tell them, "Wait a minute, you don't understand. This is a positive thing that is happening to me." It really is positive, in the sense that anyone who wants to listen to what I'm doing this year has to listen to other people's music, who they may not have a relationship with, and come to terms with whether they can deal with my relationship to those people or not. Which is exactly what you do when you're listening well, you know? "What did

I like or what didn't I like about it? Was it the piece, or was it the way they played the piece? Or maybe I just don't think he can do this; he shouldn't be doing this." All those things have no application to this point because people assume that if Keith Jarrett's going to play somewhere, he's going to play his own music. Even now if I play a concerto and the audience wants an encore, they want me to improvise.

Lange: So in addition to broadening your own musical experience, you're trying to broaden the listener's range of musical experience as well.

Jarrett: My experience has been that when you risk losing a listener, you're either doing something terrible or doing something very important. I've come to terms with when I'm doing something terrible—I'm the first person to know it's bad. If I continue to know that, then all I have to do is put those pieces together, and if I'm still risking the listening public, it's got to be a right step, you know? With the exception of pure shock value—anyway, there's no shock left.

Lange: Let's talk about the difference between writing for orchestra and writing for "jazz" quartet. You've had two well-known quartets that you've written for...

Jarrett: The hard part of writing for an orchestra is writing for an orchestra. The hard part of the quartet situation is not the writing at all—it is the question of how to make it a personal statement for everyone in the band. So that's a separate thing. In other words, if you take these four people and subtract even one and put a different person in it, the music I would write for that group should be different. And if anyone ever does a study on it, they'll see that the American quartet and the Scandinavian group and even the music I wrote for the trio at the Vanguard—I don't know if it will ever get recorded—but you could put them beside each other—and even the string music for Jan—and see how much consideration went into who was playing.

Lange: I think they sound very different...

Jarrett: Yeah, but a lot of people attribute that to the players. Like they'll say positive or negative things about, "The Swedish band doesn't exert enough pull against Jarrett's free-flowing melodic lines." Or, "Charlie Haden and Paul Motian were always pulling and stretching things, and we think that challenged Jarrett's creativity." But what they're really hearing isn't quite what they're saying.

What they're saying is true, but what they're hearing is how considerate I had to be to write for each of those bands. If I wrote the *Belonging* music with Charlie and Paul in the band, they couldn't be pulling in that way. The language wouldn't work. I'd have to stop and say, "Listen, Charlie, you gotta come down on 'one' here." If I wrote chords in a certain manner for Dewey, for example, and he was playing on changes, it would be a whole different sound. By Jan somehow changing his language, and the way the four of us played together, that worked. Someday I'm pretty sure that there'll be some serious studies of a lot of things, and I hope to be alive to see a few of them [laughs]. Just for fun, to see if it ever really happens.

Lange: So whenever you've composed something, it's been for very specific reasons or a specific situation. If you had to compose quartet music, it was for a particular group of players…

Jarrett: In jazz, yeah…

Lange:… and if it was an orchestral piece, it was because you were commissioned or…

Jarrett: Well no, actually *In the Light* was a collection of pieces I wrote with no outlet at all. But we all have youthful flows of ideas at a certain stage in our lives, and whatever happens, happens in that period of time. What happened in that period for me was I was not working, I didn't have a good instrument, I didn't have a suitable place to live, and writing certainly made some sense. It was a way of expressing something.

Lange: You've titled a lot of pieces "Hymn," even though they're different-sounding pieces in different contexts. Why "Hymn"?

Jarrett: Well, in the sense that Bach always ended his pieces with a dedication to God. It's the same thing. If I could call everything I did "Hymn," it would be appropriate because that's what they are when they're correct. I connect every music-making experience I have, including every day here in the studio. If it does not connect with a greater [long pause] power, and if I do not surrender to it, nothing happens. In that sense everything feels like a hymn, because I don't have access to this just by the fact of being Keith Jarrett and having recorded all this time. There's no reason why I should have this experience ever. Every time it's a gift. So if I want to acknowledge this gift, I would have to call it a hymn. "Ritual" was, in a way, just

another word about something perhaps surrounding a state of prayer.

Lange: When trying to describe your solo concerts, a lot of people say they hear traces of all different kinds of music: Oriental music, Russian music, Mideastern music, Scottish bagpipe drones, English folk tunes, Indian folk music and all this other stuff. I don't know if they think you've digested all this stuff, and are consciously or subconsciously throwing it in there. Why do you think that is?

Jarrett: If I were a "stylist," it wouldn't happen. If I were a self-conscious artist the way most people think an artist is supposed to be for some reason—and mostly critics seem to think that—I would be saying something only I could say, and I would always be avoiding saying anything anyone else has ever said, and I would somehow sound unique. Where to me—I've said this before—that's step number one: you finally have your sound and what you like; you have a way of making your music. Now, throw that away, and that's the beginning of being an artist. People want to stop at step one and say, "Listen, man, this sounds like everything; it's eclectic!" Call it anything you want; all I know is that step two is that you have to throw that away. And if you throw it away, then at any moment you can sound like anything, except it won't be that other thing.

Lange: Does it bother you when people use those "influences" to latch on to?

Jarrett: It bothers me how easy it is to do it, and that they choose listening to it that way because it's easier to do that. Associative listening, I guess I would call it.

Lange: Listening for recognizable events.

Jarrett: If they come to hear me, they want to hear my music, and if I come out with the attitude that none of it's mine, something's gonna go wrong. You can see how directly it leads, from improvising and not wanting to possess the music I improvise, to playing other people's music. Really, I've been feeling in the last few years, even while improvising, I am playing other people's music, or other music. It isn't mine.

Lange: So this is the reason for getting involved not only in public performances of concertos, but also the LP of standards with Jack Dejohnette and Gary Peacock.

Jarrett: Yes. Standards was, believe it or not, the opening to the classical thing, like a stop-off in American Songwriterville, trying to pay back some of my debt to the kind of music I felt Gary and Jack and I

had as a kind of tribal language that we all grew up with. We had a very serious dinner the night before we recorded. I prepared in advance of this dinner to talk about non-possessiveness, about how I didn't have any arrangements, how there was not going to be any idea of how to do these things. Just, "Do you like this song?" I had a list of songs, and we'd decide to try one, and almost without exception that was a take. Including what everyone thinks was made for the mass market—"God Bless the Child." It was absolutely nothing except that bass octave, and then Jack started to play the thing, and that was it.

Lange: When you're playing standards like that, the American popular song, do you hear the lyrics when you're playing?

Jarrett: Yes. That was the other thing I talked about that evening, although it was mainly for my benefit. I wasn't going to play a melody that was nothing but notes; I was going to play only melodies that I was familiar with verbally.

Lange: So the lyrics are part of what you relate to…

Jarrett: Well, I thought these pieces have been played in trio contexts before but not in trio contexts with utter respect for the song above everything else—above how the solos are, above anything. Just respect for the song. So when we went in there the next day, I could tell we were all thinking the same thing. I would think of a song, and Jack might start singing the bridge and the lyrics and say, "Yeah, okay." The second volume has a ballad on it that I think—not trying to sound too identified with the record since it's mine—but I think it's the best melody playing by a trio of a ballad I've ever heard. We'll see. Most likely what I'll hear about it is, "He's singing too much on this." [Laughs.]

Lange: Since so much of your creativity is concerned with process rather than the end result, how important is the piano to you, specifically? Is it just a tool that, if you could get to that source without the piano, you'd be willing to give up?

Jarrett: Well, I've created a history, you know? A kind of architecture that includes the piano, and I've created an audience who, no matter what I say about them at any time, wouldn't exist at this moment without my piano music. If I didn't feel responsibility for them, then the piano wouldn't be a necessary tool for anything—anyway, for getting into the state I spoke of previously. The other reason it's important is if I want to interpret other people's music, the piano is becoming more important than it was before. I have become a better pianist in the last year— probably three times better in the last year—than I was before by virtue of practicing and diligent discipline. But that doesn't mean I need the piano. Actually, my favorite instrument is probably the tabla drums.

Lange: That's interesting. Why's that?

Jarrett: I just think that the tablas have everything in them that you need to make music. And nothing more.

August 1984

My Dinner with Carla

by Don Palmer

To paraphrase filmmaker Jean-Luc Godard, here are two or three things you may want to know about her—Carla Bley that is. Her favorite color is green, even though she says that she doesn't look good in it. She doesn't like official holidays. "When I finish a piece of music, I have a holiday—well, not a holiday, but a celebration." She doesn't like bright, noisy restaurants with Muzak. She felt apprehensive about her first Japanese tour in late May. Her music is facing new assimilationist pressures, and from within no less.

Most of this is the sort of trivia one might expect to get over a dinner with Carla, especially from a rambling conversation at an ill-lit but comfortable Italian restaurant on New York City's Lower East Side. But this last bit of information about Bley's music taking a turn towards the mainstream is surprising. Could Carla Bley, the queen of the avant-garde composers, actually consider compromise after all these years as one of the few contemporary musicians whose work was unique, fresh and funny, and whose compositions helped jazz players add to the vocabulary of improvisation?

From the time she quit school at the age of 15 and took a job in a music store selling sheet music, Carla Bley has blended irreverence with innocence. Her religious family in Oakland did little to stunt that development, but her involvement in the church did leave Bley with a working knowledge of religious and spiritual music. She also claims that a job in her aunt's flower shop in Carmichael, Calif., where she made and placed sprays on caskets, provided some inspiration for her funereal music of later years.

When she left California for New York City in the early '60s, Bley had no problem working as a cigarette girl in jazz clubs before integrating herself into the full-time jazz scene. From 1964 on, Bley was a prime force in the formation and growth of the Jazz Composers Guild, its orchestra and eventually the Jazz Composers Orchestra Association, a nonprofit foundation to support the orchestra and commission new works. JCOA spawned another even more ambitious project, the New Music Distribution Service, which was Bley's attempt to provide an outlet and distribution network for new or non-commercial records without depriving musicians of the ownership and control of their music.

Although her current involvement at NMDS is limited to publishing a newspaper every two and a half years, Bley still gets "incredible satisfaction out of it. When we and Mike Mantler started JCOA, we only wanted to write for big orchestras. We never had any gigs, so we had plenty of time left over to tend to business. I did all the stamp licking and envelope stuffing, but now I don't have time to sneeze. When you have so many irons in the fire"—Bley pauses to check the cliché—"Is that the word? You've got to delegate responsibility among people who you hire."

Since the mid-'60s Bley has enjoyed a slow but inexorable climb to the heights of success, especially if measured in jazz terms. She estimates she has written 300 songs and 50 scores for her 10-piece band. Bley has performed on dozens of albums, and her own recordings have received far more acclaim than scorn. In addition, Bley's recent albums are distributed by ECM via the Warner Bros. conglomerate, and all her work is available by mail from the Mighty Mouse of alternative music, NMDS. Nonetheless, Bley seems torn by the notoriety and the good fortune that homage through transfiguration is not only hip but acceptable and popular. So maybe the new musical direction is Bley's typical iconoclastic, nose-thumbing response to the times having caught up with her. Or maybe, as Bley states, her new release, *Heavy Heart*, is about springtime and love.

Either answer coming from Bley the prankster could be a half-truth, but it is unquestionable that *Heavy Heart* tends toward the sentimental excesses of the New York studio scene rather than a bluesy, quirky reply to love, fulfilled or not. This is not to say that *Heavy Heart* is as unctuous as David Sancious or as vapidly, technically soulful as David Sanborn, but most of the indelible Bley trademarks have been skillfully manicured or excised. The tunes are still Bley-like, hip and exquisite; the harmonies elongated under the fluid, piping alto of Steve Slagle and the snorting, muscular trombone of Gary Valente (on "Ending It"); the solos and arrangements always take an unusual turn a phrase or two before becoming predictable; and Bley's ethnic sensibility takes the form of Latin lilts and tempo-altering shuffles. In short, *Heavy Heart* is a light, breezy album without being formulaic, and one which fabricates jazz-pop from evocations of the revived electric bands of Miles and Gil, Marvin Gaye's "Here, My Dear," and assorted sultry, sensuous tunes.

Yet fans of the eccentric Bley, the keyboardist/composer whose work can be rich and zany like Ellington's "East St. Louis Toodle-Oo," shouldn't despair, because her soundtrack for the French film *Mortelle Randonnee* is less soundtrack and more Bley recording than *Heavy Heart*. *Randonnee* finds the imagistic Bley calliope in full swing. Drunken melodies, staggered ensemble passages that are part cacophony, part call-and-response and doleful, even dissonant harmonies abound in a mélange of tangos, dirges and mock marches. Like *Musique Mecanique* and *European Tour 1977*, *Randonnee* is energetic, brassy and full of weird twists that'll make you perk up and even cackle.

On the eve of her first Japanese tour, Carla Bley was in a good mood because she "just had a burst of self-confidence about it. The apprehension I feel about Japan could be what I'd feel about anything new, so it might be just fine afterwards."

Bley went on to explain, "In the last year I've become shy of getting on the stage. And, if you figure I've had a band for eight years and for seven of those years I didn't know whether I was onstage or off, it just means I've been made to feel self-conscious recently."

By whom? The audience? Well, have you ever been pelted? "Oh yeah, I've been pelted. In France it was tomatoes; in Italy it's cans and apricot pits or half-eaten peaches. That doesn't bother me. I had played the Italian national anthem and was just being irreverent in general. It took people seven years to get used to that, and now they don't throw things."

Alto saxophonist Steve Slagle laughed and added, "Beer cans in Germany, but for no good reason." Bley continues, "And full of beer. I stopped the concert and said, 'I want the guy who threw that up onstage.' The audience ran after him, but he went over a fence. I wouldn't continue until I could pour a can of beer over somebody because that beer had splashed all over us. The promoter offered himself, and I poured an entire can of beer on his head. I love audience participation."

Getting back to the point, Bley blamed the press for making her self-conscious. "They ask me things that I don't even want to mention. They ask me questions that make me wonder why I am doing this, am I strange, do I look funny, am I not qualified?"

Certainly Carla Bley's propensity to stray from the facts, to spin tales, and her willful innocence work at cross purposes for her and the press. She's also said that critics are more interested in personalities than music, which she amended. "I should say that humans like personalities more than music. I'm that way. When a person plays, I don't listen to their notes; I listen to who they are. That's what I mean by personality.

"I think I'm getting to be well known in a wider circle, so that people aren't really music lovers. I think a lot of people who might come to a concert now are sensation seekers, and I can't provide that. I can only provide the music."

As Slagle later explained, Bley's concern over the presentation of her music was not just due to fear. The additional preparation for her Japanese tour had become necessary because Bley and the band discovered that a two-hour set was more powerful and effective than two one-hour sets, and the build-up, tension, and subsequent release, which Bley's music strongly generates for the audience, was dissipated during the intermission. But, in order to play for two hours nonstop, the band has to be "really tight."

Although Bley eschews the notion that she is motivated by a desire to appease her newer and larger audience, she has produced an album that is simpler, more

Carla Bley in Köln, Germany, 1984. (Hyou Vielz)

streamlined and accessible than much of her previous work. *Heavy Heart* should certainly get some radio airplay and attract more listeners, which in turn could make Carla Bley a tad wealthier and even more self-conscious.

Her response? "I didn't know I was gonna make that record. About a year after *Live*, I took the band into the studio, and we made a follow-up album with the pieces I'd written. The recording wasn't good, and I knew it the next day when I listened to it. I think what was wrong was that the live album had worked, and we tried to reproduce it but in a studio with no overdubs. We missed the audience—that's all it could be. I'm not talking about applause,

I'm talking about the breathing that an audience puts into a piece of music.

"If you record in the studio, you have to use a different process; it's a different art form. I'm always thinking, 'I know this,' so I said to myself, 'I know this,' and decided to make a studio album without using the guys in my band. I was going to follow the procedures and start with just the rhythm section and add the other tracks later."

Bley intended to use all studio musicians, but she ended up with her own rhythm section plus percussionist Manolo Badrena and guitarist Hiram Bullock as the add-ons. She also knew that her love for the saxophone dictated that at least one horn had to appear on the album. Her

Carla Bley.
(Roger Ressmeyer)

choice was Slagle because he's a "romantic kind of guy." Bley had Slagle come to the session to play the melodies for the rhythm section, but he wanted to play in the main studio with the band instead of being isolated in his booth. The result was that Slagle's guide tracks remained on the recording although initially they were to be erased, with new horn parts dubbed in. Later Bley added more horns, but not before deciding to use her guys "because of sentiment, and they play better." Now she calls her attempt at a studio album half-successful and a "mongrel."

Bley says that she wants to do another studio record, and she even talks about disbanding her group so that she can put more time into the effort. Surprisingly she stated, "I might quit my band in August for financial reasons. The band has been an obsession of mine. I put all my copyright royalties into it, but the band does not make money. It is a losing proposition—any big band is."

Whether from fatigue, momentary disillusionment, or the desire to see if we'll miss her when she's gone, Bley says that she's even soured some on leading a band. "You should have a band and see what it's like. If you're not an extrovert, it's really hard, particularly if you're not a virtuoso musician. If I could take one brilliant solo or something, and the audience would scream with delight, my presence onstage would mean something. I wrote the music, but why am I even there? I do a couple of hand waving things which I don't do very well, and I play an organ solo that has maybe two or three notes over a period of five minutes. I feel like I should be in a cage with a sign on me that says, 'She wrote the music.'"

Bley seems undaunted by Slagle's boast that she's a great leader because she gives musicians the freedom to express themselves within a framework. Like the great bandleaders such as Mingus, Ellington, and Basie, Bley knows how to write for and elicit strong performances from her soloists. But she'll accept no comparison between her playing and that of the other great minimalists of the keyboards.

"Ellington always had some little thing he played on the piano that was startling and wonderful. I really should try to figure out a cameo in the middle of the night, where I play something that I prepared in advance and was real flashy. I would love to be flashy, but I hate to prepare in advance. I couldn't repeat myself two nights in a row because I have an aversion to saying the same thing or playing the same thing. But next month I'll play the same set every night. I don't know if it'll happen, but I'm planning to do that."

Though Bley is obviously no Cecil Taylor or Oscar Peterson chops-wise, nor is her economical playing as skillful as Monk, Basie or Ellington, her brief and infrequent solos are expressive. On the late Clifford Thornton's *The Gardens of Harlem*, Bley plays the introduction to "Gospel Ballade," and her halting style conjures a lumber camp/whorehouse pianist playing the blues for the sanctified.

Bley claims that she has no direct influences on her writing or playing. "I just hear something and it sticks. Anything I like or hate comes out in the music. I've never studied any kind of music, and even if I were to attempt to duplicate something, I'd fail horribly." She pauses, gives an aw-schucks laugh and concedes, "Okay, fail beautifully."

She continues by describing her technique. "When I do a solo and when it's good, there's a word for every note I play. I speak the solos while I play. I played an organ solo on 'Heavy Heart' [the title tune], and there's a word for every note. They're all silly words, ordinary words, corny words, so I'd never tell you what they were.

"I'm just a composer, and I use jazz musicians because they're better. They play better, they're smarter, and they can save your ass in a bad situation. If their music falls off the stands, they can make it up. A classical musician, a folk musician, or a rock & roll musician is pretty limited in what they can do to help out the leader. I need all the help I can get."

Not only does Bley think jazz musicians are better, but she finds classical musicians are snobby, because they think there's only one way to play. Nonetheless, she had nothing but praise for the radio orchestra in Köln, Germany, where she had just performed with fellow composers Michael Mantler and Mike Gibbs. "It's a good orchestra, and the string players aren't snobby. They played right on the beat. You usually put your hand down, and they come in a few minutes later, so I was trying to match the time of the orchestra by playing real late. At the end they were matching me."

How long does it take you to finish a piece for jazz musicians? "Two months. First I write a lot of material, then I start gettin' rid of all of it. Then I've got a rough copy, and I start working on a score. That takes a lot of time, and then I have to copy the parts.

"I just wrote a new piece, and the way it happened is interesting. Five days before Marvin Gaye died, I wrote this piece that sounded just like Marvin Gaye, but I didn't want a piece like that. It was great, but it was in a field I wanted to leave behind me since I had done the *Heavy Heart* album. It's a bass solo first, for Steve Swallow because he's always raving about Marvin Gaye and says that's where he learned his phrasing. It's for the 10-piece band, but the bass has the melody and the solo. There are no other soloists, which means that I get to play the bass line all the way through on my synthesizer. That's more fun than I've ever had. I think I want to be a bass player."

April 1985

The Quincy Jones Interview

by Zan Stewart

Quincy Jones, even if you didn't know his name from Adam, even if you didn't know that he is one of contemporary music's main creative sparks, that he was 1983's Producer of the Year, that he's scored 33 films and been responsible for 30 albums, that he's won 15 Grammys, that he's been in the entertainment business for 35 years, even if you didn't know his middle name is Delight, a leisurely look around his Los Angeles office would start to fill in the picture. The walls are adorned with photographs, mementos and awards. There are pictures of heroes and friends like Miles Davis and John Coltrane, and pictures of associates, such as Quincy with Michael Jackson or Quincy with his arms around Count Basie. On a side table, next to a phone with 10 lines that never stop flashing, there are blank notepads printed with *The Color Purple*, the name of the film he's producing. There's a framed collection of platinum discs of Jackson's *Thriller*, a Jones

production which sold an unimaginable-but-true 37 million copies. More or less office center sits a Yamaha electric grand piano. Behind Jones' clutter-free, glass-topped desk is a stained-glass logo for his Qwest label, which he launched in 1981. Beyond all this, there's something intangible, and without getting too cosmic, let's just say there's a presence. After all, Quincy Jones is a man who makes things happen.

Born in 1933, Jones was raised in Seattle and began playing trumpet at an early age. Ray Charles was a childhood friend, and the two often worked and jammed together. A prodigy, Jones was employed by 14 and joined Lionel Hampton at 15. Later, he took a break and began studies at Boston's Berklee College of Music. Soon he was back with Hampton as a trumpeter and arranger, and was quickly adding his touch to sessions with Charles, Dinah Washington, Duke Ellington, Cannonball Adderley and others. He toured the Middle East and South America with Dizzy Gillespie's orchestra, then joined Mercury Records as an A&R man. There he recorded his own dates, such as *The Birth of a Band*, as well as producing pop hits like Leslie Gore's 1963 smash, "It's My Party."

The year 1963 found Jones composing his first film score, for Sidney Lumet's *The Pawnbroker*, and in 1969 he signed with A&M Records, an association that lasted 12 years and resulted in such albums as *Walking in Space*, *Body Heat*, and *Sounds... And Stuff Like That*, the latter his first platinum disc. In 1978 he scored Lumet's film of *The Wiz*, and made the acquaintance of Michael Jackson. He produced Jackson's 1981 *Off the Wall*, which was a mere prelude to the stunning success of 1983's *Thriller*. In addition to *The Color Purple*, Jones is currently working on a new solo album, which will spotlight Sarah Vaughan and organist Jimmy Smith among as-yet-unnamed others, and is due for May release.

Jones arrived to meet his visitor attired casually in faded denims, a yellow T-shirt, a cardigan sweater composed of bands of warm colors that blended softly together and tan loafers with pale blue and yellow socks. Sipping apple cider (he drinks wine as well, but only with meals, since recovering from two aneurysms in 1974), the personable, convivial Jones talked at length about his life and achievements.

Zan Stewart: I'm one of those who really enjoys your earlier albums, like

Quintessence. Yet in listening to *Thriller*, I hear a lot of basic stuff there, too, a basic bluesy feel to many tunes...

Quincy Jones: That's why I get so confused. People get all hung up with the evolution of this music and saying, "You're not into jazz anymore." Bullshit. It's all the same thing to me.

Zan Stewart: Do you feel your jazz background is essential to your role of producer of non-jazz music?

Jones: Oh, yeah, sure, in many ways. Philosophically, musically, because those skills enable you to turn on a dime. You don't get hung up with the way things are supposed to be.

Zan Stewart: You've made so many hit records. Is that something you always wanted to do?

Jones: You know, I think every musician in the world would like to make hit records—every musician that ever picked up any instrument. Even a 12-tone player wants what he puts together to appeal to a lot of people. The ideal situation is to do something you like and have everybody in the world like it and buy it, too. I think everybody feels that.

But when I started out, it was different. I have a funny kind of background. I came out of a gospel group, but I had an early interest in big bands, and also worked in an R&B band with Bumps Blackwell up in Seattle, and would go play bebop after hours. That was pure love. Ray Charles was 16; I was 14. Ray would play at clubs like the Black and Tan, and I also played all over town, and then we'd get together at the Elks Club after hours to play bop. In the clubs or at dances, you'd have to play schottisches [Scottish dances], pop songs, R&B, and so on, but when we played at the Elks Club, that was for us.

But at that time—and Cannonball [Adderley] and I used to laugh about this—we were conditioned to try to avoid having our music appreciated by a big audience, especially the young guys who were on the coattails of Bird and Diz. We were their disciples. It was very unhip to have a big following.

I remember playing with Lionel Hampton—who was really the first rock 'n' roll bandleader, even though he had a jazz background—and we were at the Bandbox in New York City, which was next door to Birdland. Clifford Brown, Art Farmer and I were in the trumpet section. We had to wear Bermuda shorts with purple jackets and Tyrolian hats, man, and when we played "Flying Home," Hamp marched the band outside. You have to imagine this—I was 19 years old, so hip it was pitiful, and didn't want to know about anything that was close to being commercial. So Hamp would be in front of the sax section, and beating the drumsticks all over the awning, and soon he had most of the band behind him. But Brownie and I would stop to tie our shoes or do something so we wouldn't have to go outside, because next door was Birdland and there was Monk and Dizzy and Bud Powell, all the bebop idols standing in front at intermission saying, "What is this shit?" You'd do anything to get away.

I was always on the edge. Even as a kid in Seattle, we'd play anything, for strippers, for comedy acts, while at the same time harboring our love for bebop. At that time you didn't want to communicate, but then you had to get it out of you. Herbie Hancock said he had the same problem. It's like that old Sid Caesar joke: "We used to have radar in the band to let us know when we got too close to the melody." It was that kind of attitude.

Stewart: Maybe you weren't asking for appreciation because it wasn't there anyway.

Jones: Well, a funny thing happened at the end of the '40s and the 52nd Street thing. I'm sure people who were closer to it might have a different attitude, but the way it looked from here was that at one point, between '44 and '46, many of the mavericks and rebels, the innovators, they left Jay McShann, Earl Hines and other leaders, and went with Billy Eckstine. It was like a sociological thing, as if they were saying, "We aren't interested in being entertainers anymore. We want to be recognized as artists. That was the first time black musicians ever took that position, at least en masse, like that.

Billy had the first crop of naturally feeling but thinking, seriously thinking musicians, people dealing with polytonals, trying to break a sound barrier, musically. But when they made that decision to not be entertainers, they were taking the risk of losing an audience. And at one point the audience fell totally out, so the musicians said, "Well, we don't care," and they withdrew. There was no interest in entertaining or communicating because there was this search for a new sound.

So we left that creative era and went into the '50s, which was the worst era for pop music. Coming from modern jazz to

that poop was horrible. Remember the radio? Tunes like "How Much Is That Doggie in the Window," "Davy Crockett" and so on. It was unbelievable [laughs]. That was the pop scene, but Elvis Presley's appearance changed that whole thing for young white America, because he opened the way for black music to come in.

But back to this hit thing. People want hits—Miles Davis, too [laughs]. To me, there's something retarded about someone saying, "I don't want anybody to like my music." That's insane. But I can see saying, "I don't care if anybody likes what I do." We've all gone through that. Music is an incredible animal. It's an absolute, like math. You can't hold it; it just floats around out there.

Stewart: Speaking of your own music, we hear you have a new album in the works. How do you start a new project?

Jones: Well, it's hard to say. It's like I sketch a physical thing in my mind—like colors, contours and shapes. I literally see pictures and colors. These undefined shapes come through first, then the secondary colors. Then I have to be patient; I have to sit and wait until it becomes clearer and clearer. I may formulate maybe 18 ideas of different things that I feel, that I really want to do and, in the end, I may use nine of them. Maybe in the last part of the project, I'll find two other things that'll divert you. But I just let it flow, let whatever happens happen, then I start boilin' and get specific. You can't capture anything until you get specific. Then you have to see if what you're hearing and seeing in your mind, you can execute in the studio. It's a funny process, man. I don't know a thing about it. I just do it.

Stewart: Will this album follow a process, like building track by track or will it be more like a "live" date?

Jones: Well, some things I start with a drum track and then add. Others won't take that form. I hope it's unlike anything I've ever done before. That's a nice feeling, to come out each time and try to pretend that you've never done any of this before. The worst thing is to say, "Well, this worked before, so we've got to do more of this." I could never get into that. But sometimes you can't help it, in that the sounds will be similar because it's your own soul. But what's great about producing your own album is that you play the orchestras, you play the singers. Nobody can tell you, "You can't do that." That's the real difference. Your own album should represent

what you want to do. It's not like working with a singer, because no matter how good the relationship is, they may say, "Well, I don't know; let's try it my way." That's why the freedom is so nice.

Stewart: What's the difference between producing Michael Jackson and producing Frank Sinatra, whom you worked with on last year's *LA Is My Lady*.

Jones: Well, Michael starts with basic tracks, then adds overdubs, then fixing—you've got to put it together like an erector set, and try to help Michael realize, or embellish, what he had. As we said, the process takes about three months. Sinatra came into the office here, and started with a list of things he wanted to do. I had two or three suggestions. He came in at 2 p.m., and in less than two hours we had rehearsed, had keys and routines on 10 songs. That's the way he's always recorded. Two months later in New York, we record. Before he gets there, the band runs down all the tunes, because Frank is one take, that's it. If the band's not in shape, he leaves them behind. And when you're recording live like he does, you can't take that chance, because when his voice is in their mikes, you can't take it out if the band sounds like shit. His booth is open, and the horns are hitting his microphone, hitting him right in the face. So, on his last session, he came in at 7, and at 8:20, baby, we went home. None of that three-month stuff.

To me, there's no such thing as good and bad in either way you record. I started recording live, but it doesn't make any difference just as long as you're capturing the real feeling of what was supposed to happen. We have this expression: leave God a little room to come through, give him 20 to 30 percent in the room. In recording, you're talking magic; for it to really happen, a lot of magic has to go down.

Stewart: What else is on the front burner?

Jones: I'm producing my first film. I've wanted to do this for a long time. There's a book that tore my heart out—it's so beautiful, written by Alice Walker, called *The Color Purple*. Reading it has been one of the most incredible experiences I've had in my life. For 15 years people have wanted me as executive producer of films, mainly to get the musical connection and just have me be a spectator. But I want to be in the physical process of making the film. That's what's nice. It's an unbelievable project, just loaded with rich music that dates from 1905 to 1940, so the music of Scott Joplin, Robert Johnson, Bessie Smith and Coleman Hawkins will be included. Imagine a film where part of the tapestry is a Hawk solo and one of the leads is just mumbling along with the solo. That turns me on.

That reminds me. There was an album, I think it was *Back in Flight*, which if you played at 45 rpm instead of 33 rpm, you'd hear a version of "There Will Never Be Another You" that sounds just like Bird. Hearing that blew me away because you could see the roots and the connection. It opened up a big door for my head; the nuances were identical, all of them.

Stewart: So the film gives you a chance to work on…

Jones: The evolution, yeah, exactly. It's amazing how things work out. You don't plan it. I started around 1970, just digging and digging—really didn't even know why, except I was just interested in it—the evolution of our music. After being in the business 25 years, I felt it would be fun to go back and see the exact sources. Research. I thought it would take two to three months, but I got hung up, ultimately going back to 479 AD to the Moors, the Spanish inquisition, then following 34 tribes from West Africa to Brazil up to the West Indies, then on to New Orleans, Virginia and so forth. It just blew me away. The whole idea of drums being banned in 1672 because the slave owners knew it was a communication device. To ban the drum did something to the music. That was in the Protestant colonies. In the Catholic colonies they were getting down—the Spanish, French—with food, music, everything. That's where it all happened. A lot of people were oppressed and restricted by the Anglicans. But when it was time to get rhythmic again, everything had to be redefined rhythmically, so a hybrid music came out of this. The film plays a role in underscoring all this.

Stewart: Any new musical projects besides the new album?

Jones: I'm going to do a musical with Mike Nichols after *The Color Purple*, and that will probably incorporate a lot of the evolutionary things. It's a piece called *Speak Easy*, so it's another thing about that time, the '20s and '30s.

Stewart: So here you are producing all this modern music like Michael Jackson, and then turn around and dig way back.

Jones: That's what's great about it—the whole menu. Why not, man? I love the notion of what that's all about, the whole

Quincy Jones.

range. It's so real and so strong. I love having the chance to go from a Michael Jackson situation to my own album to *The Color Purple*, where we have a really valid reason for using the music of that period, other than simply wanting to expose it.

Stewart: As the music changes, say from swing to bebop and so on, it seems

that the rhythm section leads the way, setting things up for the other instruments to follow. Do you agree?

Jones: Yes, I feel the major change usually comes from the rhythm section. I have always been fascinated by what's happening in the basement. The basement started with country-jazz march bands, then moved to 2/4 with Dixie and even [Jimmie] Lunceford, and so forth. Then Basie, Benny Moten, you're talking four to the floor. Then it kept accelerating into eighth notes, then triplets and 16ths and then farther, like [Billy] Cobham and Elvin Jones incorporating the African polyrhythms. Then you come back to disco, and it's just the same thing as Basie. It's always fascinating. The current rhythm section sound changes almost every six months. That pendulum really swings, going from four to the floor to the most complex things with the drum machines. You get more flexibility with them, but the machines are just a reaction to the disco thing, so when they get out of that framework, it's like escaping from prison, so you get [Herbie Hancock's] "Rockit." Music is always reacting to itself, you get to max velocity, you've got to slow down.

You can see that pendulum swing throughout all American music. I wouldn't trade that era I came up in for anything. We got a taste of all of it. There I was involved with Swing Era people like Basie, Duke, Lionel, then Dizzy, and pop people like Stevie [Wonder] and Michael [Jackson].

Stewart: Working with both jazz and pop artists seems to be quite natural for you.

Jones: I was always ambidextrous. Of course, I did *The Genius of Roy Charles* in '58, but even before that, I was double-gated. I did a lot of things with Stitt, Brownie [Clifford Brown], Art Farmer; but by the same token, I was doing projects with Big Maybelle, Chuck Willis, the Clovers, LaVern Baker. It started as a kid, because I had to have that broad range of knowledge to work in Seattle. Ray Charles used to say, "If you just deal with the pure soul of all music, everything from the schottisches to blues, you'll be all right." What a musician he is. He taught me how to read music in Braille.

Stewart: Given your wide-ranging background, what, if anything, constitutes the Quincy Jones sound?

Jones: I don't know. I know that material is the key. The song is king; melody is king. I fight strongly to have the last word on material going into an album. If somebody else picks the songs, I don't know if I really want to participate. I get called a dictator for that, but I don't care. You cannot polish doo-doo. It's very important that you're hard on everybody, including yourself, in terms of selecting material. I'm always straddling a fence to get things that will penetrate and communicate, but still have a certain musical validity, not be musically idiotic. In pop music you're dealing with anything from 300,000 to 37 million records. I don't know how to figure out what 37 million people are going to like. So far we've been lucky. We've had songs that make the hair go up on your arm. If it moves you, you're lucky if it gets to all those other people.

Stewart: While picking the songs for *Thriller*, did the hair go up on your arms?

Jones: Oh, sure. We cut nine songs, at first, and had it finished, and then threw four out to get four more that were really strong. That's a nice psychological thing to do, because you're competing with yourself. We had just come off an album that sold eight million [*Off the Wall*], and it's scary to go back in after that kind of home run. Our thinking was, "If we could just catch up with half of this thing, we'd be happy," and little did we know it'd do what it did. To me, half of commerciality is sincerity. It's gotta be real.

Stewart: How many times can you listen to a record like *Thriller*?

Jones: I can't listen to it anymore, no. The first six months after we made it, I couldn't touch it, except to listen to the singles we were going to release. We had a serious deadline on this record, since Donna Summer's album took longer than it should have, so when we got to Michael, we only had three months to do *Thriller*. That's pretty scary after a record that did eight million. On top of this, Steven Spielberg asked us to do the *E.T. Storybook*, so we had three months to do both. It almost killed us, but we made it. I had two studios going. We just rocked around the clock until we finished.

Then we had a scary thing happen. We finished *E.T.*, and Michael's record was down to mix and master. We were really tired by then, but you have to keep the enthusiasm up. So we mixed the record and were ready to have it mastered. We finished about 8 a.m., and Michael came by my house and slept on my couch. We had to be back at the studio by noon, and Bruce [Swedien, Quincy's No. 1 engineer] was going to bring the test pressing so we could listen to it before it went out. This is the record, you know? Everybody was nervous to hear what was going to happen. Well, we had been in such a hurry that we had put 25 and 27 minutes on a side, and you know that's a no-no, because it takes the sound away. We'd like 18 minutes on a side, max. That record sounded like shit, man. We knew it wouldn't hold. It was terrible. Michael cried. So we decided to hell with the deadline, 'cause they were really on our backs. So we took time off and came back, took one tune a day and brought this baby home. And that's what we did. If that record had gone out, it would have never been over, it would have been a disaster. I'll never forget that day. It was horrible.

Stewart: What was so bad about the record?

Jones: Basically the mixes were sloppy because we were hurrying. Overall, there were a lot of bad judgments from being hasty and tired. Adrenaline turns your ears into something else.

Stewart: Switching channels again, you were the first man to record an electric bass in 1953, and a synthesizer in 1964. How has the synthesizer affected modern music?

Jones: It's expanded the vocabulary. People always talk about it replacing acoustic instruments. I think that's ridiculous. If you've got that kind of an ear, maybe it can, but I think the effective usage is to have the synths do what they can do specifically. They expand the alphabet from 26 to 40 letters. They have a personality—millions of sonic designs—that can't come out of other instruments. The ear knows that the sounds aren't familiar, aren't from an acoustic instrument. By the same token, there's no synth yet that can get the sound of 24 string players with bodies there, skin on skin.

Stewart: Still, electronics seem to be the way many players are going.

Jones: It's not the same thing; believe me, it's not. I've used all the string tricks and electronic strings, and there's nothing that replaces acoustic instruments. The vibratos are not the same, for instance. They're doing a good job with samplers, but mechanically, it's very difficult to deal with that kind of humanity with an electronic instrument. A joy for me is to have the synthesized-string sound set up the fabric of what the strings are going to be, and then have a lap dissolve and have the real strings come in right underneath it. That's what I love, when they really meet each other head on in an accommodating way, join each other, strut their feathers in front of each other, enjoy being with each other. That might sound silly, but that's how I feel. I've been in the business for 35 years, and I've seen a lot of trends, but you've still got to have human beings. I don't see any machines blowing trumpet players out of work.

Stewart: Does your presence in the studio have an effect on the outcome of a product?

Jones: I think so, because I only work with artists I respect and love for what they do. Most of the time I try to put a musician in a situation where he should be comfortable. But there are times, like the world's greatest guitarist who couldn't read. You put him in a situation with 44 players, and there's a psychological tendency to freak out. I used to have that problem with Basie. I mean, he'd see seven sharps and head for the bathroom. But it doesn't matter, man, because there are guys who can read around the corner who couldn't touch Basie with two notes he'd play. So once the musician learns to trust me, learns that he can go without the net, that I won't let him fall, we have a great time. Toots Thielemans says, "You always push the right buttons on me and make me play my ass off." But that's only with someone you really love, you know. You put them in a situation where they can really be themselves.

July 1985

Henry Threadgill: Music to Make the Sun Come Up

by Howard Mandel

"You can't really talk about one thing without talking about everything. Then you know you're talking a real truth," says Henry Threadgill, the 41-year-old composer, improviser, ensemble leader, multi-reed player, and all-around creative musician—as in Association for the Advancement of Creative Musicians—who, wherever he goes, projects an enviable lightness of being.

"I hate to talk just about music. Because if you're really talking about something, it applies in every category,

across every line. Then you're talking about something. A real idea. A real generator. Like gold, silver, a mineral, the water, the air. You know you're talking about something, rather than about things, impressions, people, and that whole area. Ideas. Real ideas. There are concrete truths at the bottom, you know."

A very ordinary man works a ho-hum job and leads a hum-drum life. He lives alone and enjoys no satisfying relationships at work or in his personal life.

—from Ilyse Kazar's synopsis of *When Life Is Cheap and Death Is Taken for Granite* (Imaginary Film), libretto by Henry Threadgill 1980

Perhaps you were wondering, perhaps you aren't sure—yet—whether the art some black musicians forged in the '60s really has any substance, any staying power, any form, any significance. Ornette Coleman, later John Coltrane, Eric Dolphy, Cecil Taylor, the AACM—it's so much noise to you. Call that jazz? Those cats can't play. Too lazy to learn even the tradition, then they go mess with "classical" concepts. Who do they think they are? Their records don't sell, their proposals stretch grant guidelines. Are they too good for the club hustle? Have they tried gigging at the post office?

Threadgill walks about Manhattan's East Village, where he lives—as he did Chicago, where he was raised—limber and loose of stride, in bright, self-styled clothes, with an alert smile and a ready greeting. He's about to release *Subject to Change*, his third LP on the independent About Time Records, featuring his seven-person sextet. PBS recently aired a documentary on Panama that used his soundtrack. He's adapted Kurt Weill's Great Hall from Silverlake for 13 pieces, recorded for an A&M anthology being produced by Hal ("That's the Way I Feel Now") Willner. Of course, he's on about a dozen albums by the now-disbanded trio Air, but Threadgill's always making more music than can be documented on record. Last spring there was his dance music for an ensemble including cornetist Olu Dara and guitarist Jean-Paul Bourelly at the Kitchen's Masked Ball, his concert at Carnegie Recital Hall, his onstage appearance as a musician in the Metropolitan Opera's *Porgy and Bess*, his collaborations with choreographer Rrata Christine Jones, his Live Music/Imagination/Theatre series for his WindString Ensemble. In spring of '84, Threadgill

responded to booking agents' indifference by mounting his own month-long, coast-to-coast U.S. tour for his sextet.

"That's my will," Threadgill admits, not immodestly. He moves so fast he's become virtually invisible; the press does not know how to regard or cover such prolific activity, and Threadgill's originality of sound seems to render him "too contemporary" for regular employment in taverns that showcase jazz, though his music is based in gospel, the blues and parade marches, as well as his serious research into what's beyond. He makes a fair living—that is, he scrapes by ("All musicians live a creative life, believe me; artists, period, I don't know how anybody survives. It calls for a lot of imagination")—but he rejects the misconceptions and limits imposed on his work by the nameless world.

"I became a musician because I loved music as a kid," he explains. "Music is my game. I didn't grow up with any boundaries on music. I grew up in a ghetto in Chicago, and there was music everywhere. My grandmother took me to churches where there was music, record shops had speakers outside so you walked down the street hearing music, bands played, and still play, at the Maxwell Street flea market. Even at grammar school, teachers played records during rest periods, good music we would cool out and sleep to.

"There was never any talk of this kind of music or that kind of music. I grew up with hillbilly music on the radio, Polish music on the radio, Tchaikovsky, gospel. Radio was exciting; there was Serbian music, Mexican music, stories. We listened to all of it. And I heard music live. I would hear polka bands, then turn around to Muddy Waters or Rosetta Tharp, then go hear a choir from Romania. We listened to it all, and we heard it in the community.

"As a kid, I wanted to learn how to play all this great music, the way these great people had been doing it. It wasn't in my head to have a Mercedes or $50,000 a year; I wasn't sophisticated enough to be thinking like that. To grapple with the music was enough. And I haven't really lost that initial thing I came to music with, that interest I have. I don't need anybody to support me in that idea anymore. I can go to the grave with my ideas. I can go on through."

The man forms a belief in the existence, somewhere, of sincere human exchange... So he sets out to confirm this

Henry Threadgill.
(Teri Bloom)

faith in the potential for love and understanding. Every subsequent encounter ends in his being abused, his idealism scorned... every person and institution he deals with disappoints his faith in humanity.
    —from *When Life Is Cheap...*

"I learned through trial and error," Threadgill continues. "And some help from some good friends, and years and years in musical institutions. But I didn't get too much out of institutions, I must admit. I'm very grateful to have been able to be there, but I got more outside of them. I went to all the music schools—universities, colleges, conservatories—all around this country, on the university level for 11 years, partly on the G.I. Bill, partly on my own. I was constantly studying at these places, taking every course in music they had to offer. That was my approach; I was never interested in a degree, I was interested in the catalog. That never made any sense to me—do this for four years and you have a degree—because I said, 'No doctor would ever operate on me after four years of study; how can you be a musician in four years?'

"And here's something I want to say: it's been put out in some quarters that so-called jazz musicians don't have classical backgrounds. Now, this must be about musicians who are younger than I am, because it's impossible not to have a classical background if you're my age. There was no such thing as a jazz program, or any jazz schools then. I played Prokofiev, Poulenc and Hindemith sonatas when I was a flute major; when I was a piano major I played Beethoven sonatas, so I don't know what this crap is about only a couple people out there are special, classically trained musicians. It's a lie and a fallacy. Outside school I was in blues bands, but people wouldn't let me sit up with orchestras if I didn't know how to play Mozart and the Brandenburg Concertos. They weren't into any tokenism, they wouldn't be passing me on no color basis. I had to deal.

"I started out as a kid with piano, and when I got really interested in playing, I went to saxophone, then clarinet—that was still a very accepted thing to learn, then. I was lucky enough to have a teacher who got me into a big band, a reading band, and taught me what the second tenor part was. Just like a choir: How does the alto support the soprano? What role are you playing besides just singing your part? In these schools now, everybody knows so much, but only something specific. They don't make mistakes, and that's bad. No mistakes is bad. I'd hate to have learned how to walk without falling; I'd probably not know how to fall, and if I fell I'd kill myself. And you never learn how to jump out of an airplane if you never fall.

"My first professional experience was traveling with gospel music, church musicians, and evangelists. I was into that for a couple of years, then I came back to the secular community. That's when I started playing with blues bands. That was the first place I could play, and I had to learn to play with them. They taught me. That's some highly sophisticated music—both the emotional basis, and the technical basis, too, because the execution of every note is a highly sophisticated event.

"Howlin' Wolf was my greatest hero, my favorite. I didn't know him personally, but I loved those people. I used to play in the blues sessions on Sunday—jazz sessions on Monday—at the Blue Flame, and everybody would come to the bandstand to play. Most of the AACM cats had that kind of background; Leo Smith came up to Chicago playing with Little Milton; Lester Bowie, John Stubblefield, they know all about this. If you came up in the Midwest, you had that rhythm and blues background; that was the heart of most of your work, and you played at it for long hours.

"But one reason I stayed in that so long was the traditional guys didn't want me to play with them, didn't like the way I played because I wasn't playing bebop the way they were. They said I didn't know what I was doing, and those cats would leave the bandstand, leave you playing by yourself. When that happened, it would make me question my understanding of that music; I wouldn't take the rejection for granted, it had to be looked at. Why? I had to ask. It certainly wasn't about the feeling of what I was playing. What would generally be the case was they manipulated the licks, and I never wanted to do that. I wanted to say something.

"When I was a kid, we used to listen to Sonny Rollins; he didn't sound like he was playing somebody else's licks. Gene Ammons was one of my biggest heroes; I didn't hear Gene Ammons playing no Johnny Hodges licks, or Sonny Rollins licks, or Charlie Parker licks—his stuff was coming out of Gene Ammons. On the street, the guys would be playing those licks, and they were good at it; the reason I wasn't was that I wasn't practicing those

licks. I was trying to get through the material, the structures and the forms and the harmonies. To me, it seemed like they were all manipulating the same thing, but I was fishing. At least I knew where I was fishing; I had a clear understanding of form. I'd say to myself, if I keep my main pulse on these forms, at least I'll know where I'm at. I'll know what to do at the next juncture. Between here and there I might have some problems, but I'll know what to do when I get there.

"I had my first association with the AACM in Muhal Richard Abrams' Experimental Band in 1962, or '63. I was still playing in the blues places, and working with marching bands, with VFW post bands. I used to make a living playing parades in Chicago, in the summertime; I could play two parades a week and pay my rent and everything else. The jobs would come out of the union, and somebody might give me a big job, like a circus gig for the night. But with the AACM, I was into the circuit I really wanted to be in. I didn't really want to get out of the blues—the blues was good, is still good—but I knew where I wanted to go.

"In the AACM what was happening was an expression of what I was about, and the moment. I knew that it expressed the times, it was all intricately tied up with everything I saw about me: the revolution in America, God is dead, America shooting down its kids, the War, the questioning of traditional philosophies, Coltrane going on to an emotional base of music. I knew where I was supposed to be. I was tied into that moment. I didn't reject that moment. I didn't look back. There was nothing for me to look back to. Look back to what? My life was going on. I'm young."

And so, in the late '60s, Henry Threadgill became who he's still becoming now, who he'd been becoming all along: himself. "I don't try to play what Charlie Parker and them played; they lived through that social period, and I didn't. I learned how to play a lot of what I'm I playing by studying that music as I was coming up, but I didn't have the emotional background, I didn't understand the significance of life, to try and express what Charlie Parker and his peers were expressing. They all came out of that same context, they were contemporary, they were expressing that time. It's ridiculous for me to try to play that time I played the music of Scott Joplin, you know [on *Air Lore*], but

I had to transpose it to this moment, still.

"I've always been a composer. Basically, about 90 percent of the music for Air, I wrote it. And that music is written—down to the drum parts. There's nothing vague about it. What I was doing with Air was a scaled-down version of what I'm doing now; it had to be done with small instrumentation, so it was a harder job, more complicated, than writing for seven musicians. I'd have to allude to things. Because we only had two hands apiece, and the instruments give up only so many tones at once, I had to devise ways to imply another tone quickly, and shift, and be back in place. Here, I just stick that tone on another instrument. Before, I had to make the implication; now, I can state the fact.

"One thing I've been working towards is a larger, orchestral sound that gets away from the traditional big-band sound. I have a very large palette with the sextet. Just with the drums alone, I have 12 pitches: two floor toms, upper toms, snare drum, floor bass drum and concert bass drum—I have two percussionists, that's six tones apiece just on the drums, so that's part of my entire palette. A number of people have asked me if there's been overdubbing on my sextet records, but I'm still trying to accomplish the same thing through other means. I have on my agenda to study electronics, but I haven't finished with acoustics yet.

"Writing is a special thing to me; I haven't been able to write enough, because the vehicles aren't out there. People say, 'Oh, it would be nice if you wrote something for orchestra'—well, that's okay. But I don't write music to sit on the shelf; if I can't hear it, there's nothing for me to learn. If I just wrote stuff I completely understand, there would be no reason for me to be writing—I could just be manufacturing music, since I'd know what it's all going to sound like. But writing is a daredevil experience, you always have to go further; that's what every great writer did. There's not a great writer who ever existed who didn't keep taking chances. Beethoven took those chances, Duke Ellington, Alban Berg. That's why they remain great composers, and that's how they kept opening up new harmonies, new forms, new concepts. Because if they only kept voicing things the way they were voiced, not stretching out the binary and ternary forms, we wouldn't even be talking about them today.

"I compose through the laws of

nature. There are ways to compose that have to do with the way that life exists biologically and metaphysically. There are laws that are operating, like the laws that make the sun come out, that bring the rain. I observe the laws of acoustics, for instance, and I submit it all to my heart and my head. I don't just subscribe to a methodology. I think my approach is in line with that of people I've been fond of and studied with, like Muhal—and that's not coincidence, that's the actual fact of the transference of information.

"Of course, there are things that are notated and some things that aren't. This music we're playing comes from an improvisational base, but so does classical music; all the great composers were improvisers who could play, who could sit down and make up music on the spot. Collective improvisation, though, that's what the AACM was about, and we're still with that. But that's not all—evolution has gone on.

"One thing that happened when the music changed from the last period to the present is the shared repertoire disappeared, and a new collective repertoire did not take its place. The community of musicians in New York, they don't know my compositions. Even if they might have heard something, liked it or disliked it on record, most of them don't know how to play it. You have to understand the make-up of the piece and what the improvisation involves, if you're going to play "80° Below," or a Haydn piece, or "Donna Lee." And I don't just work in the traditional improvisational methods that occur in traditional jazz. There are no limits to improvisation; if you're going to put a limitation on improvisation, you might as well forget about it. Charlie Parker would never have gotten to where he did if he'd accepted a premise of limits, or Coltrane. What Ornette did was beautiful, too, opening up the whole arena again. Even though a lot of people—even some musicians—haven't caught up with that yet.

"You know, Blood Ulmer told me something he said Ornette used to tell him. He said that jazz is the teacher, and blues is the preacher. And I said, 'Yeah, but time is the reaper.' You can't stop it. There is a destiny that is in the genes and molecular structure of things, that has to happen. I'm really excited right now, because I find I'm stretching again; I feel like if I work, I'm going to be able to peel off another layer of skin. It's extreme, but my life has been extreme, and I love it. Ever since I was a kid, I've been interested in change, and the extremism of it. Change is good. It can hurt, but it's still good, because it's evolution. My greatest fear is the fear of not being able to go along with change, of becoming stylistic and set. There are a lot of people who don't believe in evolution, who would like to see things remain the same. And those are the people who don't want to see our music become accessible and strong, and turned over the way pop music is turned over. Because this music makes people think."

Unfailing he persists in his mission, convinced that island of goodness lies somewhere amid the corruption. In a final conflict his unyielding belief meets up with some hardcore human malevolence. The world does not conform to his interior reality. He vaporizes out of the world as we know it, but continues eternally in his mind's quest after its own truth.
—from *When Life Is Cheap...*

Blindfold Test: Carlos Santana

by Robin Tolleson

This guitar chameleon was taking his first Blindfold Test quite seriously. He sat on the floor of the music room in his home on Mount Tamalpais, a short drive from San Francisco's Mission District, where he put together the first Santana Blues Band nearly 20 years ago. His eyes were shut, his body rocking back and forth to the music. He'd laugh softly when he heard something that struck home, or growl a "Yeah."

The fusion of Latin, blues and rock that Carlos Santana has pioneered frequently hits people on a gutsy, street level. But the guitarist has recorded over the years with musicians from all across the spectrum, including John McLaughlin, McCoy Tyner, Alice Coltrane, Wayne Shorter, Herbie Hancock and Ron Carter, among others. The Santana band has just released its latest in a long line of Columbia albums, *Beyond Appearances* (Columbia 39527), a spirited pop LP produced by Val Garay (Motels, Kim Carnes), but on this day Carlos feels more like talking about the album he's working on now with Tony Williams, and about some rare Coltrane and Miles tapes he'd been given while on a recent trip to Europe.

The 38-year-old Santana, who has proven to be one of the most resilient and inspiring bandleaders in modern music, was anxious to hear some good music and talk guitarists.

1. Kenny Burrell. "Blues for Wes" (from *Night Song*, Fantasy). Burrell, guitar; Ron Carter, bass; Richard Wyands, piano; Freddie Waits, drums.

They even got the drums to sound like Grady Tate. It sounds so close to Wes, it's incredible. I can't recognize who's playing, because he never once plays himself. It's not Pat Martino. I don't think it's Grant Green either. It doesn't sound like Kenny Burrell. I've checked out a lot of his albums, but he didn't play Kenny Burrell at all. I still give him five stars 'cause he did it so well. The tone, his phrasing, even the enunciation, the language—he had it down. It was a great composition, and definitely sounds like the master, Wes.

2. John Scofield. "Filibuster" (from *Electric Outlet*, Gramavision). Scofield, guitars, DMX bass; Steve Jordan, drums; David Sanborn, alto saxophone.

That's John Scofield, right? It's his tone, and the way he's been writing lately with Miles. Like the layman's ear, I tend to get lost when people start playing too much noodle-roni, or too much improvisation without theme. But his playing lately has gotten infinitely more thematic and more melodic, and to me it's great because it keeps my attention much more closely. It's that old saying, "It's more fun to improvise than it is to listen to it," and that's a fact, unless you're close to that other galaxy of Charlie Parker and 'Trane and people like that. But I think the song is really positive, and it's a really good groove. Four stars. That's David Sanborn, right?

3. King Crimson. "Discipline" (from *Discipline*, Warner Bros.). Robert Fripp, Adrian Belew, guitars; Tony Levin, bass; Bill Bruford, drums.

I'm having problems relating to Fripp's music for some reason, I guess because I don't hear too much blues. I hear a lot of intellect, and I'm not too keen on that, or receptive, and it's probably my fault because I know the guy is brilliant. But I have to be sincere. A lot of it doesn't reach me. I'd rather hear one note that is just coated with the stuff that I need to hear than calisthenics or whatever. I don't want to sound too negative; at the same time, it's something that I'm just not receptive to yet. Some things I can claim immediately, other things take me awhile—because it's a blessing or a curse, but I come from the blues, basically. But I know the guy is important. Actually, I need some lessons from him, which would be great. I need to know a lot of the stuff that he and Adrian Belew and Andy Summers do.

4. Larry Coryell. "Rene's Theme" (from *Spaces*, Vanguard). Coryell, John McLaughlin, guitars.

I just about wore this record out. This is a classic piece, I think from *Spaces*. When I first heard it, it became very scary how much chops these people had, and how much dexterity. It's a setting like Django Reinhardt. It's extremely beautiful how both of them play. I miss Larry Coryell a lot. At one time they said he was one of the most important guitar players to come along since Charlie Christian, and it's true. In this particular session, there's a lot of magic happening between him and John. Obviously there's a lot of respect. I'm going to start checking him out again.

5. James Blood Ulmer. "Election" (from *Odyssey*, Columbia). Ulmer, guitar; Warren Benbow, drums; Charles Bumham, violin.

That sounds like something from Ornette Coleman, that kind of river. James Blood Ulmer. Sometimes I can get a little bit disinterested in this kind of music, but this one's really good. It sounds like something you could play live and definitely capture peoples' ears—they're not going to go out and get a hot dog or something. It sounds like something Jimi [Hendrix] used to do also, once he started getting too spacey or cosmic and wanted to just have fun with the stuff. Yeah, it's a really good expression, the composition and everything. To me it would be a four-and-a-half, because I would definitely play something like this live—or try.

6. Howard Roberts. "O Barquinho" (from *Guilty*, Capitol). Roberts, guitar; Dave Grusin, organ; John Guerin, drums; Chuck Berghofer, bass.

He's playing his butt off in there, man. Howard Roberts, really? His playing here is more soulful than other things I've heard

Carlos Santana.
(Jan Persson)

from him—as far as the approach and everything. Not that he's not soulful, but in this one he's really playing from his heart of hearts. That was an era that I would get confused. I'd have to listen really closely between Tal Farlow, Pat Martino, Grant Green, even Kenny for a while. Howard Roberts is really a surprise. Composition-wise, about three and a half or four. His playing is fantastic. He really got a chance to stretch in between the theme. I've got to start listening closely again to this guy.

Ornette Coleman.
(Hyou Vielz)

June 1986

Ornette Coleman and Pat Metheny: Songs of Innocence and Experience

by Art Lange

It's not easy to catch a comet by the tail, but every child has dreamed of doing it. No easier than palpably changing the world we live in for the better—yet some are able to do it, through science, through medicine, through poetry, through song. Inspiring one's fellow man to achieve excellence and individuality through the sheer strength and single-mindedness of one's chosen endeavor is no easy task, but as the poet Robert Browning said, "A man's reach should exceed his grasp, or what's a heaven for?"

I had met and talked to Pat Metheny before this particular interview, and knew of his sincerity and openness. Not having met Ornette Coleman before, I was anxious and eager to make his acquaintance and talk to him about musical topics. But, as I quickly learned, music is not the end result of Coleman's creativity; it is merely the means through which he aspires to inspire his fellow man. His responses to my questions often suggest the same Zen-like riddles that his music articulates so refreshingly.

Ornette Coleman and Pat Metheny came together earlier this year to document *Song X*, an album of sounds that seeks to, as the pair stated, create its own vocabulary, and the result is fully more than the sum of its quite remarkable parts, a mating of the innocence of experience, and the experience of innocence—songs that can't be named, only felt within that nebulous area where inspiration and imagination turn to creativity.

Art Lange: Let's start with you, Pat. Where did you first encounter Ornette's music, and how did it affect you?

Pat Metheny: One reason why I always felt good about growing up in a fairly isolated town is that there was no way to know what was "happening." I was 11, maybe 12, at the time, and in Lee's Summit, Missouri, where I grew up there was a TG&Y store—a dime store. They had a very small record collection—these were pretty much the only records available in town—and they had a deal where you could buy three or four records for a dollar. One of Ornette's records happened to be in this batch of records, and I took it home and my instant reaction to it was that I loved it. It completely captured my imagination, and I didn't know that it was "jazz" or what it was. But the nice thing about being a little kid is that you either like something or you don't. Anyway, I responded to it immediately, and started to become a jazz fan about that time through my older brother Mike, who's a trumpet player.

I started to get more of Ornette's records and always liked them; in fact, it's funny because by the time I was 13 I got a subscription to *DownBeat* and started to read that there was some kind of controversy about the way that they were playing, and I couldn't figure out what they were talking about—I couldn't imagine why people would have a problem with the music, why they couldn't just see that these guys were having a blast playing this great music. I also remember that as time went on I'd keep going back to these records, and every time I would hear them they'd sound different—which is something you can't say about too many records—in fact, they still sound as brand-new to me now as they did then.

Lange: Did hearing his music at such an early, impressionable age affect you differently as you grew older and began developing your own style?

Metheny: Not in specific ways as much as just the general feeling I got from listening to Ornette and the musicians that played with him: they're playing the music that they felt strongest about with this incredible love and joy about it, without worrying about style, or what was current. It seemed very direct to me, and while, obviously, a large part of the music that I've done over the years stylistically is not close at all, there's always that same feeling I try to play with. For one thing, I'm trying to play whatever I'm going to play with the idea of making a melody. To me, Ornette's music is about melody. There's a lot more going on besides that, of course, but it's about singing, and talking, and about the shape of the line—and to me it transcends style. It's really pure, and that, more than anything else, has been the inspiration I've drawn from listening to Ornette's music over the years.

Lange: You've always played a lot of Ornette's tunes, beginning with *Bright Size Life*, your first album...

Metheny: Well, besides all this philosophical stuff, there is also the fact that I just love the tunes Ornette writes, and I love the feeling they send up, because they make me want to play something different from what I'd normally play—which is, again, a quality you don't find in many tunes. A lot of tunes are interchangeable, especially in bebop, which is the kind of music I was playing around Kansas City at the time. It was like, when you'd make up a song list of tunes to work on, you'd have blues tunes, rhythm-changes tunes, modal tunes, and then we'd have Ornette tunes, which didn't fit into the normal definition of a vehicle for a jam session. Plus, to me, you can sing them all, and they've got hooks. I was talking to Lyle [Mays] about this just the other night, and he mentioned that in all of Ornette's tunes, the passion is in the notes—anyone could play the tunes and would get at least a chunk of that. It's all there—it's complete.

Lange: There's an amazing oneness between the two of you on this record, not just in ensemble sound, but in intent, and I think it's because you both are lyrical players, you invent melodies as you improvise instead of playing riffs or soloing on chords.

Ornette Coleman: Charlie Parker once said how he learned to play bebop based on minor sevenths—standard changes, C minor 7ths, or whatever, where you're working with A minor 7th or B minor 7th—and then you have two-beat changes, or four-beat changes, and when you have two-beat changes, with only two structures of four steps, if you start on the B side and you go to the A side... in other words, that's six whole steps on the one side and six whole steps on the other side—that makes the whole 12 tones. So in all chordal music, there's never been any movement that did not have chords with a whole step—but that whole step always had to lock into a key. Which means that if you take the best fake book in the world and look at all the keys, you'll find that maybe only three or four keys are used in the whole book. So you know what that was, it was ideas placed in a key, not a key placed in ideas.

The guitar is probably the most individual unison sound of all string instruments—I mean, it has a sound of its own no matter how many people play it, and everyone who plays it sounds like an individual unless they're playing clichéd ideas, which has to do with minor thirds and major thirds. But lots of people play an instrument for position more than for playing what they hear, and that has nothing to do with position. Now Pat, he plays from music, not from position. When he plays, you don't have to worry about the key or the idea, you just have to worry is what you're playing something?

When I was forming Prime Time, the one thing that bothered me was that [in the past] I only played music using two horns and a bass and drums, and I wasn't doing it the best because I was given other things to do. But then James [Blood] Ulmer came to my house one day and studied with me, and started playing a line on the guitar, and I found out that not only does a guitar sound like a full orchestra, but when you play a melody on guitar not only does it sound full, but it also sounds like it's moving the melody to another place—and it just happens to sound like that by the guys playing it. And I said, wait a minute—this is the way I hear the saxophone. I don't ever hear the saxophone in a key, or, if I'm playing an idea or a melody, I never hear that idea or melody on the saxophone—I only hear it because someone had made those melodies sound that way. I take those same notes and play a totally different melody.

So in other words I saw there was a relationship between the alto and the guitar. And when I started rehearsing with Pat, I was playing exactly whatever I'm playing with my band, and it's clear and it's forceful or whatever, and there was not one time when I ever felt inhibited or limited. And what's exciting to me about this session is even though it's only two horns—or two note instruments, everyone else is rhythm—it sounds like a zillion other things coming besides that. I put on a copy of the tape, and we were playing a song called "Video Games," and honest to God, I said, "Wait a minute, something is wrong with the tape recorder...." [Laughs.]

Lange: There's 12 people on that song....

Coleman: I said, "I need some batteries." That experience made me realize this idea that I've always had from the day I started to play music: that not only is it alive, but that it's endless and has no ego in it. There's something about creativity that every human being gets an equal share—and feels as intently as anything that you care about. I guess I'm talking about the quality of life. Because the quality of life doesn't tell you that you're doing something to be rewarded, as much as you're doing something that you believe is naturally going to allow you to have this experience with your fellow man. And because of the way we grow up to respect each other, and survive, we have built all of these images for someone to relate to without allowing them to participate in them. For instance, right now you can play any type of music you want, and take it to the audience, and if it's something that's real, they're going to like it. You don't have to sound like me or Pat, but it is this type of playing that makes people know that that's what's important.

Metheny: That is important.

Coleman: And the one thing that I respect about Pat—not because he's sitting here—is that he has the kind of insight and humanity that he has, and hasn't looked at his success as something that a person gave him; it's something that he actually made happen, and it's still happening. I think it's amazing to find a person with that kind of quality of humanism who wants not to worry about his success, but worry about how well he achieves what he believes. He has my highest respect as an artist and a human being.

Lange: Pat, in addition to playing with Ornette now, you previously worked with Sonny Rollins. Did you approach playing with those two saxists differently?

Metheny: Well, they're quite different. This experience with Ornette... for me to say it was the high point of my experience as a musician would be an incredible understatement. You know, playing with Sonny was way up there too, because I've admired him so much, but this wasn't just a record date. We spent about three weeks working, eight hours a day, every day, really hitting it, and talking, and really getting to know each other musically and personally.

Coleman: The feeling I got when I heard the tape... when John Coltrane decided to play from a strictly spiritual side, as on *Ascension*—he played strictly commercial music before that—and also when I first came to New York, my first

band—that same spirit was on that tape, and yet it was today's experience. That's what is so fantastic about it. I mean, you hear horns, and ideas, but also something is compelling you to realize that there is something else going on besides what you're hearing, that's causing the things that we are doing to happen. You hear that. I haven't heard that in any musician in the last 20 years.

I mean, what people call "jazz," or they say, "You've got an electric band, you've got this and that"—they can say anything, but it's not what you have, it's how you sound that's important. Like now, with Prime Time, my band is really into what I'm doing, but sometimes people read so many things and hear so many things that they hold back—and I'm always trying to get my band not to do that. But really, that same quality I've been seeking—the same thing that I heard when I first came to New York in '59, and when I heard Coltrane—is alive right now in '86, and the evidence of that to me is really on this record. Whatever the jazz person needs in this society—which means that you're an individual and you express yourself, whatever it is you feel conviction for—you don't worry about that, you stand on your own. Now that quality to me has been tamed. Everybody says, "Well, if I play some minor thirds here and some bebop here, I can get me a gig, and if I put on a green hat and have my ass out, I'll draw some people." [Laughter.] All of this has just been camouflage, to hide what the person really wants to do. And all of a sudden you realize you can't [hide it], it's either there or it isn't.

That's the one thing that I never really felt bad about. People say, "Well, this guy's still far out," or whatever. At least I realize that they didn't believe I was that way because I wanted them to say that. It's because that's how they felt about what I was doing, and I'm still trying.... The thing that I really want to achieve in my lifetime is to inspire people to be individuals. That, to me, is it.

Lange: What brought the two of you together in the first place?

Coleman: Well, Charlie Haden told me 10 years ago, "If I can only get you and Pat together; I'd get on my knees." And I said. "Charlie, you know, it's gonna happen." And last year, he said he wanted to get us together, and I said, "You tell Pat we're gonna do it this year." Charlie has been the main person to get Pat and I

together. The thing about it is I haven't really played a lot with my band, because of the fact that I don't try to get my band to support me, I try to support them. Therefore, when I do get my band going it's really what it is that I'm actually trying to achieve, and they go with me. I've never felt that I've wanted to just go out and try to survive because I had a name or I played. I only wanted to do things that are worthy of doing. And that's the thing I was really reluctant about in the past. Here's a guy who's very successful, and maybe the feeling wouldn't be right if I tried to call him and say, "Man, I want to do this and I want to do that." You know, I'm not even doing it with my own band, and I didn't feel right about that. The only thing I felt right about doing was something musical that was worthy of doing.

Lange: And Charlie convinced you...

Coleman: Yes, Charlie Haden's something else, and he was right. The thing that was amazing was that when Pat came to New York to start rehearsing, I thought we should use Denardo too, and I'm sure Pat already had the idea for the people he wanted to use. So I said, "Well, let's just try it." So Denardo came over and we rehearsed, and Pat said, "Oh man, we gotta do this," so we went down to Texas [see *DownBeat*, "Caught," *April '86*], and believe me, if you heard the stuff we did in Texas with Denardo and Charlie, you wouldn't believe it was Pat. He played more incredibly than I've ever heard. There's no words for it. And that's what you can do from someone playing with you. I mean, I always say that Denardo—not because he's my relative... well, he's really shy, but that night, what he and Pat did—they were playing so good. [Laughter.]

Metheny: Denardo is really something. That was an aspect of this whole project that I had not anticipated at all. I'd always enjoyed Denardo's playing, in particular with Prime Time, but it's hard to appreciate, in a way, the depth of what his thing is until you play with him...

Coleman: That's true.

Metheny:... because it's funny, he's got that certain thing drummers have of playing a lot—he's active all the time but he's never in your way. And it's grooving, but it's not grooving in the normal way; you can play any tempo, any feel, and it grooves.

Coleman: And that's the thing that I feel about the growth of how jazz evolved, those types of experiences when someone became aware of it. Like lots of critics say,

"So-and-so doesn't swing," or "So-and-so can't do this here," because they're comparing yesterday with tomorrow. But the thing about it is that when you hear something that makes you feel good, it doesn't matter what style or what it is, it's still having that same quality, and that's the thing I've always tried to avoid making a musician feel. I never told Denardo, "I want you to play ching-ching-ching," I never told him how I wanted him to sound so I could sound a certain way. I never told him since he was playing as a kid. That's the same way I realized when you are playing with anyone, if they have something to say, the moment you tell them what to do they can't say that anymore; they feel afraid that they're going to lose their job. I've been fired many times because the guy didn't tell me what to play, and I thought he wanted me to play what I could play, and then I found out he didn't. [Laughter.] He wanted me to play this other thing.

So what I'm saying, with the music that's called jazz, with all the incredible musicians that've played, today there's no image to carry that individual feeling into a mass expression. And there's no reason why: you have maybe 100,000 rock 'n' roll guys—why do you have that, because they're all inspiring? Right? Why couldn't people be inspired to be more creative?

Lange: Has listening to Ornette over the years—as a saxophonist and composer—influenced you as a guitarist, Pat?

Metheny: On a number of levels, very much so. One thing about guitar playing in jazz is that very few people have transcended the problem of dynamics, and Ornette is a classic example—he never plays any two notes in a row at the same volume. And, to me, that's what makes it feel so good. He's a major influence in terms of phrasing—and it's difficult to do that on a guitar, and that's what makes the so-called traditional "jazz guitar sound" not that appealing to a lot of listeners. It's very easy for the guitar to become monodynamic, and in listening to Ornette's playing I definitely got a lot of good lessons of how to make the instrument breathe, so that the phrases fall into a natural musical way, not the way they happen to lie on the instrument. I think that a lot of what Ornette plays is not saxophone music, it's music, and that's a quality that all instrumentalists should strive for—to transcend the instrument, and as he says, play ideas and sounds and thoughts rather than a pattern on your instrument.

Lange: But at the same time, since

the saxophone is an instrument that you have to breathe into to get a sound out of, there are certain limits due to its physical nature, which you don't have on a guitar or piano, that helps define its phrasing; it's like you have to stop and take a breath when you talk....

Coleman: In the Western world, whether it's American or European music, everyone uses the same 12 notes. And as people have been able to define their sensitivity through those 12 notes, calling it phrasing or dynamics or whatever, to me what they represented is the equivalent of gravity allowing things in the sky to be where they are in relation to the earth. In other words, those notes to me are the true emotional gravity. Which tells me that when you play an instrument, if someone plays a certain note, whether you like it or not, it will move you if the gravity of it is in tune with your emotional state. We are all connected to creation, and we were connected to creation long before finding out we had talent—that came second. We are not creation; we're the talent that's trying to express what creation means, and what effect it has on your nerves, on your emotions. Cyril Scott said that it took Europeans 7,000 years to accept middle C, for them to agree what middle C sounded like, so that the Germans and French and everybody said, "Okay, we're gonna use this as C." And imagine where they were before that. [Laughter.] Imagine the musicologists who designed the 12 intervals—when you think of the 12 months, and the 12 tribes of Israel, and all that. That's why I love Buckminster Fuller so much. And all of that means just the components that go into the emotions that creativity passes through you. But that doesn't mean that because they are like that they can only be used one way. Notes are like water—they take the shape of whoever's using them. Your C can make someone cry but someone else's C can make someone laugh. That's the beauty of creation, that we all don't have to be on one line to get the same results.

Metheny: Taking that one step further is the fact that it has nothing to do with "style." There's too much talk about style—and it's something that affects us as musicians on such a profound level: that's how you're defined within the musical community, what "style" you play.

Coleman: When America gets to the point that they won't have to use styles to have people express what they do in a category, then the creativeness in all popular

music is going to grow. When you think of rock 'n' roll, rhythm and blues, they're using the same notes but they say, "We're playing this, we're playing that." But in Europe years ago it was just what your name was. If your name was Jim, it was go and listen to Jim—not Jim play the blues, it was just Jim doing what he's doing. If that was the case in America, we'd all be a lot better. For instance, I never heard anyone say "white music," but I hear everyone say "black music"—and I was black before there was music. That's kind of a drag, and has nothing to do with music.

So what I'm saying is that those styles limit even the person who created the concept. And if the people involved in creative expression had the position that the people in NASA have, in their technology, all this other shit would be outdated. When you think of the shuttle *Challenger*, it was a shame, those people went up and something happened, but technology is not restricting them. They don't call it style, they call it progress. Here, you take Robert Johnson and someone else who's playing blues, and they're gonna say, "Well, this is a new style," maybe that guy didn't have style then—that was him. Someone took that and stylized it and made someone else imitate it and someone kept that alive... in fact, I think that that's one of the most inhuman things to do, to stop growth because you want someone else to be remembered. I was telling someone the other day that Mozart is more alive than some people who are playing who are alive, and yet when you saw the movie *Amadeus*, you think he's dead. But Mozart is the most-played composer in the Western world who is deceased—and that's just because of a style, not him. And when it comes to classical music, there are many performers and composers that deserve notice for what they're doing. The point is, we are all victims of the past trying to eliminate the future. And you can't do that.

Lange: As long as we brought up technology and growth, the advances in instruments have changed the way people think about what they do besides obviously affecting what they do. How much guitar synthesizer did you play on this album?

Metheny: The entire record.

Coleman: And it doesn't even sound that way.

Metheny: When we started rehearsing I had all of my guitars there—I had, what 10 guitars?—and I played each one, and I kept coming back to the guitar synthesizer, because the blend was...

Coleman: It was a marriage...

Metheny:... it just fit. Actually, the technology is becoming so sophisticated, it's becoming less technological, it's just becoming good. It's still more complicated than I would like, but there used to be so many wires and you'd have to patch 19 things together and play it. Now it's much more manageable.

Coleman: When I said I played the tape and thought that something's wrong with my batteries, it was actually the first time that I'd heard a melody played in a non-tempered design and a tempered design at the same time. And it has affected your environment. See, what technology has done for me is taken a film of space and let us know what space really is. It has made me realize that space is a container, like you put water in a jar. We're in this space right now; maybe when you go outside you're going to feel different. That's another space. That's what technology does: it starts making you aware of the quality of space which you're actually in. And when Pat was playing, it blew me away, in that it was the most perfect sound of that melody to trigger off something that makes you think of what you're not thinking about to think about what you are thinking about. [Laughter.]

Lange: And if you had played that same melody with different settings resulting in different textures and sounds, it would make you think about something different...

Coleman: Right, exactly.

Metheny: I'm convinced, more and more, that the guitar synthesizer is bringing along a situation where everything is possible as an improviser. This technology is not only making it possible, but it's so much more fun to have this range to choose from as opposed to just having one sound; now you've got any sound, and you can apply everything you've learned to that particular sound—if what you've got to play is strong enough to support that sound. That's where it gets tricky.

Lange: Does this interest you in getting a saxophone synthesizer?

Coleman: The way I've always believed in the expression of sound is whatever tool would allow you to be more natural is the best way to achieve anything. Look at the horn itself: it's a technical thing; it's no different from anything else—it's just an extension. For instance, I went out to Bell Laboratories when the first man landed on the moon, 1969, and met the guy who first invented something like a musical synthesizer. It was Emmanuel Ghent, and he had already worked with various programming, so when I played my horn through his machine it sounded like 1,000 saxophones at once. And I wanted so bad to bring that room back to the bandstand. [Laughter.] But we're talking hundreds of thousands of dollars, or I would've had that then. But economics doesn't move at the same level as intelligence and technology. So to answer your question, there's only three elements that human beings need technically: light, heat and motion. I believe that music has all three of those in it, so anything that can project that has got to be good.

Lange: What do you think you'll each take away from an experience like this one?

Coleman: I think it has reassured me that I'm on the right path, and that is to try to enlighten others to take that path out. Creative music has a very spiritual image to it, and it has allowed me to understand that success is everything that you are, more than what it is you've accomplished.

Metheny: Well, for me this has been pretty amazing on a number of different levels. For instance, when I was a kid I used to have this dream all the time, where I'm just lying on my back and look up and see this incredible sky. And I'd forgotten about it years ago. But we were into the rehearsing, playing hard every day, and during the sessions I couldn't even go to sleep—I don't think I slept but three hours during the three days that we were recording. I would try to go to sleep and just hear everything that we played. But then I started to have these dreams again, exactly like when I was a kid—and this feeling that you used to have as a child, of everything being possible.

It's funny, because so much has happened to me in a relatively short period of time, and so quickly—things that I never anticipated. I feel good, I don't have any bad feeling about it, but the fact is it's been pretty hectic the last 10 years. And this experience has been especially valuable in that it made me stop for a minute, because this has been very difficult for me. I think it's been difficult for all of us, not in a bad way, because the goals we set for ourselves were very high. I don't think Ornette or I wanted to do just a record date. Ornette said he wanted us to try and come up with a vocabulary that was unique to this particular experience. There are some moments on the record where we came very close to doing that.

Afterwards it was like a whole new ball game for me. After the project was over, I went home and sat down to write a couple of tunes and see how things would come out, and the first day I sat there with the guitar, playing notes, and listening so closely, adding C and G, taking notes out, adding E, and after about eight hours I realized I had come up with a C chord! Everything has a completely different meaning to me musically now. It was a very stimulating and exciting and inspiring experience—also as you can imagine, very humbling, in the sense that during the three and a half to four weeks we worked together, I never heard Ornette play anything less than brilliant, and I also never heard him play one note that was false.

This isn't a question where I can just come up with a glib answer, because what I'm taking away from this experience is something I'm going to be working on for the rest of my life.

December 1986

Terence Blanchard and Donald Harrison: Young, Gifted and Straight Ahead

by Howard Mandel

At a time when straight ahead seems to be the new hip direction for jazz, saxophonist Donald Harrison and trumpeter Terence Blanchard are among the most out-front and serious spokesmen of the new young lions—emphasis on young—who are revitalizing the main stem of the jazz tradition—the jazz we know is jazz—over recent decades' embrace of hybrids, far-flung influences, insistently "original" directions and a profusion of experiments.

"Anybody can be original—a baby can pick up a horn and play something original," Harrison scoffed one night outside the Village Vanguard, where he and Blanchard led their quintet for a week in early autumn. "But if you come out of a heritage, say like Coltrane did, then your original contribution will have more depth."

Pride in knowing the depth of the heritage passed down to them through such teachers as pianist Ellis Marsalis, clarinetist Alvin Batiste, trumpeter Bill Fiedler, saxists Kidd Jordan and Paul Jeffrey—knowing it on their instruments, not just recognizing it on disc—motivates the two New Orleans natives who followed their schoolmates the brothers Marsalis into Art Blakey's Jazz Messengers. They eye the high standards of musical excellence set by the original beboppers, at the same time choosing a strict regimen of post-collegiate study (Blanchard went to Rutgers, Harrison to Berklee), little drink and no drugs, which might help them endure the gig grind that's worn down so many aspiring youngbloods. If there's any truth to the claim that "jazz is back," it lies not in the record bins filled with reissues but in the renewed fervor of musicians and listeners, who are Blanchard and Harrison's age, for the real thing, rather than watered-down offshoots. See the score of rather serious, well-dressed horn players, pianists, bassists and drummers under 30 on the New York scene, and you're persuaded the future of jazz is going to be affected by folks making the most of the present from love for its past.

Blanchard and Harrison have polished their own apple with *Nascence*, their debut on Columbia after two well-received George Wein productions for Concord Jazz Records; lately, they celebrated the music of Eric Dolphy and Booker Little, working a week at Sweet Basil with pianist Mal Waldron, bassist Richard Davis, and drummer Ed Blackwell (the original rhythm team on the Dolphy/Little Five Spot date of 1961 that Prestige recorded for posterity). Blanchard used to play keyboards in funk bands, and keeps a bank of electronic equipment in his Brooklyn apartment—"I'm not going to talk about this; it's just my hobby, something I love, but it's mostly useful to compose on, a substitute for the grand piano I'd have if there was more space," the brassman insists. Donald claims he listens to "everything—African music, pop music, the whole spectrum." Together, they incorporate what

they've learned outside the jazz tradition even more subtly than Dolphy brought Bartók and birdcalls to bop rhythms and standard song forms, than Little bent Dizzy and Clifford and Miles and Kenny Dorham's contributions to his own voice and sensibility. But then, they've just begun. Who can guess where Harrison and Blanchard's careers will take them?

Howard Mandel: What does a jazz player think about while improvising?

Terence Blanchard: First of all, the musical situation you're in, and what you want to convey, musically. How you want to deal with the band—call-and-response, conversational devices, whatever. And then—it's hard to answer, man, because at different times you're thinking different things, like melody, or rhythm, or phrasing over a span of time.

Mandel: But you're pretty much focused on the immediate musical situation?

Blanchard: Oh yeah, definitely. The thing I want to get together individually and for the band is learning how to play for the moment, and understanding what to do when certain things arise. Part of trying to play jazz and being young is I have all the records. I've listened to so many things that when I start playing my first reaction is, "Oh, that's not what Clifford Brown would play, that's not what Miles would play, let me stay away from that." But now I'm trying to accept those things I'd turn away from, the musical ideas I'd naturally hear, and develop them to their highest level.

Mandel: Is that what you'd call "playing yourself," Donald?

Donald Harrison: I try to learn as much music as possible, then react on the bandstand to whatever's going on. I work on melody, say, rhythmically—trying to play a lot of meters at one time and fuse them. It's an African technique; we might be in 4/4, but I might play 6/8 on top of it, and switch into 4/4, then go to 3/4 against it. Also harmonically I'll be working on certain concepts. I think about all those things, and try to get them into my subconscious mind. Then, when I get onstage, I'm free. So when I'm playing, I'm reacting to the guys around me and playing. Basically, that's what I do.

Mandel: You've said there are things you used to play you don't play anymore; what is it you've stripped away?

Harrison: I was working on trying to have a five-octave range, and I would always try to inject that into everything I

was doing. Now I try to play exactly what's called for at a particular moment. I might have to play low and pretty, or loud and aggressive; I try to inject emotion into what I'm playing, too. But if you play for the moment, the emotion will be there.

Mandel: How do you feel about emotion in your music, Terence?

Blanchard: To me that's something that comes naturally, so my main concern is more with the content of what I'm playing. Whether I'm really saying something, and being musical in that statement. It's really hard—playing this music you're always evaluating yourself, and I guess I evaluate myself too much.

Harrison: You could never do that.

Blanchard: Even on the bandstand. I might play something and immediately say, "No, no, let me do something else," when I haven't given myself a chance to see if I could develop that. That's something I'm working on now, because when I was with Art [Blakey] I think I had a tendency to play too much, not let the music breathe. Anyway, I think the emotional thing just comes naturally.

Harrison: Yeah, I really believe what Bird said: "If you didn't live it, you can't play it." If you're a musician, you're actually telling your story. My teacher in Baton Rouge, Alvin Batiste, use to say "If you're really playing yourself, you've got to accept yourself." If you accept yourself, then you're playing yourself, and whatever you've experienced, whatever your life is about, will come through in the music. Hopefully you've experienced both emotion and intellect in your lifetime, and you can get both across.

Blanchard: If you learn as much music as you can, and you play from your heart, then there's emotion there. But intellect must become a part of it, too, because sometimes you can play from your heart and just play a lot of noise. You have to decipher whether you're being musical, and saying something that's valid, or profound.

Mandel: This must be a pendulum swinging through the music's history, because when you hear Dizzy Gillespie or Charlie Parker records, it doesn't sound like they're being self-evaluative, but rather that they're just bubbling up with ideas.

Harrison: But they had to think about the music at some point. They were taking the music somewhere, they were doing things, and you have to think about it; there's no getting around that. Otherwise, there's no intellect and it's just like the rock 'n' roll thing.

Blanchard: You know, part of the problem we have to deal with is that many people look at things that aren't jazz and call them jazz. One record company executive admitted to me that a lot of instrumental music couldn't hold its own against vocalists in that kind of music. They call it jazz so people could think they were part of this elitist subculture listening to great music. In actuality, they were listening to another form of commercial music—rock 'n' roll, or funk, or fusion, or pop. And, in turn, in the '70s the guys who were trying to play straight ahead didn't get any recognition at all, because they were being nostalgic, as far as the public was concerned. We're not being nostalgic; we're just trying to play in a certain tradition. We want to play this kind of music, and we need to uncover all the bones, to let people know what's really happening, what's jazz and what's not, so people can make an honest choice. If you lay it on the line, then the consumer can make the choice. The other way, you're talking down to people.

Harrison: In school you're taught that Beethoven and Bach were great, which is true, but you're not taught that Bird and bop were great, too—there's not the same reverence. If people knew that jazz musicians were great musicians, and what jazz really is, then people would have the knowledge to make the choice of what they want to hear.

Mandel: Do you think people in general have the patience and desire to listen to truly great music?

Blanchard: Of course.

Harrison: They're not given the opportunity; it's snatched away before they're even given the chance to know what it is.

Blanchard: When you're growing up, you're educated about European classical music, so there's a wide audience for that. Maybe not on the level of the audience for Bruce Springsteen, but it's being supported by the public and certain interest groups. We have to educate people as to what really is jazz, what's part of the tradition. Because the music has been associated with greatness only in the subculture. For a long time, and I guess even now, people thought of jazz musicians as being the clowns, the sex fiends, the drug addicts. And that isn't what was really happening. Our guys were really intelligent.

Harrison: Wynton Marsalis has proved that if jazz is brought to people in the right fashion, they'll buy it. He's sold a lot of albums—but he's almost the only one out there. That's got to turn around. We don't know how many people will listen to jazz, because nobody knows what jazz is.

Mandel: Donald, is the album you made with Don Pullen, *The Sixth Sense*, a jazz album?

Harrison: It has jazz influences in it, but I wouldn't say it's a very traditional album.

Mandel: You're on Tony William's album *Foreign Intrigue*, too—what about that?

Harrison: That's a very traditional album.

Mandel: Does Tony talk about the difference between tradition and…

Harrison: He doesn't have to, 'cause he's doing it. We shouldn't have to either, but we're put in this position. As well as being jazz musicians, we have to be educators to the people, because the scene is so messed up right now. Don't get me wrong; I had fun on Pullen's record date. But he's not trying to be traditional.

Mandel: But he's not playing what you'd call commercial music either, is he?

Harrison: No, he's not playing commercial music at all.

Mandel: So is that music as emotionally and intellectually demanding, with the same kind of potential for greatness as jazz within the tradition?

Blanchard: I don't think so. Jazz has a lot to do with depth of knowledge. We haven't had a certain generation of musicians to carry on that part of the tradition that's a level of excellence we can judge music against.

Harrison: Terence and I have a slight difference of opinion about some of this; he leans more towards playing what's traditional first, and I think it's important to know all the music you can, but play something you've developed that's your own. In the '60s many of the musicians came up with their own things, but they were still in the jazz tradition; then guys came up trying to skirt learning the whole tradition, trying to just come up with something new. And a lot of them came up with something new, but it ain't in the jazz tradition. That's what I'm saying and that's the truth. Look 20 years from now, and you'll be able to tell. There are a lot of guys who came up with experiments, and if they're not for real, they're not going to be here. We're learning from the guys who know what they're doing, who we think are saying something musically.

Blanchard: When we say tradition, we mean the evolutionary process—how the music came about, how it grew, and how it continues to grow. How you develop your craft on your instrument, first of all, and use that as your means of expression.

Harrison: When you hear Terence, you know it's Terence, but you can hear Miles, you can hear Louis Armstrong, you can hear Clifford Brown—you can hear that depth of understanding of the jazz tradition. And if you can't hear it in a musician's playing, he's not in the tradition.

Blanchard: The biggest problem is we don't establish the process of becoming a musician by getting from point A to Z. That's also part of the problem of people looking at young jazz musicians and saying, "They aren't playing anything new." They haven't even given us a chance to develop.

March 1988

J.J. Johnson: Bringing It All Back Home

by Gene Kalbacher

It's better to burn out than to fade away.… James Louis Johnson, better known as J.J., bebop's premier trombonist, was familiar with this romantic-but-deadly notion long before Neil Young invoked it as a mythopoetic maxim for rock 'n' rollers with dissolute dreams of immortality through infamy. A number of Johnson's peers during bop's heyday in the '40s and '50s did burn out, but the trombonist never bought it. Instead, he wrought a smooth, fluidly frantic trombone diction comparable to, and compatible with, the saxophone and trumpet syntax invented by Charlie Parker and Dizzy Gillespie.

Born in Indianapolis, Ind., in 1924, Johnson, like many of his contemporaries in the formative fray of small-combo bop, cut his teeth in big bands. Following a 1942 stint in Snookum Russell's territory band, the trombonist spent three productive years with Benny Carter before moving on to Count Basie's band. Johnson's stay with Basie, however, was short-lived, because the trombonist was drawn into, and inspired by, the musical maelstrom of Parker and Gillespie. Besides performing and recording with them, Johnson made lasting statements with the likes of Bud Powell, Sonny Stitt, Miles Davis, Clifford Brown, Sonny Rollins and Illinois Jacquet.

Though he forged a new stylistic standard for the trombone and achieved success, both popular and critical, he dropped out of the jazz scene periodically (owing to artistic or economic discontent, or both), the first time from 1952 to '54, when he found work as a blueprint inspector. Yet Johnson emerged from this hiatus with a healthy creative agenda and renewed vitality, as witnessed by his partnership with fellow trombonist Kai Winding, with whom he performed frequently as Jay and Kai, and cut many still-cherished sides from 1954 to '56. During the late '50s and '60s Johnson led his own, New York-based bands, large and small, and further honed his composing and arranging skills; his compositions "Lament," "Kelo," "Enigma" and "Wee Dot," along with the extended work "El Camino Real," are still favored by jazz musicians.

In 1970, at the suggestion of Quincy Jones, Johnson moved to California and concentrated on writing for movies and television. His film credits include Bill Cosby's Man and Boy, and several so-called blaxsploitation pictures (*Cleopatra Jones* and *Top of the Heap*); for TV he has worked on episodes of *The Mod Squad*, *Starsky & Hutch* and "*The Six Million Dollar Man*." Although he recorded several albums earlier in this decade for Pablo (with Joe Pass, Al Grey, Milt Jackson and Ray Brown), Johnson has remained virtually inactive as a jazz performer, save for a 1977 quintet tour of Japan and a '84 sextet trip to Europe.

This past fall, Johnson announced that he had formed a new quintet (Cedar Walton, piano; Rufus Reid, bass; Victor Lewis, drums; Tom Gullion, tenor sax), was hitting the road and was itching to record again. The month-long tour culminated with an engagement at the Village Vanguard in New York City, marking the trombonist's first week-long bash in the Big Apple since he led his own band at the long-defunct Birdland nearly three decades ago. Pianist Walton, whose association with Johnson goes back to the late '50s, remarked, "Rarely have I seen a musician

so raring to perform;" a condition reinforced by Robert Palmer's review of a Vanguard set in the *New York Times*: "One expects mastery of the trombone from Mr. Johnson, and one is not disappointed."

Gene Kalbacher: Your return to the performance scene is major news to straight-ahead jazz fans.

J.J. Johnson: Straight-ahead jazz fans? An endangered species, to be sure [laughs]. There are such people still remaining on this planet.

Kalbacher: The obvious question: why mount a comeback at the age of 63?

Johnson: In a word, my career as a jazz musician has been cyclical. And for all I know, there's nothing unique about that. It has had its peaks and valleys, its moments when things were a little fuzzy. There were times when I stepped outside the jazz arena just to take a look at it, from the outside looking in. There were times when I stepped outside to re-evaluate and to take stock or take inventory of what I'm all about—what I'm all about as it relates to what jazz is all about.

Kalbacher: How would you describe the cycle since coming to Hollywood and working on film and television scoring?

Johnson: For most of that time—except for a few tours—I had playing on the back burner and writing on the front burner. At the moment, I'm reversing that. Let's just say I began to get a powerful hankering to play again. [Laughs.] I'm using country and western street talk. There's jazz street talk, all kinds of street talk. Powerful hankerin'. Do you remember a show Anthony Newley did some years ago with the wonderful title, *The Roar of the Greasepaint, The Smell of the Crowd*? That says it all!

Kalbacher: You've dropped out, for want of a better word, from the jazz performance scene several times during your career. Can you recall the reason or reasons behind these withdrawals? Was it economics? Dissatisfaction with the scene?

Johnson: It was sometimes a mixture of everything you mentioned, sometimes just one of the items. Again, I don't think that's terribly unique.

Kalbacher: Having performed so infrequently since coming to L.A. in 1970, notwithstanding the tours you did abroad in '77 and '84, has it been difficult for you to get your trombone chops back?

Johnson: I try not to let my chops get too far out of hand. All those years when I

was film composing and whatnot, the trombone was always close by, beckoning me to pick it up and play a few notes on it, sometimes more than a few notes. I never really stopped playing completely. I'm a guy who practices anyway. I practiced a lot, and I did some minimal studio gigs, playing trombone in the band on dramatic scores.

Kalbacher: In the liner notes to *Four Trombones... The Debut Recordings*, Leonard Feather cites a statement you once made about your early experience with the trombone: "There's an innate clumsiness about it; it's a beastly, horrid instrument to play, and particularly to play jazz on. Many times I wondered, how and why did I ever pick up this horrid instrument?" Although you say your chops never got too rusty during your "Hollywood film-composer syndrome," practice chops are one thing and gig chops are another.

Johnson: First of all, don't you dare call that beastly hard instrument a beastly hard instrument—because it is a beastly hard instrument! [Laughs.] No, I'm kidding. It's just a bit more difficult than other instruments once you get the hang of it. The awkwardness of the trombone as well as its ungainliness is that it doesn't have keys and valves—you put that in your subconscious. For all the pros, you never lose sight of it, but you refuse to let it intimidate you. You function as a guy with a trumpet or a saxophone does, and you go on from there. Obviously, you can't do all the things that a saxophonist or trumpet player can do, but I've gotta tell you, this current, new crop of trombonists is gaining and breathing hard on the guys with the trumpets and saxophones. The trombonists are playing faster, faster and faster, higher and higher and higher. There will come a time, I predict, when you'll have to discard the idea that the trombone is an awkward, ungainly, difficult instrument to play because of the slide. It's getting less and less that way.

Kalbacher: Although you've gigged so little in recent years, you mentioned that you did listen quite a bit to records and jazz radio and attend jazz concerts. Who are some of the young trombonists who've impressed you?

Johnson: The most articulate performance I've ever heard on the trombone was given at Wolf Trap by Slide Hampton, when he played on a set with Dizzy Gillespie. It was a tribute to Dizzy, and I believe it will be shown on public television. Slide played "Oop-Pop-a-Da" at about 100 miles per hour with about 100 choruses. I'm exaggerating, of course, but he played all over the horn, with great virtuosity. Also, I'd be remiss if I didn't credit Slide for recommending [agent] Mary Ann Topper to me.

Kalbacher: But who are the younger, fresher faces behind the trombone?

Johnson: Steve Turre sent me some tapes, and he's awfully, awfully good. There are some trombones around now who are doing a number. Bill Watrous. I hear tell about Craig Harris, and I've heard some nice stuff from Robin Eubanks.

Kalbacher: Let's turn back the clock and recall the young, fresh-faced J.J. Johnson. Beginning in 1942, you spent three years in Benny Carter's band. How much did you, then 18, learn from this future Hall of Famer about composing, arranging, improvising?

Johnson: A lot! A lot. First of all, it was an education just to be there as a sideman in Benny's band and to witness this giant of a musician—to observe him as a man, as a musician, as a saxophonist, as a composer, as an arranger. It was invaluable. He was a stylist—as Lester Young was a stylist, as Miles Davis is a stylist, as Dizzy Gillespie is a stylist, as Coleman Hawkins.... After one bar of his improvisation, you knew immediately it was Benny Carter. No one sounds like Benny Carter, no one.

Kalbacher: One can say the same thing about J.J. Johnson. No trombonist in the '40s and, arguably, no one since then, has been able to top or equal that very fragile, fast, legato style you pioneered. Who were your influences in terms of sound and tone and textures? I hear Lester Young, but that may be presumptuous on my part.

Johnson: That's not presumptuous at all. Lester Young was a primary influence in my early years; I was a big Lester Young-aholic. There was a trombonist that not many people know about named Fred Beckett, who played with Harlan Leonard's Rockets, a Midwestern territory orchestra. They never made the big time, but Fred Beckett was the first trombonist I ever heard who played in a linear, or lyrical, style. They made one or two recordings in the early-to-mid '40s. He ended up, before he passed away, with Lionel Hampton. There are other guys. I was a very big Trummy Young fan. Trummy, again, was a stylist. I was somehow impressed by the stylists. Dick Wells, a stylist—not a lot of notes, not a lot of virtuosic situations, but pure stylistic trombone. Vic Dickenson was

a wonderful jazz performer who left his mark. And Roy Eldridge. Naturally, when I first heard Diz and Bird, I knew that's where it was going to be, and, sure enough, that's where it went.

Kalbacher: Working with Bird and Diz in the late '40s, were you aware that you were creating, in effect, a new jazz language with new syntax and vocabulary?

Johnson: I don't know how conscious we were or not. It was very controversial, it was new. The evolution of jazz is so. It has to be that way. Coltrane was controversial. Mingus was controversial. Oscar Pettiford was controversial. You're gonna have these cycles in jazz. Jazz is restless. It won't stay put, and it never will, and thank God that it never has and never will. It's forever seeking and reaching out and exploring. I don't put down this so-called fusion, these guys who are heavily into electronics, because they, too, are reaching out and searching and trying to expand the frontiers, if you will, of jazz. The same criticism, the same hue and cry, about fusion and electronic music occurred when Dizzy and Bird launched their new style of jazz.

Kalbacher: There are, however, new variables today with the burgeoning of technology. With all the synthesizers and drum computers out there, there are fewer work opportunities for straight-ahead jazz musicians. Just look at film scores today.

Johnson: I couldn't agree more. The studio musicians in Hollywood are all running scared. It's frightening that their workload is getting less because of synthesizers and synthesizers and synthesizers. Guys are doing film scores with four or five synthesizers—where the score ends up sounding like 40 musicians or 80 musicians.

Kalbacher: What stands out most in your memory about working with Bird, particularly the December 1947 sextet date you did for Dial?

Johnson: I don't remember any particular anecdotes; it's so fuzzy.

Kalbacher: What was it like to be standing alongside Bird, when he was soaring and swooping through his amazing solos?

Johnson: Well, I think the archives will bear me out that I didn't work a lot with Bird. On a few, isolated recording situations I happened to be fortunate enough to be involved with Bird or Dizzy.

Kalbacher: Then again, how many times do you have to be in the on-deck circle next to Babe Ruth to remember the experience? How did if feel, listening to

Bird laying into a solo and knowing you were next up?

Johnson: Well, your knees shake a lot [laughs], they bump up against each other. Let's not forget that by the time I got on the scene, Diz and Bird had already made their mark. I wasn't involved at the beginning. I recall, in fact, that the first time I heard Diz and Bird I was with Basie's band, and we happened to be playing in New York at the Roxy or something. I had a chance to go around to these clubs on 52nd Street and hear them. Obviously, it was a shattering experience to hear this revolutionary new music.

Kalbacher: One month before your Dial date with Bird, you cut a session with saxist Sonny Stitt [Sonny Stitt/Bud Powell/J.J. Johnson], at which three of your tunes were recorded—"Elora," "Blue Mode" and "Tea Pot." Stitt, many feel, was unfairly stigmatized, and ultimately driven to the tenor from the alto, for sounding too much like Bird. Do you feel that Stitt was unduly castigated for what may have been merely a coincidence in conception?

Johnson: There were times when Stitt sounded so much like Bird that one had to wonder. Yet, there was a subtle difference. Yes, it was controversial: "Is this the ultimate Bird clone?" There were so many clones, but: "Is he the super Bird clone?" There was a Sonny Stitt in there that was uniquely Sonny Stitt; it was Bird but it was Sonny Stitt.

Kalbacher: There were indeed many Bird clones, just as a decade or so later there were many 'Trane clones. During the '40s, many musicians believed that in order to play like Bird, one had to live like Bird—to indulge one's appetite for sex, drink, drugs. How did you manage to avoid these temptations and traps of the scene?

Johnson: Someone, in an interview, asked Benny Carter the secret of his longevity. He gave a simple, eloquent statement: "I am a survivor." I say the same about myself. I survived the scene you depicted, and I have survived the cyclical ups and downs of a jazz musician's life.

Kalbacher: In Ira Gitler's book *Jazz Masters of the Forties*, in which you are the highlight of the trombone chapter, he quotes you as saying that your previous approach to leading a band was "too rigid, too meticulous, too mechanical." If indeed that was so, how do you foresee leading your new quintet after having been inactive for so long?

Johnson: I'll just try to be much looser, take more chances, be more adventurous. Just hang loose and let if flow. That's street talk, too, that characterizes what I hope to accomplish with this quintet.

Kalbacher: Pianist Cedar Walton, a member of the group that recorded *J.J. Inc.* with you in 1960, seems to be a pivotal member of your new enterprise.

Johnson: Cedar is one of my all-time favorite pianists. I was thrilled that when Mary Ann Topper and I started putting this whole thing together, we both agreed that we should have Cedar as our key guy as far as putting the rest of the band together. Cedar and Mary Ann put the rest of the band together, except for the saxophonist, who was recommended very highly by my dear friend David Baker— one of America's foremost jazz educators at Indiana University.

Kalbacher: How is the quintet's repertoire shaping up?

Johnson: For this group I've written two original compositions and rearranged a few others. I've rearranged "Copping the Bop," which I did many, many years ago on my first recording session, and Wayne Shorter's "Nefertiti." It's a little different from the one people know from Miles. One of the new ones, "Quintergy," is a play on the two words quintet and energy. It's a very high-voltage piece that kind of goes crazy. "Why Indianapolis, Why Not Indianapolis?" is another new composition.

Kalbacher: Besides returning to the performance scene, you are also returning to your hometown of Indianapolis, Indiana. What precipitated the move?

Johnson: How much more can you come back? [Laughs.] My wife, Vivian, and I lived in New York for a number of years, and we loved every minute of it. I still think New York City is one of the great cities of the world. But there came a point in time when we felt the need for a dramatic change in our lives. That happened in 1970, when we moved to Los Angeles. Los Angeles is a wonderful city. A lot of people have complaints and gags about L.A., but I have none. But, again, my wife and I both felt the need for a significant change. The logical choice, having lived in both New York and Los Angeles, was move back to our roots. My father and mother still live in Indianapolis. My wife and I were both born there, and we went through high school together there. Even though Thomas Wolfe said, "You can't go back home," we're gonna ignore his comment.

J.J. Johnson.
(Hyou Vielz)

March 1992

The Sound That Launched 1,000 Horns

by Michael Bourne

He's not Pres-like or Bird-like, not 'Trane-ish or Newk-ish. None of the stylistic adjectives so convenient for critics work for tenor saxist Joe Henderson. It's evident he's listened to the greats: to Lester Young, Charlie Parker, John Coltrane, Sonny Rollins—to them and all the others he's enjoyed. But he doesn't play like them, doesn't sound like them. Joe Henderson is a master, and, like the greats, unique.

When he came along in the '60s, jazz was happening every which way, from mainstream and avant-garde to blues, rock and then some, and everything that was happening he played. Henderson's saxophone became a Triton's horn and transformed the music, whatever the style, whatever the groove, into himself. And he's no different (or, really, always different) today. There's no "typical" Joe Henderson album, and every solo is, like the soloist, original and unusual, thoughtful and always from the heart.

"I think playing the saxophone is what I'm supposed to be doing on this planet," says Joe Henderson. "We all have to do something. I play the saxophone. It's the best way I know that I can make the largest number of people happy and get for myself the

largest amount of happiness."

Joe was born April 24, 1937, in Lima, Ohio. When he was nine he was tested for musical aptitude. "I wanted to play drums. I'd be making drums out of my mother's pie pans. But they said I'd gotten a high enough score that I could play anything, and they gave me a saxophone. It was a C melody. I played that about six months and went to the tenor. I was kind of born on the tenor."

Even before he played, Joe was fascinated by his brother's jazz records. "I listened to Lester Young, Flip Phillips, Stan Getz, Charlie Parker, all the people associated with Jazz at the Philharmonic. This stuff went into my ears early on, so when I started to play the saxophone I had in my mind an idea of how that instrument was supposed to sound. I also heard the rhythm-and-blues saxophone players when they came through my hometown."

Soon he was playing dances and learning melodies with his friends. "I think of playing music on the bandstand like an actor relates to a role. I've always wanted to be the best interpreter the world has ever seen. Where a precocious youngster gets an idea like that is beyond me, but somehow improvisation set in on me pretty early,

Joe Henderson.
(Photo by Merci Cyr, courtesy of Verve Records)

1990s

They All Love Joe
by Michael Bourne

John Scofield

"Joe Henderson is the essence of jazz," says guitarist John Scofield. "He embodies musically all the different elements that came together in his generation: hard-bop masterfulness plus the avant-garde. He's a great bopper like Hank Mobley or Sonny Stitt, but he also plays out. He can take it far harmonically, but still with roots. He's a great blues player, a great ballads player. He has one of the most beautiful tones and can set as pretty as Pres or Stan Getz. He's got unbelievable time. He can float, but he can also dig in. He can put the music wherever he wants it. He's got his own vocabulary, his own phrases he plays all different ways, like all the great jazz players. He plays songs in his improvisations. He'll play a blues shout like something that would come from Joe Turner, next to some of the fastest, outest, most angular, atonal music you've ever heard. Who's playing better on any instrument, more interestingly, more cutting edge yet completely with roots than Joe Handerson? He's my role model in jazz."

Stephen Scott

"Joe is a master," says Stephen Scott, the young pianist on Henderson's new album. "When you first hear him, the first thing you identify with in his sound is the blues, no matter what he's playing. He'll deal with some advanced harmonic or rhythmic concept, but it all starts with the blues.... Joe uses so much space when he plays, and, as a piano player, you have to learn to play in the cracks so that you won't get in the soloist's way. Joe starts in the cracks!"

Renee Rosnes

"What's amazing about all the times I've played with him is that Joe never has a bad night, never has a bad minute," says Renee Rosnes, the young pianist with Henderson's working quartet. "He's a great improviser. Every solo has a beginning, a middle, an end. He'll play a motif and develop it, and later on you'll have forgotten it, but he'll come back to it. He can take anything and take it to the limit. That's true of all my favorite players—that they don't have any limitations. Joe inspires me to always reach for the depths of every tune."

Joe Lovano

"Joe Henderson and Wayne Shorter emerged at the same time with their own sounds and rhythms and tunes. They inspired me as a young player," says one tenor saxist, Joe Lovano. "He's always had his own voice. He's developed his own concepts with the inspirations of the people he dug but without copying them. I hear Joe in other tenor players. I hear not only phrases copped from Joe, but lately I hear younger cats trying to cop his sound. That's who you are as a player: your sound. It's one thing to learn from someone, but to copy his sound is strange. Joe's solo development live is a real journey—and you can't cop that! He's on an adventure whenever he plays."

Branford Marsalis

"Joe Henderson is one of the most influential saxophone players of the 20th century," says another tenor saxist, Branford Marsalis. "I learned all the solos on *Mode for Joe* and the records he did with McCoy Tyner, a lot of the stuff he's on, like *The Prisoner*. He was one of the few saxophone players who could really play what I call the modern music, that really came from the bebop tradition but extended the harmonic tradition further. There's a small group of guys in that pantheon: Coltrane, Wayne Shorter, Warne Marsh, Lucky Thompson, Sonny and Ornette, and Joe Hen. He's an amazing musician. I'm really jaded. I don't really go to the clubs anymore. There's not really anything I want to hear—except when Joe's in town. And when Joe's in town, I'm there every night!"

probably before I knew what improvisation was, really. I've always tried to re-create melodies even better than the composers who wrote them. I've always tried to come up with something that never even occurred to them. This is the challenge: not to rearrange the intentions of the composers but to stay within the parameters of what the composers have in mind and be creative and imaginative and meaningful."

One melody that's become almost as much Henderson's as the composer's is "Ask Me Now" by Thelonious Monk. He's recorded it often, each performance an odyssey of sounds and feelings.

"I play it 75 percent of the time because I like it and the other 25 percent because it's demanded that I play it. I sometimes have to play it twice a night, even three times. That tune just laid around for a while. Monk did an incredible job on it, but other than Monk I don't think I heard anyone play it before I recorded it. It's a great tune, very simple. There are some melodies that just stand by themselves. Gershwin was that kind of writer. You don't even have to improvise. You don't have to do anything but play the melody and people will be pleased. One of the songs like that is 'Lush Life.' That's for me the most beautiful tune ever written. It's even more profound knowing that Billy Strayhorn wrote it, words and music, when he was 17 or 18. How does an 18-year-old arrive at that point of feeling, that depth?"

"Lush Life" is the title song of Henderson's new album of Strayhorn's music. "Musicians have to plant some trees—and replant some trees to extend the life of these good things. Billy Strayhorn was one of the people whose talent should be known. Duke Ellington knew about him, so that says something. There are still a lot of people who haven't heard Strayhorn's music, but if I can do something to enable them to become aware of Strayhorn's genius, I'd feel great about that."

Lush Life is the first of several projects he'll record for Verve. Don Sickler worked with Henderson selecting and arranging some of Strayhorn's classics and, with Polygram Jazz VP Richard Seidel, produced the album. Henderson plays "Lush Life" alone, and, on the other songs he's joined for duets to quintets by four of the brightest young players around: pianist Stephen Scott, bassist Christian McBride, drummer Gregory Hutchinson, and trumpeter Wynton Marsalis. That the interplay of generations is respectful, inspirational and affectionate is obvious.

"I think this was part of it, to present some of the youngsters with one of the more established voices. This is the natural way that it happens. This is the way it happened for me. I wouldn't have met the people I met if it hadn't been for Kenny Dorham, Horace Silver, Miles Davis, people I've been on the bandstand with. They introduced me to their audience. We have to do things like this. When older musicians like me find people who can continue the tradition, we have to create ways to bring these people to the fore."

Henderson came to the fore in the '60s. He'd studied for a year at Kentucky State, then four years at Wayne State in Detroit, where he often gigged alongside Yusef Lateef, Barry Harris, Hugh Lawson and Donald Byrd. He was drafted in 1960 and played bass in a military show that traveled the world. While touring in 1961, he met and played with Bud Powell and Kenny Clarke in Paris. Once he was discharged in 1962, he settled in New York, where so many of his friends from Detroit were already regulars, and where trumpeter Kenny Dorham became a brother.

"Kenny Dorham was one of the most important creators in New York, and he's damn near a name you don't hear anymore. That's a shame. How can you overlook a diamond in the rough like him? There haven't been that many people who have that much on the ball creatively as Kenny Dorham."

Henderson's first professional recording was Dorham's album *Una Mas*, the first of many albums he recorded through the '60s as a sideman or a leader for Blue Note. This was the classic time of Blue Note, and what's most remarkable is the variety of music Henderson played, from the grooves of Lee Morgan's *The Sidewinder* to the avant-garde sounds of Andrew Hill's *Point of Departure*. Whatever was happening musically, Joe Henderson was a natural.

"That's part of what I wanted to do early on—be the best interpreter I could possibly be. I wanted to interpret Andrew Hill's music better than he could write it, the same with Duke Pearson and Horace Silver. I'd study and try to find ways of being imaginative and interesting for this music without changing the music around. I didn't want to make Horace Silver's music different from what he had in mind. I wanted to make it even more of what he had in mind."

He joined the Horace Silver band for several years and fronted a big band with

Kenny Dorham—music he'll re-create and record this year at Lincoln Center. He worked with Blood, Sweat and Tears for a minute in 1969, but quit to work with Miles Davis.

"Miles, Wayne Shorter and I were the only constants in the band. I never knew who was going to show up. There'd be a different drummer every night—Tony Williams, Jack DeJohnette, Billy Cobham. Ron Carter would play one night, next night Mislav Vitous or Eddie Gomez. Chick Corea would play one night, next night Herbie Hancock. It never settled. We played all around but never recorded. This was previous to everyone having Walkman recorders. Miles had a great sense of humor. I couldn't stop laughing. I'd be on the bandstand and I'd remember something he said in the car to the gig, and right in the middle of a phrase I'd crack up!"

Henderson's worked more and more as a leader ever since, and recorded many albums, like Lush Life, with particular ideals. He recorded "concept" albums like *The Elements* with Alice Coltrane and was among the first to experiment with the new sounds of synthesizers. He composed tunes like "Power to the People" with a more social point of view. "I got politically involved in a musical way. Especially in the '60s, when people were trying to effect a cure for the ills that have beset this country for such a long time, I thought I'd use the music to convey some of my thoughts. I'd think of a title like 'Black Narcissus,' and then put the music together. I'd try to create a nice melody, but at the same time, when people heard it on the radio, a title like 'Afro-Centric' or 'Power to the People' made a statement."

Words have always inspired Joe Henderson. "I try to create ideas in a musical way the same as writers try to create images with words. I use the mechanics of writing in playing solos. I use quotations. I use commas, semicolons. Pepper Adams turned me on to a writer, Henry Robinson. He wrote a sentence that spanned three or four pages before the period came. And it wasn't a stream of consciousness that went on and on and on. He was stopping, pausing in places with hyphens, brackets around things. He kept moving from left to right with this thought. I can remember in Detroit trying to do that, trying to play the longest meaningful phrase that I could possibly play before I took the obvious breath."

Henderson names Truman Capote, Norman Mailer, Herman Hesse and the Bible among his favorites. "I think the cre-

ative faculties are the same whether you're a musician, a writer, a painter. I can appreciate a painter as if he were a musician playing a phrase with a stroke, the way he'll match two colors together the same as I'll match two tones together."

He tells a story uniquely as a soloist and composer, and he's inspired many musicians through the years. But what sometimes bothers Henderson is when others imitate his strokes and his colors, but don't name the source. He heard a popular tenor saxist a while ago and was staggered. "I heard eight bars at a time that I know I worked out. I can tell you when I worked the music out. I can show you the music when I was putting it together. But when guys like this do an interview they don't acknowledge me. I'm not about to be bitter about this, but I've always felt good about acknowledging people who've had something to do with what I'm about. I've played the ideas of other people—Lester Young, Charlie Parker, John Coltrane, Sonny Rollins, Lee Konitz, Stan Getz—and I mention these guys whenever I do an interview. But there are players who are putting stuff out as if it's their music and they didn't create it. I did."

He's nonetheless happy these days and amused about some of the excitement about *Lush Life*, that the new album, like every new album from Joe Henderson, feels like a comeback. "I have by no means vanished from the scene. I've never stopped playing. I'm very much at home in the trenches. I'm right out there on the front line. That's where I exist. I've been inspired joining the family at Polygram in a way I haven't been inspired in a long time. I'm gonna get busy and do what I'm supposed to do."

March 1992

. . . .

No Semi, No Roadies, No Set List

by Howard Mandel

Over breakfast, members of the Bill Frisell Band interact as they do onstage. Here's

Bill Frisell.
(Hyou Vielz)

guitarist Frisell, sleepy-seeming and grayer than he's appeared before, but still the fearless leader, flashing from humble to strong statement just as his probing leads are liable to explode from lyrical linearism into a dazzling cluster. Here's stalwart and capable bassist Kermit Driscoll, supporting or expanding upon whatever comes to the fore. Drummer Joey Baron arrives late—he's nursed a terrible cold since the band's return from two almost uninterrupted months in Europe, and, suffering an abnormally high fever, fronted his trio with saxophonist Ellery Eskelin and trombonist Steve Swell at the Knitting Factory the other night. Nevertheless, Baron's chipper, uplifting, and to the point.

The Frisell band has just released *Where in the World?* on Elektra/Musician, its culmination as a quartet since cellist Hank Roberts has left to pursue his own aims. As on its suites "Some Song and Dance" (abetted by a sax trio) and "Hard Plains Drifter" (arranged by John Zorn) on Frisell's 1989 *Before We Were Born*, the band conflates aspects of jazz, rock and country musics into evocations of deeply personal experience. Composed sections retain the freshness of conviction, communal improvisations rampage with daring self-assurance and ultimate good nature.

Yet a current of dark reflection cuts through the quietism of *Where in the World?* Perhaps it's Frisell's determination to forge ahead in the face of the challenges of the '90s. As it prepares for a February concert in Brooklyn, a coast-to-coast U.S. tour in March with The President (led by keyboardist Wayne Horvitz, who produced *Where in the World?*, and with whom Driscoll now plays bass), then another European trip in May, the Bill Frisell Band reaffirms its commitments to honest, exploratory interaction—and to having fun.

Howard Mandel: I've been listening to *Where in the World?*, but I still don't have a good grip on who's doing what—the strings sound so close.

Kermit Driscoll: Yeah, I'm playing all this high stuff, sometimes Bill is playing lower than I am, and then there's Hank Roberts, whose range on cello is huge.

Mandel: Bill, back to the clustering of the strings sounds, with Hank Roberts gone—I understand he wanted to pursue his own music—is it more important for Kermit to come up to where your range is by playing a five-string fretless?

Bill Frisell: Yeah, and it's amazing what Kermit's doing. A lot of the music was written for four voices, and now we end up covering parts. His fifth string makes his bass lower than the average bass, so he's doing this weird leap-frogging, sometimes playing two completely independent lines, one the bass line and the other harmonics, at once. It's really cool.

Driscoll: But it's stuff Bill wrote, and knew was possible to do. When we go into improvisation it extends a little bit, but I try to use the same ideas. It's like music written for classical guitar.

Frisell: You figured a lot of it out; you were kind of forced into that situation, 'cause I hadn't thought of only one person playing all that.

Driscoll: You'd have to hear the band now, as a trio, to hear it. It doesn't show up on our record.

Mandel: Is there much overdubbing on *Where in the World?*

Frisell: A little bit; in one or two places, I added another guitar, but it's basically the sound of the band as it was then.

Mandel: I recognize Bill's attack, his employment of the volume pedal—and then I realize Kermit's bowing his bass...

Frisell: Oh yeah, we've been playing so much live I forgot he plays acoustic on the record.

Driscoll: I don't carry it on tour, our schedule and travel is too tough, and it's about all I can do to be there with an electric and my bag.

Mandel: The tight bass contributes to the band's acoustic aura.

Frisell: Yes, and a few of the tunes we recorded in this big space that used to be a church. The tunes with bass and cello in this room had a real acoustic sound.

Mandel: It's extraordinary that you're always playing electric instruments, but are so attentive to acoustics.

Frisell: I really like playing with acoustic instruments, and not overwhelming them. With an electric guitar, you can easily wipe them out. I like to find the place where I'm right there with them.

Driscoll: There are extremes—at moments we get incredibly loud. But whenever we set up, the goal is, "Play to this room." If the sound's bouncing around, you can't play the same as in a road club. At our sound checks we play without the club's PA system, to see what affect we have in the room right away.

Frisell: Sound checks take about an hour, and we've been lucky in the last year to have our own sound person, Claudia Engelhart, who also works with Zorn's Naked City. Last fall we did some gigs in the States without her after we'd had her for a while, and it was a drag.

Mandel: You don't carry your own sound board, do you?

Frisell: We don't carry anything but our guitars—Joey doesn't even carry cymbals. We borrow stuff everywhere, so we have different amps every night. This works better in Europe, where they're more used to it than here, but still we get some suspect equipment. It would be great to have roadies and take our own amps and more instruments with us, but I don't see it in our near future. Claudia balances our sound in the room and we don't use monitors, we set up in a semi-circle, so we play to ourselves and trust her to take care of what's out front. But over the years we've put a lot of energy into playing the room without a PA, making our own balance.

Mandel: Are you currently playing material mostly from *Where in the World*?

Frisell: No—that's what's unbelievable to me about these guys, because they know everything I ever wrote. So literally milliseconds before we start playing, I decide what we're going to hit with, and it's just BAM! It's such a luxury not to have to figure out set lists, to be completely spontaneous. I can draw from my whole compositional history.

Mandel: Do you think the trio's how it's going to be for a while?

Frisell: I feel that's it now. It's kind of frustrating after years of plugging away, and having just done a quartet record, but Hank really wanted to stay home; he agreed to go on tour, but I felt if he was going to leave, we should make a clean break. He missed our last tour, too, breaking a finger the week before we were scheduled to leave, so we'd worked out a lot of the covering of parts then, and realized we could do it. Now it's just getting better and better—especially after these two months, I'm ecstatic about what's going on. It's gotten to some sort of spiritual level for me. And last week we played in Holland with Guy Klucevik, the accordionist. He killed me—he immediately got in with what we're doing. So I've decided we're a trio, but when the chance comes to have other people… at St. Ann's in Brooklyn clarinetist Don Byron is going to play with us.

There's a singer named Victor Gazy we might do something with. We might do some things with a horn section. But it's exciting musically to have things opened up, so I don't want to try to replace Hank.

Mandel: Did you give Guy your music to study?

Frisell: We had one rehearsal, but he listened to all the records, and I gave him all the parts. He worked hard, but I think there are very few people on the planet, if there are any, who could do what he did.

Driscoll: As Bill was saying, we'd start something and he'd know just where we were. In Europe we'd play whole sections of sets where there wasn't any written music, we were playing completely free. There were even times we started and ended that way; usually we go out to link some tunes, or in the middle of a tune we abandon it.

Mandel: You do that by eye contact?

Driscoll: By ear. Guy jumped right into that playing.

Frisell: He even initiated things without getting in the way. We were playing free and went into "Rambler," and he knew what to do. I have the radio tape.

Driscoll: I want to hear that.

Mandel: Do you tape yourselves often when you're touring?

Driscoll: Now that we have Claudia, we do.

Frisell: This fall she taped everything. I don't know when we'll have a chance to listen to it, but I have a fantasy about making a record out of some of that stuff. We could never come close in the studio to some of what goes on live.

Mandel: You're more self-conscious in the studio?

Frisell: Even if you're not nervous in the studio, things happen on a gig. Every night you're thrown into something different. You're on the train for 24 hours, you get off the train and you're in some bizarre place, someone's yelling at you from the audience. Weird things occur in the music you can't artificially set up.

Mandel: If you added a horn section, you'd have to write parts.

Frisell: Right.

Driscoll: The right people might be able to jump in.

Frisell: We did that on the *Before You Were Born* record, with Julius Hemphill—that was our first attempt.

Mandel: Do you think you're limited by where you're playing, or how often, because of the type of music you're playing? I mean, because it's not in the bop tradition, because it's electric?

Frisell: Say something, Joey—you haven't said anything yet.

Joey Baron: I think people see our instrumentation before they hear what we do, and automatically think "fusion," but what we do is not fusion. Club owners or concert promoters hear what we do, or get the message it's not fusion, and they think it's too risky to take a chance on.

Frisell: But when we play…

Baron: When we play, people break down their walls. All kinds of people like it. They don't bother calling it anything. They just enjoy it.

Frisell: There's really nothing weird about the music. Everybody says, "Oh, this is avant-garde…"

Baron: I don't think there's anything weird about the music…

Driscoll: When we played the Village Vanguard, I invited a lawyer who brought his friends, people who think of jazz as Gene Krupa playing "Sing Sing Sing." They loved it. You don't have to like jazz to love this music.

Mandel: Do you even call what you're doing jazz?

Baron: I just think of it as music. If someone wants to call it jazz, I don't see what's wrong with it. From my chair, it seems like we're drawing on jazz as much as we're drawing on other elements.

Mandel: You like the association with jazz, then?

Frisell: I'm not ashamed of it, but I don't really care. It doesn't matter what it's called. It bothers me that people use these names to box things away. What we do comes out of jazz, it has a lot of stuff that attracted me to jazz in the first place. But we don't confine ourselves to a certain era; we use everything we know. That's what all the great jazz players do. Sonny Rollins plays everything that comes through his mind. Monk and Charlie Parker played popular tunes, and everything that was around them. As far as the young beboppers go, there ought to be room for everybody to do what they want. It's not their fault they're getting work, and record company support. The record companies have a tendency to jump on whatever is a hit.

Mandel: Have there ever been any suggestions from your record company [Elektra/Musician] about the kind of direction you should take?

Frisell: No. Bob Hurwitz, our producer, is a strong presence and has high standards for what we do; but if there was ever any hint of pressure, I'd be gone in two minutes. They signed me—and I went with them—because they like what I was doing. I mean, if anyone thinks I recorded "Chain of Fools" for any reason but that I love the way Aretha Franklin sings, and wanted to copy her thing... but Joey hates my version of that tune. He thinks I should have used a real drummer and not a drum machine.

Mandel: What do you like best about what your boss does, Joey?

Baron: This band is a place where I can come and not be expected to do any specific thing. I can bring whatever's in my background, and it's not judged, the way it is in straight jazz circles. It has to do with attitudes. In this band, there are no attitudes—we take whatever's there. Some nights, I'll play straight time, some nights I'll do the opposite—and whatever I do is taken seriously—which allows me to take myself seriously as a musician. This goes for all of us. It's the healthiest environment in which to create music. You know, I had professional experience when I was just turning 20 playing with Carmen McRae. Like her music, Bill's is very soulful. When most people would let out 64 notes, she'd think about it and maybe let out a hum or one phrase. Bill's like that, too—he waits for the right idea.

Driscoll: 'Til he just feels like playing something.

Baron: Kermit does that, too, and that's my background. I mean, I've learned there's something about providing solid leadership—that's what's great about this band. Bill's a great bandleader: he provides safety for us to know we can play what we feel, and talk about it if we want to. When it comes to playing the music, it's not like I'm punching a time card—instead, the time has come to put myself on the line. Sometimes when I'm playing I forget it's Bill's band, because it's just so open.

Frisell: Well, sometimes I agonize over trying to figure out something for them to play, but when I say something it usually makes things worse. It works better if I just let them go.

Driscoll: If there were lots of parts, they'd disappear after a month on the road, anyway. Bill does expect miracles—but we all want the same things. We're always serious, but we're having fun at the same time. It means we can go out there and play anything, and know we're not going to be fired for it the next day.

Mandel: When you're playing a gig,

Bill, do you ever hear something these guys do that takes you in a different direction?

Frisell: Oh yeah, that's what I live for: for these guys to surprise me.

September 1992

Stephane Grapelli
From Silent Movies to CDs
by Stephanie Stein

The small, dapper Frenchman looked up as I entered the room, put aside the earphones he had on, and smiled. He set them down on the coffee table next to a portable CD player, beside the gleaming 200-year-old violin sitting in its case. Stephane Grappelli, the world's foremost jazz violinist, had been listening to a recording he'd made with pianist McCoy Tyner. Though it was still morning, it seemed as if he'd been awake for hours, listening, practicing. He politely greeted me and thanked me for being so punctual. He recounted a media mishap, when another journalist appeared for an interview an hour late, with no apologies. The writer then asked him how many people were in the Quintet of the Hot Club of Paris (the group Grappelli formed in the '30s with Django Reinhardt, the legendary gypsy guitarist), and insisted on misnaming one of the personnel. "I simply asked him to leave," said Grappelli with a Gallic shrug. "No interview. Who needs such silly questions?"

Grappelli, who will turn 85 in January, related this incident with candor, implying that life is too short for such nonsense. Active as ever, he had stopped off in New York City before beginning his annual U.S. tour this past spring. For these concerts, Grappelli was reunited with guitarist Bucky Pizzarelli—an old friend—and Jon Burr, who often accompanies him on bass. A typical evening is generously studded with the jewels that Grappelli co-wrote with Django—"Minor Swing," "Daphnis," "Nuages." Grappelli's performances continue to amaze. His playing exemplifies improvisational mastery, his tone is crystalline, and every phrase is underscored

with sheer joy. Pizzarelli, a consummate musician himself, generates the kind of conversational intimacy that nourished Grappelli's and Django's musical union. Echoes rang from the past.

Grappelli's past coincides with many historical benchmarks, musical and otherwise. Born in Paris, he came of age as his native city was reveling in the spirit of the Jazz Age. He was raised by his father, a philosophy teacher who instilled a great love of music in his son and gave him a violin when he was 10. By the time he was 15, Grappelli began playing for silent movies. His first exposure to jazz came from a gramophone store near the cinema where he worked. In between shows, he went and listened to mediocre French versions of American tunes and the scant number of American jazz records that arrived a couple of years late.

"The first real jazz record I heard was with a group called Mitchell's Jazz Kings and the tune was 'Stumbling,'" Grappelli recalled in his fluent but heavily accented English. "When I heard that, I thought, 'That's my music and that's what I want to play.' They were all black artists on that record, great musicians.

"So my destiny changed. I had no ability as a concert artist, I'm a complete autodidact. My only chance was to play the music that comes from the skies, from heaven. So God gave us jazz music. Today you need technique to play jazz music because it is developing every year. But in those days it was easy, it was simple. And the really great thing with jazz is you can improvise, and that's what attracted me."

Grappelli spent the next few years playing with various dance bands, performing on piano and/or violin. In 1933, while changing a broken string backstage during a tea dance, he first met Django. They began playing together frequently and soon became the quintessential odd couple. Grappelli was cultivated, while Django was barely literate; Grappelli was responsible to a fault, while his new partner was moody and late more often than not. Musically, they were a perfect match. Using American jazz tunes as their catalyst, they developed a sound and concept that established them as among the first bona-fide foreign jazz musicians. Their quintet used two rhythm guitars and acoustic bass, a subtle yet emphatic foil for Grapelli and Django's inspired improvisations.

"At that time, I wanted to play jazz the same way a classical quartet or quintet

Stephane Grapelli.
(Hyou Vielz)

would play," Grapelli explained. "I hated to see people dancing in front of me when I played, or eating—music must be apart. I don't know which is worse, the dancers who dance at the wrong tempo or someone in front of you saying, 'Hey, waiter, give me some mustard!' By that time, I was disgusted. I told Django that from now on we were going to play to be listened to.

"I was lucky to start in 1937 the way I wanted. The public sat there and listened to our music. Because after all, a guitarist like Django, you can't find every day. And we got to prove our music was valid. During the French Exhibition in Paris in 1937, we were engaged by a fantastic woman called Bricktop, one of the queens of the nightclubs. She booked a restaurant for three months, for the duration of the Exhibition. The place was so small, she didn't have room for a conventional group. So she booked us and all the world came to see us. It was *incroyable*—we met Louis Armstrong and Cole Porter, who just composed a song for Mabel Mercer called 'I've Got You Under My Skin.' In those days, I was playing the violin with Django, but when Bricktop or Mabel Mercer wanted to sing, I sat at the piano. We had such incredible visitors—and high society people. You know I was born very poor, so I liked their kind of smell.

"So voila, after that, I said I will never play for dancers anymore, and we started to do concerts. The first one we did about 100 young people came. Sixty years ago, our group was considered avant-garde, it was very modern. In any case it was like a plant, maybe a rose. Why not? So more and more, we got well known. All because I was not going to play anymore for *les poupettes* who dance out of time."

The Quintet thrilled audiences, and performed and recorded extensively between 1934 and '39. They were in England at the onset of World War II, where Grappelli chose to remain, while Django and the others returned to France. Although Grappelli and Reinhardt were reunited on occasion after the war, their partnership had waned. Reinhardt's health was also failing, and he died in 1953. By then, Grappelli had already started leading his own groups, and he performed in prestigious French clubs and hotels throughout the '50s. During the '60s and '70s, his international reputation was greatly enhanced by numerous festival appearances.

As the decades keep going by, Grappelli's popularity has only increased. His flexibility, humor and irascible sense of wonder have undoubtedly helped him sustain such a lengthy and rewarding career. A perennial winner in both DB's Readers and Critics polls and a member of the Hall of Fame since 1983, his stature has been upheld by countless recordings and performances in the company of such jazz masters as Duke Ellington, Benny Goodman, Joe Pass and Oscar Peterson. The sheer variety of musicians he has worked with is astonishing. His collaborations have encompassed everyone from Stuff Smith to Yo-Yo Ma, and he's influenced everyone from bluegrass fiddler Vassar Clements to the rising young classical star violinist Nigel Kennedy. His love of anything and anyone good in music is unequivocal.

"I'm attentive to every kind of music, I love every kind of music," Grappelli said, as the interview drew to a close. "I love Chinese music when I'm in a Chinese restaurant. I can listen to a Beethoven symphony, then immediately Louis Armstrong without any preparation, because that is great music. It's a gift to be like that, we are so lucky to be like that.

"And I must say that the public is the best to me here, because you invented this music. I never forget that jazz started here in America with the great black artists. That's why you are so good here, you are encouraged to play. People scream, and sometimes they scream at the wrong time, but it is fantastic.

"Just before you came, somebody called from Chicago, and said, 'There are so many groups still imitating you!' After all these years, it's such a great compliment. That's why I keep on playing.

"So give my regards to *DownBeat*. They are so good to me, making me a winner in their polls. The others in the violin district are also very good musicians, but it's always good to be the first," Grappelli concluded, with a sly laugh. As soon as the door closed, the unmistakable sound of his violin wafted down the hall.

March 1993
· ·

Joe Lovano's Sound of the Broad Shoulders

by Howard Mandel

Joe Lovano has a sound. It's a broad-shouldered, hairy-chested and tenderhearted sound, able to bear responsibilities in big bands as well as in trios, in long-term collaborations as well as in his own more recently convened ensembles. It's a sound equally applicable to companionably interactive play and true passion without lapses into forced urgency. Lovano's sound on tenor sax, especially—but on alto, soprano, flute and the clarinet family, too—has quietly become a keynote of the '90s.

Joe now seems to be heard everywhere—in John Scofield's quartet, in Paul Motian's trio, in Charlie Haden's Liberation Music Orchestra, the Village Vanguard Monday Night Band, and the Smithsonian Institution's jazz repertory band, with Dave Holland and Billy Higgins at a memorial service for revered drummer Ed Blackwell, on hot sessions for other strong leaders, and with his most ambitious album yet, *Universal Language*, following two well-received productions, *From the Soul* and *Landmarks*, all for Blue Note Records. Lovano's sound is the sound of compassion, of hard-won, fully earned accomplishment and dependably professional maturity. No wonder in these bottom-line '90s, Joe Lovano is the man.

"I'm just trying to play, to find myself

and get next to my sound," Lovano says, earnest and soft-spoken about the mission he's taken for life. Thoughtful, modest, lately turned 40, Lovano has jazz in his blood. His father, Tony "Big T" Lovano, was a tenorist (with whom Joe recorded the satisfying *Hometown Sessions* in '86, not quite a year before he died), a central figure in the organ combos and progressive bop sessions that characterized the Cleveland scene. Joe's uncle played horn, too, and his brother Anthony is a drummer. Music is the heritage of their Sicilian family, but jazz—make that modern jazz—is the special love of its American generations. Furthermore, Joe's wife, Judi Silvano (nee Silverman), is a professional vocalist with a soprano's range, and on *Universal Language* she offers wordless lines that wrap around Joe's themes and discursions as tightly as Irene Abei's cling to soprano saxist Steve Lacy's.

Not that Joe's gone quite so European as the Paris-based Lacy, but still he's exploratory and expansive. Though he's worked (even as a teenager) and studied (at Berklee) and reapplied himself (in bands led by organists Lonnie Smith and Jack McDuff and Herdsman Woody Herman since arriving in New York in the mid-'70s) to the jazz tradition's core, he's open to whatever is genuine and substantial, to whatever leads him closer to the answer to his big question: "Who is Joe Lovano?" Music frames his ongoing investigation.

"I've primarily been focused on tenor as my main voice since I was 12 years old, but I started on alto when I was a kid. And playing with Blackwell during the last few years of his life really brought that back to me," Joe says. Drums and drummers are vital to him, as they are to any jazz player; he keeps a traps set ready in his Chelsea loft and he considers veteran Detroit/Cleveland rhythmist Lawrence Jacktown Jackson as well as youthful Billy Stewart important associates. Blackwell, best known for drumming with Ornette Coleman's circle of improvisers—though he recorded with John Coltrane, Eric Dolphy, David Murray and Archie Shepp, too—profoundly underscores Lovano throughout *From the Soul*, besides attending Holland and pianist Michel Petrucciani, whom he'd never previously met. Blackwell is also vital to Joe's recently released *Sounds of Joy* with bassist Anthony Cox. Lovano lauds Blackwell's effect.

"He was a treasure in music, and an inspiration to me. Musicians like Blackwell, who are completely original and have

40 years of recorded music in their life, really get me deep into who I am.

"I've played in a lot of bands, and I always try to find something new with the people who are right there at that moment. That's what keeps music fresh, for me. Playing with people who are their own players—like Blackwell—taught me how to find myself. I've been with Paul Motian since 1981, and joined the Mel Lewis band in '80. Being with both those drummers for 10 years, touring and everything, has been fantastic. It's grounded me in an awareness of interplay, of being creative with the other people rather than just playing my horn.

"To be an honest musician, you play from your history. As your experiences grow, the music comes out. All my favorite players developed like that. Of course, we play from the history of the music around us, too. But your history, what you experience, is what really comes out if you can get deep inside yourself, the music and the personalities of the people you play with, and not just treat your instrument like a technical thing."

Nobody's likely to accuse Lovano of being a technique head. His mastery of his horns and reeds, the perfection of his intonation and articulation, the fluency of his fingerings and phrases is unquestionable, but so is his commitment to playing feelings rather than licks or chops. The point is that Joe's experiences give him new ideas about expressing feelings, rather than simply refining his cool skills. Even his years in big bands emerge in personal ways, as becomes evident with the advent of *Universal Language*.

"Doing stuff with Carla Bley—I toured with her in '83 for a year—and Charlie's [Haden] band, which I joined in '87, and with Bob Brookmeyer in Mel's band, has helped my ensemble writing to come out a little more," Lovano explains. "*Universal Language* features a little larger ensemble, with Judi's soprano voice, trumpet by Tim Hagans, Kenny Werner on piano, Jack DeJohnette on drums, Charlie Haden and Steve Swallow on some pieces together and Scott Lee playing bass, too. It has directions and influences from all the periods of my musical growth.

"Charlie's band and Carla's band were really fun because they were looser, more open. You not only had to play your part as written but there are places in the music to create your own part. Those are concepts I'm putting into my music.

"Then, the whole idea of playing in

ensembles and blending with other horns, that's the most important thing of working in big bands, I think. A lot of the great players from the history of jazz had that one common thread, that they all played in bigger groups with five and six saxophone players. They were all in each other's face. They didn't want to sound like each other, you know, and they'd say, 'Oh, yeah, you thought that was bad? Check this out!' They had that attitude, and that's how I grew up, playing with my dad, and playing with Woody's band and the Mel Lewis' band.

"I think young players who don't have that experience miss something in their playing. They just stand there and play by themselves—they don't play with a sense of ensemble. I want to have that ensembleness in my playing even when I'm playing a duet with somebody. In my solo projects, when I accompany myself on percussion as I'm playing tenor, there's some of that, too. I'm playing with an ensemble attitude even when I play alone. That definitely comes from playing in big bands."

Solo projects where he accompanies himself on percussion—gongs and rattles et al.—while playing tenor? Oh, yes, some of *Universal Language* is like that. After all, as a Midwesterner growing up with a tenor saxist for a dad in the '60s, Lovano was privy to Sonny Stitt, Eddie "Lockjaw" Davis, Harold Vick in Shirley Scott's band, Dizzy Gillespie with James Moody and records of classic horn men like Lester Young. But there were more experimental expressions also in the air.

"I heard some of the solo records of Roscoe Mitchell and Joseph Jarman that I really dug, and solo works of Anthony Braxton—they were improvisers, they were playing. Albert Ayler was from Cleveland, and he had a lot of followers, so I was around some of those pioneers of free-jazz as a kid, attending some of their concerts.

"I never heard Albert himself, but I grew up on the music of Coltrane's bands, and Miles' bands, and Ornette's bands, and the players who played with them through all their different periods," he elaborates. "The way Billy Higgins and Scott Lafaro and Charlie Haden played, and Philly Joe Jones and Max Roach's band with Clifford Jordan and Art Blakey's bands—they're all part of my history. You might say you hear something in my playing with Scofield that comes out of Ornette, but remember: all those bands were digging and influencing each other, too.

Joe Lovano.
(Jimmy Katz)

"That was a beautiful period for creative music, given the interplay among all the players in those different groups. All the things Sonny Rollins did, Wayne Shorter, Dewey Redman, Don Cherry, Freddie Hubbard, Bobby Hutcherson, [Eric] Dolphy—every record seemed to have a lot of personality in it. Jazz is a very social music; it's a lot about your contemporaries and how everybody feeds off each other. I know Coltrane played how he did because of how Sonny was playing down the street. I really try to feel that now. Here Jackie McLean is playing at the Vanguard, while I'm with Scofield at Sweet Basil. That means something to me that's going to be in my attitude all week.

"And the Brecker Brothers at the Blue Note—it's a different kind of music, but the energy is there. Their band is really arranged. They get into different aspects of interplay within the solo spaces, though it's not as open a concept as what we're playing with John. Still, Mike's created a voice for a generation of musicians. I've always dug his playing. He's a good friend of mine. And it means something that he and Randy

are playing during the same week I am.

"See, I want to play some modern jazz. I feel that that's the music from the period that's really inspiring to me. And I mean today's modern. It's got to do with the way I play and the way people around me improvise together, but it's a growth from what modern jazz was; and modern jazz from the '60s to me was a growth from the history of jazz to that point. It didn't stop there. I think it still can carry through.

"I want to play in bands that project tomorrow, but are today, really today. I'd say the Motian trio plays some modern jazz. Bill Frisell is a complete improviser, one of the most creative players today. The trio has developed the most incredible repertoire of music, standard tunes and a lot of Monk, Paul's compositions and some of Bill's and my own. Paul plays with a complete sense of adventure and exploration, letting every sound and everything around him come through his playing into the music. That's what improvising is, for me, It's listening and reacting.

"One thing I want to put together in my playing is the collective inspiration from the history of jazz up until today. So I'm not just playing a style of bebop or fusion or hard bop, or re-creating a period of swing—but instead incorporating what swing means to me. How bebop come through my language, how the Modern Jazz Quartet's classical approach and really hard-swinging blues come through my playing.

"When you're young, you focus on some things you like. That's how you play, that's the world you try to live in. But as you grow as a player, you start to combine all the different attitudes, if you're open to that. I want to grow and change and develop my ideas with everything that inspires me.

I've always been cross-generational, but I'm speaking of international influences, too. This last year I've played in Chile, been in Europe a bunch of times, played all over Japan and Hong Kong. The different flavors of the countries and their people—if you let all that influence you, your music can go anywhere. That's what Duke Ellington did, and look at all the beautiful music he gave us. To respect different cultures and let all peoples into your life to influence you is a rich thing—it filters in through my music, for sure. I don't ever want to lose that. That's why I love living in New York City."

Maybe it's not for everyone. Nor can every good player immerse him or herself in every aspect of performance and presentation, as Lovano has. Partially funded by National Endowment for the Arts jazz grants, he staged two "these are my influences, this is my music" concerts, parlaying the one in Cleveland into an evening presented by the Tri-C Jazz Festival and eventually broadcast over National Public Radio. "As a musician, you have to create your own gigs," Lovano believes. "Musicians and artists have to be really involved in what they're doing. Then it will mean something. And I think if you are involved in the whole presentation of what you're doing, rather than waiting for the phone to ring, you're going to be able to do more things you wanted to do.

"Chick Corea's done that. Jack DeJohnette's like that, too. The deeper you're involved, the deeper you're going to play. It inspires me, especially when I get things planned and then see them running smoothly.

"Personally, I want to try to get deep inside myself through music. That's it. It's a deep love my father had and gave to me. He did warn me of the pitfalls. He was a barber as well as a musician. His situation was always changing—he'd be playing around town five nights, two nights, three nights. I saw firsthand that the money was always tight, that you had to deal with all these sad cats, club owners or whoever. But somehow, he'd always take his horn out to play down in the basement, and all that other stuff would go away.

"And for me, that's what I wanted to do. I'd hear my dad practice when I was a kid, and all I wanted to do was create that sound myself.

"It's a hard life out here. You have to be strong, you have to be organized, you've got to be on top of a lot of stuff. But I think the musicians who are really involved in their careers and the directions they go in are going to be able to live a life in music."

Coming from Joe Lovano—who's planning his next special project as a blowing session with orchestrations and compositions by Gunther Schuller, who's producing music by Judi Silvano for release on his own JSL label, who's proud to be in Paul Motian's trio and celebrating its 10th anniversary, who looks forward to his quartet's annual February week at the Vanguard, and his spring tour through the U.S. with Scofield's quartet, not to mention his own autumn tour of Europe—a life in music sounds like a worthy pursuit. It's already proved to be an attainable goal.

December 1993

Joshua Redman
Street of Dreams
by Pat Cole

What a difference a year has made in the life of Joshua Redman. Twelve months ago, Redman was a largely unknown musician in search of a dream. Today, he's a young man in the limelight. He's been showered with brisk record sales, an enthusiastic following, plenty of calls from major booking agents, too many calls at home from starstruck fans and more nights in strange hotels than he cares to remember.

Not that Redman's complaining about instant success. He's ecstatic. But a dizzying rise to fame has its drawbacks. Sleep, for one, has been hard to come by. At a concert stop last September in San Diego, the young Redman was so short on sleep, he almost collapsed.

"The only way I could stay awake was to keep playing," recalls the soft-spoken tenor player. "Every time I stopped playing, I felt like I was going to pass out."

Redman has managed to conquer the hard part of being a jazz musician: breaking through a sea of saxophonists and winning recognition as a potential torchbearer of his generation. Now, comes the momentous test of building on this quick start. Fans and critics alike wonder: Can he maintain his momentum? Will he grow musically? Can he handle instant fame or the business aspects of his new life and still thrive musically?

Understanding how he came out of the blocks helps answer some of those questions. His ascent in the jazz world has arguably been the Cinderella story of 1993. After listening to his CD or witnessing a live performance, many critics showered him with adjectives and superlatives. Within four months of its release, Redman's self-titled debut sold more than 30,000 copies and rose to No. 3 on *Billboard's* jazz charts. *Wish*, his second album, released in September, is even better. The album, with some tunes recorded live at the Blue Note in New York, let Redman fulfill his dream of playing with some of his idols. It features Pat Metheny on guitar, Billy Higgins on drums, and Charlie Haden on bass. Within a week of its release, it became the most-played jazz album on radio stations nationwide, according to the *Gavin Report*.

Redman admits that while success has happened quickly, it hasn't been easy. Upon meeting him for the first time, one would hardly know that the Berkeley, Calif., native's life has undergone a sea change. Two days after the San Diego gig, Redman took some time to unwind and catch up on sleep at his aunt's house in Los Angeles' Silver Lake district. Casually dressed, he practiced riffs in a terraced garden overlooking a valley of dated Spanish-style homes, apartments and bungalows.

When meeting a guest, Redman flashes a wide smile and offers an array of soft drinks. He begins talking about living like a gypsy on the road, the ritual musicians either love or loathe. Since June 1992, he has spent about half his life in airports, buses or cars, traveling from gig to gig.

"It's exhilarating," says Redman. "There is a real sense of freedom when you go on the road. You're not tied to a specific location. But then there is also a sense of imprisonment. Sometimes, I feel like all I do is pack and unpack. An hour a day I spend packing. There is so much else I could be doing. It's been a year and a half since I've listened to a CD from beginning to end. I feel like I lose a lot of my life on the road."

But the travel is definitely worth it, he concludes. Redman genuinely likes playing for an audience. "I like being onstage," he says. "Which is funny, because when I was young in school, I didn't like raising my hand in class, and I never got kicks from being in front of a lot of people."

Redman, 24, is by no means the first young sensation the jazz world has seen this century. In fact, his rise certainly fits a pattern. Wynton Marsalis was only 19 when he started making an impact with Art Blakey and the Jazz Messengers, and 22 when he earned two Grammys for his jazz and classical albums. Miles Davis was a mere 21 when he was anointed by *Esquire* as jazz's New Star. And Duke Ellington was in his mid-20s when he became a noteworthy band leader.

What separates Redman from prodigies past? It's an extraordinary mix of academic intellect with musical artistry. After graduating from Berkeley High School as its valedictorian, he entered Harvard University with the intention of becoming a doctor.

Then, after choosing social studies as a major, he sought to become a lawyer. "I never wanted to be a professional musician," Redman says. "I saw how hard it was for my father [tenorman Dewey Redman] to succeed."

Redman graduated summa cum laude, applied to Yale Law School, deferred his admission, then won the Thelonious Monk Institute's prestigious Jazz Saxophone Competition. It's not the normal path that serious musicians take to jazz prominence.

In addition, one would think that he spent hours and hours in a room playing riffs while hearing his conscience shout, "Practice, practice, practice." Hardly. Listen to this: "It's a bit of a losing battle right now," Redman says with some regret. "The time for personal musical reflection is deficient. I don't practice. I mean, luckily, I never really did. Before, I didn't like practicing, and I had the time to do it. Now I have a desire to practice, and I don't have the time.

"The dominant things in my life are the peripheral things: doing interviews, keeping contact with the record company.

Joshua Redman.
(Photo by Dana Lixencerg, courtesy of Warner Brothers)

That does dominate right now. And it won't continue to dominate. Because I'm definitely at a point where I have to set aside that time for personal musical reflection. If I don't, I'm going to end up being frustrated. That's what I'm grappling with right now."

To Warner Bros., Redman, though young, represents a future stalwart. "I think Joshua felt he had a chance to be nearly one of a kind here," says Ricky Schultz, Warner Bros.' vice president of jazz and progressive music. "He's happening because he's extraordinary. He's the real thing. This is the most excited I have

been about an artist in the last 15 years. The last artist I had been that excited about was Pat Metheny."

So it's clear that Redman has all the promise to be a great musician. But how will he grow and thrive? During the interview, he revealed three key paths to flourishing as a musician.

Step One: Play music from the soul.

Many critics think he has accomplished this. Redman, however, thinks he has a way to go. "People say I sound mature, and I think that's the greatest compliment you can get," he says. "But I consider myself a beginner. Also, I try to be honest in what I do. Maybe there's a direct-ness and an honesty that I have. When I hear some musicians, sometimes I feel like they're not playing from the soul. Any kind of intellectual agenda distracts from what the music is about."

Well, he may be a beginner, but believe what some critics and observers say—Redman has discovered his voice in raw form. His doesn't focus on speed, tech-nique, or copying Stanley Turrentine or Dexter Gordon licks. Instead, he says, he hones in on communicating emotions. Dur-ing the recording of *Wish*, Charlie Haden was amazed at his phrasings. "He plays very original solos," he said. "He's discov-ered his soul a lot more quickly than most musicians do. His solos are very mature and consistent with a lot of continuity. He doesn't rely on licks like a lot of people do. He makes his own licks, and I'm sure he's going to be a very influential musician in jazz as soon as he gets more experience."

How should Joshua get that experi-ence?

Step Two: play with musicians who challenge you, young or old.

Part of the strategy behind *Wish* was for Redman to play with an elite group of jazz musicians. "It was a music lesson," Redman says about the day-and-a-half recording session. "It was a chance to learn from three of my idols. I was scared shitless going into the studio. I had all these insecu-rities and doubts. But once we played the first beat, all that mattered was the music."

What did Redman learn from Pat Metheny, for instance? "He's an incredibly great storyteller," Redman says. "When he improvises, it doesn't sound like a bunch of licks. There's always a journey. It can be a far-out journey at times, but there's always a sense of structure. He always has some-thing to say. Seeing that process firsthand was like seeing a master sculptor in the actual stage of sculpting instead of just see-ing the finished product. And he really has a sense of how to communicate to an audi-ence without compromising."

While some observers think that young jazz musicians shouldn't focus on playing with their peers, Redman sees the benefits. His own band members are unusually accomplished for their age. Red-man's regular bass player, 21-year-old Christian McBride, is arguably one of the best young musicians on the scene today. Drummer Brian Blade, who is also in his 20s, wins kudos for his passionate, sensitive attack. Good musicians are good musicians.

"I think it's essential to work along-side the masters," Redman says. "I insisted to Warner Bros. that I be able to play as a sideman. And I've done a bunch. Just this year, I've recorded with Melvin Rhyne [the late Wes Montgomery's organ player], Joe Lovano, Mulgrew Miller, Paul Motian, and I'm going to record with Milt Jackson at the beginning of next year. That's going to be an ongoing part of my career. It's very, very important for me to continue to play with master musicians.

"But I think there's something to be said about playing with musicians from your own generation. Great musicians come in different sizes and shapes. Playing with Christian McBride: to me, he's one of the great bass players out there. And he happens to be 21. It's just a freak, right? Not to denigrate the masters that I've played with, but I've learned as much play-ing with him as I have with anyone else. He's an incredible musician regardless of his age. So, if you find great musicians to play with, it really doesn't matter what their age is. Something very positive hap-pens when you bring together musicians of the same generation. There is a fire, an intensity, an unbridled passion. There's that youthful exuberance that I get from playing with my peers that I don't get in the same way from playing with older musicians."

Before this year, Redman had never been exposed to international acclaim. So how do you handle fame, money and set your career on a smooth course?

Step Three: Keep a level head, and surround yourself with trustworthy people.

Redman hardly thinks he's got it made. "The music business is not an artis-tic meritocracy," he says. "The best musi-cian doesn't get the biggest paycheck. Because I've never planned for this, it's icing on the cake. It's a fantasy, really."

In his favor, money isn't a problem for Redman right now. He is constantly tour-ing and playing gigs with various bands. "I'm paying my rent, I can eat, I'm not in need, I'm not on welfare," he says. "I never had any money, I never had a lot of luxu-ries. But I'm totally aware that I don't have secure employment. I book a gig, get paid, and it's on a daily basis. There isn't a sense of security."

Redman isn't looking for a movie deal, and, no, he doesn't want Branford Marsalis' job on *The Tonight Show*. He lives in a diverse neighborhood in the Park Slope area of Brooklyn, where he can hear music played on the street. It helps him

remain anchored in the jazz scene.

"New York is the only place where there is a really vital acoustic-jazz scene," he says. "Every night, if I want to, I can go and see good players. And in Park Slope, I can get away with practicing in my apartment."

So it seems like Redman's got the for-mula down, if he can just squeeze time in for more practice. While he's still worried about his future, Warner Bros. executives are less concerned. "You hope that a person or a couple of persons like him drop in your lap during your career," Says Schultz. "It's pretty exciting to work with rare and gen-uine talent."

It certainly looks like Redman knows what he's doing—and he's only just begun.

October 1994

Hank Crawford and David Sanborn

Soul Connection
by Ed Enright

Hear them each bend a single note, and the connection is obvious: David Sanborn's primary musical influence was Hank Crawford, the alto saxophonist who came out of the Ray Charles Orchestra of the late '50s and redefined the concept of "playing with feeling."

Blending influences from blues, R&B and bebop, the Memphis-born Crawford helped lay the groundwork for the current generation of jazz-tinged saxophone roman-tics. Today, at age 59, he continues to tour and record, his attack still ripe with gut-wrenching tone, his vibrato replete with a tender sexuality. A recent Rhino reissue—*Heart and Soul: The Hank Crawford Anthology*—spans Crawford's entire career, from his beginnings as an arranger and bari-tone saxophonist with the Charles Orches-tra, through more than three decades as an alto front man on the Atlantic, Kudu and (currently) Milestone labels.

Ironically, with the exception of record reviews and an occasional live-performance review, *DownBeat* has never told Crawford's story, until now. We set up a rendezvous this summer between the master and his biggest fan and let the tapes roll in the friendly confines of 49-year-old Sanborn's Manhattan apartment. Hank had just returned from a month-long tour of Europe with organist Jimmy McGriff, a frequent groove-collaborator (their latest release as co-leaders, *Right Turn on Blue*, is available on the Telarc label). David was on a short break from a busy tour in support of his latest Elektra release, *Hearsay*. Like two old friends, Hank and David were eager to dig in and let it all hang out. What follows is an edited transcript of their three-hour chat.

David Sanborn: The first thing I ever heard that you did was "The Peeper." Was that from *From the Heart* [1962], or was that from *More Soul* [1961]?

Hank Crawford: I think it was from *The Soul Clinic* [1961]. It wasn't on the first one.

Sanborn: Yeah, it wasn't. Your first one was *More Soul*.

Crawford: Right.

Sanborn: That had "Angel Eyes" on it—"Angel Eyes" and "Misty." I don't remember if it was "Misty" or if it was "The Peeper."

Crawford: Well, those were the first two that really kind of made it.

Sanborn: That was the stuff. You know what's amazing to me about you is that you've consistently maintained your sound. A lot of guys who play over a period of years, their sound deteriorates. Your conception is refined. It's not that you're doing the same thing, but it's like the essence of what you were then is happening now.

Crawford: It's the same with you. You don't change. At least not to me.

Sanborn: I guess you just try to refine what it is that—it's like, I always talk about that emotional directness in your playing. You could say more with fewer notes than anybody I know. Your turnarounds, that was the thing. That was always the hardest thing for me to figure out how to do: how to get around those V chords.

Crawford: Yeah.

Sanborn: When I first started playing, you get to a V chord, what do you do? I just listened to you because you would just get this thing going.

Crawford: You know, I don't even know how to explain it, man, because it's just natural.

Hank Crawford.
(Clayton Call)

Sanborn: You just sang through it. It's funny because a lot of the players that I related to happen to come from Memphis. [David is from St. Louis.] I found out later that they were guys who you came up with, like Frank Strozier. And George Coleman.

Crawford: Right.

Sanborn: And I studied with George. I didn't realize when I first studied with him that he was from Memphis. And when I was studying with him, he told me that you guys knew each other.

Crawford: Yeah, and you know, we did sort of the same thing. I noticed you said you played in a lot of R&B bands.

Sanborn: R&B bands, yeah.

Crawford: It was the same with us. You played with Little Milton.

Sanborn: Little Milton, that was my first gig.

Crawford: Yeah, well, it was the same thing with me. Like George and Phineas [Newborn] and them, they were more than beboppers. Just like you, I cut my teeth on R&B.

Sanborn: Was there any reason for that? Was it just circumstances or was it something that pulled you in that direction?

Crawford: Not really. Like you mentioned Frank Strozier, and there was George, and there was a lot of other saxophone players around Memphis that aren't even waxed and stuff like that. So I grew up around those guys.

Sanborn: Gene Ammons…

Crawford: Yeah.

Sanborn:… he was the other cat for me. See, I got you first. Then you led me to all the other guys. You were the guy that started me, and then I heard Gene Ammons. And then I heard Willis Jackson and all that—Arnett Cobb and King Curtis and all the others. It's funny, I was just thinking about you and George. It's curious what led you one way and George another way, even though you're similar. I hear you play bebop, and you can play the shit out of bebop. You understand the vocabulary, and you know what's happening. Was it just an emotional thing, or was it just something that you never thought about that led you in a certain way? Or was it was Ray [Charles]?

Crawford: No, I think it's just something that happens naturally. Like listening to you play. I don't hear any heavy studying or anything. That's the way you play. You play, you know, not a lot of notes.

Sanborn: Yeah.

Crawford: That's what I think. See, I was listening to people like Ammons. And before Ammons it was Earl Bostic—I loved him for his power. And Louis Jordan. Very witty, but he didn't play a lot of notes. See, with Coleman and those guys, we would go from house to house, just practice all day bebopping. We'd play all of those Bird [Charlie Parker] solos, note for note. But actually, when we went to work at night, we'd play R&B. We'd play blues, a lot of blues.

Sanborn: There wasn't much of a chance to apply bebop.

Crawford: No.

Sanborn: That's probably the biggest thing, is the context you find yourself in. And I think for me, that was what it was. What was available to me in St. Louis was rhythm-and-blues bands. I also think that emotionally I went there because of the directness of the music. And that's what I always related to about you, was that emotional directness. To me, you were like Ray. You were doing what Ray was doing—just communicating, transcending the instrument or the voice. Just like right… [points out from his chest].

Crawford: I listened to everybody that I could. But when it came time for me to play, I just played what I felt. I just do it. But, it's like your approach to the horn. It's a vocal approach. It's a vocal thing.

Sanborn: Exactly.

Crawford: That's the way I approach playing the horn: vocally. You know, if you're playing a ballad, the people, if they know the words, can sing along with you.

Sanborn: Sometimes I think the words.

Crawford: Hey, that's right. That's what Bird said mattered. You sing sax. That's basically what I do. I don't try to go outside, and I don't think you do, either.

Sanborn: No.

Crawford: But I know your abilities could lead you into other directions.

Sanborn: Well, I do go out. Sometimes I do that, but it's in a context. I play with [saxophonist] Tim Berne a lot of times, who some people consider to be "outside." And I relate to that. But I relate to all music from the same point of view in that it's all emotional, and it's all the blues in a sense. To me, Ornette [Coleman] is a blues player.

Crawford: Right.

Sanborn: You know what I mean? When I first heard Ornette, the connection between you and him was so obvious to me. It was just that, plus the fact that I think that in my early years I associated both of you with piano-less groups. And I really like that because you could really hear the alto. And you both had that same cry, that same sound. And so in my mind, Hank Crawford and Ornette Coleman were so much more similar than they were dissimilar. Did you listen to much Ornette?

Crawford: Early Ornette.

Sanborn: Like the quartet with Billy Higgins?

Crawford: Right, but after that period, I don't know. Ornette and I, we started going in different directions. He changed almost his whole direction of playing. But early Ornette, like you said, he had a real blues sound. Even Bird, man, with all of the lines. They were based on rhythm and blues and on blues. But, like I said, I didn't follow [Ornette]. I listened to everybody and got what I could, but I basically just played myself. Then, too, I had a little knowledge of piano. Actually, that was my first instrument.

Sanborn: Well, who else did you listen to—Gene Ammons, right?

Crawford: Yeah, Gene. And I liked the Lockjaws and Cannonballs and all that, but they came later. But the early influences were blues saxophone players.

Sanborn: Did you hear Eddie Vinson early on?

Crawford: There's another one.

Sanborn: That's funny, I came to him a little later. As I got older, I started to see the chronology of all the music. But as it

happened to me, I got you, and then I got Ornette, then I got Gene Ammons, and I got Charlie Parker much later. Now, as I step back from it, and I see all the people that influenced me, I understand what it was, what that common bond was that I related to. Jackie McLean, and then Phil Woods, and Lee Konitz and…

Crawford: Hey, I listened to those guys, too. Lee Konitz, Paul Desmond.

Sanborn: Paul Desmond was so beautiful. He was so lyrical. And that lyricism, to me, that's the thing that you did and continue to do. The last time I heard you live was in Chicago at the Blackstone Hotel. This was four, five years ago, and you played "You Send Me."

Crawford: Uh-huh.

Sanborn: And it was like… [taps his hand on the table very slowly] at that tempo. And to play a slow tempo like that, that, to me, is the hardest thing musically in the world to do. Forget about notes, forget about double time, 16th notes, 32nd notes, that don't mean shit.

Crawford: All the musicians understand…

Sanborn:… that the real art is how you can play a ballad.

Ed Enright: You both are so drawn to ballads. What's their appeal?

Sanborn: You sing. You can sing them. You get involved, and it's intellect and emotion and physical and all that. For me, when I play a ballad, I'm not aware of thinking. Sometimes when I'm playing up-tempo tunes, I catch myself thinking about where I'm going to go. Or, I'll be into it, but I won't be into it in the same way as I am when I'm playing a ballad. I can just kind of surrender myself to the ballad. It's a speed thing. Like when you're driving in the Grand Prix, you're grooving and you're in the moment, you're in the zone, but you're down-shifting, you're getting into that turn, you're aware that shit's going on around you and stuff. But in ballads, it's like, fuck it.

Crawford: Ballads, they're romantic. You know, they're sensual, especially on alto. The alto is so romantic. And another thing, man: I find that most females love the sound of the saxophone, especially if it's an alto. The alto has a special kind of voice.

Sanborn: There's a cry that an alto has.

Crawford: Yeah, there's a cry. [To David.] Like when I heard your thing, I think it might have been the first thing of yours I heard. It knocked me out, and that was a solo you played on "What a Difference a Day Makes" with Esther Phillips. I said, "Wow, who's that?" And David [Newman] said, "That's the guy that we told you we saw in St. Louis. He used to come around." Of course, what I remember about you in St. Louis is, one night… I don't remember this completely… but I remember we were playing the Riviera Ballroom. Somebody said that this guy here says he likes the band, and I think you might have been with your mother and father.

Sanborn: Probably.

Crawford: And they told me you're a saxophone player. And I didn't see you for a long time. In fact, I don't think I saw you until I did your TV show [*Night Music*, February 1990].

Sanborn: Yeah, that's right.

Crawford: A lot of people compliment David about his generosity and stuff. When you had your show, you really exposed a lot of artists.

Sanborn: For me, it's a payback. Because by acknowledging what has come before you and what's happening around you, you feed your own soul. You're always going to find out something different. When Hank was on the show, just being with him in that context, I learned so much from just standing next to him playing, which I had never done before. As much of an influence as he's been on me over the years, I'd never had the opportunity of standing next to Hank.

Crawford: We should do that.

Sanborn: Listening to him, listening to the sound come out of his horn—that's like an education. That's a year of college, right there, I'm telling you.

Enright: Let's talk a little bit about that show. What tunes did you play, Hank?

Crawford: I played what he suggested I play.

Sanborn: I think Hank did it as a favor to me. I asked him to play "The Peeper" and "Don't Cry Baby." Now, I've always kind of felt bad about that because I felt like I kind of put you in a…

Crawford: No, it was proper man. I didn't have any problem with that.

Sanborn: Because the thing that's important for people to realize is that Hank is a working, evolving musician. This is not an oldies thing. That was one period of Hank's life that happened to have a tremendous influence on me, because that's when I started to play the saxophone. And it's hard when somebody covers as much ground as Hank has, to cover all the things that he has done and

David Sanborn.
(Hyou Vlelz)

continues to do. [To Hank.] I think that what's interesting about this anthology on you, is that there is stuff that's current. You see the whole line: what was great about the old music is great about the new music. It's the same Hank Crawford. [Looking at the song listings in the anthology.] The same soul that was there in 1963, that's there in 1992.

Crawford: Well, it's the same for David, too. Like I said, I feel honored that he was impressed by my playing. But, to be honest about it, you also have impressed a lot of players. [To David.] There are a lot of

players you've influenced, man. There are a lot of young players who have come up and asked me, "What do you think of David Sanborn?" This man has built his school, too. Don't you forget it. Because he comes down the tree: he dug me, I dug Louis Jordan.

Sanborn: It's all part of the same continuum.

Crawford: On David Letterman's show, he said, "I dug Hank Crawford." You know how that makes me feel to hear him say that? He didn't have to say that.

Enright: David, who are some of the

cats out of the Sanborn school of saxophone—players you're impressed with?

Sanborn: I like Kirk Whalum a lot.

Crawford: My student, raised him.

Sanborn: Really?!

Crawford: Raised him. His brother lived in St. Louis, Kenneth Whalum, tenor player.

Sanborn: No kidding?

Crawford: His mother—Ms. Whalum, we use to call her—taught Phineas. Kirk has a lot of history to tell you, too. He was right around the corner from us.

Sanborn: He's the guy who I'm really impressed with. He's got so much heart in his playing. And he's got the sound.

Crawford: It's the sound. You know I did a couple of seminars at schools, and most of the kids don't ask me how to play the horn; they ask me how I get the sound. They say, "What kind of mouthpiece are you using? What kind of reed? How do you get the sound?" And I can't explain that.

Enright: How often do you two actually see each other? Do you ever get a chance to hang out like this?

Sanborn: Not very often. Well, we're always—I don't know about Hank, I'm sure Hank is working all the time, too. I'm always on the road. I spend six, eight months of the year on the road.

Crawford: That's about the same with me.

Sanborn: So you know, we very rarely have a chance to do this.

Enright: When was the first time you actually met each other?

Sanborn: Well, the first time we physically met was—[to Hank] you probably don't remember this. But I got called…

Crawford: Yeah, this is what I need to know.

Sanborn:… and I don't even remember what it was. It was some kind of jingle, something for a commercial in New York. And I walked in the room, and it was you. I don't even remember who else was there, because I saw you there and I freaked out.

Crawford: Oh, man.

Sanborn: I had never met Hank before. I introduced myself to you. I'm sure you don't remember because it was one of those things where everybody was warming up, and everybody played. All I remember was that we were playing beforehand. The rhythm section was playing, everybody was playing the blues. And you played, and then it was my turn, and I said no. I wanted to hear you play. But that was the first time we actually met.

December 1994
· ·

Betty Carter
It's Not About Teaching, It's About Doing
by Michael Bourne

Betty Carter came out scatting. Syllables. Cascades of sound, soft and furry, easing above and around the changes. Then, words. "In the still of the night…" Cole Porter—but now it's Betty's song. And, all at once, with only a turn of her head, the rhythm rocketed! Triple time! So fast a train might've derailed—but not Betty. Betty drives a trio like Ben-Hur drives a chariot, galloping hard—but with style. And at the finish, a last "night" held high and strong, she nailed it like Pavarotti.

I've experienced the unique excitement of Betty Carter often through the years and around the world, but the performance last summer at the Istanbul Jazz Festival was definitive. She sang standards. She sang originals. I'd heard all the songs before—and yet never before. Some singers, every note, every word, every emotion, it's the same at every show. Betty Carter sings songs like Monet painted haystacks. Now yellow. Now purple. Now there's the pink of a sunset. It's nonetheless a haystack. It's that much more a masterpiece.

And she works the trio. (What drummer in Betty's band hasn't lost weight at every gig? She's downright aerobic!) Time stands still—or flies! Betty kaleidoscopes colors and moods and feelings and grooves. Some songs all rhythm. Some songs all heart.

Betty Carter sings jazz. "I'm a jazz singer, there's no doubt about it," says Betty. "I reach, and I take liberties. I do a lot of stuff—and it's mine. What you hear is me and my thinking at that moment and the musicians behind me. They're reaching and growing at the same time. There's a real energy that these young kids have and want to have. There's a real camaraderie between the audience and these young musicians that bounces off me. I really do feed off these kids."

She's worked most often since the '70s with young musicians, usually newcomers to the scene (see sidebar). She's

become the virtual godmother to a generation of musicians, especially young rhythm sections—encouraging them, fighting for them, fighting with them. It doesn't matter who they've played with before or what and where they've studied, when they join Betty's band that's when the real schooling begins.

"It's not about teaching. It's about doing and being allowed to do. What I can give them or say to them is, 'You've got to work to get better.' What I've been able to offer them are jobs. And, in the meantime, I put in a dose of skill. I can talk about what I've gone through, why this works and that doesn't. They're eager and really listen. They're in a hurry to cram it all in in a short space of time, and that's okay because things these days are in a hurry."

Her young pianists have included Benny Green, Stephen Scott, Cyrus Chestnut, Mulgrew Miller, Jacky Terrasson and now Xavier Davis. Her young bassists have included Dennis Irwin, Curtis Lundy, Michael Bowie, Ira Coleman, Ariel Roland and now Eric Revis. Her young drummers have included Kenny Washington, Lewis Nash, Winard Harper, Troy Davis, Gregory Hutchinson and now Will Terrell. She's even featured a saxophonist or two—like Don Braden and Craig Handy. And once a year at the Brooklyn Academy of Music, she gathers a whole stageful of young musicians. She'll host her third Jazz Ahead series, again with 20 or so newcomers, next spring at BAM.

"I select musicians from the IAJE [International Association of Jazz Educators] convention. I'll visit a college like Berklee and hear who's there. I listen to all the kids coming out of school. I might be told about them by musicians who know what I'm into. Or someone might send me a tape. I listen."

It's the same when she's looking for (listening for) musicians.

"You know there's something about a person when they have it. Something you can't nail down. Something you just feel inside. You know it immediately. Because of the time that I've been out here, and I've heard so many guys, I can just imagine what it would be like to have someone brand-new like this and what I can do with them.…

"I don't listen to a certain thing. You've got to listen for the time, what they do with the rhythm, what they do with their solos, how they create or how they're trying to become creative. You know they're young and don't know everything, but with time and some exposure, some steady work, they could really develop....

"They've got to have chops, but that doesn't mean their chops are necessarily right. You've got to have a feeling along with your chops. Most young players have an idea of what they want to do and what they want to be, and you can hear that. I want them to be themselves with me. I make sure they know that you do not have to be like the one who preceded you. I want something from you. I want you to feed me."

Betty Carter came out of Detroit, where the modem-jazz scene in the '40s was the most active outside of New York. She won an amateur singing contest—like Ella and Sarah—and jammed with Charlie Parker, Dizzy Gillespie, Miles Davis and other greats who'd play through Bop City. She joined the Lionel Hampton band when only 18. Hamp's band was (and is) a jump start for young jazz talent—Johnny Griffin was in the band then, also other singers like Jimmy Scott and Jackie Paris—and, while learning about music, Betty also learned about life. Gladys Hampton, the boss behind the band, became a mentor.

"I learned how to travel with men, how to be independent, how to look out for yourself, how to be in control, how to get on the stage, how to get off the stage, how to be disciplined, how to sit in a bus for hours and hours. I learned a lot from Gladys and Hamp both, not always realizing then that I was getting it."

"Betty Be-Bop" was her nickname then.

"I was disturbed at the time because I was always improvising. That's all Hamp had me doing. I thought, 'Jeez, I want to sing a love song!' I learned to do that on my own."

She was encouraged early on by Miles Davis and, after a tour with Ray Charles, the classic 1961 album *Ray Charles and Betty Carter*—with the hits "Baby, It's Cold Outside" and "It Takes Two to Tango" became her real breakthrough. She recorded a variety of albums for a variety of labels in the '60s and, when record deals were not forthcoming, established her own Bet-Car label in the '70s. She signed with Verve in 1988, and her first Verve release, *Look What I Got!*, earned a Grammy.

She's become more and more popular and acclaimed ever since. (Through to this year's Critics Poll, since '89, she's been voted top jazz singer in both the Readers and Critics polls.) And what's been her greatest strength, as an artist and as an

Betty Carter.
(Teri Bloom)

individual, through tough times and even now as she's enjoying her greatest success, is an almost fierce integrity. She's never compromised. She's always determined herself to be herself. And, finally, she's reaping triumph after triumph.

"It really is different now. I feel good. I'm much more relaxed about my music than I've ever been. It's taken all this time maybe for some people to adjust to what I'm doing, but now people know exactly what they're coming to hear when they're coming to hear me. I can let go. I can real-

ly put out. I can take all kinds of risks."

Betty's most recent "risk" was, actually, great fun. She toured with friends—drummer Jack DeJohnette, bassist Dave Holland and pianist Geri Allen—last fall around Europe. *Feed the Fire*, her newest album, was recorded in London and is highlighted by some serious interplay, an almost giddy "Sometimes I'm Happy," an impressionistic "Lover Man" and Betty's extraordinary duets with Geri on "If I Should Lose You," with Dave on "All or Nothing at All" and her quiet percussive

All The Young Dudes

by Michael Bourne

Betty Carter is an extraordinary artist, but also an extraordinary teacher. Some graduates from the Betty Carter "school" of jazz—pianists Benny Green (1983–'87) and Stephen Scott (1987–'88), drummers Lewis Nash (1981–'84) and Kenny Washington (1978–'80), and bassist Dennis Irwin (1976)—reflected on their "matriculations" through Betty's band, the first important regular gig for all of them.

Benny Green played piano with Betty from April 1983 through April 1987, his first real road gig. He eventually matriculated through the other great jazz "school" of Art Blakey.

"Betty and Art both emphasized directing my focus toward individuality, developing my own sound. That meant to not be intimidated by my predecessors in the Messengers. That meant, specifically with Betty, setting aside recordings. I was listening to records she made with John Hicks. They had such a good hookup, and I really admired his playing. Betty noticed that right away. Betty and Art both made the point about developing Benny. Betty was more verbal in her instructions. Art would drop gems of knowledge on you when he thought you were ready to hear it, but he preferred the Messengers to talk among themselves. She'd use visual imagery to convey the way she could see a piece telling a particular story. She'd emphasize the drama and the emotion in the performance and want us to relate our own experiences, like romantic experiences, to the music."

Stephen Scott became Betty's pianist after Benny Green split in 1987 and stayed through 1988. Betty's band was also Stephen's first important regular gig.

"What stands out most from working with Betty was respecting us and challenging us to take chances. I think that the basis of what she does is being original and being respectful to the music, helping the music move along. If you hear a quintet or a trio playing "Star Eyes," more than likely they'll play it like Charlie Parker did. That's great to respect Charlie Parker, but, as a musician, shouldn't you take time to think of an arrangement that stands on its own? Betty had a way of getting musicians doing whatever they should be doing in their own direction. I'd be trying to play Mulgrew Miller stuff or Kenny Kirkland stuff, and she'd say, 'Whose line was that? Is that yours?' I'd say no, and she'd say, 'Stop playing it!' That's what Betty taught me—to challenge myself and to challenge the music."

Lewis Nash was living in Phoenix when Betty was looking for a new drummer in 1981. Drummer Freddie Waits recommended him and, unheard, she flew him to New York for an audition and he stayed through 1984.

"I never played that fast before or that slow before—ridiculously slow tempos. Betty had extremes going that most people only fit in between. She also helped bring out dynamic range and control. She used to say, 'Watch me for the colors.' She'd say certain stuff or I'd have to be able to follow her hand. Betty's phrasing is unpredictable, so I had to trust my internal clock. If you waited for her lyric to know where you were, then you were lost. I learned to keep tempos myself without relying on where the lyric fell—and she expects you to be there. Betty didn't like telegraphing stuff, so that the audience would say, 'Oh, now they're setting up to…' She wanted stuff to happen suddenly, when the audience is lulled into a certain mood, and then jolted. That's one of her trademarks, being able to shift gears on a dime."

Kenny Washington was just breaking into the New York scene as a drummer when he joined Betty's band in the fall of 1978. He stayed into 1980.

"One of the things I learned from Betty was paying attention. I mean, with her body inflections; like, she might want a bass drum on the downbeat. And not only were the arrangements hard, she would constantly change them. She kept you sharp! Most singers, after you get the gig under your belt, you go to work every night and don't think about it. Betty Carter is the one gig where you cannot do that, where it's different every night. Betty used to play ballads so slow you could go to the bathroom between beats. And she would never count off the band on a ballad. We'd be doing a tune like 'Spring Can Really Hang You Up the Most,' and you'd watch her hand go way down. That's the downbeat—but you wouldn't know where that second beat was going to fall. You'd have to feel the space between the beats. And she didn't want any sweets on the ballads, no brushes on the snare drum. She wanted the first beat on the ride cymbal, the second beat on the hi-hat, the third on the ride cymbal, the fourth on the hi-hat, and that was hard. Not only did you have to feel the space, but it took a lot of control, plus you couldn't play too loud—just enough to be heard. And then she would play 'My Favorite Things' at breakneck speed!"

Dennis Irwin played bass in Betty's band right after Dave Holland in 1976. He stayed only six months but learned plenty and also more with Art Blakey.

"It didn't take long for Betty to pull my coat different ways. I've learned a lot from singers, but Betty's thing is the attack on the note. I used to try walking with alternating fingers, but she got me in the dressing room and said, 'No, baby, ding-ding-ding-ding, all with the index. Look at those old pictures of Ray Brown and Oscar Pettiford doing everything with one finger. It's too uneven if you're alternating fingers.' She was right, but I couldn't get the muscle memory together when I was with Betty. I was thinking too much about it. It wasn't until I was with Art that I was able to relax and incorporate the things Betty talked about, pacing and drama, how to put a set together, doing things very slowly, quietly so that the bass note hangs in the air. She really exposed the bass a lot, and I could've benefitted from staying longer. Betty prepared me in a lot of ways for working with Art. She stressed being yourself,. And she was so strong it was like being the bass player in a big band. It took a lot of stamina. She'd do long sets and the music had this intensity. She'd ride me the whole time. She wants the best."

vocalizing with Jack on spontaneous sparring they've titled "What Is This Tune?"

"It just happened," says Betty about the tour. "I'd worked with Jack and Dave when they were younger." Jack worked in Betty's band before his gig with Charles Lloyd back in the '60s. Dave worked in Betty's band in the '70s after his gig with Miles Davis. "I went to see Dave one night at Fat Tuesday's when he was working with Hank Jones [recently]. I decided that I wasn't going backstage. I was just going to enjoy the show and cut out. But as I was walking down the street, I heard someone calling me, and it's Dave saying how dare I leave without saying something! And he said that he wanted to work with me again."

"Betty thought it would be great," says Dave. "I thought first about just bass and vocals, and then I thought it would be great to have a trio with Jack and Betty. Betty suggested we should have Geri involved. Jack and I both admire Geri's playing a great deal, and it went from there."

"I'd always wanted to do something special with Betty, and then Dave pushed all the right buttons," says Jack. He'd reunited with Betty on her Keep the Music Movin' concerts at Lincoln Center and the Apollo several years ago. And on tour last fall, just like 30 years ago, Betty worked the band. "I think we worked each other very hard on the tour," Jack adds. "She wanted that. Usually, she's with the younger guys, and she really has to be on them for every little thing. Dave and I have gotten seasoned since our times with Betty, and it was important for Betty—and a treat for us—that she had musicians she could trust. She could take chances that she doesn't do normally with her regular trios. This tour for Betty was challenging."

"I knew it was going to be right, and it was going to be fresh with Jack and Dave because they're creative and they're going to be different all the time," says Betty. "Another difference from playing with younger musicians is that I'm often teaching them tunes and, with Jack and Dave, I'd just say, 'Let's play "Lover Man,"' and they knew it—and off we'd go! I'm the one who didn't know 'I'm All Smiles,' but Geri thought of that, and I had one of those 'fake' books and there it was."

Geri Allen first encountered Betty while attending the University of Pittsburgh in the '70s. They became friends when Geri was teaching at Howard University in the '80s. "Betty did a clinic," says Geri. "A lot of these kids were experiencing jazz for the first time. A lot of times they were looking in books or transcribing from records. To have a chance to be close to an artist of Betty's magnitude was a great moment for many of them. I remember Betty leading her clinic by singing everything to the students. And if the students had any questions, they had to improvise, to vocalize their questions. These kids had to get up on the spot and react to music like they'd never done before. It was such a great illustration of what jazz is. It was really in the moment, terrifying and exciting all at once. That was the way Betty brought the real world of jazz to the students, the jazz life as it lives onstage."

Geri recorded a duet of "Stardust" and "Memories of You" with Betty on the 1990 album *Droppin' Things* and felt the tour last fall was like her own master class. "Every time we would play, I was amazed at Betty's command, at her ability to communicate directly to each person in the audience, no matter how big or how small the venue. Every place was Betty's house. That was certainly a lesson in artistic mastership. And it's consistent. It was like that every night. She was able to connect. That was a great lesson for me to watch."

Dave and Jack were likewise inspired.

"I've really enjoyed the relationship of the bass to the singer," says Dave. "She doesn't have a format when she sings. She improvises and demands that spontaneity from the people she's with. She expects a serious contribution from everybody and draws it out of them. She gets right in your face when she sings. She comes right up and sings into your bass! It's real communication. It's a real band."

"By the end of the tour, we were worn out," says Jack. "It was hard work but enjoyable work."

Dave and Jack also recognize parallels between Betty and another master musician they worked with.

"Miles was always moving forward and developing his music," says Dave. "It never ceased during his life, and I think Betty is the same way. She's not happy to just settle back and do the set routine. Many vocalists find something that's comfortable and stick with it, but Betty is constantly looking for the next movement forward, for something that gives a piece a little something extra special."

"She's comparable to Miles in that sense," says Jack, "and loves the music with such a passion. She goes around scouting talent because she wants to give something back to the community."

Betty, Dave, Geri and Jack will play some concerts to promote *Feed the Fire*—and because they'll all have another great time together—but, otherwise, as always, she'll be on the road with her young musicians. One might presume that her young musicians keep Betty young. But, for Betty Carter, it isn't only who she plays with but who she plays for.

"Don't forget that if it wasn't for the audience, I wouldn't be here right now. I didn't have records I could depend on. All I had were my people. I've tried to give them everything I could. *The Audience With* album I did in San Francisco was thanking them for sticking with me all these years and supporting me at the door. It's been very encouraging, people enjoying what you're doing and encouraging you to go on ahead...."

July 1995

Dr. John
Temple of Big Band
by Michael Bourne

The Doctor is in... the groove. When he walks or talks or he sings, there's a cadence about Dr. John, as if there's a New Orleans second line dancing deep down in his soul. He sounds like a bear, growling but sweetly furry, especially when crooning them oldies so bluesfully or even when barking Popeye's chicken and other vendables for TV ads. He looks like a bear, cuddly but mysterious, a hoodoo teddy with his gris-gris stick always at hand.

Born Malcolm John Rebennack Jr. in 1941, "Dr. John" was introduced in 1968 on his first album as a leader, *Gris-Gris*, with the song "I Walk on Guilded Splinters" and other music inspired by New Orleans voodoo and Mardi Gras. "Right Place, Wrong Time" and "Such a Night" in 1973 were his only top-40 hits, but he's nonetheless recorded and traveled the world.

His latest project, *Afterglow*, reunites Mac with friend and producer Tommy LiPuma. It's a big-band album arranged mostly by John Clayton and offers some of his favorite songs by some of his favorite singers, especially jazz and

Dr. John.
(Photo by Kevin Mazur
for Shore Fire Media)

blues ballads of Charles Brown, Louis Jordan, Louis Armstrong and Mac's long-time partner as a producer and a song-writer, Doc Pomus. We talked about Mac's musical life (and often laughed) on a spring afternoon in Manhattan.

Michael Bourne: I've always want-ed to know what the hell are "guilded splinters."

Dr. John: It's a corruption of "gilded splendors." That's how the words got passed down in gris-gris terminology. It ain't English or French. Actually, music is our language.

Bourne: Your persona as Dr. John is often very mystical. Have you been involved in actual voodoo rituals?

Dr. John: I'm a voodoo priest. I'm not active. I'm not what you'd call a religious cat. I like the music. I had a church and a shop in New Orleans maybe 20 years ago, Dr. John's Temple of Gris-Gris. It ain't called "voodoo." That's a common denom-inator for what they got in Haiti and Brazil and other places. New Orleans has it own thing. It's called "gris-gris." It's a real mix-ture of American Indian stuff and African stuff with all kinds of other cultures' stuff.

Bourne: Gris-gris actually means grey-grey.

Dr. John: It's not black. It's not white. It's somewheres in the middle. It's what life is.

Bourne: You've lived in New York since the '80s. What do you miss most not living in New Orleans?

Dr. John: I go back there, and I get torn between all of the ways the city's changed for the worse and all of the ways the city's changed for the better. I love New Orleans. It's a deep part of my life. If I had-n't grew up there and came up with all these studio cats, I would never have become what I became. Guys passed stuff down when I grew up in New Orleans, and that was real special. All the older guys taught me and Allen Toussaint and all the young guys all that history and about how to be musicians.

We were so far behind in recording technology in New Orleans in the '50s and '60s. When the rest of the world was recording four-track and eight-track, we were still recording one-track.

When we started making one-to-one-track overdubs, it all sounded jive because what was overdubbed was louder on the fade-out. We were way behind the times technologically, but we continued making records people liked because there was a good feeling on them records. That influ-enced all of my life making records. It ain't about we get one guy in the studio and we put on one track and then bring in another guy for another track. If you want a record to feel good, get guys all together and play. Then it's gonna feel real, and it's inspiring. Guys play better when they're playing off of each other, when everybody vibes off of one another.

I still record like that. They hired two studios for *Afterglow*. They had the strings on one side where I was, the horns on the other side so they wouldn't get no bleeding. I was in the middle of it all. I could see the conductor. I could see Ray Brown and the drummer [Jeff Hamilton]. That's impor-tant to me, being right there.

Bourne: You don't usually sing with a

sound like the Basie band behind you.

Dr. John: I loved that! John Clayton arranges so special. When I first heard his stuff, I said, "Wow, this cat really thinks about everything." I told Tommy LiPuma right off, "That guy!" John wrote stuff in all kind of different zones. He reminds me a little of Ernie Wilkins and Neal Hefti but doesn't copy stuff. He uses some of their stuff to make it all have some base. I like Alan Broadbent's writing, too. He wrote a couple tunes, but John wrote the bulk of this record.

Bourne: Wouldn't you like to have Ray Brown on the road?

Dr. John: Ray is so funny. Ray said, "I can still play [the bass], but I just can't carry it no more!" Some of my most favorite sessions I used to cut in L.A. with Ray and Earl Palmer on drums, Charlie Collins the guitar player and Plas Johnson, just the five of us on a lot of little dates.

Bourne: When you first worked in the New Orleans studios, you played with and learned from the masters. Huey "Piano" Smith. James Booker…

Dr. John: Lloyd Glenn. Charles Brown. One of the first guys I ever played on a session with was Charles Brown. I was playing guitar, and I was so intimidated because Johnny Moore was one of my heroes. And I thought that I was gonna have to play guitar like Johnny Moore did on all those records with Charles. Charles was so sweet and guided me through everything.

That's how I learned to play piano, basically playing guitar with Professor Longhair and Allen Toussaint, James Booker, Huey Smith, all those guys. I'd get close to them and watch where the changes fell. That's what my guitar teachers taught me. "You watch what them piano players do!"

I learned a lot from just seeing what they did and how they approached the music. I learned from Huey Smith about playing way back in the time. If you let the rhythm section push it, you pull it and a really funky thing happens. I remember Professor Longhair playing piano like it was a percussion instrument, like it was a marimba. I used to hang out with him. I'd show him everything that I still do.

Bourne: One thing about all the music from New Orleans is a real timelessness, whether it's jazz or blues or R&B or a Mardi Gras parade, and all that music comes through in you.

Dr. John: I'm just a guy. I play what I play. I don't know what the hell it is. I try to play with good guys. I was taught that if

Resurrection and Reunion
Red Heart Beats Again

"He's the last of a breed, a genuine original, truly an American icon. I really believe that," says Tommy LiPuma about his long-time friend Mac Rebennack. *Afterglow* is the first major production by LiPuma as the new president of GRP, the fourth Dr. John album produced by LiPuma. Actually, LiPuma first heard Mac even before Mac became known as the Doctor.

LiPuma was working for A&M in 1966 when he heard a demo single produced by Rebennack. "I think it was called 'Ju Ju Man.' I'd never heard anything like it. It was insane. I dug it. I picked it up for the label. Nothing happened with it, but that's when I first met Mac. Mac was a thin beanpole at the time."

They eventually worked together when LiPuma came to Horizon in the '70s and produced two Dr. John albums, *City Lights* and *Tango Palace*. They stayed friends after both of them settled in New York in the '80s. "I heard this record called *Dr. John Plays Mac Rebennack* and he did "The Nearness of You." I'd never heard him play a standard." LiPuma produced a whole album of Mac singing standards, *In a Sentimental Mood*, with the Grammy-winning "Makin' Whoopee" duet of Mac and Rickie Lee Jones.

Dr. John eventually signed with GRP and, soon after, Tommy became the new boss. "Life seems to intertwine," says Tommy. "I said that we've got to do another album, but this time let's do all these great songs. We grew up with the same music. We were both fans of Charles Brown, Percy Mayfield, Ray Charles, Nat Cole, Louis Jordan, and big-band guys like Ernie Wilkins and Ralph Burns." *Afterglow* is a magnum opus for both of them.

It's also the first album on the resurrected Blue Thumb label. "One of the reasons that I've restarted Blue Thumb is that my musical interests are wide. I don't want to be in a narrow street," says LiPuma. He's also bringing back Impulse! as an active label—complete with the hallmark orange-and-black spines that look like punctuation in everyone's record collection.

Tommy LiPumu has worked all around the recording industry since the '60s as a musician and producer and executive. He's earned 18 gold and platinum records, also 30 Grammy nominations. LiPuma produced the classic *Breezin'* for George Benson, and they'll collaborate again at GRP (a new jazz/hip-hop release is planned for the fall). He's already signed Charles Lloyd to the new Impulse! while the Impulse! classics will be re-released. "We're going back to as many of the original tapes as we can to remaster. We're making them look like the gatefolds of the old packages. We'll also bring back the little red heart on the spine of the Blue Thumb records." And that little red heart beats again, first for Dr. John.

you play with guys better than you, you learn something. And if you ain't learning, you're dying.

Bourne: I meet with a screening committee for the Grammy Awards and we wrangle about whether a singer should be nominated in the "Jazz" category or the "Traditional Pop" category. *Afterglow* will be a tough call because it's both and also blues. "Blue Skies" is not a blues, but sounds like a blues when you sing it.

Dr. John: We do "So Long" as a tribute to Charles Brown. I've never thought Charles Brown ever fit as straight-up blues or R&B or pop or whatever. My mother

used to say her favorite blues singer was Charles Brown, but to me, when he sang "Tell Me You'll Wait for Me" [also on *Afterglow*], it's sophisticated pop like Nat King Cole or more jazzified than pop or blues. How can you put a jacket on it? It overlaps all of that. And music should do that.

Bourne: "Gee, Baby, Ain't I Good to You" is the oldest song on the album, but sounds very fresh.

Dr. John: I love that arrangement by John Clayton. It reminds me a little of Neal Hefti or Johnny Mandel. I blew two takes just listening to [trumpeter] Oscar Brashear play the intro. It was like sitting at home listening to my stereo. I forgot to come in. "Oh, okay, take two. Oscar, play it again." And he killed me again, and I blew it again! I love when music takes me out of wherever my head was. That's spiritually what music always should do.

Bourne: You selected many of these songs as tributes.

Dr. John: "I know What I've Got" is a tribute to Louis Jordan. He's one of my all-time heroes. I've always felt that Louis Jordan and Cleanhead Vinson and Earl Bostic were the most underrated guys. They killed me. "I'm Confessin' That I Love You" is a tribute to Louis Armstrong. I met him twice, and he was down-home and as hip a cat as you could get. He came from my neighborhood in the Third Ward. We were baptized in the same church. I've felt connected to him ever since I was a kid listening to old Louis Armstrong 78s.

Bourne: Your father sold those records.

Dr. John: He had this little shop and sold what they called "race" records, basically R&B and blues. And he sold hillbilly records, gospel records, pop records, but because he was right by Dillard University, the first black university in New Orleans, he sold a lot of "race" records.

Bourne: Doc Pomus was someone you worked with often, and you sing two songs you wrote together on the new album, "New York City Blues" and "There Must Be a Better World Somewhere."

Dr. John: Doc was one of the special people in my life. This guy was a very powerful example of somebody who felt that if you really work at something hard enough and long enough, it'll pay off some kind of dividend. I did a song on a tribute to Doc ["I'm on a Roll" on *Till the Night Is Gone*] that was the very last song he wrote while he was in the hospital getting ready to pass away, and his last words to me were, "Make sure it's in that Louis Jordan bag!" That was just how he thought. Doc knew he wasn't gonna hear that song, but he gave me that last instruction.

Bourne: And, otherwise, you'll carry on Doc's work, looking for that better world.

Dr. John: You know, there's two songs about a better world. Earl King wrote a song called "Let's Make a Better World to Live In." Doc wrote the song "There Must Be a Better World Somewhere." I'm trying to the best of my ability to live between those two songs. I'm trying every day to learn how to do my job a little better. I succeed, and sometimes I don't, but, hopeful-

ly, I'm going in the right direction. All I know is that when the gigs is cool, when the sessions is cool, that's all I could ever ask for. I'm blessed to be doing something that I love. I ain't always got it down, but I'll take some shots at it.

September 1995
· ·

Roy Hargrove and Kenny Garrett

Opposites Attract
by Martin Johnson

"If you're looking for controversy, you've got the wrong two guys," so says trumpeter Roy Hargrove. A slight smile creeps across saxophonist Kenny Garrett's face as he nods in agreement from across the table.

But honest, guys, we weren't shopping for controversy, we were looking for contrasts—and we found them in abundance. Garrett is one of the last musicians to do the traditional apprenticeship route. Although accepted at Berklee, he turned down the academy to go on the road in 1978 with the Duke Ellington Orchestra under the direction of Mercer Ellington; since then he's worked in bands led by Freddie Hubbard, Woody Shaw, Art Blakey and Miles Davis. The *New York Times* recently referred to him as an elder statesman at 34. Although his latest recording, *Triology*, is winning a deserved bounty of praise, he's recorded only a few times as a leader and admits to having to spend half the year doing sideman gigs.

Hargrove, on the other hand, is the product of jazz's new fast track; he very nearly burst onto the New York jazz scene a full-fledged star. Although he went to Berklee for a year and a half, he made frequent visits to New York and made a strong impression on jazz insiders. By the time he was 19, he had left Berklee and was recording his own major-label debut, *Diamond in the Rough* (1990). After five recordings for Novus, he's now working for his second major label, Verve, and sup-

porting *Family*, his second somewhat thematic release for them.

What they do share in common is musical excellence. Each man is a highly distinctive soloist. You can hear their influences, but not at the expense of hearing the players. They have earned their high regard. In fact, if we're choosing up sides for bands whose members are under 40, and you bypass these guys at trumpet and alto saxophone, then my band can kick your band's butt.

Martin Johnson: Have y'all ever worked together?

Hargrove: The first time I worked with Kenny was probably with Carl Allen on his *Manhattan Project* [December '88].

Kenny Garrett: That was the only record we did together.

Hargrove: Yeah!

Garrett: We should hook up on a date soon [both laugh].

Hargrove: I remember being so excited about getting to play with you because I had been listening to you on this one recording called *Double Take* [1985] by Freddie [Hubbard] and Woody [Shaw]. I remember listening to it and going, "Man, I never heard an alto sound like that." You have a very original sound. Man, it was deep. Then, I went over to Berklee and I heard Antonio Hart—I heard him outside a club, and I said, "Man, Kenny Garrett is playing here." It was Antonio; I thought, "Wow, I thought I was the only one on to that sound." When Carl told me about the date, I said, "Wow!"

Garrett: That's true; that was a good date.

Johnson: Do either one of you regret not pursuing the conservatory route all the way?

Garrett: I was going to go to Berklee, but then the opportunity to play in the Duke Ellington Orchestra came up, so I took that. I got to play with Cootie Williams and Harold Minerve, this guy who was a protégé of [Johnny] Hodges. I think a lot of universities turn out players that are not individual....

Hargrove: Yeah, clones.

Garrett: I felt that by being in a big band, I got a lot of firsthand experience.

Hargrove: I believe that Berklee is a place that a lot of cats go to for a short time until they get gigs. A lot of cats do that, then there are cats who go all the way and graduate. It's very easy to get caught up in the school. Basically, what they teach you is how to transcribe solos and all that. You have all this information at your fingertips, John Coltrane solos note for note. People practice that stuff and they think that's how you learn how to play; but that ain't it [shaking his head].

Garrett: It depends on where you come from. If you're from a small town, then you need that environment.

Hargrove: Yeah. I have to agree. I was traveling back and forth to New York, I was getting so much work. I played with pianists John Hicks, Kenny Barron, Harold Mabern, some others, too. Ralph Moore… Bobby Watson; yeah, Bobby! Curtis Lundy got me that gig. I was influenced a lot by Bobby's style of writing. He had a little rhythm and blues and dance and some intellectual stuff, too. Right away, being from Texas I could relate to that.

Roy was born near Dallas in 1969, a time when his hometown was in transition from being a happy confluence of Southwestern and Southern cultures to the urbane, appearance-conscious city featured on the hit television series of the same name. Hargrove is a canny amalgam of both components. His slight accent and warm, friendly manner speak to old Dallas. His stylishness speaks to the new Dallas.

If Hargrove seems bothered by the Verve high-concept approach to recording, it doesn't show. Of course, he probably knew what he was getting into; the label has specialized this approach since the "songbook recordings" of the '50s. He's planning a big-band performance for the Washington Square Jazz Festival in New York (late August). And for his next record? "I think I'm moving toward working with vocalists, maybe doing some vocal stuff myself," he said. "That would surprise a lot of folks."

Maybe, but Hargrove—like Joshua Redman—seems bent on translating jazz virtuosity into pop stardom. Even his upcoming small-group project, *Parker's Mood*, a tribute to Charlie Parker with a drummer-less trio featuring pianist Stephen Scott and bassist Christian McBride, has a distinctly market-friendly air to it. (Its release is timed to celebrate Bird's birthday, Aug. 29.) But though both Garrett and Hargrove came of age long after pop had relegated jazz to the margins, it should come as no surprise that both men want to change that situation. For instance, shouldn't jazz musicians integrate the contemporary pop vernacular into their repertoire?

Roy Hargrove (left) and Kenny Garrett.
(Teri Bloom)

Garrett: Young musicians shouldn't be afraid to take the opportunity to play popular music, and show that it's all relevant.

Hargrove: Yeah!

Garrett: There are a lot of cats that won't play popular music because their loyalty is to jazz. But we all have that; it doesn't mean you have to stay there. You don't progress [if you do].

Hargrove: That's the thing that messes me up about Sonny [Rollins]. when I heard him this year [in Europe], he was playing all these contemporary notes, and I said, "Wait a minute, where did that come from?" That just shows the whole history of it. I always thought you should be open; you got cats who say hip-hop, contemporary R&B or whatever, and they say, "Oh no, not that." At the same time, you take them to a party and they hear their song and [mimics dancing]. A lot of the great cats always stay current: Wayne [Shorter], Ron Carter. I just heard Jackie McLean doing a cover of Luther Vandross' [version of] "A House Is Not a Home."

My favorite hip-hop group is Wu Tang Clan right now. I also like Mobb Deep and Notorious B.I.G.

Johnson: Do either of you ever wanna do a hip-hop jazz album?

Hargrove: I want to do something, but I don't want to do something where it's supposed to be integrated with jazz. I would just do it to be a hip-hop record.

Johnson: Like Branford did?

Hargrove and Garrett: NO! [Both laugh.]

Hargrove: I would just come straight from the hip-hop vein and not even call it acid-jazz, hip-hop jazz or whatever.

Garrett: I think everybody is waiting for me to do it because of my association with Miles. I just did some stuff with GURU [*Jazzmatazz, Volume 2*], and I'm getting a feel for it. When the time is right, I'll do it. But one obstacle is the record companies, they'll look at it and…

Hargrove: They'll say, "Wait a second, we can't put this in a hole."

It's a problem that Garrett is probably very familiar with. If prominence were at all related to ability, Kenny Garrett would be a household name in jazz, not a so-called late bloomer, but record companies haven't known how to handle this multifaceted brilliance. The Detroit native is a quiet, thoughtful man in person. If he is frustrated by the long road toward recognition, it doesn't show. He laughs at the notion. "I'm just glad they acknowledged me. I've been out here playing a long time.

The public may be getting a very solid idea of that playing thanks to *Triology*. Already hailed by some critics as one of the year's best, it's a superb and daring recording with the virtuosic Garrett stripped down to an alto-bass-drums format. And while he possesses mind-numbing technique, he still feels an obligation to entertain. "When I go to a club, I want to be entertained. So when I got to play, I'm an artist, but I want people to be entertained. I'm always changing my compositions. I want it to be fresh. Now, we're in a society where you can just put the remote on, and people can't sustain themselves [for long periods of time]. I learned that from Miles. Coltrane messed it up for saxophone players. He played [solos] for 20 and 30 minutes, so everyone else thought that they should, too. He learned a lot by doing that, but Miles said, "We're not going to do that. You're going to play a little bit, then you're going to play, then you; we're all going to play a little bit. This is a family; we'll spring.' I'm caught in the middle, because I love to play; but by the same token, I want people to be entertained. That's the process you have to continue to work on."

By now, it's become clear that the major difference between the men refused to play a minor part—namely, experience. Kenny's got it; Roy's getting it. Will future generations only be left with the academy? Is that a bad thing?

Garrett: Five years ago, I would say it is. I think it's a way to get from point A to point B. Now, a lot of the cats [from school] are getting record dates.

Hargrove: Record dates; oh, man.

Garrett: In the long run, I feel that the music will suffer from them not having the same experiences; but every generation says that. Every generation you lose something. If the cats can find themselves…

Hargrove: Experience—that's what it is. A lot of people helped me. I got the chance to play with Clifford Jordan, Barry Harris; just being able to watch them. Otherwise, you could be at the gig and playing, and someone like J.J. Johnson comes in and just looks at you [Roy scrunches up his face, both laugh]. I remember one time I was at the gig, and Freddie walked in the door. He's my all-time hero, King Freddie of Hubbard.

Garrett: I feel very fortunate to have played with so many strong players—Fred-die, Woody, Dizzy, Miles, Donald Byrd.

Hargrove: Dizzy, Miles, gaaaaahhh-hd! That's why, sometimes, I wished I played like trombone, so I could play with some of those cats: Miles, Dizzy or even Wynton. I think I'll get me a valve trombone and play in Wallace's band, then play in Wynton's band, then play with Terence.

Garrett: I hope that a lot of the younger cats can get together. There's you and Wallace and Terence and Wynton, but because of the way things go, y'all never get to just hang out like our forefathers used to. You can't do that.

Hargrove: They've got you on a schedule, you've got to go out and do your thing—your thing. You don't have any bands any more. The band I have has been together for only three years. Back in the day, cats had bands together 20 years, 30 years. Everybody wants to do their thing. It's like you get the date and you do your thing. "Well, I got a record date, so I guess I've got to go promote my record and band."

Johnson: How do you feel about your reception from the critics?

Hargrove: They always try to make it an age thing. I don't think there should be so much emphasis on the "young lions." Of course, I guess you've got to make the story interesting, but let me tell you a story about when I was in L.A. and got reviewed. The critic said the bass player could have sounded a little more like Ray Brown. And he went around the whole band like that. Can you guess who it was?

Garrett: Leonard [Feather]? [Everyone laughs.]

Hargrove: I feel when they say stuff like "kids in suits." That's really shallow. I feel when you play, you should look your best. I have a thing about looking at photographs of jazz musicians—of Bird, Sonny, Dizzy—and how they used to dress.

Garrett: I'm kind of on the other side. I can't play with a suit on. When I played with Art Blakey, I had to play with a suit and tie on. When I looked at those pictures, I said, that's not me. But you have to keep it on a certain level.

As a matter of fact, the photo shoot highlights some differences between the musicians' personal styles. In contrast to Roy's effective, by-the-book casual duds, Kenny is casual in his own way: blue jeans, sneakers, a long-sleeved black T-shirt, occasionally covered by a jacket made of an intricately detailed Third World fabric. Garrett has made such fascinating duds a trademark. Whenever his work takes him to an exotic corner of the world, he seeks out fabrics and religious artifacts. He works with a tailor in Ohio to produce his clothing. Even seated, certain disparities stand out. Roy is very much the young whippersnapper, eager to please, anxious to have his say, and fidgety throughout the interview as if it's work for him to sit still. At the cafe we visit, he skips lunch while Garrett chooses one of the vegetarian offerings and betrays his avuncularity only when told that the cafe isn't fashionable enough to serve herbal tea.

Garrett: Did I tell you the story about when we did the second *Double Take*? Woody was killing it. Freddie was saying stop!

Hargrove: It came out, though. *Volume Two*. Right?

Garrett: *Volume Two* came out, but the stuff they was really playing, that didn't come out. Woody didn't want to step on him, but he got in the area. At one point, we had Dizzy come in.

Hargrove: [Eyes bugging, head cocked back.] Dizzy, Woody and Freddie? WOW!!

October 1995

Charles Brown
Blindfold Test
by Dan Ouellette

The "Blindfold Test" is a listening test that challenges the featured artist to identity the musicians who performed on selected recordings. The artist is then asked to rate each tune using a five-star system. No information about the recordings is given to the artist prior to the test.

Born in Texas in 1922, Charles Brown was not only trained in classical piano as a youngster but also listened to and learned from such jazz and blues pianists as Art Tatum, Albert Ammons and Jay McShann. Moving to California in the early '40s, Brown joined up with guitarist Johnny Moore in the seminal R&B trio the Three Blazers, which became the top "race" band of the time thanks to Brown's classic "Driftin' Blues" released in 1945 on Aladdin.

Brown began his solo career in 1948, chalking up several hits that influenced numerous R&B and pop artists. However, like many of his R&B contemporaries, he didn't survive the rise of rock 'n' roll. He went into semi-retirement until 1989, when Bonnie Raitt enlisted him as the opening act for her tour and Rounder Records launched it Bullseye Blue label with his comeback album, *All My Life* ('90). He recorded two more well-received discs plus an R&B Christmas album for Bullseye before releasing his superb Verve debut, *These Blues* ('94), featuring tenor saxophonist Clifford Solomon, guitarist Danny Caron, bassist Ruth Davies and drummer Gaylord Birch. His Verve follow-up is already in the can and is scheduled for release early next year. Meanwhile, Dr. John pays tribute to Brown on his latest disc, the big-band bash *Afterglow*, and Raitt enlisted Brown for touring duty once again this past summer.

This was Brown's first Blindfold Test. It was administered in the living room of his modest apartment in a senior housing complex in Berkeley, Calif.

Charles Brown. (Clayton Call)

Count Basie

"Shine On, Harvest Moon" (from *Brand New Wagon*, Bluebird, 1990/rec. 1947) Basie, piano; Waller Page, bass; Jo Jones, drums.

That sounds like a young Count Basie to me. I have to give him five stars because he has his own style from way back. He's got the genuine article. He knows his craft so well. It's not how much he plays, but the way he plays. He's got a real relaxed style, and he uses his right hand a lot. Whenever he wanted to put something over the best, he'd use his right hand. Plus, I love those little plinks to his playing that you can hear on this tune. This number sounds like "Cry for You," but it's not. Can we start it over again? [Hums along with the melody.] Of course, it's "Shine On, Harvest Moon."

Dr. John

"Since I Fell for You" (from *Goin' Back to New Orleans*, Warner Bros., 1992) Dr. John, piano, guitar, vocals; Chris Severin, bass; Freddy Staehle, drums; others.

I know who that is by the New Orleans touch he gives the piano. That's Dr. John. I'd give him a grade of four stars. He's got his stuff together. I love his playing, and I give him credit for holding on to his own style even though he uses little tricks from other people. I can even recognize some tricks he's got from me. But it's Dr. John's style. I also like the way he sings

with that Creole touch and combination Southern and French accent. When he was just a young guy, he played guitar on songs I recorded for Ace Records. He loves Charles Brown. He called me the other day and wants to record some of my tunes. He said the numbers I sing fit him to a tee.

Ray Charles

"The Midnight Hour" (from *Blues + Jazz*, Atlantic/Rhino, 1994/rec. 1952) Charles, piano, vocals; other personnel unknown.

[Laughs immediately.] That's early Ray Charles. I hear him trying to sound like Charles Brown. He said in his book *Brother Ray* that he wanted to sound like Nat Cole and me so that he could make some money, too. He even used Johnny Moore, the guitar player I worked with for so many years, on some of his records so he could get the same sound. Yeah, this is really good. We'll have to give him five stars for being able to understand so well what others did before developing his own style. Of course, he had to find the Ray Charles style because

he realized there wasn't any money to be made playing like me or Nat Cole.

Jimmy Dorsey and His Orchestra

"Green Eyes" (from *Swing Time! The Fabulous Big Band Era 1925–1955*, Columbia, 1993/rec. 1941) Dorsey, clarinet, alto saxophone; Bob Eberle, Helen O'Connell, vocals; others.

Now this is my favorite. I grew up with it during World War II. It's Bob Eberle and Helen O'Connell singing with Jimmy Dorsey. Eberle was good and Dorsey played the sweetest alto sax, but I was crazy about Helen O'Connell. When she sang, you understood every word. You got the love in her voice. This is very beautiful and deserves five stars because Helen O'Connell was someone who influenced my singing. I picked up tricks from her, like that slurring in her voice. Even though I don't sound like Helen O'Connell, some of her singing wiped off on me. It suited me. I've always felt that it was important for a man to pattern his vocals after a lady singer's style because you never have to worry about people saying you sound like her.

Misha Mengelberg Trio

"Rollo III" (from *Who's Bridge*, Disk Union, 1994) Mengelberg, piano; Brad Jones, bass; Joey Baron, drums.

I'd be a loser on this one. But if I was judging it, I'd say here's a person playing great chord structures and working at mastering his own style. I like it, five stars. Is he still living? I don't know who this is, but he sure handles those chords. Plus, I like the way he plays the melody. He's doing all these tricks from different eras, but still comes back to the melody. He has a beautiful style. He doesn't play like anyone I know, but I'd recognize his playing anywhere. If I listened to his record, I'd know him forever.

January 1996

McCoy Tyner and Michael Brecker

An Easy Marriage of Styles

by Martin Johnson

It's hard to believe, but pianist McCoy Tyner and saxophonist Michael Brecker, pillars on the scene for decades, had never played together until a gig a year ago at Yoshi's in Oakland. That evening revealed a deep rapport and good chemistry that can be heard on Tyner's *Infinity* (Impulse!), which features the finest playing both men have documented in several years. It is no exaggeration to say that Tyner is a living legend. His piano work helped elevate the John Coltrane Quartet of the early '60s into one of the finest jazz groups ever heard. In the three decades hence, Tyner has perhaps the most widely imitated approach to his instrument, a hearty romanticism powered by a huge orchestral sound. Along with his *DB* Readers and Critics Poll–winning big

band, he continues to perform with his trio of bassist Avery Sharpe and drummer Aaron Scott.

For Brecker, fame and critical recognition have been a little overdue. He made a name for himself in the '70s both as co-leader with his brother, trumpeter Randy, in the Brecker Brothers and as a sideman of choice for highbrow pop recordings. He has maintained a balance of sideman pop and jam work as well as working as a leader and for the last three years with his brother again. Although frequently associated with fusion, his brawny yet cerebral style is straight outta the jam tradition. Perhaps his lack of recognition illustrates how many jazz buffs prefer to listen with labels instead of their ears.

When Tyner and Brecker met one afternoon at the Steinway showroom in midtown Manhattan, a number of contrasts were immediately apparent. Tyner walks slowly with a regal bearing, Brecker moves quickly, and even when relaxed looks like he has a lot on his mind. But despite some obvious physical and demographic differences, they have a lot in common. They are both thoughtful men who measure their words very carefully and enjoy talking about music without dishing dirt. Once they settled in, the kind of rapport emerged that makes *Infinity* so delightful.

Martin Johnson: What attracted the two of you to the project?

McCoy Tyner: Well, I've always liked Michael's playing. But I really wasn't sure he was from Philly [looking at Brecker with a wryly raised eyebrow, both laugh] until he gave me a rundown, and I said, "Oh, okay." There are so many musicians from Philly that it's unbelievable! We had that in common and... well, I've been influenced by John [Coltrane] a lot, too. So I thought it would be an easy marriage of styles. I think he has an individual voice and plays very sincerely. I was influenced by Bud Powell and Thelonious Monk, and you can hear a little bit of that influence in my playing; but I think that I still have my own voice.

Johnson: Michael, how did you feel about it when approached by McCoy?

Brecker: It was something I dreamt about for a long time. It's hard to explain. For me, it's more than the fact that I'm influenced by McCoy and John Coltrane. I think the quartet was the reason I became a musician....

Tyner: Hmmm, that's interesting.

Brecker: And that was sort of characterized by the fact the group went beyond the strength of John Coltrane. The group consisted of four musicians and was a marriage that transcended the individual musicians. It was a powerful and musical and spiritual force. I felt it was one of the strongest, if not the strongest, group of the century, along with one or two of the Miles bands, and, just talking off the top of my head, maybe Duke Ellington. I was so strongly influenced by McCoy's playing. I never thought we would get to play together; I don't know why...

Tyner:... See, you never know. [Laughs.]

Brecker: So when the chance came, of course, I jumped at it. And the only way to characterize it is that it's the most comfortable I've ever felt in any context.

Tyner: We had lotsa fun. Yoshi's was... [Trails off and smiles, deferring back to Brecker.]

Brecker: It started the very first night, it was a tremendous amount of fun. [McCoy giggles.] It's led us to do a couple of different types of gigs, things that should be strange.

Johnson: What do you mean by different types of gigs?

Brecker: We played at a trade convention and had a great time. Not a regular audience, a lot of folks from MCA [the parent company of Impulse!].

Johnson: Whose idea was it to do "Impressions"?

[Both look at each other unsure of the answer.]

Tyner: I think it was you. I had done it on *Remembering John*. I think
you suggested it.

Johnson: Either of you fearful of inviting the ghost of Coltrane?

Tyner: [Looks at Michael.] You want to answer that?

Brecker: No, you try.

Tyner: Well [smiling], to tell you the truth, there's one thing I realized. We can never recapture anything, because it [the world] is always changing. It's always different. People leave the planet but their styles remain here. They're here in spirit. What I'm saying is that to try and duplicate anything doesn't make any sense. That's the reason why when I left John, Jimmy [Garrison] and Elvin [Jones] were ready to leave, and they said, "Let's play as a trio." I said, "No," because it's like a tree, your roots are there but you branch off. What I'm doing is like an extension of what I did with them. It's 1995, and I'm still drawing strength from those roots. The deeper the roots the higher the tree can grow. I love my roots, but, by the same token, you have to continue to grow, and try to create new ideas. But John is always present. Like Charlie Parker, he's there, and that's good. People still remember them, and you work to keep their ideas alive.

Johnson: And how did you feel approaching it as a saxophonist?

Brecker: Um, [pausing] I didn't think about it in terms of how I was going to approach it. It just so happens that I'm very strongly influenced by John Coltrane. Very much so, too, by Joe Henderson, Sonny Rollins. Those are the three, as far as saxophone players go, dominant forces, the roots of my playing. Then there is other stuff that has grown out of that. When I get up and play with McCoy, I just play. I don't think, "I don't want to sound like this." Harmonically, it has worked out wonderfully, I don't have to think about it.

Tyner: [Murmuring.] He sounds like himself, let's put it like that. That sums it up. Even with all those influences. [Clearing his throat and projecting.] Even in my case, I had a chance to meet Bud Powell, he's from Willowbrook, Pennsylvania, and he lived right around the corner from me at one point. Thelonious Monk and Art Tatum have been major influences, but I came up with something of my own. Even though someone may open the door, you have to walk in yourself.

Brecker: Well, it almost goes without saying, but McCoy has such a strong influence on the piano that it's pretty much changed the way the instrument is played. He's changed the piano harmonically forever, and that's a remarkable thing.

Johnson: Because of your influential role, do you find it difficult to listen to younger players for fear of hearing an aspect you did not want to see repeated?

Tyner: I hear influences from what I've done, but I hear their own individual personality because when you're young you're still developing. It's the same with me when I was with John. I was lucky to be in an environment where I could grow and let my own sound come out. That's what I hear in the young players, some of them seem to be working hard to be individualists. If I could play a part in that, then I'm very thankful. I'm very happy to see that some of the young people I've influenced are working hard to create their own sound. It's funny, someone opens the door for you,

McCoy Tyner and Michael Brecker. (Teri Bloom)

then you open the door for someone else, and pretty soon you have an open house!

Johnson: Let's come back to *Infinity*. Was it a mutual decision to do "I Mean You"?

Tyner: One of the things I like best about the whole feeling behind this project is that a tune can come, and we'll just do it. It doesn't really matter who suggested it. We were looking in Monk's book and we said, "Hey, this might be a good tune." I had recorded previously with [John] Scofield. When things are right, they just stick out; it [the tune] just announced itself really.

Johnson: And "Good Morning Heartache"?

Tyner: I've been playing that for a while, and I've loved it. I heard Billie Holiday sing it and... [waves his hand in amazement]. I had the opportunity to familiarize myself with the song. I think I played it a long time ago, then stopped, then I started playing it solo.

Johnson: Is that when you began picking up the tempo toward the end?

Tyner: Yeah.

Johnson: You've had a trio together for many years now. Has it been difficult to maintain the continuity?

Tyner: No, I believe in that I was with John for six years, and you become like family during that time. You can draw on that, it gives you a chance to grow and develop.

Johnson: Speaking of growing up and developing, tell me how did the Philadelphia scene differ given the decade between y'all?

Brecker: When I came up in Philly, there wasn't that much of a scene left. There were a couple of clubs; I did a lot of playing in people's houses and after-hours clubs, strangely enough, and I don't know if any of those are still there. But some of the people we have in common are still around. I grew up in the suburbs of North Philly. I come from a musical family, that's how it all started with me. By the time I was in high school, I started meeting a lot of people in the jazz community in Philadelphia, a lot of great players. It's phenomenal to me, and no one's ever been able to explain how Philly has produced so many great musicians. A lot of great musicians continue to come out of Philadelphia in spite of the fact that there are not a whole lot of places to play.

Tyner: I grew up in a basically black community, but it was a community, people were concerned with each other. I didn't have a piano from age 13 to 14—I started [playing] when I was 13. People in the neighborhood let me use their pianos. I'd alternate between three neighbors, and they were very encouraging. I'm so glad I grew up in Philly. To me, at that time, Philadelphia was a nice place to live. It had a nice domestic scene, but it had a nightlife, too. We had major jazz clubs. There were plenty of gigs for guys that played. A guy could open up a bar and put a piano in. He was supposed to have a music license, but he could get that later, once he saw how it worked. I worked in little clubs, Ridge Avenue...

Brecker: Ridge Avenue? Yeah.

Tyner: There were lots of gigs, especially on weekends. It was a great scene, and there was a lot of enthusiasm about playing and jams; we had jam sessions at people's houses. That was common. [Imitating a bystander.] "Jam in North Philly, lets go." You would have Lee Morgan, Archie Shepp, Reggie Workman and the Heath brothers. There was a lot of enthusiasm and people were serious about music. Things have changed a bit, though there are still great musicians there, but then the town had a special feeling.

Brecker: I agree.

Johnson: You wrote several of the songs on the record on the way back from a West African music festival. What was it about the trip that inspired you?

Tyner: I wrote some of it while I was there, particularly in Dakar. What I do sometimes is wait until a project comes up and I start writing. I have a tendency to do that. Sometimes I write out of pure inspiration. "Fly with the Wind" I wrote at a date in Cleveland. I went by the club in the daytime and sat down at the piano and wrote. Most of the time it's all there, I just need something to make it come out.

Johnson: McCoy, has Africa been more inspirational for you than any other place? One of my favorite records of yours is Asante.

Tyner: It's really funny; when I was growing up in Philadelphia there was a cultural affiliation through the community with Africa. We had a big parade for [scholar and Ghanian founding father] Kwame Nkrumah. I've always been interested in African culture, really all international culture, period. I travel all over the world, and it's so nice to be in the company of people who have different cultures. I take a particular interest in African culture because it's in me and it's reflected in a lot of my songs.

Johnson: You work mostly with the trio.

Tyner: Most of the time. I do big-band dates in Europe from time to time, but only a couple of times here in the States. It's expensive and I don't want to be on the road constantly. I knew Woody Herman very well and Frankie Berry, music director of his band, and he told me to be cautious about [big bands]. I met Basie, but I couldn't get close to Duke Ellington, he was always surrounded by an entourage. But I had one-on-one conversations with Woody, and he passed on some pretty good information about big bands. I watched a video of Duke Ellington and learned so much from it. So the big-band experience is really great. But it's scary. I think of all the things involved in running a big band, like paying everybody! [Laughs uproariously.] That's why we're able to do these festivals in Europe, because they have money allocated for the arts, which is great. [Wiping his brow in relief.] Whew!

Johnson: Are you on the road constantly?

Tyner: Some people, like B.B. King and Ray Charles, go out on the road for 10 months. I can't do that; I have to come home sometime to sleep in my own bed for a while. Then go back out again.

Brecker: It's less than it used to be for me. I have two small children [Jessica, six, and Sam, two], so I try to spend as much time with them as I can. It's less than half the year [that I'm out on the road]. Like McCoy, I like to go in and out. After about three weeks out, I want to come home. Five weeks is about the most I can take, and that's rare now. I like to sleep in my bed, too. I'm trying to find a balance, but it's difficult to plan.

Johnson: What is the status of the Brecker Brothers?

Brecker: We've been working pretty consistently for the last three years. We decided to make a record three years ago after not having worked together for a long time, and we liked it so much that we did another album and did a lot of touring behind it. We're going to take a break now and do some solo projects, some other things, and get together again in a couple of years and perhaps do an acoustic group.

Johnson: Do you still do a lot of sideman work?

Brecker: Not as much as I used to; I'm cutting back.

Johnson: Does it require a different perspective to come in as a sideman than come in as a leader?

Brecker: Yeah. If anything, it's a little easier. [Both laugh.] There's a lot less responsibility. I just think about the music and showing up on time. There's nothing about payroll and things like that.

Johnson: I'm sure y'all have listened to each other's work for a long time now. What changes have you noticed?

Tyner: Um, that's a tough question. [Both laugh.] I think it would be better to ask each individual about their own playing.

Brecker: Yeah, you start. [Both laugh again.]

Tyner: Well... I've done some solo-piano gigs, and that's really interesting. I'm really enjoying that; I was affected by Oscar Peterson in that regard. I think that every pianist should do that for a while. I feel that I've grown a lot doing that. Really, though, I'm less interested in analyzing how I'm playing today versus how I used to play. I think it's enough to say that I'm very happy with what I'm doing, big band, trio or solo. I see some maturity over the years, and part of being mature is being happy with yourself regardless of what anybody or the critics say. Being happy with yourself is the most important thing.

Brecker: I have to echo McCoy. If anything, what has changed is how I view my playing. I have less of a tendency to judge it; and that's something I never thought would happen. I used to be very hard on myself. Maybe it comes with maturity, but I'm grateful for those moments of nonjudgmental attitudes toward my playing. I find that I'm enjoying myself a lot more.

May 1996

Van Morrison
Jazz Revisited

by Clive Davis

So, in the words of Ira Gershwin, how long has this been going on? Van Morrison's new album for Verve— a raw-boned assortment of rhythm and blues, jazz and classic ballads—has prompted the same question from an awful lot of people. Everyone has heard of Morrison the Celtic visionary, the poet who weaves quotations from William Blake into his songs and organizes esoteric seminars on "the healing power of music."

But when news broke that the Belfast-born singer had gone into London's Ronnie Scott's Club—arguably Europe's most prestigious jazz venue—to record with a group of Britain's outstanding jazz musicians, it surprised all those listeners who thought of him as a rocker, albeit of the more mystical variety.

"Blues in the Night," "Sack o' Woe," "Centerpiece"—these are not the kind of songs that are immediately associated with the man who has been a cult figure to rock audiences since the release of that vintage slice of psychedelia, *Astral Weeks*, way back in 1968. Of all the many artists to appear on Verve in recent years, he must have seemed the most unlikely recruit. Morrison—who duetted with John Lee Hooker on the 1993 release *Too Long in Exile*—does not see it that way. In a rare interview, the normally media-shy star, renowned for stonewalling journalists with monosyllabic non-answers, was eager to explain that *How Long Has This Been Going On* marks a return to the traditions that inspired him to go into the music business in the first place, first with Irish show bands, and later with the R&B-inspired group Them. Even at the best of times, Morrison never exactly breaks into a tor-

Van Morrison.
(Photo courtesy of Van Morrison)

rent of words. But when he talks about his passion for Gil Evans, Jimmy Giuffre or Hank Crawford's arrangements for the Ray Charles Orchestra, the barriers, slowly but surely, start to come down.

"My father had a big record collection; and blues, jazz and gospel were all around me when I was growing up," he says. "People like Mahalia Jackson, Sister Rosetta Tharpe and Lead Belly. I listened to a lot of big band stuff, too. The first vocalist that made an impression on me, apart from Lead Belly, was Ray Charles. After that it was Sam Cooke and Bobby Bland. Later, when I started out, I got a chance to tour with Little Walter and Jimmy Reed.

"When I first went to New York [in the mid-'60s], I used to wander into the jazz clubs. I can remember hearing Roland Kirk at one—can't remember its name now. There were only three people in the audience, but he went ahead with the show anyway."

Singer/songwriter Mose Allison, who was originally slated to appear on the Ronnie Scott album but was unable to make the date, testifies to Morrison's abiding passion. "I've known him since he lived in California in the '70s. He used to sit in with my trio, and I still see him almost every time I come to London. There's a whole lot of kids who've never heard of me who've heard my songs through him. The story about Van is that he's hard to talk to. A lot of people have been trying to get at him

and he's had to become very protective of himself. But I've heard him talking about R&B history, and I'm astounded at how much he knows."

How Long Has This Been Going On evokes the atmosphere of a hot, perspiring night on a '60s bandstand. In effect, it is a live album with no audience. Morrison's old friend and co-producer, British jazz stalwart Georgie Fame, occasionally takes time out from his Hammond B-3 and arranging duties to sing on numbers, including "Early in the Morning," and he adds his inventive brand of vocalese to a spirited setting of "The New Symphony Sid." James Brown's longtime sideman Pee Wee Ellis—who is now based in England and often works with Morrison—also handles his share of arranging and playing tenor saxophone.

If the vocals sound ragged in places, it was mainly because Morrison was aiming to keep the session as loose and spontaneous as possible. "There wasn't a lot of emphasis on how it sounded," he says. "It was more like, 'Let's try it.' Doing it in a room like that, there was a lot of leakage and stuff. You know you're not going to get the best quality vocals, but we just wanted to go for the live thing. What you lose at one end, you gain at another."

The band—which features trumpeter Guy Barker, saxophonist Alan Skidmore, bassist Alec Dankworth, pianist Robin Aspland and the drummer Ralph

Salmins—had previously worked with Morrison on a number of concerts. But, according to Georgie Fame, the decision to cut an album of jazz and R&B material came out of the blue.

"He's always liked the music on the album, but he's never had much of a chance to play it. And being an alto player, he's always loved Cannonball [Adderleyl and [Eddie] 'Cleanhead' Vincent. When I'm playing at Ronnie Scotts, he'll often pop in to listen, or sit in on one or two numbers. He just said one day that he wanted to do this record, so we cobbled together the tunes. He knows most of these melodies anyway, and I've heard him sing them in private. I got the band together, and we ran through some ideas one quiet afternoon at the Bull's Head [a popular jazz venue in Barnes, southwest London]. That went very well, so Van said, 'Let's do it.'"

Guy Barker—who released his own acclaimed Verve debut last year—describes the impromptu mood. "When we'd played the concerts before, we'd have a set list, but it would only last as long as two or three songs. Then he'd yell at Georgie, who had an extra mike fixed up to communicate with him, and he'd pass the message along to us. The same kind of thing happened with the version of 'Moondance' on the record. We'd finished everything, and Van said, 'We ought to do this.'"

By all accounts, working with Morrison can sometimes be as stressful as interviewing him. Dr. John, another R&B veteran who produced Van's '77 "comeback" album, *A Period of Transition*, has described the frustration of dealing with the singer's mood swings and constant shuffling and reshuffling session musicians. As the good Doctor recalls in his autobiography, published in 1994: "He's probably one of the few guys that I ever felt like punching out in the middle of a session, but I didn't do it—not because I didn't feel like it, but because I respected his singing so much.... His music is powerful. He's a mystical cat, and I got to respect him in that."

Morrison has often discussed the irony of starting out as a blues singer and later being hijacked by the pop image-makers. Ironically enough, *Astral Weeks*, the so-called "sound of acid" album that essentially earned him his place in the rock pantheon, found him working with a number of New York's finest jazz musicians, among them the Modern Jazz Quartet's Connie Kay, bassist Richard Davis and Jay Berliner, guitarist on the Mingus master-

piece *The Black Saint & the Sinner Lady*. Executives at Warner Bros., then Morrison's record company, apparently thought that using top-flight jazz players was one way of keeping a lid on the budget. In these days of endless overdubs, the very fact that the entire disc was completed in two days has itself entered rock lore.

Was it intimidating for him, a 23-year-old jazz buff, to be in the same room with the likes of Kay? "No, not at all. Some of the stuff that Connie played was like country—he was very broad-minded. It was very relaxed. We got it all done in a couple of days, but that's the way you did things in those days. I like spontaneity. At a certain point, with 24-track and all that, recording became a long, drawn-out thing. People now automatically play in stages. I find it's the engineers who want to do it that way. Everyone is geared to overdubs." Some of Morrison's less-publicized jazz ventures are his occasional concerts with the Danish Radio Big Band, whose members performed on the 1985 Miles Davis/Palle Miekkelborg orchestral album *Aura*. Morrison first worked with the band a decade ago, and toured America with them in 1989. His last date with them was an open-air concert in Copenhagen last year.

Thinking of the saxophone gives him the excuse to enthuse over his early memories of Fathead Newman and the hard-driving soloists in the Bill Doggett and Bill Black bands. Coltrane is another personal favorite. Then there is the stylish Jimmy Giuffre, whose folkie hit recording of "The Train and the River" was the record that first inspired Morrison to take up the saxophone when he was a teenager.

The great attraction of Giuffre, for Morrison, was his economical style: "It was all about 'less is more,'" he explains. One reason that Morrison never took his own music-making too far in the direction of jazz seems to have been the old fear of losing his spontaneity. "I had a few lessons, but I didn't think, in the end, it would be for me. I thought I'd probably get very caught up in the technical side of things. I'd get lessons from people and they'd be doing other jobs. I thought that was odd, somehow. And I remember reading on the back of some LP that the guy who was playing was self-taught, so that kind of stuck in my head."

With the Ronnie Scott disc behind him, it would be encouraging to see Morrison making more of these full-scale returns to his roots. When the great singer/pianist Charles Brown made one of his rare visits

to England, Morrison was in the opening-night audience at the Birmingham franchise of Ronnie Scott's. Imagine a pairing between those two contrasting voices! In the meantime, Morrison is busy working through his store of unreleased tapes spanning three decades, a project that he first started, he says, about 15 years ago. "I got burned out with it that last time, but I keep going back to it, and now it looks like if it's gonna happen. There's so much stuff, so many takes, it's mind-boggling."

And what about the new, serene Van Morrison we keep hearing about in the press? The gossip columnists report that Morrison's more settled personal life has brought a new, more extroverted dimension to his public performances. The old demons have been exorcised, or so we are told. As usual he has his own view.

"More extroverted? I don't think so. I thought I was more that way in the early '70s. I used to do more movement onstage; I was more dynamic. Now, I'm aiming for more of a balance—not to be too extreme in anything—and to let the musicians play and just sit on that, rather than do a show. You give the musicians space and plenty of solos. That's why I like the jazz approach—that's where I'm at now."

December 1996

Joni Mitchell and Cassandra Wilson

Alternate Tunings

by John Ephland

Their paths had never crossed. One is from the cold and blustery fields of Alberta, Canada, the other straight out of Jackson, Miss. Joni Mitchell and Cassandra Wilson have more in common now that they've spent a long evening together, but their kinship, a musical bond thick as blood, has deep roots.

Mitchell's latest work involves drums-only accompaniment. With her arsenal of created guitar tunings, she and Brian

Blade (that's right, Joshua Redman's drummer) formed a music both spare and florid, improvisational even as it surrounds that inimitable voice.

Mitchell—whose last feature in these pages was a 1979 cover story on the occasion of her recorded collaboration with the late Charles Mingus—has been on a roll of late: among other awards, two Grammys for last year's *Turbulent Indigo; Billboard*'s Century Award, a new honor the newsweekly bestows on musicians from all genres who've made a highly significant impact on the arts in this century, also in '95; an induction into the Rock and Roll Hall of Fame this year. This fall sees the release of *Hits and Misses*, two career-spanning anthologies of her work with every label she's ever recorded for. Having just turned 53, clearly, she has much to celebrate.

While Mitchell may have worked with Mingus, Pat Metheny, Jaco Pastorius, Michael Brecker and—with the exception of one—all of Miles Davis' former mid-'60s sidemen, Wilson's jazz pedigree is better known to *DownBeat* readers. Witness her recent wins, starting with last year's Readers Poll and continuing with both the Readers and Critics polls for top female jazz singer this year. Apart from her success with *Blue Light 'Til Dawn* and *New Moon Daughter*, the 40-something singer's recent work includes guest spots on Javon Jackson's *A Look Within*, David Sanchez's *Street Scenes*, guitarist Pat Martino's next record, a duet with Dianne Reeves on the Bob Belden–produced *Strawberry Fields*, music for the soundtrack to the current film *Rosewood*, and recording and touring with Wynton Marsalis this winter as part of his ambitious *Blood on the Fields* project.

The musicians met in Los Angeles for dinner earlier this year at Adriano's, a fashionable Bel Air restaurant. The conversation/interview, which spilled over to Wilson's hotel, dealt with the mechanics of music, definitions and the relevance of jazz, "that widened harmony," and Miles Davis. Both women were earnest, robust and, at times, a tad wild, Mitchell taking the reins often in a conversation that jumped off the path more than a few times.

John Ephland: Both of you seem pretty restless when it comes to making music. What makes your music sound different?

Joni Mitchell: What opened the door for me was that my left hand couldn't get at the chords that I heard in my head. So I tuned the guitar to the chords that I heard in my head. [Folk musician] Eric Ander-

Joni Mitchell.
(Clayton Call)

son showed me open G and D modal tuning. After that, I never played in standard tuning.

Cassandra Wilson: That's what I started out doing: playing guitar and singing Joni Mitchell songs. But it was something I had stored away.

Mitchell: What years?

Wilson: It was '74, '75, '76.

Mitchell: And coffeehouses were still around?

Wilson: In Jackson, Mississippi, no less. Check that out. I figured out the tuning on [Mitchell's] "For the Roses," and that was it. I was gone. I was taken by the tunings. There was Miles, I remember, when I was four or five; then when I got to be 15, there was Joni. The tunings were the

thing. That's what opened up everything for me.

Mitchell: It's that widened harmony that they create.

Wilson: There's a resonance.

Mitchell: And even just simple bar chords. You can make instant music with them all, with those really wide chords. First of all, you can't get them on a guitar without the tuning. Its physically impossible. You widen the orchestral breadth of the instrument considerably. You've dipped it down into the upper-bass range, for one thing. You've got a lot more bottom on the music than the normal guitar. And there are inversions that it couldn't have been possible to finger.

Wilson: Unless you have really beauti-

Cassandra Wilson.
(Teri Bloom)

ful, strong, wide hands, you can't get the same kind of resonance inside of a Spanish tuning.

Mitchell: Because the strings are so tight.

Wilson: Once you find the place for it, the guitar speaks. The only problem is my bass player complains. Because when we do the open tunings, we're off into his space. We overlap.

Mitchell: Now, when I add bass, the bass player wants to go polka-dotting along on the bottom. Especially in pop music. He wants to come in and stay in. I think, "Bump, bump, bump," kind of four-on-the-floor almost, only a little more creative, but not much. So he's putting dark polka-dots across the whole thing. So I'm saying to bass players, "Do you have to stay in all the time? Couldn't you go up in the mid-range and play a countermelody?"... There's a lot

of quotes from Stravinsky in my music, if you listen. From Rite of Spring. It's a little jazzy, but it's not jazz. It's jazzy in that the harmony is wider, but jazz has its own harmonic laws.

Ephland: You're breaking up stuff, and you're making your own music.

Mitchell: According to the guy who wrote a book on jazz, [multi-instrumentalist] Victor Feldman, he defined it and locked it into harmonic laws. Victor Feldman apparently wrote a technical teaching book or some kind of book on jazz harmony [*Musicians Guide to Chord Progression*]. We were playing on a date. What was it? "Moon at the Window." Victor was playing vibes. Well, on this one, he got really uptight. I thought the words were bothering him because he's a family man, and it was about people with the incapacity to love, and he had a very loving family. I

thought the words must be bothering him. I said, "Are the words bothering you?" He said, "I hate the harmony and the harmonic movement." I had to stop and send him home. I said, "You can't play on some thing that you hate!" I played the piece for Sarah Vaughan. She had a comment on it: "That's a strange form," she said to me. I said, "It's not really a strange form, it's an old standard form. It has a verse at the beginning that never comes back, then it's got A-B-C three-part melody like most standards do. There's one chord that changes the interval as it goes into the C section that's a bit shocking. I don't know what it is, whether it's a fourth or—I don't know technically what it is. It comes in a little bit odd, but it's a good odd. It's no odder than any change in life. It's kind of like a "but." The thing is drifting off... "but." That's how I think that chord works. It sets up an alternative viewpoint.

Ephland: So you were breaking the rules?

Mitchell: I don't think there are any rules left to break. But she thought so. Wayne Shorter came in, and he's the broadest musician that I've ever worked with. He knows the numerical language, the alphabetical language, and the fly shit, yet he chooses to play through metaphor, as I do. He's the only metaphor guy I know.

Wilson: Couldn't you find a classical musician that understands?

Mitchell: I'm sure there would be somebody if you knew where to look; but a lot of times, classical musicians can't interpolate. They've always had the guidelines someone else wrote. It kind of kills their ability to improvise, in a lot of cases. Not all. But I think you have to grow up doing both.

Ephland: When you say "improvise," what does that mean?

Mitchell: Making it up [laughs], as opposed to reading it.

Ephland: What do you think, Cassandra?

Wilson: What's the Jazz Age? What is improvisation? What is jazz?

Mitchell: It's a fine line.

Ephland: We seem to live in a time where there's a hardening of terms.

Wilson: I didn't think about jazz when I started listening to Joni. I think everything we've produced in America is jazz.

Ephland: Everything we do is jazz?

Wilson: Yeah. Because we've learned how to improvise.

Ephland: That's interesting, Cassandra. Have you been thinking about this long, that everything we do in America is jazz? I mean, it swings, too. Right? Excuse me for bringing up Wynton [Marsalis], but…

Wilson: While I eat?!

Ephland: I find what both of you sing draws me in. You each ask the listener to get closer as opposed to what belters do with their singing.

Mitchell: Belters tend to be showy, not intimate. We can probably both belt, if you like that kind of theater. I'm not sure that I do. It's like grandstanding to me. I said to Mingus, "Who's your favorite singer?" expecting Bessie [Smith] or Billie Holiday. He said Judy Garland—a grander, showier kind of singing. It's an interesting question. We both could sing that way, I'm sure.

Wilson: How do you get a voice like that? And how are you able to maintain a voice like that? How can you sing night after night after night at full broth and not rip your throat out? I'm not into that. I'm a Miles Davis child.

Mitchell: Miles is my favorite singer, and probably yours, too [laughs]. So tasteful.

Wilson: The first Miles I heard was *Sketches* [*of Spain*]. That was just so damn expansive. I'm a Miles fan. I love all of his work. There's specific periods that I bond to. It's nostalgia, though. But I listen to it all. I love it all.

Mitchell: Miles was a fine, fine sonic innovator. And some of the music of the bands he inspired, and kicked into gear, that's some of the finest music I've ever heard.… The later stuff, I think, he had less inspiration. It took him longer to play. It seems like he stood around more. He was so pure. He really waited until he heard something that he felt.

Wilson: So much of it has to do with the emotions.

Mitchell: I'm at that place now, in a way. I'm almost too picky to go on. I'm still making the music, and I've got some new ideas. But you get narrower, in a way. It takes more and more to get you off. Mingus, at the end, couldn't stand anything except a couple of Charlie Parker records. He couldn't stand his own music. He'd go, "He's falsifying his emotion. That ain't shit." He heard all the effort people put forth and very little purity and sincerity. I get that way sometimes. My jive detector gets too sensitive and music just sounds awful to me. All of it.… In a certain way, we do most of our enthusiastic listening in our youth. It's the backdrop for our courtships, and you stow it, and you're sentimental. The songs with the Pioneers, Roy

Rogers' backup band, I'm just thrilled listening to those old songs. That's the music of my pre-teens. It's much better music than I realized as a child. Sentimental, kind of cornball, classic cowboy stuff. I never was much of a country-and-western fan, but I love listening to that. It swings. It's got that element of jazz in it.

Ephland: And their hearts are in it so much.

Mitchell: And every track is excellent.

Wilson: Like *Turbulent Indigo*. I heard it the other night. The song is, "You've made everything I fear and everything I…" There's this passage or this space where there are two bars and it's a repeating thing. For me, it's the epitome of the economy of motion. Two changes that just tear everything up. Tears everybody up. And it's only the space of two bars. It's in the middle of it and comes out of nowhere. It's like harmonically, how does this fit in here? Where does it come from?

Mitchell: Weird things. It comes out of the tunings.

Wilson: I know. That's you. And I'm always prepared for it. But this one, I wasn't prepared for it because it's so spare. It's only two bars.

Mitchell: Or Miles plays this flat note on the end of "It Never Entered My Mind." This is a really early recording. He draws this note flat, and he holds it flat all the way out. If he played it in pitch, it wouldn't do this to you, what it does. It's the saddest note.

Wilson: It's not a flatted fifth, is it? [Laughs.]

Mitchell: No! It's a flatted flat! Know what I mean? It is FLAT! It's like out of tune. But if he played it in tune, it wouldn't have the impact. It's the saddest note in the world. It's like he just lost it on this note. Sometimes I go through these periods where I get temporary perfect pitch and everything is driving me nuts! I go and put that thing on.

Wilson: That's why you had to find those guitars. Because of the tunings. I deal with maybe two or three tunings. I can't imagine what you have to deal with because I know you must have hundreds of them.

Mitchell: I have 60. But that's too many.

Now we're in the lounge of the Hotel Nikko. The bar band starts their set playing Thelonious Monk's "'Round Midnight."

Mitchell: [To Cassandra.] What do

you think about Monk? You're also a piano player. Does he have an influence on you?

Wilson: Definitely. Monk is the main influence. I took classical piano lessons for seven years, so that was my first introduction to music formally. But Monk, *Monk's Dream*—that album was one of the first albums, along with *Sketches of Spain*, that I heard as a kid. When I started playing piano, those were the first piano sounds I heard. Later came the classical things: Tchaikovsky, Chopin, Ravel, that whole piano tradition out of Europe. The first sounds I heard from the piano were this weird kind of [makes "tink tink tink tink" sounds]. That's the way I play piano now. Economy playing.

Mitchell: I just discovered Monk two nights ago. I knew the name. I heard all kinds of stories, like, "Monk could paint! He painted a bowl of flowers and an ax!" But I never really knew what he was about. Monk hasn't worked his influence on me, but he's going to. The first thing that caught my eye was that he played flat-fingered, like Laura Nyro, instead of with an arch, which is harder, I think, for going fast. Then, of course, the obvious, which everybody notes, is how he's always working from the top down and cross-handing. But the thing that really amazed me is the economy, the minimalism of it. How beautiful it was! I'm a chord-puller. I like hybrid colors, like triads or full-fisted chords.

Ephland: I can tell by the way you play your guitar that you do that.

Mitchell: But this guy is linear and very percussive. On the left hand, totally tonal chords, or sometimes just rocking from the black to the white to the black to the white keys. Very, very minimal, but God! When it fibers in with the other players, a lot of times, if the piano player has a lot of chops—this has been my experience in hiring piano players for my band—they get really pianissimo on you, and they start scribbling over all these intricate things, and they take up a lot of space and they over-embellish.

Wilson: That's why I don't have a piano player.

Mitchell: It's hard to find a minimalist.

Wilson: They figure, "OK—88 keys? I've got to play every one of them. Twelve notes? I've got to play every note." And it's the instrument itself, you can't really blame them. Unless you really have the serious discipline and you can focus on bringing the piano into a small space, condensing it, it's hard to do that. I think it's hard for a lot of pianists. Now the old cats, who used to comp with the singers, understood how to do that. A lot of space.

Mitchell: Leaving the vocalist room to breathe.

Wilson: And for the imagination.

Ephland: The two of you are band players as well as vocalists. But you also imply—Cassandra, you do it more than Joni—the use of space. You both imply a lot, and I sense you don't feel like you have to say everything and put everything out there. You leave stuff out so people can fill it in for themselves.

Mitchell: Speaking more for Cassandra, because of my wordiness, I am first responsible to my words. So, when I play with a band, I have to be the leader. Well, the words have to be the leader. And if there's any room for anyone to get in, well, good luck! We did a jam one time, and it was ridiculous. It was Herbie Hancock's pilot for a series. Two drummers: Vinnie Colaiuta and I forget the other one; two horn players, Wayne Shorter and David Sanborn; Bobby McFerrin and myself. And we're doing "Hejira" and "Furry Sings the Blues." Now, those are two very moody songs. You got all these guys waiting to get in the gaps. Two horn players and a scat singer, so to speak—that is to say, a wordless singer—waiting for a hole to open up for them to get an "ooh aah" out. There's hardly any. A lot of people who heard it thought it was successful. I wish sometimes I could write a song with less story. Let me try it: "The wind, the wind, oh the lovely wind. La-la. [Laughs.] You can take a lot of space between those and then give them eight bars to blow around!

Wilson: There's something about your phrasing that implies space. It's the most unique phrasing. When I first heard the way you would say all the things you would say, and when I started writing songs, I would try to do that. I would try to write poetry and sing it and I would just sort of—I couldn't get it all in! That's a special art. Not everybody has that.

Ephland: This is one of the reasons we got you two together—we kind of saw Cassandra coming from more of a jazz-oriented background and going toward pop music, however savage a description that is.

Wilson: Dangerous. Dangerous.

Mitchell: Cassandra, forgive me, but from the little I know, that doesn't sound quite accurate. She's got a classical piano background, she's listening to jazz as a young person, but she's also a singer of folk

music. Right?

Wilson: What do you call all that?

Mitchell: That's just good American fun! [Laughs.] I don't think we're coming from anything that radically different. I'm coming first from classical music, a couple years of piano where they crack you at the knuckles. I could memorize faster than I could read. I was not going to be literate, apparently. Well, as it turned out, I didn't need to. There were rare occasions that I did, but I just needed an interpreter. You hire a guy to write the lead sheets out. Then you're home free. It's an important thing. I mean, I wish I had it.

Wilson: Well, it's important to have the tools to communicate, especially in the jazz world. If you don't have those tools, there's no respect there, on a certain level. I treasure both of them now. I'm glad to have it all, but I think there's a certain kind of opening you get when you approach your instrument intuitively. The trade-off is, because you don't know the rules, you can open doors, open windows. That's what the tunings were for me. It was like a way out. When I first tapped back into it, it was like, whew!

Mitchell: It's a tool for discovery. That's the great thing about it. It's like a no-man's land. It's uncharted territory.

Ephland: You could say you both haven't gone from point A to point B. Instead, you've always been where you are all along.

Wilson: We are all complete. I like that.

February 1997

Steve Lacy
Forget Paris
by John Corbett

"My head is my only house, unless it rains." —Captain Beefheart

Road Trip: January 1996

Soprano saxophonist Steve Lacy picks up shop and hits the trail, leaving Paris, the cosmo metropolis that he and his wife and main collaborator, singer and string player Irene Aebi, have called home for the last quarter century. Their temporary new residence: Berlin. Under a fellowship from the

DAAD, the German government's arts foundation, Lacy will live and work in the reunified capital city. But this is only the latest in an ongoing string of road trips that stretch back like a freeway to the early part of Lacy's career.

Chapter One: The Road

An imperative to go where the music tells you to go. "I live on the road," muses Lacy, reclining with an espresso in his airy Berlin apartment. "I spend an awful lot of time in airports, on airplanes. And we're not even certain where the next turn will take us. I'm still on the road, man. Paris is finished for the moment. We've used up Paris. It's not a very good moment in Paris right now—they're blowing it! Maybe well go back when it swings the other way." Beyond the year-long residency, Lacy says he and Aebi will stay awhile in Berlin, a city that has quickly proven, as he puts it, "very fruitful." Indeed, already he's been the focus of FMP's five-day Workshop Freie Musik, performing with five pianists (Misha Mengelberg, Marilyn Crispell, Ulrich Gumpert, Fred van Hove and Vladimir Miller), a festival documented on the live CD *Five Facings*. And over this particular late-October weekend, he shares the spotlight (albeit in separate performances) with pianist Cecil Taylor at the Total Music Meeting, as one of "Two Portraits." (Lacy later jokes: "Let's call it 'Two Sketches.' We did what we could.")

"I've always gone where the music takes me," Lacy explains. "It isn't that I want to go here or there, it's that that's where the music is. The music has taken me all over the world. And that's also in terms of living, because I have to live where Irene and I can operate—where I can play, and she can sing, and I can write, and we can have a group and realize things. Berlin has been a refreshing change and opened up everything for me." With change of scenery comes a change of scene, and Lacy has disbanded his longest-lasting band, the Steve Lacy Sextet, paring it down to a more economical trio with bassist Jean-Jacques Avenel and drummer John Betsch. It's been a period of great development and turmoil, honors and knocks: In 1992, Lacy received the prestigious (and lucrative) MacArthur Fellowship, while in the same year, after five records, he was unceremoniously dropped from RCA/Novus, his first liaison as a leader with a major record label. In 1994, his book *Findings: My Experience with the Soprano*

Steve Lacy.
(Hyou Vielz)

Saxophone was published, a crowning achievement in his purposeful and exhaustive self-documentation.

Through triumph and pain, Lacy's main activities continue to center around composing for Aebi's voice. "We're working on an opera all this year, but we're already performing bits of it here and there," he reports. In fact, Lacy's been metamorphosing words into music since 1967, when he adapted Lao Tzu's "The Way." Ever road warriors, he and Aebi will take off the next morning—the day after his portion of the Two Portraits fest is done—to present the opera-in-progress at a French festival. Strange coincidences abound: Bangladeshi poet Taslima Nasri, whose work Lacy had already been setting to music, turned out to be the couple's upstairs neighbor when they arrived in Berlin. Now Lacy's turning her text into

the opera's libretto. "It's not a coincidence at all, it's one of those written-in-the-stars things. This is what we came to do here—though we didn't know that. It's an adventure also, and it's a dangerous adventure, so we're playing it cool." It's an adventure, of course, because opera isn't exactly en mode in the jazz world these days. "I swore I'd never do it. I swore, oh man, I never want to do that!" exclaims Lacy. "We had enough trouble with musical theater pieces and dance pieces."

Road Trip: 1970

Based in Rome, Lacy and his Swiss-born wife are frustrated playing with enthusiastic, but amateur, Italian musicians. Lacy can't find anyone whose reading skills are strong enough to perform the music he's writing. And furthermore, there are no good drummers around. "I played this fes-

tival in '69 outside of Paris, and there were all the cats from Chicago. There was Roscoe Mitchell, Anthony Braxton, Leo Smith. Here were good drummers and Bobby Few the piano player. And I said: 'Wow, these guys live in Paris, that's where I want to go.'" Go where the music tells you to go.

Chapter Two: Mixed Media

The Two Portraits pairing suggests a crossing. "Cecil and I have crossed paths for many, many years," the 62-year-old recalls. "Going back to 1953 when he plucked me out of the traditional music and threw me into the avant-garde ocean." Lacy performed and recorded with Taylor for six years. "He's a very important figure in my life; he showed me the way to find my own music. I discovered Monk through Cecil, he turned me on to dance like Cunningham and Balanchine; he clued me in on politics, films, a certain amount of literature and theater, and humanity, people." At the last minute, the whimsical and unpredictable Taylor chooses not to capitalize on a potential (and widely anticipated) mid-fest duet with Lacy, so the soprano saxophonist's sparkling solo set, full of Monk and Lacy's own compositions, leaves the crux uncrossed. "Cecil likes to leave people hanging," grins Lacy afterward, unfazed

In the four decades since joining "Cecil's gang" (his term), Lacy has immersed himself in collaborations with a wide array of different art forms. This polymorphousness is evidenced at Two Portraits, where Lacy plays with dancer/performer Shiro Daïmon and actors Hanon Reznikov and Judith Malina.

"I was inspired by Duke Ellington, who was a total arts man. His stuff involved the visual—he was a painter himself—and poetry and dance and music and theater and everything. And on the other hand, Harry Partch. Gil Evans took me to see Partch's show *The Bewitched* in '57 or '58 in New York. It was musical theater with song and dance and speech, and things were falling out of the ceiling and floor, like a happening. But it was completely controlled, it wasn't accidental or chance. A total theater piece, I saw it two nights in a row. Even before that I was taken to see Broadway shows—that's one of the things my family did for me that I'm really grateful for. Plus, I've always been interested in painting. Since I was a kid I was interested in art, in fact I used to try to make a little bit myself.

"To me it seems the most natural thing in the world is not to combine, but to employ the various media together. Why not? like Duchamp said, you can put anything you want in a work of art. That was a very important statement, and he proved it in his own work. I've always been eager to collaborate with dancers, painters, poets, actors, cinema, whatever. It makes the music move. Music has to be what it normally would not be. It requires something new of the music, and I like that urgency, that need to change, to adapt, to invent." Lacy says he can learn more from a painter, actor, comedian or clown than from another musician.

"Sports figures, too. You can get inspired watching some athletes, get ideas about rhythm, line, timing, dynamics. It's all there. We're in the same boat, we're here to entertain each other... until the ship goes down!"

Road Trip: 1966

A musical turning point comes in the midst of a misadventure in Argentina, with trumpeter Enrico Rava, bassist Johnny Dyani, drummer Louis Moholo and Irene along for the ride: "Tangled up in the tango! I learned what the tango was, down there, and it ain't funny. But since then tango has been a very deep part of the music I do—there must be hundreds of little tango-type movements in the music I write. It was a disaster. That was the wrong group at the wrong time in the wrong place playing the wrong kind of music, the wrong money and the wrong hotel. And yet it was very important. The music was incredible, but the politics... We arrived, and there were tanks in the streets; they were prohibiting the Beatles. It was a fascist jungle, and also there were old Nazis running around. And we arrived with our little free-jazz routine, and the posters advertised: 'Revolution in Jazz!' You can imagine the reaction. We were on one-way tickets, and playing off the door of the theater. It's a recipe for disaster. The rest is history. Nine months we languished down there. We played all we could, and we performed, and eventually we found a small public that appreciated what we were doing. Before the very end we recorded [*The Forest and the Zoo*]. I made that happen because I thought the music was too important to lose. It was what we'd call the 'hermetic free.' The point of no return. Where the music had the maximum calories in it. There was nothing to say, no words necessary. Just: 'play.' After that, the music went elsewhere."

Chapter Three: Various Freedoms

In the era after the harrowing visit to South America, Lacy's music took a very different turn, right into the period he calls "the scratchy seventies." "After about a year or so of playing completely free," he says, "the music started to sound the same every night. And then it was no longer free. That's when we had to start making another revolution." In retrospect, he categorizes the work after "hermetic free" into two sequential types: "post-free"—which began to put fences up in the music, to "groom" the total improvisation—and eventually "poly-free." "The G-major scale came right back. I thought I'd never see it again. But when it came back it was wide open with possibilities. We started adding melodies, written things, modes, rhythms. Sometimes it was free, and sometimes it was free not to

be free. Limits are very important. Once you know you're only going to do something for one minute, there's a certain freedom in that. You don't have to worry about the second minute."

Lacy's musical route took him deep into composition and back into performing Thelonious Monk's pieces, an obsession he first seriously initiated on his 1958 record *Reflections*, then with trombonist Roswell Rudd in the early '60s. It's a songbook he's never since tired of digging into, though at the time, as Lacy is quick to point out, nobody was recording Monk tunes. As for his own approach, he sums: "You go through the complex to get to the simple. We have an old piece called 'Bone.' We try to get it down to the bone. You want to end up with something that's easy... easy to love!" A prolific composer with a writing style as distinctive as his personal soprano sound, Lacy has carefully honed his perspective on working material. The jazz I like is a mixture of prepared and unprepared," he details. "The unprepared is also prepared, and the prepared is also unprepared. There are four edges. Improvisation is a tool, not an end in itself. It's a way of finding music that can't be found by composing. And composing is a way of finding music that you can't improvise. Maybe certain geniuses can improvise perfect structures, but in general to really make a language structure you need time to work on it, time to think about it and prepare it. And then you can play it in a minute! It's prepared. And you can play it in an unprepared manner. You can play it differently each time, in an improvised manner. This is what Monk is about, a prepared structure that can be played in an improvised manner and can be elaborated upon improvisationally. It promulgates improvisation; the tune is not complete without improvisation. And a lot of what I write is made to be improvised. It's up to you to fill them out." Lacy ponders a minute, then adds: "Monk told me: the inside of a tune is what makes the outside sound good. That's a very succinct definition of form, but it's true!"

Road Trip: October 1961

After Ornette Coleman's record *Free Jazz* was out and successful, there were demands for him to produce live concerts by his double quartet. Eric Dolphy wasn't available, so Ornette called Lacy, who was working days at a record store: "We had rehearsals in New York—Don Cherry, Bobby Bradford, Art Davis, Charlie Haden, Ed Blackwell. It was wonderful, the music was very exciting, I was looking forward to the concert, really. We got on the plane, went to a cinema in Cincinnati. On the cinema was written: 'Free Jazz—Ornette Coleman Double Quartet.' Around the cinema was a long line of people waiting to buy tickets for it. And guess what? They didn't want to pay. It was a crisis, man. 'Hey, it's free jazz, we're not gonna pay.' So they wouldn't pay, and we wouldn't play. The concert did not take place, we got back on the airplane, went back to New York, and that was the end of Free Jazz in America." And the birth of an archetypal ruse. "Now it's a joke, but it wasn't then. Everybody was hungry, broke. The chance to play some interesting music and get paid for it! To go all the way out there and find a lack of comprehension like that, it was hard "

Chapter Four: The Horn

In the end, there's the horn. The inimitable soprano sound that Gil Evans wrote lead parts for on his first record, *Big Stuff*. Back then, there was no one but Lacy—even John Coltrane, who several times asked technical advice from his predecessor, was a decade behind Lacy in coming to the straight horn. Now, of course, sopranos are as ubiquitous as, say, Monk tunes. "What do you want your instrument to do and what does your instrument want to do? Those two things are the basis of a style, really. Your own desires and the instruments exigencies. The soprano, if you take Evan Parker's playing and Lol Coxhill's and Coltrane's and my own, you can see that it can be played in a million different ways. The truth is that it hasn't been played in a million different ways, it's only been played in two or three ways. Sometimes I'm disappointed that somebody doesn't imagine something else to do with that. Maybe they'll come along.

"The main disappointment is that hardly anybody has developed the bottom of this instrument. I must be the only one that's really opened up the bottom." In fact, through tireless work he's extended his lowest note possibility down to a low G through combination of lipping and foot-muting. "I'm waiting for somebody else to really have founded something downstairs. That's perhaps the most interesting part of the horn, the most beautiful part, its most pleasant part." But Lacy points out the excruciating work that goes into such discoveries: "These things are possible if you really want them, but you've got to pay

dearly, and you've got to sound terrible, so pathetic and hopeless and hapless for a long time until it turns the corner and starts to sound better. To go through those pains, not everybody wants to do that. But the difficulty of playing a thing like that gives it expressive power automatically. It has tension because it's not easily won. It is per se dramatic because… maybe you won't be able to do it!" Lacy chuckles with the distinctive laugh of personal experience.

Head Trip: Sometime in the late 1950s

Zen was in the air, everyone was reading John Cage and thinking about sound and silence. In New York City, young Lacy had an adventure without leaving his flat: "I was practicing long notes to develop my tone. I started playing two notes. I was working on the smallest interval, the minor second. In those days I was pretty crazy, really, I could do things for long, long periods of time. So, I started rocking back and forth on this minor second, between a B and a C, and decided to stay on those two notes for a long time. I played them for maybe an hour. Of course it went through the various stages of boredom, frustration, puzzlement, and it started to get interesting because my perceptions started changing. So I stayed on those two notes, that little interval, for a long, long time, I don't know how many hours, until I started to hallucinate, to the point where that little interval had become enormous. And I had become very small. There I was, this little being in a huge room, and the room was a minor second. And it was uncanny, extraordinary, and I almost flipped because it was real, it was surreal, it was unreal, but it was for real. I found that I could hear so many things within that little interval, it had completely changed its aspects. When I came out of that room and went back to the rest of the horn, everything had changed, there was no relationship that was as previous to that experience of having gone into that little interval. My mind was blown, my ear was blown. That's a very important experience to dig into something to the point where you get beyond. Like Georges Braque said: impregnation, obsession, hallucination. Dig in, obsess, then it's a hallucination, and that's where something is revealed. And you can apply it to anything, break down a wall a day."

Epilogue: Where To?

As long as he's lived in Europe, Lacy still doesn't like being known as an expatriate.

"I've been out here for 30 years," he says, gazing out the window into the gray drizzle of Berlin. "But I don't want to be an ex-anything. If you're ex-, you're gone really. You're not there anymore!" he snickers, revealing the New York twang that's stuck with him through thick and thin. Where will the next twist in life's turnpike take him? "I feel a pull from America, and there's a time coming soon when I'll have to go back. I must, for a while, to see what's involved. It's just a question of timing, but it's coming up. I think there's something I'd like to accomplish: I hear a lot of stuff coming out of New York, and it sort of rubs me the wrong way. I may be fooling myself, but I thought maybe I could go back there and do something about it." Home from the road or just another pit stop, maybe the peripatetic jazzman will alight on these shores, set them straight like his horn.

February 1997
. . . .

Medeski Martin & Wood

Band of Gypsies
by Ed Enright

The first time you hear Medeski Martin & Wood, you'll swear that you're listening to a quartet or quintet. It's all right there: Drums, percussion, bass, organ and lead line all lock into a mysterious-sounding yet surprisingly simple groove. Count the layers of rhythmic activity, and it adds up to four, maybe even five. Then remember: That's a trait shared by some of the best trios. Together, multi-keyboardist John Medeski, drummer/percussionist Billy Martin and acoustic/electric bassist Chris Wood are probably best described as a "power" trio. And, like the finest three-man outfits, from the Bill Evans Trio to Cream, they achieve a focus and directness that's seldom found in larger ensembles. They play music thick with improvisation and group interplay, a mixture of catchy hooks and spacey extended jams bearing obvious links to jazz, blues, rock and native African rhythms. They'll hit you like a B-3 organ dropped from a 10-foot stage, but you'll still be able to get right up and spin-dance with the Deadheads who pack their live shows.

Medeski Martin & Wood have created their funky sound and bohemian fan-base by following a very definite plan. But there's no corporate or commercial marketing scheme at work here; rather, it's a mission of sorts, beautiful in its simplicity and quite in character with the group's experimental mindset.

"We set out to see just what would happen if we went out on the road," says the outspoken Medeski, 31, of an insanely ambitious tour schedule that began some five years ago. "We went out in a van and a camper, slept in campsites all across the country and found out what's going on—that's how we developed our music. If you want to build something from the bottom up, you've got to be out there checking it out. Some record label executive sitting in his New York office has no idea what's going on."

"We're out there getting the real reaction, the testing fields," adds 33-year-old Martin, the trio's most laid-back member, before the trio's recent gig at Chicago's Cabaret Metro.

Wood, the quiet one at 26, chimes in, "We're definitely proud of what we're doing. It wasn't calculated at all."

Medeski Martin &Wood have taken a step up in their touring accommodations since the early days: They travel by bus (complete with driver, bunkers, a living room and a tiny kitchen), employ a couple of support staffers and actually make a profit from their live shows. Self-declared "food snobs," they can even afford to occasionally indulge in their dinner of choice, sushi and sake. But they remain a totally independent entity, free to play exactly what and where they please. They appear frequently on the rock circuit at venues like Cabaret Metro or the Fillmore in San Francisco and open up for groups like Los Lobos and Morphine. But you're just as likely to catch them at a jazz haunt like New York's Knitting Factory, where they held a series of shows and workshops in September and October featuring guest musicians like John Lurie, John Zorn, Marc Ribot, Steve Bernstein and DJ Logic.

"Nobody finances us, nobody gives us a penny to tour," Martin says. "A lot of groups need it because it's expensive to go on the road," Medeski explains. "But nobody wants help from the label because you just owe that money back to them. We don't have that problem; we're totally self-

sufficient on the road."

Medeski Martin & Wood don't have a label now, anyway. *Shack-man*, their third CD for Gramavision/Rykodisc (which entered *Billboard*'s Top Contemporary Jazz Albums chart at No. 7 in November) marks the end of their latest recording contract. And despite a buzz about the group being ripe for major-label picking, they roll on without looking too far ahead. 'We really have no idea what's going to happen," Medeski admits, visibly pleased that he and the others are free of label expectations. "We're not working at it, not thinking about it. The priority is the music."

"Although, it is an exciting thing in the back of our heads," Martin notes. "But now we have time to think about what's important to us. We've been reveling in the fact that we're completely free right now. It's been some four to five years now. We have no obligations, no contracts with anybody…. 's wonderful."

Indeed, the group values freedom over money or major-label attention. "If we wanted to make money, we wouldn't be on a tour bus," Medeski points out. "We want to do what we need to do to make the music the best it can be, and that is not driving the RV any more. Because after three years, with the RV and the van…"

"… That's OK for a couple of weeks," Martin says, "but then when you have to tour for five weeks straight and the pressure is on every night, the responsibility is too much. It's a lot safer, and we're feeling better when we get onstage. So now it's about quality living on the road. We're more like gypsies than just musicians who do a jazz festival now and then."

With their tip-top chops and considerable experience playing with formidable improvisers on New York's downtown scene, this band of gypsies could easily be working individually as sidemen with well-known jazz names on the festival circuit. Instead, they choose to pursue their own creations on alternative circuits like the H.O.R.D.E. tour. Wood, who once played a stint with pianist Steve Kuhn, puts it simply: "We'd rather do what we need to grow and be better."

"And we could definitely be more commercial than we are," reminds Medeski, a former member of the avant Either/Orchestra and one-time collaborator with rambunctious guitarist David Fiuczynski. "We don't play funky music to be commercial; we play it because that's what we grew up listening to." James

Brown, Booker T. and the MGs, Tony Williams Lifetime, electric Miles Davis, George Clinton, Ahmad Jamal and Herbie Hancock all come to mind. At least one critic has described Medeski Martin & Wood as the best "crossover" act since Pat Metheny, another artist known for his jazz chops, extensive travels and popular appeal.

"I think in some ways our success is similar to Metheny's in that we got in a van and started touring ourselves, independently," says Martin, who, in addition working with such heavy hitters as Bob Moses, Dave Leibman and Jaco Pastorius, has played extensively with pop-jazz fluegelhornist Chuck Mangione. "But musically we're coming from a different place. In Metheny's music, I didn't hear much of the pop music of the time. I didn't hear him incorporating that as much as we're incorporating the hip-hop thing and the funk thing and all that nuance."

And what about the jazz thing? Medeski Martin &Wood have made their jazz sensibilities clear from the beginning, when they started out as a piano trio playing at New York's Village Gate. Their first album, 1992's *Notes from the Underground*, included covers of the Duke Ellington hit "Caravan" and Wayne Shorter's "Orbits" and "United," plus horn parts and some pretty serious group improvisation. *It's Jungle in Here* (1993), which saw Medeski switch to organ as his primary keyboard, also featured guest horn players and included renditions of Thelonious Monk's "Bemsha Swing" (fused with Bob Marley's "Lively Up Yourself") and John Coltrane's "Syeeda's Song Flute." And the group recorded Ellington's "Chinoiserie" on 1994's *Friday Afternoon in the Universe*. Catch a live show and you'll likely hear them play Horace Silver's "Cape Verdean Blues" or quote from Charles Mingus' "Goodbye Porkpie Hat." According to their Web site, which offers audio snippets from live performances, they've even thrown in a bit of Miles Davis' "All Blues," although they don't quite remember actually doing it.

"As far as we know, we've never played 'All Blues,'" Martin insists. "I think we were playing a tune and I just quoted 'All Blues,' and somebody stuck it on the Internet," Medeski suggests. "That's really funny."

"I heard it, and that was it," Wood claims. "I said, wow, it sounds very similar."

Medeski Martin & Wood have definitely opened the doors of jazz and other less-than-popular music forms to young listeners, as evidenced by their fan-mail postings on the Web site. But when asked if they feel like evangelists, they answer with a resounding "Nah!"

"I think it's cool that maybe our music is linked to some great jazz," says Medeski, who grew up listening to recordings by Evans and Bud Powell. "In one way, there are some really fanatical fans, and when they hear us doing 'Chinoiserie,' I know they're out there trying to find the original version. And occasionally we get to tell them, hey, that was Duke Ellington, or that was 'Lonely Woman,' which Ray Charles sang—check it out."

Medeski Martin & Wood give no explanation for the emergence of their crowd, many of them fans of the band Phish and latter-day followers of the Grateful Dead. "It's a phenomenon," smiles Martin, who claims he wouldn't recognize the Dead if he heard them. "I think we were chosen, we were adopted by a wandering lost tribe."

"It's really because of our touring," Wood says, more seriously. "'Cause these are the lands of kids that don't go to the force-fed MTV world of pop culture. They are out there to check out live bands, and unfortunately there aren't a lot of other bands with higher levels of improvisation out touring the U.S."

Phish themselves perhaps tipped the scales in Medeski Martin & Wood's favor by playing the trio's tapes at their gigs. "They'll play tapes of Monk, and they'll play us," Medeski says of the group, well known for its hep alternative scene and vast musical repertoire. "Between sets, they play the kind of music they like to listen to. And their audience, the reason they go to see Phish is they want to be edu-ma-cated."

Medeski Martin & Wood have certainly educated their unexpected and unwashed multitudes, though not in a classroom sense. And the Phishheads, in turn, seem to be an amusing source of inspiration for them. "In an immediate sense, we respond to everything that's going on around us, what's going on in the room," Wood says. "If we played every night to a European crowd that sat and listened quietly and clapped their hands politely at the end of every song, as opposed to a roomful of kids dancing, we'd play a lot differently." Medeski Martin & Wood have mined the current scene like no one else, and they offer plenty of reflection and advice to bands who feel the call of the road.

"Leave your ego in the bathroom,"

Medeski says bluntly. "You could be the greatest musician in the world, and if the promoter hasn't heard you, he doesn't give a shit, and he shouldn't because you're not going to bring people into the club. And the most important thing to remember is that it's like any business. If you're going to start a restaurant, a dental practice, you've got to sink something into it to get something out of it. Just because you sit in your room and practice doesn't mean that you deserve to make money for what you do. So you've got to get out there. Jazz musicians spend so much time studying their craft, they think they're owed something more. That's why they can't get any gigs."

The band has stuck to its philosophy of nonstop exploration, a determined openmindedness that's led them away from busier, headier forms and more toward what they call "groove" music. "We're just naturally gravitating more and more toward contemporary pop song forms," Medeski clarifies.

And as long as the musical breakthroughs and magic moments keep happening, the band will stay together and on the road. "When it stops changing, we'll stop doing it," Medeski promises. "We're trying to find a way to play grooves and song forms that have happened since 1950, and try to dig in for some more emotional depth and ambiguities in terms of the content."

"We'll keep at it as long as we continue to learn and create something that's satisfying and rewarding," Martin predicts. "Forever, you know?"

August 1997

Sonny Rollins
The Man
by Bob Belden

There's something about the sax that makes it impossible for saxmen to resist talkin' shop in each other's company. When a colossus like Sonny Rollins starts talkin', be ready for an in-depth lesson in saxology.

Rollins, who won double honors in the 1997 *DownBeat* Critics Poll as Jazz Artist of the Year and Tenor Saxophonist of the Year, took up the horn 50 years ago. He's had a long career, as both a sideman and

leader, onstage and in the recording studio—a portion of which is represented on two new boxed sets, the two-CD *Silver City* (Milestone) and the six-CD *The Complete Recordings* (RCA, due out this summer). Needless to say, what he knows about the instrument could overload the "hang" capacity of even the hippest sax enthusiast.

We caught up with Rollins in May as he was preparing to embark on a two-week tour of Japan. What follows is an edited version of what happens when two sax lovers really start talking.

Bob Belden: What drew you to the saxophone?

Sonny Rollins: What really drew me to the instrument was Louis Jordan.

Belden: The Tympany Five?

Rollins: Right, the Tympany Five. I used to hear them over my at uncle's house. He had a lot of these old country blues records. I didn't like all of them, but the Louis Jordan Tympany Five, that really struck a chord in me. So that began my liking the saxophone. I had always liked music, but I think that kind of made me conscious of that particular instrument, and I began to recognize that instrument when I heard it. I would have been around six to seven years old.

Belden: Did you have an instinct for a particular horn?

Rollins: When I first began to see Jordan (not in person, but I saw pictures of him), he had a really great King Zephyr, So some years later, when I got my first tenor, which I think was probably in 1944 or something like that, I got a King tenor.

Belden: When did playing the saxophone become a social event for you?

Rollins: Well, the music came first. Because when I was a kid, about 11… my father was in the Navy, and in the summertime I used to go down to Annapolis, where he was stationed at the academy there. There was a girl. She was older than me, actually, but I had big eyes for her. She worked at the academy. So anyway, one day Erskine Hawkins was playing there, and I went there and saw the band and everything, and then I saw this girl, Marjorie Brown, up there sort of with the musicians. And I got really crushed, because I knew, well, hey, that's…

Belden: That's where her interests lie.

Rollins: Really. Why would she mess around with a little squirt like me, you know? I wanted to be like my idols. I wanted to be like Louis Jordan. I wanted to be

Sonny Rollins.
(Jan Persson)

like Coleman Hawkins. I wanted to be up there. I wanted to be a musician playing, you know?

Belden: When did you first hear Coleman Hawkins?

Rollins: Well, I heard Coleman Hawkins, I guess, around the time of that record, "Body and Soul." I would imagine I probably heard him around the late '30s. There were some older guys on my block who were into Duke Ellington and all these people. So I sort of got a really good education, you know, as a kid growing up and liking jazz. We used to always go and listen to all these records. I'd listen to Ben Webster and all those guys, and really got a good insight into him. But I liked his playing a good deal. I thought that Coleman was really an important figure. And I liked his demeanor, sort of the pride and dignity with which he carried himself.

Belden: Did you have an instinct for discerning that one particular musician attracted you more than another musician? Then would you study this particular person more?

Rollins: I listened first a lot to Louis

Jordan, before I really even knew about Coleman Hawkins. Then when I found out about Coleman Hawkins, I was attracted, I think, to his sound (he had that great sound), and then it just seemed like he knew so much music. Just his mental thing and intellectual approach really got to me.

Belden: Because there was a moment... I don't know how you would describe the style of playing before Hawkins, but it seems to me like harmony wasn't as important as the motion, I guess.

Rollins: Exactly. Coleman had so much of that harmony down pat, and he really had it to a high art. A lot of young guys don't even really like Coleman Hawkins today. I mean, they know of him and they respect him, but I think they don't relate to him that much. But the thing I liked about him was, as you said, the harmony. I mean, the harmonic concept was so advanced. Somebody told me the other day, as a matter of fact, that Coleman was a real big fan of Art Tatum.

Belden: Do you feel that the '40s were a good time for a musician, as opposed to maybe 10 years prior or 10 years later?

Rollins: When I was coming up, I was sort of coming right around the time of the small group. As I said, I liked Louis Jordan and the Tympany Five, and then I was just getting in there while Hawkins was doing a lot of his small-band work, all of the wonderful work that those guys were doing, and of course leading right into bebop with Charlie Parker and Dizzy and those small bands.

Belden: Hawk had the first bebop session.

Rollins: That's right! In fact, do you know a guy named Scott Devoe? He's an author who is writing a book about the birth of bebop and the years before bebop. But at the center of the book is Coleman Hawkins. It's a very interesting book. He sent me a manuscript, and I endorsed it because I thought it had a lot of interesting facts in there about how Hawkins was actually a much more important figure in bebop than a lot of people recognize. So I would say, yeah, Hawkins was a very important man and he was playing a lot of chords and stuff.

Belden: Bird played chords on the

saxophone.

Rollins: Yeah, I think Bird came very much out of Coleman.

Belden: Were you much into Lester Young?

Rollins: I was. You know, what happened was that one day on my block one of these older guys that was really into music. He came down the street, and he said, "Who's the greatest saxophonist?" We all said, "Coleman Hawkins." He said, "No, Lester Young." So then we said, "Oh, Lester Young; who's this guy?" And then I began listening to Lester Young. So, yeah, I got into Hawkins first. But when I heard Lester Young, of course, he's completely phenomenal, also. So, yeah, I began listening to Lester after Hawkins, but once I heard him, I realized I was in the presence of greatness.

Belden: During this time, was there any perception that what these musicians were doing was considered art?

Rollins: Well, I think Hawkins is the one that gave me the sense that this is something beyond even the feel-goodness of music. Not that there's anything wrong with the feeling-good aspect of music.

Belden: In the '40s, did the musicians develop a sense of artistry about what they did?

Rollins: Well, I think that's probably true. There are some other social implications. For instance, Charlie Parker, I think, was one of the people who really wanted jazz to be looked at as an art music rather than as an entertainment music. That was one of the things that attracted us in our crowd to Charlie Parker, because there was a certain dignity he had about playing, about the music. So there was a social element that came in there also. People wanted to be accepted as the artists that they were.

Belden: I was going to mention a parallel of [singer/actor/political activist] Paul Robeson to Hawkins.

Rollins: Well, Paul Robeson was one of my heroes. As a boy, we used to go to a lot of Paul Robeson's rallies and so on. As you know, he was quite a political figure, as well. So, Paul Robeson was really one of my early, early heroes.

Belden: I think Hawkins might have been the first of the jazz musicians to get that kind of acclaim at that time.

Rollins: I wouldn't argue with that at all. I think Hawkins had the same kind of dignified demeanor and so on.... Yeah, that might have been one of the things that attracted me to his playing. But I also saw

him a lot, because I used to live uptown. When I saw him in person, he was always a guy who was sharp, he always had a big Cadillac and all this stuff. He carried himself in a very dignified manner, which was not always the case with well-known musicians.

Belden: This period was where you became known in the jazz world. Outside of your own desire to succeed, was there someone who made things a little bit easier for you?

Rollins: Well, I would say that I just got a reputation, word-of-mouth, you know; well, there's some young guy uptown who can play this kind of stuff. Then, I worked with Babs Gonzalez and recorded. But also, when I was in high school, the latter stages of high school, I was rehearsing with Thelonious Monk's band every afternoon. So Monk was very important.

Belden: In 1949 and '50, you started making records. How does the recording process today compare with those early dates?

Rollins: You know, in those days, when we recorded, there were two takes, maybe. I mean, I'm trying to recall, but I know we didn't do 10 takes on one song. Maybe we'd do two takes on a song, and I would say that would be the norm.

Belden: So when you went in to make a record, you were just documenting where you were at at that moment?

Rollins: No. I myself didn't think anything about that. I didn't think much about that. Actually, I was just so much in heaven to be there, playing with these guys, and to be playing and then making a record.... I mean, I was just trying to represent myself in a good way. I didn't think much beyond the actual fact of, "Well, we're making a record," and that was it. Who knows if people would even hear the record? You know what I mean. There wasn't this kind of media exposure like there is now. You would have to go and hunt up jazz records. So, I mean, so what?... I made a record with J.J. Johnson. Who knows how many people would even hear that record besides the true jazz people, you know? Or maybe it might not even be heard at all. So I didn't think of anything beyond just appearing in the studio and having a chance to make a record.

Belden: With RCA, did that period see a change in your methodology?

Rollins: In a way, it was. Because at the time that happened, you see, I had signed a long-term agreement with RCA.

So I think this was different than when I'd go in to do a Blue Note recording or something, and I'd make one record, or make two records, and that would be it until the next time Al Lion called me up again. [Laughs.] When I went with RCA, that was a sea change, because then I was signed to do, I think it was six LPs.

Belden: Of which, eight eventually came out.

Rollins: Yeah.

Belden: You had a big deal at the time. *DownBeat* reported it as, for that time, a pretty good amount of change.

Rollins: Yeah, it was a lot of money. It was a pretty nice contract.

Belden: Do you ever pick a tune because it has a feeling on the horn?

Rollins: I pick a tune, and then it sometimes has a feeling on the horn after I pick it. Or I pick a tune because I like it, and then if I'm lucky, it has a feeling on the horn.

Belden: Do you ever get into a phase where you'll play a certain tune a lot, and then eventually it disappears from your repertoire?

Rollins: Well, "Three Little Words" would be one of those songs. There's a song I used to play, "I'm Old Fashioned." I really used to play it over and over, and really liked it. And then, finally, it just seemed like I couldn't get anything going on it any more, so I stopped playing it. I tried to play it recently because it's on a compilation album they put out, and I just couldn't get into it. So, yeah, I have phases where there are certain songs which I get into, and then that's it. After a while, then you want to do something else, for some reason. I don't want to say that I've gotten everything out of this song. I hate to say that you can get everything out of anything. So let's just say that maybe my approach to the song finally reached its limit, and maybe I would have to approach it in a different way.

Belden: From '69 to '72, you were absent from the scene. Did you rest a during this time?

Rollins: Well, I wouldn't quite say "rested." I had gotten burned, I would say, by a lot of record companies, so that I was sort of afraid to get involved with the record people. I didn't want to have anything to do with the people at record companies. Also, one of the companies that I was with, ABC, I had one record for them.... I'd made several, but one of the records I'd made for them, they said, "Gee, Sonny, we can't sell this record; this is too..."

Belden: *East Broadway Rundown.*

Rollins: Right!

Belden: Of course. That's the one that sells the most.

Rollins: Yeah, so I mean, I had just gotten really [disenchanted] with record companies and these shyster people. Not just the companies, there's a lot of agencies. As most musicians are, I was at the mercy of these unscrupulous agents. So, I just got away from the business world for a while. I mean, that's the period when I went to India, and so on and so forth. So, I had sort of gotten away from the industry. I mean, I never stopped playing. I always had my horn wherever I went. And I never stopped playing myself, but I just got away from the business end of it.

Belden: So you signed with Milestone. Do you feel you've had a comfortable relationship?

Rollins: Well, you see, I had recorded for Orrin Keepnews when he had Riverside in New York. So as Orrin tells the story, I was doing a solo concert at the Whitney Museum one day, and he was there, and he says to me, "Well, gee, Sonny, why don't you start recording again?" At that time, he was with Audio Fidelity. So, then I went with him, and then shortly after that he turned the label into Milestone.... I mean, they went with the Fantasy people. Then I stayed there, and after I started producing my own things, then Orrin got out of the picture—but I just stayed out there with the company. And 25 years passed by.

Belden: You've managed for a long time to have total say over your recordings. Is that something that, when you had the opportunity, you knew this was the time to do it?

Rollins: Well, I became very self-conscious about recording around the '70s. I wanted to do a lot of takes on everything and try to put out the best representation of what I could do. Of course, I was doing that in the '60s also, so I shouldn't say that. I mean, when I was with RCA, I had access to the RCA studios up on 24th Street, and I used to go by there 24 hours a day, you know, whenever I wanted to, and practice. Then, I also was able to do a lot of different tracks. I remember I was up there with George Avakian, who was producing me at that time, and I had the option of doing as many tracks as I wanted—he deferred to me. So that was something I started doing before. But in the '70s, I also wanted to have that kind of control. I always wanted to have control, of course, over what I did,

for one thing because I wanted to make sure that what came out was the best representation of Sonny Rollins, and I thought I knew what that is. Now, I might not be perfect in that. Some people hear things in my playing that I don't hear, you know. But nevertheless, I felt that I wanted to be able to have the final say in what came out. So it was something that I had always been trying to do, and I did get that amount of autonomy at Milestone, yeah.

Belden: Is there something you haven't done yet as a recording artist or as a soloist?

Rollins: Well, I hope so. Because if not, I would probably head for the graveyard. I mean, I hope there's a solo that I haven't played yet. As a matter of fact, I am trying to get to something that I haven't done before. So as far as soloing, yes, I hope there is. As far as context, yeah, there's a lot of playing situations that I haven't been in yet—many of them. I mean, actually, it's endless.

Belden: You've done some orchestral stuff.

Rollins: Right. I did do one orchestral piece. In fact, I think I might do that again. There's been some talk about doing that again next year. So we may revisit that piece, which is OK.

Belden: The album *The Bridge* [recorded in 1962] was an incredibly influential record.

Rollins: Yeah, I like *The Bridge* a lot. A lot of people like that.

Belden: The sound of jazz at that time was harder, much harder, and *The Bridge* has an airier texture to it.

Rollins: Mmm-hmm. I think so. Yeah, I think it was.... Well, remember, when I made *The Bridge*, I was sort of away from the jazz scene for a while, so I probably didn't reflect anything really that was happening around me so much. I mean, it was strictly coming from me and the group, you know.

Belden: What is your response to the release of bootleg recordings?

Rollins: The reason why I have been so much against bootleg records is because I always viewed it as a way that unscrupulous people are profiting off of the poor, beleaguered musicians; I've never looked at it in an artistic way. Because most of these records, nobody gets paid. So I always view the whole industry as people that are just ripping off the artist. Now, that puts me in a very funny position, because I feel that way; at the same time, when I hear something by somebody that I like that was pre-

viously unrecorded, I mean, it really knocks me out. If I heard something by Art Tatum that was never released, I'd probably turn flips. So as a listener, it puts me sort of in an ambiguous position.

Belden: You recently played [the big pop venue] Tramps in New York. Is this...

Rollins:... a trend? [Laughs.]

Belden: Is this a sign of a new direction?

Rollins: Well, the thing is this: As you know, for career reasons I decided a long time ago that I wanted to play concerts because it would just be more prestigious, it would be better for jazz as a whole, not just for Sonny Rollins.... It would be better for the business if jazz musicians of some repute would do concerts, wouldn't have to play clubs all the time. So anyway, I decided to just have a concert career, and that's what I've been doing for quite a while now. However, I have been in the habit of playing the [pop-oriented club] Bottom Line in New York; I used to go down there once a year or something like that.

Belden: And the Beacon occasionally.

Rollins: Right. Well, the Beacon [concert hall] is sort of a big house.

Belden: Do you like concerts because the environment is so much more your environment?

Rollins: Yes, that's part of the reason. And the conditions, the backstage conditions are much more pleasant [at] these things, they make a difference. Being able to have a nice dressing room and all this stuff... I believe in that, even though there are always going to be people that say, "Well, gee, why not the good old conditions of being in a smoke-filled, whiskey-drenched nightclub? Boy, you guys were really playing music then." You're always going to get people who say that, or say, "Well, gee, Billie Holiday was great because she was a dope addict." I mean, this kind of mentality is going to be around all the time.

Belden: When did you really make the complete transition to concerts from the club environment?

Rollins: Well, I would say that outside of the fact that I played the Bottom Line annually for some years, I have been playing concerts probably since the late '70s. So I would say that at least 20 years, give or take a few years maybe.

Belden: So, in a sense, there were environments where you were playing that you would consider as intimate as any club in New York. Yet people seem to mis-perceive that as not playing in clubs.

Rollins: Well, you have to remember: When I did those [engagements at clubs like Bogarts, Rockefellers, the Bottom Line, Great American Music Hall], I did it for, like, one night or two nights at the most. So most people conceive of a club as like six nights a week. If I go to a place [like] the Roxy, I'll play there for two nights. I don't believe I played at the Roxy for more than that. I didn't play at the Music Hall for more than two nights. Bogart's, those places, maybe one night. Those clubs were one-night, two-night places, That's why the perception was also given credibility: "Well, he's not really playing clubs, because he's not there six nights a week." Right?

Belden: Yeah, exactly. You can play concerts all over the world; would you want to play clubs all over the world?

Rollins: Right. Well, I wouldn't want to play clubs all over the world, either. Jazz needs some dignity. It needs to be looked at as a serious, important art form. And if you're going to be playing in nightclubs, I don't care what you say, you're not going to get that kind of respect for it. Not that the respect is even the thing that's going to put jazz over the top—I don't know. But it's just the idea that if you're just playing night-clubs, it just diminishes the music in some kind of way. At this time, in 1997, I think it's just not enough to be playing nightclubs. It's just not enough, you know. It wasn't for me 20 years ago. It's not proper. If you want to do it, OK. But you shouldn't have to do it.

November 1998

Louie Bellson, Roy Haynes, Elvin Jones and Max Roach

Once in a Lifetime

by Ed Enright

Louie Bellson, Roy Haynes, Elvin Jones and Max Roach are like four giant planets.

Clockwise from top left, Max Roach, Elvin Jones, Louie Bellson and Roy Haynes. (Rick Malkin)

Fellow musicians gravitate like meteors, and hangers-on constantly orbit like satel-lites. Getting them together is like orches-trating the Harmonic Convergence—a once-in-a-lifetime celestial phenomenon.

Avedis Zildjian Co., the 375-year-old cymbal-maker, made it happen this Sep-tember when they paid tribute to these four jazz drumming heavies, septuagenarians all. Billing it the American Drummers Achievement Awards, Zildjian called on a younger generation of drummers—Steve Gadd, Terri Lyne Carrington, Peter Ersk-ine and Marvin "Smitty" Smith—to per-form in honor of Bellson (74), Haynes (73), Jones (71) and Roach (74), respectively. Proceeds from the bash, held at Berklee College of Music in Boston and hosted by Bill Cosby (himself a closet drummer), went toward scholarships in each of the honored names.

The day before the big event, *Down-*

Beat held a roundtable discussion with the foursome in the privacy of the Friends Lounge, upstairs from the Berklee Performance Center. (We also heard from the honorees during a brief press conference the afternoon of the show; a few of those comments have been integrated into the following interview.)

After posing for a quick photo session, Bellson, Haynes, Jones and Roach drank a toast of red Italian wine, sat down and were ready to roll.

Ed Enright: Have the four of you ever been together before?

Roy Haynes: I know we've all been together separately, but not all four of us.

Elvin Jones: Not at the same moment. This is the first time for that.

Enright: What does it mean to receive this honor? How does it make you feel to be together for this?

Haynes: I'm glad to be here with these guys. Somebody said I was in good company to be with Max, Elvin and Louie. I'm looking forward to it. But I would like to hear these guys play! That would really knock me out. I'd sit back and just check 'em out! We've got some youngsters playing tomorrow, so it'll be cool.

Max Roach: It brings back a lot of memories. For example, I remember the time that Louie Bellson and Buddy Rich and Gene Krupa ganged up on me because I had won this *DownBeat* poll. I was the first black musician to win a poll for the magazine. So they went to California with Clark Terry and me, and here I was on the stage with these three killers. What a night that was! When I first heard Elvin, the band with Brownie [Clifford Brown] and them came to Detroit, and I got sick and I had to stay home a couple nights. Every night when the gig was over, I'd hear them coming down the hall happy. Laughing. This is Elvin, now, so I thought, I'd better get well and get myself back to work. Quick! Elvin Jones, he was a baby at that time. Roy Haynes, every time we came to Boston, Roy was the killer in Boston. When Roy finally got to New York City, Bird [Charlie Parker] hired him. I left and went on the road with Benny Carter, and Roy took my gig and kept it! [Laughs.]

Louie Bellson: It's a very special honor for me because I consider myself a student of these three teachers. I started with Big Sid Catlett, "Papa" Jo Jones, Max Roach, Roy Haynes and Elvin Jones. These are truly my teachers. Anything I do

today is a reflection of what they showed me. Max, I recall in the '40s when we did two drum-set clinics in Brooklyn for Henry Ader. Saul Goodman was there for tympani and Burt Morales did the Latin thing. After I played, Max came to me and said, "Louie, you play so wonderful, can I add a comment?" I said, "Yeah, of course." He said, "Why don't you learn how to play melodically?" I said, "What do you mean?" He said, "For instance, if you're playing 'Cherokee,' build your solo around that tune of 'Cherokee.'" I never forgot that. It put me on a new avenue. Of course, many times I've listened to this gentleman here, Roy, and also Elvin. I'm especially honored to be one of the four honorees. And I think it's marvelous that this is happening, because what we've done so far can be a reflection on some of the students coming up: to love your craft and do the best you can and add something to this wonderful history of drumming.

Roach: Let me just say something about Louie and what an inspiration you were to me. As a composer and an arranger, you stood out in the crowd. Louie Bellson was a craftsman, one of the few people whose music Duke Ellington played. Mercer [Ellington] always complained that his father never would play his music. When we did a record dedicated to Charlie Mingus, Duke invited us all to participate and asked us all to bring compositions, and we played your music as well. We got to the studio, and Duke was at the piano—Louie, you're probably familiar with this sight—he was already writing stuff, putting stuff down. When we finished the date, we didn't play anything of Mingus', we didn't play anything of mine! [Laughs.] But we recorded Louie's. Louie to me was as much a drummer as he was a composer and an arranger. I especially remember the tune "Skin Deep."

Bellson: That was actually written in 1947. Of course in those days, Tommy Dorsey or Benny [Goodman] had their own arrangers. I just wrote to keep my hand in composition. Then when Juan Tizol and Willie Smith and I joined Duke, Tizol said, "Bring those arrangements in to Duke." I said, "Juan, are you crazy? Me bring in arrangements to Duke Ellington and Billy Strayhorn? No way!" So finally, Duke came to me and said, "Bring the music in." So, reluctantly, I brought in "The Hawk Talks" and "Skin Deep." I was just flabbergasted that he wanted to hear some of my music. Even if he just heard it during rehearsal,

that was good enough for me.

Roach: That was a great piece, "The Hawk Talks." I forgot about that one. But that was an inspiration to the few drummers who did do a lot of writing. It got me really on it. I was always trying to do something in that area. The drums are a hell of an instrument, and people don't always recognize that.

One of the things about Elvin that has always mesmerized and fascinated me was the way his mind worked on that instrument. He uses all four limbs, not just contrapuntally—not left, right and against each other—but as a composer. No matter how much you watched and listened, there was something else. And there were a few people like that: [To Bellson.] You mentioned "Papa" Jo was one of the great masters, and of course Big Sid. The track Jones set is an innovation that came out of the United States, where you charge with all four limbs, you charge. And Roy Haynes was another one who came to New York with all that stuff. Stuff was happening from every other direction. Then when I learned that Elvin played guitar, that really fascinated me. It was very musical. I had no idea about Elvin until he came to New York. He just shattered the vernacular, as did Roy.

Jones: This is the first time a manufacturer has recognized their endorsees as contributors to the musical art form. I think it benefits not just the four of us, or the next four artists, whoever they may be; but it provides a kind of inspiration for the students. It gives them a motivation. This isn't something that just gets printed in the paper. It's something that recognizes what you have done, what you have accomplished with your life as a musician. I think that's what is most important about the whole event, I think, that in the future it will even be more significant because now a precedent has been established. And I think it will be followed up in greater numbers, with more manufacturers setting up scholarships for other universities and music schools across the country.

Enright: The four of you share what seems to be an instant rapport. Would you say that's true of drummers in general, more so than other instrumentalists? Drummers of all styles seem to learn from each other and feed off each other.

Jones: You say "drummers" as if we're a different breed from anyone else. I don't think that's true. Drummers are certainly musicians, and they may even be more musical than other instrumentalists. But when they say drummers are more of a fraternity, I don't think that's true. It's just that when we're together, we know that we share something, something in common, something very essential in our life... which is a drum set. We use it for musical expression. But all musicians do that, I think: piano player, the woodwinds, the reeds. So I can't say it's anything exclusive in that way, but I think it may appear that way sometimes.

Haynes: I agree. Every time I go someplace and we have a discussion with musicians, I always learn something. That's one of the things I've been doing with the music: I try to keep my ears open because I'm learning from what he's saying. But I've often heard people—even years ago—say that drummers were closer. I mean, I heard people say that in the '40s and the '50s, so there is something to it. First of all, the drummer is the heartbeat, and there's something about drummers. I don't know what it is, but I've felt it in a lot of the older players. But I like what Elvin's saying about us all being musicians. There's a joke that I heard once, I think when I was with Ludwig. They were having a meeting, and they said all the musicians should be there at a certain time, and you drummers can come, too, if you want to! [Laughs.] That's an old one.

Roach: We had a little abuse that we had to deal with, we were discriminated against, and we had to band together, I guess, so we defend and protect each other.

Haynes: Max Roach, this guy, he was the first of the drummers, especially the black drummers, to get credit from where I was sitting, and I've been doing this since the '40s. I've watched him and Sid Catlett and Jo Jones—as great as he was, he didn't get enough credit from where I was sitting. Cozy Cole, to me, got a lot of credit. He played the drums with Cab Calloway. He did a movie, *Stormy Weather* or whatever movie it was, and he also had a drum school. But this guy [Roach] was the first person around my age to really get noted.

And this guy, Elvin... I was playing with Ella Fitzgerald in the '50s at Cafe Society, and Hank Jones was playing piano. This young guy comes in and Hank says, "This is my brother." That's when I first met him. That was in the '50s, before I went to Detroit.

Jones: I was just visiting!

Haynes: That's the first time I met you. Hank said, "He plays drums," and I said, "OK!" So later on in the '50s, I think I heard him from playing with Mingus and Harry "Sweets" Edison. I used to go to Detroit a lot, and I would always go by the Bluebird, a club where Elvin was working. I would sit and hang out with this guy. That's how we met. There's something about each of these guys that I've connected with.

Roach: This is very special because Zildjian has opted to recognize the instrument itself. As Roy just told in that funny story about drummers—we're the outcasts. The drummer is not really considered a musician.

Haynes: You guys helped change that, though.

Roach: And when I think about composition, our instrument—and I know I'm being partial here—brings a special something to the world of composition. Maxine [Roach, Max's daughter], for example, who's a string player, did a piece off a drum solo which was mine. She made the bass drum the cello, the cymbals became violins, and so on. It was a magnificent piece. She took the drum solo and just orchestrated it for strings. It showed me something about that instrument. I told her, "Now, the next one you do, listen to Elvin and put something to what he did!" [Laughs.]

Haynes: I think it's really a strong bond that's here. We're all related in some way. I filled in with John Coltrane for Elvin several times. And I replaced Max Roach with Charlie Parker. And I think it was 1952 when Louie Bellson was leaving the band and Duke had called me up. Louie, you had just married Pearl Bailey, and you were going on a honeymoon. Duke did call me, but he just talked, he didn't say, "I'd like you to join," but that's what it was all about. I didn't go with the big band, because this new music was happening, so-called bebop. Max Roach, when he left Charlie Parker, he recommended me. He said I took his gig, but he offered me the gig, [laughs] and I went with the band and started on 52nd Street at the Three Deuces. And stayed there a long time. They always had two groups on 52nd Street; I think it was Erroll Garner and Charlie Parker. Then Bud Powell came with his trio, and Max Roach was going to be on drums, and I was still going to be there. And I didn't know if I was going to have to mess in my pants or what when I learned Max Roach was going to be playing opposite me with Bud Powell.

And I think one of those nights Char-

lie Parker played a tune that I had never played before, and I didn't know what the hell I was going to do. There was a little door on the side of the drums at Three Deuces, and Max came up to the door and told me everything I should do, if it's a break here or a solo or whatever, and he always helped me. I remember when I was playing in New York at the Royal Roost with Lester Young, and we were playing "Lover Come Back to Me," and Lester gave me the bridge. And at the end, Max said to me, "That was a hell of a 16 bars," and I said, "I wasn't countin' bars." I just played. I realized then, hmmm... 16 bars, this guy's pretty good. [Laughs.]

Jones: The first time I listened to Max was on a recording. I was in the Army at the time, and we were in the barracks practicing rudiments. And this fellow, Raymond Landcaster, I asked him, "What is [Max] playing?" And he immediately analyzed everything you were doing, put it into rhythmic context and said this is what YOU were doing. And it made me aware of how much further I needed to go to reach a point where I could feel even partially satisfied with what I was playing, the way I was getting myself educated. It was that distinct identity that Max Roach had in any context. The music would start, and everybody would say, "That's Max Roach playing the drums." I think Louie Bellson has the same kind of identity as a drummer. The first time I heard him was with Duke Ellington's band, also on record, and he played a solo, and the only other person I'd ever heard at that time who could play a drum solo like that would have been Buddy Rich, but it wouldn't have been as distinctive. That was a signature of his artistry and ability as a drummer and percussionist. And I had the same experience with Roy Haynes. What fascinated me about him was that he played so many counter-rhythms and phrases, and that was his identity, to approach a rhythm from the back or from the bottom or from the side, and, to me, it was ingenious to hear that.

Bellson: I feel that drummers are the tone of life. We are rhythm, we are timing, we are pacing. Everything in life is based on rhythm: the way you talk, the way you walk, the way you express yourself on an instrument. And this group here—Max, Roy, Elvin and I—were very fortunate to come through a golden era. I'm talking about the likes of Dizzy Gillespie, Charlie Parker, John Coltrane, Oscar Peterson, Ellington, [Count] Basie, Lionel Hampton.

This is something that is monumental, and also this group represents identification. You can put a record on and I know that's Max; that's Roy; that's Elvin, that's Louie, that's Jo Jones. That mark of identification proves respect for one another. So when I hear something by Max, Roy or Elvin, I respect their ability as gentlemen of high class who know their craft. They have their identification, and that adds a lot of respect from drummer to drummer. I learned from "Papa" Jo. He told me once, "You can walk into some funky little nightclub and hear some drummer nobody ever heard of. And if you listen to him play, you can pick up something that you can add to your repertoire." Always a process of learning. Roy, you and I talked about that today. Every day is a new process.

Enright: Each of you has worked with some of the biggest names in jazz. Have you ever thought about how these artists have influenced your own playing—be it melodically, rhythmically, your soloing style or your accompaniment style?

Jones: The more exposure you have with other artists and other contacts in music, the greater the potential for you to develop. And it'll make you better. For me, when I was playing with Coltrane, I heard purity in his tone, in his discipline for study. That's what he was projecting. I think it affected me, as well as when I played with J.J. Johnson. They've got that purity. Here's a trombone player that could play with a slide that's faster than somebody could finger a trumpet, that distinct style and taste and articulation as if it were a valve. This is passed on to me. I'm already inspired, but that inspires me to be better, to make myself better so that I can be worthy of being in that kind of company. I think you can learn it from anybody. They don't have to be great, well-known artists. Like they say, you can walk into a room and here's a guy who's never made a record in his life, but he's there playing and swinging something. You'll absorb that because it's a part of you. That's what it is. It's a part of you.

Bellson: I was always taught to be an accompanist until it was time to solo. I learned that from Dizzy, too. To be able to hear a soloist, what they're playing, so that you can give them proper backing. Sometimes, in the rhythm section, if the piano and the bass and the drums are all comping at the same time, it's too busy and the soloist has to turn around and say, "Wait a minute, what's going on? Where are the

fundamentals?" I feel that I go by the music. Like when I would back Johnny Hodges. If Johnny Hodges was playing one of those beautiful things of his. I'd take great delight in having my brushes and feeling that warmth from that poet. So I play according to what the music is. If it's bebop, if it's swing, whatever music, my ears are tuned in to the band, the soloist, and I gear myself that way. That's what I learned from Max and Roy and Elvin.

Roach: This music is a very democratic art form. The fact that Elvin worked with John Coltrane, I worked with Charlie Parker, Roy worked with Sarah Vaughan and Louie worked with Ellington—what we got from these great players affected us and influenced what we did. This is a collective; you learned from everybody. We had to coexist with dancers, a variety of things that influenced us; atmosphere we came up in, the time, sociologically, politically, artistically. We were exposed to so much. And that individuality is reflected in everybody.

Enright: The last time Louie and I spoke, we talked about the importance of passing on what you learn from the musicians who come before you. Who are some of the players—drummers or otherwise—you feel you've passed your knowledge on to?

Bellson: I've been able to pass it on to anyone who comes along—students, sidemen, you name it.

Jones: That's the thing. You never know exactly who. I think a lot of people learn just because they buy a record or they come by a club. When I walked into a club and saw Max Roach playing, I'd just stand there. Or Art Blakey. Or Kenny Clarke. Any of these guys. I'd just stand there and watch. Something would hit me. It would all be beautiful, but it would just be a matter of hearing something you feel you'd be able to do. You know you can't do it all, but there's something you can pick up that will help you with part of what you do all the time.

Roach: The thing that all of us have given to ourselves and the rest of the world is hard work. Everyone has given time to develop on that instrument. When I see Louie and hear Louie, when I see Elvin and hear Elvin, when I hear Roy, I know that work has been going on. And it still goes on. Louie's always been a perfectionist, Elvin's a perfectionist, Roy Haynes is a perfectionist. Lester Young was a perfectionist. As Louie put it earlier, we inherited something that we hope everybody listens to and passes it on.

Bellson: I don't know who coined this phrase, but at clinics I always say, "You have to know where you came from in order to know where you're going." You have to know about Max Roach, Roy Haynes and Elvin Jones, then you can go ahead further. If you don't know that history, you're going to miss an awful lot. Those students who really want to play, they dig into records by Roy, by Max, by Elvin, and study that wonderful art. That history will help them get to this stage, and then further on. That's so important. If a drummer starts and plays for years and doesn't know "Papa" Jo or Chick Webb and Max Roach, Roy Haynes and Elvin Jones, you'd better go back to the drawing board.

As the conversation winds down, we gradually make our way out of the Friends Lounge. A busy weekend awaits these four friends, as does our limo. On the elevator ride down, Roy Haynes looks around and takes a deep breath. "This is very serious," he says. "I never dreamed it would happen like this. We're all in our 70s, and I love you all."

November 1999

Milt Jackson
Lessons from Bags
by Jon Faddis

Milt Jackson and I first met in 1972 at the Nice Jazz Festival, when I was playing with Charles Mingus. The Modern Jazz Quartet was at the festival as well, and I considered myself blessed just to be in Milt's presence. I admired him then, as I do now, for his extraordinary musical abilities, his powerful intelligence and his wonderful wit. When he plays the vibes, I am always surprised by the purity of his sound and the clarity of his solos. He continues to amaze in a variety of settings—big band, small group or a capella—with the emotional depth of his music and the unabashed energy and joy with which he performs.

Milt is both as down-to-earth and bluesy as one of his nicknames, "Bags," suggests. And he's as dignified and elegant as a Sunday preacher—as his other nickname, "the Reverend," testifies.

Milt Jackson.
(Hyou Vielz)

And he is always about bebop.

Milt tells some of the best jokes, the craziest stories (like the time Dizzy Gillespie sandwiched them both between a streetcar and a truck in Cleveland... but that will have to wait for another time), and he makes some of the most delicious peach cobbler I have ever tasted. He's been known to bring dishes of it to gigs, resulting in a lot of "Mmmm-hmmms," not just for his music but also for his cooking. He plays a fine game of pool, and on long airplane rides beats hand-held computer games at poker and blackjack. He and I have shared stages the world over, and for well over a decade, we both have come home to the same area of New Jersey, where we are neighbors. He is also a teacher of mine in many ways. Mostly, I am honored to say that we are friends, and I love him.

This interview is based on several conversations that took place at Milt's home in Teaneck, N.J., during the week of Aug. 9. These conversations among myself, Milt,

Milt's graceful wife, Sandy (they met at Birdland in 1957) and a friend or two who dropped by were held around the dinner table and in the living room. Surrounded by stunning photo-portraits of some of the great jazz musicians (the MJQ, Cannonball Adderley, Miles Davis, Diz, Sonny Rollins and Jimmy Heath), we talked about music, including of course, the MJQ, Diz and some great new projects of Milt's. And we talked about the rest of life too—family, growing up and food for both body and soul.

Milt has wrestled with a few health problems during the past few years. But between mouthfuls of steak with special gravy and rice and veggies, Milt, now 76, would have you know that he is "feeling very well, coming along just fine, thank you." I am proud of his endurance.

For me, the magical thing about conversing with Milt is that the more I talk with the man, and the more I listen to his music, the more I realize how much I still have to learn from him.

Jon Faddis: Bags, you're celebrating 60 years in the music business. What are some of your favorite memories as you look back over your career?

Milt Jackson: Coming into Dizzy's band as a soloist. And, believe it or not, playing one-nighters with [Dizzy's] band. I remember one time, in 1945, we did 90 one-nighters in a row!

Faddis: How did the gig with Dizzy come about?

Jackson: It was in Detroit. We played at a joint called the Bizurti Bar. All the Detroit musicians, like Yusef [Lateef] and Willie Wells would go to this bar and jam all night. Dizzy had just left Billy Eckstine's band and he came in and he heard me play and said, "Man, why don't you come to New York? As a matter of fact, if you come to New York, I'll give you a gig." And that's what I did. I packed my suitcase with my two little suits and took a train. Something else I will never forget: I had a $20 bill in my pocket. The fare was $18.63.

So you can imagine what I had left!

Faddis: $1.37!

Jackson: [Laughs.] So, when I got here, Dizzy had organized the big band. It had K.D. [Kenny Dorham] in it, by the way. Then for some reason, Diz disbanded the band. Then he turned around and reorganized it and added me as a featured soloist.

Sandy Jackson: Who was in the band?

Jackson: Dave Burns, Elmon Wright, Cecil Payne. And we had Leo Parker playing baritone—boy, what a band!

Sandy Jackson: Who was in the rhythm section?

Jackson: Kenny Clarke, John Lewis, Ray Brown and myself. Ray and I joined the band about three weeks apart.

Faddis: What was your relationship with Dizzy like?

Jackson: Oh, man! I fell in love with everything that Dizzy did. He was a teacher and there were so many things that he taught us. I learned a helluva lot from him—just being there.

Faddis: Do you have any stories about Dizzy that you would like to share?

Jackson: [Grinning.] Yeah, I have a lot of them, but I don't think I'd like to share 'em. [Laughter.]

Sandy Jackson: Most of them you can't even tell!

Faddis: You got that right!

Jackson: I lived with Dizzy and Lorraine at 2040 7th Ave.

Sandy Jackson: Lorraine kicked you out of their house… but you can't tell that one.

Jackson: It's funny. I had to move, and I moved to Brooklyn and wound up staying with Sonny Stitt.

Faddis: Dizzy's big-band rhythm section became the Modern Jazz Quartet. How many years did you spend with the MJQ?

Jackson: 44.

Faddis: When was the last time that you played together?

Jackson: Just after Connie [Kay] died in 1995. Because one year, we used Mickey Roker on drums and for some reason, John Lewis didn't like Mickey. And I never could figure it out because, to me, Mickey was always one of the most swinging drummers we had. There's a strange thing about John Lewis, though, which is that he's the only jazz musician I know of who deliberately suppressed swing. The quartet would be playing and suddenly hit a groove, and John would pull back from it. I never understood this because John had a way of playing the piano the way Erroll

Garner played in the days of swing, and nobody could play like that. We had a way of swinging that was unsurpassed and I never understood why John suppressed these elements.

Faddis: The MJQ did a lot to bring a certain type of respect to the music.

Jackson: I think the idea, at least my idea, was that we could bring another level of respect to the music and in doing so, captivate a much larger audience.

Faddis: Is there any place that you've played where you feel that you play better because of the audience or the environment?

Jackson: Well, yeah. Europe. The reason is that the European audiences have more respect for our music than audiences here in America. Europeans have a higher regard for it.

Faddis: Why do you think that is?

Jackson: Well, no matter what you're going to become in Europe, as a student, you've got to take a year of music education. It's mandatory. That gives the Europeans more insight into our music. Americans take it more for granted than Europeans. I'll give you an example: The first tour that the MJQ took to Europe was in 1956. In fact, we left the Blackhawk in San Francisco and went straight to Europe. When we came back to the States, people wanted to know what these four black dudes had done to make so much noise in Europe. After that, the Americans started paying more attention to us.

Faddis: Do you find that, as you've aged, you start thinking differently about music?

Jackson: I wouldn't say differently, but you start thinking about a lot of things that have developed and lean toward that direction, because as an artist, I like to keep up with what's going on, especially with the music from our era, the bebop era. I cannot deny that I'm more partial to that era than to any other era in my musical career.

Faddis: And what is it about bebop?

Jackson: The fact that it was so different, the way that Charlie Parker, Dizzy and [Thelonious] Monk came up with the creation. It was such a different approach. And most of us youngsters got into it right away. I guess I was able to realize the value of what it meant to the musical world. A lot of the weight was left on Dizzy because Bird died at such an early age, and a lot of things that we would have learned from him, we had to get from the extension of Dizzy because we needed someone to carry on the tradition of what they started.

Faddis: What about some of your peers that took bebop in a different direction? Like Monk and 'Trane [John Coltrane]?

Jackson: Well, Monk's conception of music in terms of his writing and playing was so different. He took things and changed them around. Monk also had a unique quality where his writing, particularly, wasn't articulate. He never used an eraser and he'd do a lot of scratching out, things like that. But he had one of the most unusual characteristics I know of in a musician. He could take an idea—actually, it would be a mistake—and he would sit there and toy with that idea so that it was no longer a mistake. He'd make it part of the piece. Very unique. 'Trane excited the players because his thing was an extension of Bird [Charlie Parker].

Faddis: You did a recording a few years ago called *Ain't But a Few of Us Left.*

Jackson: Doing that CD means that we're gradually losing so many originators of the music that I felt that I had to mention that fact. The youngsters aren't into the music the way we were, so that puts a special dimension on emphasizing bebop. 'Cause it is very special.

Faddis: Are there young vibes players who come over to hang out and talk music?

Jackson: We have Dave Pike, who I always thought was a good player. More recently, of course, is Stefon Harris, who is developing very rapidly. Also Steve Nelson and Jay Hoggard.

Faddis: How about you? How did you get started with music? Would you talk a little bit about your childhood?

Jackson: My mother was a very religious woman. And we did gospel music, A.J. and I.

Sandy Jackson: A.J. is Alvin, his older brother.

Faddis: Do you have other brothers and sisters?

Jackson: Yeah, I have four brothers. Ironic, 'cause the youngest one died first.

Faddis: Where were you in the birth order?

Jackson: Next to A.J. He was the oldest, I was next, and when I was 7, we would sing gospel duets, and I played the accompaniment on the guitar. A lot of people don't know that guitar was my first instrument. Now let me tell you something wild about that. My father's guitar would be sitting in the corner and my mother would be cooking a steak, which was a rarity in those days for a black family. And she would take the hammer and would be beating on the steak to tenderize it, and I would use the rhythm from the hammer to solo on the guitar. That's how I got started.

Faddis: After you started guitar, then what?

Jackson: Well, that was about it. I didn't get piano lessons until I was 11. I had lessons when I was 11 and 12; then my mother couldn't afford to pay for any more lessons. Let me tell you something else. There were two leading gospel groups in Detroit at that time: the Flying Clouds, and the group that I was with, the Evangelist Singers. Every Sunday, all of us used to travel to Windsor, Canada. We'd give a concert at Elder Morton's Church of God and Christ, and they would broadcast it on the radio, station CKLW. They'd take up a collection for us and I would make about $16. That was a lot of money in those days!

Faddis: Did anyone else in your family play any other instruments?

Jackson: My mother tried to play the piano, but that didn't work. Now, my father played the guitar, but strictly by ear. He had no kind of formal training. A.J. later played bass with Charlie Shavers, Hines, Hines and Dad.

Faddis: How were you introduced to the vibes?

Jackson: Mmmmm. Believe it or not, it was by singing. I discovered that by using the speed control on the vibes, I could imitate the vibrato I used as a vocalist. Man, that fascinated me.

Faddis: Who are your favorite singers?

Jackson: Oh, man, without question, Sarah Vaughan. Ella [Fitzgerald], Billie Holiday, Carmen McRae, Dinah Washington.... I just love singers! And there was this blues singer that sang with Jay McShann's band named Walter Brown. Helluva band!

Sandy Jackson: Milt, who was that guy you used to play on the jukebox every time? Charles Brown? Was it "Drifting Blues?"

Jackson: Ray Brown and I used to go into this restaurant at night, after work. Me or Ray would get a dollar's worth of nickels and just put nickel after nickel in that jukebox, and listen to him play "Drifting Blues" and "Merry Christmas, Baby." [All laugh.]

Sandy Jackson: The woman who owned the restaurant hated to see them, 'cause they kept playing the same thing, all night long.

Faddis: Milt, where did those first vibes originally come from?

Jackson: When I was 16, my father

put a down payment on my first set, and I paid it off at $5 a week. I had a job delivering beauty supplies to barber shops and beauty parlors.

Faddis: So you started playing the vibes at 16?

Sandy Jackson: But you started playing in high school. Tell Jon how you had played all the other instruments and your teacher introduced you to the vibes because you had finished before everyone else.

Jackson: Well, we had a prescribed course and a whole semester in which to do it. Half the semester was gone and I had already finished. So the teacher said, "Why don't you take up the vibes? That'll give you something to do, plus keep you out of trouble."

Faddis: Do you remember the teacher's name?

Jackson: Sure. Luis Cabrera, from Mexico.

Faddis: When you were coming up, how much of an influence did Lionel Hampton and Red Norvo have on you?

Jackson: None, truthfully. My only inspiration from them came as far as playing the instrument itself. I was fascinated by the instrument.

Faddis: Do you keep in touch with Hamp at all?

Jackson: You know, it's funny about Hamp. Hamp always had this ego thing where he was the king and it wasn't easy to reach him.

Faddis: What would you say to a young musician that would really like to become a jazz musician, but who doesn't have the support of his or her parents?

Jackson: If you love it enough, you pursue it, regardless of what your parents tell you. Because eventually, it will bring you your livelihood.

Faddis: Yet teachers and family help too, and family was and is obviously very important to you.

Jackson: I realized the value of having a stable family life at an early age. Sandy and I have been married 41 years, and we have a daughter, Chyrise, who is 34. You've got to have a family that's sympathetic to what you're doing in order to survive. My parents always preached stability—having a job where you bring home a paycheck every week.

Faddis: So you became a jazz musician?!?!

Jackson: Yeah! I had a steady day job and played vibes in a club called the Twelve Horsemen that paid $3 a night. By

leaving for New York, I got more of an outlet to do what I felt I needed to do.

Faddis: Did your parents understand?

Jackson: They didn't at first. Coming back home for the first time with a big band, I had to show my mother what it was all about, because the only people they knew anything about were Ella Fitzgerald and Louis Armstrong. So, one day, I brought Ella home for dinner. And my mother went and called up everyone and said her son was playing with Ella Fitzgerald. That was a very big thing to her.

Faddis: Sandy, what is your favorite recording of Milt's?

Sandy Jackson: *The Ballad Artistry of Milt Jackson*. It's a string album. Very romantic.

Faddis: Even at his age?!

Sandy Jackson: Even at his age!! [*Laughs.*]

Jackson: Damn!

Faddis: Don't worry, we'll edit that out.... [Louder laughter.] Bags, do you listen much to your own recordings?

Jackson: Sometimes. Now, really only the newer ones. Occasionally, I'll pull out one of the classics.

Faddis: Do you have a favorite recording?

Jackson: Well, I'd also have to say *The Ballad Artistry*. I've always been partial to big bands and strings. For example, all my string dates, the one with Jimmy Jones where we did "Feelings," I love those records. And most recently, the one that John Clayton wrote and conducted.

Faddis: That's a new recording with the Clayton-Hamilton Orchestra called *Explosive!* (Qwest). Why did you decide to do another big-band recording?

Jackson: Well, I've always loved big-band music and John Clayton is a heck of a writer. He also has what I call a special charisma for conducting and writing that type of music.

Faddis: Last thing. I hear that you're working on a new book. When is it going to be released?

Jackson: First of all, the worst thing that you can do is put a timetable on it. Because the way that I'm writing it isn't like a journalist or a writer, you know? I write as I feel it, and it takes much longer that way. And I've been approached by several publishing companies who've asked me when the book will be finished.

Faddis: Is there a title for the book?

Jackson: *Bags' Groove.*

Faddis: Amen to that.

THE 2000

October 2000

Southern Swing

A Week on the Road with the Lincoln Center Jazz Orchestra

by Paul de Barros

Lincoln Center Jazz Orchestra.

(Frank Stewart)

The dance floor of Miami's Knight Center is nearly empty, save for a drop-dead gorgeous woman in a short black dress and heels, whose black curls fly behind her as she Lindy Hops with her partner. The 3,000 theater seats sloping gently behind the flat floor are about two-thirds filled. The tune, "The Blues Train" by Andy Farber, is attractive, but the chunky tempo doesn't work for dancing. A trumpeter turns up the heat, growling a long, raunchy solo seemingly aimed directly at the girl. She throws him a broad, sidewise smile.

The band turns to something trustier—"Take the 'A' Train"—and the shell of shyness slips away. Dancers of all ages flood onto the floor, gyrating and leaping, many of them from a swing-dance club, with suspenders and bobby sox, going through rehearsed steps, others improvising boldly. One woman leaps up on the hips of her partner, then plants a kiss on

his forehead. When the band plays a slow, 12/8 blues, more dancers stream down from the seats. Their feet shush on the ballroom floor, like it was 1938 all over again.

The "For Dancers Only" tour has struck the right chord—again.

The band is the Lincoln Center Jazz Orchestra, and the suggestive trumpet player is 38-year-old Wynton Marsalis. We're on the Southern leg of a 24-date tour that started April 9 at Williams College in western Massachusetts, and will end at New York's Roseland Ballroom on May 19. And I'm spending a week with the band.

Step out of a cab onto the hot concrete in front of Miami's Hyatt Regency Hotel, as high-mast yachts float by on the canal—it's the beginning of a fascinating, firsthand look into this organization, with its concerts, education programs and audience development, as well as a behind-the-scenes glimpse into the backstage world of a big band on tour.

The LCJO was created as the Classical Jazz Orchestra in 1988 to play the music of Duke Ellington for Lincoln Center's Classic Jazz series. In 1991, Jazz at Lincoln Center became a year-round department of Lincoln Center, and, with Rob Gibson as executive producer and director and Marsalis as artistic director, the orchestra came under the aegis of Jazz at Lincoln

Center (J@LC). The band took its first tour in 1992. Since then, it has played on five continents, commissioned works by everyone from Benny Carter to Joe Lovano and produced eight recordings, including Marsalis' Pulitzer Prize–winning oratorio, *Blood on the Fields*. J@LC acquired its own, separate nonprofit status in 1996, and the organization that started out with a staff of three now has 50 employees.

But while the orchestra has proven remarkably successful, critical response has been mixed. The New York jazz establishment, in particular, has been skeptical, suggesting that a jazz band playing repertory for an institution is inimical to jazz itself.

For this tour, the 15-member band— five saxes, four trumpets, three trombones, and three rhythm—is playing dances. They even have a swing-dance couple on board—New Yorkers Janice Wilson and Paolo Lanna—who offer workshops as well as performances. To get "in the mood," band members and even J@LC staff have taken a swing-dance lesson. Marsalis says the idea of playing dances came out of a conversation he had in Puerto Rico.

"Dancing has always been a part of our music," he says. "Coming from New Orleans, playing the second line, you always see people dancing. That's part of the beauty of it, really, the communal aspect of it."

Backstage in Miami, a crush of young music students assail the trumpeter after the show, asking for autographs, lessons or simply saying hello. He seems to know half of them by name. It's a ritual that will take place everywhere we go.

"Have you been practicing?" he asks. "Yes."

"Have you been listening to any solos?" "Yes."

"What solos?"

"Well..."

"You get you some records of some solos. Get you some Louis Armstrong solos."

"Swing is the coordination of the eighth note," says reedman Victor Goines, exaggerating the accents on the clarinet line to "Anitra's Dance," as student drummer Obed Calvaire plays time on the ride cymbal. "It's important to find out how to manipulate that lilt. We sometimes call that 'the triplet inside.'"

We are sitting in a hot, second-floor classroom at Miami's New World School of the Arts. Goines and trombonist Wycliffe Gordon—who the band affectionately calls

"Pine Cone," or just plain "Cone"—are giving a five-hour workshop as part of the Essentially Ellington high school competition, which will take place at Lincoln Center later in the month.

"Every finalist received a free workshop like this," explains Laura Johnson, J@LC's education director, on hand to coordinate. Free scores went out to 1,890 schools; 176 tapes came back, and there are 15 finalists.

The students seem keen to hear about life on the road. "How do you have a family?" one asks, earnestly.

"When we get to Birmingham," Goines answers, "I'm going to rent a van and drive home to Atlanta for a barbecue. Some of the other guys in the band will come, too, and sleep on the floor, just so they can enjoy that atmosphere. We have families, and we are a family."

Inside St. Petersburg's 2,000-seat Mahaffey Theatre—a gorgeous, white-and-gold Italian Renaissance facsimile, with pillars and boxes curling around the sides—a pumped crowd anticipated the LCJO's second show on their Southern swing. Marsalis introduces two former Ellington sidemen in the audience—trombonist Buster Cooper and bassist John Lamb—then counts off "'A' Train." The room floods with color.

Trumpeter Ryan Kisor takes a plunger solo that becomes a perfect work of architecture—logical, melodic, thoughtful and swinging. Alto saxophonist Ted Nash offers a bright and sweet snapshot on bassist Rodney Whitaker's perfumed ballad "Darien Niles," and Walter Blanding Jr. offers tough, guttural tenor on A.K. Salaam's "Congo Mulense." The group's rugged texture suddenly softens down in support of Milt Grayson singing "Do Nothing Till You Hear from Me." A cartoonish original by Gordon, "Blues the Typewriter" mimics the stop-and-"ping" of a carriage return.

Suddenly, the dancers come on. Wilson wears a long brown skirt, a floral blouse tied off at the stomach and bobby sox shoes. She has a flower in her hair. Lanna wears loose tan slacks and a long-sleeved shirt, not tucked in. Their moves are natural, unrehearsed and deliberately unchoreographed.

"All my life," says lead alto saxophonist Wess Anderson, "people have been telling me, 'You have to get the dance element in your playing.' Before, it's been more like a myth, a way of getting to imag-

ine what it's like. 'OK, I'm dancing now.' Now that I can actually see it, it's improved my playing 80 percent."

Drummer Herlin Riley, who drives the band with a Buddy Rich–like fervor, describes playing for dances as being "the electricity inside of a human jukebox." He plays a steady four on the bass drum, "feathering" it with a light touch that reinforces Whitaker's supple scoop through the time.

"It's important that you don't overdo it," Riley emphasizes, "that you're not playing so hard so that it cancels out the bass notes. It's very subtle. Because when the lower frequency of the bass and the high frequency of the cymbal come together, then that really perpetuates the swing."

Swing's a religion for these guys (as are Armstrong and Duke Ellington, who they mention everywhere we go). But for all the talk of lilt and swing, there is not much air in this band. Precision, yes. Rhythmic purpose, definitely, but sometimes it sounds swamped by its own purposefulness and intentions. The feeling is a little chunky, and rarely glides.

Back in my room, I almost step on a "poop sheet" that has been slipped under the door:

3:00 a.m. Bags

4:30 a.m. Lobby Call/Check Out

5:00 a.m. Leave for Birmingham, Ala.

Morning. Diesel hum in the hotel parking lot. I climb into one of the big Prevost tour buses, divided into four sections. Up front is the private driver's cockpit, behind that, a living area, with two, railroad-style booths, large TV, a long couch, kitchen area with refrigerator and bathroom. In the middle section sit 12 bunks, three high and six to a side, each with a reading light and curtains. In back, another lounge, with another TV. I throw my shoulder bag onto a mid-level bunk and fall asleep in minutes.

When I wake up, I feel like I'm in a coffin. Utter darkness. I can hear the hum of the engine, freeway noise and some quiet breathing. When I turn on my side, my elbow hits the bunk above me. I roll out, knock on the door and it slides open with a pneumatic hiss. D Venson, the tour manager, talks on his cell phone, staring at his laptop. *Saving Private Ryan* plays on the TV monitor as I dig into the freezer and find a microwave breakfast sandwich and some fresh fruit.

"Where are we?" I ask.

"Georgia, I think." Venson lifts one of

the shutters and peeks out. "No. Too bushy for Georgia. We must be in Alabama."

This is a nine-hour ride, our longest jump of the tour.

Day off in Birmingham, Ala. Trumpeter Marcus Printup and Goines go home to Georgia, Marsalis and Riley to New Orleans. Pianist Farid Barron goes to the theater to practice. Whitaker and his young son, Langston, trot to town to see the Civil Rights Institute. Saxophonist Joe Temperley and I meet for breakfast. At 70, Temperley is the elder in the band, the only man to have actually played with Ellington's group, replacing Harry Carney after Duke and Carney passed. He commands tremendous respect. On the bus, he reads in the back lounge. Everyone calls it "Joe's Sanctuary," and they leave him alone.

"With Woody Herman," he says, with traces of his original Scottish accent, "we did a lot of riding on the bus overnight to save money on hotels. Nobody slept. They just stayed up all night drinking. But these tours are like a military operation—the buses, the plane trips, the hotels. We always stay in really nice places. Everything is timed to perfection. And everybody's well looked after. We always have meals after the sound check."

In the afternoon, Temperley goes up to his room to practice the bass clarinet part for an Ellington piece they're rehearsing tomorrow.

How do these players—mostly young—feel about playing vintage music, when they could be out playing their own stuff? Nash, whose sparkling, modernist solos add a lot to the band, says when he first got the offer in 1997, he had doubts. One prominent musician even advised him, "not to get involved with that bunch."

"I was a little worried that it would be too traditional, a little too swing-oriented, which I thought would be sort of a step backwards. But the lesson I learned out here is that you can make music accessible without selling out. People like music not because of the style, not because it's old-fashioned, or because it's harmonically simple, but because it's music that's honest and it speaks to them. You can do that in any genre."

The next day at the Alabama Theatre, Riley is late for rehearsal (he's always late). The band needs to bone up on the tunes they will record for next year's Essentially Ellington competition. Marsalis takes his place at the far end of the trumpet section,

slouching slightly to one side. With his short hair and thick-rimmed glasses, he looks like Billy Strayhorn. He calls "Blue Feeling."

"It's too slow," complains Temperley after a run-through. "I played this with Mercer's band. It's all right to play it slow, as long as you don't hang back."

"Listen y'all," says Marsalis, later, during "Rumpus in Richmond." "When people are playing solos, it's gotta be really tight. Not loud, but a lot of force."

He walks out in front to listen.

"That sounds good, but when Ryan is soloing, the trombones are too loud."

"What are we wearing tonight?" Riley asks.

"Charcoal suits," Wynton answers. "Any tie."

When the show starts, the hall is nearly empty, but slowly fills up, with a mix of middle-aged folks (including a larger percentage of African Americans here) and fresh-faced students. On "King Porter Stomp" and "Stompin' at the Savoy," the band has the muscular snap and precision of Jimmie Lunceford. The trombone section is slick, led by Ron Westray's declamatory articulation, and Gordon's tone glows like Incan gold.

Marsalis plays as if possessed. His trip to New Orleans must have been salubrious. On Westray's brassy "Mr. Personality," the trumpeter wails high, smearing out elephant roars, screaming, laughing, glissading up and down, like a kid with a new toy. Barron answers with a dissonant, smash-chord solo. When the band goes into Duke's "The Second Line," from *The New Orleans Suite*, the feeling is so good that the argument about whether or not to play jazz masterworks suddenly seems just silly. Why consign historic jazz to its frozen existence on records?

"The whole idea of 'modern' or 'contemporary'—it's time for a new concept, a new way of looking at it," Barron says. "One thing Wynton told me early on was that he heard Jelly Roll Morton in what McCoy [Tyner] did. I never would have associated the two. When I stopped perceiving the music in that dated sort of fashion, without preconceived notions of what the music was supposed to sound like, I began hearing that lineage."

After the show, a bunch of us go to Ona's, where local trumpet man Bo Berry knocks us out with his Clifford Brown–like licks. Anderson and some others sit in.

"They can't get a victory! Not one victory!" Marsalis taunts, as we stand outside the bus in the morning, lining up our luggage. The objects of this taunt are Venson and Gibson, who Marsalis waxed on the basketball court last night. (Gibson and Mary Fuss, J@LC's director of public relations, have flown in from New York.)

Marsalis is almost as obsessed about sports as he is the trumpet. Not more than 5" 9", he is thick through the shoulders, has a powerful bull neck and is in great shape. "Everywhere we go," says production assistant Nathan George, "he finds a ball court. In Burlington, Vermont, we were playing ball till 2 a.m. He can't get enough of it."

We have a short hop today, just 241 miles to Jackson, Miss. I ride with Marsalis in his Winnebago, and chat first with Gibson, then Marsalis, who at the start is sleeping at the back of the rig. Marsalis has two drivers and a personal assistant, John Miller.

Gibson has deep admiration for Marsalis.

"He's always thinking about the big picture," Gibson says. "Whenever I get bogged down or depressed by some minor little failure, some show that doesn't work out, Wynton reminds me of what we're really in this for."

Which is?

"Nothing less than putting this music in the rightful position of respect where it belongs in American society. Nothing less than the education of children about this great tradition. And I'm not just talking about America. We're taking this band all over the world this year and doing residencies with young French musicians, Australian musicians, Chinese musicians. People are hungry for this music everywhere."

"But, Rob," I argue, "wasn't that just what Arthur Blythe, Henry Threadgill and Lester Bowie also were trying to do in the 1980s, except in a lot hipper way—show the relationship between 'the tradition' and modern music?"

"The avant-garde jazz movement failed to hold its audience," Gibson says. "And the audience wasn't that big from the start. They tried, and on some artistic levels it worked. But in terms of a continuum, Lester [Bowie] quit trying. He didn't take the time or the effort to keep the tradition alive through education. My interest has always been to reach as many people as possible. You spend just as much time to get concerts done for 60 as you do for 6,000. So the opportunity to do this work in New York was something I couldn't pass up."

Gibson sounds particularly high about the $103 million capital campaign for Frederick P. Rose Hall, J@LC's new home at Columbus Circle, which will open in fall 2003. His tone is messianic, a mood Nash catches nicely: "It's sort of a mission thing. A lot of people are negative about that, because they're not getting gigs, and I can understand that. But what this band is doing is actually helping everyone, because we're creating an audience that's going to last for generations."

Everything J@LC does is part of this mission, to rescue a music Marsalis perceived 20 years ago as a dying traditional art form. Whether you agree with that perception or not, it seems ungenerous to begrudge him, or the band, credit for what they actually do.

Marsalis stirs. Dressed in jeans and a blue T-shirt, he sleepily serves himself a bowl of Honey Nut Cheerios. Does he think things are better now for jazz than when he started out?

"It's a thousand times better. You see them out there listening! I've been seeing that for 20 years. I haven't read about it, but I've seen it. You see all those kids who want to play. Everybody wants to play, everywhere you go. We who are out here understand the positive impact it has on people."

And what if J@LC fails?

"It's impossible to fail at this," he replies. "How can you fail, teaching kids whose parents want them to be taught? How can you fail at playing concerts that people want to hear? You cannot fail. It can be written that you fail, but you cannot fail. How can you fail with a kid who says, 'I put on your record when I was 12 years old and it inspired me to become a trumpet player.' A kid gives me a pen and his hand is trembling. That's not because somebody wrote a good review of my music, or a bad one. He listened to my music. How can we fail when we have the best musicians in the United States playing with us every night? We play with symphony orchestras, and they want to know, 'Where the hell did this band come from?' How can we fail?"

The Winnebago parks in front of a grassy field across the street from our hotel, the stately, wood-paneled Edison-Walthall, in Jackson. Time for touch football. Marsalis, Gibson, George and I toss the ball around. While Gibson sets up some end zones, I run out for a long one, and Marsalis fires an incredible 60-yard bomb. Right on the money. How can he fail, indeed?

At sound check in the huge, modern Thalia Mara Hall, Marsalis takes me aside. "I remember when all these guys' kids were born," he confides. "There's Langston, Rodney's kid. We were just over at Wycliffe's family's, having some food. We've been doing this for 15 years. What makes me so mad is people saying what we are doing is not real. That's what makes me so mad."

The concert tonight is a train wreck. Westray starts "Maybe Later," but the trumpets miss their cue, so he has to start over again. Marsalis calls "Stompin' at the Savoy," then sheepishly notices that Riley hasn't come back from intermission.

Yet, without question, this is the swingingest night I've ever heard the band play. When Riley finally climbs up to his drums, in blue shirt and suspenders, grinning ear to ear, "Savoy" absolutely stomps. On "Jumpin' at the Woodside," all the kinks are out. The band, loose, seems to lift off the stage. There's air between the parts, and all that dreary "purpose" has evaporated. On "C Jam Blues," Barron walks behind the bandstand and shouts to Marsalis, "Never stop! Never stop!"

After the show, I tell Westray I've never heard the band sound better, even though they screwed up a lot of stuff.

"For some reason," he says, "bands play better when they're tired."

But I've struck a chord. Later, he passionately elaborates: "I've been arguing with Wynton about this for years. We'll be rehearsing, and he'll say 'Y'all are bullshitting. You've got to be more precise.' But that just creates the fear of making mistakes. It makes people sound stiff. What this band needs to do is get loose. This is where I think there's a tension between the band and being part of an institution."

Is it possible for an orchestra driven by an institution to have a personal sound? The Cleveland Symphony Orchestra does, but can a jazz band?

Marsalis thinks it already does, but the band members are more cautious. Whitaker suggests that as more players contribute tunes to the book, the group takes on its own flavor.

"It's getting there, absolutely," Temperley offers. "When we first started people were kind of over-awed with Ellington's music, but the more we played it, Wynton encouraged people to play their own idea of it, not just copy, per se, what was on the recordings."

The proof, of course, emerges in the

listening. And when I close my eyes, I realize I would recognize this band anywhere in a minute. First off, this is no regulation swing band, with call-and-answer patterns between the sections. Much like Ellington's ensemble, the LCJO is a big band with a small-group concept and agility. Each section has a distinct hue: the saxophones, with their chewy, resonant texture, Temperley's sweet, shivering baritone on the bottom and Anderson's warm, singing tone on top; the trumpets, a brass choir with four distinct voices, heralded by lead man Seneca Black's brilliant sound; and the trombones, muscular, warm and fluid, with a very personal articulation. And the rhythm section, with the locked-up solidity of Riley and Whitaker, the unusual (for a big band) playfulness of Barron, and Riley's decidedly New Orleans chattering, in support of soloists. Yes, the band sometimes sounds like Duke, but anyone who says this band doesn't have a personal sound today isn't listening.

Jones Hall, Houston, the last stop on the week-long swing. The band has everything going for it tonight—precision and relaxation, making for the best show of the tour. They are fat and precise on Basie's "9:20 Special"—Gordon's powerful projection and attack are something to behold, as he plays an aggressive, growly solo, yelling through the horn. Blanding and Anderson nod approval after a blistering six choruses by Temperley. Marsalis catches the mood and pulls out a tune I haven't heard them play yet, Duke's sexy/bluesy ballad "Almost Cried," from *Anatomy of a Murder*. It's a perfect call, as the band sings their parts as if they were born playing them.

After the show, the "usual" crush of students backstage, and it takes Marsalis an hour before he can get away. Back in his hotel suite—with a piano in the adjoining room—he throws off his jacket, loosens his tie, flops backwards onto the bed and releases a long sigh.

"One thing Miles Davis told me," he says, "when I asked him how could he be bullshitting? He said, 'They'll wear you out, man. You'll find out. They'll wear you out.'"

Later, a bunch of us pile into the Winnebago and drive out to the suburbs, where a friend of the band has been barbecuing brisket all day. Barron plays stride piano along with a Louis Armstrong record as we munch slices of beef. I try to forget that I have to leave this all behind soon. In the morning, I'm "flying home."

As my plane takes off, I picture the band getting back on the buses down there, hugging north across Texas, like a huge Jazz juggernaut, blowing up dust behind it, leaving joy and knowledge in its wake. This is not just a band on tour, but a religious congregation, spreading the word of jazz. I'm grateful to have been along for the ride.

December 2001

Blues Hit Town

B.B. King and Buddy Guy Ride a Sanctified Musical Highway

by Frank-John Hadley

Something at once unusual and reassuring is in the air on this chilly late-September night at Boston Harbor. Singing booms out of the Fleet Boston Pavilion and ricochets crazily from one wall to another among the fish storage depots, seafood restaurants and wharves lining Northern Avenue. The sound carries past the replica of the Tea Party brig and Old Glory standing tall on to the new 10-story federal courthouse, where marshals armed with submachine guns stand guard behind concrete barriers. Now mixed with the reverberating overtones of a guitar, the voice skips across the water, out to where the historic USS *Constitution* warship is berthed out toward Logan Airport.

The shards of music decrease in volume but gain in poignancy the further one travels away from the concert tent. The blues song "Bad Case of Love" is a comforting whisper in the dark. Everything seems right again in the world, for a while anyway, when B.B. King's music catches the wind off the harbor and blankets the area.

A few hours earlier, King and his close friend Buddy Guy, both slated to perform in the Pavilion, sat down for an interview in King's big, long tour bus. The two master blues artists shared some of the wisdom they've accumulated over the past decades. Whenever King spoke, Guy paid him reverential attention, as though the 76-year-old giant of American music were giving parts of a relaxed little sermon filled with great truths. If time allowed, these uncommonly kind and polite men would have talked for hours.

This is a tough, challenging time for Americans. Does the blues have the power to heal or at least make a collective people feel better?

B.B. King: Yes. Blues does the same thing any other kind of music does. Sometimes it takes your mind off things. People think because they named it blues that everything has to be (his hands cover his face in mock distress) BOO-HOO! That's bull. I don't know who the hell named it blues. But to us, if we're singing, and usually we are about a lady, and we want to get to her, we don't paint all the pictures that Frank Sinatra or Sammy Davis or some of the other people paint. (He starts singing a love song: "I see the meadows and the crows…") We get to the point! Baby, you're looking good! I'm crazy about you! Can I see ya! (Laughs.) We're still going to the same point, if you understand what I mean, so blues can make you blue, and if you are blue, it can bring you out of it.

Buddy Guy: We've been singing about hard times and good times all our lives. We've been having tragedy since the beginning of man. So what I try to do now is go out and just be myself. I just go ahead and try to do what I've been doing all the time: sing a joyful song every once in a while and remind people that we're singing about other things that happen in life.

B.B., what's your take on Buddy Guy, the man and musician?

King: (He puts his head back and fixes his eyes on a spot on the ceiling. A long pause follows. Finally, he speaks with palpable emotion.) Well, he's one of the great, great guitarists that we have. He's one of the nicest guys that I've ever met. He has the training that we used to get. We got a word that we use down home called "mannerable." That's him. It means he respects everybody, and he likes to treat people like he wants to be treated. I've known him for many more years than he looks. (Guy's a young and handsome 65 years old.)

Guy: I've learned most of what I've learned from you, B.

King: (Nodding at Guy.) He took good care of himself when a lot of us didn't, that's why he looks so damn meow. He's a fine man and a fantastic musician.

Buddy, how about the gentleman on my right?

Guy: You know, it would take me too long to try to explain it. I met him in 1958, and the first thing he said to me was: "I want you to come to my room tomorrow." I was shaking: "Wait a minute! B.B. King asked me to come by!" B.B. King was the guitar player that was squeezing the strings. There were young guys in Chicago, Earl Hooker and them, but he was the one everyone knew about when you turned your radio on. He had to put me out that day, when he got tired of me, because I wasn't going to ever leave. (Laughs.) I'll never forget it: I came back again to his room and found him [listening to] a new [recording] on a reel-to-reel tape. He went to sleep on me. I put the sheet on him and locked the door. I just cried when I left. I've never told him that.

King: The Pershing Hotel. (Laughs quietly.)

Guy: I said then, "There'll never be another [B.B.], as long as I live, I don't care how many guitar players." I got one of my guitars with two Bs on it. I tell Eric [Clapton] and them all they should put them Bs on their guitars. Eric said he will. I heard Lonnie Johnson and I heard Lightnin' Hopkins and I was in love with it all, but when B. made "Three O'Clock in the Morning," I said, "Now, who in the hell is this? Whoever it is, I don't want to ever go to school no more. I just want to play guitar." That turned my whole life around!

Who's been the most important person in your life? Musician, teacher, family member, anyone.

King: My mother. She died when I was about 9. I spent from 9 to 14 alone. I was what they called a "house boy" for a white family down there [in Mississippi]. I think about her and the training she'd given me from time to time. I used to be very skinny, and I guess my mother knew that, and she used to tell me that if I'd always be nice to people there would be someone to stand up for me. You know, they still do. People speak up for me if I'm in trouble.

Guy: I would say the same. I probably would have been in trouble if it hadn't been for my mother. My mother had had a stroke for like 19 years and I went to visit her. I had partied all that night. She could hardly walk, and she had this cane, and she says, "You're tired, ain't you?" And I said, "No." She just whopped me across the chest with the cane. (King laughs heartily.)

Buddy Guy
and B.B. King.
(Mark Wilson)

And I fell back across the bed, and when I woke up, it was 9:30 the next morning. She said, "When I tell you you're tired, you go to bed!" I'm like 24-years-old, and I didn't fight back.

King: You better not fight back!

How important is religious faith to you?

King: That's another thing that was instilled in me. My mother was very religious. The church we belonged to, the Church of God in Christ, had a guitar player. In fact, the pastor played guitar. Reverend Archie Fair had this guitar, and I had never seen the likes of a guitar before, never heard one before. So when I grew up I wanted to be like him. I was around five and I wasn't looking at the girls then. I was enjoying the music and the singing. Sanctified people could sing so good. I felt a certain way then that I've never felt again until I met the Pope two or three years ago. I felt like I really wanted to give God a message. There's got to be somebody stronger than us, and that's who we pray to. (Pause.) But when I was about 15, I'd sit on the street corner in Indianola, Mississippi, and I'd start off with a gospel tune. People would always like it and pat me on the head and say, "Keep it up, one day you're going to be great." But they never put nothin' in the hat. People who asked me to play a blues would always put something in the hat, and that's why I became a blues singer!

Guy: Oh yeah, my mom brought me up like that, man. I was put here by God for a mission—to make people happy.

Buddy, your new album *Sweet Tea* connects with your early years in the rural South, around Baton Rouge. You have a strong sense of tradition.

Guy: Muddy Waters. B.B. King. Howlin' Wolf. Those shoes will never be filled. Look around, just B.B. and me are still out there. If you had interviewed me 15 or 20 years ago, I'd have said there's a handful of us. Now the hand's not full. Actually from that area down south, B.B. and I are about the only two that's traveling now since we lost John Lee Hooker a few months ago. Junior Wells, Jimmy Rogers, all of them [gone].

You miss them?

Guy: (Softly and sadly.) Oh yeah. It's like a ball team almost. If you don't have the whole team out there, you can't win. Everybody has to pitch in.

When you're onstage, are you playing for yourself? For your musicians? The crowd? God? A combination?

Guy: When I go out there tonight, my whole soul and body are for the audience.

They've taken the time to pay a fee and come and see me when they could have been somewhere else, so I owe everything there tonight to them.

King: I'm a little bit different. I play to enjoy myself, but it's like cooking a good meal. Buddy brought me some gumbo the other night—and he was very concerned that I had enjoyed it. Well, I'm like that with my music. I'm on the stage playing, and I'm having a good time, but I wouldn't have such a good time if I was looking at the audience and nobody's moving. I'm not like the superstars with the people reaching up and screaming—OOOOHHH! AAAH-HHH!—I never had that, but if I can see one person moving their head, seeing one of them doing this here (pats his foot), then I know I got someone else enjoying what I'm doing, too. If I'm just going to play for me, I'll go and get in my room. When I put on a new set of strings, that's when I play for me. (Laughs.) You follow?

Buddy, describe your guitar style.

Guy: If you pay close attention, you'll hear B.B. King, Muddy Waters, those guitar players that I learned everything I know from. Buddy Guy never did have anything. The first time I saw B. in Baton Rouge when he came through there (c. 1950), I was about 14 or 16, and I was at the club waiting about two hours before he got there. This was right after that record ["Three O'Clock Blues"] I fell in love with so much. I saw him play, and I say, "Well, I can't sing like that, and I'll never be able to shake my left hand like that, but I'm going to get something out of it—and I did.

B.B.?

King: I don't really know how [to describe my playing.] Like Buddy, I had my idols. Lonnie Johnson was my favorite of all. Lonnie seemed to be that one guitarist that was the link between all kinds of music. He could play with Duke Ellington, he could play with Lightnin' Hopkins, he could play with Muddy Waters and Mahalia Jackson. He could play with anybody! And it seemed to fit in. I wanted to be like him. But I could never hear lows, when I say lows I mean bass sounds. I could never hear bass sounds very well. So when I finally did get an electric guitar, I'd always turn the treble up on it a lot. See, this is the first time Buddy ever heard me say this. (Laughs.)

Guy: I told him I was going to shut up and let him do the talking.

King: So I started to play the very first guitar that I had that was electrified. It wasn't an electric guitar, it had a pickup on it, and I would turn all the treble up on it, then I could hear the lows. Even today, I can't hear the lows real good. My bass player's played with me so long because he plays the way I want to hear it. It's sort of a twingy sound. So if you say, "How do you play it?" My answer is, "B.B. King twings it!"

B.B., people point to you as the person responsible for first bending guitar strings.

King: Yeah, I hadn't heard nobody do it before I started, but there's another reason, the same darn thing I just got through telling you, you hear something that ain't there and you push it up to where it is there. (Laughs.) I've always been crazy about the sound of the steel guitar. I've always been crazy about the Hawaiian sound, guys playing Hawaiian and singing, and the guitar seems to blend right in. And boy, these country musicians, they just kill me the way they play steel guitars. I could never do it. I only know of two or three black guys that ever played them. Buddy and them can use the bottleneck, but I can't do that for nothin'.

Guy: I can't get much out of it. I threw [my slide] away.

King: Yeah, but you do it some. I've seen you!

Guy: When I saw Earl Hooker, I threw it away. (Laughs.)

King: You and anybody else. Earl Hooker and Robert Nighthawk! You stop! And now you know who's so good at it? Bonnie Raitt. Because I could never do that, I would trill my hand. (He puts his hand out, palm up, and wiggles his fingers.) It sounded a little like the steel, the Hawaiian sound, when I trill it like that. I kept doing it so much, now I can't pick up the guitar without doing it. It was nothing that I had planned. It'd be a good story to say, "I did that because I knew it was." That's bull. It just sounded good to me and I kept doing it.

You both love jazz, don't you?

King: Yes! (Guy nods his head in agreement.) Even though I know what I like to play, I like to hear the guitar of any of these great people, Charlie Christian and Django Reinhardt, that were doing things that I wished I could do.

Buddy, you recorded Bobby Timmons' "Moanin'" in the '60s?

Guy: When I first went to Chicago [in 1958], I was looking for Muddy Waters and Little Walter, and I got the chance to meet Bobby in person there. I didn't think there was that much jazz in Chicago, but they had many jazz players and clubs. Dinah Washington was around before she died, and Buddy Rich and others had a big jazz club called the Blue Note.

King: I was friends with Dizzy Gillespie and Charlie Parker. I wished I could play bop. I was friends with Jay McShann. I knew Duke Ellington pretty well, and I did some tours with him. To me, Duke was the great teacher. When it comes to swinging, oh, it's hard to sit still and listen to Count Basie without moving your feet. I knew him very well. We used to play Keno together. A lot of the great ones I knew. And it's a funny thing: It seemed like they were the nicest people. Sassy Sarah Vaughan was one of the nicest people to me. Most of the great, great, great people in jazz were sweet as pie. If you were trying to learn, I swear, they'd help you. All you had to do was ask.

Guy: Did you ever do "Everyday I Have the Blues" with Basie?

King: With the Count Basie Band? Yeah! Memphis Slim, his name was Peter Chatman, wrote it and recorded it, but he didn't call it "Everyday I Have the Blues." Then later a guy called Lowell Fulson did it and he had it very slow. (King sings part of the first verse while keeping time with his hand on the couch.) He had a hit on it. Then I did it with my band about '56, and we had a hit on it. (He hums it at a faster clip.) Then later on Count Basie and Joe Williams did it, they had it "up," and, I don't know about Buddy, but the rest of us said, "OOOOHHH! HOOOO! HOOOO!" We finished now! Don't bother me with that one no more!"

January 2002
· ·
Tony Bennett
The Art of Being Bennett
by Michael Bourne

Tony Bennett approaches his music with the same passion that he brings to his painting. He dives into both with sincerity, commitment and integrity. And at 75 years old, the artist occupies a unique space in the music universe, his singular voice effortlessly straddling generations and genres.

See, in the foreground, the lines are heavy," said Tony Bennett, looking at a landscape drawn by Bruegel. "But then, as he draws back, the lines get lighter and lighter. It's the lighter lines that create depth."

"It's like when you sing without a microphone," I replied. "In the actual acoustics of a Radio City Music Hall, your voice isn't loud, but you project it, and an audience feels it much more intimately."

"The public is so used to hearing it miked and with the mechanical Reverbatron or all that," Bennett explained. "It's a shock to hear a voice when it's natural. When it's raw. No glitz. And funny thing, that's the one thing I do that people always remember."

"Because they have to listen harder."
"Because it's real."

When we're together, at a jazz fest or back home in New York, Tony Bennett and I don't talk much about singing. We talk much more about art. I showed him my sketchbook in Copenhagen. He hipped me to a Mondrian exhibit in The Hague and gushed about the medieval paintings in the town hall of Perugia. Or about how Chinese perspective is the opposite of how Western painters see a focal point.

If you only know Bennett as a phenomenally popular singer of the American popular songbook, you only know half of the cat. Bennett is also Anthony Benedetto, a successful painter of landscapes, cityscapes and portraits of his favorite musical artists—from Louis Armstrong and Frank Sinatra to Duke Ellington and Dizzy Gillespie.

He's been exhibited at various galleries through the years, including a 1994 retrospective at the Butler Institute of American Art in Youngstown, Ohio. He's presented many of his paintings in a 1996 art book, *What My Heart Has Seen*, and in the introduction, Bennett's long-time musical director, Ralph Sharon, wrote that "painting is becoming his second profession, but remains his first love."

Every day, wherever he's singing, he's painting. And according to his 1998 memoir, *The Good Life*, he's been doing both since he was a teenager. Now, at age 75, he's giving back to the music. He's spearheading a unique public high school, the Frank Sinatra School of the Arts in Queens, which opened its doors in a temporary home in

Tony Bennett.
(Jan Persson)

September (a permanent home is scheduled to open in 2003 in Astoria). After a rigorous audition process, 250 New York City ninth and tenth graders were selected to enroll in the school, founded by Bennett in the memory of his good friend and colleague Sinatra. In addition, Bennett has recently opened Bennett Studios with his son Dae. It's a state-of-the-art production center in a beautifully redesigned railroad station in Englewood, N.J. Besides serving as a professional recording studio, Bennett Studios also will feature the Tony Bennett Center for Media Arts, which will provide education opportunities in the recording arts to local students.

And yes, he's still singing great.

Playin' with My Friends: Bennett Sings the Blues (Columbia) is his newest album, a collection of stellar duets with Diana Krall, Sheryl Crow, Billy Joel, Stevie Wonder, Ray Charles, B.B. King, Kay Starr, Natalie Cole, Bonnie Raitt and k.d. lang. Bennett toured last summer with k.d. lang, which climaxed with a Sept. 29 concert at Radio City Music Hall—a crowded and much-needed revitalizing concert just two and a half weeks after the terrorist attacks.

And yes, he sang "Fly Me to the Moon" without a microphone, and his voice resounded to the highest balcony.

Earlier that week, Bennett and I did something we've talked about for years. We went to the Metropolitan Museum of Art together on a Monday—when the museum is closed to the public but open for him. We joined some Met members and patrons for a preview of an exhibition of 50 drawings by the 16th-century master painter Pieter Bruegel the Elder.

Bennett knows my passion for the Dutch masters, and I couldn't resist asking

if we could do an interview upstairs in the Dutch galleries of the Met. It was cool with the Met. And where better for two art-heads to talk than on a bench in front of a masterpiece, the painting that in 1961 was the first to be bought for a million dollars: Rembrandt's *Aristotle Contemplating the Bust of Homer.*

Do you feel a difference, a real physical change, when you're in a place like this looking at a Rembrandt?

Absolutely. Seeing the work of great masters, you learn from them more than you could ever learn from a constant study of painting. When you see a Rembrandt or a Velasquez, they inspire you.

Is there a split between the painter and the singer? When you look at this painting, is "Rags to Riches" or "When Joanna Loved Me" somewhere else in your consciousness?

I can simplify it by saying that I paint in the daytime and I sing at night. I'm very consistent, because I do both every day.

Does your life as a painter influence you as a singer?

Painting made me fall in love with life. By painting nature, you become startled by it. Everything that's alive becomes interesting, becomes fascinating. You can't believe the universe and what a gift it is. You just soak it all in, but you can't soak it all in, because the more you know, the less you know. Life becomes a complete mystery, and you fall in love with every aspect of it, and with the beauty of it. You can't understand why people descend into the lowest form of human behavior, which is fighting.

You also sing songs about life and your life. You've said that, like a "Method" actor

who looks to connect his own emotions with his character's, you're a "Method" singer and want to connect to the songs autobiographically.

That was my training. I applied the Method technique to singing. Telling stories with the songs. I came out of the Second World War on the G.I. Bill of Rights, and they gave us the best teachers. The American Theatre Wing gave me my acting teacher. His name was Zhilinski, and he was the secretary to Stanislavsky (creator of the Method). I enjoyed watching him more than any Broadway show I've ever seen. He could show you 13 different ways to cry or to laugh, 13 different ways to play a drunk. I applied the Method technique to singing. Telling stories with the songs.

Besides the acting, they gave me a bel canto singing teacher, and also a vocal coach, Mimi Speer, who was right on 52nd Street. That was when Art Tatum was there, and Billie Holiday, Erroll Garner, George Shearing, Stan Getz. All the greats were playing on that strip.

So you're learning bel canto, a very classical style of "beautiful singing" by day, then every night you're in the jazz joints of Swing Street.

Yeah!

I asked before if your painting has any influence on your singing, but what about the other way? Does your being a singer impact on your being a painter? Do you see parallels in your artistic lives?

It's not just music and painting. All of the arts have basic rudiments—form, color, what to leave out, the economy of line, simplicity. The same basic rules apply to cooking or playing tennis or any craft. But art and music are also quite different. With music, you're involved with other musicians. With painting, it's more introverted. You stand alone in front of this stark white canvas and you see what happens. And if you happen to get a successful painting, it's a victorious feeling.

I love when you sing "Speak Low," and I've heard you sing it at many concerts. There's one line: "Love is pure gold and time's a thief!" I've heard you suddenly shout "Thief!" as if in anger. I've also heard you whisper that same word with a haunting sadness. There's an impact to that moment however you sing that word.

It's like a strong line in a painting. But it's hard to compare painting and music. They're different, and yet there are the basic rules.

You've said that the first singer who

knocked you out was Al Jolson, and the first singer you wanted to emulate and learn from was Bing Crosby. Your favorite entertainers of all time have been Frank Sinatra, Louis Armstrong and Jimmy Durante. All five of these singers were wonderfully unique.

Right. That's the thing. I feel we've lost individualism. That was always the American style. It's like when Duke Ellington searched for musicians who were completely different. If someone played drums just like Jo Jones, he'd say that guy was just one of the chorus. He wanted to hear something different from each drummer, each saxophonist. Johnny Hodges was different, and so was Ben Webster, and right down the line. Coleman Hawkins. Charlie Parker. John Coltrane. Each one was an individual. That's the beauty of this American art form—to show that individualism. Not to become cattle with rings in our noses and we're all going this way.

But that's true of all art. To create something uniquely of yourself. I look around this section of the Met and see paintings that could only have been painted by these 17th-century Dutch masters. Character in a face only Hals could paint. Joyous folly in a Steen. Tranquil moments of time in a Vermeer. Drama but also whimsy out of Rembrandt's shadows.

If you go to a classroom, like at the Art Students League, you see everybody at their easels painting a model. If you walk around and look at the paintings, you can be impressed or unimpressed, but everybody is painting that model differently. Right from the beginning, art is a statement that we're all different.

To be successful as an artist you have to appeal to an audience.

You still have to be yourself. Looking for a style, or having a design to be different from the next guy, you can't do it that way. That becomes fashion, premeditated. Just by being yourself makes you different. Manet said to paint what you see. Just try to get a clear picture of what you see, and you paint that, and I guarantee it'll come out differently from anybody else's.

Each of us in an audience also responds differently to art. Each of us hears music differently, or sees something in a painting differently, and it might not be what you were seeing as you painted.

Rembrandt's *Aristotle* is a good subject to look at. It's so perfectly balanced because of the light. That's the most important thing when I paint. I just look for light. If the light is right on something, that's

what catches my eye. Another thing is that the hand [hanging to the side] is very faulty. If I'd done that hand, I'd say that I hadn't done it right, because it looks superfluous. And yet it isn't, because Rembrandt puts a tiny diamond on the pinkie and the light bounces like crazy from that dot. It's just a dot. The gold chain that comes down [across the torso] looks absolutely like gold and exquisite jewelry, but when you get up close to it, it looks like a complete mess. It's all kinds of bizarre and scruffy colors all mixed in, but as you step back from it, you feel the gold is right there in the painting.

Hearing and seeing are different senses, yet both connect to one's brain and heart and soul. What do people see of you in your painting or hear of you in your singing that is most truly yourself?

That's a difficult question. I have just one premise. About six months before Bill Evans died, he called me in some remote little town I was in, and he said, "I just want to tell you to keep it up." I knew he was talking about the record we'd just done. He said, "Just go with truth and beauty, and stay away from all the other stuff." Right there my life changed, because he gave me a premise to live by. I can't really answer your question, except to say that when you hit it, you know when it's truthful, and when it's right, it becomes beautiful. And it's always a search.

Now that I've arrived at 75, it's beautiful that what I've been doing is being accepted more and more, because I committed myself to never compromising, not with any song, not with any painting. I'm just out to do nothing but the best that I can.

You said in your book that the one song you never wanted to sing again was "In the Middle of an Island," but maybe now you could find truth and beauty even in that stinker.

You never know. There are lots of people out there who have different tastes, and my job is no less to entertain them, so I might end up doing that after all.

Even at the outset of your career, you said that you wanted always to find honesty in what you were doing. I hear singers all the time singing ornamental filigree all over a melody, but they can't sing one true note—when one true note can be so powerful and beautiful.

That's why I love Billie Holiday so much. She was so completely honest with herself. You heard it right away. It's a matter of finding yourself and accepting yourself and feeling comfortable with yourself.

The singers I've always been impressed with have been honest in that way.

Goethe said that a critic should always ask first what the artist is trying to do, but too many critics blather about what they think an artist should do.

Fred Astaire told me all he ever wanted to do was knock people out of their seats. Duke Ellington, Count Basie, Woody Herman, Frank Sinatra, all they wanted to do was knock people out. That's a cute way of saying it, but what it really is, is you've got to love your audience. If you don't love your audience, stay home and practice. I know there are guys out there who say, "I don't care what the audience thinks! I want to play what I feel and to hell with them!" OK, that's fine. But if you're on a stage, I still think we're servants to an audience. Not that there aren't other ways and styles to be able to say what you have to say, but I think you always should perform. Stravinsky was far out, but he moves you, he grips you, he gives you great performances. You can be as far out as you want to be, but you can still entertain an audience. If you don't dig the audience, don't do it.

Do you feel the same as a painter? Do you paint for an audience?

I do. The audience has to participate in a painting. It's like the hand in this Rembrandt. It isn't finished. So the audience has to fix that hand for themselves. You leave out something for the audience to see for themselves. Like in a Matisse or a Picasso, there's a lot of emptiness, or just white canvas. You might do a portrait and leave the whole top of the head out, or an ear at the side out, but you can still see that ear in the way the composition comes together. What you leave out the audience fills in with their own eyes. The audience contributes to the performance.

We meandered among the European paintings to the museum's Trustees Dining Room for lunch. Tony wanted to see some of my recent drawings and showed me his own ever-present pocket sketchbook, including a pencil portrait he'd just done of his drummer, Clayton Cameron. He also gave me a drawing lesson, showing me a way to anchor my hand while drawing short lines from point to point.

Then we drew each other.

My drawing of Tony was a nervous doodle, but in his drawing of me, I look quite serene. I have several of Tony's pieces hanging in my apartment, now proudly including a Benedetto Bourne.

Tell me about the Frank Sinatra School of the Arts.

I've acquired $70 million from the City of New York and Astoria, my hometown, and we're building a school there. Queens College gave us a whole floor as a temporary site. We've started now with 260 students.

Studying what?

All of the arts. We have great advisors. Paul Newman and Joanne Woodward. Eli Wallach and Anne Jackson. Annie Leibowitz. Wynton Marsalis. Alan King. Carol Burnett. Harry Belafonte is going to be one of the main advisors. It's a public school, but we're also going to have a foundation called "Exploring the Arts." We'll bring in artists to perform for the students.

One difference with this school is that we'll have the students go into the field before they graduate. We'll have them serve apprenticeships with Peter Max, LeRoy Neiman, or commercial studios. We're going to teach them form, whatever the art is, so that whatever they want to do when they get out, they'll have a leg up. We're teaching them basics. How to read music. How to paint properly. All the basic rules. The performers will go into the field and entertain, for the blind or at old age homes or at any benefits that have to be done, like now with this war effort.

Some new performers, they're manufactured, and they're out on a stage before they've ever been on a stage. Our students will get their feet wet. They'll be contributing even before they graduate.

I usually ask jazz musicians to name five favorite records, but I'm much more curious about your five favorite songs.

"All the Things You Are." "Last Night When We Were Young." "Remind Me." "My Ship." "Soon It's Gonna Rain."

Can you name your five favorite painters?

Rembrandt. Velasquez. Matisse. Van Gogh. Bonnard. Bonnard could fantasize in such a beautiful way. He could take an ordinary thing like a dirty bathroom and make it look like an Egyptian castle. Van Gogh I like because of the feeling. You can feel what he felt. The same with Rembrandt. You can feel his joy of painting. Velasquez, just like Rembrandt, conquered the art of painting.

Matisse is great for me because he stayed optimistic to the end of his life. His paintings became more and more simple yet symphonic. He actually graduated to a higher plane. Matisse was like Joe Venuti. The older he got, the better he played. I hope I can get better as I'm getting older.

What's your favorite color?

I don't have a favorite, but Duke Ellington said to me, "Your color is blue." I had a wonderful art teacher, John Barnicort, who told me Bonnard sketched a painting out, and before he put all the colors on, he painted it all ultramarine blue, so that when he painted the other colors together, the blue would still come out in various places. A lot of times, the base of my paintings is blue.

Same for jazz. The base of jazz...

The blues! Yeah!

Which brings us to your new album, Playin' with My Friends: Bennett Sings the Blues. *People don't think of you as a blues singer, but when you started singing in the Army, blues is what you were mostly singing. "Don't Cry Baby" on this new album, you were singing more than 50 years ago. A whole new generation is hearing these great songs that you've been singing all along, and you're singing duets with a whole new generation of singers, including k.d. lang.*

I was thrilled. They all hit home runs. Diana Krall is terrific, and Sheryl Crow. These contemporary singers on the album are the singers who've been able to sustain more than one or two records. They've become the real pros at what they do. Stevie Wonder is like the Irving Berlin of today. I've been so impressed by him. He's so prolific and always plays what he feels. He's very uninhibited. He's really a jazz player.

It's also nice that people today are getting to hear Kay Starr several generations since "Wheel of Fortune."

We did a show years ago called *The United Nations of Music.* We had George Shearing, Harpo Marx, Louis Armstrong and Kay was the President [Lester Young]. It was an experience I've never forgotten. It was a wonderful TV show. Louis Armstrong was hilarious, and he had a jam session backstage with Harpo! I remember that Harpo's son (pianist Bill Marx) was giving him modern chords to play. I was thinking, "Why isn't somebody recording this?" It was unbelievable, to hear that horn with Harpo.

Kay was so wonderful to me, and I just wanted to return the favor. Basie once told me, "You should make a record with Kay Starr," so I put the two of them together, with Kay doing Basie's "Blue and Sentimental."

One highlight on the record is much more emotional now, you and Billy Joel singing "New York State Of Mind."

My God, who could've dreamed...

You said in your memoir that, "New York has always been a creative force in my music and my art."

Anybody who ever communicated, like 99 percent of anybody who became world famous, would not have done that unless they made it in New York. Elvis Presley, Woody Allen, Johnny Carson—they all made it on *The Ed Sullivan Show.* Judy Garland's greatest performance was at Carnegie Hall. Benny Goodman changed the whole world of music at Carnegie Hall. The whole history of jazz emigrated from New Orleans to Chicago to New York.

What do you think is New York's greatest strength?

It's an open university, and we have the best teachers. Whatever your profession is, you have to rise to it and become a master, and that happens in New York more than anywhere else.

(Tony opens his book of paintings to an impressionistic view of 6th Avenue with a blur of yellow cabs streaming by Radio City Music Hall and flags flying all around.)

See all the different flags? All these flags of all these countries are in this city. The madness of it all, what these terrorists did, is that they didn't only attack New York. They didn't only attack America. They attacked the whole world. And one thing I love about New York is that the whole world is here!

January 2003

Reality Lessons

The Unofficial Mentor-Disciple Relationship of Andrew Hill and Jason Moran

by Greg Osby

Facilitating a conversation between two expressive and innovative artists is a rare and wonderful occasion. And the satisfaction of being part of such a meeting is magnified when you are the person who, in part, served as the bridge responsible for the union. This was the scenario in which I found myself while interviewing Andrew Hill and Jason Moran.

I was fortunate enough to be invited into Andrew's inner circle in 1988, when I was closer to Jason's age. At the time, Andrew had resigned to Blue Note Records (He's now on Palmetto and just released a big-band album, *A Beautiful Day*). During this period, Andrew and I shared many all-night one-on-one rap sessions and lengthy train and bus rides. I was the eager and willing recipient of advanced, and classified, information on matters of composition, concept and application—all with Andrew's personal philosophies regarding ensemble and performance logic. I have benefited immeasurably from Andrew's advice and examples, and now it's proper and timely that a "passing of the information torch" be documented.

I met Jason Moran in 1996 at the recommendation of his fellow Houstonian, drummer Eric Harland, who was a member of my band at that time. After a lengthy telephone discussion, which revealed a shared affinity toward perpetual development and lofty musical aspirations, I hired Jason and took him out on tour without even hearing him play a note—a risky move but not a regrettable one. It has been my pleasure to witness his development into one of the most distinctive voices on the contemporary scene.

Although I wouldn't characterize this as an official mentor-disciple relationship between Jason and Andrew (although Jason has taken lessons from Andrew), I will attest to the power of Andrew's influence on Jason, as well as on myself. Because of the information that can be culled, meetings like this should take place on a regular basis. So much can be learned from them, essential information that can't be absorbed in a classroom. Elements of the music must be passed on orally or, even better, by example. So what better example than Andrew Hill, with whom Jason Moran and I sat down to talk at a cozy bistro in Jersey City, N.J., on a September afternoon. Here's part of what transpired.

Andrew, you've influenced a lot of people and inspired even more. From your perspective, what do you hear in Jason's playing?

Andrew Hill: Sometimes you hear what might sound like a mature player, but

they're staggered—they'll be at that point for the rest of their life because they don't have a certain type of anxiousness and openness. What impressed me about Jason when I first saw him was that he wanted it. He really wanted it. It's like a voice from God.

Jason, tell me about Andrew's playing, concept and approach.

Jason Moran: The first time I read his name was in reference to somebody else. This is before I really knew about a lot of music, so I was listening predominantly to Thelonious Monk. Horace Tapscott came to Houston and they said, "This guy is like Andrew Hill and Thelonious Monk." Monk, I knew his music, but I didn't know Andrew Hill. Not a lot of people come through Houston, so a friend of mine gave me *Point of Departure*. It didn't sound like anything I had checked out. I was 15.

I don't know many 15-year-olds affected by something on that level.

Moran: I liken it to listening to Monk first, because he did a lot of things "kind of wrong." That was the first thing I learned as "right." He was really sincere. Andrew had things in *Point of Departure* that I thought could be sampled in rap songs. I was listening to parts. You know that part you wrote for bass clarinet on the second piece? I can't even think of the name of it. I thought, "This is so bad!" It was the phrasing, the band. How you picked musicians. Or how you didn't pick them! And they all came together and were able to perform your music in a manner that immediately drew me in. Then I'd buy all his records and they all sounded different. They weren't rehashed from record to record.

The one thing that captured my attention is the way you both approach solo piano. What do you think about when you're compensating for the lack of accompanying instruments?

Hill: It's a matter of getting synthesis with the audience. Sometimes I used to prepare numbers, and by the first 10 minutes I'm out of things to play. But then there's the magic of that moment, just playing piano and reaching that point where you can get the feeling. There's no way to prepare for a solo performance. You have this audience and then you have to become comfortable with yourself.

Moran: That was the rough thing when I did this last record (*Modernistic*, Blue Note). I was used to being in the studio with a bunch of other people, then I was in there by myself and it took three or four hours to get used to that, just playing

your song. But like you were saying, I can't really prepare for that.

Hill: You just have to realize you're ready for it.

Jason, as a young bandleader, what do you expect from your sidemen?

Moran: First is that I can actually talk to them on a personal basis before we hit the bandstand. I've never had good experiences with people I didn't like. When you meet somebody that you get along with and your personalities click: That's how you and I met, Greg—basically on the phone, before we played any music.

Then, when they start to play, there needs to be sincerity and truth. They're not trying to please me, but they're playing exactly who they are. Do your thing, if you have a thing. A lot of people don't necessarily have a thing that they play. Tarus Mateen actually has a style, a very aggressive style of playing bass. He switched from upright to acoustic electric: That's part of his thing, that he can play both of those instruments very well.

Hill: Have empathy and some type of professionalism.

What best describes a good composition?

Hill: One that other people can play and out of which they can bring something new.

Can it be incomplete and still be great?

Hill: Yeah. It depends on the artist. Sometimes you can give people a sketch and they come up with something more dynamic than one of your finished compositions.

You've written a lot of open-ended pieces that have taken on a different character each time they're performed.

Hill: In any group of people, different persons perform a composition. Each are radically different.

But there have been people who have fallen short of your expectations. What did you do to compensate for the lack of creativity?

Hill: I try to join in to get a common ground. It hasn't happened that much, but it goes back to the principle of the old jam sessions. You play on the level of the person if you can't go up. And I can't insult a player. I try to work with him.

Do you both have any determined approaches to composition?

Moran: No. I just choose whatever it is at the current time. Most recently I was transcribing people's voices for compositions. One time before that, I sat down and thought, "This is the mood I want to create,

Andrew Hill and Jason Moran.
(Lourdes Delgado)

or this may be loosely based off of a painting." I don't have a structured way of composition. If I hear one of Andrew's pieces, and I hear Andrew playing it, I know it's an Andrew piece. But if I hear somebody else playing an Andrew piece, I'm not going to know if it's an Andrew piece. If you hear somebody playing a Ravel piece, you're going to know it's a Ravel piece, almost because it always stays the same. It's written out so much that it's not going to change. In this music, you have a lot more liberties.

Do you have a host of characteristics, like themes, modes, voicings, anything that would identify your pieces?

Moran: I tend to loop sections, meaning I sample myself. It's basically a vamp, a James Brown vamp is all it is. But I tend to utilize that, even in other people's compositions, whether it's Brahms or "Planet Rock." I find a section I like and play over a certain section, to a certain point where it doesn't get boring. But I can't really listen to my music objectively and say, "This is what this is." I listen to it critically.

What strikes you about Andrew's music as an identifiable characteristic?

Moran: It changes so much. Most of the time I hear Andrew's music, Andrew is playing it. So that's the one thing. The

performer performing his own composition is a lot different than me playing Andrew's piece.

Andrew plays with such a personal touch. It's almost like the keys go five or six inches deeper than he actually plays it. When you see a key go down, it's about an inch, but the tone and the touch is so deep and soft and not cutting and abrasive. It's so deep and padded. A piece like "Ashes" is basically half notes and quarter notes, but the way the harmony moves and the way it resolves at the end is baffling.

Both of you approach playing with a heightened sense of percussion.

Hill: I haven't really thought about the percussive nature of the piano for six months. The piano has so many different things, you're always a student of it. One year you try to perfect your percussion. Now I'm trying to go into my dexterity. I'm still into rhythm. It's a natural response. I'm instinctively working on that stuff now.

So dexterity as a means for more explicit expression?

Hill: No. I used to be able to go one week without practicing and everything would be fine. But as I get older, there's a need to practice, because I'm not as pliable as I used to be. It's just like going to the gym for me. If I don't practice that way, I

find myself in an embarrassing situation.

Jason, your passion for hip-hop factors into your compositional approach. You performed the classic hip-hop piece "Planet Rock" on your current solo CD, Modernistic. *What can be done to make that a part of contemporary repertoire?*

Moran: In my teens, when I was getting heavily into jazz, I was also really into rap music. I would hear the same themes in the music. They're both African music. They have a lot of the same tendencies, but are expressed in totally different ways. I would see a relationship between a Public Enemy beat and Thelonious Monk's left hand. What I decided to try to address in this piece was to have that same feeling, but most of those rap pieces are so predominantly based on a hard, driving drum beat. How can you create that on a piano? My method was to prepare the piano. To put paper in it to make it sound like a snare drum, put clothespins on the bottom strings to make it sound like a bass drum. So you could actually have that feel, but it wasn't mean and sinister. And it still had a natural melody.

How much have you experimented with alternative keyboards?

Hill: When I was young I had an organ, a harpsichord and a piano. I experimented with electricity, but I just don't have the feeling for it, because it moves too much. That's why I wasn't much of an alternative keyboard person.

Organ, keyboard, synthesizer, computer laboratories—the sound moves too much to really deal with it. Like the piano, whenever you hit it, a certain sound comes out at a certain place. With electricity, I can't get used to the temperament because the temperament is never the same as it was before.

Moran: When those instruments started to really creep into the scene, were a lot of your peers flocking toward it? Or were they kind of blocking themselves?

Hill: It was well received, so everybody tried to play it. I had dealt with it earlier and couldn't deal with it, and didn't want to deal with electricity.

What new studies or directions would you like to involve yourself in that you haven't had time for in the past?

Hill: I'm open for anything. I'm having opportunities to do things I dared not dream of for decades. I've done things for big choral groups, symphonic orchestras, the string quartet; more so than anything, I just would like to continue to have the enthusiasm I have now.

And a steady pace.

Hill: I don't need that much work. When I was younger, it could be steady, but now it can be sporadic.

So what are you studying?

Hill: I'm doing remedial work on the piano. I have to relearn how to use the pedal. The sound pedal is a technique in itself. There's so much that can be done with it. I'm beginning to hear a lot of new things, so I need a different facility to get to what I'm hearing now.

How about you, Jason?

Moran: Two things: Playing solo, which in itself is a continuing study. Someone once remarked that one of my faults was using the sustain pedal too much. And I remember in one of my early lessons with Ellis Marsalis, he said, "Put your feet away from the pedal." It was hard for me to handle a natural legato in my playing. I quickly abandoned that taking my feet away! I need that crutch of the sustain. But there's a lot of things. Like Andrew was saying, small things like left hand. Returning to the art of finger dexterity. Because your technique is also an ongoing process.

We always have that discussion that "You are what you eat"; and if people practice scales and arpeggios, then their approach to improvisation is directly reflected in the way they practice. It cultivates their thinking in a certain way. Do you sense any danger in adopting a regimen?

Moran: Yeah, I do. I have a sign that says, "Routine Is the Enemy" on my wall. It's an old poster of these guys from the Depression era walking in order, and then there's one guy walking out of the line. I believe that to a certain degree. But I also believe that you should devote time to your art.

Hill: I notice most of the younger players, all they have is technique. Most musicians may not have feeling, but they do have the technique. You have to come up to a certain level, but once a person reaches that level, they should work on different things, especially on piano. You've got trick fingering on other instruments, but with piano, you've got to hit it! It's not like you can change a lot of stuff, create your own scales, which is interesting in itself.

There are certain techniques on piano where you can imply notes, you can "ghost" some sounds without necessarily hitting it, right?

Moran: Yeah, there are overtones where you play certain notes and the third will ring without you actually playing it.

But you have to be listening really close to actually hear that. It's so subtle that you might not actually hear it.

Hill: And with a band, that's lost anyway.

Moran: But there's a richness that should be investigated. One time I was watching you at Lincoln Center outdoors and I noticed you playing more below middle C than I had ever seen before. Not like I'd seen you play a billion times, but from the times I'd seen you, there was more of a devotion to a certain area of the keyboard that was almost forgotten. Everything tends to be up on the right side instead of the left side of the keyboard where you can get into some dense structures. I remember a lot of people saying, "Don't play or comp down there because it's muddy." I took offense at first because how dare you tell me where I should play. You have to learn to play the right combination of notes to where it all actually sings. Those are the things I'm thinking about.

Moving on, let's talk about the creative climate in the '60s. Was there a widely vibrant and abundantly collaborative spirit in the music, or is that an idealization and myth?

Hill: It's part reality, part myth. When we talk about the '60s, we have to go back to the '50s. It enabled us because instruments were so cheap, so from that there was an abundance of people who had instruments who could play them. Then you had all these great artists. Most musicians didn't have any other skills than what they did. People would get together, and bebop had grown so tired and stagnant that it was a pleasure to get together with different people and play. It was something that created itself from a need of its own. People were getting together with their ideas. Then the clubs started closing, so the only thing the musicians had was getting together and playing with each other.

So did you get together on a regular basis and talk shop with your peers?

Hill: In that time, you could. It's amazing when you think about it, how we got together, talked about your life, who played it right, how a note should be, how it should sound. You heard more music. People talked more about music then than now.

How about you, Jason. Do you get together with your peers and talk shop?

Moran: Shop? Not really. I talk to you. We talk about music. We rap on a fairly regular basis, whether it's about music or what happens in the band or what happens

personally. Yeah, to a certain degree. But not specifically with many other pianists. I talk to pianists like James Hurt or Vijay Iyer, but we talk less about piano than about a concept. They have a study, or a science to what they're talking about. But sometimes when you hear the science, it doesn't make sense to you.

Who did you go to for sage-like advice, Andrew? We come to you.

Hill: There was really no one to go to. You could go and they'd be more generalized in conversation. You might meet someone like Eric Dolphy. Eric was good to talk to. That's the good thing about jazz being more institutionally oriented. It creates more people to talk to about jazz. It produces a certain type of generalness about it. When you're by yourself, you're almost forced to come up with a different approach. That's why I say going from the '50s to the '60s was a different thing because this type of information wasn't available in a school. You would always have to talk to the musician and do your observances yourself.

Moran: I didn't really realize how what he just said was so profound until we just did a session with Sam [Rivers], and he was saying when he and Jaki [Byard] lived together and they would just find some composition book and they would go through the book together to actually create music. There was no institution teaching you how to play jazz.

Hill: People were eager to learn and share knowledge. So consequently, you've got all these different techniques and styles at one time. It's not like today where you say, "That's new school." Everyone had to come to a certain point on their own. That's the difference.

Universities are good for general knowledge, but they really don't do this job of creating freedom. Most people who go to these universities don't really start playing until two or three years after they get away from them. And there's still nobody to talk to. Like I told you in our first lesson together, "I'll take your money forever..."

Moran: (Laughing.) Yeah, you said, "Man, I took your money, then you didn't come back!" I didn't want to bother you. The lesson was so deep, what you were saying. I was still young and what you were saying was heavy.

Hill: You've got to find your own way, do your own researching, investigation and do things that you're interested in. One person may do something this way, but it may not work for you. But if you can hear it, it may be something you can bring out yourself.

February 2003

The Heath Brothers
Blindfold Test
by Dan Ouellette

Three's a crowd? Not when the Heath Brothers hang together. When the three (Percy, 79, Jimmy, 75, and Tootie, 67) took the stage at the live *DownBeat* "Blindfold Test" at last fall's Monterey Jazz Festival, they had the crowd in stitches with their wicked humor, highly opinionated observations and articulate critiques. But above all, the trio displayed a fraternal camaraderie—they enjoyed riffing with each other and thoroughly engaged the audience. At the beginning of the session, Tootie quipped, "Percy's gonna mess around and get a television show out of this." If a scout had been in attendance, the Heaths would be starring in a second season replacement program right now.

John Lewis
"Lyonhead" (from *Kansas City Breaks*, Red Baron, 1992, rec. 1982) Lewis, piano; Frank Wess, flute; Howard Collins, guitar; Joe Kennedy Jr., violin; Marc Johnson, bass; Shelly Manne, drums.

Tootie: (Immediately.) I hate it. Get that off. (Fakes snoring.) That's the Turtle Island String Quartet and some other guys (laughs). (When the piano swing part hits.) Ooh, yeah.

Jimmy: John Lewis, Percy Heath and the Modern Jazz Quartet.

Percy: That does sound a little Quartet-ish once they got going. That is John Lewis.

Tootie: That's Lewis. Is that Stephane [Grappelli]? I think they were all in Europe someplace and drunk when they made this.

Jimmy: Frank Wess, too. It's all right, but it took too long to get to the swing.

Percy: I wouldn't put this down. It's nice music. But it was too elaborate in the front.

Tootie: I hated it. It had no feel. Who's on bass?

Percy: It wasn't me. I wasn't there. That's Marc Johnson? That was John's boy back when he was the musical director of Monterey. Who's on drums? Is that you, Tootie?

Tootie: Oh, no. I made a lot of 'em that were nothing, but this wasn't one of 'em.

Stefon Harris and Jacky Terrasson
"My Foolish Heart" (from *Kindred*, Blue Note, 2001) Harris, marimbas; Terrasson, piano; Tarus Mateen, bass; Idris Muhammad, drums.

Tootie: It's Milt Johnson and Dave Blubleck (laughs).

Percy: It's Bobby [Hutcherson].

Tootie: These two guys can't decide whose solo it is.

Percy: That's called interplay.

Jimmy: Or counterpoint.

Tootie: This is awful. I hate it. Take it off!

Percy: People express themselves the way they see fit. It's a xylophone or marimba instead of vibes. That was interesting to combine with the piano. I'm not going to criticize a record I've never heard before. But I couldn't hear the drums in this mix. I wanted to hear more accents. And the bass player was like in a monotone. I wanted to hear more accents from him too.

Jimmy: Is this Gary Burton? I can't identify these guys. They were doing collective improvisation, which goes back to Dixieland and New Orleans music, just modernized. But it's not my cup of tea.

Percy: Me neither, but I would listen to it.

Tootie: I wouldn't buy it or listen to it. And I wouldn't recommend it. I hated it. There was no groove in it. I'm a drummer. I like having a beat in the music. That's why I listen to hip-hop, because they have a serious beat.

Jimmy: And it didn't have a melody. I'm a saxophonist and a single-note player, and I like melody. You start off with the melody and then improvise off of that. This just started with the improvisation. That was Stefon Harris? Oh, yeah, I know him, but I don't like this tune.

Benny Goodman Quartet
"Say It Isn't So" (from *Together Again!*, Bluebird, 2002, rec. 1963) Goodman, clarinet; Teddy Wilson, piano; Lionel Hampton, vibes; Gene Krupa, drums.

Tootie: I love this and I don't even know who it is.

Jimmy: And it's got a melody: "Say It Isn't So."

Tootie: From jump street, you can hear the beat. Hey, there's Lionel Hampton.

Jimmy: And Teddy Wilson. It's Benny Goodman and Lionel Hampton.

Tootie: Now that's jazz. There's nobody with a doctorate in symphonic music playing here. This comes from here (pats his chest). All those doctors are OK with me as long as they're the kind who are in the hospital.

Percy: These are the real guys. But I can't hear the drummer.

Jimmy: The drummer was miked down in those days. I knew all these guys, from that generation. I like this because it puts you in a certain mood. It's romantic. You don't have to intellectualize this to understand it. You feel it.

Tootie: I like the song and the beat.

Percy: That was wonderful. I enjoyed it. I knew all those guys, too. I admired all of them. The Heath family grew up listening to music like this, so this was perfect for me.

Misha Mengelberg Quartet
"Hypochristmutreefuzz" (from *Four in One*, Songlines, 2001) Mengelberg, piano; Dave Douglas, trumpet; Brad Jones, bass; Han Bennink, drums, percussion.

Tootie: [The trumpeter] is at home practicing. This is right out of the book. This has a beat but it's too fast. You can't pat your foot to it, you can't dance to it, so what good is it?

Percy: I don't know, but that piano keeps going on and on and on.

Tootie: And the trumpet sounds like a mosquito. I sure hope these guys aren't in the audience because we're gonna get beat up once they hear what we have to say.

Percy: This guy could play the trumpet. But everyone who plays doesn't necessarily qualify as a jazz musician. You've got to convey some experience. Maybe he hasn't had much except in school. But as a musician matures, he knows what to leave out. You have all those notes to use, but you choose which ones to play to tell a little story.

Jimmy: Was that Dave Douglas? Yeah, he's the media wonder, the favorite. They rank him as being very special. But I find his playing to be emotionless. It's like Tootie said. This sounds like he's practicing exercises. But I'm spoiled because I remember Fats Navarro, Dizzy and Miles. They had technique, but they also had feeling and emotion. I hear Clark Terry play one note and I know it's him. This guy played hundreds of notes and I didn't know who he was.

Illinois Jacquet

"Illinois Goes to Chicago" (from *Savoy 60th Anniversary—Timeless*, Savoy Jazz, 2002, rec. 1946) Jacquet, tenor saxophone; Emmett Berry, trumpet; Bill Doggett, piano; Freddie Green, guitar; John Simmons, bass; Shadow Wilson, drums.

All: Oh, oh.

Tootie: Now, those are our boys.

Percy: That's sweet. This is a good one.

Tootie: (At the tenor solo.) That's better than sex right there.

Percy: Or good accompaniment.

Jimmy: Sounds like the Beast. Illinois Jacquet. (At the trumpet solo.) And that sounds like Sweets.

Tootie: No, it's Russell Jacquet. No? It's Emmett Berry?

Jimmy: I never heard this. But I knew who it was right off. It swings and has a nice melody. Illinois Jacquet has always been one of my favorite saxophonists. I like his breath control, the way he sings and sustains notes. He has a beautiful sound and he's always in tune. He's a great saxophone player. I heard him just a few weeks ago playing at a dance at Lincoln Center. He was sitting down when he was playing, but man, could he play.

Von Freeman

"If I Should Lose You" (from *The Improvisor*, Premonition, 2002) Freeman, tenor saxophone.

Jimmy: (After a few guesses.) It's Von Freeman? He's got 80 years of experience and expression that he gave in that one song. I like this so much. I like his tone, his expression. He took some liberties that a younger player would take. Von is free of the chords. He's been in Chicago for all these years, back there with Gene Ammons. He has that warm tenor saxophone sound. To play this song as complete as he did without accompaniment is quite a challenge. I'd give him tops.

Percy: It was beautiful. The first few notes sounded Hawkish to me with the big tone. But some of his notes and the way he played chords was not Coleman. Von is talented. So is his whole family.

Tootie: This definitely had a beat. I could feel it. And I could identify with the melody. His sound was warm and wonderful. He fooled me because I thought he was

The Heath Brothers. (Teri Bloom)

a younger guy as he did some things that the younger kids are doing today, like playing outside the chords, the melody and the key. The name of the tune is "If I Should Lose You" and it sounded like he was losing it on purpose there for a minute.

Percy: But he found it again.

October 2003
· ·

Béla Fleck and the Flecktones
Expanding Worlds
by Jason Koransky

For the experienced touring band, the road can offer a font of creative inspiration. Béla Fleck and the Flecktones have toured relentlessly since forming in 1989, so for them, being away from home doesn't invoke stress. Rather, getting out of Nashville and onto a tour bus offers the band some time to relax and create a fertile songwriting environment.

When Fleck, Victor Wooten, Roy "Future Man" Wooten or Jeff Coffin come up with a song idea on the road, it's easy

for them to turn this seed over to the band. On tour, the quartet lives in close quarters; they focus on the band and the music at hand; and oftentimes, sound checks become rehearsals.

Take the evolution of "Puffy," for example. The song—the third track on the band's new triple CD, *Little Worlds* (Columbia)—bears a distinct similarity to *Black Market*-era Weather Report. The opening bass riff jumps with the exuberance of Jaco; the underlying rhythm and harmonic structure bears a distinct African sensibility, just like Zawinul would create; and over the top of this, the saxophone dances with the band in a Wayne Shorter–like melody.

This resemblance comes as no coincidence.

"This song started after we were watching a live Weather Report video on the bus," says Victor Wooten, the Flecktones' fleet-fingered virtuoso bassist. "The next sound check, I started playing that groove, thinking about Jaco [Pastorius], but playing it in a thumb way to give it a little different sound than how Jaco would have done it. But it still has his flavor. We just all started playing and it was slamming."

"That melody just spilled out of me at the sound check," says goatee-sporting, free-spirited Flecktone multi-reedist Coffin about the genesis of "Puffy."

"Once we started working on it, it had that Weather Report vibe going on," agrees

Béla Fleck and
the Flecktones.
(Paul Natkin)

Future Man (he jokingly—sort of—claims to come from 2050), Victor's brother and the Flecktones' rhythmic machine, who at times plays the acoustic kit and various percussion instruments, but usually is heard on the synth-axe drumitar, a guitar-shaped electronic percussion instrument of his own invention.

"While still being respectful to Weather Report, the song just lent itself to going all the way as a Flecktones creation," says five-string banjo player and bandleader Fleck. At face value, this comes across as an inconsequential comment. But really, it speaks volumes about the confidence that Béla Fleck and the Flecktones have in the integrity and nature of their music.

Just like Weather Report, the Flecktones possess a distinct, instantly recognizable sound; they may emulate, but they don't duplicate. They have recorded a body of work that, in addition to retail success (and similar waves of positive and negative criticism from the press), documents a group progression. And as a live act, they have ascended to almost unprecedented commercial success, just as Weather Report achieved in the '70s, playing to hundreds of thousands of devoted fans every year.

"People come out to hear improvised instrumental music, and our popularity just continues to grow," Coffin says. "There are one or two vocal tunes a night. But that's not why the fans are there. It's amazing to us every time we play."

Obviously, the Weather Report comparison should not be carried too far; the bands are two distinct animals. But the fact remains that the Flecktones are one of the best bands in improvised instrumental music today, just like Weather Report was in the '70s and early '80s. With only one per-

sonnel change since its formation—original Flecktone harmonica player Howard Levy left the group at the end of 1992, and the band continued as a trio for a few years until Coffin joined the fold—they defy the free agent trend in instrumental music. Sure, they all pursue active careers with their own bands and side projects, but Fleck, Wooten, Future Man and Coffin all return to the Flecktones as their primary gig.

This consistency has allowed the band to evolve to the point where *Little Worlds* was possible. It stands as a milestone, and coming in at well over two hours of music, featuring more than two dozen guests on songs that span three CDs, it offers the best songwriting and production of the Flecktones' recording career.

"The question is, Are you going to make something worthwhile out of the music, or is it just going to be a chops display?" says Fleck, 45. "For me, it's taking these fresh musicians and trying to make music that we all like. There are no other combinations of these instruments and these players in the world. I know we're not copying anyone. People can decide if it's an innovation or just a retread. What we have to do is express ourselves as musicians and people in our music, and make the music that we care about."

"Let me show you the real reason why I bought this house," Fleck says a few minutes after I arrive at his new home on the south end of Nashville.

The house rests near the top of a tree-lined hill, in an area that's more country than urban, where many successful Nashville musicians live. It's modest in comparison to the estates nearby, but by no means is Fleck's modern home unimpressive. Traces of music abound—open and

closed banjo cases, a piano, CDs and sheet music don't clutter, but are ubiquitous. One room and a closet are filled with dozens of banjos and guitars (including many of his pre-War era, 1932–'41 Gibsons), some of which he uses, others he never plays and are just part of an extensive collection.

"I'm kind of embarrassed to have all of this; I just play the banjo," says Fleck, a modest, soft-spoken New York native who possesses a dry wit and quick sense of humor. But being the most respected banjo player on the planet—a man who can traverse the worlds of jazz, bluegrass, classical and pop and add something significant to each—has its just financial remuneration.

We descend a staircase to the basement, down to the reason why Fleck bought this place. On the stone walls are numerous photos and concert posters, a gold record given to Fleck by Warner Bros. with all the albums he did for the label when they were trying to re-sign him (they lost him to Columbia) and more.

The key word here is stone: Almost all Fleck had to do was carpet the basement, and he had a perfect environment in which to record. So he has a full studio in his basement; this is where he spends almost all his time when not on the road. In the middle of the room sits a full Pro Tools rig and a multitude of recording equipment. Banjos and guitars are set up on stands; mike stands and cords are everywhere. There are couches, chairs, side rooms to isolate when recording and a pool table.

This is an environment that studio junkie Fleck cannot live without. *Little Worlds* exists on two levels. First, there are the raw performances from the quartet and the contributors. Then there's the mixing, mastering and manipulating of these parts: Having instruments seamlessly switch back and forth between acoustic and electric on "Latitude"; solos from various band members morph into each other on "Sherpa"; a 4/4 loop being inserted at the end of the 5/4 song "Sleeper"; and more. This is an area in which Fleck has developed quite an expertise, as he was an early devotee of Pro Tools.

"For a year and a half, when I came home, I'd come off the bus and start working on the album," Fleck says. "Maybe I have to learn to let someone else do some of the mastering, and my energy should be put into the overview of a project. But why would I give all the fun to someone else? The music comes alive while editing.

"There's a dichotomy between live and

studio playing. The counterpoint to our studio stuff is that we allow all of our live shows to be taped, and anyone can trade those for free. There are thousands of tapes of us playing together live. So how are we going to make a CD that appeals to people?"

The Wooten brothers arrive when we're downstairs, and they've brought along a couple of friends who they're going to take to the NAMM convention that starts later in the day. Coffin is not yet back from a tour with the jazz band he leads, the Mu'tet, and can't make the interview this Friday morning.

We go upstairs to discuss the making of *Little Worlds*. (I caught up with Coffin in Nashville two days later.) The album is the band's third recording for Columbia—following 2000's studio CD *Outbound* and the 2002 concert release *Live at the Quick*, which features a live 2000 recording of the Flecktone "big band" with bassoonist Paul Hanson, reed player Paul McCandless, tabla player Sandip Burman, steel pan player Andy Narell and Tuvan throat singer Congar ol'Ondar. The previous Columbia recordings (following six albums on Warner Bros.) showed a band whose rapport was reaching new levels of simpatico. *Little Worlds* appears to be the maturation of this process.

How did the concept for Little Worlds *come together?*

Future Man: It started with the idea that it would just be the band in the studio. It just organically grew, friends coming into town.

Fleck: We were supposed to go to Europe after 9/11, but nobody felt good about going then. So we had some time off and started recording. We figured we'd just record everything we had going that we liked, and some new stuff as it came up.

Wooten: We were taking our time. It wasn't like previous times when we would do a record in two days. With this album, we could record, leave, come back in a day or two, do some fixes.

Fleck: Everything was set up at my house, so all we'd have to say is, "Would you come over tomorrow night? The stuff's all set up."

Your songs are not simple—they weave together complex parts in odd time signatures. How does a Flecktones arrangement come together?

Fleck: Each guy makes up their own parts on 90 percent of the music. Because of this, we're not sitting around trying to figure out what the other guy wanted them to

play. We're using our creativity to create the parts we're going to play night after night.

Wooten: A lot of times there's trial and error. We're in a sound check, and we throw out suggestions as to what we should do. Everyone has the freedom to put forth their ideas. That's the cool thing why a song sounds like a Flecktones song, not a Victor song or a Jeff song. It really has a band sound.

Coffin: Anything we want to try, we try it. Regardless of what it is. And we try it until it's right. If at the end we don't like it, we discard it. But we won't discard it until that inspiration has been tried.

Fleck: And if it's not working, we know that. Or at least the leader of the song knows. Even if he doesn't love what's going on, he still doesn't tell the other person what to play. It's all about respect.

Future Man: Another subtle but important ingredient is that a lot of the stuff we play is free time. We are in the age of perfection where you have click tracks. But the time here is moving all over the place. It may start slower and pick up toward the end. You have the imperfection of the line, the ebb and flow. It breathes. Like on "New Math," there's a lot of time stuff happening.

What is happening?

Future Man: "New Math" doesn't sound like a big deal. It sounds natural and organic as we superimpose the times. We are in three and five at the same time. Béla's rolling in groups of fives. It's different than an Earl Scruggs roll.

Wooten: I hear the song start in 3/4. When my bass comes in it's 5/4. The whole song is like that.

Fleck: But they're all overlaying the same basic pulse. What's different about this tune than the other ones on which we've done counting in odd meters or combinations of meters is that it's all over the same pulse. In the same place where you're hearing three notes, later on you're hearing five, later on you're hearing seven. But the basic groove is not changing. We meet at the downbeat. It's just a three-beat bar, and everything else is being jammed into that space.

Future Man: "New Math" represents a new concept, that I'm establishing something and building off of that. I want to be able to play in whatever number you want to, wherever you are. So, if you're in 4/4, and you want to go into 7, you should be able to know where that 7 fits over the 4, in an organic way.

Fleck: [Future Man] has been teaching this to anyone who will listen, because it's an interesting concept. For 12 years my reaction was, "It sounds cool, but it sounds like math. How can we make music out of it?" It's taken this long just for it to click in my head.

It sounds as if the band has really reached a comfort level with Jeff as a band member on this album.

Wooten: Definitely. It was a stretch for him when he started to play with us, with all these odd time signatures. And we play fast. He had been doing mostly straight-ahead. That's been a nice element for us, because we hadn't been doing a lot of straight-ahead.

Coffin: When I hooked up with these guys six years ago, I was jumping into their stream. It was important to me to really make the transition in a way that wasn't changing their music. I wanted to become part of what they were doing, but retain who I am.

All the stuff [on *Little Worlds*] was written since I've been in the group. Béla's a very open musician. I bring in a lot of stuff, like Radiohead, Tortoise, Malian singer Oumou Sangare. When Béla heard the Tortoise album *TNT*, there were a lot of loops going on. He said it was tailor-made for the banjo.

Fleck: Jeff has really come into his own as a band member. He plays so many instruments. If you ask him what's his main instrument, he would probably say tenor sax. It's the one that if you compare him to other players, you'd say he's one of the great tenor sax players. But listen to him play the clarinet. It's beautiful. And he's a beautiful melody writer.

How has the band achieved such a synthesis with jazz, bluegrass, classical, African music and so many other musical elements?

Future Man: In the beginning, I remember that Béla wanted to do a jazz record. At the time the prevailing thought was that the banjo should just be in bluegrass. But that's not correct. If you look at all the early Louis Armstrong records, there was always a banjo. So if anything, this is bringing it full circle.

Fleck: Initially, we tried deliberately not to do bluegrass. If you listen to the first album, there is no bluegrass. It wasn't until the third album that we said, we have a banjo in the band. I shouldn't be ashamed of my bluegrass heritage. I should be proud of it.

Future Man: The first time we started

doing bluegrass, people in the crowd would be satisfied. People would hear the jazz side, the folk side, the classical elements. Different people would hear what they were listening for. That makes for a certain chemistry.

Fleck: I've heard lots of combinations over the years of disparate elements put together that I don't like. All through the '80s, you would hear these world music combinations that weren't working. We heard things in our music that didn't work. It takes an instinctive reaction, when the needle is going into the suck, you better change your part!

Wooten: All that's happening is you get high-level musicians, and we play music. This guy's instrument just happens to be banjo, this guy's instrument just happens to be the drumitar. We are all intelligent and speak English. So we can have a great conversation. It's the exact same thing with music. It's not the instrument that's making the music, it's the person. So if you get the right person, you can put any instruments together.

Future Man: That was one of the secrets of Miles Davis. He would put these people together based on their capabilities. A lot of times it's just what a musician sees in another musician.

Wooten: Bluegrass is an overlooked medium of music for most of us jazz guys. I recommend that jazz guys listen to some of this stuff, and try to play it. I've learned a whole new repertoire. That's the fun thing about the Flecktones. We get to play jazz festivals and bluegrass festivals, Bonnaroo and world music festivals.

Are the Flecktones innovators?

Wooten: When I look back at it now, even if I just take myself for an example, I realize, and I don't think it's too egotistical to admit, when the song "Sinister Minister" came along, the bass solo that I took, nobody was playing that way when it came out. But now there are people playing that way. I wasn't trying to be innovative. But that's just how I play. I see more banjo players now. I see electronic drums. I see the way that people say that the Flecktones started something new. But that wasn't the thought. That's the best way to innovate, when you're just doing what you do.

Fleck: What the band originally was, when I was looking for guys to do this television show *Lonesome Pines*, I was looking for guys who were innovating on their instruments. We had never even played together before the TV show. There's

nothing to be coy about. We're doing something new.

What's in the future for the band?

Fleck: I did the classical album (*Perpetual Motion*), and I've been writing a double concerto with [bassist] Edgar Meyer, commissioned for the Nashville Symphony. The Flecktones have done some symphony dates. For these, we just had a few charts that we dashed out, did two or three things with the orchestra, did our set, and they'd play some stuff. It was so much fun, and it sounded great. But we have not written the "Flecktone Concerto" yet. We need to write a great piece of work that we can go out and do with orchestras.

Future Man: I can see the drum set like a piano. And I see the piano like a drum kit. I use my fingers like sticks. I can get the complexity that you get with a piano, but you can get different harmonics. I was able to do some interesting things on the record with my new instrument, the RoyEl piano. I'm going to take everything I know about the drums and fuse it into a harmonic statement. When I was a kid, I saw Buddy Rich play, and I know that there's a way to express everything he did harmonically and melodically. Miles Davis said that the melody will be found again through the drums and the bass. I believe this, and am working on it.

November 2004

Godfather of... Jazz?

James Brown Reveals the Behind-the-Scenes Details of His 1969 Big-Band Gem with Louie Bellson and Oliver Nelson

by Aaron Cohen

James Brown jumps at the chance to talk about his voice. Internationally known through a string of titles—Soul Brother No. 1, Hardest Working Man in Show Business and, of course, Mr. James

Brown—he's America's most influential living musician. So that voice, whether singing, speaking, screaming or announcing one of his trademark accented grunts, has a considerable amount of weight. Today, as he sits on a couch in his sprawling estate that sits on an even more expansive few hundred acres in South Carolina, Brown wants to talk about how his shout connects to earlier days in the backwoods outside his window.

In 1969, when Brown's career was peaking, he took a detour from the funk to visit an old musical love. Recruiting one of the top big bands and arrangers, the singer made a jazz record called *Soul on Top* on King Records. The album was recorded in a couple of days, released but buried when Brown climbed different artistic and commercial heights with "Sex Machine" and "Soul Power." But collectors, and Brown himself, never forgot it. The reissue this year of *Soul on Top* (Verve) stands out as prominently among the current wave of jazz vocalists as it must have 35 years ago.

This album's plan was straightforward. Brown would interpret some standards, rework some of his earlier hits and sing an original that bandleader/drummer Louie Bellson wrote for the occasion. Arranger Oliver Nelson would help shape Brown's famous delivery so his rhythms would flow with the swing-based orchestra. Everyone also knew that the singer could only sound like James Brown, and it is this distinctive voice that makes *Soul on Top* far more than just a novelty.

Through his own take on free improvisation, Brown ties together funk's explosive first beats with Bellson's expertise on swing's divided pulses. *Soul on Top* is also one of the few jazz vocal recordings where a real American regional dialect is pronounced. Then, as now, such roughness was frequently polished away (or, in the case of Nina Simone, transformed into something else entirely). On this record, Brown's accent is as thick as the tar that his father scooped out of the South Carolina trees.

"The way we sing, 'gwine' is correct and 'going' is not correct," Brown explains from his red living room couch. "The Southern way was what got me through— I was real! And I don't perspire, I sweat.

"Just to show you what I'm saying, there's an African woman over there," Brown continues as he points to a statue across his living room floor. "And that piece of wood is harder than Italian marble. You can't cut through that wood. That's the motherland. It's down there, it's nature. That's what jazz is about. It carries a lot of history."

Brown's involvement with jazz stretches back to his childhood just over the nearby state line in Augusta, Ga., where his operations are based today. In his 1986 autobiography, *The Godfather of Soul*, he talks about singing gospel as well as rhythm and blues. He also watched the big bands pass through the region. A particular early challenge for Brown came when he tried to play Count Basie's "One O'Clock Jump" on the piano. Years later, he joked about that with Basie when the bandleader opened for Brown at Madison Square Garden.

As Brown began churning out his own hit singles in the 1960s, jazz informed several of his recordings. Sometimes jazz standards or arrangements appeared on his albums or records he produced for his colleagues. Many of these sides are still awaiting reissue. Several musicians who were trained in jazz have passed through his band—such as trombonist Fred Wesley. Brown adds that he constantly listened to jazz records while traveling to and from hundreds of one-nighters, even to the point where he had a turntable installed in his car.

"I used to drive a station wagon, a 1960 Mercury," Brown says. "And I'd listen to the Modern Jazz Quartet, Art Blakey, all those people. I couldn't get with those three-chord blues things. I had to go on."

Part of this progression were the instrumental records that Brown released under his own name, or under the names of his bands (such as the JBs). At a time when jazz singles were appearing on the same jukeboxes as soul 45s, veteran arranger Sammy Lowe conducted a big band that featured Brown on organ. Sometimes Brown played drums.

"I don't play [these instruments] well," Brown says. "I play them artistically."

By 1969, Brown had gone further than anyone could have predicted. The singer was selling millions of records, had personally cooled down the rioting in Boston during the wake of Dr. Martin Luther King's assassination and had entertained the troops in Vietnam. So Brown not only held the commercial clout to make a jazz album, he already had experienced genuine risks.

An admirer of singer Pearl Bailey, Brown also got to know the work of her husband, Bellson. "Louie Bellson—I didn't know that man could play that much

drums," Brown says. "That man has forgotten more than most guys know."

As their bands crossed paths on the touring circuit, they talked about collaborating, but nothing came of it until 1969, when Brown appeared on Joey Bishop's TV show in Los Angeles, where Bellson was in the band. Plans solidified at that meeting.

"James realized he was getting a together band," Bellson says today from his home in California. "I didn't have any problems playing R&B and gospel. Married to Pearl Bailey, going to gospel churches and being a die-hard Christian, all that came easy for me."

But what made Bellson realize that this would be a jazz project was when Brown told him on the telephone that Nelson would be the record's arranger and conductor.

Nelson brought his diverse experiences to *Soul on Top*. The late saxophonist had studied with composer Elliott Carter before working with Basie, Duke Ellington and Bellson in the 1950s. When Nelson recorded such albums as *Blues and the Abstract Truth*, he found new ways of combining the freedom of modern jazz with complex notated scores. He also used a distinctive blend of strings and French horns for the arrangements on Etta Jones' 1961 record, *So Warm* (Jones had once been signed to King).

Since Brown is not one to shy away from pronouncing his own individual abilities, it was somewhat surprising to hear him talk about his reliance on Nelson for this project. "I need somebody to collaborate with," Brown says. "I give them the basic idea of what I want and then they put it where it should be. Then I say, 'That should have been a seventh, that should have been a diminished to give me this kind of out sound.'

"Oliver Nelson was one of the greatest arrangers who ever lived," Brown continues. "That man was baaaad!"

When the band convened during two night-long sessions in November 1969 at Hollywood's United Recorders studio, Brown brought only tenor saxophonist Maceo Parker from his own group. The singer says he wanted almost all of the instrumentalists to be members of Bellson's 19-piece orchestra so *Soul on Top* would be seen as a jazz album. He also says Parker was initially uneasy about being thrust into a new situation.

"It was a strange thing," Brown says. "Maceo was afraid to play because of all those great musicians. But I said, 'Man,

just go and be yourself!'"

Ernie Watts, who played alto saxophone at the session, laughs when he is asked if he recalls Parker's trepidation.

"Maceo is one of the great players," Watts says. "So we had a nice time."

Like many jazz musicians of that era, Watts was a big fan of Brown's own songs. He was somewhat taken aback by the set list on the recording sessions. "I was pleasantly surprised that he did standards. He did tunes, and I was used to his R&B thing. But his inflection, sound and the way he hears melodically worked great."

As Brown and Bellson had predicted, it became clear early on that Nelson's arrangements were ideal. "Oliver knew how to write for singers as well as instrumentalists," Bellson says. "Some guys write great instrumentals, but don't know what to do with singers. He left a lot of holes open for James. Some arrangers write too many notes and the singer has to strive to hit all those high notes, especially with brass. But Oliver was perfect. We didn't have to change anything at all, it went down perfectly."

Blaring rhythmic declarations underpin everything on *Soul on Top*. This vitality is strongest on some of the ballads that the group transformed, especially the 1930s ballad "That's My Desire" and Hank Williams' country weeper "Your Cheatin' Heart," which becomes a boogaloo in the hands of this band. A sense of determination is underneath the insouciant surface of "For Once in My Life," which was a pop hit for Stevie Wonder a year earlier.

The mighty rhythm section on the date is a reason for this relentless push, especially with Bellson working alongside percussionist Jack Arnold and bassist Ray Brown. "Ray Brown was too good," James Brown says. "That's how good he was. He had no competition, ever."

"With Ray, you didn't have to worry, you had that anchor," Bellson says. "Ray rose to any occasion. I don't care what you were playing. If he was in there playing, you knew it was going to be right."

What's different about this recording is that Ray Brown plays electric bass. Bellson says that plugging in was not out of the ordinary for him, since he frequently had to do so for his television work. But bassist Christian McBride, who says Brown "played his ass off on electric," contends that the bebop legend told him he never liked the Fender.

Bellson remembers that James

James Brown.
(Charles Stewart)

Brown's own command of musical tempo made "Every Day I Have the Blues" such a success since timing is crucial on that song, even as this version is completely different than Joe Williams' performance. The group also recast some of Brown's more famous tunes into 4/4 swing, including "It's a Man's, Man's, Man's World" and "Papa's Got a Brand New Bag." Through his phrasing, Brown reinvented these songs with a unique take on vocal improvisation. Rather than scatting to get away from words, he gives new dimensions to familiar phrases. Since the LP truncated many of these performances to fit the allotted time, the unedited versions on the CD reissue offer the full dimensions of his delivery.

Two new pieces were also included in the sessions. Brown's production manager, Bud Hobgood, wrote "The Man in the Glass," which Bellson says was the only *Soul on Top* track in 12/8. The drummer also wrote "I Need Your Key (to Turn Me On)," where Brown delivers a seemingly extemporaneous mid-song speech about the double meaning of the title.

"The *'ki'* is like in aikido," Bellson says. "Unlike judo, you don't hurt anybody, you use your brain for positive thinking and James got a big kick out of that. I said, 'I wrote this for you, James, because I know you use *ki* all the time.'"

Leonard Feather, who observed the recording for the *Los Angeles Times*, report-

ed that the group worked together with impeccable discipline and by 6 a.m., "Nelson walked to the control booth tired but strangely relaxed."

"Watch what happens after this record hits the market next month," Brown told Feather 35 years ago for the *Times* story. "Everyone will be looking for jazz singers and jazz musicians to play for them. I haven't had a record in 10 years that didn't make the national charts; this one will start a trend away from those weird sounds and sloppy musicians, the ones who've been standing in the doorway keeping music out."

"We finished the record date," Bellson says. "We hugged and said we hoped we could do something like this again."

Nothing like *Soul on Top* ever did happen again. Brown tried out some of the material from the album in Las Vegas and demonstrates how he sang "It's Magic" in a voice that sounds a few octaves higher than his raspy conversational tone. The performance did not go over there, nor did it work in front of his fans in New York.

"I went to the Apollo, and I thought it would kill the people, but they didn't applaud," Brown says. "I went back to do my old show that was supposed to be greasy because it was alive and rough. I was trying to get away from the grease, and you can't get away from the grease, period. They're in the Middle East trying to find the grease, that oil!"

By 1970, the whole world was dancing to the deep funk of "Sex Machine." *Soul on Top* would have seemed like an anachronism.

About 25 years later, McBride was planning to record with James Brown. Alongside this project, he began working with Harry Weinger at Polygram to reissue *Soul on Top*. As they went through the vaults together and sifted through the tracks, McBride also remixed the record.

"We brought Ray Brown up a little bit," McBride says. "I thought that at certain points on the album, [the guitars] started stepping on each other. So we brought one guitar back, brought one up a little more, and brought the horns up a little more to make them more in your face. What we did was make it nice and even all around."

With record industry mergers a few years later—Polygram and MCA combining into Universal—the *Soul on Top* reissue was shelved. When McBride learned that Verve reissued it this year without his remix, he expressed his chagrin through a barbed essay on his Web site.

Bryan Koniarz, who produced the edition of *Soul on Top* that was released this year, agrees with McBride that, "In the merger, [the reissue] got lost in the shuffle." But he says that there was no reason to change the overall sound quality from the original LP release.

"When we listened to the vinyl here, we thought the vinyl sounded great," Koniarz says. "We tend not to remix things if we have the opportunity. Because we like to offer historical accuracy. If it sounds great, there's no reason to fool with it."

The key players on *Soul on Top* are just glad to see it out. "Sometimes you do something 40 years ago, you hear it again and say, 'That was good, but that was then,'" Bellson says. "Not so with this thing. It has the same spark and excitement."

At the end of the conversation at his home, Brown talks about trying his hand at jazz again. Perhaps as a singer, perhaps through starting his own label. He'd rather not divulge the details. Then Brown says that if he were to sing jazz, it will be "smooth, but funky" and launches into "Straighten Up and Fly Right."

"It will fit anywhere," Brown says about his possible future in jazz. "No boundaries. Anywhere we want to take it, it will go that way."

June 2005

Hank Jones

Family Legacy

Hank Jones on His Famous Brothers (Elvin and Thad, of course), Art Tatum, Coleman Hawkins, Melodic Integrity and Finding the Soul of a Song

by Joe Lovano
(with Ted Panken)

At the end of his photo session at the club Smalls in Manhattan, Hank Jones sat by himself at the Steinway. All of a sudden, the lid of the piano came crashing down, and Jones screamed, "Oh, God! It hurts! I broke my finger! Call a doctor!"

Consternation reigned. Joe Lovano rushed over, a look of concern on his face. Jones grabbed his hand, moaning, writhing, his face a mask of agony.

Suddenly the 86-year-old pianist smiled. "Gotcha!" He threw his head back and laughed.

A sigh of relief spread over the room, and the tone was set for an insightful interview. Jones is both a historical figure and a consequential tonal personality of the present day. A prime influence on generations of pianists—Oscar Peterson, Tommy Flanagan, Kenny Barron and Mulgrew Miller among them—for the logic and clarity of his conception, his playing projects energy, mischievous humor and joie de vivre. When stimulated—as he is on the 2004 Lovano–Jones collaboration *I'm All for You* (Blue Note) and this year's follow-up, *Joyous Encounter*—there is no fresher voice in jazz.

—Ted Panken

Hank Jones: I want to know from where you get your energy. Give me your secret.

Joe Lovano: I'm trying to feed off of you. The first time we played together was in Moscow, Idaho, at the Lionel Hampton Jazz Festival.

Jones: Ten years ago.

Lovano: At least 10 years ago. Elvin was playing drums. It was incredible to play with you and Elvin in that jam-session setting, call a few tunes and explore. Your feeling, sound and touch has taught me so much about orchestration—spontaneous orchestration within a quartet, for example.

Jones: Each player feeds on the other player. You gain something from every experience. Working with you has been especially beneficial because you have such a wealth of ideas. Your stamina is always there. I'm trying to follow you and at the same time give you some support. Sometimes, if I get a chance, I'll try to lead. But as an accompanist, I can't afford to lead. I have to follow what you're doing.

Lovano: You hit such a groove when we play, no matter what tempo and structure we're playing on. My playing has grown incredibly by interacting with you. And listening to you play with Charlie Parker, or Miles Davis, with Cannonball Adderley on *Something Else*, or the way you play on *Bags and Trane*. Growing up listening to those recordings gave me a sense of what this music is about, the communication within a band.

Jones: You should be trying to find your own groove. Accompanying is basic. It's a question of playing in your spaces. Support, but don't go ahead. Don't lead. Unless there's a big open space and you can make a suggestion.

Lovano: Listening to you with Charlie Parker, or behind John Coltrane or Milt Jackson, it's like you're feeding voicings and rhythms and sounds that are leading. In your accompanying style, you do lead.

Jones: Sometimes you have to.

Lovano: It might be an unconscious thing. You're not jumping out and saying, "Oh, follow me."

Jones: No, no. You lead according to where the soloist is going, because you can identify the progression that he's going to take. It's inevitable. It's a matter of logic. If you play a certain chorus, it's got to go a certain other place.

Lovano: Your playing has developed around a lot of your relationships with people, and listening to your recorded history is amazing. Can you talk a little about before you came to New York, and growing up around Pontiac, Michigan, and Detroit, and some of the key players you played with at the beginning—Lucky Thompson, Wardell Gray—with whom you played early on and then played with again years later.

Jones: That happened particularly in the case of Lucky Thompson. We worked together in a small band in Lansing, Michigan, led by a drummer named Benny Carew, who was a fine drummer, a good singer and a dancer. He was related to the baseball player Rod Carew. I had previously played with Lucky in that small band. Later he came to New York (he came before I did) and played with Hot Lips Page. In fact, he got me the job. That's how I came to New York. Lucky and I did two recordings in New York. His idol was Don Byas.

Lovano: I loved Don's playing. Did you play with him at any time?

Jones: One time. I was working with Hot Lips Page at the Onyx Club, right across the street from the Three Deuces on 52nd Street. Don Byas was working there. He came over to the Onyx Club on his break, and he played "Sweet Georgia Brown" with us. He played 40 choruses that night; he played until it was time for him to go back on the bandstand across the street. Every chorus was different.

Lovano: That period intrigues me. There was so much energy, and people were feeding off of each other. Today we have this incredible library of music that everybody studies. But back then, you had to be in a room with someone, and feel their tone, presence and energy. What was it like to sit in a room with Art Tatum, to watch him and hear him play?

Jones: His playing boggled the mind. He was so advanced, you couldn't believe what you were hearing. You could sit there and watch him for hours, as I did. When he finished his work at McVann's in Buffalo, he would go to a nightclub, or someone's home, and play until 11 or 12 the next day. He did things on the piano that were impossible, but he made it look so easy. As long as he had that case of Pabst Blue Ribbon beer alongside the piano, he could just keep on playing forever. He used to accompany singers. A lot of people don't know this, but he was a master accompanist. When he was playing with, say, Edna Day, who was the vocalist on this band with which I worked, he would accompany her in a manner that didn't require him to play solo.

Lovano: Some players would be intimidated by such a virtuoso like Art Tatum. Whereas you took that, and it inspired you to become yourself, to reach for his clarity without trying to play what he did.

Jones: Exactly. That's a mistake that some younger players make: They try to imitate. I've heard pianists play Art Tatum's solos practically note for note. That's fine, except that Art played it first. Pianists should concentrate on developing their own ideas. Imitation is good to a point, but not to the point where you're doing it note for note. You learn to have that same harmonic train of thought. The technical part is something else, but if you can imagine these things, if you can think of them, at least you can use your own harmonic interpretation, without playing it exactly like Art or any other soloist.

Lovano: The players that you heard all fused together, in a way—Fats Waller, Teddy Wilson, Tatum, Nat Cole. I've had conversations with colleagues of yours, talking about hearing you play in the '40s and '50s, and how you put things together from your own experiences and your inspirations. How did you feed off others and then let your own imagination work?

Jones: I've always listened to great pianists—all musicians, but particularly pianists—and adapted from their styles what I can put into my own thing without doing it note for note. Your mind automatically either accepts or rejects things. Your

preferences will take over. If you like something, you will try to adapt it, or use it for your playing and adapt it into your playing style in a manner that means you're not imitating, but in the same idiom.

Lovano: Did you hear a lot of music before you came to New York?

Jones: Quite a bit. I heard Teddy Wilson, Fats Waller, some Earl Hines, but I didn't hear Tatum until later. I patterned my style after Teddy Wilson and Fats Waller early on. They both played two-handed piano. When I arrived on the New York scene, I wasn't playing the way I play today. I was only playing in that style that I had been more accustomed to; that is, the Teddy Wilson–Fats Waller style. Then I heard the "bop" style. I've never been happy with that term. But when I heard that style, I thought there were portions of it that I could adapt into my own playing. I tried to integrate these things into my playing without becoming over-balanced one way or the other. I wanted to maintain the two-handed playing style.

Lovano: When did you first encounter Thelonious Monk?

Jones: I heard him at Minton's. His harmonic voicings were so different from anybody else's—and they still are. He always played everything with that stylistic approach, whether it was a ballad, or whether there was a bounce to it. It's a difficult style to emulate. His harmonics were so different.

Lovano: You play with such a beautiful searching feeling. Your harmonic rhythm is incredible, the way you place the changes and lay things within the structures of what we play. Playing with Elvin through the years had that same feeling—his harmonic rhythm, where he put the beat, where the chords fell. For me, it's coming from your approach.

Jones: That may be the key to Elvin's playing. His playing was musical. He approached everything from a melodic standpoint. He played the melody on the drums and the accompaniment at the same time. That's why his style was so complicated and complex. He was doing a lot of different things at once. Buddy Rich was one of his idols, as was Jo Jones.

Lovano: I was playing with Elvin at Ronnie Scott's club in London in 1987, the week that Buddy Rich passed, and it affected Elvin a lot. Gene Krupa and Buddy Rich were part of Jazz at the Philharmonic when you were touring with that unit. Who were some of the folks who were

on that with you?

Jones: On trombone you had Bill Harris. Charlie Parker did one or two tours.

Lovano: Was that the first time you played with Bird?

Jones: I think that was, except I'd heard him play at the Three Deuces. There was Coleman Hawkins, Lester Young, Harry Edison, Charlie Shavers, Roy Eldridge, Barney Kessel.

Lovano: Was Flip Phillips part of that?

Jones: Yes, and Ray Brown was on bass.

Lovano: When you first played with Ella Fitzgerald, was it part of that tour, or were you playing in her groups prior to that?

Jones: I had joined Ella as an accompanist during the time I was doing JATP. Later, Ella joined JATP. When I first joined JATP, Helen Humes was the vocalist. We did two tours a year, one in the spring and one in the fall. So it was a lot of traveling. Most of the big cities.

Lovano: There have been periods where you did a lot of touring and other periods where you were just in New York.

Jones: Those times were when I worked at CBS. I joined the CBS Orchestra in 1957. I was there for 17 years, and wanted to make it to 20 years so I could make the 20-year club, but the orchestra went out of business.

Lovano: You were doing studio work, and playing and recording some of the masterpieces of jazz. The ones I learned and studied were the Charlie Parker Verve albums, Lucky Thompson's *Tricotism*, *Bags and Trane* and Elvin's first record as a leader.

We actually recorded one of the tunes that you did as a trio with Elvin on *Joyous Encounter*. Thad was incredible on that record. He was one of the great trumpet players in the music, as well as a composer and arranger. I played with the Mel Lewis Orchestra right after Thad moved to Copenhagen. One of the first times we met, you came and sat in with us once during one of the band's anniversary weeks at the Vanguard. Can you talk a little about Thad, and the Thad Jones–Mel Lewis Orchestra?

Jones: Thad was an arranger who never studied the craft, per se. He never took a formal course in arranging, harmony, counterpoint or anything like that. He had this natural ability. Of course, he played with the high school orchestras and band. In fact, he and I went to Ann Arbor once on a trumpet competition. We played "Flight of the Bumblebee"—I was his accompanist.

Thad was a genius. A lot of people don't give him credit for being the trumpet player that he was. Everybody recognized that he was a great arranger. But he relegated the solo work to the guys in the band. In the Thad Jones–Mel Lewis Orchestra, there were four trumpet players, and they were all soloists. So they got to play the solos, and Thad just conducted.

Lovano: I learned so much playing his music, being at the Village Vanguard every Monday night for those years. Did you play in the band at the beginning?

Jones: Roland Hanna started with the band. Thad lived in the next little town over from where I lived, but I never got to see him. My schedule at CBS was pretty heavy. I was doing a lot of those shows, like Jackie Gleason and Ed Sullivan, and sometimes my day would start at 7 a.m. for a rehearsal. Well, if you're up until 5 a.m., it's pretty hard to make it at 7. So I had to leave the band. But it was a great experience.

Lovano: During the CBS period, were you also gigging around town?

Jones: It was difficult to do anything else except for recording dates. Generally, the recording dates took place during the daytime, so I could do some freelance recording.

Lovano: When did you start playing more as a leader? Was it after this period with CBS, or prior to that?

Jones: Prior. At Savoy Records, I did a lot of records with other people who were the leaders, like Sonny Stitt and Paul Gonsalves. Cannonball Adderley and his brother, Nat. Kenny Clarke was the drummer, and sometimes Shadow Wilson played drums.

Lovano: The things with Coleman Hawkins I'm sure propelled you to become a leader.

Jones: Working with that group was an experience. Coleman was a great player as well as an inspiration. He believed in doing something right. He set a great example for us. Miles Davis was in that band, Max Roach, J.J. Johnson at one time, and Fats Navarro. At Savoy, there was a time when I became the leader. That meant my name was on top; a leader in name only.

Lovano: But did you organize the sessions as far as arrangements or picking the repertoire?

Jones: When I was the leader, yes. You had a lot of freedom during those days. Ozzie Cadena used to be the A&R man there. We did a lot of things, sometimes with a quartet, sometimes with a trio, a

Hank Jones.
(Jimmy Katz)

quintet, and so forth.

Lovano: Thad and Elvin came to New York in the early and mid-'50s. You'd already been in New York for 10 years. When Elvin first was playing with Sonny Rollins and then the John Coltrane Quartet, did you go hear them? Did Elvin surprise you by the way he emerged?

Jones: He never surprised me, because he was playing that way before I left Pontiac. I knew that sooner or later he would connect; but I heard him play with Coltrane one time. I did a recording with Coltrane when he was playing with the band. For some reason, the pianist wasn't

able to be there—McCoy, I guess.

Lovano: I don't think that ever came out.

Jones: It may not have. But it was interesting. I never heard him play with Coltrane in a nightclub engagement. Our paths never crossed. Unfortunate, because Thad, Elvin and I should have recorded a lot more.

Lovano: You only did a few with the three of you. Elvin's record was in 1961, and it was during the period when he was playing with Coltrane. He was playing with such an explosive approach within the spaces of the rhythm. You, Thad and Elvin

Hank Jones.
(Jimmy Katz)

ly didn't inhibit their careers in the least. Thad and Elvin have had a great influence on a lot of people, and I hope that something I have played might have had an influence on somebody for the better. A positive influence. That's what you try for. Because you're not just playing for yourself, you're trying to raise the level of the art, actually.

Lovano: Can you say something about your parents, and the home life that nurtured all three of you to embody these principles in your art?

Jones: My father played guitar and my mother played piano, and my two older sisters, older than I. There were two older sisters, and I was the third one in the family. I'm the oldest male in the family. But both my sisters played piano, and everybody sang. Of course, I played for the church choir. Everybody in the family was musical. I had one brother who wasn't particularly musical, but he had a great musical memory. He had memorized all the solos on all the records we had. He could have been a great musician if he wanted. I had another brother named Paul who also played piano. You never hear about him, but had he wanted to continue as a pianist, he would have been a fine pianist.

Altogether there were 10 of us. Elvin's twin died as an infant. His name was Alvin Roy. Elvin's name was Elvin Ray. I always believe that Elvin in some way, psychologically or spiritually, was playing for his brother and himself. That may be a strange concept, but it seems likely to me, because he must have been conscious of his brother, even though his brother died as an infant. They were twins.

Lovano: That had to be tough for the family at the time.

Jones: It was. Music was a big part of our lives. It might have been the one thing that held the family together in the early years, because it was a common denominator we had.

Lovano: How old were you when you first left the Pontiac area?

Jones: I was about 20 or 21. I went to Cleveland, worked in a band that had Caesar Dameron.

Lovano: He was good friends with my dad. My dad played with Tadd Dameron.

Jones: He and Caesar were fine musicians. Caesar played alto and Tadd played piano.

Lovano: Did your folks ever hear you at Jazz at the Philharmonic, Coleman Hawkins or these other groups?

all seemed to have the same ideas with the harmonic rhythm, the melodic clarity and swing. There have been some other jazz brothers who have had similar empathy and feelings—Montgomery, Heath, Marsalis. But it seems like they've all been trying to keep up with the Joneses.

Jones: We all had a similar approach, maybe with some differences based on the types of groups we were exposed to or associated with. A lot of my playing when I first came to New York was studio work. Even

before I went to CBS, I used to do a lot of recordings where the only people you saw were the guys who did that kind of work exclusively. So it was a different musical approach. But basically, we had the same general idea, except that Thad and Elvin had a lot more talent and ability than I had.

I wish Thad and Elvin had lived longer, and I wish even more that the three of us had done more things together. We could have done some great things, but it just didn't happen that way. But it certain-

Jones: Unfortunately, my mother and father had both passed away. But both my mother and father heard me play in church. My father was like a musician himself, but he thought that jazz was evil, and he felt that certainly nightclubs were. So if you played jazz in nightclubs, you were in an evil environment. You couldn't play on Sunday. I was on a job once on a Saturday, and he yanked me off the bandstand at 11:30 p.m., because I couldn't play on Sunday. He was a deeply religious man. He didn't allow me to have even a pack of cards in the house.

Lovano: By the time you went to New York and started to travel and play, what did they think about your journey into the world of music?

Jones: My mother thought it was a good idea. I don't think my father was too thrilled with it. But eventually he acquiesced, because he knew that was the direction that I had to go.

Lovano: You've recorded thousands of songs. It seems like every song feeds you ideas, and you make it your own. Did you always have that approach?

Jones: Everybody hears things differently. I might hear a ballad like "Don't Blame Me" as something I'd like to emphasize. Or maybe I can take an excursion on a certain harmonic progression that nobody else would take because that's my approach. If everybody played things the same way, things would get monotonous.

Lovano: Has playing ballads through the years deepened your expression?

Jones: I think so. In a ballad, with the slow tempo, you have a chance to understand some of the nuances of the harmony, so you can explore some different harmony. Sometimes I even change the harmonic progressions. Maybe that's not a good thing, but I always try to maintain a certain integrity as far as the melody is concerned. The melody is the reason this song was written. Nobody writes a tune with just chords. The chords relate to the melody. So you have to be true to the melody if you're going to express what the composer had in mind when he composed the tune.

But you can change a lot of the harmonic progressions without damaging the melody. What I like to keep in mind is that if you can't help it, don't hurt it. This is the musical Hippocratic Oath. If you can't improve it, leave it alone. Many times you cannot improve on harmonic progressions unless you use a completely different harmonic approach that would change the

character of the melody. You don't want to change the character of the song; that is, to the extent it's not recognizable.

Lovano: Your approach with reharmonization is free. The first recording we did was a ballads project. I felt that to do a recording playing ballads, I had to have Hank Jones, the greatest accompanist of all time, be part of that rhythm section, with George Mraz and Paul Motian. It was a thrill to explore playing ballads that encompassed all keys, in a certain way, and all tempos. Everyone played with a free approach within whatever tempo we were in, and whatever song we were in harmonically.

Jones: Every group that is musically successful is successful because the members have an affinity for each other's harmonic approaches and in their general approach to music. You're on the same page. You hit from the first tune, and it takes off and stays in the air.

Lovano: You're free in the music. I love the way you play intros. When you set up a tune by itself, the tempo, the feeling and the way you lead into the melody is fantastic, and everybody has tried to cop that through the years.

Jones: The tune itself suggests whatever you do at the beginning. I think of the melody. I never think of the words because I never learn words. But the melody itself suggests what to use for an introduction. The idea that the composer expresses in the first four or eight bars, or someplace in the tune, gives you an idea about what sort of introduction would be appropriate for that particular tune.

Lovano: I'd like to address one thing about your touch and the sound you get on the piano. The piano sits there, you can have 100 different people come up to that same piano, and most of them will just sound like a piano player or the piano. Then you have people like Herbie Hancock, Chick Corea, Keith Jarrett, Bud Powell, Thelonious Monk or yourself, who can sit at that same piano and sound like themselves and have their own sound and their own feeling. Can you address some of your secrets?

Jones: I'm not sure there are any secrets. I'm always reacting to what I hear. That's why I say that the personnel of the group is extremely important. It permeates down from the leadership. It doesn't happen if the leader isn't there to set the tempo. By tempo, I mean the feeling of the tune itself.

There are lots of ways to play tunes. But there is always the best way to play a

tune. Every tune has a soul, a central thought. It's like a poem. Every poem has a central thought. If you can then identify that central thought, then you can appreciate what's being explained. The same thing applies to music. Every tune has a central thought, a musical idea, a form, an entity that lives. If you can then identify with it, then you can be part of it, and make it come to life. You have to live with it.

Lovano: Our new recording is called *Joyous Encounter*, and that's exactly what it is. It's unique because of the different generations within the group. Our music is multigenerational and multicultural, and the way we are gelling and putting things together freely throughout the repertoire that we're playing is inspiring.

Jones: When you say it's multigenerational, nothing could be more true. What happens in every generation is that people who are able to achieve that, who can move to that level, they tap into a stream of consciousness. It's there, and if you can tap into it, then you can produce music at that level. It seems like all the great players, like you, Coleman Hawkins and Lester Young, who have reached that level, all play that way because they've reached that level. It's not the easiest thing in the world. I'm still trying to get there myself. Just give me a little more time. Maybe another 100 years.

June 2006

Flowing Collaboration

Elvis Costello and Allen Toussaint Travel to New Orleans for the City's First Major Post-Katrina Recording

by Dan Ouellette

Allen Toussaint's house still stands, but remains uninhabitable. His recording studio is gone, swept away. The diaspora to which he belongs persists. And his city's music endures, even if its musicians have been scattered by last fall's maelstrom. But New Orleans, presently a hint of its former glory, will be fine in the future, says Toussaint, the city's 68-year-old maestro of popular music.

The soft-spoken, refined Crescent City native—who's temporarily residing in New York while waiting for his house to be refurbished—has a positive outlook. "I've heard people worry about the city becoming a Disneyland when it's rebuilt," he says. "That'll never happen. New Orleans has something about it that says, 'I'm this.' That will prevail. The baptism of Katrina didn't kill that."

Toussaint smiles and nods across the hotel suite at the W in Union Square to Elvis Costello, the pop music omnivore who shares his passion—and optimism—in restoring the New Orleans soul that sired the heart of American music. Costello also served as the catalyst to their collaborative CD project, *The River in Reverse*, which was the first major recording project tracked in New Orleans after Hurricane Katrina and the subsequent floods. It serves as a poignant and joyful testament to the city's cultural legacy.

"Popular music wouldn't be what it is today if New Orleans was only about Louis Armstrong," Costello says. "People think I'm exaggerating when I say something like this, but it's true. The music there is so deep, wide, rich and beautiful."

As for *The River in Reverse* (Verve Forecast), Costello says, "I don't want people to think of this as a grandstand statement. This album began as a way to celebrate Allen's songbook and his voices—as a piano player, arranger and singer—that have been underestimated."

But he acknowledges that the recording of the album became something bigger. It's a symbol of hope that the spirit of New Orleans will again shine vibrantly in its homeland. As for his role in the recording, Costello says, "I can't adopt the legends of the Mardi Gras and be credible. I had to find my own way to express how all the music that has come from that city has affected me over the years."

Both looking dapper in suits and sipping cups of licorice tea, Toussaint and London-born, New York-based Costello are preparing to perform a showcase of music from *The River in Reverse*—a mix of obscure Toussaint tunes, collaboratively written new songs and a fresh Costello number written in the aftermath of Katri-

na—in the intimate Joe's Pub later this evening. It's mid-February, a few months after the plethora of benefit concerts for hurricane relief and fundraising CDs, when the attention to the cause has waned.

It's no surprise then that the Costello hookup with Toussaint has been suspect in some camps and chastised by detractors who question the former's motivation. In its capsule preview to the show at Joe's Pub, *Time Out New York* wrote that "Costello's late-breaking buddy-buddyship with... Toussaint to us smacks of opportunism. Moreover, the pairing just doesn't make sense."

On the surface, the Costello–Toussaint team does seem like an odd partnership. Personality-wise, the two couldn't be more different. Costello, 51, talks fast and beams in boyish enthusiasm as if he were living his wildest dream every day as a musician exploring beyond pop-music constraints. His mother, who worked in future-Beatles manager Brian Epstein's record store in Liverpool, once said that when she was pregnant she listened to all kinds of music—from jazz to pop—so that her son could learn to appreciate music in the womb. The jovial Brit is a classic extrovert.

In contrast, Toussaint is a reserved introvert with a gentlemanly manner who speaks slowly and quietly in a slight Southern drawl. He's steeped in the A-through-Z of New Orleans music, and comes from the Big Easy piano school of Professor Longhair. "I'm a Fess disciple," he says. "He's my patron saint, my Bach."

While Costello and Toussaint come from different planets, they're both on the same page when it comes to music. Each admires the other for his sensitivity to song craft.

As for Costello seeking out a "late-breaking" friendship with Toussaint, the allegation lacks substance. In fact, the two worked together twice before, dating back to 1983 when Costello sought out Toussaint to produce his rendition of Yoko Ono's song "Walking on Thin Ice" for an album of interpretations of her own compositions she was releasing.

"I heard Allen's songs before I knew his name," says Costello, who remembers well the fondness of the Merseybeat bands of his youth for Toussaint's song "Fortune Teller." He was also a fan of R&B singer Lee Dorsey, who was a hit-maker with many of Toussaint's tunes, including "Ride Your Pony" and "Working in the Coal Mine."

"Lee Dorsey's music was when I start-

ed to pay attention to who was behind the songs," Costello says. "It was like a good secret. Little by little I got the story that he wrote or arranged this and that and that."

When he was becoming established as a rising-star pop artist, Costello was also seeking out his heroes in vital outposts of American music such as Memphis and New Orleans. "When we'd tour, on our days off, I always tried to plot out a way to get to those towns that I wanted to visit," he says. "For Yoko's song, I knew I could only record it on the road. I thought of making the impossible request—getting either Willie Mitchell or Allen Toussaint to produce the track. I called Allen up and he said, 'Let's do it.' We went to New Orleans and spent three days at his Sea-Saint Studio. It was difficult interpreting a song as unusual as Yoko's, but we did a good job. Plus, it was magical working with Allen. It was like a dream."

In 1988, a couple of years following his 1986 *King of America*, Costello began working on *Spike* with his co-producer T Bone Burnett. Recording sessions took place in Dublin, London, Hollywood and, because Costello "was hearing some different sounds in my new songs," New Orleans, where he enlisted Toussaint. "I felt completely confident working with Allen again," he says.

In the liner notes to the expanded version of *Spike*, Costello wrote about recording with the Dirty Dozen Brass Band and Toussaint at Southlake Studio: "[Allen] pretty much set the scene for 'Deep Dark Truthful Mirror' with his colossal piano part [while] the Dozen played off his performance.... It was like seeing a sketch turn into a painting."

Toussaint didn't know much about Costello before they met. "I just knew there was an Elvis Costello," he says. "But I was stationary in New Orleans. New Orleans was cut off from the rest of the world in many ways. What was common knowledge to other folks, well, you'd have to leave New Orleans to check that out. I didn't know his music."

But once Toussaint got to know Costello, he recognized him as a "scholar" of all stripes of pop. "Once I started to hear his world of music, I didn't know how I could have been sheltered from it that long," he says. "I'm glad I'm wide awake now."

Costello regrets that he lost contact with Toussaint, but was pleased to run into him when they both performed on the same stage at the 2005 New Orleans Jazz and Heritage Festival.

Their next encounter came in the wake of catastrophe. Costello was on holiday on Vancouver Island with his wife, Diana Krall, when Katrina hit New Orleans and the levees were breached. One of his first concerns was for the well-being of Toussaint. He contacted his friend Joe Henry, who told Costello that he heard Toussaint was fine, that he had vacated New Orleans for New York at the urging of Joshua Feigenbaum, who co-founded NYNO Records in 1996 with Toussaint to record music from the Crescent City.

The next day, Sept. 4, Costello played the Bumbershoot Seattle Arts Festival main stage as a solo act. "I wanted to sing what was in my head and heart," he says, "so I closed the show with Allen's 'Freedom for the Stallion.' I sang it to remind people of what was happening in New Orleans."

As Katrina approached the Crescent City, Toussaint figured he'd weather the storm. "I had been through hurricanes, and I thought I knew the nature of them," he says. "They come and wreak a little havoc, then you take your boards back down and put 'em back behind the garage. I've had 12 inches of water in my house more than once. I knew how to handle that. I wanted to stick it out. But this was quite different."

Toussaint checked into the Astor Crowne Plaza Hotel on Bourbon Street, but as the city's plight worsened, he took a bus to Baton Rouge and caught a flight to New York. Feigenbaum called Toussaint the day before the storm hit. "Allen refused to leave, but then came here when he could get out of the city," Feigenbaum says. "He stayed up here, but got depressed every day watching CNN. So I asked him if he wanted work, and he said sure."

Feigenbaum contacted Bill Bragin, who programs Joe's Pub and who had been the founding general manager of NYNO Records. "I asked Bill if maybe Allen could open up some shows on the piano, and he said, 'We can do better than that,'" Feigenbaum says.

Bragin recalls a conversation he had with Dan Melnick, the artistic director of Festival Productions, about what the music community could do to help in the aftermath of Katrina. "Our conclusion was that [since] we produce concerts, we should produce concerts," Bragin says. "The best way to help New Orleans musicians was to let them do what they do—make a living and support their city by making music."

Since Joe's Pub's evening shows were

Allen Toussaint and Elvis Costello.
(Jimmy Katz)

booked, Bragin inserted a couple of solo-piano weekend matinees featuring Toussaint. Remarkably, this was the first time he had ever performed solo. They were immediate sellouts. Meanwhile, Wynton Marsalis had asked Costello to perform at the Jazz at Lincoln Center Frederick P. Rose Hall benefit to raise hurricane relief funds. Costello told Marsalis about his Bumbershoot tribute, that Toussaint was in New York and that he wanted to perform the song with him. Costello and Toussaint hooked up and rehearsed.

"We followed McCoy Tyner and Harry Belafonte," Costello says. "McCoy played this mind-bending music, then Harry came on and it's like hearing Moses speak. All I could do was sing the best I could."

The performance was not only moving, but it also planted a seed. With the wheels turning inside his head about putting together a Toussaint songbook album, the next day Costello caught his Joe's Pub matinee. "I didn't know what the album would look like, if I could produce it or maybe sing on it. But I knew that Allen's

songs and the tradition he comes from are so central to jazz and popular music."

Around the same time Costello and Toussaint performed together again at the Madison Square Garden "From the Big Apple to the Big Easy" benefit, Verve Music Group A&R exec John McEwen contacted Costello with a similar recording concept. "Allen and I started discussing what this record would look like," Costello says. "We agreed to record selections from his songbook that were not the obvious ones that everyone knew—songs that were close to the heart. And we discussed the possibility that we could write some songs together."

For Toussaint, everything in his musical life was suddenly converging at a whirlwind tempo. "I always make the distinction between the pace of New Orleans and everywhere else in America," he says. "We sort of mosey along in New Orleans. I've been coming to New York for years—for business and I have family in the Bronx—so I know the pace here. You have to hold your hand out and catch it. That's what I understood about Elvis' exhilaration. As fast as the pace of New York is, the pace of Elvis is even faster. There's a lot going on with Elvis."

After a tour in Europe, Costello returned to New York in early November, and the pair met up in Feigenbaum's apartment. "It was a comfortable place for them," Feigenbaum says. "I got the piano tuned up and made sure they had plenty of tea. Then I got out of the apartment and let the two professionals work."

Nothing jelled at first. "It seemed like the piano was antimagnetic," Costello says. "We couldn't touch it for a long time. It was like we had never heard music before."

The icebreaker was Toussaint's minor-key version of Professor Longhair's classic "Tipitina," which he had played at Joe's Pub. "A door opened with that onto a whole [musical] history that never gets talked about," Costello says. "I wanted to catch something of the feeling of what Allen was playing, to write lyrics that fit with the melancholy and reflection of this piece. It's a presumptuous thing to add new lyrics to something as indelible as 'Tipitina,' but I wanted to adopt the signature of Allen's music, like the hymnal cadence in the chorus."

The next day Costello sang the lyrics of the retitled "Ascension Day" to Toussaint. "Allen liked it. We couldn't get on the piano fast enough," Costello laughs. "I was playing the guitar, Allen was playing the piano, and then sometimes we were both on the piano at the same time, our two hands crossing over. You know you're getting to something when you're saying to each other, 'It's this chord,' 'No, it's this chord.' I could never presume to tell Allen how to phrase anything, but sometimes I would come up with a voicing or harmonic idea. We went from having nothing to different kinds of collaborations. When we wrote 'Six-Fingered Man,' we were completing each other's sentences musically."

Toussaint had never experienced a songwriting collaborative session like that before. "Elvis came so well equipped," he says. "He comes with ideas. Elvis was the general leading us to the hill."

Toussaint songbook tunes, including the funked-up "On Your Way Down," the gospel-tinged "Nearer to You" and the soul cooker "Tears, Tears, and More Tears"—all newly relevant in light of Katrina's ravages—are open to interpretation, Costello says, then adds, "But why change something that's already perfect? Allen's arrangements already have all these nuances that were integral to the composition."

Soon after working up a batch of tunes, Costello and Toussaint, who both sing on the project, headed into the studio to have, in Costello's words, "a dialogue between people from different parts of the world."

Pegged to produce the sessions was Henry, who had also produced the Toussaint tracks ("Yes We Can Can" and "Tipitina and Me") for Nonesuch's *Our New Orleans* 2005 benefit album. He had been in conversation with Toussaint about recording an album of his material for his *I Believe to My Soul* series when Costello came up with his songbook-album idea. "Elvis didn't want to get in the way of something I had planned, but I felt that Allen should have the opportunity to do whatever he should pursue," Henry says. "So, we all decided to do this together."

Henry first became friendly with Costello when he produced Solomon Burke's comeback album, *Don't Give Up on Me*, in 2002. "When I hit problems bringing the concept together of *I Believe to My Soul*," Henry says, "I used Elvis as my sounding board and champion."

When his original pianist for the project bowed out, Costello suggested contacting Toussaint, who jumped at the last-minute invite. "I was flabbergasted that he agreed," Henry says. "He pulled the project together. I keep his picture on my wall as a reminder."

Even though he knew Costello and Toussaint, Henry still felt nervous about his role in *The River in Reverse*. "I'd never produced artists and their bands before," he says. "I always saw myself as a smart casting director—putting a band together and then directing the proceedings to try to make the magical and unique happen during the conversing and collisions. But here I was being asked to bring my point of view to a project where Elvis had his group and Allen had his people. As it turned out, they needed someone to take charge, to take the wheel and drive."

Henry found Costello to be "an open-hearted collaborator who was trusting" of suggestions and Toussaint to be "the producer's producer and the closest person alive that has the open-mindedness and transcendence of Duke Ellington." The first day's session was daunting in preparation, Henry recalls. "But the apprehension evaporated once it became clear how respectful everyone was to each other and how much we were on the same page philosophically with the material. The first day's sessions produced three masters and provided the template for the rest of the recording."

The group at the session consisted of Costello's rock band the Imposters (Steve Nieve, who switched from piano to B-3, bassist Davey Faragher and drummer Pete Thomas) and Toussaint's electric guitarist (Anthony Brown) and horn section (baritone saxophonists Brian Cayolle and Carl Blouin, tenor saxophonist Amadee Castenell, trumpeter Joe Smith and trombonist Sam Williams).

The first week of the *The River in Reverse* sessions took place in late November at Sunset Sound in Los Angeles, then moved to Piety Street Recorders in New Orleans in early December. Nearly the entire album was performed live with minimal overdubs. "You listen to the mix back, and you hear how much life there is in the music," Costello says. "That's where the vitality of interpreting songs comes from. You can hear it in Allen's song 'Who's Gonna Help Brother Get Further?' I can't think of a better question to ask right now, but not in a heavy-handed way."

Costello beams at Toussaint's lyrics and recites the last verse: "What happened to that Liberty Bell I heard so much about? / Did it really ding dong? / It must have dinged wrong / It didn't ding long." He loves those lines: "That's why we sing the verse twice. I like the idea of handing the words back and forth, playing it like a little group having a conversation."

Also on the CD is the urgent and angry title track that Costello penned the afternoon before he appeared at *The New Yorker* magazine's benefit event at Town Hall in September. The lyrics in the chorus are pointed:

"Wake me up
Wake me up with a slap or a kiss
There must be something better than this
I don't see how it can get much worse
What do we have to do to send the river in reverse?"

"I wrote the song in 10 minutes," Costello says. "I had all these images floating around in my head for a week and they suddenly solidified into that song."

While the album has its Costello–Toussaint-composed moments of gloom, including the funerary march-beat "The Sharpest Thorn" and the disgrace-in-darkness "Broken Promise Land," *The River in Reverse* also buoys in celebration of the

New Orleans sound. The up-tempo "International Echo" is spiced by Toussaint's Longhair-like breaks and drenched in images of how the power of music cannot be denied. "That's a song about how music comes from one city, travels around the world and then rebounds back," Costello says. "I wanted to show the joy of that. I'd never written a song about music before."

Toussaint notes that the entire project was Costello's brainchild. "I was the yes man," he says of the project, which will be featured at festivals across the country this summer. "I enjoyed the journey, especially how the tunes would grow from one day to the next. We arrived places. It wasn't just wishbones and feathers everywhere. We took every step with integrity and faith, belief in what we were doing."

Before the hurricane and flood, there were nine recording studios in New Orleans. Only two were in business at the time *The River in Reverse* was recorded. "It was wonderful [going back]," Toussaint says. "Elvis was insistent about recording the project there. He wanted the authenticity because I'm from there. But we also wanted to show that there's life in the city, that this isn't a total dead zone."

Costello experienced the city in a different way. Going to New Orleans wasn't a homecoming, but a shock of reality. "It was emotional," he says. "You arrive at an empty airport and then see blown-down signs everywhere. The first day I was there I walked around the streets and all the franchise businesses were closed. They'd just left town. Local businesses were struggling to keep going because of a lack of patrons. The first day at Piety I asked my driver if it would be too morbid to drive me to where the flood hit the hardest. He drove me to where the breach in the levee had occurred in the Lower Ninth Ward. It was horrifying seeing the destruction at eye level after having seen it through a television lens."

Toussaint adds, "We'll all be coming back. Elvis wanted to bring that musical life into the album. That was the thing to do and he followed through on it. It was the right thing to do, to breathe life into the area."

It's a first step, though Toussaint is a realist. He soberly says, "It's going to take a lot of money to rebuild, but it'll also take a lot of guidance. You can't just take the money [for rebuilding], throw it out there and see where it winds up."

But he remains hopeful about New Orleans' revival. "The city is the cradle of American music," Toussaint says. "Babies are still being born, they'll pick up a trumpet and tap into the tradition, and the music will prevail."

August 2006

. . . .

Mastering His Music

Dave Douglas Solidifies Control Over His Adventurous Career

by Steve Coleman (with Dan Ouellette)

While Dave Douglas won top trumpet honors in the Critics Poll, his influence in the past year has been manifold. His Greenleaf Music, a joint effort with Chicago's Michael Friedman, continues to evolve as a pioneering artist-run independent label. Through this label Douglas has pursued ambitious projects, such as last fall's *Keystone*—which features scores for Fatty Arbuckle silent films—and this spring's *Meaning and Mystery* quintet disc. He directs the Festival of New Trumpet Music, with its fourth season in New York running Sept. 15–Oct. 15, and he's artistic director of the Banff International Workshop in Jazz and Creative Music. He also continues to explore ever deeper compositionally.

In early May, Douglas, who lives in New York's Hudson River Valley, and fellow creative artist Steve Coleman, who resides in Allentown, Pa., rendezvoused at a friend of Coleman's apartment in the Bronx to converse about the creative process, the recording industry and life as an expressive jazz musician.

The two exchanged e-mails before the session, though Coleman piloted the back-and-forth with freewheeling improvisation. "I didn't want to plan this out much by sending you all of my questions," he told Douglas, then joked, "If you knew the questions, you'd already have your answers, so I wouldn't be necessary."

At the close of their 110-minute dialogue, which ranged in subject from eso-teric music philosophy to the nuts and bolts of staying artistically fresh, the two agreed that they'd like to keep their conversation going in the future. "This could go on for days," Douglas said, to which Coleman replied, "Yeah, let's hook up again."
—Dan Ouellette

Steve Coleman: Why did you decide to record with a major (BMG) after your success with several smaller labels?

Dave Douglas: I was on 10 different labels before BMG/RCA—great independent labels that gave me the opportunity to do what I wanted. In 1999 some majors approached me. I wasn't sure if I wanted to go that way, but I decided that giving creative music worldwide exposure was an opportunity I couldn't pass up.

Why BMG?

Back then the head of the label was Steven Gates, to whom I was introduced by Steve Backer and Bob Belden. I had conversations with a bunch of labels, but Steven was the only person who nodded when I said that I wanted each record to be a different band, a different project, a different vision. The way I work is defining a new direction with each set of music.

And the execs at the other labels?

One literally laughed at me when I said that. I don't want to name names. RCA was excited about working this way and wanted to support it. And they did. I made seven radically different records for them in a fairly fast amount of time, and they supported them all. I can't say that was the hippest business decision. Maybe that side of me shoots myself in the foot, but I did it.

What happened at the end with BMG?

When I was finishing my contract, BMG was merging with Sony. Nearly everyone was getting fired. In fact, there were five different label heads in my six years with the label. I wanted to continue working the way I had been, but I had a few arrangements I wanted to amend. After the merger, I knew those negotiations weren't going to happen. So I had two options. One was to buy RCA myself.

(Laughing.) Yeah, that's one choice.

But I looked at my bank statements and I thought, not yet. I decided not to go back into a relationship with myriad independents. I wanted to be in one place. Plus, I wanted to own my own masters, which is what every artist who really thinks about it wants. I would love when I'm a great-grandfather to still see my recordings out there. During this time, I was talking a lot with Mike Friedman about the direction of the recording industry and how it was going through this huge transformation that could be to the benefit of independent artists doing music off the beaten track. If you look at sales figures overall, jazz is definitely off the beaten track. Mike and I talked about formulating a label that would be successful and not lose money. You know the old joke: How do you make $1 million as a jazz record label? You start with $3 million. I wanted to avoid that model.

I talked with Mike recently when I was in Chicago to see Von Freeman play. He told me that the vision of Greenleaf Music would also include other people beside yourself.

That's true, and it was important to have a 50–50 royalty agreement between label and artist. Why should the investment of years of an artist's life be less valuable than the money a label puts up to support the artist? I was certainly inspired by what John Zorn has done with his 50–50 profit sharing with Tzadik. So we have this great band from L.A. called Kneebody on Greenleaf, and we're talking with other people.

How's Kneebody doing?

It's been OK, but it's tough to break a new artist.

As an independent label, how do you go about marketing, which is what the majors are supposed to be better at because they have more resources?

After the first year of Greenleaf's existence, we radically changed our take. We were doing the traditional brick-and-mortar distribution, but then we started to see the chains and independent record stores closing down. We also noticed that people who listen to alternative music are much more involved with searching out an artist they're interested in. We shifted to a much more Internet-based distribution. We found that easier, but the one concept that's not going to change through all this record industry shifting is an artist having contact with an audience at live shows. We sell a ton of records at shows.

Frank Zappa said that he made more money through his own Barking Pumpkin label than he ever made with the majors, even though he was selling smaller numbers. And Tim Berne, who plays very individual music, has his own label, not quite like ArtistShare, and does everything himself.

It's interesting you mention ArtistShare. You can't ignore what they've done with Maria Schneider and Jim Hall. That

model has had an influence on the industry. During this shift, at this moment, there are dozens of new models. It'll be interesting to see what happens.

Especially with the new technology.

Yeah, and also the delivery of the music. But we've found that downloads aren't that big a part of the business yet. We sell 90 percent to 95 percent of our CDs by mail order. But Greenleafmusic.com is also a central location where I can put up my essays and even do radio streams where we get an artist to program two hours of their favorite music, then we pay the rights for the music to stream. That's increased sales at our online store, and now we even house other musicians' albums that they've made themselves, like Marcus Strickland, Maurice Brown and Michael Moore from Amsterdam.

But the one thing about these new business models is that listeners and people who love music also have a responsibility to support the artist. It doesn't take a lot. With an artist-run Web site, you assume the goodwill of people—that they will buy the CD but not copy it for their friends. I see it at gigs. With a group of college guys, where once I'd sell five CDs, now I just sell one. How you purchase music is a political decision. To perpetuate the music, people have to pay back into the system. It's only happened a few times, but I've been approached by fans asking me to sign a CD-R. They don't understand the humor of that.

As far as playing for live audiences, do you think your success has had anything to do with touring a lot? I think of someone like Charlie Hunter who got grassroots notice by traveling around the country in a van and then got signed by a major as a result.

Charlie, yes, and The Bad Plus today. And Medeski Martin & Wood. They got in an RV and crisscrossed the country for years. People used to complain: How did they get so big? Well, they went on the road. If you're willing to put in that kind of work—and it ain't easy playing 200 gigs a year with everyone in the band willing to commit—it's a no-brainer.

Do you feel there are too many CDs, that every high school student, college student and professional musician is putting out an album even if they can't write, can't play and haven't developed musically yet? I'm wondering about the quality or originality of ideas.

We're certainly saturated. I get so many CDs—in the mail, at concerts—I

can't listen to them all. I make an effort to listen to everything, at least a little. But I do respond to every e-mail—fan mail or a question.

I do, too. It takes a lot of time.

Yeah, but I'm wrestling with what you're saying about saturation. I hear you, but I also think if people have the opportunity to say something, it's good. But in hindsight, music of value will stand out. Look at the '40s and '50s. There was a lot of clutter then too, but the great figures are who we think of now. Of course, there were probably musicians we don't know about who were important then.

So you feel like it's a free market thing where some cream will rise to the top.

The market is too free. We should have more support for artists and composers. It's a bigger question: How can we support artists versus having too many people recording CDs?

When you compose, do you create for yourself or think about people in your audience?

If music is a communication, then you've got to communicate to somebody. When I compose, I don't just play anything. But there is that element of intuition or magic that's unexplainable, mystical. There's an interior place where you go and communicate with the entire universe.

But do you write for real people, with somebody in mind—of course, not naming names?

(Laughs.) Yeah, like my friend Billy from the fourth grade.

I read a quote from Michael Jackson once where he said he wanted to make music that touched everyone in the whole world. And I immediately thought, that's not me. That sounded bad to me.

(Laughs.) And he made a record called *Bad*. Seriously, everyone who reads this magazine loves music and has a strong opinion on what they hear. It's about what moves you. When I hear a piece of music I like I want to capture it so that I can share it with someone. Composing is sharing those moments with somebody who is moved by sounds. That's what I want to communicate. When I write, I try to find those places of spark. My happiest moments come when I'm onstage performing a new book of music and the band plays a tune the way I heard it and the audience hears it too.

Does the band change the vision of your composition during a performance?

Absolutely. The ultimate is to reach a

piece of music in a different way each night. Music I write has to be open enough for each musician in my band to add his own voice to it.

Do you write songs with lyrics?

Very few. I find it difficult to communicate with words. I've taken poems and written music to them, but it's dangerous because music is so powerful it can change the meaning of the words. The greatest songs are when the music and words come together and you're equally affected by both. I performed in a setting where five composers were asked to write music to Stanley Kunitz poems. It was hard because his poems have the rhythms built into them, so I composed based on a piece of prose he wrote that, paraphrased, said, "I aim for art that's so transparent you can see through it and see the world." That made it easier for me to write tunes to other poems. It was the key that unlocked the door, so I did a book of music for Andy Bey to sing that we performed at the Village Vanguard and later at the Guggenheim Museum.

Tell me about that piece I saw you perform recently, "Blue Latitudes."

It's music for a chamber orchestra and three improvisers. I used a specific tonal language derived initially from a 12-tone row but developed with a set of chords and pitch sets and then from working on a way of phrasing.

We're all familiar with the 12-tone language, but not everyone is familiar with it conversationally.

But the general listener can put their ear to it and get it. I've been using it for more than 15 years, and you're one of the reasons why I'm using it.

Me?

Yeah, you. I went to Visiones in 1990, and Greg Osby asked me to sit in. So I played on a tune. Then you came up, and I got my ass kicked around the stage by you guys throwing the M-Base language at each other. I went home and was so impressed that you guys had this language I couldn't speak. That was enlightenment. That's when I decided I wanted to come up with my own language for improvisation, which was using 12-tone lines and writing tunes for my bands with that. That's led me to play lines that are not clichéd, not overused.

Some musicians, especially younger ones, are not concerned with cliché. I've had conversations with some who say, "I don't care. I just want to be the best player I can be."

That's great as long as you put yourself into it. It's like the [Lennie] Tristano school. You pick one hero and play every note they ever played and model yourself on them. And that's how you become a musician.

Who told you that? Lee Konitz?

No, Mark Turner. He picked Warne Marsh and he doesn't sound anything like him because he's Mark Turner. My goal has been to reach out and expand my language. I identify that in your music. I hear that in your bands. The way you use rhythm is unique.

It's something you develop.

It's what makes the music succeed. There's a deeper lived experience behind it.

Those are the reasons why you're attracted to certain music in the first place.

Right. The most frequently asked question I get is why I studied Balkan folk music—in the late '80s before the fall of the Berlin Wall and before the records were widely available. I honestly don't know. I wish my family had Balkan ancestry, but it doesn't. I found the music fascinating and I wanted to bring that language into jazz. I discovered rich, meaty stuff by listening to the brass bands of Macedonia, and looking into the Balkan musical language spoke to my language of playing in odd meters. It was like learning how to play modal jazz, with which I now have a mixed relationship.

We can't let that slide by. What do you mean by that?

In 1987, Horace Silver told me and Vincent Herring, "You young musicians all got the wrong musical lesson from John Coltrane."

(Laughs.) Now, that's a hell of a statement.

Horace's point was that people who listen to 'Trane play all that stuff over a D-minor seventh chord. They want to know how to superimpose and put the most complex substitution in. In Horace's musical world, what was hip in music wasn't what you played over one chord, but how you got from one chord to the next—voice leading. That lesson has stayed with me. If you look closer at what Coltrane played, the reason all those superimpositions worked was because they were so brilliantly rhythmically voice-led.

So, where does the mixed feeling come in now?

I've been focusing more on voice leading. I've been studying 15th- to 18th-century counterpoint and looking at Bach chorals a lot. I'm not saying that's what music should be, but I'm fascinated by the voice leading in that. It's definitely not modal music even though it came out of modal music 100 years earlier with chants.

There's an energy that exists in place and time that affects all of us. That vibe goes through each of our filters and comes out. Graham Haynes told me that he could hear what Wynton [Marsalis] was doing as similar to us. I said we're all in the same era and we're all responding to the same stuff.

But it's also important to note that different people are picking different parts of the history to emphasize. Certain things are going to get lost, while other things will take on more importance than they should.

It's all in the details, living moment by moment. There's a lot of detail you don't see by just looking to the past. Looking back to the '40s and '50s is like seeing the highlights of a basketball game on ESPN versus seeing the entire game. We're not hearing conversations that Charlie Parker was having. In the future, no one's going to be writing books about this. It's just a moment, but it may be an important moment to you or me or both. It may be an important energy node in our lives that has a grand effect.

Looking back to the '40s and '50s is fascinating, but looking back to the recent past is just as fascinating.

How recent?

The whole era of the '70s and '80s, between the so-called golden age of free jazz in the '60s and the re-emergence of mainstream jazz in the '80s. That middle period is a hazy area that doesn't get talked about much. A lot of artists from that period have not become part of our generally accepted history of the music.

Like Henry Threadgill.

And Julius Hemphill and even Woody Shaw. I had a conversation with Anthony Braxton about how many mainstream histories are leaving him out. The official histories being told are not reflecting those viewpoints. I wish somebody would write a book about the post–Vietnam War jazz scene. Not necessarily a history that takes a position, but a real survey.

You don't want to do a Ken Burns thing.

Not really. (Laughs.) This is a book by someone who knows about these great Braxton records with George Lewis, Kenny Wheeler and Dave Holland that are out of print and have never been issued on CD. That stuff is revolutionary. If we could hear that music now.

What about someone like Serge Chaloff, the baritone saxophonist?

Unbelievable.

And all that contrapuntal stuff he did from 1954, '55. You listen to it and realize how many rehearsals they must have done to get that stuff together. And then just think of how many other little movements in the music are not even in the footnotes. They just end up as names.

Booker Little.

Died at 23.

But left a great legacy. I recorded the album *In Our Lifetime* in 1996 in homage to him. He meant so much to me as a composer that it was important to share his relevance.

Booker's music is a little more known than Serge's.

Maybe. But there are only these Booker Little resurgences every few years. I would hope he would be talked about as mainstream. Serge is a whole other time. Think about all those lost scenes and important musicians not heard of. Being on the road I think about how much endurance it takes night after night keeping your chops together, your sanity together, your family together, paying the bills. How many genius musicians in the 20th century couldn't cut that, for one reason or another? They might have had a weekly gig in a local town and not have been able to make it on the road.

Then, on another level, I know extremely talented musicians who don't stretch out more and take chances with their music. I ask them why, and they say, "Look at Coltrane and Bird. I know what it takes to do that. I'm not willing to make that final sacrifice." Those are the choices you have to make. If you want to be well known and popular, you make certain choices in your music. I wish everyone could be at the same level, make the same amount of money and have the same popularity. That's some kind of utopia.

You're talking about Scandinavia. But let's talk less hypothetically. There needs to be a safety net in our society for artists, so that they can be taken care of— their families, health care. That's the kind of society I'd like to see pushed forward.

Do you think about those kinds of things when you do your music?

No, I've been fortunate enough. I don't have those pressures. The big pressure on me is to keep coming up with things in music that I believe in, new truths. Luckily, because of who I am and my personality, I've been led to places where I have an audience. It's not a given. That's why I thank God every day.

September 2006
· ·

Booker, Fess and Beyond

Harry Connick Sits at a Piano to Riff on His Home City's Piano Legacy

by Michael Bourne

Harry Connick Jr. walked onstage shirtless, and all around the American Airlines Theater women (and some men, this being Broadway) screamed. Traditionally, the curtain call of *The Pajama Game* is a parade of the cast all wearing pajamas— with the two leads each wearing half. Her the top, him the bottom. And so it was for Kelli O'Hara and Connick in the Tony-winning revival earlier this year.

"When I moved to New York, that is the one thing that I did not envision myself doing, taking my shirt off in public," Connick said.

Twenty years ago in New York, Connick was a kid fresh out of New Orleans, being touted as "the new Bill Evans." This he wasn't, but he did have the goods. Connick quickly became a star, playing piano—which he's done since he was a young child—and singing. All the while he's frequently whipped out his New Orleans piano chops, especially on two instrumental albums: *Other Hours*, which features a quartet, and *Occasion*, featuring duets with his friend Branford Marsalis.

Later in this evening in early June he would be taking his shirt off in public again for another staging of *The Pajama Game*. But this afternoon, Connick was sitting at a piano in the Rachmaninov Room in Steinway Hall on 57th Street, eager to discuss the New Orleans piano tradition, especially the work of one of his great inspirations, James Booker.

Talk about this great New Orleans culture that you grew up in. What's the first song you remember playing?

"When the Saints Go Marching In." It's the most popular traditional jazz song down there. From the time I was three,

when I started playing, it was that melody I would plunk out on the piano. As I got older, maybe five, I remember being fascinated with the combination of notes that could make a chord. If you put a C, E and G together, you had a chord, and it sounded pretty good. And the rhythmic element in New Orleans was so powerful. It's almost more important making music that makes you want to dance than music you want to listen to.

I remember my dad was trying to get me to listen to Erroll Garner. When I actually listened, when I was about 12, he was the meanest piano player. I heard Erroll doing this four-on-the-floor left hand, and my first thought was, "Man, that guy's stealing my style!" I'd never heard anybody do that.

When I came along, the purpose of a piano player was not a rhythmic one, at least not in the jazz world. Guys like Professor Longhair, Dr. John, James Booker, Allen Toussaint and Art Neville played rhythmically. But jazz musicians—that was the bass player and drummer's job, and the [piano player's] left hand would play chords. But a guy like Erroll Garner, whether he played solo or in a trio, that left hand kept pounding four out. That was always attractive to me.

I've always felt that the secret of New Orleans piano was the left hand. What does your left hand do?

My left hand has evolved over the years. I play different types of things. Professor Longhair was truly the father of that new wave of New Orleans piano playing. I don't think that anyone would say he was a great technician in a classical point of view, but rhythmically he was so strong. He played these rumba bass lines, and he put these things on the top. That bass line, for a small person like me, eight, 10 years old, was easy to relate to. Anybody could play that. I couldn't play it as well as Fess, and I still can't, but technically that wasn't hard for me to do.

One of the people he had the most influence on was James Booker, who I had a direct contact with. Booker, on a technical level, is unsurpassed. I put him up there with people like [Art] Tatum and [Duke] Ellington. True, unbelievable technique, like [Thelonious] Monk. Such an incredible sound on the piano. Booker's technique was personal. He could play classical music or play the piano functionally as well as anybody else, but he started doing things his own way. And I wanted to play like Booker.

He was a nice guy. He loved my mom and dad. He would come by my house, just stop by and say hello. He would always sit down at the piano for an hour or two and show me things. The problem was that my hands were not big enough to play the types of things he had to show me, so he'd modify them for my hand size.

It wasn't until after he died, when I was 14, that I started digging into what he was doing. That is the time musically when you're the most impressionable. You want to figure things out. In life, too. I started going back and realized, that is what he was doing!

As any jazz musician can tell you, your own style doesn't happen until later. You spend years emulating and imitating the artists you admire. People used to say, "He's copying Monk," or, "He's copying Booker." Absolutely. When you're 18, that's what you do. I used to copy Booker's things, but as time went on, it was like that game Telephone. When 10 people sit around, the first person whispers in the next one's ear, "I went to the store and I bought some milk," and that person whispers it to the next, and then the next, and by the time it gets back to you, it's something like, "I went down to the 7-Eleven and I got a Coke." It changes. It's human nature. That is the way my piano playing has changed. I go back and listen to the early Booker things and [my playing] sounds totally different now.

There's a real power to New Orleans music. So much is played at a party or in a saloon where you have to play loud.

If there's a room full of people and they want to dance, and there is only a piano player there, you got this going… (he thunders a groove on the piano and just about blows the mike out). It's big, man! You play that for hours and hours. You're going to develop a big sound after a while.

And some muscles on your fingers.

You know what's funny? Physically, I'm a much bigger man than Booker was. I'm about 6' 2", 200 pounds. Booker was maybe 6', 155 pounds. The way he played was way different than the way I play, but his sound was huge. It wasn't because of any upper body strength. If I need to make the room rock and roll, I'm going to put my body into it. But he didn't have to exert a lot of energy. When he played, he was still. I move a lot when I play. That's the way I'm made. But if you listen to his records, his sound was tremendous. That's just what God gave him.

A young Harry Connick Jr. with James Booker.
(Michael Smith)

When you were a kid and he'd come by, were you aware how much of a lesson you were getting?

When I got to be 12 years old, I remember him coming. A year before he died (1983) there's a record he did called *Classified*, and he's on the cover in this brown polyester suit. He came to the house in this suit, and he was proud of it. He was proud that he'd cleaned up, or at least he said that he had. He acted as if he was fairly lucid at the time. Those were some of my best memories of him. I could get a straight answer out of him. I'd say, "Hey, James, how did you do this?" and he would answer

me succinctly and clearly as opposed to when I would get phone calls, like at 2 a.m., and he'd ramble and ramble, or I'd go see him play and he was incoherent.

But the music was absolutely solid as a rock. It was just his personality. Not to imply that he had any imbalance, but it would seem that he did. And compounded with the huge amounts of drugs and alcohol that he consumed, it was almost impossible to have a conversation with this guy.

The stories about this guy are endless, from going onstage naked to going onstage with a loaded gun, threatening to kill himself if nobody gave him a tip or because his lover had left him. It's crazy. Why he took such a liking to me I will never know. New Orleans is full of piano players and young musicians. I genuinely cared for him, as did my mother. She died when I was 13. Booker died when I was 14. When he found out she was sick, when I was 10 or 11, he was saddened by that. I don't know why my family knew him so well. I remember my family talking about [getting] him into a studio: "We need to produce a record with him. We need to get him to play."

He would show up at the house and his phrase was just, "Pour me a glass of mineral water and some Seagram's." When I tell you some Seagram's, I mean like 30 percent of the bottle, just straight. Bang, he'd hit that and he'd chase that with that water, and he'd start playing.

Booker's performances were legendary. Did you learn show business from him?

No, not at all. Booker was almost the antithesis of what I wanted to be. I wanted to be what Louis Armstrong was. Pops was my idol as far as show biz. Had Booker not done any drugs or alcohol, he probably would have been a quiet person. Keep in mind that this is a 14-year-old's account. People who really knew him, like Ellis [Marsalis] — who knew him when he was 12—may differ. But I was always under the impression Booker was a shy person, that he was introverted, while I was extremely extroverted. I loved to perform. I loved to look at the audience and smile at them and include them in what I was doing. Most New Orleans performers are like that.

I don't think the things Booker did onstage were necessarily to please the audience, but to please himself. Almost like the way Monk would get up and dance around in circles. I don't think he was doing that for applause. I just think that he needed to dance. Booker did stuff because he felt that he had to do it.

I read that he once spent all the money for the gig on a spectacular entrance, like the time he drove onto the stage in a Cadillac like a triumphant Roman general.

What's crazy is that he could back that up. There's a lot of people who do that today and do not have the talent to back up that kind of pomp. James Booker did.

He was in jail for a time, in Angola, one of the world's toughest jails.

I've been there many times. That's not a place you want to be. Back in the '70s when he was there, Angola was considered the bloodiest prison in America, and he was

not of the physical or mental stature to handle that kind of environment. If you're going to a place like Angola, you'd better be big and strong physically or mentally, and I don't think he was either. I don't know how he survived at all.

Did you learn from his troubles not to do the things that troubled him?

No. I have two main influences in my life. One was my parents. My father was district attorney of New Orleans from when I was five until about two years ago. My mother was a judge. Doing drugs would've been the stupidest thing in the world. I steered clear of that. Also, my immediate mentors were the Marsalis family: Ellis, who doesn't drink, doesn't smoke, doesn't do drugs, and all of his sons. Wynton and Branford were the two I idolized most because they were in New York doing exactly what I wanted to do. They were playing jazz music and had successful careers. That was the last thing on their minds: getting high, drinking. They just didn't do it. And when you're 14, you want to do exactly what your heroes do. If Wynton and Branford had been big coke heads, maybe I would have become a coke addict. They were intent upon studying hard and practicing hard. Everybody from that school, the New Orleans Center for the Creative Arts, did that.

James was the manifestation of all the things as a person that you didn't want to happen to yourself. You strive to be a person who has peace of mind, which he didn't have, which he probably did not have any control over.

What was the best musical lesson you learned from him?

I used to get restless a lot onstage. We were like an amateur version of the Jazz Messengers. We called ourselves the Jazz Couriers. When the alto player was taking a solo, or the drummer, or even me, there was a piece of me that used to get restless. I wanted the song to end because, No. 1, we weren't that good. Also, the audience wanted to like it, but they were getting restless. As a performer, I don't like any downtime. I like it to be exciting, fulfilling for the audience.

Booker didn't care. He would go onstage and play exactly what he wanted to play. He had no inhibitions about it. [He'd play] a ballad. If it were outside at a jazz festival, people were screaming and hollering, and it was when you would think he would play some rocking boogie, he didn't care. He played what he needed to play

at that time, what needed to be said at that time. That comes with age.

I'm 38. I'm getting to the point when people respond to truth more than anything else. I need to make myself happy first, and audiences can respect that. They can sense when you're trying to manipulate them, and James never did that. He always played what he wanted to play. That's a real good lesson.

How much did you study other New Orleans piano masters? Did you go back to Jelly Roll Morton?

I never studied Jelly Roll's stuff as much as I just listened to it. There were so many piano players. When I was in New Orleans growing up, from when I was five to 13, there were 50 piano players that I heard any day. I heard Booker. I heard Tuts Washington, Armand Hug, Phamous Lambert, Walter Lewis, Jeanette Kimball, Sweet Emma. I didn't need to hear people on records, because I was going down all of the time and listening to them in person. Art Neville, Allen Toussaint, Dr. John—there's a million of them down there. Or Ellis. Think about that—one city! You could hear any of those people on any given night. Earl Vuiovich. Ed Frank played more with one hand than most people have played with four.

When I got to be 13, I started studying with Ellis at NOCCA, that's when everything changed. Ellis started hitting me with people I'd never heard of, much less heard. I'd never checked Herbie [Hancock] out, or Bill Evans out. McCoy [Tyner], Chick [Corea], Horace Silver. I remember when Ellis said that Monk died. I was 14. I didn't care. "This guy sucks. He makes a lot of mistakes. He's real sloppy." I didn't know.

I hated Monk when I was an early teenager. But over the years, as I started listening to him, Wynton would come through town and say, "You should listen to Monk." I got every Monk record. I transcribed every Monk solo. I started listening to Earl Hines. I went back as far as James P. Johnson, Meade Lux Lewis, Albert Ammons, Fats Waller, but I didn't take that extra step to go even further back and listen to a lot of Jelly Roll. For some reason, I was not interested. Jelly Roll was a big part of our culture, but I never transcribed a lot of Jelly Roll stuff.

Still, you knew him as a part of New Orleans culture. There are great music scenes in New York, Chicago and elsewhere around the world. But nowhere like New Orleans, where the whole culture is alive.

You don't have to go and hear it, you're hearing it always.

It's incredible. The tradition is there. Only after I moved to New York did I realize that I have never seen a city like New Orleans.

It's as if the whole city's got a musical genius.

It does. Even people who know nothing about music. There's a dance that we do around Mardi Gras, or any time, called the second line. There are people who have not an ounce of music or rhythm in their bodies, but they pull out a handkerchief and they dance. That's our culture. New Orleans has its own genius. When I think about it in depth, it's overwhelming. You don't see it when you grow up, but when you step back, it's wild.

It's the heart of this culture that will rebuild New Orleans.

Absolutely. They knocked us down for a while, but you can't keep us down as a community. All of the efforts should be applauded. It's a situation far bigger than anybody could have even dreamed of. Now that we've got our bearings back, things are being done. New Orleans is going to come back, and in a profound way. In light of all the suffering, tragedy that was unimaginable, we will gain so much with how we look at our society, how we treat our people, how we set up plans for the future in case this kind of stuff happens again. A lot of good things are going to come out of the rebuilding process, and New Orleans is going to be a better and stronger place for it.

January 2008

That Old Cowboy

by David French

"Do you know this tune?" Dave Brubeck asked. "Who made it popular?" I responded, shaking my head no.

"Nobody," deadpanned Brubeck, evoking laughter all around the room.

The song in question was "I'm Alone Because I Love You," an obscure ballad from 1930. Brubeck was listening to it at a recording studio on the west side of Manhattan. It was a playback of one of the tunes that would comprise his latest album, *Indian Summer* (Telarc), a solo piano outing of standards and a few originals, rich with a meditative, twilight intensity.

Behind the mixing board in a tan poplin suit, pockets stuffed with eyeglasses, pens and mechanical pencils, Brubeck clearly did not feel great. Although he could still joke around, he had put in a full day of recording, and two days before, on tour with his quartet in Texas, he had gashed his ankle badly on a hotel bed frame, requiring a trip to the hospital. As his wife, Iola, arranged a scarf around his neck, he admitted that the pain had kept him from sleeping the past couple of nights and made traveling from Texas difficult. As soon as the playbacks ended and the course of the next day's work was decided upon, the Brubecks stood to get ready for the drive to their house in Connecticut.

"I haven't been home in two months," Brubeck said. He sounded spent, like he wanted to fall into bed and pull the covers over his head. Watching the 86-year-old pianist make the slow, painful walk to the elevator, it was hard not to wonder why he keeps working so hard.

"I've asked him a bunch of times, 'Why don't you slow down? Why don't you retire?'" said saxophonist Bobby Militello, who has been a member of the Dave Brubeck Quartet since 1982. But the answer is always the same. "He wants to play. Playing is as much his life's juice as breathing."

Brubeck has been one of the most famous—and busiest—jazz musicians in the world for more than 50 years, since at least 1954 when his portrait appeared on the cover of *Time* magazine. Brubeck's place in jazz history would have been assured if he had retired in 1960, the year that his album *Time Out* sold more than 1 million copies. It sells well to this day, and in addition to being popular, it stands as one of the most influential jazz albums ever. It showed jazz musicians that a whole world existed beyond 4/4 and waltz time.

But Brubeck, unlike his old quartet mate Paul Desmond, who went into semi-retirement after the classic Brubeck band broke up in 1967, has never stepped away from performing, or even slowed down. He has kept up a ferocious level of activity over the years, amassing an immense discography of jazz and classical works, spending most of his life on the road and filling in the gaps between gigs as produc-

tively as possible, often holed up in his hotel room with an electric piano and manuscript paper.

In 2006, however, after a grueling tour that left him "about as near exhaustion as I've ever been," Brubeck finally made a concession to age and announced that he would no longer tour Europe. Nevertheless, with travel time, his current schedule of 60–80 performances a year keeps him on the road more than he is home.

"He's something else," Militello said. "He's not laying back at all. He wants to keep himself sharp and try to push himself to the edge of what he can do. And he doesn't stop growing. Every day, every time we play a gig, it's, 'Be ready for what he's gonna do. Keep your ears open.'"

A few weeks after the studio sessions for *Indian Summer*, Brubeck returned home to Connecticut following a tour of California. The highlight of the trip was a stop at the Brubeck Festival at the Brubeck Institute in Stockton, Calif., founded by the University of the Pacific to honor their famed alumnus. He made this tour with his characteristic determination, because prior to the trip, the cut on his leg had become infected and for a week he went in and out of the hospital. He had to cancel several concerts.

At the festival he took part in a performance of the "Brubeck Songbook"—a set of songs he wrote with Iola—sung by Roberta Gambarini, and his recent "Cannery Row Suite," a jazz-meets-12-tone opera based on the John Steinbeck novel *Cannery Row*, with Gambarini and Kurt Elling in the lead roles.

The following day he attended the San Francisco Ballet's performance of "Elemental Brubeck," a work choreographed by Lar Lubovitch to Brubeck's music. After this, his quartet, augmented by a big band of top West Coast players, performed his 1963 suite "Elementals" at the San Francisco Masonic Auditorium.

"For our 50th wedding anniversary, we celebrated at the Claremont Hotel in Berkeley and I invited the guys that used to play with me," Brubeck said, recalling his visit to San Francisco, his old hometown and the original base for the Brubeck quartet in the 1950s. "Seven different bass players came in and played that night. Now, 16 years have gone by, and I was ready to see a lot of old friends. And almost all of those guys are gone. Wyatt Ruther, Norman Bates and Bob Bates. There were four Bates brothers—if you wanted a bass player you called their house. And Bob Skinner. On and on it goes. Oh boy. It's tough when you don't see guys again. I never saw my brother again after that anniversary. That's tough when you go back."

Balancing this sense of loss from the California trip, to some extent, was the enormous pleasure he takes in contact with younger musicians.

"I hear some of the Brubeck Fellows at the Institute, and they're so far ahead of where I was at their age," he said. "There's no comparison with how great they are. Like the band that was assembled in San Francisco to do 'Elementals.' Four of them came up and said, 'We play with your son Matthew.' That made me feel so good. That tradition is still going on with a set of new players. Matthew is a great classical cellist who can improvise or play with a symphony orchestra. My kids are doing so much."

Four of Brubeck's six children— Matthew, Darius, Dan and Chris—work as professional musicians and have played with their father. They have established impressive careers as performers, composers and educators. Brubeck's voice thickens with pride when he recounts their accomplishments.

Even with all of the awards Brubeck has received over the years, his greatest honors come from seeing new generations carrying on what he started. "That's significant," he said. "When the San Francisco Ballet was doing the piece based on 'Elementals,' we sat in the audience, and the audience went ape for the ballet. That's the kind of award that brings me joy. To hear my music played one night by a jazz band, and then the old quartet recording of 'Elementals' being danced to. They asked me to come backstage. All those young dancers saying how great it is to dance to and hear your music—that's what I want to hear more than awards."

To record a solo piano album at his age could be considered a gutsy move. With no rhythm section to hide behind or lean on, he sits alone, inviting comparison to recordings he made more than half a century ago.

Brubeck's playing has changed. It is more simple. Whereas playfulness and curiosity once defined his playing, emotion comes through most on his recent work. When he's onstage, pure joy leaps out through bits of old songs and snatches of stride and bop as he time travels through all the jazz history he has helped shape.

A deep, resonating mood of reflection,

beauty and loss emerges on tracks like Kurt Weill's "September Song" and the old Harry James weeper "You'll Never Know." "I'm Alone Because I Love You"—the tune nobody made popular—is one of Brubeck's favorites from the album.

"That's an old song," he said. "I've never played it since I was playing in a band in the '30s. But I've always liked that tune."

Two of the tracks recall other piano players for Brubeck. "'Memories of You' by Eubie Blake was one of the first tunes I ever played, and I did a song that I associate with Nat Cole, 'Sweet Lorraine,'" he explained. "Knowing him before he was a singer, I've always loved his playing. He was such a great pianist I almost was sorry he could sing so well because he didn't do as much with his trio."

Tucked in with the covers are originals like "Summer Song," a recent composition with a 12-tone row melody, and a new version of a song he first recorded in the '50s, "Thank You," originally titled, "Dziekuje." Brubeck wrote the classical-influenced piece after a visit to the Chopin museum in Poland. "It's dedicated to my mother," Brubeck said, "because she loved Chopin."

Brubeck didn't choose the title *Indian Summer*; Telarc President Bob Woods suggested it. "I went about it thinking about my growing up on a cattle ranch with a lot of Indian friends," Brubeck said. "So Iola said, 'You're on the wrong track. He's thinking about the Indian summer at the end of people's lives. At the end of your life.' So [then] I approached it a little differently."

"He recorded 'Indian Summer' 50 years ago," said Russell Gloyd, Brubeck's longtime manager, musical director and conductor. "Now he understands what an Indian summer is, whereas before, 50 years ago, he played it more as a composition, not necessarily a life statement."

Brubeck thinks his playing has become more emotional with age. "Hardly a week goes by that I don't lose an old friend, or somebody close to me is having a heart attack," he said. "I couldn't tell you how many great pianists are having physical problems—guys who I've admired my whole life. What's happening to us? We've always been strong and could take a lot—a lot of hard life, and bounce back and go the next day. I can't accept it. I can't accept that I'm not strong. So you play a little differently when you're not as strong as you used to be."

A message from Brubeck on the Brubeck Institute's Web site says that he

would like to be remembered as "someone who opened doors." When asked about which doors he opened most changed jazz, he quickly offered "polyrhythms and polytonality"—simultaneously playing more than one rhythm or time signature and in more than one key.

In 1949—before many outside of San Francisco knew who he was—Brubeck wrote an article for *DownBeat* called "Jazz's Evolvement as an Art Form." In that piece, basically an artistic manifesto, he urged musicians to explore beyond familiar jazz harmonies and 32-bar form. He suggested that in the future jazz would absorb many elements of modern classical music such as counterpoint, polytonality and polyrhythms. He also speculated that jazz would easily accommodate such then-exotic musical elements as Chinese scales and African and South American rhythms.

"I knew that jazz should go in this direction," he said. "You read that old *DownBeat* and you'll see how I point to world music. That's what I mean about opening doors. There weren't many guys pointing that way. Maybe Dizzy [Gillespie] more so than anybody else.

"Pianists from Poland and Russia, when they see me they go into this thing, 'I grew up in my country playing odd time signatures. I didn't know I could do it in jazz. When I heard you, I knew if you did it, I could probably do it better,'" Brubeck laughed.

And yet, as influential as Brubeck clearly was as an idea man, as a player he never inspired many obvious followers or a cult of personality, like such more romantic figures as Miles Davis and John Coltrane. Reflecting on his legacy, Brubeck exudes a slight sense of disappointment—that on some level, compared to his peers, he has been misunderstood or taken for granted by the jazz establishment.

"If you knew all the guys who never say anything too good about me who secretly know I opened the door for them, or have said it, but it isn't picked up by the jazz police," he said. "If I told you all the guys you'd be surprised. At the same time the critics are saying I'm not playing jazz, I'm influencing a whole bunch of guys who play so great.

"I'll give you one example," he continued. "One of my favorite piano players was Bill Evans. When he was young, he made a lot of good remarks about me. In the fake book, he gets credit for recording 'Alice in Wonderland' and 'Someday My Prince

Will Come.' But where did Bill hear it? Maybe five years before? I know where he heard it, he knows where he heard it and he would tell me where he heard it. But it dies right there.

"I won't name any more. But look at some of the best, far-out guys, you'll find that the guy they heard who set them off in the right direction was that old cowboy Dave Brubeck."

If jazz tastemakers have at times slighted Brubeck, he also hasn't needed their support. He has often chosen to leave jazz behind entirely. Beginning in 1967, with the release of his sprawling, double-LP oratorio *Light in the Wilderness*, Brubeck has divided his time between touring and recording with a jazz combo and writing and performing his classical pieces. These range from intimate chamber music to massive orchestra-plus-choir timber-shakers. Experimenting with forms beyond the jazz norm was something Brubeck had always done.

"I wrote my first ballet in 1946," he said. "I was saying, 'Dance music—ballet—should be possible.' Gradually it became possible. I traveled for years with a ballet company doing ballet music with a quartet onstage. Then the first year at Monterey we played with the Monterey Symphony Orchestra, and nobody expected that. I won't say we were the first, but we were out there in the early '50s doing that."

Today, writing and performing the large classical pieces excite him the most.

"I get a lot out of that challenge, hoping I can come up to the challenge," he said. "I'm always afraid that I won't. And yet, I'll take on the next one and say to myself, 'How can I think that I can do this?' But I'll work on it, plodding away."

One of the greatest days of his long career, he said, was the performance of his "Gates of Justice" at the 2004 Newport Jazz Festival with his band, a brass ensemble, choir and two vocalists. "People thought this was going to be the biggest turkey we've ever done," he laughed. "But amazingly, we had to repeat three sections of the mass because the audience loved it so much."

He was delighted last year when the Pacific Mozart Ensemble in Berkeley, Calif., asked him to supply the missing "Credo" section from Mozart's Mass in C Minor; and an October performance of his pieces "Canticles" and "Upon This Rock" at the University of Notre Dame in South Bend, Ind., featured a 200-piece choir.

Dave Brubeck.
(Jimmy Katz)

As he recounted all the things he had on the horizon, Brubeck sounded like an excited teenager. "There are always great things coming up—in the next phone call or the next e-mail—and boy, are they coming in hot and thick!"

When asked about life on the road with Brubeck, Gloyd described a typical night away from home for the bandleader.

"We can pretty much guarantee two standing ovations a night when Dave performs," he said. "The first one is the stand-ing ovation that the audience gives out of respect for all that Dave has accomplished in his life and given to them. That is a moving, heartfelt tribute. The second standing ovation is the one that I always laugh about because it's after he plays for two-and-a-half hours and they're screaming for more encores. You see this frail man walk to the piano and sit down. Suddenly this alchemy takes place and this young firebrand takes over. You literally see the years disappearing through each piece."

Permissions

Grateful acknowledgment is made to the following writers for permission to use the material specified, all of which was previously published in *DownBeat* magazine.

Bob Belden: "Sonny Rollins—The Man," August 1997. Reprinted by permission.

Larry Birnbaum: "Milt Hinton—The Judge Holds Court," Jan. 25, 1979; "Weather Report Answers Its Critics," Feb. 8, 1979; "Clark Terry—Big B-A-D Brassman," September 1981. Reprinted by permission.

Steve Bloom: "Freddie Hubbard—Money Talks, Bebop Walks," November 1981. Reprinted by permission.

Michael Bourne: "Joe Henderson—The Sound That Launched 1,000 Horns," March 1992; "Betty Carter—It's Not About Teaching, It's About Doing," December 1994; "Dr. John—Temple of Big Band," July 1995; "Tony Bennett—The Art of Being Bennett," January 2002; "Harry Connick Jr.—Booker, Fess and Beyond," September 2006. Reprinted by permission.

Aaron Cohen: "James Brown—Godfather of... Jazz?," November 2004. Reprinted by permission.

Pat Cole: "Joshua Redman—Street of Dreams," December 1993. Reprinted by permission.

Steve Coleman: "Dave Douglas—Mastering His Music," August 2006. Reprinted by permission.

John Corbett: "Steve Lacy—Forget Paris," February 1997. Reprinted by permission.

Clive Davis: "Van Morrison—Jazz Revisited," May 1996. Reprinted by permission.

Paul de Barros: "Tony Williams—Two Decades of Drum Innovation," November 1983; "Jazz at Lincoln Center Orchestra—Southern Swing," October 2000. Reprinted by permission.

Jon Faddis: "Milt Jackson—Lessons from Bags," November 1999. Reprinted by permission.

David French: "Dave Brubeck—That Old Cowboy," January 2008. Reprinted by permission.

Frank-John Hadley: "B.B. King and Buddy Guy—Blues Hit Town," December 2001. Reprinted by permission.

Martin Johnson: "Roy Hargrove and Kenny Garrett—Opposites Attract," September 1995; "McCoy Tyner and Michael Brecker—An Easy Marriage of Styles," January 1996. Reprinted by permission.

Gene Kalbacher: "J.J. Johnson—Bringing It All Back Home," March 1988. Reprinted by permission.

David Less: "Al Green—Soul Reborn but Sales Waste Away," April 5, 1979. Reprinted by permission.

Joe Lovano: "Hank Jones—Family Legacy," June 2005. Reprinted by permission.

Howard Mandel: "Henry Threadgill—Music to Make the Sun Come Up," July 1985; "Bill Frisell Band—No Semi, No Roadies, No Set List," March 1992; "Joe Lovano—Joe Lovano's Sound of the Broad Shoulders," March 1993. Reprinted by permission.

Bill Milkowski: "Brian Eno—Excursions in the Electronic Environment," June 1983. Reprinted by permission.

Greg Osby, "Andrew Hill and Jason Moran—Reality Lessons," January 2003. Reprinted by permission.

Dan Ouellette: "Charles Brown—Blindfold Test," October 1995; "The Heath Brothers, Blindfold Test," February 2003. "Elvis Costello and Allen Toussaint—Flowing Collaboration," June 2006. Reprinted by permission.

Don Palmer: "Carla Bley—My Dinner with Carla," August 1984. Reprinted by permission.

Zan Stewart: "Quincy Jones—The Quincy Jones Interview," April 1985. Reprinted by permission.

Robin Tolleson: "Carlos Santana—Blindfold Test," August 1985. Reprinted by permission.

Lee Underwood: "Maynard Ferguson—Rocky Road to Fame and Fortune," July 1980. Reprinted by permission.